BETWEEN ROME AND CARTHAGE

Hannibal invaded Italy with the hope of raising widespread rebellions among Rome's subordinate allies. Yet even after crushing the Roman army at Cannae, he was only partially successful. Why did some communities decide to side with Carthage and others to side with Rome? This is the fundamental question posed in this book, and consideration is given to the particular political, diplomatic, military and economic factors that influenced individual communities' decisions. Understanding their motivations reveals much, not just about the war itself, but also about Rome's relations with Italy during the prior two centuries of aggressive expansion. The book sheds new light on Roman imperialism in Italy, the nature of Roman hegemony and the transformation of Roman Italy in the period leading up to the Social War. It is informed throughout by contemporary political science theory and archaeological evidence, and will be required reading for all historians of the Roman Republic.

MICHAEL P. FRONDA is Assistant Professor in the Department of History and Classical Studies, McGill University. He has published a number of articles on topics in ancient history and has contributed to D. Hoyos (ed.), *The Blackwell Companion to the Punic Wars*.

BETWEEN ROME AND CARTHAGE

Southern Italy during the Second Punic War

MICHAEL P. FRONDA

McGill University

CAMBRIDGE
UNIVERSITY PRESS

937.
04

CAMBRIDGE
UNIVERSITY PRESS

University Printing House, Cambridge CB2 8BS, United Kingdom

Cambridge University Press is part of the University of Cambridge.

It furthers the University's mission by disseminating knowledge in the pursuit of education, learning and research at the highest international levels of excellence.

www.cambridge.org
Information on this title: www.cambridge.org/9781107689503

© Michael P. Fronda 2010

First published 2010
First paperback edition 2014

A catalogue record for this publication is available from the British Library

Library of Congress Cataloguing in Publication data
Fronda, Michael P., 1970–
Between Rome and Carthage : Southern Italy during the
Second Punic War / Michael P. Fronda.
p. cm.
Includes bibliographical references and index.
ISBN 978-0-521-51694-5 (hbk.)
1. Punic War, 2nd, 218–201 B.C.–Campaigns–Italy, Southern. 2. Punic War, 2nd, 218–201 B.C.–Social aspects–Italy, Southern. 3. Punic War, 2nd, 218–201 B.C.–Political aspects–Italy, Southern. 4. Italy, Southern–History–To 535. 5. Italy, Southern–History, Military. 6. Hannibal, 247–182 B.C.–Military leadership. 7. Rome–Relations–Italy. 8. Italy–Relations–Rome. 9. Carthage (Extinct city)–Relations–Italy. 10. Italy–Relations–Carthage (Extinct city) I. Title.
DG247.33.F76 2010
937'.04–dc22
2010009141

ISBN 978-0-521-51694-5 Hardback
ISBN 978-1-107-68950-3 Paperback

For Joseph D. Fronda (1935–1985)

Contents

Acknowledgments

It is perhaps clichéd for a scholar to open his or her first academic book by noting that it started as a PhD dissertation and took final form after a long period of development and revision. Yet some clichés become so because they are true. This is certainly the case with the present book, which did in fact begin as a dissertation written in fulfilment of my doctoral degree at The Ohio State University. Indeed, the core of the book – the basic question, why did some allies revolt during the Second Punic War? – had its roots in a seminar paper that I wrote in 1994 in my early days as a graduate student, the central thesis of which the professor for the course deemed 'ingenious but ultimately unconvincing'. The work has grown and developed a great deal since then, just as has my own thinking on Roman Italy and ancient history in general has evolved and matured. New arguments and ideas have been added, others have disappeared. This book is the end result. It was written and revised at three different academic institutions – The Ohio State University, Denison University and McGill University – and has benefited immensely from thoughtful criticisms, corrections and suggestions by many colleagues and friends whom I have been fortunate to meet. Any remaining weaknesses, fallacies and errors are my own. I leave it for the reader to determine whether the final product is ingenious or convincing.

It is impossible to name everyone who has helped me directly and indirectly along the way, but the following individuals must be acknowledged. First, I thank Nathan Rosenstein, my dissertation supervisor and the professor who commented on that original seminar paper. He is a formidable scholar, a careful critic and one of the finest professors I have ever had. He more than anyone else taught me how to be an ancient historian. He has been and continues to be both a mentor and a friend. I am indebted as well to the other members of my dissertation committee, Timothy Gregory, who first introduced me to the world of archaeology, and Barry Strauss, who rightly urged that I look at political science and international relations theory to help unpack my ideas. Fellow graduate comrades Bill Caraher and Jack Wells read various drafts of my dissertation and continued to give welcome suggestions as that dissertation grew into this book. From Ohio State I should also thank Will Batsone for helping me to become a more sensitive reader of ancient texts, and Jack Balcer (†) for his gentle guidance. Garrett Jacobsen and Tim Hofmeister, my friends and colleagues in the Classics Department at Denison University, provided both moral support and practical advice. The influence of Lisa Fentress, John Dobbins and Darby Scott, whom I met during my wonderful summer at the American Academy in Rome in 2000, can be found in the more archaeological sections. My colleagues in the Department of History and Classical Studies at McGill University helped me immeasurably during the major revision stage. Hans Beck attentively read through and commented on the entire manuscript. He also provided invaluable insights on Roman historiography and the sources for early Roman history, which greatly improved Chapter 1. He has been a great friend and ally. John Serrati read drafts of Chapter 7. Discussions with Bob Morstein-Marx, Claude Eilers, Rene Pfeilschifter, Craige Champion, Martin Jehne and most of all Art Eckstein have helped to clarify and strengthen arguments throughout the book. Art also showed me the manuscript of *Mediterranean Anarchy, Interstate War, and the Rise of Rome* before its publication. Stephen Oakley graciously allowed me to see drafts of volumes III and IV of his *Commentary on Livy Books 6–10* before they were published.

I am grateful to the staff at Cambridge University Press for their diligence, assistance and especially patience in seeing the manuscript through various revisions to final production. I thank especially my editor, Michael Sharp, and also the anonymous readers whose comments and suggestions invariably improved the work. Student research assistants at McGill, Sarah Limoges and Robert Eisenberg, did a great service by aiding with proofreading and typesetting.

I would be remiss not to mention my wife Jennifer Brecht. She has, among other things, proofread texts, offered pointers on prose style and taken part in innumerable one-sided discussions of interstate relations and the Roman alliance system. But most importantly, she has been there with love and support throughout the long and often trying process of writing and publication. Without her, this book would not have been written. Finally, I dedicate this book to my father Joseph Fronda (†), whose love of history made a deep impression on me as a child, though I did not realise it at the time. I only wish that he could be here to read it.

Note on abbreviations

The abbreviations used throughout this book are those of the *Oxford Classical Dictionary*, 3rd edn (for references to ancient literary sources and inscriptions) and of *L'Année Philologique* (for the titles of scholarly journals), with the following additions and variations:

All references to Dionysius of Halicarnassus (Dion. Hal.) refer to the *Roman Antiquities* unless otherwise indicated.

Beck and Walter, *FRH*	Beck, H. and Walter, U. (eds.), *Die frühen römischen Historiker* (2 vols.). Darmstadt, 2001.
Cauer²	Cauer, P. (ed.), *Delectus Inscriptionum Graecarum*, 2nd edn. Leipzig, 1883.
DNP	Cancik, H. and Schneider, H. (eds.), *Der neue Pauly: Enzyklopädie der Antike* (16 vols.). Stuttgart, 1996–2003.

Maps

Maps

Map I Italy, third century BC

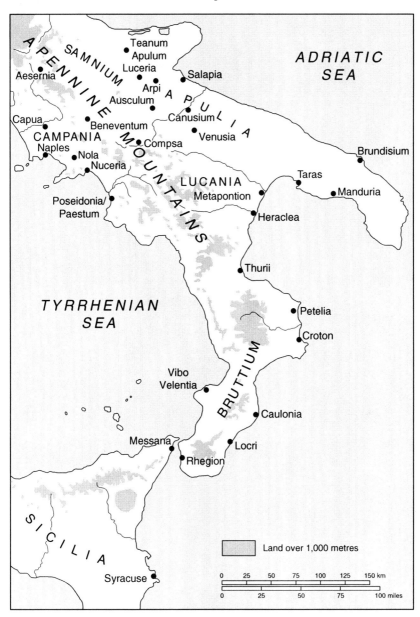

Map 2 Southern Italy, third century BC

Maps

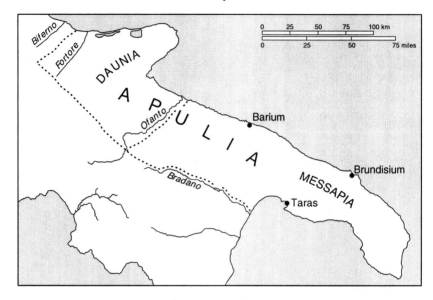

Map 3 Apulia, Daunia and Messapia

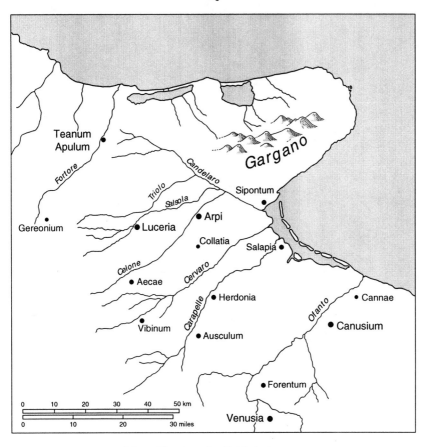

Map 4 Northern Apulia/Daunia

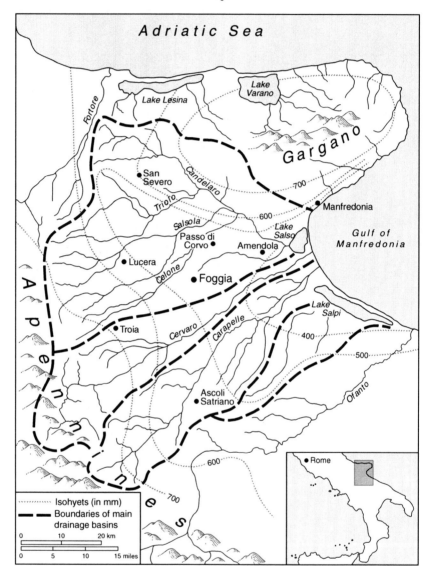

Map 5 Northern Apulia/Daunia: hydration systems (From G. Jones 1987)

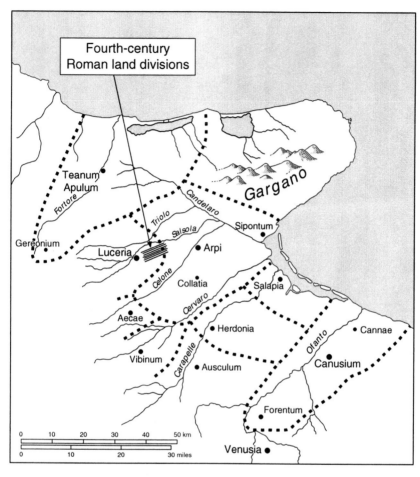

Map 6 Northern Apulia/Daunia: approximate boundaries between cities

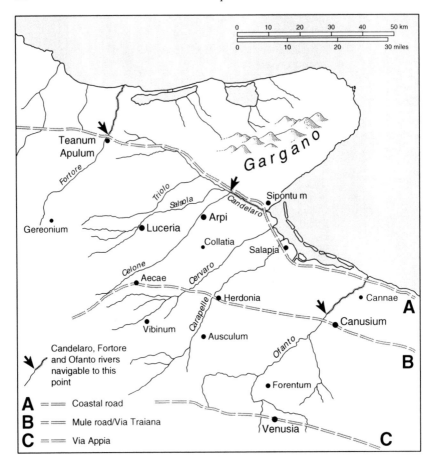

Map 7 Northern Apulia/Daunia: roads and navigable rivers

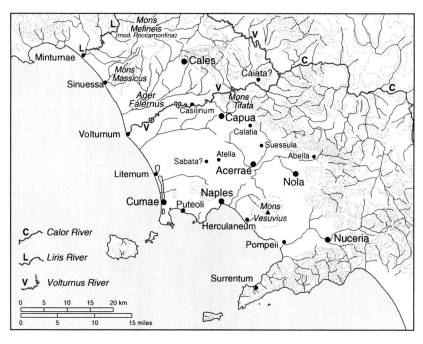

Map 8 Campania

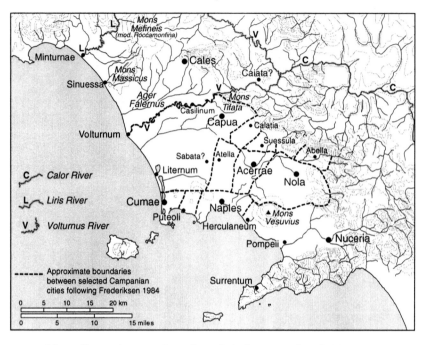

Map 9 Campania: approximate boundaries between selected cities

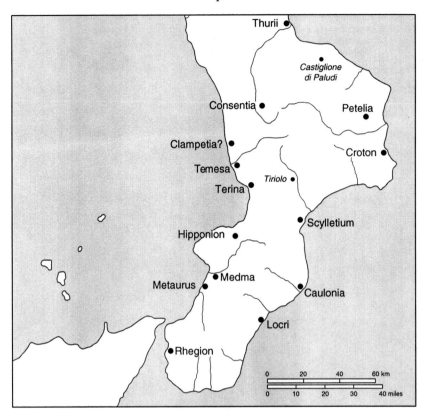

Map 10 Bruttium and SW Magna Graecia

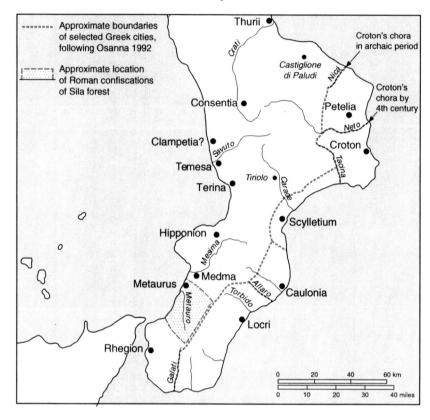

Map 11 Bruttium and SW Magna Graecia: approximate boundaries between selected cities

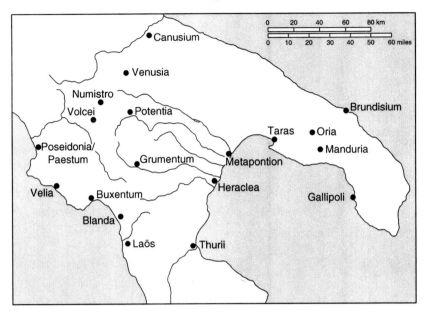

Map 12 Lucania and SE Italy

Maps

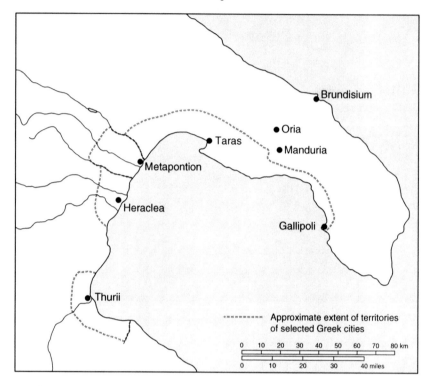

Map 13 SE Magna Graecia: approximate boundaries between selected cities

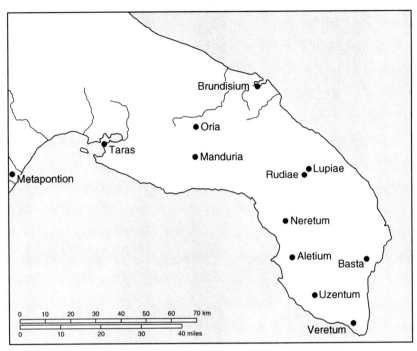

Map 14 Taras and the Sallentine Peninsula

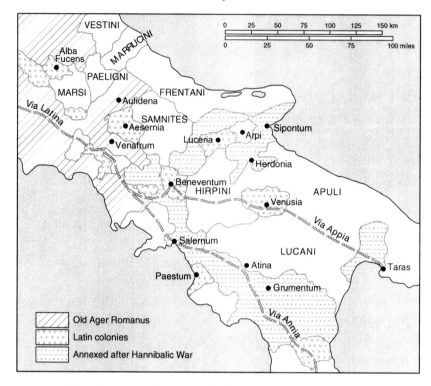

Map 15 Roman confiscations and colonisation, *c.* 200–100 BC

Introduction

PROLOGUE

At the end of a single, fateful day in the middle of the summer of 216 BC[1] – 2 August according to one Roman tradition, but perhaps sometime in early July if the Roman calendar was running ahead of the solar months[2] – near the small Apulian town of Cannae, Hannibal stood seemingly on the brink of victory over the Roman Republic. He had just exacted a crushing defeat upon the largest Roman field army mustered to that day. At least fifty thousand Roman and allied soldiers lay dead on the field of battle; thousands more were captured. One consul perished, while the second managed to gather survivors and seek refuge in the neighbouring city of Canusium. Perhaps most importantly, within a few days a significant number of communities in southern Italy, hitherto allied with and loyal to Rome, began to defect. The battle of Cannae was indeed a major turning point in the Second Punic War, marking the end of its first stage, typified by large-scale clashes between Hannibalic and Roman armies in Italy, and the beginning of its second stage, a war of attrition whose outcome hung in the balance at least until 211, when the tide of war turned decidedly against Hannibal.

Viewed in a broader context, the battle of Cannae and the subsequent defection and reconquest of Rome's Italian allies can also be understood as a significant point of transition in a much longer development. That is, the last two decades of the third century, occupied largely by the Second Punic

---

[1] All subsequent dates are 'BC' unless otherwise noted.

[2] According to a fragment of Claudius Quadrigarius (Beck and Walter, *FRH* 14 F52 = fr. 53 Peter, from Gell. 5.17.5; see also Macrob. *Sat.* 1.16.26) Cannae was fought on 2 August 216. This book adopts the position that the Roman calendar was running well in advance of the seasons in the early years of the war, with 2 August on the Roman calendar probably equating to around 1 July on the solar calendar in 216 (following the calculations of Derow 1976). Although the accuracy of the Roman calendar during the Second Punic War is highly debated, few if any of the arguments in this book rest on the outcome.

War, stand in many ways as the closing act in the Roman conquest of the Italian peninsula south of the Po and Rubicon rivers, a process that had begun in earnest in the middle of the fourth century. From this perspective the Second Punic War was not only a 'global' conflict between two powerful Mediterranean states; rather, the war also shaped the local diplomatic and political context, providing an opportunity for Italian communities to exercise independent foreign policy and to break free from Roman rule. At the 'global' level, Rome's ultimate victory after Hannibal's crushing success in the early stages of the war paved the way for its conquest of the Mediterranean. Rome entered the Second Punic War as the dominant city in Italy and a regional hegemon, yet emerged as a 'world power'.[3] At the local level, Hannibal's strategic failure essentially signalled the end of Italian independence. Disloyal Italian states were reconquered and in many cases severely punished, and the post-war settlement allowed the senate to consolidate its position vis-à-vis the Italian allies. For more than a century Roman hegemony in Italy was unchallenged by local threats or outside invaders until the time of the Social War and the final political integration of the peninsula.

The purpose of this book is to examine the Second Punic War from the local perspective of Rome's Italian allies, in particular the specific factors (military, political, economic, etc.) that convinced some allied states to remain loyal to Rome while others decided to defect. My analysis focuses, therefore, primarily on diplomacy. Certainly Hannibal's defeat (or, if one prefers, Rome's victory) can be explained at least in part by looking at tactics, strategy, logistics, command, military and political institutions, and so forth, and I will outline some of these approaches below. In addition, however, Hannibal's and Rome's relative successes in conducting negotiations with Italian cities, the policy decisions of those cities, and interstate relations between different Italian communities also shaped the course and outcome of the war. Put simply, Hannibal's inability to win over more Italian communities – a diplomatic concern – contributed significantly to his overall strategic failure in the Italian theatre of the war, and thus ultimately to Rome's victory over Carthage. Yet, as indicated above, Hannibalic–Italian (and Roman–Italian) diplomacy during the

---

[3] For a summary of Rome's rise from hegemon of Italy to Mediterranean power, see Crawford 1978: 43–57; Goldsworthy 2000: 316–21; see also Errington 1972: 119–28, according to whom, 'The seventeen years of the Second Punic War which led to the defeat of Carthage was the most decisive single phase of Rome's rise to world power' (p. 119). It should be noted that Rome was still consolidating its hold in the area of the Po Valley by placing colonies in northern Italy in the early second century (see Chapter 7, pp. 309–10).

Second Punic War cannot be divorced from the longer-term development of Roman power in Italy. Thus, this book situates the critical policy decisions made by the ruling classes of various Italian cities, especially in the wake of Cannae, in the context of interstate behaviour and patterns of diplomacy between the communities of the peninsula stretching back to the emergence of Rome as the hegemonic state in Italy in the fourth century. It is hoped that this analysis not only contributes to our understanding of the Second Punic War – a pivotal event in Mediterranean history – but also sheds light on Roman–Italian (and intra-Italian) relations during the period of the Roman conquest of Italy.

This book is organised broadly into three parts. Chapter 1 presents a series of related background discussions. I will briefly analyse Hannibal's strategy – his plan to break up the system of alliances between Rome and the cities in Italy – and various solutions proposed by modern scholars for why and how his strategy did not bring about a favourable outcome in the war. As we will see, such previous scholarship has gone a long way in explaining Hannibal's defeat in the Second Punic War, but it has not accounted adequately for the diplomatic aspect of his strategic failure. Chapter 1 also discusses the Roman conquest of Italy and the nature of Roman–Italian relations in the fourth and third centuries, thus foregrounding the events of the Second Punic War in the major developments of the preceding century. The nature of the ancient evidence is examined as well.

The core of the book, Chapters 2 to 5, deals with the pivotal phase of the Second Punic War. Each of these four chapters presents a regional case study: Apulia (Chapter 2), Campania (Chapter 3), Bruttium and western Magna Graecia (Chapter 4) and southern Lucania and eastern Magna Graecia (Chapter 5). The organisation follows Hannibal's path, both geographically and chronologically, throughout southern Italy as he tried to elicit allied defections after the battle of Cannae (between 216 and 212). In all four regions Hannibal's diplomatic success was in some way limited. Between 216 and 215 he and his lieutenants convinced a significant number of cities in Apulia, Campania and the 'toe' of Italy to rebel from Rome, but at no point did all of the cities in any of these regions defect. He was more successful in southern Lucania and eastern Magna Graecia, as every major city between Thurii and Taras switched sides. Yet this success was belated, since he did not begin to win these cities over until late 213 and early 212, and even then he was never able to control the citadel of the region's most important city, Taras.

That Hannibal's diplomatic success in these regions was mixed makes them intriguing subjects for analysing what particular conditions, factors and considerations convinced individual cities to choose different courses of action in the middle years of the Second Punic War. For each region I attempt to identify, as much as the sources allow, the specific and in some cases unique circumstances that shaped the decision of each city to remain loyal to Rome or to ally with Hannibal. What emerges is a picture of individual self-interested communities responding to the immediate internal and external pressures brought on by a changing military, diplomatic and political landscape. As I will discuss below, this is rather more nuanced than typical interpretations of Italian (dis)loyalty, which tend towards blanket explanations. At the same time, attempting to understand the Second Punic War from the perspective of these individual communities requires tracing, as much as possible, longer-term local political and diplomatic developments, which were often complex and multipolar. Thus, my analysis maps out the history of each city in a given region and especially that city's relationships with surrounding communities to see how local intercity rivalries, bonds or other diplomatic patterns informed its disposition in the Second Punic War. Such an approach is made possible by the fact that many of the communities in the regions studied in Chapters 2 to 5 were involved at various times in Rome's campaigns against the Samnites and against Pyrrhus, for which we have a good deal of literary evidence. Moreover, ancient literary sources also make occasional reference to tensions and conflicts independent of Rome between various cities and groups within the four regions under examination. Finally, significant archaeological research in southern Italy in the last thirty-five years or so has revealed much about long-term economic and demographic developments, which further adds to our understanding of the 'back story' to these cities in the Second Punic War.[4] Overall, therefore, while the case studies appear to be concerned only with events within a narrow chronological period in the late third century, they explore and elucidate a much larger swathe of the historical canvas.

The third part of this book, Chapters 6 and 7, considers how events played out after the cities in these four regions made their initial policy decisions following Cannae, responding either positively or negatively to Hannibal's overtures. Both long-term and short-term implications are considered, so once again this third section operates on two levels. Chapter 6 is a synthetic discussion of the difficulties Hannibal faced after he achieved only partial success in these four regions, focusing on the years 214 to 204,

---

[4] The problematic nature of the ancient literary sources and the methodological difficulties in relating archaeological data to the literary evidence will be discussed below (pp. 5–13).

by which time nearly all of the defecting cities had been reconquered by Rome, forcing Hannibal to operate in an increasingly restricted corner of the peninsula. He was never able to lure the Romans into another potentially decisive battle after 216, nor to elicit enough allied revolts to force Rome to the bargaining table, so the conflict in Italy turned into a war of attrition that played increasingly to Roman strategic advantages. At the same time, some of the very same local conditions that Hannibal successfully manipulated in order to win over some of Rome's Italian allies, such as local intercity rivalries and intra-city political factionalism, contributed, ironically, to his inability to hold those cities.

Chapter 7 points ahead to how the Roman response to the cities that defected during the Second Punic War shaped developments in Roman–Italian relations in the second century.[5] The post-war settlement included the punishment of local elites who had promoted revolt, but also rewards for those members of the same class who convinced the Romans of their fidelity. This environment encouraged local aristocrats to forge stronger ties with members of the Roman aristocracy in order to secure their own political standing, which over time promoted fuller incorporation and unification. I will also consider what circumstances and policies allowed Rome to overcome the sorts of interstate tensions that bedevilled Hannibal and discuss what Hannibal might have done differently to win over more Italian allies, especially in those areas that remained more firmly loyal to Rome throughout the war (e.g. Etruria and Umbria).

SOURCES, PROBLEMS AND METHODOLOGIES

It is necessary to discuss briefly the problematic nature of the primary evidence brought to bear in the pages that follow. Of course, any ancient source, be it a literary text or not, should be approached with a cautious and critical eye, but this is especially true when dealing with the highly inconsistent sources for Roman (and Italian) history in the fourth and third centuries. Indeed, technical discussions weighing the relative historicity of individual passages or considering the relevant significance of archaeological data are found throughout this book; they are too numerous to be listed and summarised here, and the reader will have to judge the merits of the specific arguments as they are confronted. Still, it is appropriate to discuss in more general terms some of the major challenges posed

---

[5] For more on these relations see now Bispham 2007: esp. 74–160.

by the ancient evidence for this period, both literary and material, and the respective approaches that will be taken in this book to deal with them.

It must be admitted that the surviving relevant ancient texts for the period in question were written considerably later than the events they describe in the fourth and third centuries, though they contain occasional fragments of contemporary or near-contemporary sources. This is particularly the case with the surviving accounts of Rome's wars against the Samnites and the corresponding spread of Roman power into Campania and Apulia (*c.* 340–290), which provide much of the critical information for our reconstruction of the regional histories and long-term patterns of interstate behaviour that shaped events later in the Second Punic War. For this era we must rely heavily on the second pentad of Livy's *Ab urbe condita*, the only unbroken narrative source for Roman Italy in this period, supplemented by the accounts of Diodorus Siculus, Dionysius of Halicarnassus, Cassius Dio/Zonaras and Appian, as well as a host of references gleaned from other, non-narrative sources (such as Strabo). Yet, despite the wide range of literary sources cited, Livy ultimately provides the backbone of the narrative, and thus also of our analysis of the later fourth and early third centuries.

The trustworthiness of Livy's account of this period is not a given: he wrote three centuries after the fact, relying on sources that were themselves late, derivative and problematic. The following are just some of the weaknesses of Livy and the historiographic tradition on which he based the narrative found in Books 6–10.[6] Livy (or his sources) tends both to glorify the achievements of Rome and to exonerate the Romans from any blame in the many wars they fought. It is assumed that he at least occasionally magnified, if not entirely fabricated, Roman victories, while downplaying or even suppressing altogether Roman military setbacks. Roman sources are also guilty of anachronism and retrojection, imposing later events, developments and concerns onto Rome's earlier history. Since Roman historiography began only with the work of Fabius Pictor (*fl. c.* 210–200), we need to ask what sorts of information, accounts and documents for the fourth century were available to Livy, either directly or through the sources that he consulted. Thus, we are left to ask: just how much genuine fourth- and early third-century material is preserved in the surviving accounts of Livy (principally) and the other ancient authors?

---

[6] For a thorough discussion of Livy's sources and the literary techniques used by authors of the 'annalistic tradition', see Oakley 1997–2005: I.13–108 (esp. 72–99), on which much of the following discussion is based. See also Briscoe 1971; Oakley 1997–2005: IV.473–92.

This question has generated a spirited scholarly debate, which has intensified in the last decade or so with renewed scholarly interest in the history
of the early (and 'early middle') Republic. Historians have tended to adopt
one of two opposing approaches, the 'conservative' and the 'sceptical', to
borrow Oakley's terminology.[7] Among recent scholars writing in English,
Cornell (1989c, 1995b) and Forsythe (2005), respectively, represent these two
approaches, though neither to the extreme. For Cornell, the ancient literary
tradition for Rome's early history (down to the First Punic War) preserves a
significant historical core – kernels of truth that form the narrative framework – upon which additional layers of narrative detail and embellishment
have been superimposed. This approach, while not uncritical, tends to be
more trusting of the narrative sources than the 'hypercritical' approach of
past generations, who assumed that ancient authors invented the bulk of
early Roman history. While Forsythe does not completely follow in the
footsteps of the hypercritics, he is far more doubtful about the historicity
of the literary tradition. Thus, he tackles the sources for the same period
through a hermeneutic of suspicion: assuming rather more Roman chauvinism, embellishment, manipulation, and outright invention and fabrication within the literary record than do his more trusting colleagues.[8]

This book in general follows the 'middle path' between these two
approaches. It would be naïve to accept every narrative detail in the
ancient sources at face value.[9] Livy's account in Books 6–10 contains
obvious cases of invention, such as lengthy speeches ascribed to famous
Roman (and some non-Roman) generals. At the same time, the analysis
in this book assumes that the sources have preserved a good deal of fac-
tual information, including the names of magistrates and the locations of
battles and captured cities, some of which are so obscure that their very
mention argues against fabrication.[10] As indicated above, Livy's narrative
is the main source for much of the present discussion of the fourth and
early third centuries. He relied on as many as six early Roman sources for
this period; these include Fabius Pictor, who was born in the middle of

---

[7] Oakley 1997–2005: 1.100–4, citing Beloch 1926 and Salmon 1967 as 'too critical' while commend-
ing the balanced methods of De Sanctis 1956–69, Harris 1971 and Cornell 1989a, 1989b, 1989c; see
also Cornell 1995a: 1–30, 2004. For a similar approach, see Ogilvie and Drummond 1989.

[8] Also highly critical: Wiseman 1979, though see reviews by Briscoe 1981b and Cornell 1982.

[9] Thus, for example, in her analysis of Rome's foreign policy in the era of the Pyrrhic War, Hof
2002 tends to assume the reliability of such sources in the absence of explicit counter-evidence.

[10] For arguments on the authenticity of references to such obscure places, see Harris 1971: 60;
Oakley 1997–2005: 1.63–7. Indeed, Livy's account appears on the whole much more trustworthy
for the period dealing with the Samnite Wars, especially from the outbreak of the Third Samnite
War.

the third century and would probably have known men who were alive or even active during the Third Samnite War, and whose fathers and grandfathers lived during the Second Samnite War and earlier.[11] Moreover, such information as the names of magistrates and triumphators, the foundations of colonies, the creation of new tribes, and so on, were probably recorded in official records, such as the Pontifical Tables.[12] Roman aristocratic families kept records of their ancestors' deeds, though the historical quality of these family histories must have been uneven and especially liable to intentional embellishment.[13] In addition, Rome's urban landscape was littered with monuments, both public and private, with inscriptions (including the consular and triumphal *fasti)* and in some cases even visual depictions that provided information about deeds of the past. Livy's sources may even have had access to occasional local histories or chronicles of locales in the Greek-speaking part of Italy. Overall, a good deal of genuine material must have passed from archival and oral sources into the early annalistic sources, and eventually into the accounts of later authors.[14] Livy himself comments (6.1.1–3) on the improved quality of his sources for the period after the Gallic sack of Rome in about 390. In a number of places he preserves multiple versions of the same event, which allows the modern reader a chance to evaluate his sources and select the more plausible.[15] We are fortunate that Appian, Dionysius

[11] I follow the traditional convention in employing the terms First, Second and Third Samnite Wars as a matter of convenience. The terminology is, however, problematic: see below n. 31. On Fabius Pictor and the potential pathways for the preservation and transmission of authentic information, see Luce 1977: 139–84; Ungern-Sternberg and Reinau 1988; Cornell 1995a: 1–30; Oakley 1997–2005: 1.21–72; Beck and Walter 2001: 1.17–52, esp. 27–37; Forsythe 2005: 59–77. Livy explicitly cites Fabius Pictor, Piso, Claudius Quadrigarius, Licinius Macer and Aelius Tubero as sources for Books 6–10, and he probably also consulted Valerias Antias: Oakley 1997–2005: 1.13–16.

[12] Whatever one thinks about when the Pontifex Maximus stopped keeping annual records, or whether the *Annales Maximi* were published by P. Mucius Scaevola or some later author, there is little doubt that the Pontifical Tables were recorded from an early date (perhaps the fifth century if not earlier), probably transcribed into a chronicle or onto more durable material (also at an early date), and were an important source of information for the early Roman historians: see Rawson 1971 (who is more pessimistic about the survival of Pontifical material in Livy's narrative); Wiseman 1979: 9–26; Bucher 1987; Drews 1988; Oakley 1997–2005: 1.24–7; Frier 1999 (originally published in 1979); Beck and Walter 2001: 1.32–7.

[13] On falsehoods and exaggerations in family histories, which may have crept into the literary historical record, see especially Ridley 1983.

[14] Note for example Rich's (2005) recent re-evaluation of Valerias Antias, emphasising his archival research and use of archival material, contra Badian 1966 (among others). Rich also observes that '[m]uch of Livy's domestic material must derive ultimately from archival sources, particularly the routine material on such matters as provinces, armies and prodigies. The most important archive for this purpose would have been the reports of the senate's decrees …' (p. 156).

[15] Oakley 1997–2005: 1.13–16 provides a list of all variants that Livy cites, though he notes that they rarely differ greatly. In some cases, however, the versions differ significantly, such as 8.37.3–6,

of Halicarnassus, Diodorus Siculus, Valerius Maximus, Cassius Dio/ Zonaras and Polybius contain relevant passages that are either parallel to or even independent of Livy's account; in both cases they offer potential external checks on the dominant Livian narrative.[16] Indeed, it is remarkable how often Oakley's magisterial four-volume commentary on Books 6–10 of *Ab urbe condita* – a work of inestimable value to the research and writing of this book – demonstrates the plausibility of the core Livian narrative.[17] Overall, therefore, although the second half of the fourth century lay at the very fringes of the Roman historical tradition, we need not despair entirely at the quality of our sources, even though they must be dealt with cautiously.

In contrast to the rather abundant, albeit problematic literary source material for the period down to about 290, there is a relative lacuna in our sources for events in Italy during much of the middle of the third century, the period from the end of the Third Samnite War to the outbreak of the Second Punic War. However problematic Livy's extant history may be, the loss of Books 11–20 (covering the years 292 to 220) is regrettable, as we are left to rely instead on the rudimentary outline provided by the *periochae* of these books. Similarly, Diodorus Siculus' account breaks off in 302 except for a few fragments. Dionysius' Ῥωμαικὴ ἀρχαιολογία originally covered the period down to 264, but all that survives concerning the third century are significant fragments dealing with the Third Samnite War and the Pyrrhic War. In addition, Plutarch, Cassius Dio/ Zonaras and Appian offer detailed if tendentious accounts of Pyrrhus' invasion of Italy. The fragmentary narrative of Cassius Dio/Zonaras does cover the Roman activities in the northern and southern peninsula in the 270s and 260s, though from 264 it focuses almost exclusively

---

where his sources disagreed whether a Roman army was sent to fight the Apulians or to defend them against the Samnites.

[16] For example, Livy (8.22–3) and Dionysius (16.5–6) record parallel accounts of the events surrounding Naples in 328/7. According to Oakley 1997–2005: 1.38, Dionysius' version is derived ultimately from a Greek source. This episode will be discussed at greater length in Chapter 3.

[17] In fact, the overall tenor of Oakley's introductory chapters on Livy's sources and the early Roman historical tradition is, perhaps surprisingly, one of cautious optimism regarding the preservation of authentic historical material. It should be noted that Oakley amends some of his specific arguments in the relevant section of his *addenda* and *corrigenda* (1997–2005: IV.474–92), but his overall position on the survival of some authentic historical material even from before the third century remains relatively unaffected by his additional arguments. Indeed, in the *addenda* and *corrigenda*, Oakley calls attention to the potential role of aristocratic funerals and dramatic performances in forming a Roman national story that included at least some historical material, especially from the late fourth century, though he expresses overall scepticism about oral tradition as a channel for conveying 'reliable facts' from a much earlier period (1997–2005: IV.478–9). His most recent thoughts on the topic are found in Oakley 2009.

on Roman–Carthaginian relations at the expense of Italian affairs.[18] Similarly, Polybius effectively starts his history with the events leading up to the First Punic War, but he glosses briefly over the war with Pyrrhus and otherwise makes only a few passing references to Italian cities (other than Rome) before the Second Punic War. Overall, Italian affairs in the third century, particularly the fifty years or so after Pyrrhus left Italy for good, are rather unevenly documented.[19]

This gap in the narrative sources for the middle of the third century poses a formidable but not completely intractable problem. The various sources for Pyrrhus' Italian campaign do provide evidence for local politics and interstate relations in southern Italy, especially among the southern Italian Greek cities, in the early third century, even if the coverage of Italian matters between Pyrrhus and Hannibal is spotty at best. In addition to the major narrative texts already discussed, some information about the third century can be gleaned from a range of minor literary sources, such as Strabo's *Geography*, Pliny's *Natural History*, Justin's *Epitome of Pompeius Trogus*, Orosius' *Histories against the Pagans*, and the enigmatic, anonymous *Liber coloniarum*. Although these additional sources are generally very late, tralatitious in nature, of uneven historical scope and sometimes belonging to genres outside those typically associated with historical narrative, some genuine third-century nuggets may be extracted through a critical reading, on a case-by-case basis. It is the contention throughout this book that enough authentic material survives for us to be able to combine it with the fuller evidence for the late fourth and late third centuries and thus interpolate processes and developments in the early and middle part of the third century.

Source material for the later third century, composed primarily of accounts of the Second Punic War, is much more abundant: for this period we have at our disposal Polybius and Livy, supplemented by Appian, Cassius Dio/Zonaras, Plutarch and scattered notes in other sources. Unfortunately, Polybius' continuous narrative of the Second Punic War breaks off after his account of the battle of Cannae, so that, with the exception of a few fragmentary passages, we are forced to rely mostly on later sources of often lesser quality for Italian affairs in the middle and later years of the war. Therefore, Livy's narrative (especially Books 23–9) once again provides the bulk of the data for our analysis of the internal politics and policy decisions of Rome's allies from the wake of Cannae until the

---

[18] Interestingly, Bleckmann 2002 has recently argued that Dio/Zonaras is a superior source to Polybius for the period of the First Punic War, but see the critical review by Hoyos 2004b.
[19] The fragmentary sources for 292–265 have been collected by Marina Torelli 1978.

Roman reconquest of all states that chose to defect, and these books suffer from many of the same deficiencies that I have discussed above.[20]

All the same, the events of the Second Punic War took place much closer to when Livy's sources wrote, and there is reason to believe that a good deal of authentic information made its way into his account. He drew either directly or indirectly on contemporary and near-contemporary authorities, including Fabius Pictor (who fought in the war), Cincius Alimentus (a Roman senator captured by Hannibal), Coelius Antipater (who wrote an account of the war around 130), Silenus and Sosylus (Greek historians who accompanied Hannibal in Italy) and Polybius.[21] In particular, Cincius Alimentus, Silenus and Sosylus probably recorded important information about Hannibal's diplomacy and the situation within the walls of the cities in southern Italy.[22] There is also evidence that some Roman archival material, potentially containing information about local politics in some of the cities that defected, survived into the first century – Livy or (more likely) his sources may have consulted these documents.[23] Finally, we are not totally dependent on Livy's narrative for the years after 216: Appian, Cassius Dio/Zonaras and a few fragments of Polybius record some additional information and in some cases different details from Livy, perhaps representing variant source traditions.[24] Obviously, narrative details should not simply be accepted at face value. Yet it seems excessively sceptical to assume that all narrative details in Livy and other later sources are necessarily distorted or fabricated unless proven otherwise. When determining the veracity of a piece of information from an ancient source, we must consider if it is inherently plausible, if it forms part of an internally coherent

[20] The deficiencies of Livy's third decade are laid out in concise and sobering fashion by Walsh 1982.
[21] Burck 1971: 26–8; Luce 1977: 178–81; see also Huss 1985: 284–5; Astin 1989: 3–11; for the argument that Livy used Polybius for Sicilian and African affairs, and even for some Italian affairs, Luce follows Klotz 1951 contra Tränkle 1972. For Cincius Alimentus, see Frier 1999: 206–7, 238–9; Beck and Walter 2001: I.137–8; Habinek 2007. For Coelius Antipater, see Tränkle 1977: 222–8; Beck and Walter 2001: II.35–9.
[22] See Walbank 1970: I.26–34, esp. 28–9.
[23] Two examples will suffice. First, Livy (28.46.16) states that Hannibal erected an altar near the temple of Lacinian Juno (near Locri) and set up an inscribed record of his achievements in Greek and Punic; Polybius also mentions the inscription (3.56.4; cf. 3.33.18). The inscription probably was first recorded by Silenus, though it is unclear whether his notice came to Livy via Polybius or Coelius: Walbank 1970: I.364–5. Second, Cicero (*Leg. agr.* 2.88) mentions the existence of records of the senatorial debate in 210 about the fate of Capua; see also Chapter 3, pp. 102–3.
[24] For example, Appian and Livy give different reasons for the revolt of Thurii; see Chapter 5, pp. 223–4. For general a discussion of Appian, see especially Brodersen 1993. Hahn 1972 argues that Appian's major source for the Hannibalic War was Fabius Pictor, while Leidl 1996: 299–304 holds that Appian's account of the Second Punic War in Spain can be used judiciously to supplement Polybius and Livy.

narrative, if it finds confirmation from an independent source and/or if it is consistent with the ancient author's broader themes.[25] The approach in this book is to make such evaluations on a case-by-case basis.[26]

Finally, we must consider the challenges posed by interpreting and integrating different types of evidence. The material remains of human cultural activity, such as coins, inscriptions, ceramics and even the traces of buildings, defensive walls or other monumental architecture, hold great potential to enhance our understanding of ancient history; indeed, archaeological evidence is vitally important for examining periods for which the literary record is particularly inadequate or even non-existent. This book has benefited from the sustained archaeological research conducted in southern Italy since the middle of the twentieth century, which has unearthed an enormous quantity of data.[27] Yet the interpretation of the data is not without its own particular obstacles. There is on the one hand the temptation to stitch together disparate bits of archaeological data simply to fill the gaps in the literary record, or to use archaeological evidence merely to confirm the picture drawn in literary sources. On the other hand, there is the danger in seeing archaeology as a sort of independent check on literary evidence, and thus attempting to draw conclusions based on material evidence studied in isolation from literary evidence.[28]

[25] That is, if an ancient author tends to treat a subject in a particular fashion, for example Livy's theme (23.14.7, 24.2.8) that the lower classes always supported Hannibal and the elite favoured Rome, references in the author's work that are potentially embarrassing to his thesis may represent authentic historical data that slipped through the editorial process or were simply too widely accepted to leave out.

[26] This is especially the case for the central section of this book, where sources are brought to bear that reveal the internal politics of Italian cities during the Second Punic War. For these episodes we may speculate on how authentic notices may have worked their way into Livy's (and others') narrative. Perhaps sources close to the events had gained some knowledge of Italian affairs (Cincius, for example, was active around Locri) and this material was transmitted indirectly to Livy or others. In most cases, however, we simply do not know what Livy's sources were for Italian affairs, and thus we must judge on its own merits each of the relevant episodes that he narrates.

[27] It would be impossible to list all of the excavations and surveys conducted in the last thirty or forty years, or to make reference to all of their associated publications. For an overview of trends in archaeological research in southern Italy, see Curti, Dench and Patterson 1996. There have been numerous regional studies (such as Salmon 1967; Frederiksen 1984; Mazzei 1984a; Volpe 1990; Arthur 1991a; Lamboley 1996; Isayev 2007) and city/settlement studies (Small and Buck 1994; Mertens and Volpe 1999; and the now nearly forty publications from the *Forma Italiae* project of the Università degli Studi di Roma 'La Sapienza').

[28] For recent discussions of some of the methodological difficulties in integrating literary and material evidence, and the unfortunate tendency of ancient historians and classical archaeologists to assert the primacy of one or the other sort of evidence, see Herring 2000: 46–7; Williams 2001: 185–7; Dench 2004: 13–18.

As with the use of literary evidence, this book steers a middle path in its reliance on archaeology. For the period under examination, it is nearly impossible to divorce material evidence from literary evidence, since the very gathering and interpretation of archaeological data from any historical era tends to be informed by the interpretive framework provided by literary sources. Indeed, there is no need to seek such an explicit division between types of evidence. Instead, this book adopts Finley's view that the relationship between history and archaeology is not one of 'two distinctly different disciplines but [rather] two kinds of evidence about the past, two kinds of historical evidence'. Depending on the specific context or question, material evidence or literary evidence may take precedence, but there are also many 'contexts in which the two types of evidence have to be deployed together so closely that in a sense neither is of much use without the other'.[29] Since this book tends to focus on political and diplomatic affairs, it will more often employ literary texts as the major source of evidence. Nevertheless, political decisions are not infrequently informed by economic, demographic or cultural developments, which archaeological evidence may be more instrumental in elucidating. Thus, it is not my intention to relegate archaeology to the role of 'handmaiden of history', nor to establish the general primacy of one sort of evidence over another, but instead to marshal all available evidence to shed light on Italy in the fourth and third centuries. It is to this period, the century or so before Hannibal's invasion of Italy, that we now turn our attention.

ROME AND THE ITALIANS, *CIRCA* 350–220

As suggested above (pp. 1–4), the varied responses of Rome's allies to Hannibal's invasion of Italy must be placed in the broader historical context of the Roman conquest of the peninsula and subsequent consolidation of power in the late fourth to third centuries. On the one hand, this dynamic revealed itself differently from region to region and city to city, such that the specific local history of a given community produced a unique set of circumstances, which in turn yielded particular reactions to Hannibal's overtures. Thus, to understand why a city acted as it did

[29] Finley 1986: 7–26 (both quotations on p. 20); see also Finley 1971. Dench, Herring and Williams (see n. 28) suggest, broadly, a similar methodological approach. Attema 2000 is an interesting exercise in synthesising literary and archaeological evidence, which concludes that Livy's description (in Books 1–10) of the central Italian landscape and Rome's early expansion against the Latins and Etruscans is consistent with recent archaeological findings. See also various essays in Sauer's (2004a) volume, *Archaeology and Ancient History: Breaking down the Boundaries,* especially Sauer 2004b.

during the Second Punic War, we need to consider its distinct story within the broader narrative of the extension of Roman power in the previous century or so, when Rome gradually transformed scattered regional affairs into a series of bilateral relationships. For each Italian community, therefore, we must examine its particular bilateral relationship with Rome and its interaction with surrounding states at least as much as the sources will allow. On the other hand, a number of general patterns can be observed, albeit with specific local variations. Thus, I will briefly trace the course of Rome's conquest of Italy and highlight some of the important themes in the development of Roman–Italian relations from around 350 to 220. These general themes and patterns will re-emerge throughout this book, finding their particular local expressions in the regional case studies comprising the central four chapters.

The first half of this period down to around 270 saw the Romans engaged in sustained fighting, leading to the subjugation of nearly all the communities of the peninsula south of the Po and Rubicon.[30] This era is dominated in the extant sources by the so-called Samnite Wars – the First (343–341), Second (327–304, with a truce 321–316), and Third (298–290) – and the Pyrrhic War (280–275).[31] The first three were a difficult series of conflicts that pitted the Romans against a coalition of Samnite communities in the south-central Apennines, and also brought Rome into increasing contact with the inhabitants of Campania and Apulia, who all (or mostly all) submitted to Rome by the end of the Second Samnite War. Starting around 311, the Romans also turned their attention to Etruria and Umbria and defeated a number of cities lying along the Chiani, the upper Tiber and Lake Trasimene, including (probably) Volsinii, Perusia, Cortona, Arretium and Clusium. By the end of the fourth century Rome extended its hold across the central Appenines, as the Hernici, Aequi, Marsi, Paeligni, Marrucini and Frentani submitted to Rome, whether peacefully or by the sword. Roman alliances with at least some of the Lucanians may have triggered the Third Samnite War, during which the

---

[30] The following outline of the Samnite Wars and the conquest of northern Italy follows Cornell 1989a: 351–91; for additional details, see also Salmon 1967: 187–279; Cornell 1995a: 345–63.

[31] This division of the nearly annual hostilities between the Romans and Samnites into distinct 'wars' is to a great degree a modern construct; the ancient sources do not neatly divide events in this way but rather refer to a single great conflict between the two combatants lasting for half a century; see Cornell 2004: 121–3. I will retain these terms, however, as a matter of convenience. The historicity of the details of the First Samnite War, as presented in surviving ancient accounts, has been doubted (for example, Beloch 1926: 371; Salmon 1967: 197–201), and indeed Adcock 1928: 588 denied that the war took place at all. Such scepticism is extreme, and most scholars accept that some conflict (or conflicts) took place, even if the events have been distorted in our Roman sources.

Romans were able to defeat – with difficulty – a coalition of Samnites, Etruscans, Umbrians and Gauls. While the Samnites were conquered by 290, fighting continued in Etruria and Umbria at least sporadically into the 260s. Sometime between 290 and around 285 the Sabines and Praetuttii were incorporated as 'citizens without the vote'; the inhabitants of Picenum joined them by about 270.

Rome's growing power drew the attention of the Italiotes, citizens of the Greek cities of southern Italy.[32] Rhegion and Thurii appear to have appealed to the Romans for protection against neighbouring Lucanians and Bruttians, and Rome's willingness to oblige brought it directly into Italiote affairs. In 282 the Romans went to war against Taras, the most powerful Italiote city. The exact reasons for the conflict will be discussed in greater depth in Chapter 5, but for now it will suffice to mention only that the coming war with Rome encouraged the Tarentines to appeal to Pyrrhus, the king of Epirus, for protection. Pyrrhus subsequently invaded Italy and, along with the Tarentines, joined forces with a variety of peoples already at war with Rome, including Samnites, Lucanians and Bruttians. Pyrrhus' invasion and early success encouraged additional defections by a number of Italiote cities and perhaps some Oscan-speaking communities.[33] Although Pyrrhus enjoyed initial success against Rome, he eventually conceded Italy by 275, leaving his allies to fend for themselves. Rome, capitalising on his departure, subjugated the southern Greeks, including the Tarentines in 272 and the Samnites, Lucanians and Bruttians by around 270 (or soon thereafter). The latter peoples appear to have suffered

---

[32] The following outline of the Pyrrhic War and the subsequent Roman conquest of southern Italy follows Franke 1989; Staveley 1989: 420–5; Cornell 1995a: 363–4; see also Salmon 1967: 280–92. Ancient sources for the Pyrrhic War: Diod. Sic. 20.1–11; App. *Sam.* 9.1–12.2; Plut. *Pyrrh.* 16.1–26.2; Dion. Hal. 19.8–20.12; Liv. *Per.* 12–14; Zon. 8.4–6; Cass. Dio 9–10.

[33] The Romans had already begun campaigns against the Lucanians, Samnites and Bruttians by 282, before the arrival of Pyrrhus: Liv. *Per.* 12; Dion. Hal. 19.6, 16; App. *Sam.* 7.3. It is unlikely that the Romans were at war with *all* of the Lucanians, Samnites and Bruttians in 282–280, so it is possible that some previously quiescent communities rose up only after Pyrrhus' arrival and initial military success. Plutarch (*Pyrrh.* 17.5) reports that 'many of the Lucanians and Samnites came to [Pyrrhus] after the battle' (ἀφίκοντο δ᾿ αὐτῷ Λευκανῶν τε πολλοὶ καὶ Σαυνιτῶν μετὰ τὴν μάχην) of Heraclea, whom he chastised for showing up late. These may refer to the allies (οἱ σύμμαχοι) who had not yet joined him when he decided to engage the Romans at Heraclea (Plut. *Pyrrh.* 16.3), in which case these Oscan-speaking groups had already allied themselves with Pyrrhus before the battle. Yet Plutarch calls attention to the fact that Pyrrhus defeated the Romans with only Tarentine aid (*Pyrrh.* 17.5). Among non-Greeks, only the Messapians are named specifically as offering him assistance (when his ships supposedly ran ashore: *Pyrrh.* 15.5). Italiote cities besides Taras appear to have allied with Pyrrhus only after his victory at Heraclea (Plut. *Pyrrh.* 18.4). Some of Plutarch's late-arriving Samnites and Lucanians may, in fact, have included those who decided to defect only after Pyrrhus had won the battle. Or, it is possible that they were nominally allied with Pyrrhus but decided to hold back until the outcome of his first clash with the Romans was known.

particularly harsh territorial confiscations as a penalty for challenging Rome. The Roman conquest of Italy was essentially complete.

This sequence is fairly well known, and it is unnecessary at this time to elaborate on the narrative – the events as they pertain to the communities of southern Italy will be analysed in greater detail in the following chapters. Rather, I will focus briefly on the nature of interstate relations in this period, not only between Rome and the various cities that it eventually conquered, but also among the Italians themselves. Scholars have tended to emphasise Roman bellicosity and unilateral aggression, seeing these events as fitting into a narrative of the inexorable spread of Roman power at the expense of the communities of peninsular Italy, who in this version of the story are either reduced to helpless victims or elevated to a status of noble but doomed resistance.[34] This book assumes, however, that interstate relations in the late fourth and even the early third centuries were rather more contingent and multipolar. Rome was not the only aggressive and hegemonic state in the Italian peninsula, even though it found itself the most dominant by the time that Pyrrhus landed at Taras.[35] Instead, it would be more accurate to envision Italy as an 'international system' marked by endemic warfare, with all states engaged in fierce competition and some emerging as hegemons with the ability to project power and influence over neighbouring states.

This approach draws heavily on so-called Realist theories of international relations, and is particularly indebted to Arthur Eckstein's recent work, which applies Realist paradigms of state behaviour to the ancient Mediterranean world.[36] According to the Realist school of thought, international systems tend to be 'anarchic': no effective policing mechanism

[34] For the extreme bellicosity and aggression of Rome, the classic formulation is Harris 1979 (covering the period from the late fourth into the first century) and Harris 1990 (covering the period down through the fourth century). Harris' thesis has had profound influence; see, for example, Oakley 1993; Raaflaub 1996. For supposed Roman unilateral aggression, see, for example, Cornell 2004: 'In fact it is clear from an unbiased reading of the sources ... that the Samnites cannot be shown to have attacked the Romans or their allies except as part of a defensive response to Roman imperialism' (p. 128, citing Harris 1979: 177). For a discussion of the tendency of some scholars to heroicise the resistance of Italic peoples, such as the Samnites, to Rome, see Dench 2004: 18–21 (referring in particular to Salmon). Roman particularism is a running theme in the recent edited volume by Dillon and Welch 2006; see Fronda 2007b.

[35] For example, Tarquinii and Volsinii attacked Sutrium in 311: Liv. 9.32–3, 9.35; Diod. Sic. 20.35.5; cited by Eckstein 2006: 128, who notes that even Harris 1971: 53, 58 accepts the Etruscans as aggressors in this case.

[36] See especially Eckstein 2006, but also Eckstein 2003, 2008; Champion and Eckstein 2004. Perhaps the most prominent exponent of Realism in the last half-century has been Kenneth Waltz (1959, 1979, 1988, 2000). Mearsheimer 1995 offers a very good introduction to the various sub-schools of international Realism. For an excellent, concise summary, see Eckstein 2006: 12–36.

exists above the level of the individual state; there is no authority such as international law or world government that controls or regulates in a meaningful way how states treat each other. The only instruments regulating how states interact, therefore, are the states themselves. The second important Realist assumption is that states behave more or less as rational, unitary actors. Third, the primary motivation behind state behaviour is security, which most states try to achieve through the protection and accumulation of resources. Thus, neighbouring states will often find themselves at odds over access to natural resources. This competitive environment will frequently produce hierarchies wherein relations between states are shaped by their relative power: major powers will compete with each other at the top of the hierarchy, while smaller states will often join together to balance against a more powerful, aggressive neighbour.[37] Such alliances are driven by necessity and self-interest, and they last only so long as the perceived common threat exists. In more extreme cases, very weak states will be compelled to submit to a more powerful state in order to maintain their own survival. In all cases, states generally attempt to maximise their resources and security within a limited menu of options dictated largely by the amount of relative power each can bring to bear.

The Realist approach to interstate relations applies well to Italy in the late fourth and early third centuries.[38] Although the ancient sources tend to focus on Rome's growing power and its relations with the various communities, they also indicate clearly that Italian states fought each other, with local conflicts frequently predating Roman involvement in a given area; this will be discussed in greater detail in the following chapters.[39] Undoubtedly much of the warfare resulted from territorial disputes, since land was the most important natural resource for pre-modern agricultural societies. Moreover, there appears to have been significant change in settlement patterns throughout much of southern Italy by the end of the fourth century, which points to a generally higher degree of communal organisation. Some areas, especially those in close contact with nearby Greek

---

[37] The tendency is for small states to balance somewhat more frequently than to 'bandwagon' (to join forces with an aggressor): Walt 1987; see Eckstein 2006: 65–6 (for application to the ancient Greek context) and 66 n. 122 (for additional bibliography).

[38] It must be stressed that this book is the work of a historian, not a political scientist. The analyses found in the following chapters will not repeatedly refer back to Realist or other political science theories, nor will they make frequent use of cross-cultural comparisons. The basic tenets of the Realist paradigm, however, inform my understanding and interpretation of the ancient evidence.

[39] Intense internecine rivalry has long been recognised in Campania; see, for example, Cornell 1989a: 358–9. Specific local rivalries in Campania and the rest of southern Italy are discussed throughout Chapters 2 to 5.

colonies, such as Messapia and Apulia, witnessed the development of large nucleated centres not unlike *poleis*. In other areas, such as Lucania, emerging 'centre places', though probably not cities in the classical sense (that is, a *polis* or *urbs*), nevertheless exhibited a high degree of sophistication and social organisation: for example, massive stone fortifications, in some cases enclosing large areas and containing public buildings.[40] At many sites there is also evidence for a corresponding emergence of very wealthy, possibly hereditary elite families, such as monumental tombs containing multiple graves and wealthy burial goods. Overall, there appears to have been an increase in population throughout southern Italy in the fourth century.[41] All of these developments point to a more extensive and thorough exploitation of a community's surrounding territory, as the local population was compelled to extract surplus goods and food to support the political elite, the building of monumental architecture, and their own growing numbers. This process of urbanisation (or perhaps better, centralisation) certainly led to intensified conflict, as communities fought fiercely for limited resources while, at the same time, their greater level of organisation would have given them increased capacity to marshal resources for common projects, including war-making.[42] Furthermore, the ruling elite, whose political legitimacy was tied to wealth and success in war, would have been encouraged not only to protect their own lands but also to enrich themselves and their city by leading armies to conquer neighbouring cities, extend their own city's territory and bring back moveable wealth such as slaves and booty.

Finally, there were few, if any, institutions in place in this period to limit conflicts or to resolve them peacefully. There were a number of federal organisations: leagues or confederacies, such as the so-called Samnite League, Bruttian League and Etruscan League. These often served primarily religious functions, though they also provided mutual defence for league members. It is not clear how formally or efficiently these multi-state entities functioned, and in any case they do not seem to have eliminated

---

[40] For 'urbanisation' or 'centralisation' in southern Italy, see, for example, Gualtieri 1987; Volpe 1990: 36–45; Lomas 2000; Fracchia 2004; Gualtieri 2004; Barker 1995b: 181–212; Isayev 2007. This process varied greatly from region to region, and it would be misleading to imply that there was any one type of 'Italic' settlement, let alone one supposedly modelled on the *polis*-type.

[41] Fracchia 2004: 80–1.

[42] On urbanisation in Roman and pre-Roman Italy as an aggregative effect of warfare, see Cornell 1995b. Even if we do not call fortified places such as Samnite hill forts 'cities', the widespread building of artificial fortifications in the fourth and early third centuries not only shows that communities were investing resources in defence but also suggests real or at least perceived threats to the communities' security.

conflicts between league members.[43] In addition, as Eckstein notes, throughout the ancient Mediterranean world, interstate diplomacy was primitive, with negotiations generally taking the form of one or both sides publicly listing grievances and making demands.[44] Such 'public diplomacy of compellence' more often than not ratcheted up tension between states, leading almost inevitably to war rather than to peaceful resolution. The overall picture, therefore, is of a highly combustible interstate environment in which both internal and external factors promoted endemic competition, conflict and war.

As mentioned above, international systems will tend towards hierarchies featuring one or more dominant states: in a unipolar system a single superpower asserts hegemony over the entire system; bipolarity refers to a system with two powerful states, each of which asserts hegemony over the less powerful states in its own domain within the larger system; multipolarity refers to a system with many powerful states each asserting regional hegemony while at the same time competing for system-wide dominance. Until Rome finally defeated Pyrrhus and (re)asserted control over the bulk of the peninsula, Italy would be most accurately described as a multipolar system. We should not see Rome, then, as the only expansionist hegemonic state, but rather as one of a number of powerful states and coalitions competing to dominate the system. Also, Lemke (1996) has observed that within any international hierarchy there exist numerous regional or local hierarchies, each with its own unipolar, bipolar or multipolar arrangements. So even after Rome began to emerge as the most powerful state in Italy, pushing the entire system towards unipolarity – certainly by around 300 if not earlier – the peninsula as a whole could still be seen as a series of local or regional interstate systems within which one or a few states asserted, or attempted to assert, their own hegemony. For example, Arpi, Canusium and perhaps Teanum Apulum each dominated

---

[43] Indeed, the emergence of federal leagues in the late-classical Greek world further complicated interstate affairs. A hegemonic power within a federal structure might use the league's resources for its own imperial aims, either to defeat other hegemonic rivals or to subordinate further the weaker 'allies' within the league. In practical terms, such leagues may have led to *more* conflicts rather than fewer. See Beck 2008.

[44] Eckstein 2006: 59–63. Among the primitive features of diplomacy shared by all states in the ancient Mediterranean: states maintained no permanent diplomatic corps or group of experts; the general lack of information about foreign states' intentions and capabilities led to high levels of mistrust, as each state operated on 'worst case scenario' assumptions; diplomatic missions tended to be carried out only when a conflict reached a crisis point, when war was essentially unavoidable; diplomatic language tended to be blunt and confrontational, rather than sensitive or tactful; diplomatic exchanges tended to take place in public and amounted largely to grievances, counter-grievances and demands for redress.

a cluster of smaller communities in Apulia while vying with each other for regional supremacy.[45] Thus, a major theme in this book is that hegemonic aspirations and the desire by regional powers to extend their influence and acquire more resources in order to maximise security lurk behind the actions taken by the larger Italian cities, such as Capua, Taras or Arpi, and were not distinctly Roman motives for behaviour. Meanwhile, the behaviour of the other communities in a region must have been informed by the aggressive posture of powerful neighbours.

We can also speculate that competition and armed conflicts between regional hegemonic states, especially those with shared borders – such as Arpi and Canusium, mentioned above – surely led to grudges, mutual hatred and intense and often unresolved rivalry, even if this dynamic is not always noted explicitly in the primary sources. Such rivalry would have added to mistrust between states, lessening the chances that subsequent disputes between them could be solved peacefully. When one local hegemonic state gains a strategic advantage, it makes sense for its rivals to seek outside assistance in order to 'balance' against the emerging dominant power. This might lead to the development of a long-standing alliance between two or more states against the threat of a powerful rival. Such enduring alliances do not contradict the Realist paradigm, as the basic motivation behind their formation remains security.[46] In certain cases a local hegemonic power might severely threaten the security or even survival of its neighbours, which might compel its rivals to look for help from outside the local (or regional) system. Literary sources contain numerous examples of communities appealing to Rome for help against their local enemies, which should not be dismissed lightly as pro-Roman propaganda, for they fit squarely within the Realist model that we are assuming.[47] This is not to say that Rome was dragged unwillingly into local disputes. Rather

---

[45] For regional interstate hierarchy and hegemonic rivalry in Apulia, see Fronda 2006 and this book, Chapter 2.

[46] In the strictest Realist terms, alliances are expected to last only as long as the shared threat exists. In ancient Italy, as I have argued, the environment was highly competitive, leading to endemic conflict. If a rivalry developed between two states – or two clusters of states – it is possible they would become locked into a cycle of mistrust and conflict such that the perceived threat would never disappear. The alliances formed in response to the perceived threat could, therefore, also endure so long as the other conditions within the system did not change drastically. For a more thorough discussion, see Chapter 7, pp. 281–7.

[47] For example: the Sidicini supposedly tried to place themselves under Roman protection against the Samnites (Liv. 8.2.5–6); some Lucanians appealed to the Romans for protection against the Samnites (Liv. 10.11.11–13); the people of Thurii sought protection against the Lucanians (Liv. *Per.* 11). Livy's (7.29.4–7) account of the outbreak of the First Samnite War is particularly illustrative: the Samnites attacked the Sidicini, who sought protection from the Campanians; when the Samnites proved too formidable, the Campanians turned to the Romans for help.

the opposite: the Romans were undoubtedly as opportunistic as any other community in Italy, manipulating and exploiting local rivalries in order to justify their interference and extend their influence. Rome's intervention probably exacerbated local rivalries – perhaps favouring one state over its rival, leading to additional local tension and subsequent conflict, which in turn encouraged more Roman involvement. In any case, a second theme is the importance of local interstate rivalry in shaping how Italian communities interacted with each other and reacted to intervention by 'outside' powers, such as Rome, Pyrrhus and Hannibal.

Related to the foregoing discussion is a third important theme that recurs throughout the present work: that the cities of Italy remained generally disunited, competitive, mutually mistrusting, and lacking in common identity, even long after Rome had brought the entire peninsula under its control and suppressed, as far as we know, warfare between local states. This theme warrants additional attention, since the opposite – the apparent cohesiveness of Rome's Italian empire – is often assumed.[48] In order to evaluate this theme, I need to summarise briefly how Rome dealt with subordinate communities, whether they were conquered or came more willingly within its orbit.

According to Livy (8.14), the Romans reorganised this relationship in 338, though it is more likely that the settlement developed over a number of years. In any case, by the time the whole of the peninsula was conquered, certain general patterns were in place.[49] First, Rome made treaties or otherwise dealt with individual states; leagues and confederacies were

---

[48] For example, Cornell 1995a: 364–8 emphasises that Roman rule brought the allies certain benefits with relatively light burdens, concluding: 'By drawing up this kind of balance sheet it becomes possible to understand the loyalty of the allies to Rome, and to explain both the dynamics and the cohesiveness of the system' (p. 368). For David 1996: 35–53, Italy became unified under Roman rule because of the economic and cultural effects of the shared Hellenisation of the elite classes, so that in the third century Italy was transformed into a unified state – 'transformation de l'Italie en un état territorial' (p. 53 in the 1994 original French version, p. 43 in the 1996 translation in English). Salmon 1982: 57–72, esp. 71–2, however, downplays the cohesiveness of the 'Roman Commonwealth' of the third century.

[49] The following brief summary of the organisation of the subordinate Italian states is based on Staveley 1989: 420–36. It has often been assumed that the arrangement of allied states formed part of a project, more or less planned, to unite the peninsula under Roman hegemony. There has been the temptation, therefore, to assume that the organisation of the Italian states into a strict hierarchy of legal and/or treaty statuses was more systematic and intentional than may have been the case. This assumption can be traced back to nineteenth-century scholars such as Beloch 1880. Indeed, it is not at all clear that the status of *civitas sine suffragio* (for example) was 'higher' or 'more prestigious' than Latin citizenship or vice versa, and it is best to reject the notion of a 'strict hierarchy' of alliances. More recently, Hantos 1983 has argued that the Italian states can be grouped according to five patterns of obedience and integration, which Rome applied according to specific circumstances, not as part of a long-term plan to unite Italy, but rather in order to control and dominate the allies. Still, Hantos' five categories are themselves overly schematised.

dissolved, or they continued to function at the local level but their member states were tied to Rome by separate, individual treaties (or by other arrangements). Second, all subordinate communities were obliged during times of war to supply troops for the Roman army (or navy). In addition, some cities, usually those whom Rome had defeated, were forced to give up part of their territory, which was incorporated into the growing *ager Romanus*. Third, all subject peoples fell into one of a range of relationships with Rome based on the legal status of their community: full citizenship (*civitas optimo iure*), citizenship 'without the vote' (*civitas sine suffragio*), Latin-right cities, and allied cities. Communities with full citizenship included a number of cities in Latium that were incorporated into the Roman state but remained self-governing *municipia*,[50] and a series of small garrison colonies manned by Roman citizens (*colonia civium Romanorum*). All other subordinate cities were also self-governing. The inhabitants of cities possessing *civitas sine suffragio*, located mostly but not exclusively in Campania, were technically Roman citizens (*cives*); they possessed the rights of *commercium* and *conubium* and were obliged to serve in the Roman legions, but they could not vote in Roman assemblies or hold office in Rome. Latin cities possessed nearly identical rights to those of the *civitates sine suffragio*, including *conubium* and *commercium*. Unlike the cities without the vote, Latin cities were technically foreign (*peregrini*), so the troops that they contributed to the Roman army served not in the legions proper, but in associated allied contingents (*socii*). The Latin cities included some towns in Latium that were not incorporated as citizen *municipia*, as well as a string of strategically placed colonies, founded by former Roman citizens and probably some allies on land confiscated from the conquered. Finally, the allies (*socii*) were technically free communities whose citizens possessed neither Roman (in its various forms) nor Latin rights, so they did not enjoy the associated privileges. They were bound to Rome by individual treaties, which laid out the specific obligations and conditions of their relationship. It is likely that these terms varied from city to city, although this is not certain, but (as mentioned above) all allied cities were obliged to provide Rome with troops. This arrangement of dependent communities bound to Rome by treaties and various shared rights, privileges and obligations has been given various names, such as

---

[50] I use the term *municipium* to refer to any incorporated, self-governing community whose citizens possessed some form of Roman citizenship. Whether these communities were called *municipia* or something else (e.g. *oppidum civium Romanorum*) in the period before the Social War does not bear on the present discussion. In general, see: Sherwin-White 1973: 38–94, 200–14; Galsterer 1976: 64–84; Humbert 1978: esp. 1–43; Bispham 2007: 13–16, 103–12.

the 'Roman Commonwealth' or 'römische Bundesgenossensystem'. Either term implies too formal an organisation, so perhaps looser terminology, such as the Roman alliance network (or similar), is to be preferred.[51] Whatever term we choose to use, it might be expected that the Pyrrhic War marked a significant moment in the development of the relationship between Rome and its subject allies. For the first time Rome fought a major war against a Hellenistic king and, after a difficult struggle, emerged victorious and able to stake its claim as a major player in the broader Mediterranean world.[52] At the same time, there is some indication that the Romans increasingly saw Italy – the peninsula south of the Po, including lands that were not technically part of the *ager Romanus* – not as a collection of subordinate yet independent communities, but rather as a coherent entity, under Roman authority, and defined against outsiders such as the Epirotes and, especially, the Gauls.[53] Indeed, Polybius (1.6.6) states that at around the time of the Pyrrhic War the Romans began to attack the rest of Italy that had not yet been subdued 'not as if it were a foreign country, but as if it rightfully belonged to them', and he later (2.20.10) mentions in passing that the Romans fought against Pyrrhus 'for Italy' (περὶ τῆς Ἰταλίας). A series of new Latin colonies were founded far from Rome, which not only helped to secure distant subjugated lands but also perhaps

[51] Throughout this book I adopt the orthodox position that Rome's Italian allies were typically bound by formal treaties. In a recent, stimulating article Rich (2008) argues that treaties between Rome and the Italian allies were not the norm. I am not entirely convinced by Rich's thesis. It is admitted that there are only a limited number of explicit ancient references to treaties between Rome and individual communities in Italy, but given the patchy nature of the sources, especially the loss of Livy's second decade, it is not surprising that any list of treatied states will be incomplete. Moreover, I believe that Rich is overly sceptical in dismissing several potential examples of *foedera*. For example, he doubts the authenticity of Livy's (9.20.8) reference to a treaty between Rome and Teanum Apulum, following the latter's defeat in 318–317, a passage whose historicity I have defended elsewhere (Fronda 2006: 399–402; see also Chapter 2, pp. 80–1). Finally, if making treaties with the allies was the normal Roman practice, it is not surprising that the ancient historians (especially Roman authors) did not always explicitly mention treaties following Roman conquest: such an outcome would have been assumed. Rich's thesis is attractive, however, in as much as it emphasises the likelihood that affairs between Rome and the Italians were widely varied and rather unsystematic, a position that is consistent with the present discussion. In the end, this debate does not bear heavily on the main arguments in this book, for Rich agrees that what he terms 'treaty-less allies' would still have been under Roman sway and obliged to provide troops according to a fixed schedule (2008: 67–70). Thus, the arrangement that he argues for would be functionally similar to what I have described. For further discussion, see also Oakley 1997–2005: III.271–4, who concludes that 'a firm decision on this matter is not possible' (p. 274).

[52] Crawford 1992: 45–6: 'With the Pyrrhic War, Rome faced for the first time an enemy from the civilised core of the Mediterranean world and, with his defeat, that world began to take note of Rome.' Forsythe 2005: 358: 'Rome's defeat of Pyrrhus was a clear declaration to the rest of the ancient Mediterranean world that the Romans had arrived on the world scene of warfare and power politics, and recognition of this fact was no long time in coming.'

[53] See for example, Williams 2001: 128–30.

symbolised the extension of Roman control over the length and breadth of the peninsula: Cosa (273) and Ariminum (268) to the north, Paestum (273) and Beneventum (268) to the south.[54] The consul P. Sempronius Sophus is supposed to have vowed a temple to the god Tellus during his battle with the Picentines in 268; the temple was built soon thereafter and, according to Varro (*Rust.* 1.2.1), contained a painting of *Italia* (*in pariete pictam Italiam*). If this depiction of *Italia* was part of the original temple construction, then by the first half of the third century the Romans had some concept of Italy and understood it to be their domain.[55] Finally, references to two treaties support this point. Appian (*Sam.* 7.1) mentions an 'ancient treaty' between Rome and Taras that bound the Romans not to sail beyond the Lacinian promontory. The treaty was contravened by a Roman fleet in 282, providing a *terminus ante quem*, but it may have been signed as early as 330.[56] Polybius (3.26.2–4) states that the historian Philinus recorded a treaty between Rome and Carthage stipulating that the former would keep away from the whole of Sicily, the latter away from the whole of Italy. Polybius himself doubted that this treaty ever existed, and some scholars have agreed with his assessment.[57] Serrati (2006: 120–9) most recently argues, however, for the historicity of the 'Philinus Treaty', associating it with the renewal of a treaty between Rome and Carthage in 306, mentioned by Livy (9.43.26).[58] If historical, both the 'Philinus Treaty' and Appian's 'ancient treaty' show that the Romans considered all (or mostly all) of the Italian peninsula to be within their exclusive sphere of influence perhaps as early as the turn of the third century. Rome's victory over Pyrrhus and the subsequent post-war settlement would have reinforced this belief.[59]

---

[54] The Romans had already placed a colony in south-eastern Italy, at Venusia in 291. Venusia and the four colonies founded between 273 and 268 effectively marked off the 'corners' of Italy, establishing a line between Roman and Gallic Italy in the north, while leaving furthest southern Italy free of colonies for the time being. See Purcell 1990: 10.

[55] On the symbolism of the depiction, see Wiseman 1986: 91; on the temple, see Flor. 1.14; Val. Max. 6.3.1; Dion. Hal. 8.79; Platner and Ashby 1929: 511. Roth 2007 argues that the *picta Italia* described by Varro was a real artefact, but one that probably dated to the restoration of the temple of Tellus in the first century BC. He leaves open the possibility, however, that this supposedly later image replaced an earlier depiction of *Italia*.

[56] See Liv. 8.17.10; on the historicity and date of the treaty: Oakley 1997–2005 II.681 n. 1; Forsythe 2005: 350; Fronda 2006: 414 n. 79 and this book, Chapter 5, pp. 197–8; contra Barnes 2005: 88–9.

[57] Walbank 1970: 1.354; Eckstein 1987: 77–8; Scullard 1989: 530–7 is less certain; Hoyos 1985 ultimately argues against the treaty but presents an excellent summary of both sides of the debate. For a more complete bibliography, see Serrati 2006: 120 n. 25.

[58] See also Liv. *Per.* 14; Serv. *ad Aen.* 4.628.

[59] So Williams 2001: 129 concludes: 'By the 260s BC, then, it seems from the available evidence that Romans considered that Italia was geographically equivalent to the peninsula, that Gallia (i.e.

But did the allies share this view and thus, more importantly, see themselves as members of a greater, shared, political entity rather than as individual and autonomous sovereign states? In other words, did the allies develop stronger feelings of Roman and Italian unity during the third century? Certainly some modern scholars assume that such a sense of shared identity and purpose was well in place by the Second Punic War,[60] and the nearest contemporary literary source seems to lend support to the idea. Polybius, in his description of the outbreak of the war against the Boii and Insubres (2.23–4), which is probably drawn from Fabius Pictor, juxtaposes the 'inhabitants of Italy' with the Gallic invaders, claiming that the Italians no longer saw themselves as allies of Rome, nor did they think that the war was for Roman hegemony.[61] In response to the Gallic invasion, the Romans called upon their allies, who reacted with alacrity, allowing the Romans to field three armies totalling over 60,000 Roman and over 90,000 allied soldiers. In the same famous passage he lists the total number of men able to bear arms for Rome, enumerating not only the number of citizens of military age but also the potential contribution from each of various allied peoples throughout Italy. Polybius' description of Roman manpower in 225 will be discussed at greater length below (pp. 37–9). For the moment, it suffices to note that Polybius/Pictor implies a closeness between Rome and its allies; the inhabitants of Italy united against 'foreign' enemies such as the Gauls or, later, Hannibal.[62]

Yet at the same time there is strong evidence that the Italian allies still did not embrace the notion of a unified Italy under Roman leadership, even after the Pyrrhic War. First, it must be stressed that the peninsula south of the Po remained a war zone for a decade after the defeat of Pyrrhus, with Roman generals celebrating fourteen triumphs between 275 and 264 over various Italian communities, in addition to M'. Curius Dentatus' triumph over 'the Samnites and Pyrrhus' in 275. In some cases, these campaigns can be seen as mopping-up operations extending naturally from the Pyrrhic War: the Samnites, Lucanians, Bruttians and Italiote cities had sided with

everything beyond Picenum) was not included within it, and that they regarded Italia as in some sense theirs, insofar as they had come to exercise their hegemony over all of it.'
[60] See above, n. 48. For additional discussion, see below (pp. 27–8).
[61] For events surrounding the Gallic invasion of 225, Polybius probably used Fabius Pictor as source, and he would have been interested in presenting Italy united under Roman leadership against a fearsome Gallic threat. Polybius' depiction is problematic, therefore, as it most probably contains pro-Roman exaggeration of the cooperative spirit between Rome and the allies. See Walbank 1970: 1.184, 196; cf. Beck and Walter, *FRH* 1 F30a–b (= fr. 23 Peter, from Eutr. 3.5 and Oros. 4.13.6–7), with commentary.
[62] So too Livy (23.5.11–13, 24.47.5), in reference to Hannibal.

Pyrrhus and were subsequently punished. But some of the defeated appear to have been brought under Roman authority for the first time, including the Picentines (over whom two triumphs were celebrated in 268), Sarsina in northern Umbria (triumph in 266) and the Sallentines and Messapians in the 'heel' of Italy (two triumphs in 266). In other words, there were still communities within the peninsula that were objects of conquest rather than willing participants in the Roman commonwealth.[63] Indeed, that the Romans founded a Latin colony at Brundisium in 244 suggests that the region was still not secure more than twenty years after the Sallentines and Messapians had been defeated initially, or at least this is what the Romans believed.

More intriguing are the campaigns recorded against two communities in Etruria, Volsinii and Falerii, in the middle of the third century. According to Zonaras (8.7), the citizens of Volsinii appealed to the Roman senate for help to suppress members of the freedman class who supposedly had seized all the land and magistracies.[64] The Romans sent an army, besieged Volsinii for a year, executed the men who had seized the magistracies, razed the city to the ground and refounded it at a new site with the surviving Volsinian citizens. The *Fasti Triumphales* record a triumph over the *Vulsinienses* in 264, and resettlement is at least consistent with the archaeological evidence.[65] The remaining details, however, are suspicious.[66] A more plausible explanation for Rome's heavy-handed response to the Volsinian situation is that the city defected (or at least some of the ruling elite were fomenting rebellion). More striking is reference to a campaign in 241 against Falerii, a mere thirty miles from Rome, which ended in a crushing Roman victory: allegedly 15,000 Faliscans were killed, half of their territory was confiscated, the original hill-top town was destroyed

[63] Zonaras (8.7) claims that the Romans justified their invasion of the Salentino by claiming that the communities had sided with Pyrrhus, but in reality they wanted to seize the strategic port of Brundisium.

[64] For the Volsinian affair, see also Val. Max. 8.1 ext. 2; Flor. 1.16; Oros. 4.53; *De vir. ill.* 36; John of Antioch fr. 50 (= *FHG* 4.557).

[65] Resettled Volsinii is identified with modern Bolsena. The original site was probably located at modern Orvieto (= *urbs vetus?*), some twelve miles away, though some argue that both the old and new cities were located in the vicinity of Bolsena. For the location of old Volsinii at Orvieto, see Harris 1965: 113–14; Camporeale 1970, 2002; Staccioli 1972; Barker and Rasmussen 1998: 100, 266; contra Raymond Bloch in a series of publications (1947, 1950, 1953, 1963, 1973) and Scullard 1967: 126–32. The location of old Volsinii is a good example of the challenges posed by integrating archaeological and literary evidence, as discussed earlier in this chapter (pp. 12–13). Short of a remarkable new discovery, there will be no way to confirm the location, and the various proposed sites, which show signs of abandonment in the third century, have been proposed only because of literary references to Volsinii's destruction/resettlement.

[66] Capozza 1997 argues that the sources' emphasis on the alleged laziness of the Volsinian aristocracy and the resulting political ascendancy of freedmen derives ultimately from concerns in the first century AD over the influence of imperial freedmen.

and resettled in the nearby plain, and both consuls celebrated a triumph.[67] The exact causes of the Faliscan war are unknown but, whatever the case, it stands out as a powerful example of resistance to Roman hegemony and assertion of autonomy by a state situated close to Rome rather than at the fringes of the peninsula, in the middle of the third century. In the same year (241) the Latin colony of Spoletium was founded in southern Umbria, close to the eastern border of Etruria. Overall, the Romans appear still to have been consolidating their hold on Etruria and southern Umbria even as they were fighting a war overseas against the Carthaginians.

Finally, let us return to Polybius' discussion of Italian sentiments just prior to the Battle of Telamon in 225. I mentioned above that his account implies a sense of Roman–Italian unity in the face of the massive Gallic incursion, but a closer reading of the text suggests that the evidence is rather ambiguous. It is best to look at the passage (2.23.11–13) in full:

συνηργεῖτο δ᾽ αὐτοῖς πάντα καὶ πανταχόθεν ἑτοίμως. καταπεπληγμένοι γὰρ οἱ τὴν Ἰταλίαν οἰκοῦντες τὴν τῶν Γαλατῶν ἔφοδον οὐκέτι Ῥωμαίοις ἡγοῦντο συμμαχεῖν οὐδὲ περὶ τῆς τούτων ἡγεμονίας γίνεσθαι τὸν πόλεμον, ἀλλὰ περὶ σφῶν ἐνόμιζον ἕκαστοι καὶ τῆς ἰδίας πόλεως καὶ χώρας ἐπιφέρεσθαι τὸν κίνδυνον. διόπερ ἑτοίμως τοῖς παραγγελλομένοις ὑπήκουον.

On every side there was a ready disposition to help in every possible way; for the inhabitants of Italy, panic-stricken by the attack of the Gauls, no longer reckoned that they were fighting as allies to the Romans, or that the war was begun for their [the Romans'] hegemony, but each man considered the danger being brought upon himself and his own city and country. So there was great alacrity in obeying orders.

Polybius emphasises that fear of the Gauls, not closeness to Rome, convinced the allies to obey orders and make the appropriate war preparations more quickly. The passage does hint that the extreme danger of the situation led the Italians to feel that they and the Romans were 'all in it together' defending against a common threat, rather than subjects fighting to further Roman interests.[68] But notice the fundamental motivation behind the

---

[67] Zon. 8.18; *CIL* I² p. 47; Frederiksen and Ward-Perkins 1957: 128–36; Uggeri 1998b. Terrenato 2004: 234 suggests that the town was not destroyed by the Romans and that the change in settlement patterns indicated by the archaeological evidence can be explained as a local response to shifting lines of communication and changing economic conditions, such as the building of the Via Amerina (cf. Terrenato 1998a). Yet Terrenato still accepts the Faliscan War as historical, and thus even if one adopts his archaeological interpretation, the conflict remained an intriguing case of late Italian resistance to Roman power.

[68] The ethnic angle of the struggle also should not be overemphasised. Various 'Italian' peoples had cooperated with the Gauls in the past, sometimes at the urging of the Italians themselves: the Gauls and Etruscans allied against Rome in 299 (Polyb. 2.19.1–2; Liv. 10.10.6–12); Samnites, Etruscans, Umbrians and Gauls formed a coalition against Rome in 295 (Liv. 10.18.2, 10.21.2;

remarkable Roman–Italian cooperation: each was thinking about himself and his own city. If his characterisation of the Italians' mindset can be trusted, Polybius seems to be saying that the severe threat brought out intense localism and particularism, not feelings of unity. Given the above previous discussion of the Realist theory of interstate relations, this case of remarkable cooperation between Rome and the allies should not be surprising: they worked together to defeat a shared threat, but the underlying motivation was still the self-interest of individual states.

We cannot conclude, therefore, that a strong sense of unity between Rome and its subject allies surfaced in the fifty years between the Pyrrhic War and the Second Punic War, whatever ideas the Romans themselves may have believed or promoted. Indeed, the Romans were still fighting wars of conquest and consolidating their power within the peninsula as late as the second half of the third century, at times just a short distance from their own walls. The picture of the so-called 'Roman Commonwealth' that comes into view, then, is far from a sort of proto-nation, but rather a collection of individual sovereign states motivated, as late as 225, by their own self-interest and exercising their own autonomy, in so far as it was possible given Rome's dominant position in the peninsula. That we have relatively few cases of Italian states acting autonomously and resisting Roman hegemony can be explained partly by our sources, which after the Pyrrhic War tend to focus on Rome's dealings with the broader Mediterranean world.[69] It can be understood mostly, however, as the predictable outcome of Rome's emergence as the hegemonic power in a steeply unipolar hierarchy of Italian states. In this environment the smaller states – Rome's subject allies – still valued their own sovereignty and autonomy yet had little choice but to cooperate with the dominant state until the hierarchy was radically altered. In such a case, the competitive tendencies of Rome's allies would be expected to resurface as each state struggled to maximise its resources and position itself within whatever new balance of power developed.

But how did Rome come to occupy such an ascendant position vis-à-vis the other states and communities in Italy, with essentially unchallenged hegemony from Pyrrhus' departure in 275 until Hannibal's invasion in 218? What were the mechanisms of Roman control? I have already touched

---

Zon. 8.1); the Gauls appealed to the Etruscans for help in 283–282 (Polyb. 2.19–20; see also Cass. Dio 8.38.1). If we can trust Polybius, the Italians were afraid of the Gauls in 225, but their fear is better explained by the ferocity of this particular invasion, and not because the Italians felt a strong sense of common identity with the Romans (or each other).

[69] Fighting during the First Punic War took place mainly in Sicily and Africa, and as a result we hear very little about Italian affairs during the war. For Hamilcar Barca's efforts at raiding Italian coastal communities, see below, pp. 45–6.

on some of these in passing. One cannot overstress the importance of the practice of absorbing some conquered territory into the *ager Romanus*, extending forms of Roman citizenship to various Italian communities, and in all cases obliging subordinate states to contribute troops to the Roman army. This threefold policy allowed for the citizen population of Rome to grow so as to dwarf any single potential peninsular competitor, even the largest (such as Capua or Taras).[70] Also, the Roman citizen population, combined with the military obligations of all of the subordinate allies, meant that Rome could draw on a vast reservoir of manpower to fight its wars. Thus, the Romans could overwhelm any single Italian state and easily defeat even small coalitions. Only an organised and concerted effort by numerous smaller states could ever challenge Roman supremacy, unless an outside force altered the equation, while Rome's policy of dealing formally only with individual states, rather than leagues or confederacies, presumably limited the chances for such a widespread coalition forming.

The placement of colonies and garrisons at strategic locations throughout the peninsula also tightened Rome's grip. Garrisons appear to have been used infrequently: we find Roman garrisons in a few of the Italiote cities, including Taras and Metapontion. A handful of small Roman colonies, composed of no more than a few hundred colonists, were situated mostly along the Italian coast, probably to 'safeguard ports and adjacent coastline either against the neighbouring natives (Volscians at Antium, for instance) or against enemies, whether pirates or others, coming from the seas'.[71] Of greater strategic importance were the Latin colonies, larger settlements of between 2,500 and 6,000 adult men and their families, of whom at least some were

---

[70] If surviving census figures can be trusted, Rome possessed more than 150,000 men of military age by the middle of the fourth century, and the total may have been much higher by the end of the fourth century (Brunt 1971: 26–33). Assuming 150,000 men of military age, the total Roman citizen population, including women, children and older men, would have been in the neighbourhood of 500,000 persons (assuming that adult males made up approximately 30 per cent of the population: Lo Cascio 1994). Afzelius 1942: 153, extrapolating the Roman population from the size of the *ager Romanus*, came up with a somewhat lower figure of around 350,000 free persons after 338. By 225 the number of Roman citizens (adult males) had swelled to 300,000, the total free population to over 900,000 persons, according to Brunt's (1971: 44–60) conservative estimate. By comparison, Taras at its height in the fourth century had a total population of only 110,000 to 150,000 persons (Pani 2005: 22). It should be noted that Lo Cascio 1999 argues for even higher population figures for Rome, estimating *at least* 1,000,000 adult males (3,500,000 total free persons) living on the *ager Romanus* in 225. I am sceptical of such high estimates but, according to any estimate, the population of Rome (i.e. the number of citizens) was already huge in comparison with other Italian cities by the middle of the fourth century, and it grew larger by the last quarter of the third century, dwarfing other large communities in Italy. We will return to this topic in Chapter 7.

[71] For the function of coastal Roman citizen colonies (so-called *coloniae maritimae*) founded before the Punic Wars: Salmon 1955 (quotation at p. 67).

Roman citizens until they were enrolled as colonists. In a recently founded colony many of its inhabitants would have once possessed Roman citizenship or have descended from Roman forebears. Presumably, Rome could expect a higher degree of loyalty from the Latin colonies than from other allied states, and indeed, these colonies did show remarkable constancy.[72] At the same time, Latin colonies were located at sensitive points, overlooking areas that had recently come under Roman control or that commanded natural lines of communication. Cicero (*Leg. agr.* 2.73) famously claimed that the Romans in prior generations 'placed colonies thus in suitable locations against the suspicion of danger, that they seemed not to be towns of Italy but *propugnacula imperii* (bastions of the empire)'.[73] There is no doubt that Latin (and Roman) colonies served not only to protect the frontiers of Roman expansion, but also to keep an eye on – and in some cases geographically divide – the allied states among which they were interspersed.[74]

Italy was not contolled through compulsion alone. In addition, Roman rule relied heavily on collaboration by the political elite of the allied states, generally the local aristocratic class.[75] No doubt some local aristocrats were seduced by the shared profits of Rome's successful wars: allies certainly received booty, and they were probably allotted land from territory confiscated from the defeated and were enrolled as citizens in Latin colonies.[76] But the Romans also provided support for local aristocrats, either backing the entire ruling class of a community or promoting specific individuals, families or groups either directly or (more likely) indirectly. [77]

---

[72] There is only one known example of the defection of a Latin colony before the Social War: Fregellae revolted around 125, though the circumstances are nebulous (Liv. *Per.* 60; Vell. Pat. 2.6; Obsequens 90; Val. Max. 2.8.4; Asc. 17 C; Plut. *C. Gracch.* 3; *De vir. ill.* 65.2). There is also the famous instance during the Second Punic War, when a number of Latin colonies failed to meet their troop obligations; the colonies were publicly rebuked in Rome, and later in the war were forced to send additional troops as a punishment (Liv. 27.9.1–10.10, 29.15.1–15). Still, there is no evidence that any of the colonies defected.

[73] *[Maiores] colonias sic idoneis in locis contra suspicionem periculi collocarunt, ut esse non oppida Italiae, sed propugnacula imperii viderentur.*

[74] See now J. R. Patterson 2006a.

[75] Münzer 1920 remains a foundational work for the interconnection of Roman and Italian elites.

[76] In some cases, indigenous populations may have coexisted with colonists though possessing a subordinate status; natives may also have been granted smaller plots of land. Yet there are examples of locals entering into the colonial elite. See Cornell 1995a: 366–8; Bradley 2006: 171–7; contra Brunt 1971: 539–40. Venusia is widely cited as an example of a colony-foundation that included large numbers of indigeneous persons: see Chapter 2, pp. 61–2, 98.

[77] In the period between about 270 and 220 the loyalty of the local ruling classes was probably easy to maintain, since there was no realistic alternative to obeying Rome. Their loyalty could not be assumed, however, in periods when Roman hegemony was seriously tested, such as at points during the Samnite Wars, the Pyrrhic War and the Hannibalic War, or when the geopolitical situation was more ambiguous, such as it probably appeared to local states when the Romans first

In particular, the Romans seem to have rewarded local aristocrats who actively advanced the Roman cause or who in some way forged close ties to the Roman aristocracy.[78] In some cases Roman backing must have taken the form of financial support, such as gifts of money or land with which a local aristocrat could enrich himself. But, of course, such economic benefits had a political dimension, since wealth was a prerequisite for political advancement in most ancient Mediterranean societies. Other gifts and honours may have added to a local aristocrat's symbolic capital and thus contributed to his status. A local aristocrat with close personal ties to the Romans – close friendship or intermarriage between their families – may have possessed greater credibility in his home town. An aristocrat with relatives or close friends among the Roman *nobiles* would presumably have had some leverage in Rome, giving him more influence among his fellow citizens, who would turn to him as an expert on Roman affairs or simply to act as a trusted intermediary. Pro-Roman aristocrats occasionally may have requested (or at least been given) military support to suppress local opposition, whether an uprising of the 'lower classes' or some sort of aristocratic factional violence. One imagines that in many cities certain individuals or families enjoyed high or even dominant political standing in large part because of their association with Rome.[79] At the same time, this probably fostered a certain amount of disaffection among aristocrats who 'lost out' as a result of growing Roman influence. For example, the Romans certainly punished aristocrats who were disloyal or who were the leading figures in their city's resistance to initial Roman conquest, perhaps executing members of certain families, or confiscating their property (which in

made inroads in a given region. In such cases it was vital for the Romans to win over a critical mass of the local elite and convince them that cooperating with Rome was the better option. See Terrenato 1998b, arguing that the local aristocrats mediated Roman power, using the Etruscan elite as a case study,

[78] Zonaras (8.6) preserves an intriguing example of such personal ties between Roman and local elites. During the Pyrrhic War, after the city of Croton had defected, some Crotoniate aristocrats attempted to hand their city over to the Roman consul P. Cornelius Rufinus, who was campaigning nearby. The plan failed when opposing aristocrats learned of it and sent for help from Pyrrhus' commander, Milo. Zonaras states explicitly that the pro-Roman aristocrats were the 'friends' (τῶν ἐπιτηδείων) of Rufinus. See also Frontin. *Str.* 3.6.4.

[79] Consider the Cilnii of Arretium, a very powerful family (*genus praepotens*) whose great wealth engendered such jealousy (*divitiarum invidia*) that their fellow citizens tried to exile them (Liv. 10.3.2). The Romans, undoubtedly at the request of the Cilnii, sent a dictator with an army to quell the disturbance, who allegedly reconciled the Cilnii with the people (Liv. 10.5.12–13). One suspects that this was not simply a case of class conflict, but instead involved other aristocratic families. Whatever the exact circumstances, the Roman 'reconciliation' seems to have left the Cilnii in power. Similarly, when the Romans resettled Volsinii and Falerii (discussed above, pp. 26–7), favoured families must surely have received choice lands.

turn may have been given over to openly 'pro-Roman' families).[80] There may have been occasions when the Romans, either by the prompting of the senate or by the decision of an individual magistrate, simply backed one side over another in a local factional struggle. At the very least, some families would have found their local influence and prestige diminished vis-à-vis their political rivals who had Roman backing. Thus, the extension of Roman hegemony would have produced both 'winners' and 'losers' among the aristocracies in many cities.[81]

One final, remarkable and probably representative example demonstrates this dynamic. Livy (23.1.1–3) reports that a certain aristocrat named Statius Trebius from the Samnite town of Compsa contacted Hannibal after the battle of Cannae and promised to turn over his city should Hannibal bring his army near. Trebius was a leading aristocrat (*nobilis*) who had been opposed by an aristocratic faction of the Mopsii, a family who held power because of the favour or friendship of the Romans (*factio Mopsiorum familiae per gratiam Romanorum potentis*). Compsa was one of the principal towns of the Hirpini, who had been conquered around 290 or 270.[82] So, about two generations after Roman conquest, an aristocratic family's political power was strongly linked to their association with Rome. Either the Romans placed the Mopsii in power or in some way favoured them in 290/270 and that initial support was enough to solidify their political position for two generations, or Rome provided ongoing (or at least more recent) support for the Mopsii, thus guaranteeing that this loyal aristocratic party could keep a hold on the reins of power.[83] At the same time, Trebius and presumably other rival Compsan aristocrats appear not to have shared equally in the benefits of Roman rule.

---

[80] For example, according to Livy (10.1.3) the Frusinates were involved in some sort of conspiracy with the Hernici in 303. The Roman consuls conducted investigations then scourged and executed the leaders of the conspiracy. An example from the Second Punic War is particularly illuminating: when Scipio recaptured Locri (in 205), which had defected earlier in the war, he executed the authors of the revolt (presumably aristocrats) and 'gave their property to the leaders of the other party on account of their outstanding loyalty to the Romans' (*de auctoribus supplicium sumpsit bonaque eorum alterius factionis principibus ob egregiam fidem adversus Romanos concessit*): Liv. 29.8.1; see Chapter 7, pp. 313–14.

[81] On the range of personal and familial connections between Roman and allied elites, focusing more on the second century, see now J. R. Patterson 2006a.

[82] The Hirpini were defeated near the end of the Third Samnite War and again after siding with Pyrrhus. Compsa presumably fell sometime in this period. See Salmon 1967: 275–6, 285–90.

[83] It is possible that the Mopsii's rise to power had been relatively recent, having earned Roman favour sometime closer to the Second Punic War. Even this situation supports my case, for it would still indicate some form of Roman intervention on behalf of a local aristocratic family albeit long after 'first contact'. It seems more likely, however, that the Mopsii benefited from Rome's post-conquest settlement in 290/270, and their position was perhaps reinforced periodically over the subsequent half-century.

Just as I argued with regard to local interstate rivalry, the Roman promotion of individuals, families or groups within a city may have broken down along factional lines and thus exacerbated pre-existing political rivalry: that is, by favouring one group over their rivals, the Romans may have intensified competition and enmity between the groups. Or perhaps the Roman backing of certain local individuals or groups gave rise to new jealousies and factional rivalry. In the Compsan example that was cited above, the families of Trebius and the Mopsii may have been political rivals for generations, or their rivalry only emerged once the Romans favoured the Mopsii and thus tilted local political competition in their favour. This need not have been a conscious policy – though the Roman senate may have decided at times to back one family over another – so much as the natural consequence of *ad hoc* decisions and personal relationships arising from specific circumstances. Whatever the case, an ongoing theme in the following chapters is how the dynamic of Rome's indirect rule through collaboration by the local governing classes intersected with personal and political rivalries within those local aristocracies, and how these internal divisions came to the surface when Rome's position was threatened by Hannibal's early military success. Those aristocratic individuals and groups who perceived that they had lost out to their rivals as a result of Roman rule would have been more likely to see Hannibal as a more attractive alternative; it is around these disaffected local aristocrats that 'pro-Hannibalic' (or 'anti-Roman') movements could crystallise.

To summarise briefly, Italy in the late third century, on the eve of the Second Punic War, consisted of scores of autonomous, competitive states dominated by Rome – a single, large, hegemonic power. Rome bound these states to itself through a series of bilateral treaties, as well as other formal obligations. The Italian states were technically Rome's sovereign allies, though in reality they were unable to exercise their own foreign policy. Using the terminology of international relations, this situation is best defined as a unipolar international system. Rome was able to maintain its position at the top of this hierarchy of states in part because it had overwhelming military advantages, such as vast resources in the form of territory and population, which discouraged or even prohibited the smaller states in the system from challenging Roman authority. Roman hegemony was also based in part on cooperation from the local ruling classes. These local aristocracies were, however, riven by political competition and factionalism, which in some cases appears to have been the product of – or at least exacerbated by – the relationship between the Roman *nobiles* and members of the local elites. It was this arrangement that confronted Hannibal in 218; he needed to develop and execute a strategy that could break the bonds between the Roman and local ruling elites and detach the subject allies from Rome. This discussion will now turn to the nature of Hannibal's strategy and to some previous explanations for why it failed.

HANNIBAL'S STRATEGY

Military historians have pored over the strategies, tactics, armaments, logistical dispositions, and quality of commanders of the two combatants in the Second Punic War.[84] Attempts to explain the failure of the Hannibalic strategy have likewise produced voluminous scholarship. But what, in fact, was Hannibal's strategy? Although at least one scholar has argued that Hannibal had no clear strategic objective when he marched into Italy and therefore never pursued a single coherent strategy,[85] it seems clear that he did formulate a strategy to achieve a specific objective. Hannibal did not expect to capture or raze the city of Rome but rather envisioned the war concluding with the Romans offering or accepting acceptable peace terms.[86] A treaty between Hannibal and Philip V of Macedon in 215, preserved in a fragment of Polybius (7.9.2–17), contains provisions for future dealings with the Romans, indicating that Rome's

---

[84] 'In the history of the art of warfare the Second Punic War is epochal', concludes Delbrück 1975: 311; for analysis of the Second Punic War primarily from the perspective of military history, see, for example, Dodge 1891; Thiel 1946: 32–199; Montgomery 1968: 89–98; Delbrück 1975: 311–90; Lazenby 1978; Caven 1980: 85–258; Bagnall 1990: 155–299; Peddie 1997; Goldsworthy 2000: 143–328; for a recent treatment of logistics in ancient warfare, with a specific analysis of the Second Punic War, see Erdkamp 1998; for the mechanics of battle in the Second Punic War, see Sabin 1996; Daly 2002. The Second Punic War looms large in a wide range of topics in Roman social and political history, generating an expansive bibliography. For example: on the outbreak of the war and Roman imperialism, see Dorey 1956; Errington 1972: 96–101; Eckstein 1987: 169–77; Rich 1996 (with lengthy bibliography); on the war and Roman politics: M. L. Patterson 1942; Crake 1963; Develin 1985: 82–8, 117–25, 153–64; Rosenstein 1990, 1993. On the economic and demographic effects of the war in the second century and beyond: Brunt 1971; contra Toynbee 1965 (arguing that the effects of the Second Punic War were felt in southern Italy as late as the nineteenth century); Cornell 1996 (for an excellent summary of the debate). A wealth of archaeological evidence has contributed to the study of Hannibal's legacy, at times calling into question the image presented in the literary evidence that the Second Punic War caused profound and long-term damage to agricultural production and a large-scale decline in population in southern Italy; see, for example, Lomas 1993: 115–23.

[85] Peddie 1997: 5–6, 199–200.

[86] Lazenby 1978: 85–6; Briscoe 1989: 46; Lazenby 1996b: 41–2; Lancel 1999: 109. Groag 1929: 79–96 argued that Hannibal hoped to establish a balance of power in the western Mediterranean by reducing Rome's hegemony to central Italy. There is no need to posit such specific war aims, though Hannibal surely figured that a defeated Rome would be compelled to accept a significantly downgraded status.

destruction was not the assumed outcome at that time.[87] According to Livy (22.58.3), Hannibal told his Roman captives after Cannae that he was not fighting a war for the death of the Romans (*non internecivum sibi esse cum Romanis bellum*), but rather for dignity and empire (*de dignitate atque imperio*). After the speech he sent ten captured *equites* to the Roman senate in order to discuss the ransom of Roman prisoners, as well as a Carthaginian representative named Carthalo to discuss peace terms (Liv. 22.58.6–7). The wording of the passage suggests that Hannibal (in Livy's view) suspected the Romans would have desired peace after suffering such a significant defeat at Cannae.[88] As Lazenby (1996b: 41) noted, Hannibal marched on Rome only once, in 211, not in order to seize, besiege or destroy the city, but rather to draw the Romans from their siege of Capua. It was difficult in the Hellenistic period for one large state to utterly destroy another in war, so the strategic objective of warfare usually meant compelling an enemy to surrender or seek peace.[89] In this regard, Hannibal's aim to force Rome to accept terms conformed to contemporary practices and expectations.

Wars in the Hellenistic period also tended not to be protracted affairs – although there were exceptions – and the winning side could hope to force the losing side to seek terms in a relatively short time. A state could compel its enemy to seek terms by marching into its homeland and defeating its army in one or a few pitched battles, or it could break its enemy's will to continue fighting by capturing enemy cities or ravaging their land. Larger states often controlled a number of subordinate or 'allied' states that felt varying degrees of loyalty towards the dominant power, and an aggressor could attempt to pry loose an enemy's subordinate allies. Eliciting defections could be achieved either by seduction or by compulsion. On the one hand, representatives of a powerful Hellenistic state could make appeals to these smaller subordinate states, assuring them that switching sides would

---

[87] The key terms are found at 7.9.12–15. They guarantee that any peace terms between Hannibal and Rome would include certain protections for Philip, and also that in the case of any *subsequent* war with Rome, Philip and Hannibal would help each other. See also Liv. 23.33.5, 23.33.10–12, 23.33.34.4; App. *Mac.* 1; Zon. 9.4.2–3; Eutr. 3.12.3; Walbank 1970: 11.42–56; for the authenticity of the document, see Bickerman 1944, 1952; Barré 1983.

[88] Carthalo was commissioned to offer terms *si forte ad pacem inclinare cerneret animos* ('if by chance their [the Romans'] minds were inclined towards peace'). Hannibal of course could not be certain the Romans would surrender, but he suspected his victory at Cannae had broken the senate's will. Versions of the history of the ten prisoners and Hannibal's peace offer appear in a number of sources (Polyb. 6.58.2–13; Cic. *Off.* 1.39–40, 113–15; Gell. 6.18.1–9; Val. Max. 2.9.8), apparently all tracing back to Gaius Acilius (*FRH* 5 F5 = fr. 3 Peter, from Cic. *Off.* 3.115).

[89] Goldsworthy 2000: 156. For general discussions of Hellenistic warfare, see Garlan 1994; Hamilton 1999; Chaniotis 2005; Launey 1949 remains a fundamental work.

yield some benefits. Hellenistic monarchs frequently promised freedom and autonomy (ἐλευθερία καὶ αὐτονομία) to woo smaller states to their side.[90] On the other hand, bringing force to bear directly against an enemy's weaker allies might leave them little choice but to defect. Defeating an enemy's army in a pitched battle or ravaging their territory with impunity could also encourage allied defections by emboldening disaffected allies and convincing even loyal allies that the dominant state could no longer protect their interests. In turn, the combination of battlefield defeat and the rebellion of subordinate allies could place further pressure on a more powerful Hellenistic state to seek terms quickly.[91]

Although there is no explicit evidence that this was Hannibal's strategy, a number of references in literary sources strongly suggest that he planned his campaign, at least initially, along the aforementioned lines. According to Livy (34.60.3; cf. Polyb. 3.34.1–5), Hannibal recognised that the key to defeating Rome was to march into Italy and disturb its alliance system, and he appears to have expected his invasion to yield a quick victory rather than a war of attrition. In 217 he marched into northern Campania and laid waste to the *ager Falernus*, either to elicit a pitched battle with the Roman army under Fabius Maximus or to expose Rome's inability to defend its own territory.[92] Polybius (3.90.10–13) implies that Hannibal decided to march into the *ager Falernus* at least in part out of frustration that his victories at the Trebbia and Trasimene had yet to yield allied revolts. This suggests that Hannibal had thought that only a couple of victories were necessary to bring the war to a conclusion.[93] Carthalo's embassy to Rome after Cannae also suggests that he expected the Romans to capitulate after such a crushing defeat. It is striking that only after Cannae did Hannibal both send a legate to Rome and address Roman prisoners in congenial terms, when previously, after the battles of both Trebbia and Trasimene, he freed non-Romans but treated Romans badly.[94] The change in tactics may indicate Hannibal's frustration at Rome's

---

[90] On 'freedom and autonomy' and similar slogans and propaganda, see Gruen 1984: 132–57.

[91] Goldsworthy 2000: 155–6.

[92] The *ager Falernus* had previously been part of the territory of Capua, but it was confiscated after the Capuans sided with the Latins during the Latin War (340–338). The territory was initially distributed to Roman citizens in viritane allotments, who by 327 were organised in the newly formed *tribus Falerna*: Liv. 8.11.12–13, 8.22.7, 9.20.6; see Chapter 3, pp. 122–3.

[93] Hannibal was frustrated that Fabius would not offer battle, and his decision to invade the *ager Falernus* was made in response; it had not been planned long in advance. Polybius states explicitly (3.90.11–12) that Hannibal hoped that if the Romans would not defend the *ager Falernus*, their allies would revolt. He further explains (3.90.13) that although the Romans had been defeated in two battles, the allies had yet to revolt, and he ties this to Hannibal's decision to invade the *ager Falernus*.

[94] Liv. 22.58.1–7; Polyb. 3.77.3–7, 3.85.1–4.

refusal to have sought terms sooner, implying that he expected to conclude the war relatively quickly. He also appears to have made use of liberation propaganda.[95] Overall, then, Hannibal's strategy in the Italian theatre of the Second Punic War can be summarised rather simply: march into Italy, win pitched battles and detach Rome from its allies. He figured that the war would end through diplomacy, with the Romans accepting terms dictated by him. He hoped to achieve this by overawing the Romans and their allies with his military prowess, while at the same time breaking up the so-called Italian confederacy by weakening the resolve of Rome's Italian allies. The latter was to be achieved in two ways: first, by defeating Roman armies Hannibal would undermine Roman credibility and shake the image of Rome as the dominant city in Italy; second, Hannibal would attempt to convince the allies that siding with him was more beneficial than remaining loyal to Rome.

HANNIBAL'S STRATEGIC FAILURE: PREVIOUS EXPLANATIONS

Why did this strategy fail? The starting point for any discussion of this question must be the great advantage Rome enjoyed in manpower. It is generally agreed that Rome's manpower reserves and its ability to field army after army profoundly shaped the course of the Second Punic War, with some citing this as the critical factor in determining the war's outcome.[96] In fact, the Romans did enjoy a significant advantage in manpower relative to the forces under Hannibal's command at the outbreak of the war and maintained that advantage throughout the course of the conflict. According to Polybius (2.24), the total number of Roman and

---

[95] Guarantees of freedom, autonomy, or similar phrases can be found in Hannibal's treaties with Capua (Chapter 3, pp. 114–16), Locri (Chapter 4, pp. 164–7), Taras (Chapter 5, pp. 215–16), and 'the Lucanians' (Liv. 25.16.7). Similarly, Hannibal spoke in kind terms after both Trebbia and Trasimene to allied prisoners of war (but not the Roman prisoners), promising to restore their territory and free Italy from the Romans (see above, n. 94). Erskine 1993 has suggested that Hannibal did not use Hellenistic liberation terminology, and the aforementioned references to liberation propaganda are Polybian projections. His main evidence is that Livy does not mention Hannibal's promise of freedom after Trebbia and Trasimene in Books 21 and 22, which, according to Erskine, were less reliant on Polybius as a source and can thus be used as a 'check' on Polybius' version. Yet Livy *does* mention other instances in Books 21–2 of Hannibal's operating in the tradition of Hellenistic diplomacy, for example offering arbitration to settle a dynastic dispute in Gaul (Liv. 21.31.6–8; cf. Polyb. 3.49.8–13). Overall, the ancient sources strongly attest to Hannibal's pose as a Hellenistic liberator.

[96] Lazenby 1978: 235; Briscoe 1989: 74–5; Goldsworthy 2000: 315–16. Of course, this argument rests on the assumption that not only the allies but also Roman citizens would remain loyal and thus allow the Roman state to enjoy a manpower advantage when prosecuting the war.

allied men capable of bearing arms in 225 exceeded 700,000 infantry and
70,000 cavalry. Brunt adjusted Polybius' figures and estimated that the
population of Italy, not including Greeks and Bruttians, exceeded 875,000
free adult males, from whom the Romans could levy troops.[97] Rome not
only had the potential to levy vast numbers of troops but did in fact field
large armies in the opening stages of the war. Brunt estimates that Rome
mobilised 108,000 men for service in the legions between 218 and 215,
while at the height of the war effort (214 to 212) Rome was able to mobil-
ise approximately 230,000 men. Against these mighty resources Hannibal
led from Spain an army of approximately 50,000 infantry and 9,000 cavalry. By the time Hannibal reached the Rhône his force had dwindled to
about 38,000 infantry and 8,000 cavalry, and when he descended into the
Po valley, the Carthaginian general commanded perhaps 20,000 infantry
and 6,000 cavalry. Even the addition of 14,000 Gallic troops (if Polybius'
figures are to be believed) left Hannibal outnumbered at the battle of the
Trebbia.[98]

Rome's manpower reserves allowed it to absorb staggering losses yet
still continue to field large armies. For example, according to Brunt, as
many as 50,000 men were lost between 218 and 215, but Rome continued
to place between 14 and 25 legions in the field for the duration of the war.
Moreover, as will be discussed below, Roman manpower allowed for the
adoption of the so-called Fabian strategy, which proved to be an effective response to Hannibal's apparent battlefield superiority. Put simply, the
relative disparity in the number of available troops at the outset of the
conflict meant that Hannibal had a much narrower margin for error than
the Romans.

Yet it also should be recognised that Hannibal's Italian strategy had
the potential to counteract, at least partially, Rome's manpower advantage. Hannibal might have figured that rebellious allies, dissatisfied with

---

[97] Brunt 1971: 44–54, 416–22 also estimated the potential manpower at over 940,000 if the Greeks
and Bruttians were included. Baronowski 1993 argues that Polybius double counted contingents
who were actually under arms in 225, so he estimates a somewhat lower figure of around 600,000
total Roman-allied manpower available (combining cavalry and infantry). De Ligt 2004 argues
for more or less the same order of magnitude. Lo Cascio 1999 on the other hand argues for significantly higher totals (though see above, n. 70). Scheidel 2004: 3–4 has raised serious questions
about the accuracy and usefulness of Polybius' manpower figures, but no one would deny that the
Romans had at their disposal a significant reservoir of their own and allied citizens, thus enjoying
a vast advantage in potential manpower over Hannibal's invading army.

[98] For estimates of the troop strength of Hannibal's army at various stages during his march from
Spain to the Po valley, see Lazenby 1978: 34–48, 50–1; see also De Sanctis 1956–69: III.2.81–2;
Walbank 1970: 1.361–7. The route of Hannibal's march also remains a constant topic of debate; for
a comprehensive treatment, see Proctor 1971, though more recently Lancel 1999: 57–80.

Roman rule, would provide reinforcements for his own army; in fact, as noted above, he quickly acquired thousands of Gallic troops. Even if disaffected allies did not furnish troops for his army, the rebellious states would have deprived the Romans of potential soldiers for the legions. Returning to Polybius' report on the number of potential and actual men under arms in 225: of the 770,000 available men (combined infantry and cavalry), about 275,000 were Romans and Campanians, and 85,000 were Latins. The remaining (approximately) 410,000 would have been citizens of allied cities. Polybius' 'Campanians' probably included all *cives sine suffragio*, who represented perhaps 20 per cent of the total number of 'Romans and Campanians,' or more than 50,000 men. Since a number of communities with *civitas sine suffragio* did defect during the Second Punic War, their loyalty to Rome cannot be taken as guaranteed. Thus, they represent an additional 50,000 allies whom Hannibal might hope to detach from Rome. We know from hindsight that no Latin communities defected during the Second Punic War, and although this does not mean that disloyalty among Latin communities was unthinkable, I will assume that no Latin colony would ever rebel, and that likewise Roman *cives optimo iure* would never defect in large numbers. This means that Hannibal could have hoped to deprive Rome of 460,000 potential soldiers, leaving around 300,000 Romans and Latins to man Rome's armies – still a significant reservoir of men, but much more manageable given Hannibal's tactical excellence.[99] Meanwhile, if significant numbers of Italian allies joined forces with Hannibal – say half of them – Rome's manpower advantage would have been completely nullified. The Hannibalic strategy, if successful, would have at least levelled the playing field in terms of manpower; in the best-case scenario vast numbers of Italian allies would revolt, significantly augment Hannibal's forces and leave the Romans outnumbered.[100]

[99] Baronowski 1993: 190–2 estimates that *cives optimo iure* accounted for *at most* 83 per cent of the total number of Romans and Campanians mentioned by Polybius; I have assumed an 80–20 split. An exact figure is impossible to ascertain, though minor differences will not much affect the present argument. Baronowski also estimates that Roman manpower reserves were actually somewhat lower than Polybius' total of 770,000 infantry and cavalry since he double counted the Romans, Campanians and some allies (see above, n. 97). A lower figure would actually strengthen my point, since we would have to lower the number of citizens who (it is assumed) would never defect (Latins and *cives optimo iure*), to somewhere around 250,000 men according to Baronowski. In other words, Hannibal's army would have been less outnumbered by Romans and Latins, so he would have required fewer allied defections to level the playing field or even to achieve numerical superiority.

[100] Scheidel 2004 and 2006 has argued that Polybius' figures contain a number of peculiarities and may be fatally flawed as a source of information for the population of Rome or Italy. Still, his own recent estimates do not contradict the conclusions drawn here: he estimates that the allied population outnumbered the Roman population by about two to one throughout the entire

Hannibal's strategy appeared to be working, at least in the first few years of the war. From 218 to 216 Hannibal was unchallenged in Italy; he won a series of stunning victories over Roman armies and, after Cannae, inspired a number of Rome's Italian allies to defect. Indeed, all or most of the communities in Campania, Apulia, Bruttium, Samnium, Lucania, Magna Graecia and the Sallentine peninsula revolted at some point during the war, and many had defected by 215. But after 216, although he was still capable of exacting painful defeats on opposing armies, the war stalemated, and by 211 fortunes had clearly begun to turn against him.[101] He never forced the Romans to the bargaining table, nor (and perhaps more interestingly) did he bring about a total disintegration of the arrangement of alliances between Rome and the subordinate states in Italy. While Roman manpower undoubtedly shaped the Second Punic War, further analysis is required to explain the failure of the Hannibalic strategy, especially the question of why Rome's *socii* did not revolt in greater numbers in the critical period after Cannae.

Rome's effective military and diplomatic response after Cannae was greatly responsible for Hannibal's defeat. Scholars have correctly recognised that after initial failure, Rome adopted counter-strategies that played to its strength in manpower, while limiting Hannibal's opportunities to take advantage of his apparent tactical superiority, though they vary in the degree to which they credit individual Roman commanders and politicians for deciding on a war of attrition, or structures in Roman society that allowed it to endure such a war for nearly two decades.[102] De Sanctis

---

Republican period, and by nearly three to one in 225 (see Scheidel 2006: 208–9, 213 Table 1). Thus, according to Scheidel, had Hannibal elicited more massive allied revolts, he might have been able to draw on significantly greater manpower than the Romans would have had at their disposal.

[101] The most complete narrative account of the Second Punic War remains De Sanctis 1956–69: III.2 (originally published in 1916), though see now Huss 1985 and Seibert 1993b; in English: Lazenby 1978 and Goldsworthy 2000: 143–328.

[102] Errington 1972: 77 credits the competence of key Roman commanders such as Fabius Maximus, Marcellus and Tiberius Sempronius Gracchus with the defeat of Hannibal's strategy. Goldsworthy 2000: 227, 314–15 suggests that there was 'far more continuity in the Roman command', and that Roman commanders were generally superior to Carthaginian commanders except Hannibal. Goldsworthy also praises the Roman senate for committing troops to distant theatres while enduring a war of attrition in Italy and lauds the willingness of all classes of Romans to endure difficult campaigning. Caven 1980: 156–7 calls attention to the senate for its willingness to prosecute the Fabian strategy. Bagnall 1990: 201–3 also praises the senate for strategic far-sightedness, based, however, on the highly questionable argument that the crisis of Cannae was a 'national catharsis' that cleared Rome of 'political lumber', and that Roman military commanders after 216 were no longer chosen because of politics but rather on the basis of merit. Dorey and Dudley 1972: 68–70 credit the senate for following the appropriate strategy after Cannae. Cottrell 1961: 146–53 commends the senate both for silencing talk of surrender

(1956–69: III.2.209–14) perhaps best articulated this position, arguing that strict adherence to the 'Fabian strategy' ultimately saved the Roman cause and led to Hannibal's defeat. Fabius Maximus advised that Rome should not meet Hannibal in the open field, unless the Romans clearly held the advantage.[103] Meanwhile, the Romans would be able to field many armies and not only wear down Hannibal's forces but also prevent further defections while punishing allied states that had rebelled. In fact, during the critical window of opportunity after the battle of Cannae, when some allies began to break away, the installation of Roman garrisons in a number of wavering cities was probably decisive in dissuading them from following suit.[104] Caven (1980: 148–9) argued that Hannibal's incomplete success in encouraging allied revolts actually contributed to the success of the Fabian strategy, since Hannibal's new allies were potential targets for Roman reprisals. Thus, Hannibal faced the dilemma of having to divide his army in order to protect his allies or be shown incapable of protecting them.[105] Pursuance of the Fabian strategy produced subsidiary benefits for the Roman cause. Goldsworthy (2000: 314–15) has argued that the stalemate in Italy allowed Rome's legions and their commanders to become

and for 'developing in full the harrying tactics of Fabius'. According to Cottrell (p. 147), 'The factor which, in the end, defeated the invader was not the ability of Rome's generals, but the strength and vitality of its political institutions.' Of course, the idea that Roman strength lay in their institutions is part of a long historiographic tradition stretching back to Polybius.

[103] Strictly speaking, the 'Fabian strategy' should refer only to the military posture (supposedly) adopted by Q. Fabius Maximus during his dictatorship in 217, following the disaster at Trasimene. I will use the term more loosely, as a label for the more cautious approach that the Romans adopted, in general, after the battle of Cannae. Erdkamp 1992 is certainly correct that Livy over-schematises the dichotomy between Fabius' wise caution and his opponents' reckless aggression. In reality, Fabius probably did not advocate avoiding combat altogether; rather, he advised that the Romans should avoid battle only for the time being, until the circumstances were advantageous for the Romans to fight. In fact, Fabius' unsuccessful attempt to cut off Hannibal in the *ager Falernus* shows that he was willing to engage the Carthaginian in pitched battle if he felt the situation was favourable. Erdkamp summarises (p. 137): 'Fabius' intention was not to keep on avoiding battle forever, but to alter the circumstances disadvantageous to the Romans first and to fight only on the right kind of terrain.' It was risky to avoid combat even for a short period, since Hannibal's unhindered devastation of the allies' lands created allied unrest and discredited Rome, pressuring the Romans to respond. This helps to explain Rome's adoption of a more aggressive posture in 216: the Romans were compelled to save face in the eyes of their allies, so they had raised a very large army and attempted to bring the war to a close under (hopefully) favourable battlefield conditions (Erdkamp 1992: 140–2; Beck 2005: 287–9; see also Scullard 1973: 47; Briscoe 1989: 49–52). After Cannae the Romans adopted a more cautious strategy in the middle years of the war, generally avoiding pitched battle with Hannibal while focusing their efforts on preventing allied revolts and recapturing cities that had defected. Even then, some Roman commanders (for example, Marcellus) appear to have been more willing to engage Hannibal in the field.

[104] For example, Nola in Campania (Chapter 3, pp. 135–8); other examples are discussed throughout Chapters 2 to 5.

[105] See also De Sanctis 1956–69: III.2.214; Goldsworthy 2000: 313.

more experienced and skilled at facing Hannibal in Italy, mitigating his initial advantage, while Roman armies demonstrated increasing superiority over other Carthaginian armies and commanders. Peddie (1997: 110) suggested that as the war dragged on, Hannibal faced not only the loss of manpower, but also the loss of 'junior command', which crippled the battlefield effectiveness of his army. Perhaps the most important result of the Fabian strategy was that it deprived Hannibal of the opportunity to follow up Cannae with another stunning victory in a pitched battle, which might have yielded even more defections and further pressured the Roman senate to capitulate.

It is appropriate, therefore, to praise Rome's long-term strategy and its decision to pursue a war of attrition. But this decision was reached only after a string of crushing victories by Hannibal shook the image of Rome's invincibility and brought about a large – but not critical – number of allied defections. Indeed, the Fabian strategy was made possible because massive allied defections never materialised: there would have been little point in pursuing the strategy if there were very few allies left to prevent from defecting. Had more *socii* revolted after Cannae, Rome might have been convinced to seek a diplomatic resolution to the war, or the Romans might have felt it necessary to meet Hannibal in pitched battle in order to save face, rather than let him roam freely throughout southern Italy. Even if the conflict evolved into a war of attrition, more allied defections after 216 could have erased the disparity in manpower, giving Hannibal a better chance to withstand protracted hostilities. The question remains, therefore, why more allies did not revolt immediately after Cannae.

Critical errors in the prosecution of the war probably contributed as well to Hannibal's ultimate defeat in the Italian theatre, though to what degree is a matter of debate. It has been argued that Hannibal failed to capitalise on this battlefield victory at Cannae, echoing Livy's sentiment, placed in the mouth of Maharbal, that Hannibal knew how to win battles but did not know how to use those victories to win the war.[106] Thus, Montgomery (1968: 97) and Shean (1996) have argued that Hannibal should have marched immediately on Rome after Cannae, though most scholars agree

---

[106] Liv. 22.51.1–4; this statement appears in an alleged conversation between Hannibal and Maharbal after the battle of Cannae, during which the latter boasted that Hannibal could dine on the Capitoline within five days if only he ordered his cavalry immediately to ride against the city. The episode is reported in one form or another in a variety of sources besides Livy: Val. Max. 9.5 ext. 3; Flor. 1.22.19–20; Amm. Marc. 18.5.6; Plut. *Fab. Max.* 17.1–2; Sil. 10.375–6. The story appears to come originally from Cato (Beck and Walter, *FRH* 3 F4.13–14 = frs. 86–7 Peter, from Gell. 2.19.9, 10.24.7, and commentary), so it was presumably in circulation soon after the Second Punic War.

that such a manoeuvre would have been impractical, both because of the distance and because of his lack of preparation for a lengthy siege.[107] Still, there is some merit to the notion that Hannibal failed to capitalise as much as he could on his victory. On the one hand, Goldsworthy (2000: 216) has recently suggested that he should have marched on Rome, not with an eye to besieging or capturing the city, but to coerce the Romans to seek terms, or at least to further erode their credibility by marching into Latium. On the other hand, perhaps he should have remained in southern Italy rather than marching into Campania, as he did in the summer of 216. Thus, Peddie (1997: 198–9) chastises Hannibal for not pursuing the remnants of the Cannae legions more robustly, claiming that this cost him the military initiative. He might also have chosen to march towards Taras and win the support of the Greek cities along the southern coast of Lucania, securing south-east Italy before trying to elicit revolts in Samnium, Campania and Bruttium. If successful, he could have created a more unified southern bloc, rather than the resulting checkerboard of loyal and disloyal states that proved difficult to protect. Yet there was significant military and symbolic value in marching into Campania, a wealthy and strategic region, and attempting to detach those communities – some of which possessed a form of Roman citizenship – from Rome. It is intriguing to speculate on some of the choices Hannibal did and did not make – and we will revisit this particular discussion in Chapter 7 – but it must also be stressed that had a greater number of allies defected immediately after Cannae, such decisions would probably have been far less critical to the war's outcome.

Another factor that is often invoked in explaining Hannibal's defeat was his inability to receive adequate reinforcements after 216.[108] On this point, Roman naval superiority is sometimes cited as critical in cutting off reinforcements by sea from Carthage, though again the degree to which Hannibal or the Carthaginian political elite should be faulted for failing to recognise or address the imbalance in naval power is a matter of some debate.[109] The explanations advanced for Carthaginian maritime

---

[107] Errington 1972: 74–5; Delbrück 1975: 337–9; Lazenby 1978: 85–6; Lazenby 1996b: 41–2; Peddie 1997: 97–101; Lancel 1999: 109; Goldsworthy 2000.

[108] Dodge 1891: 382, 403–4, 632; Caven 1980: 149–52. Hoyos 1983: 175 argues that 'powerful reinforcements to Hannibal might have brought decisive action … [and] provided at least the opportunity for greater achievements' in Italy; see also Hoyos 2004a: 127–32.

[109] De Sanctis 1956–69: III.2.212 mentioned Roman control of the seas. Montgomery 1968: 97 blamed Hannibal for not recognising the importance of sea power, though Lazenby 1996b: 46, 1978: 235 observed that his repeated attempts to capture ports show that he had a keen awareness of the importance of sea power. Thiel 1946: 192–3 blamed the Carthaginians for not providing vigorous naval support for Hannibal's offensive: 'the maritime failure of Carthage decisively contributed to Roman victory'. Hoyos 1983, however, argues that Hannibal had full command

failure are not entirely convincing,[110] though it does appear clear that the Carthaginian navy rarely played a significant role in the resupplying of Hannibal's army. Along similar lines, a number of scholars see Hannibal's defeat in Italy as closely linked to Roman successes in other theatres of the war, which used up or cut off resources that could have been used in Italy.[111] Here too, however, scholars are often at odds over exactly how developments in Spain[112] and Sicily[113] related to the Italian campaign. Lazenby (1996a: 106) credits the Romans with a good grasp of long-term strategy for committing significant resources to the Sicilian and Spanish campaigns even though Hannibal remained unbeaten in Italy. Carthaginian failure in these theatres certainly contributed to Rome's ultimate victory

of military operations, so he, not the Carthaginian government, should be held responsible for the allocation of reinforcements. Delbrück 1975: 312, however, asserted that it would have been foolhardy for Hannibal or Carthage to waste money building up a fleet since they could never outstrip Roman naval superiority. More recently, Rankov 1996: 49–58 has suggested that 'naval superiority' must be understood within the context of ancient naval warfare: since ancient fleets could spend only short periods of time at sea and were forced to hug the coastline during operations, Roman naval superiority was the product of their control of Italian coastline communities and the island of Sicily (for much of the war), which made it hard for fleets to sail from Africa and land safely in Italy.

[110] Failure to obtain a port cannot be the sole reason for Carthaginian maritime failure, since Hannibal did, in fact, gain a port early in the war (Locri in 215) and received reinforcements via that port (see Chapter 4, pp. 166–7 and Appendix B). One must also question if an ancient fleet really needed a port in which to land, since the Romans were able to pick up sailors around Croton and Thurii after those cities had fallen to Hannibal (Liv. 26.39.7; see Chapter 5, p. 230), and they were able to beach their ships near a hostile city during First Punic War (Polyb. 1.29.1–3). Despite the fact that Rome recaptured Syracuse and therefore essentially controlled Sicily, a Carthaginian fleet was able to cruise the waters off Taras as late as 209 (Liv. 27.15.7). Finally, one must question the 'superiority' of the Roman navy: it is unclear how successful the Romans were at preventing enemy ships from landing or raiding towns along the coast, while Roman fleets did not necessarily prove effective in combat (consider the defeat of a Roman fleet at the hands of the Tarentines: Liv. 26.39).

[111] On this point, Hoyos 1983 argues that potential reinforcements were wasted in Spain and Sicily.

[112] Peddie 1997: 198 blamed Hannibal for failing to secure Spain adequately before marching on Italy, thus allowing the Romans to make gains there and preventing him from using Spain as a source of resupply; but Caven 1980: 155–6, 256–7 argued that the Carthaginian senate was *too* concerned with Spain and Sardinia and thus wasted time and resources on campaigns there rather than making a concerted effort to resupply Hannibal until it was too late. For the importance of the Spanish theatre: Dorey and Dudley 1972: 96–118; Errington 1972: 80–92; Richardson 1986: 21–61, esp. 31–5; Briscoe 1989: 56–61; Barceló 1998: 73–83; Lancel 1999: 102, 133–51.

[113] De Beer 1969: 233, 240 argued that the Carthaginians wasted their efforts in Sicily and should have focused on sending supplies and reinforcements to Italy, yet Rankov 1996: 55 argues that Rome's victory at Syracuse was the turning point in the war because it cost the Carthaginians control of Sicily and essentially cut off the routes of resupply by sea from Africa to Italy. According to Peddie 1997: 199, Hannibal should have changed 'his command structure when the fighting spread to Sicily', and even taken over direct command on the island, since its importance outweighed that of his dwindling holdings on the Italian peninsula. Lazenby 1996a: 115 likewise sees Roman control of Sicily as critical, but he emphasises that the major turning point – the Roman capture of Syracuse – came about 'largely by accident', not because of negligence or strategic short-sightedness on the part of Hannibal or the Carthaginian senate.

in the Second Punic War, but their importance must remain secondary to the war in Italy. If Hannibal had elicited massive allied defections in Italy and the Romans had had to rely on only their own citizens to man the legions, then there would have been fewer troops to spare for overseas military actions. At the same time, Hannibal might have been less reliant on resupply and reinforcements from overseas, since much of Rome's man-power advantage would have been eliminated and he could have recruited more soldiers from those areas of Italy now free from Roman control. In other words, greater Carthaginian success in the Italian theatre could have potentially rendered Sicily, Spain and Roman naval superiority relatively unimportant.

Some scholars have criticised Hannibal as a poor student of history, for not learning from the Pyrrhic War and, more recently, the First Punic War, that the Romans would fight on in the face of adversity.[114] It would be foolish to deny that the Romans were tenacious and resilient. At the same time, Hannibal may have drawn different – and not unreasonable – conclusions from Rome's first two great Mediterranean conflicts.

Although the First Punic War was a protracted struggle in which Rome repeatedly suffered major setbacks without surrendering, the lessons of that conflict are not unambiguous. Consider, for example, Regulus' campaign in Africa in 256. After defeating a Carthaginian fleet off Ecnomus, Roman forces sailed to Africa and landed at Cape Hermiae. Regulus' army captured Aspis and Tunis, plundered the surrounding countryside and captured a large number of cattle and slaves, meanwhile defeating a Carthaginian relief force and storming their camp. At this point, he entered into negotiations with the Carthaginian senate, and although accounts differ with regard to the specifics of the negotiations, all sources agree that the Carthaginians were inclined to accept terms but refused to surrender because Regulus' offer was too harsh. The Carthaginians regrouped only after the timely arrival of the Spartan mercenary Xanthippos, who badly defeated Regulus in a pitched battle; the Roman survivors withdrew from Africa later that same year.[115] In other words, Regulus' invasion of the enemy's homeland, coupled with battlefield success, nearly brought the Carthaginians to their

---

[114] For example, Dorey and Dudley 1972: xv–xvi criticise Hannibal for failing to learn from the example of the Pyrrhic War that the Romans could never be compelled to seek terms in a short war. Lazenby 1996b: 43–7 argues that Hannibal probably anticipated a lengthy war of attrition because he must have learned from the example of the First Punic War that Rome could and would fight on for years.

[115] For the Roman invasion of Africa in 256 and 255: Polyb. 1.25–36; Liv. *Per.* 17–18; Diod. Sic. 23.11–15; Flor. 1.18.21–4; Cass. Dio 11.22–3; Zon. 8.12–13; Oros. 4.8.6–9; Eutr. 2.21; Walbank 1970: 1.89–92; Lazenby 1996a: 97–110; Goldsworthy 2000: 84–92.

knees within a couple of campaign seasons. Meanwhile, the Romans never faced a significant Carthaginian invasion of Italy, but were fortunate to fight the war for the most part in Sicily and Africa. Yet when Hamilcar Barca took over command of the Carthaginian war effort in 247, his first operation was a raid on Bruttium and the territory of Locri, and over the next few years Hamilcar continued to raid the Italian coast, reportedly as far north as Cumae (Polyb. 1.56.2–11). Though he lacked the resources to mount a full-scale invasion, Hamilcar appears to have recognised that Italy was the key to defeating Rome.[116] It is tempting to speculate that Hamilcar's campaigns had a great influence on his son, so the lesson that Hannibal took from the First Punic War was not that the Romans would never surrender, but that one had to fight the Romans in Italy.[117]

The example of Pyrrhus' invasion may have reinforced this lesson. In 280 Pyrrhus defeated a Roman army in a single pitched battle near Heraclea. The outcome of the battle encouraged further defections from the southern Greek cities (and possibly some Samnites and Lucanians),[118] and for a brief period thereafter there was coordination between numerous Roman adversaries.[119] Pyrrhus sent his trusted adviser Cineas to Rome, who carried out extensive negotiations with the Roman senate. The majority of senators, noting the defeat and the allied defections, were anxious for peace, and Cineas' proposed treaty was rejected only after the venerable Appius Claudius Caecus made an impassioned speech against it.[120] Later the Romans took the initiative and sent an embassy to Pyrrhus in

---

[116] Perhaps Hamilcar focused his efforts on the coastal communities because he was trying to disrupt the contributions that the Romans received from their naval allies, or perhaps he desired to encourage widespread revolts of Rome's Italian allies but simply lacked the resources and manoeuvrability to bring this about.

[117] The behaviour of Syracuse early in the First Punic War is also instructive. A Roman army under the command of Ap. Claudius Caudex invaded Sicily in the first year of the war (264). He relieved the Carthaginian siege of Messina, defeated the Syracusans and Carthaginians in pitched battles and began to besiege Syracuse, to where the Syracusan army had retreated. In the following year (263) the consuls M'. Valerius Maximus Messala and M'. Otacilius Crassus, invaded Sicily with four legions, and most of the cities allied with Syracuse and Carthage promptly switched sides and sided with the Romans. When Hiero, the tyrant of Syracuse, recognised the situation, he immediately sought peace terms with the Romans (Polyb. 1.11.3–1.12.4, 1.16.1–11). Thus, a Roman invasion of Sicily, coupled with victory in pitched battle, brought about the rapid disruption of the alliances between the most powerful state (Syracuse) and its allies, which in turn compelled Syracuse to seek terms. The sequence follows the general patterns of Hellenistic warfare, which were discussed above (pp. 35–6), and also may have confirmed the notion that Hannibal could only hope to defeat Rome by invading their 'homeland'.

[118] See above n. 33.

[119] Thus Dionysius of Halicarnassus (20.1.4–8) depicts Pyrrhus in command of a fairly organised, multi-ethnic force at the battle of Ausculum.

[120] Ancient accounts of Pyrrhus' negotiations with Rome are at points contradictory and certainly have been retouched to make the Romans look better. Still, there is good reason to believe the basic

order to negotiate the ransom of Roman captives.[121] The next year, in 279, Pyrrhus again defeated the Romans at Ausculum.[121] After the battle Rome and Carthage agreed to a treaty (Polybius 3.25.3–5): the Carthaginians promised to provide the Romans with naval assistance, and each party agreed to help the other if either made a συμμαχία πρὸς Πύρρον.[122] Terms of the treaty seem to suggest that the Carthaginians were concerned that Rome was about to cave in and leave Pyrrhus free to invade Sicily. In fact, Pyrrhus did receive an embassy from Syracuse, Agrigentum and Leontini asking for help against the Carthaginians, and by 278 he had quit Italy and sailed to Sicily. He sailed back to Italy in 276 with a fleet of 110 warships and numerous cargo vessels. Along the way a Carthaginian fleet destroyed the bulk of his warships, though his army escaped on the cargo ships; the Romans defeated his army, however, at Beneventum in 275, convincing him to abandon Italy once and for all. If Hannibal had studied the Pyrrhic War,[123] he must have observed that the Romans were brought to the brink of accepting terms after one or two pitched battles and the defection of

---

narrative that the Roman ruling elite wavered after Heraclea. The story is plausible enough on the surface. Moreover, Appius Claudius' speech survived in some form and was still read in Cicero's day (Cic. *Brut.* 61, *Sen.* 16), lending credence to the account – after all, there would have been little need for his speech unless the senators were earnestly debating a negotiated peace. Finally, while the story is highly dramatic and ultimately emphasises Roman resolve, it contains the rather unflattering picture of the majority of the Roman senate as afraid to meet Pyrrhus again in battle.

[121] According to Plutarch (*Pyrrh.* 21.1–4) another round of negotiations may have followed after Ausculum, with Cineas making a second trip to Rome, though this may be a reduplication of the negotiations after Heraclea: Broughton 1951–52: 1.193; Lefkowitz 1959.

[122] The precise meaning of συμμαχία πρὸς Πύρρον is difficult to determine. 'An alliance *against* Pyrrhus', as some scholars have translated it, would seem at first glance to make more sense. Walbank 1970: 1.350–1 argues that the phrase means 'alliance *with* Pyrrhus'; according to Walbank, the treaty was designed to encourage the Romans to keep fighting, while leaving the door open, if that failed, for Roman assistance should Pyrrhus invade Sicily (even if the Romans had made peace with him).

[123] In the anecdote of a famous meeting in 193 between Scipio and Hannibal, the latter expressed great admiration for Pyrrhus' generalship (Liv. 35.14.5–12; App. *Syr.* 9–10; Plut. *Flam.* 21). The account is almost certainly spurious (Holleaux 1957: 184–207; Lancel 1999: 195), but it may reflect a tradition that Hannibal possessed knowledge of Pyrrhus' campaigns. Stronger evidence is provided by Polybius' (3.22–7) list of Romano-Carthaginian treaties signed between 509 and the so-called Ebro Treaty in (probably) 226 or 225. One of the treaties was an extension of a prior treaty with specific clauses added regarding Pyrrhus and should be dated to 279/8, after Pyrrhus' victories at Heraclea and Ausculum, but before he invaded Sicily (Polyb. 3.25; see also Diod. Sic. 22.7.5–6; Liv. *Per.* 13; Walbank 1970: 1.349). Hannibal's brother-in-law Hasdrubal orchestrated the Ebro treaty (Polyb. 2.13.7, 3.27.9). Although Polybius (3.26.2) states that most older Romans and Carthaginians in his own day were unaware of the prior Roman–Carthaginian treaties, this observation probably did not apply to Hannibal's family, since presumably Hasdrubal made sure that neither his activities in Spain nor (more importantly) the Ebro Treaty contravened any previous agreements. Since Hannibal inherited Hasdrubal's diplomatic arrangements, he probably learned about earlier Romano-Carthaginian treaties, including the treaty of 279, and perhaps knew of the events that surrounded its signing. Finally, since Pyrrhus engaged Carthaginian forces in Sicily, there were probably Carthaginian records and accounts of this conflict. The

a number of its allies. Also, viewing the war from the Carthaginian perspective, he would have noticed that Punic military assistance was instrumental in Rome's victory over Pyrrhus. He may have concluded, therefore, that the Romans could be compelled to surrender if he invaded Italy and stayed there (unlike Pyrrhus), and a third power (such as Carthage) did not present itself to help Rome.[124]

But if Hannibal's reading of the Pyrrhic and First Punic Wars led him to this conclusion, then perhaps, as has been suggested, his strategy was doomed from the start because Rome simply did not behave like other contemporary states. Thus, it has been argued that Hannibal could never have worn down the Romans' resolve to such an extent that they would seek terms. The reasons cited for extreme Roman doggedness vary from such nebulous concepts as Roman character to the far more plausible assertion that the confidence of the Roman senate was bolstered by its knowledge of its great manpower resources.[125] It is hard to believe the Romans could *never* have been forced into a situation when they would surrender. For example, had Hannibal elicited more widespread defections, the senate's confidence to continue the fight would have been badly shaken. But even if they still never gave in under such circumstances, Hannibal at least could have greatly mitigated Rome's strategic advantages, as discussed above, and thus been in a better position to win a long war. In other words, Hannibal need not have been concerned with the Roman reaction to his strategy so long as the Italian allies had responded more positively to his overtures.

But perhaps Hannibal was foolish to believe that he could bring about a collapse of Rome's system of alliances, or maybe he completely misunderstood the nature of Roman–Italian relations, given the relative loyalty of the allies during the war. It has been suggested that Rome and the allies

---

Ebro Treaty has generated considerable scholarship; for brief analysis and bibliography see for example Walbank 1970: 1.168–72; Richardson 1986: 20–8.

[124] This fits with Hannibal's treaty with Philip V of Macedon (Polyb. 7.9; see also Liv. 23.33–4), since the alliance protected against this powerful Hellenistic state's entering the war on Rome's side. For additional strategic implications of the treaty, see Chapter 5, pp. 211–14, Chapter 7, pp. 298–9.

[125] For the intransigence of the Romans, see Crawford 1978: 'The war was settled by Roman persistence, a characteristic which had already helped defeat Pyrrhus and which was about to defeat Hannibal ...' (p. 50) and 'It was clear in the aftermath of Cannae that Rome had no intention of ever surrendering ...' (p. 52); Caven 1980: 256–7: 'Hannibal either did not consider, or ignored, that Rome would not surrender after shattering defeat'; Baker 1929: 150–1 argues that Rome adopted a 'victory or death' posture after Cannae. See also Briscoe 1989: 53: 'the firmness with which the crisis was met prompted Polybius to devote the whole of book VI [to extolling Roman virtues]'. For the view that the Romans' stubbornness after Cannae was based on their knowledge of their manpower advantage: Goldsworthy 2000: 315.

shared a 'community of interest', with the allies enjoying the perceived benefits of Roman hegemony; along similar lines, it has been argued that close cultural and ethnic bonds convinced the allies to choose the Romans over Hannibal, whose army was composed of Carthaginians, Iberians and Gauls.[126] Yet, as was discussed earlier in this chapter, it is by no means certain that the allies appreciated the supposed advantages of living under Roman dominion, nor that they felt particularly strong bonds of common unity.[127] As will be discussed in the next four chapters, the Italian allies harboured a number of grievances against Rome; some complaints were common across communities, while others were specific to individual communities (or even to particular groups and individuals within communities). It is not clear that the Carthaginians would have appeared much more foreign than the Romans to some groups in Italy, for example the Italiote Greek communities. But even if the Carthaginians *were* culturally and linguistically alien to many of Rome's Italian allies, this does not mean that Hannibal would not have been more politically appealing.[128]

A more cynical argument emphasises fear of Roman reprisal as a chief reason for Hannibal's failure to elicit more allied revolts.[129] This position has some merit, though Hannibal also treated intransigent states poorly, and it is hard to believe that the ruling class of a city was always significantly more concerned with Rome's response down the road than with Hannibal's army outside their city's wall. Some scholars have questioned whether Hannibal's self-portrayal as a Hellenistic liberator was credible, since his brutal punishment of intransigent Italian communities contradicted his promise of 'freedom', or even because the Italians simply would not understand Hellenistic diplomatic language.[130] By the late

---

[126] For example, Hallward 1930: 56; Badian 1958: 143–5; Toynbee 1965: 272–80 (arguing that Rome's generous enfranchisement of the conquered helped to unite the Roman commonwealth); Dorey and Dudley 1972: xvi (making the anachronistic claim that Hannibal was challenging not a city-state but a nation-state); Crawford 1978: 52–3; Lazenby 1978: 87–8; Salmon 1982: 80–2 (more cautiously arguing that the allies acted out of self-interest, but still emphasising Hannibal's foreignness); David 1996: 57.

[127] See above, pp. 25–8. See also Mouritsen 1998, 2006, who critiques the idea that there was a growing sense of Roman and Italian closeness during the second century BC, and thus argues *a priori* against such a development in the third century BC. Furthermore, Lazenby 1996b: 42 and Goldsworthy 2000: 222–4 observed that the communities who joined Hannibal did not have a common identity or purpose.

[128] Consider the willingness of some Italians, especially Etruscan communities, to make alliances with the Gauls; see above n. 68.

[129] Briscoe 1989: 75–8; David 1996: 57; Goldsworthy 2000: 226.

[130] Erskine 1993 suggested that either Hannibal posed as a Hellenistic liberator but the Italians were confused by the propaganda, or that ancient authors, especially Polybius, Hellenised Hannibal and portrayed his actions in terms of Hellenistic diplomacy. Errington 1972: 69–71, 76–7 argued

third century most communities in Italy had exposure to Greek culture,[131] and there is evidence that at least some of the states in southern Italy had experience with liberation propaganda (see, for example, App. *Sam.* 10.1). In any case, it is implausible that the ruling elite of the Italian states could not grasp Hannibal's pledge that they would be free from Roman rule.[132] Moreover, Hannibal does not appear to have merely made generic offers of freedom, but rather he seems to have tailored his diplomacy from state to state in response to specific local concerns.[133] Finally, that a significant number of allies did in fact defect after Cannae – and continued to defect as late as 213/12 – speaks against the notion that Hannibal's foreignness was an insurmountable obstacle.

LOCAL CONDITIONS AND THE FAILURE OF HANNIBAL'S STRATEGY IN ITALY

Hannibal's diplomatic failure was that he could never elicit enough allied defections at one time, and the reasons for this are to be found in the specific contexts of each city. Unfortunately, however, although scholars frequently make reference to the loyalty of the Italian confederacy, there has been no comprehensive study aimed at the question of why some allies revolted but others remained loyal during the Second Punic War since J. S. Reid's (1915)

that the release of prisoners after the battles of Trebbia, Trasimene and Cannae probably had little effect in convincing the Italians that Hannibal was a legitimate liberator, while his treatment of intransigent communities completely undermined his promise of freedom. On Hannibal's potentially cruel treatment of Italians: Polyb. 3.86.8–11 (massacre of adult men from communities seized in Umbria and Picenum in 217) and Liv. 23.15.2–4 (destruction of Nuceria).

[131] See Lomas 1993: 46–8; Cornell 1995a: 86–92.

[132] Contra Erskine 1993.

[133] Compare the terms of the surviving treaties between Hannibal and Italian communities: Capua (Liv. 23.7.1–3; see Chapter 3, pp. 113–17), Locri (Liv. 24.1.9, 13; see Chapter 4, pp. 166–7), Taras (Polyb. 8.25.2; Liv. 25.8.8; see Chapter 5, pp. 203–4, 215–16) and the Lucanians (Liv. 25.16.7). The treaties share a number of terms, including the guarantee that Hannibal's new allies would live under their own laws. This has led some to conclude that the treaty terms represent generic promises and thus do not reflect the particular concerns of individual cities (for example, Ungern-Sternberg 1975: 56–7; Frederiksen 1977: 183, 1984: 240–1). There are, however, a number of differences and unique provisions. The treaty with Capua dictated that Hannibal would hand 300 Roman hostages over to the Capuans. The Tarentine treaty contained the unique clause that the Carthaginians could seize any houses or property that the Romans possessed. Only the Tarentine and (perhaps) the Locrian treaties compelled the city to hand over its Roman garrison to the Carthaginians. Only the Locrian treaty contains a proviso dealing with control of the city's port. Overall, the differences in the treaties indicate that Hannibal tailored his negotiations in response to specific local demands. Indeed, as will be discussed in Chapter 3, Hannibal's negotiation with the Capuans included specific promises that he would extend Capuan hegemony. Hannibal must have expected to encounter some difficulty in convincing the allies to revolt (Lazenby 1996b: 43–5), so it is not surprising that he tried to accommodate local interests.

lengthy article, itself not without weaknesses.[134] As we have seen, when scholars discuss Italian loyalty, they tend to invoke overly broad explanations for Hannibal's failure to quickly elicit large-scale revolts – indeed, Reid concludes that Roman beneficence towards their allies limited the effectiveness of the Hannibalic strategy. It is necessary, therefore, to study closely why many allied states remained loyal to Rome even after Hannibal's awesome victories and his promise of freedom, for this loyalty resulted in the war's lasting perhaps longer than Hannibal had anticipated, and once the conflict became a war of attrition, other factors undermining Hannibal's chances for success came into play. One of the goals of this book is to provide such a study.

As I have already indicated, detailed analyses of the specific local factors and conditions shaping the decisions of individual cities to revolt or remain loyal after 216 will occupy much of the next four chapters, and it would be impossible to summarise all of the specific discussions here. Still, it is worth pointing out briefly a few general patterns that emerge from the regional case studies. First, the individual communities in Italy acted out of self-interest and responded to the immediate pressures and opportunities brought about by Hannibal's entry into Italy. These cities – or rather, their ruling elites – were not much motivated by abstract notions of Italian unity or loyalty to Rome (or to Carthage, for that matter). Second, the decision to revolt was also informed by longer-term internal political and external diplomatic conditions, which point back to some of the overarching themes and developments of the fourth and third centuries discussed in this chapter. Hannibal's early victories in the war disrupted Rome's control of the peninsula – Roman unipolar hegemony – which in turn allowed local tensions, political divisions and especially regional intercity rivalries to rise to the surface. Hannibal had difficulty eliciting allied rebellions because each community made the decision whether or not to rebel based on the unique history of relations with its neighbours and the specific ways in which the larger events of the war affected these local rivalries. Thus, the decision of a state to remain loyal or to defect was born of a specific set of circumstances. Third, no single diplomatic strategy or single promise would work for all Italian communities. It seems that Hannibal was successful in winning over the most powerful city in

---

[134] In the main, I disagree strongly with Reid's adoption of the position that the allies remained generally loyal because the Romans were more or less benevolent overlords. As such he downplays, again wrongly in my opinion, the degree of allied disaffection and the severity of the rebellions. In addition to the bibliography cited in n. 126, analysis of allied motivations can be found in Groag 1929: 79–96 and De Sanctis 1956–69: iii.2 *passim*. Kukofka's (1990) short monograph on southern Italy in the Second Punic War is unfortunately brief and does not explore in much detail specific allied motivations.

each of the four regions under investigation. As mentioned previously in this chapter, Hannibal explicitly promised to extend the power of Capua, which was the largest and strongest city in Campania; whether he made similar promises to other large states (such as Arpi or Taras) is unknown, but their ruling classes were motivated to side with Hannibal by aspirations to (re-)establish their city's local hegemony. But when a potential local hegemonic power accepted Hannibal's offers, it had the effect of limiting his success among neighbouring communities, especially those that had a long-standing rivalry with – and so feared the emergence of – the aspiring regional power. Thus, age-old intra-regional competition helped to undermine the effectiveness of the Hannibalic strategy.

Fourth, for cities that did defect, local political rivalry and aristocratic competition undermined Hannibal's war effort. Hannibal was initially able to gain control of some cities by playing on political factionalism. In all cities the local ruling aristocracy appears to have harboured a wide range of sentiments towards Rome, with a core group of aristocrats strongly in support of the Romans. Such aristocrats probably owed their position, at least in part, to Roman backing. Meanwhile this presented Hannibal with the opportunity to win the support of rival aristocratic families who saw in the elimination of Roman rule the opportunity for their own political ascendancy. But such support proved difficult to maintain, for when Hannibal's fortunes appeared to waver or when he seemed unable to deliver on his promise of political power, pro-Hannibalic aristocrats lost credibility and fell out of power, or they reconciled themselves with Rome, and Hannibal lost control of their cities. Also, taking control of cities in this way left in place a built-in opposition, as resistance to Hannibal could crystallise around those who had formerly held power. Thus, the very conditions that helped Hannibal win over a good number of Rome's allies in southern Italy ultimately contributed to his diplomatic, and thus strategic, failure.

Put in this light, it is perhaps not surprising that Hannibal was unable to navigate the complex tangle of interstate ties and rivalries, political factionalism and unique local circumstances, and thus bring about the collapse of Rome's Italian empire. Indeed, what may be more remarkable is how the Romans had been able to overcome the same sorts of localism, particularism and factionalism that vexed Hannibal. We will come back to this question, which was touched on earlier in this chapter, in Chapter 7. For the moment, however, we will return to the plains of Apulia in the summer of 216, where Hannibal's strategy first began to bear fruit – and where some, but not all, of Rome's allies in the region began to defect.

CHAPTER 2

Apulia

INTRODUCTION

This chapter will examine the application of the Hannibalic strategy in Apulia, its mixed results in the summer of 216 and Hannibal's ultimate strategic failure in the region. Apulia in the Second Punic War is an interesting case study because Hannibal did in fact enjoy a great deal of success there. He won over the most powerful city in the region, Arpi, as well as many smaller communities including Salapia, Herdonia, Aecae and probably Ausculum. It was in Apulia, moreover, where Hannibal's strategy first began to produce results, as these revolts occurred immediately after the battle of Cannae and before Hannibal departed for Samnium and Campania. Yet he was not completely successful in eliciting allied revolts in Apulia, even though the battle of Cannae took place there and should therefore have had the most dramatic effect in undermining Rome's reputation among nearby communities. Two Latin colonies remained Roman strongholds, Luceria and Venusia. More interestingly, a few Apulian communities remained loyal to Rome, including Teanum Apulum and Canusium, the latter situated very close to where the battle of Cannae was fought. Ultimately, of course, Hannibal failed to hold Apulia; in fact, Arpi fell to the Romans within only a few years, in 213, making it the first of Hannibal's important allies to be recaptured.[1] Since Rome had maintained control of Luceria, Venusia, Teanum Apulum and Canusium, Hannibal's Apulian allies were essentially isolated, and since he was unable to protect them, the Romans slowly but surely reconquered all of the rebellious cities. Thus, Hannibal's enterprise in Apulia fell prey to Rome's long-term strategic advantages. The fundamental question remains, however, why Hannibal did not convince more Apulian cities, especially Canusium and Teanum Apulum, to revolt after the battle of Cannae.

---

[1] Compared, for example, with Capua (recaptured 211), Syracuse (211), Taras (209) and Locri (205).

Even though Apulian affairs during the Second Punic War are intriguing – the Apulians supplied Hannibal with his first Italian allies and provided the Romans with their first major reconquest in the war of attrition – there has been very little attempt to analyse why some Apulian cities defected while others remained loyal to Rome. The revolts of Arpi, Salapia, Herdonia and Aecae are typically mentioned only in passing as evidence that the Hannibalic strategy had begun to work after the battle of Cannae, but there is rarely any effort to explain how particular local conditions shaped the varying decisions of Apulian cities to revolt or remain loyal.[2]

Yet even prior attempts to focus on such specific local factors in Apulia have proven insufficient. For example, some scholars have argued that fear was the decisive factor: the combination of Hannibal's victory at Cannae and, perhaps as significant, the proximity of his army persuaded many nearby communities to defect.[3] While there is certainly some truth to this assertion, it cannot account entirely for the revolts of Apulian cities. The people of Gereonium rejected Hannibal's overtures and ultimately chose to be massacred rather than surrender, suggesting that Carthaginian threats were not necessarily menacing enough to convince a community to revolt. More importantly, this assertion explains only why a city would revolt; it does not explain why other cities such Canusium, having witnessed the battle of Cannae and with Hannibal's army nearby, did not follow the same course of action. Canusium is a particularly striking example because the battle of Cannae occurred within its territory and yet the Canusians remained loyal Roman allies.

Other explanations emphasise local ethnic tensions in limiting the success of the Hannibalic strategy in Apulia. Reid (1915: 108) argued that there was little sympathy for Hannibal because there had been strong Greek influence in the region, so Apulians would have been wary of his 'barbarian' army. This argument is fundamentally flawed, as it assumes that there existed a general Greek sentiment antithetical to allying with a 'foreign' invader. Yet events during the war seem to undercut this notion. For example, the Greek city of Locri allied with Hannibal in 215 and remained his ally until 205, while the neighbouring Greek city of Rhegion remained a staunch Roman ally. There is, moreover, strong evidence to suggest that

---

[2] For a typical example, Lazenby 1978: 89 states: 'But in other respects, his strategy at last began to bear fruit: some of the Apulian communities, including Arpi, Salapia, Aecae and Herdonia, seem to have gone over to him immediately after Cannae …', yet he provides no further analysis. Kukofka 1990 oddly does not mention the revolt of Arpi and makes only brief reference to other Apulian communities when they intersected with Rome's counter-efforts in south-eastern Italy during the middle years of the war.

[3] See Reid 1915: 106; Caven 1980: 141; see also Ciaceri 1928–40: III.132–46.

Rhegion and Locri were bitter rivals, and the Locrians may have seen Hannibal as a means to assert hegemony over neighbouring Greek cities.[4] The people of Taras also had a long history of allying with various Italic peoples in order to assert their hegemony, in some cases over neighbouring Greek cities.[5] Livy (25.15.7) states that Thurii did not share a strong sense of kinship with Metapontion, though both were Greek cities. These examples caution against assuming that there was a strong sense of unity among the Greek communities in Italy, or that the Greeks were inherently opposed to allying with 'barbarians' to further their own interests.[6] Thus, even if the Apulians were highly 'Hellenised', this fact in itself would probably not have contributed significantly to Hannibal's failure in Apulia.

A more plausible explanation calls attention to the long-standing hostility between the communities of Apulia and the nearby Samnite communities. It has been argued that some Apulian communities had originally allied with Rome because they hated the Samnites. By the time of the Second Punic War, however, the Samnites had been subjugated and ceased to pose a threat. Thus, enmity towards the Samnites was outweighed by growing resentment against Roman domination, which in turn motivated the Apulians to revolt.[7] The cities of northern Apulia, on which we will focus in this chapter, appear to have shared certain cultural practices, perhaps indicating some sort of common identity. For example, Apulian cities often display similar monumental architecture, while epigraphical and onomastic evidence suggests that Messapic continued to be spoken in several of the major centres such as Arpi and Canusium.[8] It is possible that there was ethnic tension between the Messapic Apulians and the Oscan Samnites, and indeed this chapter will argue that Apulian–Samnite hostility did influence the effectiveness of the Hannibalic strategy. Yet during the Second Punic War, Arpi revolted while Canusium remained loyal, indicating that the Apulians were not a unified bloc responding equally

---

[4] For Locri and Rhegion, see Chapter 4, pp. 167–71, 183–4.

[5] See Chapter 5, pp. 193–7.

[6] For a more general discussion of rivalry and envy (*phthonos*) shaping Greek interstate relations, see Hornblower 1983: 13–31, citing the specific example of Thurii and Croton 'who hated each other' (p. 16).

[7] De Sanctis 1956–69: III.2.201; Caven 1980: 141.

[8] On Messapic language in Apulia, especially in northern Apulia (so-called Daunia): Parelangèli 1960; De Simone 1988, 1992; Untermann 2000. Literary sources make reference to several individuals with Messapic names in the Apulian cities of Arpi and Canusium (among other places): below, n. 29. Messapic names also appear in Greek script on coinage from Apulian cities: below, n. 149. Some northern Apulian cities had massive earthen walls that enclosed extensive territories (below, pp. 76–7), and the local elites appear to have adopted Hellenised burial practices (below, pp. 77–8). Some cities, however, such as Teanum Apulum, display evidence of Oscanisation: below, p. 95.

to the same motives and pressures. Neither hostility towards the Samnites nor resentment against the Romans can account for the particular disposition of each city in the region during the Second Punic War; other factors have come into play.

It is necessary to examine more closely the conditions that contributed to Hannibal's defeat in the Apulian theatre, by focusing on the local level and analysing the specific economic, political and diplomatic factors – many of them independent of the conflict between Rome and Carthage – that shaped the choice of each Apulian city's ruling elite to revolt or not. This decision was rooted in a complex matrix of political rivalries, economic tensions and diplomatic interests, and for Hannibal the critical moment came immediately after the battle of Cannae, when he was unable to win over all the Apulian cities precisely because of these local factors.

As we will see, the city of Arpi sided with Hannibal because the Arpians wanted to extend their local hegemony and knew their opportunities for expansion were limited so long as Rome dominated Italy. After Arpi revolted a number of less powerful cities that shared traditional ties and economic links followed suit, thus gravitating toward Arpi's hegemony. Meanwhile, Canusium and Teanum Apulum were also powerful cities but both maintained rivalries with Arpi. The Canusians and the Teanenses would have perceived the new Arpian–Hannibalic axis as an immediate threat to their interests. The Arpian revolt, therefore, probably strengthened the resolve of the Canusians and the Teanenses to remain loyal to Rome. This chapter will emphasise regional and sub-regional history in order to demonstrate not only that such longer-term relationships existed between various Apulian cities, but also how they influenced events in the Second Punic War, thus allowing us to view the conflict from the local perspective.

Before proceeding to the main analysis I must define what I mean by 'Apulia', for the purposes of this chapter. The boundaries of Apulia, especially its border with Samnium, are difficult to determine with certainty, and even the ancients found it hard to disentangle.[9] By the time of Augustus, Apulia was part of the administrative *Regio II*, which encompassed the entire 'heel' of Italy between the Bradano (Bradanus) and Biferno (Tifernus) rivers and included areas and communities that had little association with 'Apulia' or the *'Apuli'* in previous centuries. The southern half of the *Regio II*, which had been known variously as Messapia,

[9] See, for example, Strabo's shifting definitions (6.3.1, 6.3.5, 6.3.8); for modern attempts to define the boundaries: Salmon 1967: 23–7; Volpe 1990: 13–14.

Calabria, Iapygia or the land of the Sallentini, will not be discussed in this chapter (see Map 3).[10] Rather, we will focus on the northern half, especially the communities from around the Ofanto (Aufidus) to the Fortore (Fertor) rivers; this area was also called 'Daunia' in antiquity.[11] The western limit is the base of the Samnite Apennines, following roughly the modern western border of the *provincia di Foggia*. The communities discussed in this chapter include Arpi, Herdonia, Salapia, Aecae, Vibinum, Teanum Apulum, Canusium, Ausculum and Luceria. Venusia (which straddled Samnium, Apulia and Lucania) will also be included (see Map 4). This cluster of communities formed a relatively coherent international system with intensive interactions, both peaceful and hostile, from at least the fourth century. The same cities were also much involved in the action of the Second Punic War and they receive a fair amount of attention in the literary record. Thus, we have the possibility to examine in closer detail how they responded to Hannibal's overtures. The actions of other bordering communities will also be discussed when relevant.

THE REVOLT OF ARPI, 216

Arpi was the most important city in Apulia,[12] and the Arpians had a long history of loyalty to Rome that stretched back to the fourth century. During the Second Punic War, however, the city defected. Indeed, as I will argue, Arpi was probably one of the first communities to abandon Rome, when it willingly invited Hannibal into an alliance. The revolt of Arpi was significant because it encouraged other Apulian cities to defect in turn. In this section I will analyse the reasons for the Arpian revolt, in particular how local hegemonic interests were an important consideration.

In order to analyse both the specific circumstances surrounding the city's defection and its impact on neighbouring cities' policy decisions, we need to establish when exactly the Arpian revolt took place.[13] Ancient

---

[10] I will discuss the communities of the Sallentine peninsula briefly, in terms of the interaction with the powerful Greek city of Taras, in Chapter 5.

[11] In this chapter, I will use the terms 'Daunia' and 'northern Apulia' interchangeably in a geographic context. Even though Pliny lived at a time when Apulia included administratively the entire heel of Italy, he describes Apulia as beginning (from the south) at around the Aufidus and including two sections: the Apulia of the Daunians and the Apulia of the Apulians (*HN* 3.103–4). Polybius (3.88.4–6) calls approximately the same area 'Daunia', which comprised the northern part of Iapygia. Strabo (6.3.8) places the southern extent of Apulia/Daunia as far as Bari (Barium), though in the same passage he also calls attention to the Aufidus as an important topographical marker.

[12] Arpi as the pre-eminent city in Apulia: see below, pp. 76–7.

[13] There is some disagreement whether Arpi revolted soon after Cannae (De Sanctis 1956–69: III.2.201; Seibert 1993b: 212) or sometime the following year (Reid 1915: 106).

literary evidence suggests that it occurred immediately after Cannae, in the summer of 216. Polybius states specifically that the Arpians approached Hannibal soon after his victory at Cannae, while Livy reports more generically that some of the Apulian cities, presumably including Arpi, switched sides in the wake of the battle.[14] Both passages, however, contain anachronisms, so references to the immediacy of the Apulian defections must be treated with some caution.[15] In the same passage Polybius emphasises that Arpi did not surrender to Hannibal but rather invited him to come to them, suggesting that the two sides reached some sort of negotiated agreement. It is most likely that such negotiations were carried out while Hannibal was in the area, probably when he rested his army in the days after the battle of Cannae before marching through Samnium to Campania. This fits with later reports that a local aristocrat named Dasius Altinius had led Arpi into revolt soon after the battle of Cannae.[16] Livy (27.1.4) claims that the nearby city of Herdonia revolted immediately after the battle.[17] Taken together, the ancient evidence strongly suggests that Arpi and neighbouring Apulian communities defected in the summer of 216, in the brief window after the battle of Cannae but before Hannibal set off for Campania.

It also appears, as I have just mentioned, that Hannibal gained Arpi through peaceful negotiations rather than by storming or besieging the city. Although we lack a detailed account of these initial negotiations, accounts of the Roman reconquest of Arpi indicate that Hannibal won over the loyalty of a party of local aristocrats.[18]

At first glance, Livy paints a picture of Arpi beset by political *stasis*, with the lower classes in support of Rome and the aristocrats in favour of Hannibal.[19] Thus, when Roman troops besieged and stormed Arpi in 213,

---

[14] Polyb. 3.118.3; Liv. 22.61.10–12, 23.11.11.

[15] For perhaps the most obvious anachronism, both Livy and Polybius state that Taras revolted soon after Cannae; in fact Polybius claims that the Tarentines 'immediately surrendered' (Ταραντῖνοί τε γὰρ εὐθέως ἐνεχείριζον αὐτούς). However, Taras did not revolt until the winter of 213/12; see Polyb. 8.24.4–8.31.6; Liv. 25.1.1, 25.7.10–10.10; App. *Hann.* 32–3; see also Chapter 5, pp. 189–90. De Sanctis 1956–69: III.2.201 n. 1 resolves the anachronism in Polybius by emending Ταραντῖνοί to Σαλαπῖνοι.

[16] Liv. 24.45.2; App. *Hann.* 31.

[17] However, see Lomas 1996, who places the revolt of Herdonia in 214 with no explanation; Sirago 1992: 71–4 assumes the cities of Apulia revolted in 216; he allows for the possibility that Herdonia revolted later (p. 74 n. 4). Again, no explanation is given.

[18] The reconquest of Arpi (213) is narrated at length by Livy (24.45–7) and in briefer form by Appian (*Hann.* 31). The city was taken by Q. Fabius Maximus (cos. 213), the son of the more famous Cunctator, who served as his son's legate (or proconsul according to Claudius Quadrigarius *apud* Gell. 2.2.13 = Beck and Walter, *FRH* 14 F56 = fr. 57 Peter). It is tempting to speculate that later accounts of Arpian affairs in 213 are derived at least partly from family records of the Fabii transmitted through Fabius Pictor.

[19] It is worth noting that this is the opposite of Livy's usual portrayal of the *principes* in support of Rome and the mob loyal to Hannibal; see Chapter 1, p. 12 n. 25.

they found a Carthaginian garrison of 5,000 troops alongside 3,000 Arpians, but the local troops quickly turned on the Carthaginians and blamed their own government for selling them out to the foreigners.[20] The political situation must have been more complex than this, and the Arpian ruling elite was probably not uniform in its support for Hannibal. The ancient sources do suggest that Hannibal had the support of a party of aristocrats, including the aforementioned local *princeps* Dasius. When Hannibal later suspected that the Arpians were going to submit to Rome, he investigated charges of sedition and executed other members of Dasius' family.[21] When the Romans and Arpians parleyed, the local citizenry compelled the city's chief magistrate (Livy refers to him as a 'praetor') to discuss terms with the consul. This unnamed aristocrat had presumably been in Hannibal's good graces, given his pre-eminent position in 213, so it is likely that that he too promoted the initial move to side with the Carthaginians.[22] Finally, the Arpians complained that their city was betrayed not by the entire ruling class, but rather by a few leading men (*principibus … paucis*).[23] Thus, a closer analysis of the episode reveals that Hannibal had the support of at least a small party of the local aristocracy, of whom some were related to Dasius Altinius.

It is not surprising that Hannibal gained Arpi by winning over the loyalty of a critical mass of the local aristocracy, and indeed pro-Hannibalic (or anti-Roman) aristocrats were also instrumental in the defection of other Apulian cities, including Herdonia and Salapia. As with the case of Arpi, we do not possess detailed accounts of the internal political conditions in Herdonia and Salapia during the lead-up to their revolts, but the relatively detailed narratives of their recapture later in the war at the hands of the Romans allow us to reconstruct the political context.

In his account of the situation in Herdonia, Livy (27.1.3–15) again presents the political situation as one of *stasis*, with the lower classes in favour of Hannibal and the leading men leaning towards the Roman cause. When Hannibal learned in 210 that the Herdonian nobility had been plotting with the proconsul Cn. Fulvius Centumalus to betray the city, he executed the ringleaders, burned the town to the ground and

[20] Liv. 24.47.3–6.
[21] Liv. 24.45.11–14; App. *Hann.* 31. Livy specifically refers to Dasius as '*principe*' and mentions his great wealth.
[22] Liv. 24.47.7.
[23] Liv. 24.47.6. Of course, one would expect the common citizens facing Roman soldiers to blame the ruling class for the revolt, but it is interesting that Livy does not have the citizenry blame the entire aristocracy, which would have better fitted into Livy's general theme of *stasis*. Rather, they accuse only a few leading men, a core faction within the ruling elite. This slight detail is certainly plausible and may reflect genuine historical information.

transferred the remaining population to Thurii and Metapontion. It is
doubtful, however, that the entire local aristocracy was unified in its loyalty to Rome. In fact, some Herdonian aristocrats were courting Fulvius
while at the same time others informed Hannibal of the plot.[24] Livy's
report that only those leading men who had negotiated with the Romans
were put to death further suggests that the entire local aristocracy was not
involved in the plot.[25] We can surmise that aristocratic loyalty was also
divided when the city rebelled in 216 following Rome's crushing defeat at
the battle of Cannae.[26] Hannibal was thus able to win over a core group
of local aristocratic supporters at this critical juncture in the war, though
we will never know if the decision to revolt caused the local ruling class to
splinter, or if Hannibal manipulated pre-existing political rivalry.

   A more striking picture of local political division is seen in the case
of Salapia, which the Romans also retook in 210. Both Livy (26.38.6–14)
and Appian (*Hann.* 45–7) record the names of two leading citizens of
Salapia – Blattius and Dasius, bitter political opponents whose personal
rivalry extended to their loyalties during the Second Punic War: Blattius
remained loyal to Rome while Dasius sided with Hannibal. The two
accounts of how their rivalry played out during the Roman reconquest
of Salapia differ in some details, but they largely agree in terms of the
general outline of events. Salapia was under firm Carthaginian control,
garrisoned by 500 Numidian cavalry.[27] Blattius hoped to betray the city
to Rome but reckoned that his plan could not succeed without additional
support, including Dasius' help. After sending messengers to the consul
M. Claudius Marcellus, Blattius approached his rival to strike some sort
of deal. Both Livy and Appian agree that Dasius initially rejected Blattius'
offer, and Livy states explicitly that Dasius refused primarily because the
two were rivals for high political honours.[28] The political rivalry between
Blattius and Dasius was long-standing (ἐκ πολλοῦ, according to Appian),

[24] Liv. 27.1.6.
[25] Archaeological evidence is broadly consistent with the Livian narrative. Herdonia's city walls
   and gates show signs of repeated repairs, including some haphazard reworkings in cruder material that can be dated to the last quarter of the third century. Mertens 1995b: 143–5 associates this
   construction with Hannibal's siege in 210. Similarly, Mertens and Van Wonterghem 1995: 155–9
   identify significant rebuilding in the second century, which is consistent with the city's destruction during the Second Punic War. They also conclude from the construction that the site was
   reoccupied soon after the events of 210. Surely some elements of the population (including those
   who favoured the Roman cause or were at least ambivalent) had managed to flee the city and
   came filtering back after Hannibal left the area. Stauncher supporters of Hannibal may have
   accepted more readily their transfer to safer Carthaginian strongholds such as Metapontion and
   Thurii. For the impact of these 'exiles' on Thurian affairs in particular, see Chapter 5, pp. 229–31.
[26] Liv. 27.1.4.   [27] Liv. 26.38.11; App. *Hann.* 47.
[28] Liv. 26.38.6–8; App. *Hann.* 45.

certainly predating the events of 210 and probably tracing back to before
the Second Punic War. The sources mention only these two men by name,
but the fact that they came from old, powerful families and the fact that
Blattius needed Dasius' help both imply that the two men had political
allies. The Salapian episode must have involved more aristocrats than the
two men whose names we know, though Blattius and Dasius may have
been the leaders or most prominent members of different aristocratic 'factions'. If so, Hannibal was able to win over Salapia in 216 by winning
over a critical mass of disaffected local aristocrats, including the party of
Dasius.

Let us return to Arpi. The city sided with Hannibal peaceably in 216.
The local ruling elite was probably divided when their city revolted, and
Hannibal succeeded in winning over the loyalty of a party of aristocrats, allowing him to control the city – a similar sequence to that which
unfolded in other Apulian communities, as just discussed. That Hannibal
relied on the cooperation of at least some local elites to secure the loyalty of Arpi is predictable. But why a group of aristocrats would risk siding with Hannibal is a more difficult question. I have just discussed how
intra-aristocratic political competition in Arpi, as well as in other Apulian
cities, seems to have involved long-standing feuds and personal rivalries.
I suggest that the local ruling party would tend to be pro-Roman (or at
least be more hesitant to defect) because the Romans had supported them
in the past, or simply because they benefited from the political status
quo. Aristocrats who were closed out would have been less satisfied with
the current political order and thus would have been more likely to find
an alliance with Hannibal an attractive option. Ultimately, a rival faction may have seen Hannibal as a means to further its own interests or to
seize power. Ancient evidence, albeit scattered, provides support for this
dynamic in Apulia.

Literary sources preserve the names of a number of elite families, including the Dasii (in Arpi, Salapia and Brundisium), the Blattii (in Salapia),
and the family of Busa (in Canusium),[29] who all lived during the Second

---

[29] The name 'Dasius' was Messapic, and its ubiquity throughout a number of Apulian cities has led
some to argue that it once referred to a function, title or status rather than a personal name. Given
the name's widespread use, there is no need to argue that all Dasii, especially those in different
cities, were related or members of the same 'clan'. Rather, it may simply have been a common
name deriving from an older word or title. On 'Dasius', see Schulze 1966: 38–9, 44–5; Salmon
1969: 55 n. 65; Mazzei and Lippolis 1984: 226; Volpe 1990: 44; Sirago 1992: 73. Busa was also a
Messapic name, with forms appearing in inscriptions throughout Apulia: Schulze 1966: 38 n. 2
contra Klebs 1889: 1072–3 (who assumed it was Oscan). According to Schulze 1966: 423, 'Blattius'
may be related to the Oscan name 'Blossius', though he later (p. 519) lists it as Messapic.

Punic War. We do not know when these families achieved elite status, but at least some of them must have possessed it for generations, perhaps even predating the Roman conquest of Apulia. Such endurance of native Apulian elites is implied in Dionysius of Halicarnassus' account of the foundation of the Latin colony of Venusia in 291. Dionysus records that the colony was founded with 20,000 settlers, a figure often rejected as improbably high.[30] Others have attempted to reconcile Dionysius' report by arguing, for example, that the large figure represents the total number of inhabitants, a fusion of settlers and the native population.[31] Regardless of the original number of colonists, some may have been enrolled from the local population. Native aristocratic elements probably survived the colonial foundation and were still visible in the late third century.[32] This theory gains support from references to Dasius of Brundisium,[33] who commanded the garrison of Clastidium and betrayed it to Hannibal in 218. Brundisium had been refounded as a Latin colony in 244.[34] That Dasius was placed in charge of a garrison shows that native aristocratic families could survive a colonial foundation and achieve high political honours within a generation or so. We might also consider comparative evidence from Campania, where literary and epigraphic sources show that the Calavius family had been prominent for over a century, possibly since before the initial Roman conquest.[35]

Some local aristocrats benefited from Roman conquest and furthered their own local standing through their relationship with either the Roman senate or individual Roman aristocrats.[36] Again, we can look at the striking example of Dasius of Brundisium, who had been entrusted with commanding the garrison in Clastidium.[37] Dasius' position as *praefectus praesidii*

---

[30]   Dion. Hal. 17/18.5.2. For the foundation of Venusia, see also Vell. Pat. 1.14.6. Dionysius' figure of 20,000 colonists is far higher than the typical number of settlers sent to a Latin colony, usually between 2,500 and 6,000 men (see Gargola 1995: 56). Salmon 1969: 60–2 n. 80 emends the number to 6,000; Bernardi 1947 lowers the number to 2,000.

[31]   For example, Bottini 1981: 153; Mario Torelli 1984: 325–36, 1992: 608–19; Marchi and Sabbatini 1996: 19.

[32]   On the potential integration of local elites into a colonial ruling class, see Bradley 2006: 174–5.

[33]   Polyb. 3.69.1–4; Liv. 21.48.8–9.

[34]   Cic. *Att.* 4.1.4; Salmon 1969: 64.

[35]   Livy (9.7.1–3) mentions a Capuan aristocrat named Aulus Calavius, son of Ovius Calavius, who supposedly made a speech after the Caudine Forks (321). Aulus was, according to Livy, an old man. If there is a kernel of historical truth in this passage, Ovius and probably Aulus would have been adults before Rome granted the Capuans *civitas sine suffragio* in 338. Members of the Calavius family were accused of heading an aristocratic conspiracy in 314 (Liv. 9.26.5–7); Pacuvius Calavius held the office of *meddix tuticus* in 216 (Liv. 23.2–4); and an unspecified number of Calavii were accused of arson in 210 (Liv. 26.27.7). See also *CIL* 8.2564, 10.3787; Schulze 1966: 138, 351–2.

[36]   Volpe 1990: 35–7; Sirago 1992: 75.   [37]   Polyb. 3.69.1–4; Liv. 21.48.8–9.

indicates not only the survival of indigenous elites, but also the achievement of high office by indigenous aristocrats within a Roman framework.
Busa of Canusium, after providing food and shelter for the survivors of
Cannae at personal expense, was bestowed honours by the Roman senate,
illustrating that Rome rewarded loyal local aristocrats.[38] Blattius of Salapia
may have had close personal ties with members of the Roman aristocracy,[39]
which could account for his more persistent loyalty. The case of Blattius is
very similar to Lucius Bantius of Nola (in Campania), to whom Marcellus
gave money and prestige gifts in order to secure his loyalty. Presumably
receiving public honours and gifts had symbolic value that enhanced a
local aristocrat's status.[40] For another piece of comparative evidence,
Livy states explicitly that the Mopsii, an aristocratic family in Compsa in
Samnium, were powerful thanks to the Romans.[41]

While some elite families survived and profited from Roman rule, others
may have lost out or perceived that Roman rule limited their chances to
further their own political standing. Indeed, it is likely that the Romans
punished local aristocrats who resisted Rome's initial conquest of their city.
Thus the consul L. Postumius Megellus (cos. 291) captured Venusia and
killed thousands of the native population, including presumably members
of the local elite class.[42] In around 315 a Roman garrison was holding the
city of Luceria; the local population betrayed the garrison and handed

---

[38] Liv. 22.50.11–12, 22.52.4–7, 22.54.4–7; Val. Max. 4.8.2; cf. App. *Hann.* 26; Polyb. 3.117.1–4. The
basic story of Busa is plausible, and in particular there is no reason to assume that the granting of
honores is fanciful. As we saw above, Busa was a common Messapic name. Livy (22.52.7) records
that she was granted honours by the senate (*ab senatu honores habiti sunt*). Presumably, such a
grant would have been preserved in records or even a public inscription, which explains how
such a detail made its way into Livy's sources. Valerius uses Busa as an *exemplum* in his section on
friendship, probably drawing on Livy as his source. It is impossible to know whether Livy derived
this story from Polybius, since his account of the Roman recovery after Cannae is largely missing.
Polybius does not mention Canusium specifically, but refers to Venusia and 'neighbouring cities'
(εἰς τὰς παρακειμένας πόλεις) to which the survivors fled. Appian mentions Canusium, but does
not repeat the Busa story. I will discuss this episode in greater detail later in this chapter.

[39] Appian (*Hann.* 46) preserves a speech in which Blattius claimed that he was friends with a
Roman general: ἔστι γάρ μοι φίλος ὁ στρατηγὸς ἐκείνου τοῦ στρατοῦ. Of course, speeches in
ancient sources are highly suspect historical evidence, and indeed in Appian's version Blattius'
speech is a deception. On the other hand, the version is broadly consistent with Livy's account
(26.38.6), in which Blattius sends messengers to Marcellus to negotiate terms for Salapia's surrender: *Blattius quantum ex tuto poterat rem Romanum fovebat et per occultos nuntios spem proditionis
fecerat Marcello.* It may be that Appian and Livy are both drawing from a tradition that emphasised some sort of personal relationship between Blattius and Marcellus, though it is unknown
whether that relationship predated the war or resulted from it.

[40] Liv. 23.15.7–15, especially 14–15. On Bantius of Nola, see Chapter 3, p. 109 n. 40.

[41] Liv. 23.1.2: *Mopsiorum factio, familiae per gratiam Romanorum potentis.* The example of the Mopsii
of Compsa was discussed in Chapter 1, pp. 32–3.

[42] Dion. Hal. 17/18.5.1; Vell. Pat. 1.14.6.

their city over to the Samnites.[43] The Roman reaction was harsh, and Livy (9.26.2–5) states specifically that treacherous Lucerians were punished. Again, it is likely that aristocratic ringleaders were among them. In some cases, the Romans took hostages, undoubtedly from aristocratic families, in order to ensure the loyalty of defeated Apulian communities: hostage taking is mentioned with the conquest of Teanum Apulum, Canusium and Forentum (318–317),[44] and they may have been taken in other cities. Even if the Romans did not directly punish local aristocrats who were disloyal or resistant, they certainly would not have rewarded them either. At the same time, as we have seen, the Romans probably rewarded loyalists and collaborators, and probably worked to maintain their friendship and support. Through such practices the Romans shaped and influenced the local political environment in Apulian cities.

As Rome consolidated its power in Apulia, therefore, some local aristocratic families benefited from Roman rule (or at least perceived that was the case) while others felt that Roman rule had limited their local political standing. Certain families may have become entrenched in power through direct Roman backing or, more frequently, by benefiting from the political status quo. Rival families, on the other hand, may have been closed out. Indeed, the imposition of Roman hegemony probably led to the formation of new political rivalries, while at the same time contributing to ongoing local political tensions. Hannibal's invasion of Italy introduced a new factor into the local political competition within Apulian cities and opened up new possibilities for rival factions to challenge dominant aristocratic families whose power was bound up, at least in part, with loyalty to Rome.

The clearest evidence of this process occurring in Apulia is provided by accounts of politics in Salapia, namely the aforementioned rivalry between Blattius and Dasius. One suspects that Dasius' willingness to join forces with Hannibal resulted, at least partly, from his disaffection with the local political order. Meanwhile, the local political landscape before Hannibal's arrival probably favoured Dasius' political rival Blattius, and we may speculate that Blattius' family had benefited directly or indirectly from the growth of Roman power in the area. This in turn helps to explain Blattius' pro-Roman sentiment once Hanibal arrived. Indeed, the tendency for local aristocratic loyalties during the Second Punic War to split along the lines of factional and/or family rivalry is visible in other Italian cities.[45]

---

[43] Liv. 9.26.1; see below, pp. 81–3.   [44] Liv. 9.16.1, 9.20.4; Diod. Sic. 19.10.2.

[45] The *locus classicus* is the revolt of Compsa in Samnium, where an aristocrat named Statius Trebius invited Hannibal to his city and promised to turn it over to him (Liv. 23.1.1–2). Trebius was

This dynamic probably played out similarly in less well-documented Apulian communities, such as Arpi, where immediately after the battle of Cannae there emerged an anti-Roman party led by Dasius Altinius, which sided with Hannibal. Altinius sought to re-establish relations with Rome only after he perceived the Romans were recovering and Hannibal's power was waning.[46] Livy states that Rome's recovery went against Altinius' hopes and expectations, suggesting that his original attraction to Hannibal was bound up with his desire to overthrow Roman hegemony. He also states that Altinius promised to restore Arpi to the Romans on the condition that he be given a reward, explicit evidence that he was motivated by personal gain rather than by 'global' or ideological concerns.[47] Indeed, both the Romans and Hannibal appear to have recognised that Dasius Altinius was a political opportunist.[48] Overall, the actions of Dasius Altinius fit with the present suggestion that the anti-Roman party in Arpi saw its own interests tied to the rejection of Roman rule and the subsequent overthrow of the current ruling party. Hannibal enjoyed the support of Dasius Altinius' party, at least as long as his own fortunes were good.

Hannibal capitalised on local political factionalism by gaining the support of Apulian aristocrats who expected to benefit if he overthrew Roman hegemony. But this only solves part of the problem. It does not explain why the pro-Hannibalic movement won in some Apulian cities, such as Arpi and Salapia, but not in others. The aristocracy of Canusium, for example, appears to have been similarly divided yet maintained its loyalty to Rome throughout the course of war. After Cannae remnants of the Roman army gathered at Canusium and the Roman colony of Venusia. As mentioned above, in Canusium the survivors, numbering as many as 10,000 men, received food, clothing and money from a local aristocratic woman named Busa.[49] Livy in particular contrasts the

---

opposed by the Mopsii, a family that, as mentioned above (n. 41), enjoyed power because of the Romans. The situation clearly suggests that Trebius (and presumably his supporters) and the Mopsii had been rivals for power before Hannibal came to Italy, and that Trebius saw Hannibal as a way to overthrow the Mopsii. In fact, Livy (23.1.3) also says that after Cannae Trebius advertised Hannibal's coming to the Compsan citizenry, suggesting that Trebius was confident that a pro-Hannibalic platform would prove popular since Rome had been discredited by its crushing defeat at Cannae. The Mopsii fled the city, indicating that they anticipated they would suffer under Hannibalic domination – especially if their political rivals were placed in power.

[46] Liv. 24.45.1–3; see also App. *Hann.* 31.

[47] In other words, Dasius Altinius did not care who won the war, so long as he could maximise his own position. His connection to one side or the other was based on pragmatism rather than ideology; the global nature of a war between Rome and Carthage was of less importance than local politics.

[48] The Romans did not trust Altinius, so they arrested him (Liv. 24.45.8–9); Hannibal had long suspected him (Liv. 24.45.12).

[49] See Polyb. 3.117.2–3 and above, n. 38.

munificence of Busa with the poor hospitality that her fellow townsmen showed the Romans.[50] Even if Livy has exaggerated the singularity
of Busa's contribution, and the Romans received aid from other aristocratic families (or at least other members of Busa's family), the episode
implies that loyalty to Rome was neither uniform nor particularly strong
among the local elite. Busa's extraordinary act of generosity may have
been an attempt to curry favour with the Romans and advance her family's standing,[51] or it may reflect strong pre-existing loyalty because her
family had received support from, or forged bonds of friendship with,
Rome. In either case Canusian politics would conform to the general
picture I have drawn of local aristocracies: each composed of individuals and groups possessing varying degrees of loyalty towards Rome and
divided by political rivalries that were themselves shaped by Roman contact. That Canusium did not defect shows that the existence of political
divisions, of the sort that Hannibal successfully exploited in Arpi, was
not enough by itself to guarantee the emergence and ascendancy of an
anti-Roman (or pro-Hannibalic) party.

What particular factor enabled anti-Roman sentiment to prevail in
Arpi? Before tackling this question, it should be emphasised that choosing to defect during the Second Punic War must have been a huge step
for a local ruling class to take, one with the potential for, if not certainty
of, severe consequences. Such a decision must have been arrived at with
difficulty, after considerable debate and the weighing of various considerations. Moreover, in any ruling class, opinions and political calculations
would have varied widely. There must have been more groups than the
two about which we hear the most, the 'anti-Roman' (or 'pro-Hannibalic')
and 'pro-Roman' factions, though the wartime conditions and stark
policy choice probably tended to polarise local aristocrats in these two
directions. Thus, we can imagine the Arpian ruling class debating the
relative merits of revolt. There was probably a vocal group of aristocrats
who argued strongly for revolt, while a core group of aristocrats cautioned
against revolt and called for staunch loyalty to Rome. Many aristocrats
would have fallen somewhere in the middle, a swing group whose support
was necessary for the success of either the pro-Roman or pro-Hannibalic

---

[50] The Canusians, according to Livy (22.52.7), afforded the Romans only shelter and protection from
Hannibal, while Busa gave the men food, clothing, and money for their journey home.

[51] In fact, Livy says that the senate voted high honours for Busa as a reward for her generosity (see
above, n. 38). Presumably honours granted in Rome would have been advertised in Canusium,
perhaps with parallel inscriptions or on some sort of honorific monument. Whatever its form,
honours granted by Rome and publicised locally would have added to the symbolic capital of
Busa's family.

parties.[52] What were the decisive considerations that urged this swing group in Arpi to support the pro-Hannibalic position?

Certainly Hannibal's victory at Cannae discredited both the Romans and any local aristocrats who voiced strong pro-Roman sentiment. The battle occurred in Apulia and it is highly likely that local soldiers were killed serving alongside Rome's legions, perhaps fostering additional feelings of resentment. At the same time, the battle's outcome and Hannibal's presence nearby made revolt a real possibility. The close proximity of both the battle and his victorious army might have simply stunned the Arpians into revolting, with the aristocratic swing group falling quickly in line with the more vocal anti-Roman party. Polybius' statement, however, that the Arpians invited Hannibal implies that the move was relatively calculated and that Arpi was not just cowed into surrendering to Hannibal.[53] A stronger objection has to do with where the battle was actually fought: within the territory of Canusium. This territory stretched from the coast inland to the territory of Venusia[54] and straddled the Ofanto River, on which the people of Canusium maintained an emporium, according to Strabo (6.3.9). Ancient Cannae (near modern Canne) was a small hilltop settlement situated a short distance to the north-east of the urban centre of Canusium and lying within this territory. Cannae appears, therefore, to have been a subordinate *vicus* of Canusium rather than a politically independent *civitas/polis*.[55] Thus, the battle of Cannae took place in the 'backyard' of Canusium. If the proximity of both the battle and Hannibal's army were the decisive factor encouraging revolt, then we would expect Canusium also to have revolted.

Throughout the Second Punic War, Apulia suffered from depopulation, loss of crops and destruction of farms on a scale at least as severe as any region in Italy, including the most devastated areas of Campania.[56] In the war's critical early years, when many Italian communities were

[52] This scenario is most visible in the cases of Capua and Nola, which will be discussed in Chapter 3 pp. 106–8, 135–6.

[53] Polyb. 3.118.3; in fact, the suggestion that Arpi made a calculated invitation to Hannibal supports the assertion that the decision to revolt followed a debate similar to those observed among the Capuan and Nolan elite.

[54] Moreno 1981; Grelle, 1992: 35, 1993: 20–6; Volpe 1990: 14–15 n. 17, 28–9, 108–10.

[55] Strab. 6.3.9; Liv. 22.43.10, 22.49.13; Flor. 2.6.15; App. *Hann.* 3 all imply that Cannae was a *vicus* or refer to it explicitly as such, though Polyb. 3.107.2 refers to Cannae as a *polis*. For the archaeological evidence, see De Juliis 1985; De Palo and Labellarte 1987; Volpe 1990: 28–9; Grelle 1992: 40–1. Ashby and Gardner 1916: 156 suggest that modern-day Canne is the emporium of Canusium to which Strabo refers, though this seems unlikely.

[56] Erdkamp 1998: 286–7. For the supposedly devastating long-term effects of the war on southeastern Italy, see Toynbee 1965: II.10–35, with critique by Brunt 1971: 269–77 and, more recently, by Mario Torelli 1993c and Cornell 1996.

making their decisions to revolt or not, Apulian towns repeatedly endured Hannibal's devastation tactics at the same time that the Romans also exacted supplies from Apulian communities.[57] In particular, as will be discussed below, Hannibal devastated the territory of Arpi.[58] The relative thoroughness of Hannibal's devastation, Rome's inability to defend its allies and the added burden of Roman consumption of local grain must have encouraged the Arpian elite to side with Hannibal. These probably were not, however, the decisive considerations.

The regional economy of Apulia in the third century was based primarily on agricultural production, mostly the cultivation of cereal crops, though wool was also important.[59] The northern part of Apulia, the focus of this chapter, corresponds roughly to the broad plain of the Tavoliere, which at more than 4,000 square kilometres is the largest expanse of flat land in peninsular Italy.[60] The plain itself is broken up into a series of 'platforms' separated by low, flat valleys. Each lower-lying area contains a river or torrent that runs more or less east–west, emptying into the Manfredonia Gulf (these rivers include the modern Ofanto, Carapelle and Cervaro), and each thus functions as a separate drainage basin (Map 5). In addition to its less rugged topography, plentiful water sources and warm

---

[57] Polybius (3.107.1–4) states that the Romans had collected supplies from around Canusium and stored them at Cannae.

[58] There has been a great deal of scholarly debate on the nature of 'devastation' in ancient warfare, in particular questioning how much damage, both long term and short term, actually resulted from such practices. On this topic I am largely in agreement with Cornell 1996: esp. 107–11. Large armies, both Roman and Hannibalic, often spent significant periods of time in southern Italy. These armies were relatively mobile and could do considerable damage to the crops themselves as well as to farmhouses and heavy equipment. More importantly, 'devastation' must have entailed the disruption of agricultural patterns, which included menacing, killing, driving off or capturing farmers during key periods such as sowing and reaping. In addition, Hannibal captured a large amount of livestock. See for example, Polyb. 3.86.8–10, 3.92.4–5, 3.93.10. Armies surely consumed local food stocks when possible, putting a further burden on nearby communities. For pre-modern subsistence farmers who lived at or near the margins, any such disruption could have profound consequences. Devastation also had a psychological dimension: there are numerous literary references to plunder being paraded in front of a city's walls in order to weaken the inhabitants' resolve or anger them into fighting. In such cases, an opponent need not have devastated a city's territory in its entirety to achieve the desired goal. Regarding long-term consequences of devastation, I am sceptical that the Second Punic War led directly to massive depopulation in southern Italy. It is likely that many of the farms that had been destroyed or abandoned during the war were reoccupied after the fighting was over, in many cases by refugees returning home. Yet some communities must have suffered long-term repercussions.

[59] There is less literary evidence for the cultivation and the production of wine, oil and other non-cereal crops, though amphorae from Greece, found in wealthy graves, indicate at least some importation of wine into Apulia before the second century. Local production of wine and oil from the fifth to third centuries was on a relatively small scale; see Volpe 1990: 30–3, 60; Mazzei 1991: 111; Mertens 1992: 95–6; Small 1994.

[60] For the topography: Delano-Smith 1967.

climate, the region also possesses rich soil. Indeed, Spurr notes that the soil of Apulia remains among the most fertile in Italy for cereal production.[61] Such conditions were conducive to agricultural production, and ancient references confirm that grain was grown in surplus in the fourth and third centuries. Livy mentions that the Arpians supplied grain for the Roman army besieging Luceria in the fourth century,[62] and during the Second Punic War Hannibal captured large amounts of grain in Gereonium and Cannae.[63] Strabo mentions the region's fertility and comments on the export of grain to Sipontum and Salapia;[64] Strabo most probably derived these observations from Artemidorus of Ephesus, showing that Apulia remained fertile and productive through the second century BC.[65] It is not surprising that Hannibal not only devastated Apulia but also wintered his army there in three out of four years beginning in the winter of 217/16.

Despite the fertility of the region, Apulia was thinly urbanised in antiquity: de Ligt (1991: 51–5) calculates that the average distance between cities in northern Apulia in antiquity was more than twenty-three kilometres, much further than the normal distance a rural inhabitant would be willing to travel on a regular basis. Although de Ligt focuses on Italian settlement for a later period, the *density* of urban centres in northern Apulia – that is, the number of cities – had not changed much from the third century.[66] Northern Apulia was dotted, therefore, by cities that were generally more than twenty kilometres from each other, with each city in possession of a relatively extensive territory. Within the territories of individual Apulian cities the population was clustered either in the urban centre or in rural *vici*. By the third century several *vici* appear to have been abandoned, presumably as the population concentrated in the emerging urban centres. The remaining rural population lived almost exclusively in scattered *vici*. Archaeological research has identified very few isolated rural settlements, and the majority of these lay along major rivers or roads – that is, lines of communication to urban centres.[67] Unfortunately, the exact

[61] Spurr 1986: 7–8 cites Varro, *Rust.* 1.2.6, 1.57.3, 2.6.5; Columella, *Rust.* 3.8.4.

[62] Liv. 9.13.9–12.

[63] Polyb. 3.100.1–8, 3.101.1–4, 8–10, 3.102.1–4, 3.107.1–4; Liv. 22.52.7, 22.43.5–6.

[64] Strab. 6.3.9.

[65] Even though Strabo discusses the region's fertility in the present tense, he starts the next section (6.3.10) by naming Artemidorus as his source for the distances between cities in northern Apulia; see also Small 1994: 546–7. For a more general discussion of how Strabo's 'present' spans the whole of the first century BC and early first century AD, see Pothecary 1997; Clarke 1999: 281–93.

[66] See Volpe 1990: 13–14.

[67] Volpe 1990: 35–49, 101–8. As many as 428 rural sites have been identified dating from the fourth century BC through late antiquity. Of these, only twenty-four can be dated to the fourth to third centuries. Systematic survey has been carried out for only a fraction of Apulia, however, so the

relationship between Apulian urban centres and rural *vici* is unclear, though this settlement pattern may suggest that communication between the urban centre and the outlying rural population would have been less intensive than in more densely urbanised regions such as Campania or Latium.[68]

Such a pattern may have limited the effectiveness of Hannibal's devastation tactics, since the destruction of outlying farmlands would not have brought as much political pressure on the urban elite. This suggestion is consistent with the literary evidence. Ancient sources report no reaction by the Apulians to Hannibal's devastation tactics, unlike the cities of Campania, where either actual or threatened Hannibalic devastation prompted responses from the local populations.[69] This is not to deny that the interests of the urban elite were connected to rural conditions. They probably possessed or otherwise derived wealth from rural estates and thus would have been affected by the devastation of outlying farms or the destruction of rural *vici*. But perhaps these rather extensive territories meant that the urban elite possessed more scattered rural holdings, so the partial devastation of a community's hinterland may have acutely harmed relatively few elite families. Or, if an invader only devastated the furthest reaches of a city's territory, the psychological impact may have been less severe than seeing an enemy parade virtually beneath the walls. One suspects a more important factor was political: in a more densely urbanised environment, where communication between town and country is more intensive, devastation of the countryside would be followed by rapid reports in the city, a significant percentage of rural denizens would be able to flee to the city, and the ruling elite would feel increased political

results may be skewed. The number of rural sites increased in the second century BC and later, as much of northern Apulia was confiscated and colonised. Antonacci Sanpaolo 2001: 27–9 identifies a similar process occurring specifically in the territory of Teanum Apulum, with the 'population gradually concentrating around settlements in strategic locations', though many rural farms scattered throughout the territory remained in use through the second century BC.

[68] There was a somewhat different settlement pattern around the two Latin colonies in Apulia, Luceria and Venusia: older rural settlements and *vici* were almost completely abandoned, while the number of small settlements immediately surrounding the urban centres of the colonies increased. There are also clear traces of Roman land divisions around Luceria. The colonies may have had a different agricultural economy. For example, there is evidence that olives and grapes were cultivated on a somewhat larger scale and at an earlier date in the territory of Luceria than in Apulian cities that were not colonised. It is likely that similar patterns existed around Venusia. See Bottini 1981:151–4; Volpe 1990: 46–9; Mario Torelli 1993b: 141–54; Marchi and Sabbatini 1996: 19, 111–15.

[69] For example, the Neapolitans sent a cavalry contingent to prevent Hannibal from plundering farms, while the Nolans talked openly of negotiating with Hannibal under the mere threat of devastation; see Chapter 3, pp. 132–3, 135–7.

pressure to respond. In a relatively less densely urbanised region such as Apulia, rural denizens living far from the urban centre may have chosen to seek refuge in remote yet defensible or fortified sites, or even to melt into the countryside rather than attempt to flee to the urban centre, thus limiting the political pressure. In any case, there is nothing to suggest that the Apulian cities in general, and Arpi in particular, were *more* susceptible to Hannibal's devastation tactics.

Hannibal moreover appears to have devastated the territories both of Apulian cities that revolted and of those that remained loyal to Rome. For example, both Livy and Polybius state explicitly that in 217 Hannibal devastated Arpi,[70] which would later revolt. He also repeatedly devastated the territory of the Latin colony Luceria, both before and after his march into the *ager Falernus* in 217,[71] yet it did not revolt. More striking is the fact that Hannibal devastated Teanum Apulum (Teate), which was an allied city rather than a Latin colony, yet it too remained loyal throughout the war.[72] After the battle of Trasimene Hannibal marched from Etruria, through Umbria and Picenum, until he reached the Adriatic coast.[73] He continued to move at a leisurely pace to the area around Luceria, Arpi and Vibinum.[74] This route would have taken him through the territory of Teanum Apulum, which he presumably also devastated at this time. Later in the same year Hannibal gathered grain from around Gereonium after he destroyed the settlement. At first Hannibal tried to seduce the inhabitants of the town into forging an alliance by promising them unspecified advantages; when the Gereonians rejected his overtures, the Carthaginian general successfully besieged the town and massacred the remaining inhabitants.[75] The ancient site of Gereonium has been located at Masseria Finocchito, near Castelnuovo della Daunia, about equidistant between ancient Luceria and Teanum Apulum.[76] Despite references in the ancient sources to walls around Gereonium, the settlement was almost certainly

---

[70] Polyb. 3.88.6; Liv. 22.9.5.　　[71] Polyb. 3.88.5, 3.100.1; Liv. 22.9.5.
[72] On the loyalty of Teanum Apulum, see below pp. 92–3.
[73] Polyb. 3.86.8–10; Liv. 22.9.1–4; Zon. 8.25.　　[74] Polyb. 3.88.1–6; Liv. 22.9.5.
[75] Polyb. 3.100.1–8; Liv. 22.18.7, 22.23.9; App. *Hann.* 15. Polybius describes in some detail the negotiations and siege, while Appian claims only that the town was captured. Livy first states that the town was already deserted when Hannibal captured it but later claims that he left a few buildings standing after burning the city, implying that the city was invested and thus defended by someone. It is possible that some of the population had fled upon news of Hannibal's approach, or that some fled when part of the town's defences were compromised but before Hannibal seized it. Indeed, this is consistent with Livy's initial claim (22.18.8) that Gereonium was abandoned after part of its walls collapsed: *urbem metu quia conlapsa ruinis pars moenium erat ab suis desertam.*
[76] For the identification of Gereonium with Masseria Finocchito, see A. Russi 1976: 208–9; V. Russi 1982: 181–4; Volpe 1990: 133. The site lies south of the Fortore River and has revealed extensive archaeological remains. See also De Sanctis 1956–69: III.2.123–5 and Walbank 1970: 1.432–4, who both

a *vicus* and not an independent *civitas*.[77] Gereonium/Masseria Finocchito
is situated within the Fortore River valley, and since the territories of the
larger Apulian centres tended to correspond to rivers and main drainage
basins, topography suggests that this *vicus* was dependent on Teanum
Apulum rather than Luceria.[78] Thus Hannibal not only devastated the territory of Teanum Apulum but also destroyed one of its rural *vici*, yet this
failed to convince the local aristocracy to defect.

The territory of Canusium was also ravaged. Hannibal wintered in
Apulia in 217/16, and he remained in winter quarters throughout much
of the spring. When he broke camp, he then decided to march from
Gereonium to the Roman supply base in Cannae,[79] a strategic *vicus* of
Canusium situated near major lines of communication: the littoral route
that stretched from Sipontum through Salapia and south along the coast,
and also the Ofanto River.[80] Both the coastal route and especially the river
were important as well from an economic perspective, as they appear to
have played a vital economic role in Canusium's longer-distance trade.[81]
The sight of Hannibal's army only a few miles from Canusium, consuming

also suggest a location between Castle Dragonara and Casalnuovo Monterotaro, to the south of
the Fortore. Alvisi 1970: 68–70; De Felice 1994: 145–9; and Lloyd 1995: 197–200 tentatively identify
Gereonium with Gerione, a hill situated well north of the Fortore, about 8 km from Larinum. The
identification of Gereonium with Gerione rests partly on onomastic considerations, though traces
of rough polygonal walls have also been found there. But Polybius clearly locates Gereonium in
or near the territory of Luceria, and Polybius, Livy and Appian all place it in Apulia. The *Tabula
Peutingeriana* (6.2/3) identifies a *Geronum* on the south side of the Fortore River. A location between
Luceria and Arpi, rather than one near Larinum, corresponds better to the literary evidence.

[77] For walls, see Polyb. 3.100.4; Liv. 22.18.7, 22.23.9. For the identification of Gereonium as a *vicus*,
see Volpe 1990: 40; Grelle 1992: 40.

[78] Volpe 1990: 14–15, 28–9; see Map 5 and Map 6. De Sanctis' discussion, while not explicit on the
matter, implies that Gereonium was in the territory of Luceria, interpreting Polyb. 3.100.1–3 to
mean that Hannibal planned to forage in the territory of Luceria. However, the exact text of
Polyb. 3.100.1 indicates that the territory of Gereonium was separate from that of Luceria: ἐν τῇ
περὶ τὴν Λουκαρίαν καὶ τὸ καλούμενον Γερούνιον χώρᾳ. A. Russi 1976: 210–14 cites two inscriptions found near the Masseria Finocchito as his main evidence for placing Gereonium in the
territory of Luceria. The inscriptions are badly preserved but may contain references to the *gens
Claudia* and the *legio prima*, both associated with the colony of Luceria. The inscriptions date,
however, to the last half of the first century BC at the earliest. Keppie 1983: 164–5 suggests that
they belong to veterans of one of Pansa's legions, raised in 43. In any case, the inscriptions should
not be used to determine the status of Gereonium in the third century.

[79] For these and following events: Polyb. 3.107.1–6; Liv. 22.43.5–10.

[80] Cannae as a *vicus* of Canusium: above, n. 55. Its strategic value: Polyb. 3.107.5.

[81] For Canusian trade along the Ofanto, see Strab. 6.3.9. Commercial amphorae from Greece, datable to the fourth to third centuries, have been found in Canusium, and the Ofanto was navigable
in antiquity as far as Canusium. It is likely that imports from Greece would have been conveyed
by ship, first to the coastal ports of Apulia, then upriver to inland cities; see Volpe 1990: 60–2,
93–4. For a discussion of the overland routes in Apulia, see Volpe 1990: 86–90; Strabo (6.3.10)
mentions the coastal road, which may have been the same route taken by the Roman army during
the Second Samnite War (Liv. 9.2.6); see also Map 7.

Roman supplies that had been collected from the surrounding countryside and stored there and occupying such a sensitive position, must have made the Romans appear powerless.[82] These circumstances surely undermined Rome's credibility from the perspective of the Canusian ruling elite. Yet even though Hannibal had marched through the heart of northern Apulia, passing a number of cities all the while unmolested by the Romans, we hear of no reaction on the part of Canusium, and the city remained loyal after the battle of Cannae.

In fact, Hannibal does not seem to have elicited much of a response from any of the Apulian cities whose territories he ravaged. Perhaps, as we have seen, the pattern of settlements and the relatively low density of urban centres rendered Apulia less susceptible to devastation tactics. Whatever the explanation, no Apulian city defected until after the battle of Cannae, when some, but not all, of the cities whose territories were devastated rebelled. Meanwhile, Hannibal's devastation of Teanum Apulum appears to have been particularly painful, since he not only gathered supplies from the city's territory but also massacred the inhabitants of its rural *vicus*, Gereonium. Still, the Teanenses did not revolt after Cannae. Overall, Hannibal's relatively thorough devastation of Apulia does not explain why anti-Roman sentiment prevailed in Arpi but not in other cities nearby.

Animal breeding was another important component of the Apulian regional economy from at least the fifth century. Strabo mentions the breeding of sheep and the production of fine wool in Apulia,[83] which is supported by archaeological research in the area of Herdonia.[84] Cattle and pigs were also grazed on the Tavoliere,[85] and both northern Apulia and the Sallentine peninsula were famed for horse-breeding.[86] Arpi and Canusium were said to have been founded by Diomedes, and the cult of Diomedes, a figure strongly associated with horses, was widespread in the region.[87] Arpi

---

[82] Hannibal's primary goal was to elicit another pitched battle with Rome, and he figured that capturing Cannae would achieve that objective (Polyb. 3.107.2). Roman commanders in Apulia kept sending messengers to the senate asking what to do, because they were greatly bothered by Hannibal's manoeuvring and uncertain about the loyalty of the allies (Polyb. 3.107.6).

[83] Strab. 6.3.9.   [84] For example, see Iker 1995: 45; Volpe and Mertens 1995: 318–19.

[85] Volpe 1990: 30–1.   [86] Volpe 1990: 30–1, 71–2; Iker 1995: 45.

[87] Strabo (6.3.9) comments on the horse-breeding of Apulia, and the founding of Canusium and Arpi by Diomedes. The cult of Diomedes was diffused throughout Apulia, in Canusium, Aecae, Arpi, Salapia, Sipontum, Venusia and Luceria, and it persisted despite the Oscanisation of some of these cities. See Beaumont 1936: 194–5; Musti 1988: 173–95 (who argues that the strong association of Diomedes with northern Apulia/Daunia is the product of Roman propaganda from the late fourth century, as the Romans tried to contrast the Daunians and their enemies the Samnites); Mario Torelli 1993b: 142–3. See also Volpe 1990: 30–4 for the importance of the horse in the formation of the Daunian elite during the pre-Roman period.

supplied 400 cavalry to the Roman cause against Pyrrhus,[88] and Polybius' description of available Roman manpower in 225 shows the Apulians supplying a disproportionate number of horses.[89]

Transhumance also was practised in Apulia during the third century, though its extent has been debated.[90] It is likely to have been a source of tension between farmers and passing herders, or even between cities or tribes competing for control of drove roads.[91] The imposition of colonies by Rome may have exacerbated these tensions, though the picture is far from clear. There were three important overland routes through Apulia.[92] I have already discussed the coastal route. The second was probably more or less the same route as the later Via Traiana, which from Beneventum followed the Calore river valley to Aecae, then bent south connecting to Herdonia, Canusium and Brundisium.[93] The third was the Via Appia, which by the middle of the third century ran from Beneventum to Taras and Brundisium. The Latin colony of Venusia was located on this major line of communication, perhaps altering local migration and pasturing patterns. Indeed, any Roman confiscation of land may have blocked local transhumance routes and therefore interfered with grazing patterns.[94] Not only the colonial foundations of both Luceria and Venusia but also any mulcting of land from conquered Apulian cities had the potential, therefore, to disrupt this element of the Apulian regional economy.

The evidence for Roman interference in local stockbreeding and transhumance, however, is scant, and there is little to suggest that the Arpian economy suffered disproportionately from Rome's disruption of local grazing

---

[88] Dion. Hal. 20.3.2.

[89] Polyb. 2.24.12, following the interpretation of Polybius' figures by Baronowski 1993; see also Lepore 1984: 321; Mazzei and Lippolis 1984: 229; Volpe 1990: 71–2; and additional bibliography in Chapter 1, n. 97.

[90] Grenier 1905: 293–328 argues that transhumance was not practised in Apulia until the second century, but others argue that it was practised by the middle of the third century (Toynbee 1965: 11.286) if not earlier (Salmon 1967: 68–70). Volpe 1990: 72–3 compromises, suggesting that large-scale and long-distance transhumance was probably not feasible until after the Second Punic War, when the Roman state could take an active part in regulating the practice. This does not preclude, however, the existence of small-scale transhumance at a much earlier date: Garnsey 1998a: 169–73; contra Pasquinucci 1979: 92–4.

[91] Salmon 1967: 68–9; Skydsgaard 1974: 11–12. Livy (9.8.6–7) implies that unsettled Samnite highlanders encroached upon the territory of the settled Apulian plains-dwellers, but the picture is certainly over-schematised and probably reflects cultural stereotyping and marginalisation of highlanders and nomadic peoples; see Dench 1995: 111–16; Horden and Purcell 2000: 80–8; see also Dench 2004.

[92] For a discussion of overland routes in Apulia, see Volpe 1990: 86–90; see also Map 7.

[93] The road was built during the Imperial period, though it probably followed a pre-existing route. In fact, Strabo (6.3.7) mentions the existence in his day of a 'mule road' that connected Canusium and Herdonia. The mule road certainly predated Strabo, and the much later Via Traiana probably followed the same course. See Ashby and Gardner 1916: 108–11.

[94] Salmon 1967: 70.

and transhumance patterns. Livy's statement that the Arpians particularly resented Samnite encroachment may indicate that they would have welcomed Roman interference with or alteration of local transhumance patterns. In any case, there is simply not enough evidence to conclude that the foundation of nearby Latin colonies or Roman confiscations of land from neighbouring committees and the resulting disruption in regional transhumance made the Arpians more inclined to revolt than neighbouring communities.

Indeed, the revolt of Arpi is all the more puzzling when we consider that the Arpians had come willingly into an alliance with Rome (318) and had shown themselves to be particularly loyal to Rome in previous conflicts against the Samnites and Pyrrhus.[95] I suggest that the solution to the question of why Arpi revolted – why the anti-Roman party won out over their political opposition – may be found by looking at the local diplomatic context, in particular the long-term pattern of intercity rivalries and sub-regional hostility, and Arpi's history as a regional hegemonic power. Since Apulia was an important theatre during the Samnite wars, we are fortunate to possess a good deal of literary evidence for Apulian interstate relations, albeit from a Romanocentric perspective of that period. A growing body of archaeological evidence contributes further to our understanding of the region.

Throughout the fourth and third centuries there was a radical change in settlement patterns in Apulia, as the less nucleated settlements typical of the late Iron Age gave way to urban centres. Many Apulian cities erected stone defensive walls around their urban centres, replacing earlier earthen works that had enclosed much wider areas.[96] Such Apulian centres also eventually contained planned, paved streets,[97] and many cities began to mint coins, suggesting both centralisation and the assertion of political autonomy.[98] By the start of the Second Punic War a number of Apulian communities emerged

---

[95] The Arpians invited the Romans into an alliance to counter Samnite aggression (Liv. 9.13.6). Later, Arpi helped to provision the Romans during their siege of Luceria (Liv. 9.13.9–12), and the Arpians are the only Apulians specifically named in the sources as supplying troops to help Rome fight against Pyrrhus, a very large contingent of 4,000 infantry and 400 cavalry (Dion. Hal. 20.3.2; Plut. *Pyrrh.* 21.9). On the alliance between Rome and Arpi, see Fronda 2006.

[96] Liv. 24.46.1–6; 27.28.9–12 describes the walls and gates of Arpi and Salapia. There are archaeological remains of the defences of Salapia, see Tinè and Tinè 1973. A series of walls have been excavated at Herdonia, which clearly show an earthen wall replaced by a brick wall at the beginning of the third century. For a detailed discussion of the walls and gates of Herdonia, see Mertens 1995b: 139–49; for a more general discussion of the late Iron Age and Republican defensive works of Apulian cities, see Volpe 1990: 27–30, 36–40.

[97] Liv. 24.46.3, 24.47.3 mentions the streets of Arpi; Liv. 26.38.8 implies a forum in Salapia; see also Volpe 1990: 36–40.

[98] By the third century, the following cities had minted coins: Canusium, Arpi, Teanum Apulum, Ausculum, Hyrium, Luceria, Salapia and Venusia. See Stazio 1972; Crawford 1985: 52–74; Volpe 1990: 36; Grelle 1992: 39–40; Rutter 2001: 76–83.

as politically independent entities; they are identified by their urban form, by the coining of money and by literary references to their conducting independent diplomacy.[99] It is not exactly clear when this process began, but the last half or quarter of the fourth century through to the first quarter of the third century appears to have been a critical period.[100]

Arpi was clearly a regional hegemonic state, probably the most powerful city in the region. Aerial photography has revealed that the circuit of Arpi's Iron Age earthen rampart ran approximately thirteen kilometres, the longest such defensive work in Apulia.[101] It also controlled a broad territory stretching from the Sipontine coast inland to the foothills of the Apennines perhaps as far as Aecae, south to the Cervaro River basin, and north along the Candelaro basin as far as Casone, including settlements along the Gargano.[102] The Arpian population has been estimated at around 30,000 free inhabitants.[103] As stated above (see n. 95), the Arpians aided the Romans at the battle of Ausculum with a very large military contingent, further suggesting that the city was a local hegemonic power.[104] Strabo claims that Arpi and Canusium were once the largest cities in the region and he comments on the formidable walls of both.[105] Livy portrays the Roman recapture of the city in 213 as a major victory.[106]

[99] Liv. 9.13.6–12, 9.20.4, 9.20.9, 9.26.1–5; Diod. Sic. 19.10.1, 19.65.7, 19.72.8–9; Dion. Hal. 17/18.5, 20.3.2 imply various Apulian cities acting independently. These cities include Arpi, Herdonia, Salapia, Aecae, Teanum Apulum, Canusium and Ausculum as well as the colonies of Venusia and Luceria; see Volpe 1990: 35–40 for summary and bibliography.

[100] Mazzei and Lippolis 1984: 185–210; Volpe 1990: 36–40; Mazzei 1991; Grelle 1992: 29–38; Mertens 1995c; Lomas 2000: 80–90.

[101] Volpe 1990: 27–30. The earthen defences around Teanum Apulum were on a similar scale; see below: n. 108.

[102] Livy (34.45.3) implies that Sipontum was under Arpian control until Rome confiscated the area after the Second Punic War and planted a colony there. The exact relationship between Aecae and Arpi is unclear. Aecae seems to have been an independent city by the Second Punic War but may have acted in the previous century as an outpost for Arpi against the Samnites. Volpe 1990: 28–9; Grelle 1992: 35–6.

[103] Pani 1979: 100; the estimate is arrived at by working from troop figures for Arpi's contribution in the war against Pyrrhus. There is no reason to assume that the Arpian population declined in the third century, at least before the Second Punic War.

[104] For Arpi at the time of the Pyrrhic War, see also Mazzei and Lippolis 1984: 185. Evidence from the Pyrrhic and Second Punic Wars may be anachronistic, and it is dangerous to project Arpi's situation in the third century back onto the fourth century. Still, all evidence points to the conclusion that Arpi was the most powerful state in northern Apulia from the late Iron Age, through the fourth century and third centuries, down to the outbreak of the war with Hannibal.

[105] Strab. 6.3.9. He claims that the walls were still visible in his own day, though it is likely that Strabo took over this observation from his sources. Livy (24.46.1–6, 22.52.7, 22.54.6) indicates that stone defensive works were certainly in place at Arpi and probably in place at Canusium at the time of the Second Punic War.

[106] Liv. 26.41.15 ascribes to Scipio a speech in 210 to veteran troops, in which Scipio compares the victory over Arpi to the capture of Capua and Syracuse.

Although Arpi was probably the most powerful Apulian community, there were several other large and presumably formidable cities in the region. As Strabo's comment suggests, Canusium was also a powerful city that probably rivalled Arpi for regional hegemony. The territory of Canusium was sizeable, though not as extensive as Arpi's, and the population of the two cities was probably about the same.[107] Likewise, Teanum Apulum, near the northern border of Daunia, was also one of the more powerful cities in the region.[108] Diodorus (19.72.8) mentions that Luceria was a very noteworthy city (πόλιν ἐπιφανεστάτην), and the difficulty of the Roman siege of Luceria conforms to the image of the city as large and well defended.[109] Overall, in the period immediately preceding Roman contact and during the initial phase of Rome's conquest of the area, Apulian settlements were in a transitional phase with a number of urban or proto-urban hegemonic centres around which smaller, subordinate settlements gravitated.[110]

The process of centralisation corresponded to what appears to be the rise of, or at least the persistence of, an oligarchic, landed elite, also mentioned in the literary sources and visible in the archaeological record.[111] Even though there is strong evidence for increasing state identity by the fourth century, Apulian communities remained highly stratified, and a few powerful kin groups probably maintained political and social domination of their communities.[112] Greek culture clearly penetrated even northern Apulia by the fourth century, and Apulian elites seem to have adopted some of its elements.[113] The importance of the cult of Diomedes in Apulia, mentioned above, suggests

---

[107] Territory of Canusium: see above, p. 67; population estimate: Pani 1979: 100.

[108] Its Iron Age defences were extensive on a scale similar to those of Arpi, with a circuit of about 11 km, suggesting that, like Arpi, it had been a powerful settlement. Teanum Apulum maintained a large territory in the third century, which stretched from the middle of the Fortore River basin north to the border of Larinum, east to the coastline near the Lago di Lesino and the Lago di Vesano, and along the Gargano, south along the Candelaro to the border of Arpi and the Triolo, and west to the foothills of the Apennines. It also controlled the *vicus* of Gereonium. See A. Russi 1976: 197–214; Greco 1981: 192, 259; Volpe 1990: 14 n. 17; and above pp. 71–2.

[109] The exact chronology is difficult to disentangle, but Livy mentions that the Romans needed to bring in supplies from nearby Arpi in order to maintain their siege (9.8.9–10), that the Romans were compelled to garrison the city, and that the Lucerians betrayed the garrison (9.26.1–2). Livy also suggests that Luceria was walled (9.15.5).

[110] Volpe 1990: 29.

[111] Bottini 1981: 151–4; Mazzei and Lippolis 1984: 185–210; Volpe 1990: 35–45; Grelle 1992: 29–42; Mertens 1995c: 135; Antonacci Sanpaolo 2001: 33–5. Archaeological evidence from tombs – different burial techniques and differentiation of grave goods – and excavations of settlements indicates increased social stratification in the fourth and third centuries.

[112] Volpe 1990: 35–40; Mario Torelli 1999: 90–102; Lomas 2000: 82–7.

[113] See among others: Beaumont 1936 (noting that Greek influence in northern Apulia was less visible before the fourth century); Fischer-Hansen 1993 (comments on the cultural contacts

Hellenisation,[114] and it appears that Taras was a major agent in spreading Greek culture into Apulia.[115] So, at approximately the same time as Rome was coming into increasing contact with northern Apulia, the communities of that region were in the process of urbanising and Hellenising, and while Roman contact may have accelerated the process, the culture of Apulia was already influenced by relations with Magna Graecia.

Thus, we see in Apulia in the late fourth century (or perhaps a little earlier) landed, Hellenised aristocracies who dominated increasingly urbanised communities. These city-states (or proto-city-states) and ruling elites would probably have functioned in ways similar to their counterparts in the Graeco-Roman world. As such, we would expect the ruling elite to derive political legitimacy from both wealth and military success. But even wealth would not have been completely separate from warfare, since Apulian aristocrats would have been economically dependent on lands targeted by opposing armies. Increased urbanisation implies that communities exploited the surrounding countryside more thoroughly, as the elite converted meagre pre-modern surplus into such projects as defensive works or ostentatious displays of wealth. This environment would have encouraged frequent warfare between Apulian and non-Apulian communities and internecine warfare between Apulian communities, especially the larger, hegemonic powers, as they competed for control over limited resources.

Our available evidence confirms the general picture. That a number of Apulian communities built impressive defensive walls suggests either the reality or perceived threat of warfare. Ancient literary sources report that the Samnites raided the plains of Apulia, and urbanisation, especially the building of defensive walls, may have been in part a response to Samnite encroachment.[116] Indeed, Livy (9.13.6) clearly states that Arpi and other (unnamed) Apulian communities originally treated with the Romans more because of their hatred towards the Samnites than because

---

between Magna Graecia, Apulia and Etruria); Lomas 2000; Antonacci Sanpaolo 2001: 31–2. See also Gallini 1973 and, more recently, Curti, Dench and Patterson 1996: 181–8 for cautionary, theoretical discussions of the problematic terms 'Hellenisation' and 'Romanisation'.

[114] Beaumont 1936: 194–5; Antonacci Sanpaolo 2001: 31–2.

[115] De Juliis 1984a: 166–72; Fischer-Hansen 1993; Poulter 2002: 112–26; see Head 1977: 43–51 on the circulation of Tarentine coins in Apulia.

[116] Liv. 9.13.6–7; Strab. 6.3.9; Varro, *Rust.* 2.1.16, 2.2.9; Diod. Sic. 20.35.2; for Samnite attacks as a catalyst for Apulian urbanisation and construction of defensive walls, see Salmon 1967: 231. For intriguing *comparanda*, a number of sites along the border of Lucania and Samnium display traits of increasingly complex settlements by the third century, a development which has been linked to the building of fortifications in response to the Samnite conflict with Rome (Gualtieri 2004). Increased urbanisation in Apulia is therefore consistent not only with Roman, but also with Samnite incursions.

of any *beneficia* that the Roman people afforded their allies. Livy (8.37.3–6) also states that one of his sources for Roman campaigns in 324/3 reports fighting between the Samnites and Apulians.[117] Teanum Apulum was originally of Daunian foundation and it became Oscanised by the fourth century,[118] while Luceria clearly succumbed to Oscan Samnite pressure.[119] Even if the picture of loyal and civilised Roman allies (the Apulians) beset by uncivilised hill-people (Samnites) is over-schematised,[120] both literary and archaeological evidence are consistent in suggesting Samnite pressure and Samnite–Apulian conflict.

Taras, the most powerful Greek city in southern Italy, may have posed a threat to the Apulians even before Rome interfered in the region.[121] Taras solicited the aid of Alexander of Epirus, who invaded Italy, attacked the Apulians and seized Sipontum, and finally signed a treaty with the Apulians.[122] As we have seen, Sipontum lay within Arpian territory. Thus,

---

[117] Livy preserves alternate versions of Roman campaigning in Apulia under the consul Q. Aulius Cerretanus in 323. Livy accepts that the Romans laid waste to the land of the Apulians who had allied with the Samnites against Rome. He also records, however, that some of his sources report that the Romans were defending their Apulian allies against Samnite attacks. The confusing nature of the sources may reflect the certainty that not all Apulian communities, or even all of the northern Apulian communities, were firmly allied with Rome.

[118] The double name, Teate (or Tiati)-Teanum, reflects the Oscanisation process. Teate was the original Daunian/Iapygian name, while Teanum (Oscan *Teianud*) is the later Samnite name. 'Tiati' appears on coins dating from the late fourth century, though early coins also bear Oscan inscriptions. See Head 1977: 48–9; Rutter 2001: 81–2. For the Oscanisation of Teanum Apulum, see A. Russi 1976: 1–3; Antonacci Sanpaolo 2001: 27–35; see also Mario Torelli 1993b: 141–3 (mentioning also the Oscanisation of Larinum and Ausculum). Mario Torelli 1999: 90–2 argues for early Samnite penetration into northern Apulia/Daunia by the middle of the fourth century, especially in the strategic area of Lavello. Samnite influence brought significant social and economic changes in the years preceding the Roman conquest.

[119] At some point the Samnites occupied Luceria, until the final Roman conquest and colonisation of the town (Liv. 9.26.1–5). *CIL* I².401 contains a number of Oscanised words; Peruzzi 2001 argues that the inscription dates to around the time of the foundation of the colony Luceria and suggests the synthesis of local Oscan and Latin culture, contra Lazzeroni 1991, who argues that the Oscan forms are archaisms and the inscription should be dated to the late third or second century.

[120] Livy (9.13.7) also portrays the conflict as one between village-dwelling Samnite hill-people and the Apulians who cultivated the plains. For the ancient historiographic tradition of the Samnites as *montani atque agrestes*, see Dench 1995, 2004. There is a long Mediterranean tradition of marginalising and stereotyping 'mountain dwellers' practising pastoralism; see above, n. 91.

[121] On Taras as a regional hegemonic power, see Lomas 1993: 35–7.

[122] Liv. 8.3.6, 8.17.9–10, 8.24.1–4; Strab. 6.3.4; Just. *Epit.* 12.2.1, 12.2.5–6. Livy is rather confused in his narrative, alternately having Alexander sail too early to Italy (340) and still campaigning too late (326). Alexander probably invaded Italy around 333 and died on campaign there sometime about 330; see Lomas 1993: 42–3; Oakley 1997–2005: II.406–7, 664–7. The Romans also made a treaty with Alexander (Liv. 8.17.10), probably about the same time as they agreed to a treaty with Taras that forbade the Romans from sailing past the promontory of Lacinium (App. *Samn.* 7.1). For the historicity and date of the Tarentine–Roman treaty, see Oakley 1997–2005: II.681 n. 1; Fronda 2006 414–15 n. 79; contra Barnes 2005: 89–94, who argues that the treaty is an Appianic invention.

its seizure may reflect ongoing hostility between Taras and Arpi, or this event may have sparked new tensions between these powerful cities.[123] Relations between Alexander and the Tarentines broke down, forcing Taras to seek closer ties with the Samnites.[124] In 326 Taras tried to manipulate members of the Lucanian elite to take up arms alongside the Samnites against Rome.[125] Later, the Tarentines tried unsuccessfully to arbitrate between Rome and the Samnites before their battle near Luceria.[126] It is plausible that Taras employed the Samnites against various Apulian communities. In any case, growing ties between Tarentines and Samnites posed a legitimate threat to Apulian communities, and even powerful cities such as Arpi would have been concerned.

Besides facing outside threats, Apulian cities almost certainly fought against each other, though there is less direct literary evidence. We have already seen that the Arpians aided the Roman siege of Oscanised Luceria,[127] and it is tempting to see their help as the product of some local rivalry or conflict, probably rooted at least partly in Samnite–Apulian hostility. Indeed, Rome's Apulian campaigns in 318 and 317 strongly hint at intra-Apulian rivalry. According to Livy, the Romans forcibly captured Canusium, Teanum Apulum and Forentum in addition to Luceria;[128] only Arpi is mentioned as being peaceably disposed towards Rome in 318–317. The Romans may have exploited such divided loyalties by siding with the Arpians against their local rivals in order to win their support and gain a foothold in Apulia.[129] Roman campaigns in the 320s also suggest intra-Apulian conflicts, with some Apulian cities (perhaps Oscanised cities such as Teanum Apulum) aligning with the Samnites against neighbouring Apulian communities.[130]

---

[123] The Tarentines may have recognised the strategic and commercial importance of controlling the southern Adriatic coast of Italy, and in this context the seizure of the port at Sipontum makes sense. Taras may have been moved in part by mercantile concerns. Sipontum as an Arpian possession: above, n. 102.

[124] Oakley 1997–2005: II.680.

[125] Liv. 8.27.6–11.   [126] Liv. 9.14.1–16.

[127] Liv. 9.13.9–12.

[128] Liv. 9.20.4–9; for the general historicity of these campaigns, see Fronda 2006.

[129] See Salmon 1967: 228–33 for Roman strategic intentions to surround the Samnites with allied states.

[130] Liv. 8.37.3–6; 8.38.1–8.39.15, 8.40.1; App. *Sam.* 4.1; *De vir. ill.* 32.1 (reading *Lucerinis* for *Nucerinis*); Degrassi 1947: 70–1, 542 (with commentary); Oakley 1997–2005: II.757–8; see also above n. 117. Livy reports that his sources are conflicting as to whether the Romans were fighting the Samnites, the Apulians, or both in these years. Although Livy tries to portray the Apulians as steadfast allies against the hated Samnites, the general confusion in his sources betrays a more fluid and complicated diplomatic situation. Indeed, the *Fasti Triumphales* record separate triumphs by the consuls over the Samnites and Apulians, the anonymous *De viris illustribus* reports a triumph over Luceria, and Appian says that the Romans captured both Samnite and Apulian towns.

The Arpians' decision to seek an alliance with Rome must be understood in the context of this muddled diplomatic milieu. Apulian–Samnite
hostility almost certainly contributed to Arpi's decision, especially if we
consider that neighbouring Luceria and Teanum Apulum were heavily Oscanised. Canusium, however, appears to have generally resisted
Oscanisation in the fourth century,[131] so there must be other factors in play.
If we look at the Apulian cities that Rome attacked in 318–317, Forentum
is described as a strong town (*validum oppidum*), though it does not appear
to have been a major state in the fourth century;[132] Teanum Apulum and
Canusium were, however, regional hegemonic powers. It is likely that Arpi
allied with Rome also to protect its regional hegemonic status, and thus
maintain or even improve its position vis-à-vis the powerful states that
surrounded it. This may have been particularly the case with the Arpians'
assistance in defeating Luceria. When the city fell, the Romans took
a great deal of plunder,[133] and for the moment Luceria must have been
severely weakened. The Arpians probably hoped to exert influence over
the city when the Romans left.[134]

But the Romans never did leave Luceria; rather, they garrisoned the city
and used it as a base of operations for raiding into Samnium.[135] The city
seems to have fallen back into Samnite hands until the Romans finally
captured it for good in 314, at which time it was converted to a Latin colony with 2,500 settlers to ensure future loyalty.[136] Over time the colony

---

[131] Oscanisation/Samnitisation of Apulia: Bottini, Fresa and Tagliente 1990; Volpe 1990: 33–4;
Mario Torelli 1993b, 1999: 90–2; Curti, Dench and Patterson 1996: 188. Canusium was originally
a Daunian settlement: Plin. *HN* 3.104. Canusium resisted Oscanisation: Bottini 1981: 151; Greco
1981: 249–64; De Juliis 1990; Mario Torelli 1993b: 142–3.

[132] The site of ancient Forentum is probably modern Lavello, though a case can be made for nearby
Gaudiano. Mario Torelli discovered an inscription in the area of Lavello that mentioned
Forentum, suggesting this was the location of the ancient city: Torelli 1969: 15–16; Bottini and
Tagliente 1986: 70. A. Russi 1992 notes that Horace (*Carm.* 3.4.13–16) refers to the town as *humile
Forenti* and both Porphyrio Pomponius (ad loc.) and the Scholiast (ad loc.) state that Forentum
was *humile* because it was situated in a valley. Thus, Russi concludes that archaeological remains
in the low-lying area of Gaudiano, slightly to the north-east of Lavello along the Ofanto River,
mark the location of Forentum. Roman conquest probably resulted in a shift in the main population centre, thus at least partly accounting for the archaeological signature (see now Mario
Torelli 1999: 99–101). Placing Forentum near Lavello is topographically consistent with accounts
of Roman campaigns along the Ofanto *c.* 315, whatever the precise location of the ancient town.
For a brief discussion of the debate, see Gargini, 1998; de Cazanove 2001: 162. Previous identification of Forentum with modern Forenza (Weissbach 1909; Beloch 1926: 402–3; Nissen 1967: 11.831;
Salmon 1967: 23; De Sanctis 1956–69: 11.304), was based mostly on onomastic evidence.

[133] Liv. 9.15.7.

[134] The Arpians already controlled the Cervaro and the Calore river valleys to the foothills of the
Apennines as far as Aecae, and they may have desired to extend their control over the Triolo valley.

[135] Liv. 9.26.1; Diod. Sic. 19.72.8–9 for its garrison and subsequent use as a base for raiding.

[136] Liv. 9.26.1–5; Diod. Sic. 19.72.8; for the date, see below, n. 168.

must have come to represent Rome's virtual control of this strategic territory, probably engendering local resentment, especially on the part of the Arpians.

Despite the Roman (or colonial) presence, ancient sources record continued Samnite attacks on Apulia after Luceria's foundation.[137] Thus, alliance with Rome against the Samnites failed to satisfy Arpian expectations. The Arpians, moreover, gained nothing, at least in terms of territory, from siding with the Romans, since the very city and territory over which the Arpians and Samnites had been fighting fell under the control of first the Romans, and then Latin colonists.[138] In fact, the Arpians may have perceived that they actually *lost* territory when Rome sent colonists to Luceria. Survey archaeology and aerial photography have uncovered a series of centuriation patterns around Luceria, including traces of *strigatio et scamnatio* datable to the foundation period of the colony. These divisions lay directly between Luceria and Arpi, so early colonial lots may have overlapped with Arpian territorial claims.[139] Even if the colonists did not occupy land that the Arpians claimed – and presumably the colonists did not make raids into the territory of Arpi – the placement of the colonial lots would have blocked Arpian territorial expansion against its former enemy. Finally, the Arpians must have understood the colony as a symbol of growing Roman hegemony at the expense of their own power.[140] This is consistent with Diodorus Siculus' statement that the Romans used Luceria as a base for operations against neighbouring peoples, implying that the colony was instrumental in controlling Apulia as well as for raiding Samnium.[141] Even after Luceria

---

[137] Diod. Sic. 20.35.2.

[138] Some of the native Samnite population of Luceria probably survived the colonial foundation and continued to inhabit the city. While it is unlikely that the Arpians still considered Luceria a 'Samnite' city after the introduction of Latin colonists, we cannot rule out the possibility that even occasional prominent colonists of Oscan descent could have been the source of bitterness for individual Arpians.

[139] For centuriation around Luceria, see Schmiedt 1985: 260–2; Volpe 1990: 209–13; Mazzei 1991: 112; see also Map 6.

[140] The imposition of a Latin colony in Luceria, occupying a strategic location at a great distance from Rome, must have had a powerful impact on local observers. The arguments of Laurence 1999: 11–26 concerning Roman road building offer an intriguing comparison. The construction of long and impressive military roads, for example the Via Appia in the fourth century, 'would seem to be both symptomatic of Rome's hegemonic leadership and at the same time to be actively reinforcing or establishing that leadership' (quotation at p. 13). For further discussion on the practical and symbolic impact of Roman roads and colonies in the period after the Second Punic War, see Chapter 7, pp. 308–11.

[141] Diod. Sic. 19.72.9: ἀλλὰ καὶ κατὰ τοὺς μετὰ ταῦτα γενομένους ἕως τῶν καθ' ἡμᾶς χρόνων διετέλεσαν ὁρμητηρίῳ χρώμενοι κατὰ τῶν πλησίον ἐθνῶν ('But also in the [wars] that came about after these events down until the present time they continued making use of this base of operations against the peoples nearby').

became a colony, therefore, tension between Luceria and Arpi probably continued through the third century and contributed to Arpian discontent.

Of course, we should not envision Arpi immediately becoming restive, chafing under Roman dominion soon after the imposition of a Latin colony on its border. Rather, one suspects that for the short term, so long as the Samnites or rival Apulians continued to threaten, the Arpians saw their alliance with Rome on the whole as beneficial. Although the narrative sources for the Samnite Wars switch their focus after the colonisation of Luceria from Apulia to other regions, as the major theatres of the Samnite–Roman conflict shifted, scattered literary references support this suggestion. I have already mentioned that Samnites attacked Apulian communities in 309; Diodorus specifies that they targeted those Apulians who supported the Romans.[142] Diodorus implies that some Apulian cities had yet to be brought under Roman control. Apulian loyalty remained divided in the early third century: according to Livy, early in the Third Samnite War the consul P. Decius Mus marched against 'the Apulians' to prevent them from joining forces with the Samnites.[143] One can only speculate as to which Apulians still took up arms against Rome, though they presumably included communities that had yet to be conquered, such as Venusia.[144] Rome campaigned along the Samnite–Apulian border again in 291, when Venusia was finally conquered and resettled as a Latin colony.[145] Lastly, Apulia saw fighting during the Pyrrhic War. It is not clear if any Apulian cities sided with Pyrrhus, but the Samnites and Tarentines, traditional Arpian foes, did. Arpi, meanwhile, did not revolt during the Pyrrhic War; in fact, it is the only Apulian city specifically mentioned in the sources as providing military assistance to Rome.[146] The

---

[142] Diod. Sic. 20.35.2: οἱ δὲ Σαυνῖται κατὰ τοῦτον τὸν χρόνον μακρὰν ἀπηρτημένης τῆς Ῥωμαίων δυνάμεως ἀδεῶς ἐπόρθουν τῶν Ἰαπύγων τοὺς τὰ Ῥωμαίων φρονοῦντας ('The Samnites at that time, when the force of the Romans was removed a long way away, fearlessly attacked those of the Iapygians (Apulians) who were inclined towards the Romans').

[143] Liv. 10.15.1–2: *Samnitibus Apuli se ante proelium coniunxissent, ni P. Decius consul iis ad Maleventum castra obiecisset, extractos deinde ad certamen fudisset.* Livy generalises by using the term *Apuli*, though it is highly unlikely that all Apulians were prepared to take arms against Rome. Instead, the reference probably reflects divided Apulian loyalties. For the probable historicity of Roman campaigns near Beneventum in 297, see Oakley 1997–2005: IV.182–4.

[144] Costanzi 1919: 195–7.   [145] Dion. Hal. 17/18.5.1–2.

[146] Taras solicited help from Pyrrhus, promising that he would find allies among the Bruttians, Samnites and Lucanians (Plut. *Pyrrh.* 13.5–6; Dion. Hal. 19.8.1; App. *Sam.* 7.3; Polyb. 1.7.5–7; Liv. *Per.* 10; Cass. Dio 9.39.1/Zon. 8.2 (claims that the Tarentines were already in league with the Samnites); Just. *Epit.* 17.2.11, 18.1.1 (claims the Samnites and Lucanians also appealed to Pyrrhus)). Whether the Tarentines were already in negotiations with these peoples is unknown, though a coalition of Rome's opponents appears to have formed soon after the battle of Heraclea in 280: Plut. *Pyrrh.* 17.5; Dion. Hal. 20.1.1–5; Liv. *Per.* 13. According to Appian (*Sam.* 10.1), Pyrrhus next offered the Romans a treaty if they agreed, among other things, to restore lands

local diplomatic context through the first quarter of the third century, therefore, resembled the situation when Arpi first appealed to Rome.

By the late third century, however, the Arpians re-evaluated their position. Half a century had passed since Pyrrhus was driven from Italy and Rome suppressed rebellious states in the south-east of the peninsula. Thus, while local hostilities and rivalries probably persisted, there was little opportunity for the Arpians (or any Apulians) to act on them. Arpi had been a regional hegemonic power in the late fourth century, but Roman rule prevented further Arpian expansion and so limited the opportunities for the Arpian elite to obtain glory through war. The ruling elite may even have felt that the status of their city as a hegemonic power had slipped since the end of the Pyrrhic War,[147] despite the Arpians' strong display of loyalty. We may conjecture that Hannibal exploited Arpian frustration, perhaps promising to expand Arpi's territory if they sided with him, or perhaps the Arpians simply reckoned that Hannibal offered them a chance to exert regional hegemony. In any case, the Arpian decision to side with Hannibal after Cannae is best understood in light of the city's history as a regional power.

There is admittedly little direct literary testimony for the Second Punic War to support this hypothesis, but numismatic evidence may lend support to the contention that hegemonic ambition weighed heavily in the Arpian decision to revolt. Arpi and the much smaller, neighbouring city of Salapia minted a series of nearly identical bronze coins. The issues are the same size, display a laureate Zeus (obverse) and Calydonian boar (reverse), and bear legends in Greek characters identifying the respective city (ΑΡΠΑΝΩΝ, ΣΑΛΑΠΙΝΩΝ) and the names of the local magistrate. Among the names, 'Dasius' appears on issues from each city, perhaps

to the Samnites, Bruttians, Lucanians and Daunians. If historical, it may imply that Pyrrhus had won over some Apulian communities, though it may simply have been a blanket demand aimed at restricting Roman power to Latium (Erskine 1993: 58 n. 6 doubts the exact terms of Pyrrhus' proposed treaty). In 279 Pyrrhus defeated the Romans at Ausculum in Apulia, where he probably hoped to gather more allies. Zonaras (8.5) claims that he gained many Apulian cities by both force and agreement: καὶ πολλὰ μὲν βίᾳ, πολλὰ δὲ ὁμολογίᾳ. Some Apulians helped the Romans, but only the Arpians are specified in the sources, perhaps indicating that other Apulian cities either sat out or actively supported Pyrrhus: Dion. Hal. 20.3.2; Plut. *Pyrrh.* 21.9; Zon. 8.5.

[147] Aecae (modern Troià) probably did not emerge as a politically independent state until the third century, before which it may have functioned as an outpost of the Arpians against the Samnites. Aecae is invisible in the sources before the Second Punic War, despite its strategic location, which must have come into play during the Samnite Wars. The lack of references may be taken as evidence that Aecae was not independent but rather was politically subordinate to Arpi, and thus came into a Roman alliance at the same time (Volpe 1990: 38–40; Grelle 1992: 35–6, 39 n. 37). If so, Aecae's political autonomy, achieved during the third century, may indicate a corresponding loss of Arpian control or influence. It must be stressed, however, that the evidence is not conclusive and Aecae's subordinate political status must remain a plausible speculation. For its location, see De Santis 1966.

confirming literary references to Dasius Altinius of Arpi and Dasius of Salapia. The great similarity between the Arpian and Salapian coins points to a close association between the two cities. Arpi was clearly the more powerful of the two, so we may speculate that Salapia was in some way a subordinate partner.[148] Moreover, these coins have been dated to the period of the Second Punic War. If this dating is accurate, and given Arpi's history as a local hegemonic power, we may conjecture that the joint issues symbolised an assertion or reassertion of Arpian regional authority during the period of revolt in the Second Punic War.[149]

Thus, hegemonic aspirations and the desire to restore or even extend Arpian power contributed to the local aristocracy's decision to revolt after Cannae. This is not to say that other strategic considerations did not factor in, or that the idiosyncratic motives of individual players (such as Dasius Altinius) were not important. But when Arpi's divided ruling class confronted this difficult policy decision, the opportunity to restore Arpian hegemony drew a critical number of aristocrats into Dasius Altinius' camp.

THE REVOLT OF ARPI'S 'SATELLITE' ALLIES, 216

The revolt of Arpi created a domino effect, whereby Hannibal was able to gain control over a number of the surrounding small cities including Salapia, Herdonia, Aecae[150] and Ausculum. The status of Ausculum during the Second Punic War is implied by an important passage in the *Liber coloniarum*:[151]

Vibinas, Aecanus, Canusinus. iter populo non debetur. in iugera n. CC. || Item et Herdonia, Ausculinus, Arpanus, Collatinus, Sipontinus, Salpinus, et quae || circa

---

[148] Afzelius 1942: 163–4 also suggests that Salapia acted under the sway of a local hegemon but does not conclude whether the hegemon was Arpi or Canusium, though the numismatic evidence obviously points to Arpi.

[149] For the Arpian and Salapian coins, see Head 1977: 43–9; Crawford 1985: 64 and fig. 19; Parente 2000. See now, however, Rutter 2001: 76–7, 80–1, who dates the similar Arpian and Salapian coins to the late fourth or early third century. This revised chronology would still indicate a long-standing relationship between Arpi and Salapia. There is no reason to assume that the Dazos (Dasius) found on coins from Arpi, Salapia and Rubi are, as Rutter states, 'clearly members of the same clan' (p. 76). See above, n. 29.

[150] We know Hannibal possessed Salapia, Herdonia and Aecae from accounts of their recapture: the Romans stormed Aecae in 214 (Liv. 24.20.8); Salapia was still under Carthaginian control, including a garrison of 500 Numidian cavalry, in 210 (Liv. 26.38.6–14; App. *Hann.* 45–7); Hannibal controlled Herdonia as late as 210, when he executed a number of aristocrats for plotting to surrender to Rome and transferred the population to Metapontion and Thurii (Liv. 27.1.3–15).

[151] The *Liber coloniarum* is a notoriously difficult text, but it probably contains accurate information as far as the location and size of centuriation, and possibly the laws that created the various

montem Garganum sunt, centuriis quadratis in iugera n. CC., lege Sempronia et
|| Iulia, kardo in meridianum, decimanus in orientem. || Item Teanus Apulus. iter
populo non debetur. (*Lib. colon.* 1.219.10–14 Lachmann = 1.164.26–30 Campbell)

The land of Vibinum,[152] Aecae, Canusium. A right of way is not due to the people;
(they were divided into units) of 200 *iugera*. Likewise also Herdonia, the land of
Auseulum, Arpi, Collatia, Sipontum, Salapia, and those [cities] which are around
Mount Garganus, the centuries having been arranged into 200 *iugera* (divisions),
by a *lex Sempronia* and a *lex Iulia*; the *kardo* faces south, the *decumanus* east.
Likewise, the land of Teanum Apulum. A right of way is not due to the people.

Since Auseulum is grouped with other cities that broke from Rome during
the Second Punic War, it too probably suffered confiscations after the war,
presumably for disloyalty.[153] Livy implies that Herdonia, like Arpi, revolted

colonial or viritane allotments. It is less reliable with respect to the legal status of the communities mentioned. The work was probably first compiled around the time of Augustus, with other
notices added over time. The current text is generally divided into two books, the first compiled perhaps in the early fourth century AD, and the second somewhat later. For discussion, see
Keppie 1983: 8–12; Gargola 1995: 158–9, 241 n. 42; Campbell 2000: xl–xliv. Gargola defends the
general historicity of the *Liber coloniarum*, following Pais 1920, Thomsen 1947 and De Martino
1984, contra Mommsen 1967. Keppie 1983 and Campbell 2000 are more cautious.

[152] Vibinum (modern Bovino), mentioned only briefly in literary sources (Plin. *HN* 3.105; Ptol. *Geog.*
3.1.72), is probably the Οἰβώνιον where Hannibal camped and ravaged the territory of Arpi in
217 (Polyb. 3.88.6). Some scholars (for example, Volpe 1990: 40–2; Pani 1991: 126–7) assume that
Vibinum defected in the Second Punic War; this is based on (1) its inclusion in this section of the
Liber coloniarum, and (2) an inscription discovered in Brundisium that may indicate Vibinum
was besieged during the Hannibalic War, perhaps by Fabius Maximus. The data, however, are
not secure. (1) Vibinum is included on the same line in the *Liber coloniarum* as Aecae (which we
know revolted) and Canusium (which we know did not revolt), so the line does not seem to refer
to confiscations imposed for disloyalty during the war. (2) The aforementioned inscription has
been heavily restored by Vitucci in 1953 to read Vibinum:

PRIMUS SENATUM LEGIT ET COMITI[a instituit M. Iunio Pera M. Aemilio]
BARBULA CO(n)S(ulibus). CIRCUM SEDIT VI[binum bello Punico secundo praesi-]
DIUMQUE HANNIBALIS ET PRAE[fectum eius cepit. Virtute in rebus]
MILITARIBUS PRAECIPUAM GLOR[iam sibi comparavit.]

The subject of this *elogium* may be Q. Fabius Maximus, who was censor in the consulship of
M. Aemilius Barbula (230) before winning fame as the *cunctator* during the Second Punic War.
But Develin 1976 and now Muccigrosso 2003 argue that it is Ap. Claudius Caecus, who was still
censor when Q. Aemilius Barbula was consul in 311. Gabba 1958 argued that the subject of the
elogium was a local official, not a Roman magistrate. Thus, this heavily restored and often-debated
inscription may deal with an individual who had nothing to do with the Second Punic War.
Overall, we must conclude that while Vibinum *may* have defected, the question remains open.

[153] I have already shown that Arpi, Salapia, Herdonia and Aecae were at some point in Hannibal's
possession. Livy (34.45.3) states that Rome confiscated Sipontum from the territory of the Arpians
and founded a Roman citizen colony there in 194, presumably as punishment for Arpi's revolt
in the Second Punic War. The reference to *Collatinus* is more obscure. Pliny (*HN* 3.11.105) mentions the *Collatini* in the vicinity of Arpi, and another passage in the *Liber coloniarum* (2.261.3–4
Lachmann = 2.202.1–2 Campbell) mentions that *Conlatinus* was the same as *Carmeianus*, near
Mount Gargano. Thus, Marin 1970: 24 and A. Russi 1976: 222 place Collatia to the north-east of

immediately after Hannibal's victory at Cannae,[154] and it is likely that all of the cities in question broke from Rome at about the same time, in the summer of 216. Although Hannibal remained in Apulia after the battle while his troops recovered and his envoy, Carthalo, made a round trip to Rome, he does not seem to have stayed long before marching through Samnium into Campania.[155] Both his brief stay and the scattered references to local aristocrats who negotiated with Hannibal[156] suggest that the cities were not besieged or captured but revolted more or less willingly. This brings us back to the question of why these cities rebelled and why other Apulian cities remained loyal to Rome.

The alignment of Apulian cities during the Second Punic War bears a striking resemblance to alliance patterns during the Samnite Wars. I have already discussed Arpi's role in helping Rome during the Second Samnite War; Salapia and Herdonia also concluded alliances at the same time.[157] Less can be said about Aecae and Ausculum, though if Aecae was politically subordinate to Arpi in the fourth century,[158] then we might suppose that it also sided with Rome against the Samnites. The similarity between alliance patterns in the late fourth and late third centuries, summarised in Table 1 (p. 89), suggests some sort of long-term bonds or common conditions that linked these cities.

There is evidence to suggest that at least some of these same cities enjoyed strong economic ties, with Arpi and Herdonia acting as major hubs in a regional economic system. Strabo (6.3.9) states that Salapia was the port of Arpi and that many goods, including grain, were traded between Salapia and Sipontum. Strabo's sources for Apulia were probably not written before the second century, but one suspects that local trade routes and lines of communication did not differ much from the third century. Even though the sites of ancient Salapia and Sipontum are now

Arpi, at the base of the Gargano and possibly in the territory of Teanum Apulum. But if the additional information in the second *Liber coloniarum* passage is accurate, then Collatia should be located near Carmeia, which is more securely identified with modern S. Lorenzo in Carignano, about 10 km south of ancient Arpi; see A. Russi 1976: 223, 1980: 96–7; Volpe 1990: 220. It is likely that Collatia and Carmeia were two small, nearby settlements within Arpian territory that was confiscated after the Second Punic War. Teanum Apulum did not, however, revolt during the Second Punic War (see below pp. 92–3).

[154] Liv. 27.1.4: *[Herdoniae] quae post Cannensem cladem ab Romanis defecerat.*

[155] For Hannibal's actions around Cannae, see Liv. 22.51.1–22.52.7, 22.58.1–9; Livy later states (23.1.1) that Hannibal left Apulia immediately (*confestim*) after the battle of Cannae and the plundering of the Roman camps; while probably an exaggeration, the reference reflects the likelihood that Hannibal did not stay long in Apulia.

[156] For local factionalism and aristocrats negotiating with Hannibal, see above pp. 64–7.

[157] Afzelius 1942: 163–4; Toynbee 1965: 1.146.

[158] On the relationship between Arpi and Aecae, see above, n. 147.

landlocked, modern coastline studies prove that they did have access to the sea in Roman times.[159] It is plausible that goods travelled along the Cervaro or Carapelle rivers, with some either exiting or entering via the ports of Salapia and Sipontum (then part of Arpian territory). Interesting archaeological finds are consistent with this picture. Examples of Corcyran A and B amphorae, datable to the late fourth or early third century, have been discovered in tombs at Arpi, Sipontum, Salapia and Herdonia – the largest concentration at Arpi – but not elsewhere in northern Apulia, suggesting that these cities imported wine from Corinth and Corcyra. Graeco-Italic (Type Will A) amphorae have been found along the Apulian coast as far north as the Gargano, including in Sipontum and Salapia, and inland along the Candelaro (in the direction of Teanum Apulum) and the Carapelle as far as Herdonia.[160] It is particularly interesting that contemporary amphorae produced in Magna Graecia have been found in Salapia and Canusium, but not in other Apulian locales. The ceramic evidence suggests a local trade network involving Herdonia, Salapia, Sipontum and Arpi. The important city of Canusium, however, does not appear to have been as active in this network, perhaps instead trading more intensively to the south.

Numismatic finds from the extensive excavations at Herdonia display a similar distribution. If excavation finds are at all representative, over the course of the third century the people of Herdonia increasingly used coins minted in northern Apulia, especially from Arpi and Salapia. This is especially true of coins datable to the Hannibalic era, of which the greatest proportion (more than 60 per cent) was produced at Arpi and Salapia.[161] Arpi thus appears to have defined the dominant horizon for Herdonia's monetised transactions, at least for the third century. The Carapelle River again seems to mark the southern fringe of a local economic system, along which cities such as Herdonia and Salapia tended to orient their economic activity more to the north (towards Arpi) than to the south.

This is not to suggest that Arpi and neighbouring towns operated under some sort of exclusive trade agreements, or that the distribution of coins and amphorae suggests any sort of federal political arrangement. The

[159] For example, see Delano-Smith 1978: 25–33.
[160] Will 1982; Volpe 1990: 60–2, 229–30, 235–7.
[161] Coins from Taras or from Apulian communities that had adopted the Tarentine style dominate the finds from the end of the fourth century and beginning of the third century. Neapolitan and Campanian coins appear around the time of the Pyrrhic and First Punic Wars. While most Arpian and Salapian coins found in the excavations at Herdonia date to the Second Punic War, some are from as early as the First Punic War. For a discussion of the numismatic discoveries at Herdonia, see Scheers 1995.

Table 1. *Summary of alliance patterns among select Apulian cities (fourth–third centuries BC)*

City	Second Samnite War		Pyrrhic War		Second Punic War	
	Rome	Samnites	Rome	Pyrrhus	Rome	Hannibal
Arpi	X		X			X
Aecae	[X]					X
Salapia	[X]					X
Herdonia	[X]					X
Ausculum						X
Teanum		X			X	
Gereonium					Xα	
Canusium		X				
Forentum		X			X	
Cannae					Xα	
Luceria		X			Xβ	
Venusia		X			Xβ	

X Strong evidence for alignment   α Destroyed before the battle of Cannae
[X] Probable alignment   β Latin Colony

apparently close economic ties meant, rather, that the ruling elite in these cities may have had a particular vested interest in the well-being of other towns, or that aristocrats in different cities may have maintained more or stronger personal bonds. The decision of one of the cities to side with Hannibal – especially a powerful neighbour such as Arpi – may have made some aristocrats in other Apulian towns more sympathetic to the idea of revolt.

Local cultural or ethnic bonds may have reinforced individual personal ties. For example, Ausculum, Aecae, Salapia and Arpi may have been bound together by their hostility toward the Samnites.[162] I have already mentioned that Aecae was probably once an Arpian outpost in the fourth century, so the city may still have maintained close ties with Arpi through the third century. Also, the similar coinage minted by Arpi and Salapia during the Second Punic War (or earlier) suggests that these two communities were especially closely linked.

Finally, one suspects that in times of duress smaller cities might gravitate towards a more powerful neighbour, either because they willingly sought protection or more probably because the neighbouring hegemon pressured

[162] Livy (9.13.6) mentions that all in the area of Arpi were peaceably disposed towards Rome because of their hostility towards the Samnites, though he does not mention other cities by name. We may conjecture that Arpi's allies felt the same way about the Samnites.

them. The rebellious states that bordered Arpi were politically independent – they do not appear to have synoecised or sacrificed local political autonomy as members of a formal league – but they were almost certainly weaker. The territory of Salapia stretched along the coast from the border of Canusium to the location of Sipontum, originally in the territory of Arpi. It is not clear how far inland its territory ran, though it clearly straddled the Carapelle River, between the territories of Canusium and Arpi, until abutting the territory of Herdonia in the central Tavoliere.[163] Herdonia and Salapia controlled territory of approximately the same size, neither area being as extensive as that of Arpi or Canusium.[164] Both Salapia and Herdonia were, therefore, probably less powerful than Arpi. Similarly, both the small size of their territories and their relative anonymity in the sources indicate that Ausculum and Aecae were also weaker states than Arpi.[165]

The status of Ausculum, Salapia, Aecae and Herdonia – smaller states bound to the Arpians by economic ties, mutual hatred of the Samnites and perhaps even the simple fact that Arpi was close and powerful – helps to explain why these cities rebelled during the Second Punic War.[166] It is likely that Arpi took the lead among these cities in the area of foreign policy. In fact, the ancient sources imply as much since only Arpi is mentioned by name as forging an alliance with Rome during the Second Samnite War and supplying troops to Rome during the Pyrrhic War.[167] In turn, the smaller cities would tend to fall in line with the Arpians. Perhaps Ausculum, Salapia, Herdonia and Aecae were drawn to Arpian hegemony out of self-interest – for example, as protection against the hated Samnites or for economic motives – or perhaps the Arpians asserted hegemony and imposed their influence on the weaker states. In any case, when Arpi revolted during the Second Punic War, its smaller neighbours unsurprisingly followed as well, conforming to long-standing patterns of state behaviour.

The decision of these cities to revolt after the battle of Cannae, however, should not be seen as a simple round of follow-the-leader. Local ruling

---

[163] Volpe 1990: 14–15 n. 17.

[164] Volpe and Mertens 1995: 291–8. Herdonia did not mint its own coinage in the third century, also suggesting its subordinate status.

[165] De Santis 1966; Volpe 1990: 14–15 n. 17.

[166] The geographic distribution of rebellious states is also suggestive. The Apulian cities that defected form a band from the Sipontine–Salapian coast to the foothills of the Apennine mountains (E–W), between the Calore and Carapelle river valleys (N–S). That Apulian cities came over to Hannibal in a block rather than a checkerboard pattern implies that their revolts were interrelated. If Vibinum defected, it would fit within the geographic block that I have described, but again, the evidence for Vibinum is inconclusive (see above, n. 152).

[167] Liv. 9.13.6; Plut. *Pyrrh.* 21.9; Dion. Hal. 20.3.2.

aristocrats faced a difficult choice, wherein, as the preceding analysis suggests, powerful local political, economic and diplomatic factors proved decisive. Smaller Apulian cities would have been driven by aristocratic factionalism and political competition, exemplified by the Blattius–Dasius rivalry in Salapia. The arrival of Hannibal in Apulia, his victory over Rome and the revolt of Arpi would have opened up new opportunities for rival aristocrats. We can speculate that, after Arpi revolted, Dasius called to mind the traditional bonds between the Salapians and the Arpians, or he pointed out the impossibility of resisting Hannibal and Arpi. Hannibal's victory and Arpi's secession meanwhile would have undermined the credibility of pro-Roman aristocrats such as Blattius. The Salapian aristocracy probably calculated that siding with Hannibal and Arpi was preferable to remaining loyal to Rome, thus a critical mass of aristocrats began to favour Dasius' party over Blattius', and the Salapians threw off their allegiance to Rome. One imagines a similar process playing out in all the smaller Apulian cities that revolted.

HANNIBAL'S INCOMPLETE SUCCESS: CANUSIUM, TEANUM APULUM, LUCERIA AND VENUSIA

Not all cities in Apulia revolted in the summer of 216. Loyal cities can be categorised into two groups: Latin colonies (Luceria and Venusia) and allied Apulian cities (Canusium and Teanum Apulum).

Venusia and Luceria were situated at the edge of Apulia and both had been Latin colonies since at least the early third century. Luceria straddled the boundary of Samnium and Apulia, and according to Diodorus Siculus (19.72.8) was one of the most noteworthy cities in Apulia. Rome's early relationship with Luceria before its resettlement as a Latin colony is difficult to disentangle, but by 314 it had been conquered and colonised.[168] As mentioned before, by the Third Samnite War the Romans used Luceria as a base for raiding Samnium, a precursor to Roman strategy in the Second

---

[168] Livy (9.2.1–8) records that the Lucerians were *socii* of the Romans as early as 321. He claims it was the Roman desire to relieve a rumoured Samnite siege of Luceria that brought the legions to the Caudine Forks. Salmon 1967: 223 doubted this and saw the claim as a Roman fabrication to justify their careless march through Caudium. Velleius (1.14.4) states, however, that the colony of Luceria was founded in 326. This date is clearly too early, but Velleius' notice may refer to the date of diplomatic contact or even an initial treaty between Rome and Luceria. If so, then Livy's report of Roman concerns about Samnite pressure on Luceria in 321 may be broadly historical; see Oakley 1997–2005: III.35 n. 3 and III.283. In any case, Luceria fell under Samnite control, with the Samnites possibly even holding Roman hostages (Liv. 9.12.9). The Romans successfully besieged Luceria with help from Arpi (Liv. 9.12.9–11, 9.13.9–12, 9.15.2–7; see also Diod. Sic. 18.44.1; Cass. Dio fr. 36; Zon. 7.26) and garrisoned it. The city switched hands twice more before

Punic War.[169] Venusia was situated at the intersection of the Bradano
trench and the upper Ofanto River valley, in the area now known as the
Melfese, on the borders of Apulia, Lucania and Samnium. Like Luceria,
Venusia was a sizeable city[170] that had been controlled by the Samnites and
used as a bastion for their raids into Apulia.[171] Rome finally conquered and
colonised it only in 291.[172] Luceria and Venusia each remained loyal after
being resettled with Latin colonists.

While it is not unexpected that the two colonies did not revolt during
the Second Punic War, their displays of loyalty despite Hannibal's success in Apulia were indeed remarkable. For example, Livy (22.14.1–3) comments on Venusia's handsome treatment of the defeated Cannae legions.
Also, in 209 neither Luceria nor Venusia was listed among the twelve Latin
colonies that refused to fulfil their manpower obligations but rather were
commended by the senate for their service to Rome.[173] Ultimately, Venusia
and Luceria would prove instrumental in Rome's reconquest of Apulia.

Canusium and Teanum Apulum also remained loyal to Rome in the
wake of Cannae and throughout the remainder of the Second Punic War.
Concerning Canusium's loyalty, the sources are explicit. The Canusians
helped to shelter – albeit grudgingly – the remnants of the Roman army
after Cannae,[174] Hannibal failed to make the city revolt in 209,[175] and he
marched there again in 207, again with little effect.[176] The disposition of
Teanum Apulum is harder to evaluate since there is essentially no historical record of the city during the Second Punic War. Some scholars posit
that Teanum Apulum rebelled during the war,[177] based primarily on the
same passage from the *Liber coloniarum* that was discussed above.[178] The
ambiguity of the passage, however, does not allow any conclusions about
the loyalty of Teanum Apulum.[179] The narrative sources also do not mention either the defection of Teanum Apulum or its recapture, and it is

---

the Romans, after some debate, decided to settle 2,500 colonists there in 314 (Liv. 9.20.1–5). For
the date, see also Broughton 1951–2: 1.157.

[169] Liv. 10.11.13.

[170] Dionysius of Halicarnassus (17/18.5.1) records that 10,000 inhabitants of Venusia were killed and
over 6,000 were captured in the final Roman assault, though the numbers are likely to be exaggerated; Strabo (6.1.3) comments on Venusia as a noteworthy city.

[171] Salmon 1967: 246–7; Marchi and Sabbatini 1996: 99–100; however, Bottini 1981: 151 argues that
Oscan pressure stopped at the limits of Apulia in the Melfese.

[172] See above, n. 30.   [173] Liv. 27.9.7, 27.10.7–10.

[174] Liv. 22.52.7.   [175] Liv. 27.12.7–8.

[176] Liv. 27.42.16; see also Liv. 27.47.1.

[177] For example, Volpe 1990: 40, 220–1; Pani 1991: 127; Grelle 1992: 42.

[178] *Lib. colon.* 1.219.10–14 Lachmann; for the full text, see above, pp. 85–6.

[179] The exact text is *Item et Teanum Apulus. Iter populo non debetur. Item* refers probably to the size
of the land divisions and possibly to the governing laws, which are mentioned in the previous

unlikely that the revolt and recapture of such an important city would go unnoticed in the sources. Strabo implies that the city remained loyal, though the passage is, admittedly, problematic.[180] Numismatic evidence may provide an additional clue; Teanum Apulum appears to have minted coins on the Roman reduced uncial system, possibly for payment of the Roman army stationed in the vicinity. Rome went to this system in 217, suggesting that at that time or later the city was under Roman control.[181] Overall, based on the lack of positive evidence that Teanum Apulum revolted, combined with the circumstantial evidence that it did not, it is better to conclude that the Teanenses remained loyal to Rome during the Second Punic War.[182]

As I noted above, it is not surprising that the two Latin colonies did not revolt. But explaining why Canusium and Teanum Apulum, two important Apulian cities, did not revolt in the wake of Cannae, poses more of a challenge, especially when we consider the defection of Arpi, a comparable Apulian city. Whereas Arpi, moreover, had allied willingly with the Romans and had a history of loyalty to Rome before the Second Punic

---

sentence (*centuriis quadratis in iugera n. CC., lege Sempronia at Iulia. kardo in meridianum, decimanus in orientem*). In other words, the territory of Teanum was also divided into 200 *iugera* centuries, possibly as the result of a reorganisation under a *lex Sempronia* or *lex Iulia*. The sentence does not necessarily mean that its land was initially confiscated at the same time as that of the other Apulian cities. Rather, the fact that Teanum was mentioned in a separate sentence from Arpi, Herdonia, Ausculum, etc., may suggest that the territory was mulcted under separate circumstances, probably when the Romans conquered Teanum in the late the fourth century. Ultimately, the *Liber coloniarum* alone cannot provide enough evidence to justify the inclusion of Teanum in the ranks of the rebellious cities during the Second Punic War.

[180] Strab. 6.3.11; in this section Strabo describes the area around the Gargano, which according to him was inhabited by the 'Apuli' (Ἄπουλοι); the only city that he specifies for this area is Teanum Apulum. He claims that the whole region was once prosperous, until it was devastated by Hannibal and 'the later wars' (οἱ ὕστερον πόλεμοι) – presumably the Social and/or Civil Wars. The picture is consistent with references to devastation around Gereonium: Polyb. 3.100.4–8; cf. 3.88.5–6, 3.107.1–2; Liv. 22.23.9–10. The implication is that Hannibal laid waste to Teanum's territory, suggesting that the city resisted him and remained loyal to Rome. Strabo's sources may refer, however, to devastation that occurred before the battle of Cannae, which tells us nothing about Teanum's disposition after Rome's allies began to defect. Strabo also claims that Cannae took place here, rather than near Canusium, which he describes in his discussion of the area inhabited by the 'Daunians' (6.3.9). This error underscores his confusion over Apulian geography and may cast doubt on where exactly his sources meant for Hannibal's devastation to have occurred.

[181] Crawford 1964, 1985: 57–61; Marchetti 1978: 479–82; Antonacci Sanpaolo 2001: 27.

[182] I have already discussed whether Gereonium was a subordinate *vicus* of Teanum. Hannibal tempted the people of Gereonium to switch sides, then he besieged the village and finally massacred at least part of the population. Gereonium remained loyal in the face of Hannibal's army, apparently with no Roman garrison present. The remarkable loyalty of Gereonium may also reflect upon the loyalty of the Teanenses, though this suggestion is certainly not conclusive. Polyb. 3.100.1–5; Liv. 22.23.9; App. *Hann.* 15; contra Liv. 22.18.7; see discussion above, pp. 71–2.

War, Canusium and Teanum Apulum did not boast the same explicit record of loyalty in the Samnite and Pyrrhic wars. Specific local conditions, especially intercity rivalry, may help to explain their decision to remain loyal.

Unlike Arpi and (probably) its subordinate neighbours, both Canusium and Teanum Apulum were forced unwillingly into an alliance with Rome. Indeed, the two cities enter the historical record as Rome's enemies during the Second Samnite War. According to Livy, in the years following Caudium, the Romans carried out military operations in Apulia, capturing Canusium and Teanum Apulum in 318, and Teate and Forentum in 317.[183] Diodorus Siculus confirms the general picture of events, albeit with some differences in the details, recording that Canusium was captured in 317 and 'Ferentum' (Φερέντην) in 316.[184] Both Diodorus and Livy report that the Romans took hostages after defeating the Teanenses and the Canusians, which is consistent with the suggestion that these cities had been forced into submission, rather than willingly seeking a Roman alliance. Overall, we can conclude that both Teanum Apulum and Canusium (and Forentum) were initially hostile to Rome during the Second Samnite War, even if the sources exaggerate the magnitude of the Roman conquest of these two cities.[185] This is summarised in Table 1 (p. 89), which shows that the alignment of Apulian cities during the Second Punic War was very similar to alliance patterns during the Second Samnite War. The relative consistency of the alignments suggests that there were intercity rivalries and hostilities between important local states such as Arpi, Canusium, Teanum Apulum and Luceria.

[183] Liv. 9.20.4–10. For the general historicity of Livy's account of these campaigns, see Oakley 1997–2005: III.268–71; Fronda 2006; contra Beloch 1926: 401–2; Salmon 1967: 230–3. Livy seems not to recognise that Teanum Apulum and Teate were the same city; Marcotte 1985; A. Russi 1987; and Grelle 1992: 33–5 argue that the first reference is to the *deditio* and the second to the *foedus*; Oakley 1997–2005: III.269 (with discussion and bibliography) argues that it is more likely that Livy has taken over the doublet from a single source rather than creating the doublet by using more than one source.

[184] Diod. Sic. 19.10.2, 19.65.7. Diodorus commonly garbles the spellings of Italian place names and chronological discrepancies are not uncommon; see Oakley 1997–2005: III.270–1.

[185] Liv. 9.20.4; Diod. Sic. 19.10.2. Hostage taking could have followed either military or diplomatic activity. Hostages are not mentioned, however, in Rome's negotiations with Arpi. The implication is that Rome did not trust Canusium or Teanum to remain loyal, suggesting that they came into alliance with Rome under different circumstances from Arpi. Livy (9.20.8) does mention that the Teates sought a *foedus*, but this reference is clearly a doublet of the campaign that he mentions a few lines earlier, as Livy has failed to notice that Teanum and Teate are the same city. The Romans probably attacked Teanum in 318, which compelled the Teanenses to seek a treaty in 317: see above, n. 183. Even if we assume that the scale of the Roman military activity has been magnified, it does appear that Canusium and Teanum were compelled unwillingly to sign treaties with Rome.

Samnite–Apulian enmity helps to explain a rivalry between Teanum Apulum and Arpi. Although Teanum Apulum was originally of Daunian foundation, it became Oscanised by the fourth century.[186] Teanum Apulum had probably succumbed to Samnite pressure by the time Rome penetrated this region, which is consistent with the entry of the Teanenses in the Second Samnite War on the side of the Samnites, against Rome and its Apulian allies (including Arpi). Indeed, in light of the traditional hostility between the Samnites and Apulians, it is predictable that Teanum Apulum and Arpi would have shared mutual antagonism. Ethnic tension was probably exacerbated by the two cities' geographic proximity and status as regional hegemonic states. The territories of Teanum Apulum and Arpi abutted, and the two must have competed for land and resources, especially as they emerged as urban centres in the fourth century.

But if this picture is accurate, why did the Teanenses remain loyal to Rome rather than seek help from Hannibal? Teanum Apulum's aristocracy must have suffered some punishment as an outcome of Roman conquest, including the giving-up of hostages; staunchly anti-Roman aristocrats were probably executed or at least had their land and property confiscated. On the other side, Rome also probably favoured any pro-Roman aristocratic families. Ironically, this reshaped ruling class, whose status was bound up closely with Roman rule, might have felt closer to Rome than their Arpian counterparts, who do not seem to have suffered a similar purge. Over time, the Teanenses may also have recognised that their alliance with Rome protected them from any Arpian aggression. Lastly, short-term events would have shaped how the Arpi–Teanum Apulum rivalry expressed itself. Put simply, the Arpians revolted first, followed in short order by neighbouring communities. When the Arpian bloc sided with Hannibal, the Teanenses may have suspected that this new alliance posed an immediate threat to their interests. Thus, in the critical period immediately following Cannae, the Teanenses preferred to hold out with Rome rather than face the prospects of Arpian regional hegemony.

Canusium presents a more interesting case, as there is more literary evidence for Canusian attitudes in 216, allowing us additional insight into their decision-making. The evidence shows that Canusium was not uniformly pro-Roman in the days after Cannae, when remnants of the Roman army, numbering in the thousands, began to gather in Venusia

---

[186] A. Russi 1976: 2–3 suggests that the double name Teate-Teanum reflects the Oscanisation process. Teate was the Daunian/Messapic name, while Teanum (Oscan Teianud) is the Samnite name.

and Canusium.[187] About the same number of survivors arrived at each city, yet the reception at Canusium was relatively cooler.[188] Indeed, Livy's anecdote about the generosity of Busa,[189] while probably overdramatic, may contain a historical core that indicates a general reluctance on the part of the Canusian elite in welcoming the Roman survivors and, possibly, even ill-will towards the Roman cause after Cannae. Roman requisitions in the days leading up to the battle probably exacerbated any pre-existing animosity,[190] while the battle's outcome must have further undermined Roman credibility. Nevertheless, why did emerging discontent and anti-Roman sentiment not blossom into a full-blown revolt?

In part, the Roman military response in the weeks after Cannae may have been crucial in suppressing a potential revolt. Despite Varro's handsome treatment in Venusia, the consul decided to unite the Cannae legions at Canusium. Later, M. Claudius Marcellus was hurried to Canusium to take over command of those troops.[191] Canusium was a very large city with impressive defensive walls that could more easily withstand a siege, and fear of a follow-up attack by Hannibal certainly influenced the Roman decision to regroup at Canusium.[192] Varro's decision to muster in Canusium may also have been designed to check any faltering loyalty in the closest allied city to the battle.[193] The Roman decision may have had the additional effect of bolstering the pro-Roman elements of the local aristocracy.[194] Indeed, once inside the city walls, the Roman commanders may have promised rewards to the Canusian elite in order to encourage loyalty.[195] Whatever the reasons for stationing the troops in Canusium, their presence surely limited the chances of a successful revolt.

---

[187] Polyb. 3.116.13; Liv. 22.49.13–14, 22.52.4–7, 22.54.1–6; see Walbank 1970: I.440.

[188] By contrast, Varro and 4,000 survivors were treated with great hospitality in Venusia. They received clothes and food, presumably from aristocratic families.

[189] See above, n. 38.

[190] Polyb. 3.107.2–4: supplies were collected from around Canusium, stored at Cannae and conveyed to the Roman camp.

[191] Liv. 22.52.7, 22.54.1–6, 22.57.7–8.

[192] Strab. 6.3.9 for the walls of Canusium. Hannibal was still nearby as the Romans regrouped, so Varro probably expected the Carthaginians to try to rejoin battle as soon as possible in order to press their advantage.

[193] De Sanctis 1956–69: III.2.202 also suggests that Varro's decision helped to secure the loyalty of Canusium.

[194] Like Teanum Apulum, Canusium did not willingly ally with Rome in the fourth century, and it was forced to hand over hostages upon Roman conquest (see above, n. 185). We may assume that the Romans likewise punished resistant Canusian aristocrats while forging strong bonds with favoured members of the local elite.

[195] Returning to the example of Busa, it is unlikely that the senate spontaneously granted honours only after the fact. Rather, it is far more likely that a magistrate on the spot would have made public gestures of friendship, including open promises of rewards and honours in return for past or even future acts of loyalty. Compare with the affairs in Nola (Chapter 3, pp. 108–9 and n. 40).

But this explanation only goes so far; the depleted and divided Cannae legions could not have hoped to storm Canusium had the townsfolk kept the gates closed, especially considering their formidable defences and the proximity of Hannibal's victorious army. Indeed, the Canusians could have chosen to invite Hannibal into the city, just as the people of Arpi had done. Other factors must have come into play.

If we consider once more the historical alignment of Apulian cities (see Table 1), we observe that Canusium tended to oppose Arpi, suggesting that Canusium, like Teanum Apulum, maintained a long-standing rivalry with Arpi. Samnite–Apulian hostility does not appear, however, to be the source of this rivalry. Canusium, like Arpi, was a Daunian city, and archaeological evidence suggests that it resisted Oscanisation.[196] Rather, it was probably rooted in unusually intense competition for local hegemony. Indeed, Canusium and Arpi were the two most populous and expansive cities in Apulia in the third century.[197] The aristocracies of both cities continued to accumulate significant wealth and presumably status throughout the third century, resulting in highly stratified communities.[198] This highly competitive environment would have encouraged rivalries both within and between communities;[199] one suspects the dynamic was particularly acute in the case of Arpi versus Canusium.

But unlike Arpi, whose hegemonic aspirations were frustrated by the network of Roman alliances and, especially, the creation of Luceria on contested land, Canusium's local influence may have expanded after Roman conquest. This conclusion rests on archaeological material from Lavello, at or near the site of ancient Forentum,[200] which Bottini and Tagliente have discovered and published.[201] In the fourth century Forentum appears to have consisted of about half a dozen nucleated, unwalled villages, each with its own cemetery located within the settlement; burial patterns and grave goods mirror those found in Daunian centres. Around the middle of the fourth century, however, a number of graves begin to reflect Samnite burial customs, contemporaneous with new types of monumental houses. These changes suggest the Oscanisation of the area. Finally, by the end of

---

[196] See above, p. 81 n. 131. [197] See discussion above, p. 77.

[198] This can be seen in the continuous use of opulent hypogeum tombs through the third century at Canusium, or at Arpi, impressive *dromos* tombs and an aristocratic house with peristyle and mosaic floors; see, for example, Mazzei 1984b: 27–43; Mazzei 1990: 58–62; De Juliis 1990; Mazzei 1991: 115–24; Mario Torelli 1999: 98–104; Mazzei and Steingräber 2000.

[199] So concludes Mario Torelli 1999: 102.

[200] Discussed above, n. 132.

[201] The following discussion of archaeological material follows closely Bottini and Tagliente 1986; 1990: 220–30; Bottini, Fresa, and Tagliente 1990: 245–7; see also Volpe 1990: 27–9; Mario Torelli 1999: 89–118.

the fourth century, most of the nucleated settlements were abandoned, with inhabitants now concentrated in a single, well-defended village. The data correspond to the period of Roman conquest, from when Rome first captured Forentum (318 or 315) until the conclusion of campaigns in the area and the foundation of Venusia (291). Graves dating from this period through the third century exhibit remarkable features. Burials were now located outside the settlement, in large underground tombs – presumably for members of the wealthy elite – similar to those found in Canusium. Tombs contained Canusian-style pottery and, in some cases, fine equestrian armour, again similar to grave goods found in Canusium. One tomb (no. 669) contained an equestrian panoply with a Roman-style helmet. From the Canusian-style pottery is the noteworthy 'Catarinella *askos*', whose decoration depicts Roman funeral iconography. The evidence strongly suggests that the elite of Forentum in the period immediately following Roman conquest adopted Romanised Daunian (specifically Canusian) cultural practices.

It has been suggested on the basis of this evidence that after Rome conquered Forentum, it was in some way placed under the administration of aristocrats from Canusium.[202] This would help to explain the unusually large number of colonists (20,000) that Dionysius reports for the founding of Venusia – the total would indeed include Latin colonists as well as natives (whether *incolae* or *adtributi*), including the 'Canusian' aristocrats stationed in Forentum, now incorporated into Venusia's territory.[203] It is, however, problematic that Rome would hand territory over to Canusium, since the city had only just been forced into the alliance system and its loyalty must have been suspect. A better explanation is that the Roman assault on Forentum greatly weakened the small community, and in the unsettled decades that followed the Canusians simply seized the territory – their expansion stopping only with the final Roman settlement after the colonisation of Venusia. Or, perhaps the archaeological evidence reflects the adoption of (Romanised) Canusian culture by the local elite of Forentum. In any case, it does appear that Rome's conquest of Forentum and, subsequently, the defeat and colonisation of Venusia coincided with an expansion of Canusian influence along the Ofanto River valley. This is very different from the situation in Arpi, which, as I argued, saw Arpian influence stunted by the implantation of Luceria.

To return to the Second Punic War, Canusium's status as a powerful city contributed to its rivalry with Arpi, and this rivalry influenced the

---

[202] Bottini and Tagliente 1986: 73; Volpe 1990: 29; Bottini, Fresa, and Tagliente 1990: 246.
[203] Dion. Hal. 17/18.5.1; Mario Torelli 1999: 94, 98; see above pp. 61–2 and n. 31.

decision by the Canusian elite to remain loyal to Rome. The two cities probably competed for regional hegemony in northern Apulia, and the long-term ramifications of the Arpian–Hannibalic alliance must have given the Canusians pause. As has just been discussed moreover, Canusium seems to have benefited despite its reluctant entry into the Roman alliance system, because Canusian influence extended in the third century as far as the confines of Venusia. These two factors probably made the Canusian aristocracy more inclined to the Roman cause and thus limited the degree of aristocratic discontent after Cannae. As a result, pro-Roman aristocrats maintained control of Canusium and allowed the remnants of the Roman army to enter the city. From this point onwards Canusium remained securely in the Roman camp.

CONCLUSION

By the end of 216, then, Hannibal had been partially successful in winning over Roman allies, including the formidable city of Arpi and a number of less powerful communities, such as Herdonia, Salapia, Aecae and probably Ausculum. Thus, Hannibal controlled a band of territory through central Daunia and could hope to have use of the port of Salapia. But a combination of local factors, in addition to Rome's military response after Cannae, prevented the defection of more Apulian cities. Winning over Arpi, the local hegemonic power, probably compelled its rivals Teanum Apulum and Canusium to remain loyal. Two Latin colonies, Luceria and Venusia, also remained steadfast in their loyalty to Rome. Thus, Roman allies essentially surrounded Arpi and its satellites, and Rome still controlled most of the major lines of communication to Arpi. We will pick up the story in Chapter 6, where I analyse how Hannibal's imperfect success left his new allies vulnerable, while long-term Roman strategic advantages came into play and allowed Rome to slowly recapture the rebellious Apulian cities.

In the next chapter, however, we will turn our attention to Campania, the region where Hannibal achieved perhaps his most dramatic diplomatic success – securing the loyalty of Capua. Patterns observed in the analysis of Apulia, such as the interplay between the local condition and the decision to revolt and the persistence of intercity rivalries, are even more visible in Campania, where Hannibal not only provided an opportunity for autonomy and local hegemony but, as in the case of Capua, actually promised it.

CHAPTER 3

Campania

INTRODUCTION

Campania, from the revolt of Capua in 216 to its surrender to the Romans in 211, was a decisive theatre of the Second Punic War. For Hannibal, the region would showcase his Italian strategy of eliciting allied revolts.[1] He was able to win over the region's most important city, Capua, as well as a number of smaller towns. Moreover, since the Capuans possessed *civitas sine suffragio*, Hannibal managed to win over Roman citizens instead of exclusively allied peoples, as he had in Apulia. He also captured an important stronghold where the Via Appia crossed the Volturnus River (at Casilinum), allowing him potentially to march north into Latium. Even at the height of his power, however, Hannibal achieved only partial success, as a number of Campanian cities (including Naples, Cumae and Nola) remained loyal to Rome. Meanwhile, the Romans committed vast resources, usually four or six legions, to hold the line in Campania. Upon its recapture, Capua's punishment was severe, and Hannibal's ultimate failure to defend the city undermined his legitimacy vis-à-vis his remaining Italian allies and marked a major turning point in the war.[2]

Rome's military response – its yearly commitment of multiple legions to Campania and the strategic placement of garrisons in key Campanian cities – accounts in large part for why Hannibal was unable to build on his initial success in the region.[3] It should be noted, however, that Rome failed to provide military support for some cities that did not revolt in the face

---

[1] Hannibal invaded the *ager Falernus* in northern Campania to awe the Italian allies (Polyb. 3.90.10–14), and the struggle in Campania was apparently an object of attention throughout Italy (Liv. 26.5.1–2).

[2] For Rome's treatment of Capua, see Liv. 26.14.9, 26.15.7–9, 26.16.5–13, 33.12–14, 34.2–13; Cic. *Leg. agr.* 2.88; App. *Pun.* 43; Zon. 9.6; Val. Max. 3.8.1. Some conditions of the punishment may not have been enforced: Frederiksen 1984: 244–50; see also Briscoe 1973: 132, 1989: 77. Hannibal appeared powerless to defend his allies after Rome's capture of Capua: Liv. 26.16.13.

[3] Especially Frederiksen 1984: 242; see also Lazenby 1978: 90–124; Lancel 1999: 127–30; Goldsworthy 2000: 223–9.

of Hannibalic pressure. For example, both Nuceria and Acerrae chose to be sacked rather than submit to Hannibal, and neither city received military assistance from Rome.[4] Rome's potential military response does not, therefore, fully explain the persistent loyalty of such communities, nor does it reveal much about why some Campanian cities decided to revolt at all. Rather, to answer these questions we must focus on specific, local conditions that shaped policy decisions in 216.

Thus, the analysis of Campania will build on the methods and themes developed in the previous chapter. This chapter will look closely at the reasons why individual cities chose to remain loyal to Rome or to revolt and, in particular, how local political factionalism and intercity rivalries limited the effectiveness of Hannibal's strategy and contributed to his long-term military failure. Much of the analysis will be devoted to the case of Capua, the most important Campanian city, whose revolt shaped policy decisions in neighbouring cities. Like Arpi in Apulia, Capua had a long history as a local hegemonic power. Hannibal's entry into Italy afforded the Capuans a chance to reassert not only their autonomy but also regional hegemony. Once Capua revolted, smaller surrounding communities that had traditional bonds with Capua also revolted. However, the threat of an expansionist Capua allied with Hannibal played a part in the decision of Capua's traditional regional rivals to remain loyal. In effect, Hannibal's success with Capua contributed to his long-term failure in Campania.[5] Moreover, unlike the above analysis of Apulia, we possess explicit evidence both that the Capuans chose to side with Hannibal out of hegemonic considerations, and that neighbouring Campanian cities feared the alliance between Hannibal and Capua.

It is necessary to establish a few definitions before advancing to the main analysis. First, 'Campania' will be used to designate the area bounded approximately by the natural topographical barriers of the Mons Massicus and the modern-day Monte Roccamonfina (to the north), the foothills of the Apennines (east), the rugged Sorrentine peninsula (south) and the sea (west),[6] encompassing the cities of Cales, Volturnum, Casilinum, Capua, Atella, Abella, Calatia, Sabata, Suessula, Acerrae, Nola, Nuceria, Surrentum, Pompeii, Herculaneum, Naples, Puteoli and Cumae (see Map 8).[7] Second, we must confront the ambiguous meaning of *Campanus*

---

[4] Liv. 23.15.3–6, 23.17.1–7.

[5] Reid 1915: 117 and David 1996: 58–9 also observe that intercity hostility helped to confirm the loyalty of Capua's traditional rivals, such as Cumae and Naples.

[6] Frederiksen 1984: 1–3; see also Salmon 1967: 23–7.

[7] For ancient literary references: Polyb. 3.91; Strab. 5.3.11, 5.4.3–11; Plin. *HN* 3.60–70. The exact location of Sabata is unknown, though it surely lay in the *ager Campanus*. Modern Forum Sabati (near modern Aversa) has been suggested, and I have tentatively followed this identification. It should

(Καμπανός) in ancient sources. Since the term could mean either the inhabitants of Capua or the Oscan-speaking denizens of Capua *and* its neighbouring communities, simply translating it as 'Campanian' will not suffice.[8] The specific context, therefore, must be considered to tease out to whom *Campanus* (Καμπανός) refers in a given passage. For our purposes, 'Capuan' will specify the citizens of Capua, and 'Campanian' will refer to the entire region or its inhabitants.[9]

We are fortunate to possess a great deal of ancient literary evidence for Campanian affairs in the Second Punic War, including Livy's detailed descriptions of Capuan politics and decision-making in the wake of Cannae, the effects of the Roman siege, and the debate over, and punishment meted out against, Capua once it fell. This material must be approached cautiously, as the Capuan revolt was a great shock to the Romans, and they could never again write dispassionately about the city or its people. Capua became a byword for the twin vices of *luxuria* and *superbia*. As late as the middle of the first century BC, Cicero could make a speech, apparently without embarrassment, characterising Capua as a sort of 'anti-Rome', willing and able to rise up and overthrow Roman power if its political autonomy were restored.[10] But the information provided in the Livian account is not without merit. His account of the Capuan revolt, for example, appears to rely heavily on Coelius Antipater, rather than more dubious later sources. The Second Punic War was a relatively recent event, and Capua's punishment generated serious senatorial debate, so it is likely that real evidence

be noted, however, that Frederiksen 1984: 36 n. 29 rejects the identification of Sabata with Forum Sabati.

[8] Greek authors frequently use Καμπανός in a broader sense than just the people of Capua. Indeed, a number of specialised words preserved in Greek sources refer explicitly to the Capuans: Καμπανός (Polyb. 9.5.2, 9.5.6), Καμπανήσιος (Polyb. 7.1.1, quoted in Ath. 12.528a), Καμπηνός (Diod. Sic. 26.10.1, 26.12.4), Καμπαῖος (App. *B Civ.* 1.90). The Latin term *Campanus* frequently, though not always, refers to Capua. It should also be noted that the earliest coins associated with Capua (dated to the late fifth century) bear the legend in Greek letters ΚΑΠΠΑΝΟΜ or ΚΑΜΠΑΝΟΜ. See Rutter 1979: 81–3, 178–9; Frederiksen 1984: 137–9; Musti 1988: 219–22; Pobjoy 1995: xii–xiv, 216–18.

[9] Although I will use 'Campanian' for the entire region, there are times when *Campanus* or Καμπανός means Capua and nearby Oscan communities (such as Atella) but not all of the cities in the region. In these cases, I will add appropriate modifiers such as 'the Capuans and their neighbours', to avoid ambiguity.

[10] In his speeches against Rullus' land law, Cicero repeatedly calls attention to the threat that Capua posed to the Roman Republic, citing its size, fertility and wealth, and the pride, arrogance and cruelty of its citizens (for example *Leg. agr.* 1.18, 2.76, 2.91, 2.95). He also claims that Capua was still capable of organising and making war (2.77), and that the Romans' ancestors wisely voted in 211 to deprive Capua of political institutions lest the city be able to provide a seat for empire (*urbem ipsam imperio domicilium praebere posse*) and strike fear into future generations of Romans (1.19, 2.88). The Capuan threat is of course greatly exaggerated to serve Cicero's specific political agenda, and there was no real chance that Capua could seriously have challenged Rome in the middle of the first century (Jonkers 1963: 45–9, Bell 1997). For Cicero's characterisation of Capua as 'anti-Rome' (*altera Roma*), see Vasaly 1993: 231–42.

was available to Coelius and even to later authors.[11] Indeed, Cicero remarks that public records concerning Capua were still available in his day.[12] Thus, while the Livian evidence most certainly contains exaggeration and distortion, it also probably preserves valuable historical artefacts, which an overly critical or dismissive treatment risks overlooking.

We may now pick up the story where we left off in Chapter 2, with Hannibal about to leave Apulia after the battle of Cannae. He marched into Samnium at the request of Statius Trebius, a member of the elite from Compsa who was the political rival of a pro-Roman aristocratic family, the Mopsii. Hannibal successfully exploited this local political rivalry and gained access to the city, though he was compelled to leave a garrison to protect his new allies.[13] According to Livy, Hannibal next marched into Campania and directly to Naples.[14] If Livy is accurate here, then Hannibal must have bypassed Nuceria along the way. This is not implausible: Hannibal apparently was anxious to gain a port, and he probably did not want to expend his time and resources investing a recalcitrant inland city, at least at this point.[15] After his unsuccessful attempt to capture Naples, Hannibal turned to Capua, where he found the inhabitants more receptive to his overtures.

THE REVOLT OF CAPUA, 216

According to Livy, the people of Capua were already agitating to revolt before the battle of Cannae. In 217 three Campanian *equites*, who had been prisoners after the battle of Trasimene and whom Hannibal had set free,

---

[11] Livy (23.6.6–8) dismisses a story, reported also by Cicero (*Leg. agr.* 2.95) and Valerius Maximus (6.4.1), that the Capuans demanded one of the consulships each year, in part because it did not appear in Coelius' account. This suggests that Coelius was his preferred source for the Capuan revolt. For support for the Livian evidence, see Frederiksen 1977 contra Ungern-Sternberg 1975; see also De Sanctis 1956–69: III.2.342–65; Frederiksen 1984: 255–61. For the relative merits of Coelius Antipater, see Badian 1966.

[12] Cic. *Leg. agr.* 2.88: *de Capua multum est et diu consultatum; extant litterae, Quirites, publicae, sunt senatus consulta complura … Itaque hoc perscriptum in monumentis veteribus reperieti …* ('It was much debated, and for a long time, concerning Capua; there are public records, Romans, and many senatorial decrees … And so, you will find this registered in the ancient records …').

[13] Liv. 23.1.1–4. Statius Trebius promised to hand over his city to Hannibal; the Mopsii fled at news of Hannibal's approach. The Mopsii family had held power because of Roman favour: *Compsanus erat Trebius nobilis inter suos; sed premebat eum Mopsiorum factio, familiae per gratiam Romanorum potentis* (23.1.3). As discussed in Chapter 1 (p. 32), this is striking and explicit evidence that at least some local ruling families received Roman backing. For a later example: in 175 the Roman senate responded to a legation from Patavium requesting help to suppress internal political discord that Livy (41.27.3–4) describes as a struggle between factions (*certamine factionum*); presumably the Romans backed one faction over the other(s). See also Chapter 7, pp. 314–16.

[14] Liv. 23.1.5–10.

[15] For Hannibal's desire to gain a port, see Liv. 23.1.5, 23.15.1–2, 23.36.1. See below (pp. 145–6 and n. 201) for the chronology of the attack on Nuceria.

informed Hannibal that Capua would revolt if he drew his army near the city, and this convinced Hannibal to march into Campania and devastate the *ager Falernus*.[16] If this is true, then the Romans lacked complete loyalty from the Capuan nobility as early as 217, though this anecdote may be Livy foreshadowing their actual revolt in 216. Likewise, Livy may also anticipate the events of 216 when he describes the actions of Pacuvius Calavius during his year as Capua's highest magistrate (*meddix tuticus*) in 217.[17] Livy informs us in his main narrative on the Capuan revolt that Pacuvius suspected that the common people would kill the local senators, seize power and revolt from Rome. Pacuvius thus manipulated the situation and, through a complicated ruse, made himself both leader of the 'people's party' and master of the now-subservient Capuan senate.[18] We later hear that Pacuvius was the leader of the party that brought Hannibal to Capua, implying that he was not only a proponent of the revolt but also its chief architect.[19]

Livy continues: after Cannae disaffection with Roman rule grew, and only two factors prevented immediate revolt. First, widespread intermarriage had united a number of Roman and Capuan aristocratic families; indeed, Pacuvius Calavius had marriage ties to prominent Roman aristocrats.[20] The second and more important reason, according to Livy (23.4.8), was that 300 young Capuan *equites* were serving in the Roman cavalry in Sicily. The Capuans understood that these young men were in effect hostages, and their families were so concerned that they convinced the Capuan senate to send a delegation to the consul Varro at

---

[16] Liv. 22.13.1–5.

[17] Ungern-Sternberg 1975: 26–45 accepts that Pacuvius Calavius was *meddix tuticus* in 217, but either rejects many Livian details about Capuan politics in that year or moves them to 216, after the battle of Cannae. Frederiksen 1984: 238–9 accepts that Capuan loyalty was already wavering before Cannae, as well as the report that Hannibal had been in communication with Capuan prisoners after the battle of Trasimene. Lazenby 1978: 66 and Goldsworthy 2000: 193–4 cautiously accept Livy's reference to Capuan prisoners informing Hannibal after Trasimene.

[18] Liv. 23.2.3–4.4.

[19] Liv. 23.8.2; see also Diod. Sic. 26.10. The tradition is accepted by Reid 1915: 112; De Sanctis 1956–69: III.2.207; Ungern-Sternberg 1975: 26–33; Frederiksen 1984: 239.

[20] Livy (23.4.7) states that 'long-established *conubium* had mixed many famous and powerful [Capuan] families with the Romans' (*conubium vetustum multas familias claras ac potentis Romanis miscuerat*), and he mentions (23.2.5–6) a couple of examples: '[Pacuvius Calavius] had children by a daughter of Appius Claudius and he had given a daughter in marriage to Marcus Livius' (*quippe qui liberos ex Appii Claudii filia haberet filiamque Romam nuptum M. Livio dedisset*). The former is perhaps to be identified as Appius Claudius Pulcher, cos. 212, the latter as Marcus Livius Salinator, cos. 219 (Lazenby 1978: 89; Frederiksen 1984: 232). Livy mentions widespread intermarriage again (23.33.3) when he describes the punishment that was meted out after Capua fell to Rome, and he notes (26.34.3) that when a number of Capuan aristocratic families were sold into slavery, daughters who had married outside their paternal household (*enupsissent*) – that is, either into loyalist Capuan families or into families from other communities, including presumably

Venusia, presumably in order to have the knights returned from Sicily.[21] Varro treated the embassy poorly,[22] and during their return to Capua the leader of the embassy, Vibius Virrius, convinced his colleagues that if the Capuans made a treaty with Hannibal they would recover land they had lost and they would be in a position to become masters of Italy. This proposal was brought before the Capuan senate and was received enthusiastically by most in attendance. The legates were sent thence to Hannibal, who had in the meantime marched into Campania, and the legation and Hannibal concluded a treaty that guaranteed Capuan sovereignty.[23] At the same time Roman citizens and magistrates were seized, imprisoned in a public bath and suffocated to death.[24]

Livy concludes his narrative: some vocal opposition to allying with Hannibal remained, led by Decius Magius, who protested, especially when he heard the city would have to accept a Carthaginian garrison.[25] When Hannibal learned of the opposition, he arranged to come to Capua in person and address the Capuan senate. Marius Blossius (*meddix tuticus* for 216) helped to orchestrate the meeting, making sure the Carthaginian general was received with appropriate fanfare.[26] When he arrived, he first dined with prominent Capuan aristocrats, including Sthenius and Pacuvius Ninius Celeres and Pacuvius Calavius.[27] The next

---

Rome – were exempt from this punishment. It could be argued that Livy exaggerates the degree of intermarriage from the couple of specific cases that he cites. On the other hand, it seems highly implausible that a century of *conubium* had produced only a handful of marriages. Livy's second reference to widespread intermarriage is found in his discussion of senatorial debate and acts concerning the fate of Capua, the records of which, as we have seen (above, pp. 102–3), were still available in Cicero's day. Livy claims that punishment was exacted on a family-by-family basis, with too many decrees to be worth mentioning all of them (26.34.2). Presumably, family ties factored into how surviving aristocratic families were treated. Overall, there is little ground not to believe that a number of Rome's and Capua's great houses were connected by marriage (see also Frederiksen 1984: 231–2).

[21] Liv. 23.5.1. The embassy may have been to find out the extent of the disaster so that the Capuans could better calculate their decision; see Ungern-Sternberg 1975: 29; Frederiksen 1984: 239–40.

[22] Liv. 23.5.2–15.   [23] Liv. 23.6.1–5.

[24] Liv. 23.7.1–3.

[25] Liv. 23.6.4–6: the majority of the senate wanted to side with Hannibal immediately after Vibius Virrius' proposal, but the older senators were able to delay the decision for a few days. This sounds like Livian rhetoric, juxtaposing wise and cautious elders against the reckless juniors, though it may preserve a kernel of historicity – the decision to revolt, as Livy's narrative reveals, was not arrived at lightly, and there most probably would have been a sizeable contingent of senators who were more hesitant.

[26] Liv. 23.7.7–9. The population of the city 'went out in great numbers, with their wives and children, to meet Hannibal on the way' (*ut frequentes cum coniugibus ac liberis obviam irent Hannibali*). This detail is plausible, for as Oakley 1997–2005: III.100 notes, 'in the ancient world it was customary for the populace to come out of a town (often spontaneously, sometimes induced by the authorities) and greet the arrival (*adventus*) of a famous figure'.

[27] Liv. 23.8.1–9.13.

day Hannibal addressed the Capuan senate, thanked the Capuans for allying with him and reiterated his promise that Capua would be master of Italy.[28] Finally, he ordered Decius Magius to be brought before him. The full senate voted unanimously for the proposal; Decius was sent in chains to Carthage, and only then was Capua firmly in the Hannibalic camp.[29]

Livy posits a number of factors that contributed to the Capuan decision to revolt, the most important of which is that the 'masses', led by the popular leader Pacuvius Calavius, were naturally inclined towards the Carthaginian cause while the Capuan *nobilitas* tried to remain loyal to Rome. Livy's second reason is that the Capuans were motivated by pride – to make their city the equal of Rome, if not the unchallenged master of Italy. Scholars have generally disregarded much of Livy's analysis as pro-Roman chauvinism that reflects a long tradition of stereotyping the twin Capuan vices of *luxuria* and *superbia*.[30] Although the Livian narrative is complicated and at times confusing, we should not be so quick to dismiss all of the details that he records. It is true that Livy emphasises political stasis, with the poorer classes hostile to Rome and inclined to side with Hannibal,[31] and that he blames Pacuvius Calavius as leader of the 'people's party' for ultimately bringing the Capuan state to the side of the Carthaginians.[32] But a close reading of the narrative reveals a much more complex struggle of interests among the Capuan elite, which was fractured by deep political divisions, competing interests and shifting loyalties.

Pacuvius Calavius' marriage connections to prominent Roman families and his attainment of Capua's highest office in 217 both suggest that he was a prominent figure in the local aristocracy rather than a recently elevated popular leader. Despite Livy's depiction of him as the chief architect of the Capuan revolt, Pacuvius appears to have favoured Roman rule at the

---

[28] Liv. 23.10.1–2.

[29] Liv. 23.13.3–10. Decius is reported to have escaped: see Chapter 7, n. 98.

[30] De Sanctis 1956–69: III.2.207 n. 19; Ungern-Sternberg 1975: 46–9; Lazenby 1978: 89–90; Frederiksen 1984: 240, 256–7.

[31] Thus, the masses wanted to destroy the Capuan senate in 217 and hand the city over to Hannibal (23.2.3); Vibius Virrius' proposal won over the masses immediately while the senate delayed a few days (23.6.4); the whole population turned out enthusiastically to see Hannibal when he approached the city (23.7.9); and the Capuan commoners were responsible for seizing and killing Roman citizens (23.7.3).

[32] This is clearly Livy's attempt to force Capuan politics to fit his general statement that Hannibal garnered support from the lower classes in all Italian cities (23.14.7), but which his own account contradicts, for example, in the case of Arpi (23.30.8), Locri (24.13.3) and Taras (24.47.6); see Lazenby 1978: 88.

beginning of the war, since he initially opposed siding with Hannibal.[33] Nor was Pacuvius alone in supporting the Roman cause, at least until 216. Pacuvius' son remained loyal to the Romans even after the Capuan treaty with Hannibal, and Decius Magius also supported them. The *meddix tuticus* for 216, Marius Blossius, was instrumental in arranging a public meeting between the Capuan citizenry and Hannibal. Since Blossius held Capua's highest office, he may have received Roman backing, or he at least benefited from the political status quo and thus would probably have promoted the Roman cause at the beginning of the war. If so, his appearance in 216 in the Hannibalic camp shows that he had switched sides. Although Livy mentions only these few men by name, presumably Roman rule rested on the loyalty of a core 'party' of pro-Roman aristocrats.[34]

At the same time, it is clear that widespread opposition to Rome emerged after the battle of Cannae, if it had not already existed before. After Varro rebuffed the embassy seeking the restoration of the 300 'hostages', Capuan dissatisfaction came to the surface. An anti-Roman party formed around Vibius Virrius who argued openly that the Capuans should seek an alliance with Hannibal. Hannibal was received at the household of the brothers Sthenius Ninius Celer and Pacuvius Ninius Celer, suggesting they were aligned with Vibius. As discussed above, Marius Blossius seems to have come over to the anti-Roman position. So too Pacuvius Calavius, who had cautioned against allying with Hannibal, since he dined with Hannibal *apud Ninnios Celeres*.[35] By the time the Capuans agreed to terms with Hannibal, only a few aristocrats appear to have remained openly pro-Roman – or at least anti-Hannibalic. Decius Magius remained committed to Rome, but Livy's account suggests that he took this stance mainly because he heard that the Carthaginians were going to place a garrison in Capua.[36] Thus Decius Magius appears to have been more concerned with Capuan autonomy than with any particular attraction to Rome.[37] When Capua fell to the Romans in 211, over seventy Capuan senators were arrested for their part in the revolt or killed themselves in order to avoid Roman reprisal, suggesting the breadth of aristocratic disaffection.[38]

---

[33] Liv. 23.2.5–7. Livy reports that Pacuvius Calavius made a speech citing his marriage ties to the Roman aristocracy as the main reason why he did not favour revolt, though Livy tries to gloss over his opposition by making the speech part of his ploy to control the senate.

[34] Perhaps these are the senators who successfully delayed for a few days the decision to send legates to Hannibal; see above, n. 31.

[35] Liv. 23.8.1–2.   [36] Liv. 23.7.4–6.

[37] Livy (27.8.2–9.13) also reports that Pacuvius Calavius' son was in Decius Magius' party, but that Pacuvius was able to convince his son to silence his pro-Roman rhetoric.

[38] Liv. 26.14.3–9. It is possible that not all seventy were committed anti-Romans from the start, but rather timeservers or opportunists.

Overall, Livy's narrative reveals a complex political milieu in which the aristocratic ruling class was greatly divided in its loyalty to Rome in the early years of the Second Punic War. Some aristocrats were more willing to break with Rome, while others remained loyal and continued to caution against siding with the Carthaginians even after Hannibal and the Capuan senate signed a treaty. There appears also to have been a swing group of aristocrats, such as Pacuvius Calavius and, possibly, Marius Blossius, who switched their allegiance from Rome to Hannibal as events developed. In any case, a number of Capuan aristocrats were motivated more by personal concerns and family connections than by an ideological attachment to either the Roman or Carthaginian cause. When the military landscape had changed dramatically after Cannae, the factors that contributed to Capuan frustration with Roman rule began to outweigh the factors that cautioned against rebellion, enough of the 'swing' aristocrats changed from the 'pro-Roman' to the 'pro-Hannibal' position, and Rome lost the support of enough of the ruling class to lose control of the city.[39]

This does not, however, explain why Capua revolted yet other cities in Campania did not. In other words, the fact that the Romans had been utterly routed at Cannae should have undermined Roman military credibility not only in the eyes of the Capuans, but also in the eyes of citizens in other cities in Campania and throughout Italy. Hannibal successfully took advantage of political divisions within the Capuan senate, but Capua must not have been the only Campanian city with a rivalrous ruling class, or with aristocrats more willing to break with Rome. Indeed, the evidence that we do possess suggests that such political divisions were not specific to the Capuans.

For example, in the same summer that he secured the treaty with Capua, Hannibal marched to Nola, where some Nolans wanted to revolt from Rome. Livy (23.14.7) claims that the ruling class remained steadfast in its loyalty and that the seditious elements came from the lower classes. In the same passage, we hear that the leading members of the Nolan senate were especially loyal to Rome (*maxime primores eius [senatus] in societate Romana cum fide praestare*). Livy (23.15.7) also claims that Nola remained

---

[39] Zonaras (9.2) and Diodorus Siculus (26.12.1) appear to confirm this general picture. According to Zonaras, even before the battle of Cannae some Capuans favoured Hannibal while others were more confirmed in their loyalty to Rome: οἱ γὰρ τὴν Καπύην οἰκοῦντες Καμπανοὶ οἱ μὲν τῇ Ῥωμαίων φιλίᾳ ἐνέμειναν, οἱ δὲ πρὸς τὸν Ἀννίβαν ἀπέκλιναν. After Cannae, the Capuans reconciled themselves and allied with Hannibal: καὶ καταλλαγέντες ἀλλήλοις ἐσπείσαντο τῷ Ἀννίβᾳ, though Zonaras is silent about the exact process. Diodorus reports that the loyalty of cities swayed as public opinion shifted between Rome and Hannibal: Ποικίλη δέ τις ἀνωμαλία κατεῖχε τὰς πόλεις, ὡς ἂν τῆς ὁμονοίας δεῦρο κἀκεῖσε λαμβανούσης τὰς ῥοπάς.

loyal because of the will of the leading men (*voluntate principium*) at least as much as because of the strength of the Roman garrison under Marcellus. Yet Livy states explicitly that the leader of the movement to revolt, Lucius Bantius, was a member of the *equites Nolanorum*, though his characterisation of this individual is confusing.[40] More telling is the fact that Marcellus conducted trials and executed over seventy Nolans for conspiring to revolt; presumably these men included members of the ruling class.[41] Nola's loyalty was not, however, solely the result of Roman military coercion in the form of Marcellus' garrison, since members of the Nolan aristocracy requested the Roman garrison only *after* they learned of possible sedition.[42] Overall, the Livian narrative reveals that the ruling class of Nola was divided in its loyalty towards Rome and that Hannibal's military success encouraged some aristocrats to break with Rome. In the end, the dominant forces within the Nolan aristocracy remained loyal to Rome despite the course the war had taken. Thus, political divisions among the ruling aristocracy, combined with Hannibal's victory at Cannae, are not enough to explain why Capua revolted and other cities did not.

Presumably, all Campanian cites were impressed with Hannibal's military success, and likewise all cities probably harboured some aristocrats who were more disposed to open rebellion. It is necessary to isolate conditions specific to Capua that explain why enough Capuan aristocrats either immediately or eventually concluded that it was better to side with Hannibal, while in other Campanian cities, the critical mass of aristocrats opted to remain loyal.

Hannibal's entry into Campania, and the approach of his army towards Capua, seems to have strengthened the anti-Roman movement within the

---

[40] Liv. 23.15.7–15. According to the story, which is also recounted by Plutarch (*Marc.* 10.2–11.1), Hannibal captured Bantius at Cannae and won him over through clemency and bribery. At Nola the young man became the head of the people's party and worked to betray his city to the Carthaginians. Marcellus recognised the man's excellence and won back Bantius' allegiance through clemency and gifts of his own – a 'fine horse' (*equum eximium*) and 500 *denarii*. Bantius goes on to be a steadfast ally, even (in Plutarch's version) levelling accusations against members of the pro-Hannibalic party. Frederiksen 1984: 257 argues that this is a moralising tale from a late annalistic source. While Livy clearly spins the story to highlight Marcellus' clemency and judgment, it is interesting that the tale retains some unsavoury and thus possibly historical elements, such as the fact that this excellent young man is wooed by Roman bribery. In Plutarch's version Bantius becomes, essentially, an informer. While the Bantius story is not impossible as it stands, it is more likely that he was, in fact, an informant who somehow had ties to Marcellus. This explains Livy's report that Marcellus gave commands that Bantius should be allowed access to him whenever he wished (23.15.15), and why Bantius was spared when Marcellus put to death seventy Nolan conspirators. Still, the fact that Marcellus had to secure Bantius' loyalty through bribery, together with the prospect that he informed on Nolan conspirators, underscores that loyalty among the ruling elite of Nola was not as uniform as Livy claims.
[41] Liv. 23.17.1–2.   [42] Liv. 23.14.7–12.

city. If we are to believe the reference to Hannibal's meeting with three Capuan *equites* after Trasimene, as early as 217 the Capuans were willing to revolt if Hannibal's army drew near. Even if we reject the reference, it is clear that the Capuans did not revolt immediately after they heard about Cannae, but rather only after Hannibal's army arrived in Campania. This makes sense, as his nearby army would have offered support for anti-Roman elements within the city and guaranteed protection from Roman reprisal.[43]

Yet if the proximity of Hannibal's army and the military threat that it posed were the decisive factors in encouraging a city to revolt, then we should expect all of the cities in a given region to have revolted once his army was nearby. Yet the evidence from Campania shows this was far from the case, as a number of Campanian cities remained loyal to Rome despite, in some cases, repeated Hannibalic threats and overtures, including cities that did not possess the military strength to withstand being stormed or besieged. Acerrae and Nuceria chose to be sacked by Hannibal's army rather than renounce their allegiance to Rome.[44] It would be surprising if the Capuans, who were able to withstand a Roman siege for five years, felt so threatened by Hannibal that their loyalty evaporated at his mere presence. Finally, a close look at Livy's narrative suggests that the Capuans did not act primarily out of fear of a military threat: he initially states that Hannibal marched to Capua once he was rebuffed at Naples (23.2.1), but he later reports that it was the Capuans themselves who sent legates to invite Hannibal before he marched to the city (23.6.5).[45] This implies that the Capuan decision to revolt or remain loyal was not based solely on the immediate military context.[46]

---

[43] For the general thesis that Hannibal successfully elicited allied revolts only when his army drew near and thus applied immediate military pressure, see Kahrstedt 1913: III.443; Ciaceri 1928–40: III.132–46.

[44] Liv. 23.15.2–6, 23.17.1, 23.17.4–7, 23.43.13–14; Sil. 12.424; Val. Max. 9.6. 2; Zon. 9.2; De Sanctis 1956–69: III.2.226 suggested that the cities surrendered more or less freely; however, Liv. 27.3.6–7 shows that the citizens of Acerrae and Nuceria still held favour with the Roman senate in 211. It is unlikely that the senate would have granted their requests had the Nucerians and Acerrans not displayed loyalty in 216. It is striking that both cities succumbed to Hannibal after Capua had revolted. Therefore, the Acerrans and the Nucerians chose to remain loyal despite the fact that Rome's military strength in Campania had been further weakened.

[45] See also Zon. 9.2.

[46] Diodorus (26.10) preserves a different tradition in which 'Pancylus Paucus' (Παγκύλῳ Παύκῳ) led the revolt by arguing that there was no reason to support Rome since they had no chance of winning and the enemy was at their gates. This would appear to support the conclusion that the Capuans revolted because of the immediate military pressure applied by Hannibal. It is not clear, however, that we should prefer Diodorus to Livy here, especially considering how badly he appears to have garbled Pacuvius Calavius' name. But if we do accept this version, notice that [Pacuvius Calavius] promotes rebellion not just because Hannibal is at the gates, but also

It has been suggested that its topography and economic conditions rendered Capua particularly susceptible to Hannibal's military pressure. For example, perhaps 'with its wide territory and unprotected villages, [Capua] was peculiarly vulnerable' to Hannibal's devastation techniques, so that the city was more likely to revolt.[47] Ancient sources do not report, however, that Hannibal's army devastated Capuan territory when it approached the city in 216 – as it did around Naples[48] – so the Capuan revolt does not appear to have been a response to Hannibal's devastation tactics. Still, the question remains whether Capua was in fact more susceptible to devastation and therefore would have been more willing to revolt than to face the *potential threat* of devastation.

We would certainly expect that there was intense interaction between town and country in Capua.[49] A few passages from ancient literary sources suggest, for example, that some Capuan farmers may have lived in the town and walked to their farms. After the Romans recaptured Capua in 211, the Roman senate decided that the Capuans would lose their citizen rights, their land was to be leased, all buildings within the city walls became public property, the city itself was to function as a granary and market, and the houses would be used by the farmers and field labourers.[50] Later, in 210, Roman soldiers quartered in houses in the city were ordered to construct huts along the city walls because the senate wished to lease parcels of Capuan territory along with houses inside the city, forcing the soldiers to find new quarters.[51] Both Cicero and Livy expect, therefore, that these farmers would have lived in the city and walked to their fields. But even if Capua were not an 'agro-town' in the third century, certainly rural inhabitants would have frequently come to the city to attend periodic

---

because, in his mind, Rome had no chance at all to recover and win the war. The implication is that the Capuans could have held out for some time, or at least were willing to do so, provided that Rome still possessed a credible military capacity. It was not merely the case that Hannibal arrived and the Capuans rebelled.

[47] Quoted from Frederiksen 1984: 241. Reid 1915: 93 argued, however, that 'ravaging of the Campanian plain in 217 [probably] delayed the accession of Capua to Hannibal's side'. Reid here is referring to the *ager Falernus*, which was the object of Hannibal's campaign after Trasimene, and, according to his argument, Hannibal's heavy-handed devastation tactics would have encouraged not rebellion, but Capuan loyalty to Rome. But the *ager Falernus* was Roman territory and had been mulcted from the Capuans over a century earlier, so it is questionable whether the devastation of this land would have been relevant to the Capuan decision to revolt.

[48] Liv. 23.1.6–7.

[49] The fertility of the *ager Campanus* and the nearby *ager Falernus* was legendary (Liv. 22.14.1, 22.15.2, 23.2.1, 26.16.7; Polyb. 3.91; Plin. *HN* 3.60; Strab. 5.4.3; Varro, *Rust.* 5.1.2.3–6; Cic. *Leg. agr.* 2.76–91; see also Frederiksen 1984: 31–53). Campanian soil and climate conditions are ideal for the production of the varieties of wheat most important to the Roman farm (Spurr 1986:7–8).

[50] Liv. 26.16.6–11, 26.34.4–11, 27.3.1; Cic. *Leg. agr.* 2.88–90.

[51] Liv. 27.3.1–3.

markets and sell their surplus produce.[52] Such intense interaction between town and country suggests that the threat of devastation would have factored into the Capuan decision to revolt, since any disruption of agricultural patterns, such as the burning of farms or the interrupting of sowing and harvest, would result in political agitation within the urban centre by urban-dwelling landowners, by those involved in trade with the rural population, and by rural citizens who took refuge in the urban centre.

But this situation was hardly unique to the Capuans, as communities throughout Campania would have experienced the same military and economic pressures. Although Hannibal did not devastate Nolan territory, the mere threat of devastation caused some of the Nolans to propose siding with Hannibal.[53] When Hannibal again attacked Nola in 215, the town was protected by a Roman garrison under the command of Marcellus. After failing to capture Nola through treachery and after a few days of skirmishing with the Romans, Hannibal ordered his men to plunder Nolan territory. Marcellus immediately ordered his troops to give battle, suggesting that he was concerned about the political consequences of Hannibal's plundering.[54] Nor were coastal cities, which presumably benefited from seaborne trade and fishing, immune to the devastation of their territories, as the example of Naples demonstrates.[55] In 216 Hannibal ordered his men to plunder Neapolitan farms and display the booty before the walls of the city, the sight of which encouraged the Neapolitans to sally out of their city walls into an ambush that Hannibal had prepared.[56] The average distance between urban centres in Campania was only about eleven kilometres,

[52] Garnsey 1998b: 117–19 is sceptical of the existence of ancient 'agro-towns' in Campania, where inscriptions and archaeological evidence indicate dispersed rural settlement (see also Frederiksen 1976: 350–2). This does not preclude, however, that some farmers lived in the towns and walked to the countryside. It is also possible that some farmers maintained shelters or cottages in the country, allowing them to remain away from the city for an extended time during periods of intense labour rather than walk to and from the city each day. Other rural agricultural settlements would have been owned by wealthy families who lived in town and administered their holdings through foremen (Frederiksen 1959: 123). For peasants frequenting urban markets in Campania, see Arthur 1991a: 44–5; de Ligt 1991: 53–7.

[53] Liv. 23.14.5–7.

[54] Liv. 23.44.3–8; Plut. *Marc.* 12.2–3; Zon. 9.3. Livy reports that Marcellus defeated Hannibal in a pitched battle, though this may be an exaggeration. Plutarch and Zonaras both record that Marcellus attacked when Hannibal's troops were dispersed and foraging. In either case, Marcellus still responded to Hannibal's devastation tactics rather than simply staying behind the city walls. See Lazenby 1978: 96–7.

[55] Polybius (3.91.1–2) comments in general on the high quality of ports in Campania; Naples was a strategic port and apparently had a significant fishing industry (Liv. 23.1.6–10, 23.15.1); Minturnae was involved in a flourishing wine trade as early as the third century (Reugg 1988: 209–28; Arthur 1991a: 57–8); Puteoli was possibly the most important Campanian port in the third century (Liv. 24.7.10, 25.20.2, 25.22.5, 26.17.2; see also Frederiksen 1984: 39; Laurence 1994: 321–5).

[56] Liv. 23.1.5–8.

the smallest ratio of any region in Italy, so even the most remote rural denizens would have been within walking distance of an urban centre.[57] We would expect that communications between town and country were similar for cities throughout the region,[58] so overall there is little to support the thesis that Capua was more susceptible to the threat of devastation by Hannibal's army than were other neighbouring communities.

It is possible that the decisive factor in the Capuan decision to revolt was less the result of Hannibal's military ascendancy – his victory at Cannae, his march into Campania or his actual or threatened devastation of Campanian territory – than the product of a specific act on the part of the Romans that engendered strong Capuan disenchantment.[59] Indeed, there was grave concern about the 300 young *equites*, sons and relatives chosen from the noble Capuan families, whom the Romans selected to garrison cities in Sicily.[60] So great was their families' worry that they convinced the Capuan senate to send a legation to Varro to seek their return, as discussed above.[61] The Capuan treaty with Hannibal contained a clause that guaranteed the Capuans would receive 300 Roman *equites* as hostages to be used in exchange for the 300 *equites Campanorum*.[62] Both the legation to Varro and the terms of the Capuan–Hannibalic treaty indicate that the security of the young men was an important matter for the Capuans, and it is plausible that Rome's decision to station them in Sicily generated additional resentment against Roman rule. It is unlikely, however, that this resentment would have encouraged the Capuans to revolt, but rather, if anything, apprehension for the safety of these young men probably blunted the desire for revolt.[63] Indeed, Livy's narrative (23.4.8) is explicit: when the Capuans were first discussing revolt after Cannae, the strongest bond (*maximum vinculum*) staving off revolt was not intermarriage between Capuan and Roman aristocrats but rather the 300 *equites*. The 300 Roman hostages may have been intended not only for a hostage

---

[57] De Ligt 1991: 53–5.

[58] Rivers, roads and other lines of trade and communication in Campania created a regional trade network of interconnected coastal cities, inland cities and *chorai*, so any economic disruption of one community may have been felt throughout the region (Laurence 1994: 321–5; Morley 1997: 51–4).

[59] Compare with events in Taras, where the city revolted in immediate response to the flogging and execution of Tarentine hostages under house arrest in Rome (Liv. 25.7.10–8.3).

[60] Liv. 23.4.8.   [61] See above, pp. 104–5. See also Allen 2006: 185–7.

[62] Liv. 23.7.2.

[63] Again, the chronology of the Tarentine revolt is suggestive of how hostages could be an effective security against an allied community's disloyalty. Outraged friends and relatives of the hostages formed the conspiracy that eventually turned Taras over to Hannibal only *after* the hostages had been killed. This implies that as long as the hostages were kept alive (as collateral), the Tarentines would be discouraged from revolting.

exchange – which in fact never occurred[64] – but also as security against
Roman maltreatment of the Capuan *equites*. The aforementioned treaty
clause may have been added to quieten concerns of those whose sons were
held by Rome and who therefore *opposed* revolt. If so, then the critical reason for the Capuan decision to revolt is probably not to be found in resentment over the 300 Capuan 'hostages'.[65]

It has been suggested that the Capuan revolt resulted from long-standing grievances against the Romans and a general resentment of Roman
rule, with Hannibal's march into Italy and his stunning victories against
Rome merely providing the spark to ignite rebellion in those communities
most aggrieved by Roman hegemony. These grievances would include such
impositions as tribute, military obligations or Roman interference in local
politics.[66] Indeed, the terms of the treaty, which Livy (23.7.1–2) preserves
in some detail, presumably indicate the foremost issues in the Capuans'
minds and suggest that autonomy weighed heavily in the Capuan decision. Besides the clause guaranteeing 300 Roman hostages, the bulk of the
treaty dealt with self-rule: no Carthaginian general or magistrate would
have authority over a Capuan citizen, no Capuan citizen would be forced
to perform military or any other kind of service, and Capua would have its
own laws and magistrates.[67] The terms resemble those of the treaties that
Hannibal forged with other communities in Italy, guaranteeing that his
new allies would live under their own laws. This has led some scholars to
conclude that the treaty is formulaic, reflecting rather Hannibal's generic
promises of freedom to all of Rome's allies than any particular situation
in Capua. Minor differences between the treaties, however, indicate that

---

[64] In 215 the senate granted the Capuan *equites* Roman citizenship and transferred their municipal
rights to the city of Cumae (Liv. 23.31.10).

[65] There is, unfortunately, no additional evidence to check whether the people of other Italian towns
similarly felt that their citizens who served in or alongside the Roman legions were essentially
'hostages', or if this discontent was particular to the Capuans. It is possible that since the *equites* were stationed in Sicily, their relatives and fellow citizens perceived that they were especially
distant and isolated, and thus more like hostages, but this is pure speculation. Indeed, we might
suspect that similar anxiety was experienced among many of Rome's allies.

[66] Mommsen 1888–94: 1.613; Badian 1958: 144 n. 4 citing the Capuan–Hannibalic treaty as 'making
grievances clear by implication'; De Sanctis 1956–69: III.2.204–8.

[67] *ne quis imperator magistratusve Poenorum ius ullum in civem Campanum haberet, neve civis
Campanus invitus militaret munusve faceret; ut suae leges, sui magistratus Capuae essent; ut trecentos
ex Romanis captivis Poenus daret Campanis, quos ipsi elegissent, cum quibus equitum Campanorum,
qui in Sicilia stipendia facerent, permutatio fieret* ('[They agreed to conditions that] not any general
or magistrate of the Carthaginians should have any right against a Capuan citizen, nor should a
Capuan citizen serve as a soldier or perform a service unwillingly; that Capua should have its own
laws and its own magistrates; that the Carthaginian [Hannibal] should give 300 from the Roman
prisoners to the Capuans, whom they themselves [the Capuans] had picked out, with whom an
exchange be made of the Capuan *equites* who were performing military service in Sicily').

Hannibal tailored his negotiations in response to specific local demands.[68] The treaty with Capua may shed light, therefore, on factors specific to the Capuan context that contributed to the decision to revolt.

The terms guaranteeing Capuan laws and magistrates and protecting Capuan citizens from the authority of foreign magistrates emphasise civil autonomy, suggesting that the Capuans harboured long-standing bitterness over Roman interference in internal civil affairs. But to what degree had Rome interfered in Capuan internal politics and judicial affairs? Livy reports that the Romans first sent prefects to Capua in 318.[69] Whether this marks the beginning of annual Roman magistrates in Capua remains open to debate, though it is more probable that Roman magistrates were sent only irregularly in response to specific disputes.[70] This view gains some support from the only literary reference to Roman interference in Capuan politics after 318: the Romans sent a dictator, C. Maenius, to Capua in 314 in response to rumours of conspiracies on the part of the local nobility.[71] This event does not tell us anything about the role of the Roman *praefecti*, but it does demonstrate Rome sending a magistrate to

---

[68] See Chapter 1, n. 133.

[69] Liv. 9.20.5: *Eodem anno primum praefecti Capuam creari coepti legibus ab L. Furio praetore datis* ('In that same year for the first time prefects for Capua began to be elected, with the laws having been given by the praetor L. Furius'). Livy later states (26.16.7–10) that annual prefects were sent to Capua beginning in 211 (see also Cic. *Leg agr.* 2.84, 2.88; Festus, *Gloss. Lat.* p. 262 L), and the historicity of the prefects in 318 has sometimes been doubted (Beloch 1926: 386; Toynbee 1965: I.244–5; Brunt 1971: 529) as a retrojection of these later prefects. But the *praefecti* in 318 need not be taken as having the same function as those from 211, while the reference to the praetor L. Furius suggests the historicity of the passage (see Oakley 1997–2005: II.555–6, III.266–7). Thus, there is good reason to accept that Rome did send prefects to Capua in 318.

[70] Humbert 1978: 355–80 accepted that this event marks the appearance of annual *praefecti iure dicundo*. Sherwin-White 1973: 43–5 is more persuasive, arguing that these were not *praefecti iure dicundo* but rather an example of infrequent magistrates sent by Rome to deal with specific issues.

[71] Liv. 9.25.2–3, 9.26.5–8; Diod. Sic. 19.76.2–5. Livy claims that Maenius was sent to conduct investigations and execute the conspirators, who instead committed suicide. Diodorus reports, however, that the dictator commanded an army, though he also mentions that the conspirators killed themselves while awaiting trial. The appearance of a dictator carrying out a typical task (commanding an army) makes Diodorus' version more likely. It is also plausible that the leaders of the conspiracy were killed (or committed suicide). It might be tempting to see this episode as a retrojection or foreshadowing of the Capuan revolt in 216 meant to underscore Capuan perfidy, especially considering that two of the ringleaders named by Livy were from the Calavius family (like Pacuvius Calavius in 216). But it would be peculiar for Livy simply to insert such a retrojection in this particular year, so one suspects that he has instead elaborated on a historical core. The fact that Livy introduces the Capuan affair at separate points may indicate that it appeared in at least two different sources that he combined; the added details in Diodorus may point to a third source tradition mentioning rumours of a Capuan revolt. Some political disturbance in Capua makes sense in light of the military pressure applied by the Samnites in that same year. The reference to the Calavii (Ovius and Novius) may be suspicious, but it is also plausible that an aristocratic clan remained prominent for generations. Livy's longer version of events probably contains some invention, perhaps the transfer of trials to Rome and certainly the lengthy speech

Capua only in reaction to a specific crisis. Thus, there is little evidence that Roman magistrates interfered much in Capuan affairs before the second century.[72] When the Capuans revolted in 216, they committed acts of violence against private Roman citizens and against the Roman military magistrates (*praefecti socium*) in the city, but nothing is said of any civil magistrates.[73] Moreover, the Capuans continued to elect and be ruled by their own chief magistrate, the *meddix tuticus,* an Oscan institution, whose existence into the third century suggests that Roman rule did not greatly impact on Capuan political autonomy.[74] Finally, other Campanian cities had possessed *civitas sine suffragio* since the fourth century and were thus presumably subject to the same interference by Roman magistrates, whether they were annual *praefecti iure dicundo* or occasional arbiters. Yet not all of these cities revolted during the Second Punic War.[75] Although the Capuans must have preferred no interference from Roman magistrates, intervention in local juridical proceedings was not the critical factor compelling Capua to revolt.

The treaty term freeing the Capuans from military service against their will does appear to reflect a real grievance, since their military burden seems to have been particularly heavy. According to Roman manpower figures in 225, reported by Polybius (2.23–4), the 'Campanians' (Καμπανῶν) contributed about 28 percent of the infantry available to them to the Roman legions, while Roman allies who did not have *civitas sine suffragio* contributed a somewhat smaller percentage (about 24 percent of their available infantry).[76] If these figures are accurate, then the Campanians,

---

by Maenius (9.26.8–19), but there is no good reason to reject a revolt (or attempted revolt) in Capua in 314 (see Oakley 1997–2005: 11.555, 111.300–1).

[72] Indeed, Frederiksen 1984: 241 argued that Capuan resentment against foreign civil magistrates was not very strong because Rome never seriously interfered in Capuan judicial affairs. Even Humbert 1978: 390–2 suggested that *praefecti iure dicundo* performed a solely juridical role and would not have otherwise interfered in local administration, though there is no evidence for their specific role in the third century.

[73] Liv. 23.7.3.

[74] De Sanctis 1956–69: 111.2.206 n. 17; Toynbee 1965: 1.214–15; Salmon 1967: 77–93; Humbert 1978: 369–70; Frederiksen 1984: 240–1.

[75] According to Festus (p. 262 L), Capua, Cumae, Casilinum, Volturnum, Liternum, Puteoli, Acerrae, Suessula, Atella and Calatia were all under the authority of a Roman prefect, though it is not clear when all of these cities were combined into a *praefectura.* Still, Cumae and Suessula were incorporated with *civitas sine suffragio* in the fourth century, as were the Campanians (Liv. 8.14.10–11), so we may assume that Rome had been sending *praefecti* (either annually or irregularly) to Cumae, Suessula and the cities of Campania long before the beginning of the Second Punic War. Cumae and Suessula remained loyal during the Second Punic War. For a discussion of *praefecti, praefecturae* and the autonomy of *civitates sine suffragio,* see Oakley 1997–2005: 11.552–4.

[76] Polybius' figures are difficult to reconcile. These estimates are based on Baronowski 1993. See Toynbee 1965: 1.214–16; Brunt 1971: 19 n. 4; see also Chapter 1, n. 99.

who included the people of Capua, appear to have endured a greater burden of military obligation in 225 than did other Italian allied communities (Latins and *socii*). Moreover, some communities with *civitas sine suffragio* did not supply troops in 225. Thus, the Capuans may indeed have suffered a disproportionate military burden, perhaps contributing to greater dissatisfaction with Roman rule. The attack on Roman military magistrates by the Capuan citizenry is consistent with this suggestion.

But one must not push this point too far. Polybius' Καμπανῶν probably refers not only to the Capuans but also to citizens of other cities in Campania, thus spreading the military obligation between a number of cities. Troop contributions also would have varied from year to year, so it is not clear that the Capuans always contributed a disproportionate number of young men to the Roman military. Perhaps more importantly, any Roman demand for soldiers – no matter how large – was a serious infringement of Capuan sovereignty, which, as mentioned above, weighed heavily on the minds of the Capuans. However, all of Rome's allies would have suffered the same sort of infringement, so while the military obligation certainly caused discontent, this discontent was not specific to the Capuans and cannot explain why the Capuans revolted and other Campanian allies did not.

Finally, it has been suggested that the Capuan revolt resulted directly from the Capuans' ambiguous political status as *cives sine suffragio,* which carried similar military obligations to full Roman citizenship without all of the associated political privileges.[77] According to this argument, the Capuans revolted in 216 because they had grown increasingly frustrated by their unrealised desire for full political integration.[78] There are, however, a number of objections to this line of reasoning. First, it is not clear that Rome's allies, regardless of their technical political status, actually desired the privileges that came with *civitas optimo iure.*[79] Second, there was widespread intermarriage between Roman and Capuan aristocrats, affording some of the latter the opportunity to promote their local

---

[77] While some scholars have held that the granting of *civitas sine suffragio* represented, at least originally, either a lenient settlement or even a reward bestowed by the Romans on states that (presumably) allied with Rome relatively willingly (see, for example, Sherwin-White 1973: 39–58), a strong case can be made that *civitas sine suffragio* always resulted from the aggressive Roman incorporation of smaller states (see Humbert 1978; Oakley 1997–2005: II.544–52). There is general consensus, however, that *civitas sine suffragio* became increasingly burdensome by as early as the late fourth century for those it was bestowed upon.

[78] De Sanctis 1956–69: III.2.205–7; Toynbee 1965: II.200–9.

[79] See Mouritsen 1998: 87–108 and Pobjoy 2000: 187–211, who argued that the desire for Roman citizenship did not motivate Italians to revolt in the Social War, and hence it is unlikely to have motivated them in an earlier period. Livy (23.20.1–2) reports that some Praenestine soldiers, who

political standing by marrying into prominent Roman families.[80] Such intermarriage was possible because the Capuans were *cives sine suffragio*,[81] so perhaps the Capuan ruling class was satisfied with their citizenship status. Third, and most importantly, other communities with *civitas sine suffragio* in Campania (Cumae, Suessula and Acerrae) did not revolt during the Second Punic War, and indeed, the Acerrans allowed their city to be sacked rather than turn against Rome.[82] This all suggests that possession of *civitas sine suffragio*, along with the frustration that it may have engendered, was not the critical factor in a city's decision to revolt.

It is best at this point to summarise the discussion so far. There is little doubt that a number of factors, including the military burdens imposed upon a state possessing *civitas sine suffragio* and possible Roman interference in local political affairs, contributed to Capuan dissatisfaction with Roman rule. Rome's recent losses, especially the devastating rout at Cannae and the immediate threat posed by Hannibal's army, would certainly have undermined Roman military credibility, promoted anti-Roman sentiment and compelled more Capuans to question their loyalty to the Roman cause. It is in this context that the Capuans voted to send a delegation to the Roman consul Varro in order to seek the restoration of the 300 *equites* serving in Sicily, and the consul's brusque treatment of the Capuan embassy in turn engendered more hostility. However, as we have seen, all of the cities in Campania would have faced similar circumstances, and most of the arguments given for why the Capuans rebelled could have been applied to other communities in Campania, yet not all of

had shown particular bravery in defending the town of Casilinum against Hannibal's siege, were offered Roman citizenship and refused. This is clear evidence that Roman citizenship was not necessarily an attraction to the Italian allies. Livy's report is located in a short passage that contains a number of remarkable details: the Roman senate also voted the Praenestine soldiers double pay and exemption from military service for five years; their commander was a certain Marcus Anicius, whose statue once stood in the forum of Praeneste; the statue had an inscription commemorating a vow made by Anicius. Livy's account of the fate of the Praenestine soldiers seems to be derived ultimately from actual records or eyewitness accounts of the inscription. Allied (Italian) motivations during the second century are discussed in Chapter 7.

[80] See above, n. 20.

[81] It is possible that the ruling class possessed full Roman citizenship: Livy (8.11.13–16) claims that 1,600 Campanian *equites* received Roman citizenship in 340 because they did not join the rest of the Campanians in siding with the Latins against Rome. Humbert 1978: 172–6 accepts the historicity of this report and takes it to mean that the *equites* became full citizens. Sherwin-White 1973: 39–41 accepts the reference but assumes that it refers to *civitas sine suffragio*. It is possible that some Campanians received favoured status as a reward for loyalty, but it is more likely that Livy has garbled some of the details and mistaken the original reasons for the granting of *civitas sine suffragio*. See below, pp. 122–3, 128–9. Whatever the case, possessing some form of Roman citizenship allowed for intermarriage between the Roman and the Capuan elite, and there is nothing to suggest that citizenship status was a major source of Capuan discontentment.

[82] Liv. 23.7.4–7.

these cities chose to revolt. The one condition specific to the Capuan context – the *equites* in Sicily – may have done as much to discourage revolt as to generate the sort of resentment that contributed to the revolt. Moreover, a number of factors, such as Romano-Capuan aristocratic intermarriage and Capua's relative ability to withstand a potential Hannibalic attack, should have left Capua less likely to abandon its allegiance to Rome.

One aspect of the Livian tradition, however, has not been discussed so far: Livy's statements that the Capuans were motivated by the desire not only to restore confiscated territory but also to assert their own hegemony in Italy. A close look at the sequence of events in the wake of Cannae reveals that Capuan hegemonic aspiration was a distinct and decisive factor in convincing the ruling elite to side with Hannibal.

Returning to Livy's narrative, only after the unsuccessful legation to Varro did a member of the Capuan aristocracy, Vibius Virrius, openly promote allying with Hannibal (23.6.1–2). He argued that if the Capuans allied with Hannibal they would be able to recover land they had lost since becoming Roman allies and the city of Capua would be able to assert hegemony over the rest of Italy (*sed imperio etiam Italiae potiri possint*). Vibius made his proposal to the Capuan senate and convinced the majority, after some debate, to send legates to Hannibal in order to seek terms (23.6.3–6). The argument that siding with Hannibal would yield an extension of Capuan territory and power must have resonated with the Capuan ruling class, since they voted to send the legation despite the fact the Romans still held 300 potential Capuan hostages. Even after the Capuans agreed to terms with Hannibal, there was still vocal opposition to the alliance, so the Carthaginian general arranged to make an appearance in the city and address the Capuan senate (23.7.4–9). Only after he spoke in person and reiterated his promise that Capua would be the 'capital of all Italy' (*caput Italiae omni*) was opposition finally silenced (23.10.1–2). Indeed, although Livy places these events after the ratification of the treaty, the fact that Hannibal had to come to Capua suggests instead that the treaty itself was not ratified until he made his appearance before the senate. In either case, the sequence of negotiations strongly implies that Hannibal's promise of hegemony was a key factor in the Capuan senate's decision to revolt.

Scholars have generally downplayed or even entirely rejected the Vibius Virrius tradition, which emphasised the Capuan desire for hegemony.[83] On the one hand, there may be some exaggeration in Livy's portrayal. For

---

[83] Ungern-Sternberg 1975: 58–9 posited that the Vibius Virrius tradition is an elaboration on the Roman stereotype of Capuan *superbia*, and he suggests that the Capuans were probably not motivated by the desire for hegemony. Similarly, Frederiksen 1984: 240 argued that although

example, it may be unrealistic that the Capuans expected to control all of
Italy, and even Livy hints at this when he describes Hannibal's promises
as *magnifica*.[84] On the other hand, it is not unreasonable that the Capuans
expected to restore their former regional pre-eminence, and perhaps even
expand their power at the expense of a greatly reduced Rome. Cassius
Dio also mentions that Hannibal won over the Capuans by promising
them hegemony.[85] More intriguing is Cicero's characterisation of Capua
in his speeches against the Rullan land laws, specifically his statement that
the Romans' ancestors wisely voted in 211 to deprive Capua of political
institutions lest the city be able to provide a seat for empire (*urbem ipsam
imperio domicilium praebere posse*) and strike fear into future generations
of Romans (*Leg. agr.* 1.19, 2.88).[86] Clearly, Capuan hegemonic ambitions
were deeply embedded in Cicero's characterisation, and even though the
threat is greatly exaggerated to serve Cicero's specific political agenda, it is
possible that his sentiment reflects a distant historical core. Indeed, in the
same passage (*Leg. agr.* 2.88) Cicero says that records and decrees concerning the senatorial debate over Capua's punishment were still extant. Thus,
Capuan hegemonic aspirations may have been part of the discussion only
a few years after the revolt, introduced perhaps in the testimony of the
aristocrats who appealed their punishment in 210, or of resident Romans
who might have fled Capua in 216.[87] Overall, there is no reason to dismiss
out of hand that there are genuine historical touches in the Vibius Virrius
tradition, and (as we will see) there is good reason to accept that hegemonic desires influenced Capuan policy in 216.

If so, then Vibius Virrius becomes the real mover behind the Capuan
revolt, rather than Pacuvius Calavius, contradicting Livy's statements
that Pacuvius was the head of the party that brought Hannibal to Capua.

Hannibal's promise to establish the Capuans as the hegemonic power in Italy is plausible, he
never meant these promises to be taken seriously. Whether Hannibal actually meant what he
said, however, is much less important than if the Capuans believed his promises and acted on
them. Goldsworthy 2000: 224 and David 1996: 57–8 allow for Capuan hegemonic motivation but
do not stress its importance; Reid 1915: 112–13 says that the Capuans wished to recover land they
had lost, but he otherwise casts doubt on the entire Livian narrative as rather fanciful; De Sanctis
1956–69: III.2.204–8 ignores Vibius Virrius, mentioning only that he was among the twenty-three
Capuan senators who committed suicide in 211 rather than surrender to Rome.

[84] Liv. 23.10.2: *et inter cetera magnifica promissa pollicitus est brevi caput Italiae omni Capuam fore …*
    ('and among the other lofty promises, he promised that Capua would shortly be the capital of all
    Italy …').

[85] Cass. Dio/Zon. 9.2: τὴν ἡγεμονίαν σφίσι τῆς Ἰταλίας δώσειν ὑπέσχετο.

[86] See above, n. 10.

[87] For the Capuans' unsuccessful appeal, see Liv. 26.33.1–3, 26.34.13; for its historicity, see Frederiksen
    1984: 260–1. Both Roman magistrates and private citizens appear to have been residing in Capua
    at the time of its revolt (Liv. 23.7.3).

The two versions can be reconciled, however, if we assume that Pacuvius Calavius was not originally in the pro-Hannibalic camp, but later switched sides and supported revolt more fervently. Indeed, as noted earlier, Livy first presents Pacuvius Calavius arguing against revolt, which the ancient author awkwardly explains away as part of Pacuvius' devious plan to dupe the senate into coming under his authority.[88] Since Pacuvius was *meddix tuticus* in 217 and was related to the Roman aristocracy by marriage, he seems an unlikely candidate to want to upset the political establishment, so it makes sense that he was originally against revolt, even if his loyalty to Rome was not resolute. Yet Pacuvius ended up in the pro-Hannibalic camp, so at some point he switched his allegiance. Indeed, the Capuan senate as a whole wavered in the days following Cannae, but only after Vibius Virrius' proposal did the pro-Hannibalic position win out. At this point, a critical mass of aristocratic 'swing voters' joined those who were already calling for an alliance with Hannibal, and Pacuvius appears to have been among that swing group. This solution is plausible, reconciles the two main traditions in Livy's narrative and is internally consistent.

Capuan expansionism in the Second Punic War also corresponds to the long-term historical context of Capua as a powerful state in the region. Livy (7.31.1) describes Capua of the fourth century as *urbs maxima opulentissimaque Italiae*. Livy later reports (23.11.11) a speech made during the Second Punic War in which it is named as the most powerful city after Rome.[89] Zonaras also records that Capua was a great city in the late third century: τὴν πόλιν τὴν Καπύην μεγίστην. Florus calls it the *caput urbium* and claims that it was once considered one of the three greatest cities in the world. Livy refers to Capua as the capital city of Campania (*caput Campaniae*), and both Pausanias and Strabo call it ἡ μητρόπολις.[90]

---

[88] According to Livy, Pacuvius Calavius recognised that if the masses seized power they would massacre the senate and lead the state to perdition. Therefore, he convinced the senate that the only way to save itself would be under his authority, and to make himself sound more credible he started off his speech by saying that he in no way backed any plan to revolt. Livy is clearly at pains to explain this contradictory behaviour, even going so far as to say (23.2.4) that Pacuvius was shameless, but not entirely corrupt (*improbus homo sed non ad extremum perditus*); see Frederiksen 1984: 239.

[89] Mago made a report to the Carthaginian senate in 216, after the battle of Cannae and the revolt of Capua. Mago argued that since Rome had lost so many battles, Capua was now the most powerful state in Italy, implying that Capua had been the second most powerful city in Italy. While the speech is certainly fictitious, it is probably accurate enough in its general description of the power of Capua.

[90] Zon. 8.25; Flor. 1.11.6; Liv. 23.11.11; Paus. 5.12.3: ἡ μητρόπολίς ἐστιν ἡ Καπύη τῶν Καμπανῶν; Strab. 5.4.10: Ἐν δὲ τῇ μεσογαίᾳ Καπύη μέν ἐστιν ἡ μητρόπολις. The wordplay of *caput*–Capua in

Archaeological evidence confirms that Capua's territory was far more extensive than those of neighbouring communities in Campania.[91]

Most scholars agree that Capua was the hegemonic power in Campania, dominating a cluster of subordinate or satellite cities including Atella, Calatia, Sabata and Casilinum;[92] the Capuans may also have influenced Cales and Cumae in the fourth century.[93] This group of cities – Capua and its satellites – are often referred to as the 'Capuan League',[94] though it is not clear whether we should understand their relationship as an organised federal state with a formal constitution, or a more fluid arrangement of communities bound by traditional, albeit less formal ethnic, tribal, military or political ties.[95] In any case, there is strong evidence for a close association between these cities. For example, Atella, Calatia and Capua minted similar coinage during the third century. From the second half of the century Atella and Calatia struck *trientes* bearing the head of Zeus (obverse) and

Livy and Florus may hint at etymology. Strabo (5.4.3, 5.4.10), presumably drawing on a Roman source, also says that Capua was derived from *caput*. Elsewhere, Livy (4.37.1) claims that 'Capua' was derived either from Capys, a legendary Samnite leader who supposedly seized Capua from the Etruscans, or from the city's location on a broad plain (*campus*); Pliny (*HN* 3.63) also makes the *campus*–Capua association. Such etymologies are almost certainly fanciful, but in any case, the *caput*–Capua wordplay makes sense only in the context of Capua as a principal city. See Heurgon 1942: 8; Frederiksen 1984: 138; Musti 1988: 219–26; Pobjoy 1995: 218–20.

91 According to Frederiksen 1984: 36–41, the *ager Campanus* in the fourth century stretched north beyond the Volturnus (including the *ager Falernus*) as far as the Sidicini, to the east to the sea, to the south to the relatively restricted territories of Cumae, Puteoli and Naples. Rome confiscated the *ager Falernus* in the fourth century; Capua's coastal lands were confiscated after the Second Punic War and resettled as the colonies Liternum and Volturnum. Chouquer *et al.* 1987: 183–231 reconstructed various stages of Roman centuriation in the *ager Campanus* and *ager Falernus* (which Capua once possessed). While some of the stages date to later periods, the extensive centuriation around Capua probably indicates the approximate size of its broad *chora* at the time of its surrender in 211, when the Roman senate voted to confiscate this land.

92 The Romans reorganised these communities at the same time, after the fall of Capua in 211 (Liv. 26.33.11–13, 26.34.7, 26.34.11–13).

93 Cales was the principal community of the Ausones. It allied with the Sidicini against Rome between 336 and 334. The Sidicini had previously been allied with the Campanians, so it is possible that the Campanians and Ausones were also allied. After the Romans defeated the Sidicini–Ausonian alliance in 334, however, Cales was resettled as a Latin colony with 2,500 colonists (Liv. 8.16.1–14; Oakley 1997–2005: II.571–5). If Cales had been a Capuan satellite, it certainly ceased to be once Rome planted a colony there. For the location of Cales and archaeological evidence for this early colony, see Chouquer *et al.* 1987: 191–5; Arthur 1991a: 27–35; Oakley 1997–2005: II.582–3. Though there is no explicit evidence for an alliance between Cumae and Capua, the two cities received *civitas sine suffragio* in the same year (340), suggesting perhaps that Cumae had fought alongside Capua (Liv. 8.14.11; Cic. *Leg. agr.* 2.66; Oakley 1997–2005: II.569).

94 The term 'Capuan League' (or 'Campanian League', 'Campanian Confederacy', etc.) has been widely used: for example, De Sanctis 1956–69: III.2.206 n. 17; Toynbee 1965: 1.139–41; Salmon 1967: 195 n. 5; Frederiksen 1984: 140–2; Cornell 1989a: 357–60, 1995a: 346–7.

95 Frederiksen 1984: 141 thought that 'Capua's position seem[ed] to lie half-way between the leading state of a federation and the centre of synoecised dependencies', though some scholars are increasingly sceptical about the formality of Oscan leagues. See Letta 1994: 387–90, 404–5; Cornell 2004: 126–8.

Zeus in quadriga (reverse), with the name of the respective city in Oscan. All three cities minted *unciae* with the head of Zeus (obverse) and Nike crowning a trophy (reverse), with Oscan legends. Frederiksen calls attention to a remarkable issue of *sextantes* from Atella and Capua, struck probably during the Second Punic War, showing Zeus (obverse) and soldiers taking an oath and sacrificing a pig (reverse).[96] Finally, the Capuan *meddix tuticus* in 214 was named Cn. Magius Atellanus.[97] His cognomen indicates either that his family was originally from Atella and had obtained Capuan citizenship, or that a single *meddix* could be elected from any of the cities who had jurisdiction over all of the whole league – both suggest close ties between the cities.

But the Capuans appear to have lost power and influence since they became Roman allies, as the Romans had mulcted the Capuans of the productive *ager Falernus* and planted a Latin colony at Cales, a possible Capuan ally or even former member of the Capuan League.[98] Whether or not the league was ever a formal organisation, the imposition of Roman rule and the incorporation of various Campanian communities into the Roman state (through *civitas sine suffragio*) would have limited Capua's ability to assert authority over neighbouring satellite cities or expand its power over other towns. Hannibal's entry into Italy and his early victories temporarily suspended Roman hegemony, allowing local bonds to rise to the surface. More importantly, a Hannibalic victory presented the Capuans with real long-term advantages: not only the restoration of lost territory but also the chance to re-establish Capua as a regional hegemonic power.

Three specific events during the Second Punic War subsequent to the Capuan revolt lend further credence to the argument that the desire to extend Capuan territory and hegemony motivated their decision. The first and perhaps most striking is bound up in the Roman failure to relieve Hannibal's siege of Casilinum, a strategic stronghold that overlooked the crossing of the Volturnus River at the juncture of the Via Latina and Via Appia. After Hannibal had secured Capua, he received word that a Roman army was making its way to Casilinum,[99] where a small garrison of Roman allies held the town.[100] Hannibal tried to win the town peacefully in order to prevent the Romans from utilising the crossing, and when negotiations

[96] Crawford 1985: 62–4; see also Head 1977: 30–5; Marchetti 1978: 443–6; Frederiksen 1984: 242–3; Rutter 2001: 63–6.

[97] Liv. 24.19.2.   [98] Liv.8.11.12–13; 8.16.13–14.

[99] Liv. 23.17.7.

[100] Liv. 23.17.10–12. For additional details about the garrison, see below, n. 117.

failed, he first tried to take the city by storm and then blockaded it over the winter months.[101] Meanwhile, the Roman general Marcellus was encamped in the mountains above Suessula, near Nola, in order to protect the cities of southern Campania.[102] In the winter of 216/15 Marcellus tried to aid the beleaguered allied garrison at Casilinum but was prevented from doing so. Livy (23.19.1–4) reports that he was held back both because of flooding of the Volturnus River, and because the citizens of Nola and Acerrae requested that he keep his army near Suessula. More importantly, Livy states explicitly that the Nolans and Acerrans made their request because they feared the 'Campanians' if Marcellus withdrew his garrison.[103] It is remarkable that the people of Nola and Acerrae feared the threat posed by Capua (and possibly the other cities in the 'Capuan League'), with no reference to Hannibal. The implication is that the Nolans and Acerrans believed that the Capuans would attack them if they had the chance (as the Capuans subsequently would do against the people of Cumae). If true, Livy 23.19.4 provides direct, explicit evidence that at least some of the surrounding communities feared Capuan expansion.[104]

The second event provides compelling evidence that the Capuans both recognised that an alliance with Hannibal was an opportunity to extend their hegemony and acted on that chance. Early in 215 the Capuans decided to subjugate the nearby city of Cumae. They first tried to convince the Cumaeans to revolt from Rome, and when this attempt failed, they arranged to ambush the Cumaeans at a pan-Campanian religious festival at Hamae.[105] The Cumaeans suspected a trap and sent word to the Roman consul, Tiberius Sempronius Gracchus, who commanded the Roman army at Sinuessa. Gracchus used this intelligence to ambush

---

[101] Liv. 23.18.1–10.   [102] Liv. 23.14.5–13.

[103] Liv. 23.19.4: *Marcellum et ipsum cupientem ferre auxilium obsessis et Vulturnus amnis inflatus aquis et preces Nolanorum Acerranorumque tenebant Campanos timentium si praesidium Romanum abscessisset* ('Both the Volturnus River – which was swelled with water – and the entreaties of the Nolans and Acerrani – who were fearful of the *Campani* should the Roman garrison leave – were holding back Marcellus, who was himself desirous of bringing aid to the besieged'). The context strongly suggests that *Campanos* refers here only to the people of Capua, since Livy clearly uses the word a couple of paragraphs earlier, in his account of the affairs at Casilinum, in reference to the citizens of Capua (23.17.7, 23.17.10). It could also mean, however, the citizens of Capua and its neighbouring satellite towns. In either case, the present argument is not significantly affected.

[104] The detail might be interpreted as an annalistic or Livian fabrication meant to highlight stereotypical Capuan *superbia* or exonerate Marcellus' failure to act. Livy mentions the detail in passing, however, without calling attention to it or elaborating on Capuan vices, so overall, this offhand comment has the appearance of an accurate report.

[105] Liv. 23.35.1–4, 23.35.13, see also 23.36.2. Although Livy says that Hamae was only three miles from Cumae, it has been identified fairly securely two miles further north nearer ancient Liternum, in the area of modern Torre San Severino (*CIL* 10.3792; Heurgon 1942: 381–3; Nissen 1967: II.715; Frederiksen 1984: 33–4).

the Capuan army and inflicted heavy losses on the Campanians.[106] The Capuans decided on their own initiative to capture Cumae without assistance from Hannibal[107] and thus appear to have been conducting an independent foreign policy, and not merely acting at Hannibal's request. Indeed, Hannibal's reaction to the Capuan defeat confirms this. When Hannibal heard that his allies had been routed, he hastily marched from his winter camp near Capua to catch Gracchus off guard and convey the wounded Capuans back home.[108] Hannibal's troops brought only arms and not supplies, so they were unable to attack Cumae, suggesting that his decision to leave winter quarters was spontaneous and reactive.[109] He returned to winter quarters but was compelled to march out again and attack Cumae, and Livy makes it clear that once again the Capuans were behind the enterprise.[110] Ultimately, Gracchus was able to defend Cumae against Hannibal's attack, so the Carthaginian again returned to winter quarters.[111] During the entire affair, Hannibal was reluctant to leave winter quarters, while the Capuans were highly motivated to capture Cumae. The Capuans would not have been able to attack Cumae as long as Rome dominated Italy, and their repeated attempts to subjugate Cumae are strong evidence that the Capuans did in fact see Hannibal as a means to restoring and extending Capuan power.

The third event is Hannibal's settlement after the siege of Casilinum. In late winter 216/15 or early spring 215, he resumed the siege in full force, captured Casilinum and garrisoned the stronghold with 700 of his own men.[112] His decision to sacrifice troops for the purpose of garrisoning Casilinum underscores the strategic importance of the town. More relevant to the present argument is Livy's statement (23.20.1) that Hannibal restored Casilinum to the Campanians (*Casilinum oppidum redditum Campanis est*) after he captured the city, suggesting that Casilinum had at some point been politically associated with, or subordinate to Capua.

---

[106] Liv. 23.35.4–19. Florus' report (2.6) of a failed conspiracy to assassinate the consuls at the Feriae Latinae in 91, which does not appear elsewhere, bears some resemblance to Livy's account of the planned ambush at Hamae. It is not clear that Florus got this story from Livy, since the *periocha* of Book 71 mentions only vaguely that '[the Italians'] gatherings and conspiracies and speeches in the meetings of their leading men were reported' (*eorum coetus coniurationesque et orationes in consiliis principum referuntur*).

[107] Liv. 23.35.2.   [108] Liv. 23.36.1.

[109] Liv. 23.36.2–5.

[110] Liv. 23.36.6–7: *[Hannibal] fatigatus Campanorum precibus sequenti die cum omni apparatu oppugnandae urbis Cumas redit* ('[Hannibal] was worn out by the entreaties of the Campanians [and] on the next day he returned to Cumae with all the siege equipment for attacking a city').

[111] Liv. 23.36.8, 37.1–10.

[112] Liv. 23.19.1–20.1; Frontin. *Str.* 3.14.2–15.3; Strab. 5.4.10.

Hannibal may have decided to turn the town over so that he would appear to make good on his promise to restore Capuan territory and extend its hegemony. Indeed, one of the reasons he had tried to capture Casilinum in the first place was because he was afraid that the Capuans would again switch sides back to Rome if the consul would encamp nearby.[113] Holding Casilinum and preventing the Romans from camping in the *ager Campanus* thus made obvious military sense. But in light of the present discussion, Hannibal's concern over Capuan loyalty, his decision to invest Casilinum and his gesture of 'restoring' the town to the Capuans appear closely related. They strongly suggest that Hannibal wanted to convince the Capuans that his promise of power was serious, and also that the Capuans perhaps expected such proof.[114]

Overall, then, we can conclude that a decisive factor in the Capuan decision to revolt was the calculation that allying with Hannibal would bring about the restoration of lost territory and the reassertion, and possibly expansion, of Capua's hegemony. This conclusion is consistent with Livy's narrative of the events leading up to the Capuan revolt, with a number of events in 216 and 215, and with the long-term historical context of the fourth and third centuries, when Capua was a powerful city that exerted hegemony over a number of satellite communities.[115]

THE REVOLT OF CAPUA'S 'SATELLITE' ALLIES, 216–215

Hannibal's success in winning over this important city appears to have encouraged a number of other Campanian cities to revolt. The smaller neighbouring communities of Atella, Calatia and the otherwise unattested Sabata revolted, and while there is limited evidence for the chronology, it would seem most likely that their defections followed on the heels of the Capuan decision. Indeed, Zonaras (9.2) implies as much: Μεταστάσης δὲ τῆς Καπύης καὶ ἡ ἄλλη Καμπανία κεκίνητο ('Once Capua revolted the rest of Campania also became incited').[116] Even though Casilinum did not fall

---

[113] Liv. 23.17.7.

[114] Hannibal may also have desired to free up his own troops rather than occupy them with garrison duty. Of course, the military and political benefits of handing over Casilinum and placating the Capuans are not mutually exclusive.

[115] I have discussed the motives behind the Capuan revolt elsewhere: Fronda 2007a.

[116] Livy (22.56.11–13) lists the *Calatini*, the *Atellani* and the *Campani* (Capuans) among the peoples who rebelled from Rome in the wake of Cannae, though the list contains anachronisms. Calatia, Atella and Sabata all surrendered immediately after Rome recaptured Capua in 211, so it is likely that they also revolted soon after the Capuans did (Livy 26.16.5–6, 26.33.12, 26.34.6–13; but see also Zon. 9.6, who states that all pro-Hannibalic communities in Campania surrendered after

into Hannibal's hands until 215, it still fits the general pattern. Allied contingents from Praeneste and Perusia garrisoned the town, thus preventing its immediate defection after the Capuan revolt.[117] The garrison suppressed plots by the people of Casilinum to turn over the city to the Carthaginians, and they eventually massacred part of the local citizenry and seized control of the section of the town lying on the north bank of the Volturnus. This extreme act came only after the garrison learned of the Capuan negotiations with Hannibal, implying that anti-Roman sentiment intensified once Capua revolted.[118] The whole affair suggests that the loyalty of Casilinum was connected to and influenced by Capua's decision. Thus, in each of these cases, Hannibal's capture of Capua brought about additional defections.

At the same time, many cities in Campania refused to break their alliances with Rome in the wake of Cannae, despite, in some cases, repeated attempts by Hannibal to seduce or intimidate them. These included the important cities of Nola, Naples and Puteoli, as well as the coastal towns of Sinuessa and Cumae, inland towns of Acerrae, Nuceria and Suessula, and colonies of Cales and Minturnae. Roman garrisons in or near Nola, Suessula, Sinuessa, Naples, Puteoli and Cumae,[119] together with Rome's ability to station at least four legions in Campania in five of the six years from 216 to 211,[120] must have deterred further revolts. But such Roman responses were not felt until after loyal cities witnessed the Capuan revolt and had their own chance to defect. So the question remains why only certain cities decided to revolt during the critical window of opportunity after Cannae.

the fall of Capua except for Atella, whose citizens abandoned their city and went in a body to Hannibal). Whatever the exact behaviour of the Atellans in 211, the sources agree that Capua's status influenced the actions of the surrounding cities. Finally, after Capua revolted, Hannibal tried to win over Nola and Acerrae, besieging the latter city. Livy (23.17.5–6) states that some of the men of Acerrae fled while Hannibal prepared to invest their city, and sought refuge in other cities in Campania that had not changed sides (*in urbes Campaniae, quas satis certum erat non mutasse fidem perfugerunt*). This statement may imply that some cities had changed sides, suggesting that cities besides Capua had already revolted.

[117] Liv. 22.15.3, 23.17.8–12; see also Polyb. 3.92; Walbank 1970: 1.427–9. According to Livy, the Romans held the town initially with a small garrison of 500 troops from Praeneste who were late in joining the Roman army destined for Cannae. When news of Cannae reached the company, they decided to return to Casilinum. This may have been at the command of the Romans, since Livy mentions that a few Romans and Latins had joined the Praenestines, perhaps including Roman military magistrates. The garrison was eventually joined by a contingent from Perusia, bringing the total garrison to nearly 1,000 men.

[118] Liv. 23.17.10.

[119] For the garrisons, see Liv. 23.14.10, 23.15.2, 23.31.4, 23.35.5, 24.7.10, 24.12.4, 24.13.7. But even the presence of a Roman garrison was no guarantee that a city would not revolt, as shown by the examples of Taras (Liv. 25.8; Polyb. 29.12; App. *Hann.* 32–3), Thurii (Liv. 25.15.7–17) and Metapontion (Liv. 25.15.5–7; App. *Hann.* 35).

[120] Six legions (216, 215, 212 and 211), four legions (214), and two legions (213) when the war effort was focused on Taras (De Sanctis 1956–69: III.2.614–19; Toynbee 1965: II.647–51).

As demonstrated in Chapter 2, loyalty and defection of Apulian cities in the Second Punic War can be explained, at least in part, by traditional, local alliances and hostilities. Similar patterns of alliance and rivalry existed among various Campanian cities as well, which are visible in the historical record from the fourth century. Thus, for example, the smaller communities of Atella, Sabata, Calatia and Casilinum (members of the Capuan League)[121] had a long history of following Capua's lead in foreign policy. Before the First Samnite War (343–341), the Capuans placed themselves under Roman protection against increasing military pressure from the neighbouring Samnites. Capua and Rome remained allied during the First Samnite War; indeed, their alliance appears to have been the reason why the Romans and Samnites were drawn into conflict with each other.[122] Livy's terminology makes it difficult to determine whether Capua alone was involved in the First Samnite War, or whether other members of the Capuan League also sided with Rome. But he later mentions that a Roman garrison was distributed during winter 'among the cities of Campania' (*praesidia hibernatura divisa enim erant per Campaniae urbes*),[123] implying that more cities than just Capua had been placed under Roman protection. We may conclude that Capua and the other members of the league probably came under the protection of Rome in 343.[124]

During the Latin War Capua and presumably the members of the Capuan League sided with the Latins against Rome. From Livy's narrative, one can reconstruct a basic sequence of events: the end of the First

[121] The nature of the Capuan League has already been discussed (see above, pp. 122–3); the term will continue to be used as a matter of convenience.

[122] Liv. 7.29.6–7.31.12, especially 29.6–7. Oakley 1997–2005: 11.284–9 accepts the basic structure of Livy's narrative, arguing that Capua's *deditio* should not be compared to the typical surrender of Rome's conquered enemies, but rather to numerous examples in both Greek and Roman history of one state's placing itself under the protection of another. The historicity of the *deditio* and, by implication, the historicity of the First Samnite War have also been accepted by Salmon 1967: 194–206 and Frederiksen 1984: 181–5; contra Toynbee 1965: 1.123–4, 400–3.

[123] Liv. 7.38.4, 7.38.9–10. The reference to the Roman garrisons in Campania is bound up in a broader narrative in which Roman troops mutinied and marched on Rome, faced an army led by either a dictator or the consuls and were ultimately reconciled without combat: see Liv. 7.38.4–7.42.7, with parallel accounts in Dion. Hal. 15.3.1–15; App. *Sam.* 1.1–2; Frontin. *Str.* 1.9.1; *De vir. ill.* 29.3. The narrative of the mutiny is problematic, and indeed Livy preserves two lengthy versions of the story. He does state (7.42.7), however, that while his sources were confused, all agreed that there was some sort of sedition. Livy's references to the passing of an otherwise obscure *lex sacrata militaris* (7.41.4) and of the Genucian laws (7.42.1–2) both suggest that there was both military and civil unrest of some type: see Beloch 1926: 371; De Sanctis 1956–69: 1.224–5; Oakley 1997–2005: 11.361–5; Frederiksen 1984: 184–6. Whatever one makes of the mutiny and its relation to the Genucian laws, there is little reason to doubt that the Romans garrisoned towns, at times for lengthy periods, in the late fourth and early third centuries – consider, for example, the Roman garrison at Luceria (Liv. 9.26.1). See Oakley 1997–2005: 11.365–6.

[124] So argues Salmon 1967: 195 n. 5.

Samnite War resulted in the restoration of a Romano-Samnite alliance and to combat this alliance, the Sidicinians and Campanians joined with the Latins, who had revolted from Rome.[125] After the Latins and their Campanian allies were defeated, Capua was mulcted of the *ager Falernus*, and *civitas sine suffragio* was imposed on the 'Campanians', Cumaeans and Suessulans.[126] Festus (p. 262 L) lists in his definition of *praefecturae* most towns known to have been incorporated with *civitas sine suffragio*; the list includes Casilinum, Atella and Calatia, showing that these towns came to possess *civitas sine suffragio*. It is likely that Rome incorporated them at the same time as Capua, as part of the settlement of the Latin War, in either 338 or 334.[127] If so, then these communities also probably allied with Capua and the Latins against Rome.

The Second Samnite War provides clearer evidence. Rome seems to have had the support of the Capuan League at the beginning of the war: the Romans used Calatia as a base for their operations for the Caudine campaign, and after the disaster at the Caudine Forks the Capuans lent support to the defeated Roman army; Atella also probably started the war on the Romans' side. Atella and Calatia, however, switched sides in the middle of the war.[128] According to Diodorus, Capua also revolted during the Second Samnite War, but Livy reports only that the Romans investigated a conspiracy by members of the Capuan elite, thus preventing a full-blown rebellion.[129] A number of factors probably contributed to disaffection among Rome's Campanian allies: the growing Roman presence on previously

---

[125] Liv. 8.1.1–3.2. Livy claims (8.2.7) that Capuans were motivated more out of hostility towards the Samnites than out of concern for the Romans. It is plausible that the Capuans would have feared further Samnite aggression once the Samnites and Romans had reconfirmed their alliance, but it is not clear whether this detail is Livy's conclusion or a genuine artefact from his sources, so the point should not be pushed too far. See Oakley 1997–2005: II.393–5.

[126] Liv. 8.11.12–14, 8.14.10–11.

[127] Oakley 1997–2005: II.552–4 concludes that 'so high a percentage of the towns known to have been incorporated with c.s.s. are included that one is forced to believe that all *civitates sine suffragio* became *praefecturae*'. Capua's neighbours had to be incorporated as *civitates sine suffragio* at some point, and the settlement of 338 (or 334) – with Livy's 'Campanian' in this case a blanket term for the 'Capuan League' – makes more sense than these small communities being incorporated anonymously at some other point. For the date, Livy (8.14.10–11) gives 338, but Velleius (1.14.3) says that the Campanians were given *civitas sine suffragio* in the same year that Cales was founded as a colony, in 334. Oakley 1997–2005 II.539–40, 554–5 argues for the later date, but it does not bear much on the present argument, as it is clear that the Campanians fought against Rome during the Latin War regardless of when the final Roman settlement was imposed.

[128] Liv. 9.2.2, 9.6.5–10, 9.28.6: the last passage reports that the Romans recovered Calatia and Atella (emending *Atinam* to *Atellam*: see Salmon 1967: 238 and Oakley 1997–2005: III.334), implying that they both had started the war allied with Rome but switched sides in the middle of the conflict.

[129] Capua: Liv. 9.25.1–2, 9.26.5–9, 9.27.1–5; Diod. Sic. 19.76.1–5; Calatia and Atella: Liv. 9.28.6; Diod. Sic. 19.101.3 (reading Καλατίαν for Καὶ λείαν: Frederiksen 1984: 213 n. 59). The defection of

Campanian territory probably generated local resentment;[130] meanwhile, in 315, the Romans suffered a defeat at the battle of Lautulae;[131] finally, the Samnites tried to capitalise on the situation by encouraging sedition.[132] Whether or not the Capuans actually revolted, the evidence suggests that the various members of the Capuan League made comparable policy decisions when faced with similar pressures during the Second Samnite War.

Finally, this pattern of alliances repeated itself during the Second Punic War. Capua revolted, followed soon thereafter by Atella, Calatia and Sabata; the people of Casilinum probably would have revolted immediately after the Capuans treated with Hannibal, but the garrison of Roman allies prevented any possible revolt. Hannibal successfully besieged the town, after which he turned Casilinum over to the Capuans. (These patterns are summarised in Table 2, p. 131.)

The relative consistency with which the cities of the Capuan League tended to align helps to explain the decisions of the smaller states to revolt during the Second Punic War. Literary evidence clearly suggests that the smaller cities in the Capuan League were encouraged to revolt because the Capuans revolted. Once Capua allied with Hannibal and began to assert independent foreign policy, the less powerful satellite communities faced a choice between Rome and Capua as hegemon. In this landscape, old bonds proved stronger, and the members of the Capuan League broke their alliances with Rome.[133]

HANNIBAL'S INCOMPLETE SUCCESS: NAPLES, NOLA, CUMAE, ACERRAE AND NUCERIA

We now turn our attention to the rest of Campania, where a number of cities chose not to break with Rome. This not to say that defection did not have its adherents among at least some of the political elite. Rather, pro-Hannibalic (or anti-Roman) movements were not able to achieve a

---

Capua, whether actual or only attempted, should be accepted as historical: see above discussion, p. 115 n. 71.

[130] In 318 the Romans created the *tribus falerna*, presumably in which to enrol settlers living on the *ager Falernus* (Liv. 9.20.5–6). Rome had mulcted the *ager Falernus* over two decades earlier, and the decision to create the new tribe may indicate that large numbers of settlers had only recently begun to claim the viritane allotments (see Arthur 1991a: 35).

[131] Liv. 9.22, 9.25.2–5; Diod. Sic. 19.72.7–8.

[132] Liv. 9.25.1–3, 9.26.5–12, 9.27.1–3.

[133] This is not to say that the decision to revolt came easily. Rather, aristocrats in Atella, Sabata, Casilinum and Calatia probably were not unified in their willingness to revolt, and in fact, Livy (26.15.5) reports that the Romans punished more harshly those aristocrats who were the leaders of revolt, suggesting that not all supported Hannibal as enthusiastically.

Table 2. *Summary of alliance patterns among select Campanian cities (fourth–third centuries BC)*

City	Neapolitan War		Second Samnite War (before 315)		Second Samnite War (from 315)		Second Punic War	
	Rome	Naples	Rome	Samnites	Rome	Samnites	Rome	Hannibal
Capua	X		X			Xα		X
Calatia	[X]		X			X		X
Atella	[X]		X			X		X
Sabata	[X]		[X]					X
Casilinum	[X]		[X]					Xβ
Naples		X		X	X		X	
Nola		X		X		X	X	
Cumae	[X]						X	

X Strong evidence for alignment   α Rome may have prevented Capuan defection
[X] Probable alignment   β Rome prevented defection but Hannibal captured

critical mass, and thus the ruling classes in these cities made the calculation to remain loyal to Rome. Such a decision is in some cases difficult to
understand, especially for smaller states that risked – and in some cases
suffered – dire consequences for their loyalty. The rest of this chapter will
consider what conditions and factors influenced the policy-decisions of
loyal Campanian states, and, as we saw in Chapter 2, local intercity rivalries and alliances appear to have been part of the equation.

Hannibal made a number of attempts to secure Naples between 216
and 214, but despite his persistence, the city displayed remarkable loyalty
to Rome. Over the winter of 217/16, the people of Naples sent ambassadors to offer forty gold bowls as a sign of thanks and friendship to the
Romans.[134] This appears to have been a spontaneous act on the part of
the Neapolitans, underscoring their strong loyalty. Hannibal made at least
two attempts on Naples in the summer of 216.[135] During the first attempt,
the city's impressive defences discouraged Hannibal from embarking on
a siege, so he instead settled for plundering their farms and parading the
booty before the gates of the city in order to elicit an attack from those
within the city. Hannibal successfully lured out and captured a number
of the Neapolitan cavalry, whom he could have used as leverage in negotiations, but he was unable to compel the city to surrender. Hannibal's
second attempt came later that summer, after the revolt of Capua, but he
quickly conceded after learning that a Roman prefect, M. Junius Silanus,
who probably commanded a garrison, now protected the city.[136] It is clear

[134] Liv. 22.32.4–9. Hannibal's incursion into the *ager Falernus* in 217, which was meant to overawe
Rome's allies and to show the Romans incapable of protecting their own territory, apparently
had little effect on the Neapolitans.

[135] Livy records three separate attempts to take Naples in 216: the first is placed before the revolt
of Capua (23.1.5–10), the second after the Capuan revolt but before his first attempt on Nola
(23.14.5–6), and the third after Marcellus arrived at Nola but before Hannibal attacked
Nuceria (23.15.1–2). The first, which is also reported briefly by Zonaras (9.2), and the second
are probably historical. The third version resembles the first, so it may be a doublet (De Sanctis
1956–69: III.2.224 n. 44; Frederiksen 1984: 257); its location in the narrative can be explained if
one of Livy's sources conflated the first and second attempts on Naples, placing both after the
defection of Capua, and Livy took over this reference as a third attack on the city.

[136] Silanus is mentioned only in Livy's third report of Hannibal's attack on Naples. If the third
episode is a doublet and conflation of the first two, as argued above, then it is necessary to determine where Silanus fits in. Livy's account of the first attack on Naples is relatively detailed yet
makes no mention of a Roman presence in the city. Indeed, the picture of the Neapolitan cavalry
riding out to drive off Hannibal's foragers assumes that the people of Naples were acting on their
own. Livy's second report is very brief, providing almost no detail except that the attempt came
after Capua had defected (*Capua recepta*). Livy's third report clearly is placed after the Capuan
revolt. If the third report is a doublet and conflation, the reference to Silanus must relate to
the report of Hannibal's second attack (contra Frederiksen 1984: 257, who argues that the third
episode is a doublet only of the first episode; see below, n. 201). This detail about Silanus was

that the Neapolitans requested assistance from the Romans, and that they did so after Capua had revolted. Thus, the Neapolitans remained loyal to Rome even in the face of Hannibal's increasing success. Finally, their loyalty did not evaporate as the war in Campania dragged on and Rome's allies faced repeated attacks by Hannibal and his Campanian allies, including a final attack in 214, when Hannibal made one last sweep against the coastal cities of Naples, Cumae and Puteoli.[137]

Nothing suggests that the Neapolitans boasted a significant pro-Hannibalic movement. Livy's account does not mention any dissent or the typical *stasis*, while Plutarch comments explicitly on the steadfastness of Neapolitan loyalty.[138] Their resolve is all the more striking if we consider the particular factors urging its revolt. We have already seen that Hannibal's devastation tactics successfully elicited a Neapolitan counter-strike. He not only defeated the Neapolitan cavalry but also captured a number of cavalry troopers, who would have belonged to aristocratic families; it is surprising that Hannibal could not generate significant discontent among the Neapolitan aristocracy despite the fact that he had captured members of their rank. Finally, Hannibal may have been seen as a Hellenistic liberator, a guise that would have been particularly attractive since Naples preserved strong elements of Greek culture well into the Imperial period.[139]

Naples' firm loyalty has been explained by the supposedly lenient terms of its alliance with Rome in 326, and by the long period of peace and prosperity that followed.[140] The Neapolitans debated seriously whether to accept the rights granted by the *lex Iulia* because they preferred 'the freedom of their own treaty to [Roman] citizenship' (*foederis sui libertatem*

---

probably mentioned in one (or some) of Livy's sources for the second attempt on Naples, but not in the source he followed at 23.14.5.

[137] Liv. 24.13.6–7.

[138] Plutarch (*Marc.* 10.1) states that Marcellus did little to encourage the Neapolitans' loyalty because they were steadfast on their own accord; he contrasts the unwavering fidelity of Naples with the shaky loyalty of Nola, which was maintained only with difficulty.

[139] For Hannibal as Hellenistic liberator: Chapter 1, pp. 35–7. For Hannibal's attractiveness to the Neapolitans: Lomas 1993: 63. For the 'Greekness' of Naples: Strabo (5.4.7) comments on the persistence of Greek customs and culture in Naples despite the Oscan conquest of many of the Greek cities in Campania. Some sort of Oscan–Greek integration was occurring by the end of the fourth century BC, evidenced by Hellenistic-style rock-cut tombs bearing inscriptions in Greek letters. In some cases, individual tombs display both Greek and Oscan names written in Greek, suggesting Oscan–Greek intermarriage or the 'Hellenisation' of elite Oscan families. Greek continued to be used in inscriptions until the third century AD, and Greek names appear in large numbers of inscriptions into the second century AD. See Leiwo 1995: esp. 58–87, 165–72; Lomas 1995b: esp. 111–12.

[140] For example, see Toynbee 1965: 1.261; Salmon 1967: 219; De Sanctis 1956–69: III.2.224. After allying with Rome in 326, the Neapolitans remained loyal allies throughout not only the Second Punic War but also the Social War.

civitati anteferret),[141] so presumably, their treaty with Rome during the Second Samnite War contained rather favourable terms. It is not clear, however, what made the treaty so attractive. Naples appears to have been a *socius navalis*,[142] but this does not necessarily mean that the military obligation was unburdensome.[143] It was common for *socii navales* to supply not only ships but also crews and rowers,[144] and some were probably obliged to supply both naval forces and land forces.[145] Thus, one cannot deduce that Naples' military obligation was light simply because it was a *socius navalis*. Moreover, we cannot tell how the Neapolitans perceived their military obligation in the summer of 216, regardless of how relatively light or heavy it might have been.[146] While Naples may have enjoyed relatively favourable conditions under its treaty with Rome, other factors must have contributed to the Neapolitan decision to remain loyal.

Cumae also remained loyal, though there are some hints in the Livian narrative that the Romans were concerned that it might defect. As discussed above, the Cumaeans requested help in 215 from the consul Ti. Sempronius Gracchus in order to foil a Capuan ambush of the Cumaean aristocracy, which would subjugate Cumae.[147] When Gracchus arrived from Liternum, he ordered the Cumaeans to bring in their goods from their farms and stay within the city walls. Meanwhile, he moved his camp outside the walls of Cumae and placed guards at the gate to prevent news of his plans from getting out.[148] With these precautions in place, Gracchus managed to defeat the Capuans at the site of the planned ambush and then repulsed Hannibal's follow-up attack on Cumae itself.[149] It is at this point that Gracchus probably garrisoned Cumae,[150] which surely helped

---

[141] Cic. *Balb.* 21; see Toynbee 1965: 1.261.

[142] Polyb. 1.20.14; Liv. 26.39.5, 35.16.3: Naples, Rhegion, Taras, Locri, Velia and Paestum are mentioned as contributing vessels for the Roman fleet.

[143] Contra Leiwo 1995: 22–3, for example.   [144] Brunt 1971: 50.

[145] Toynbee 1965: 1.491–2; Ilari 1974: 112–14; Livy (24.13.1, 25.10.8) mentions that Hannibal captured troops from Taras at the battle of Trasimene, supporting the idea that *socius navalis* and an ally under the *formula togatorum* were not necessarily mutually exclusive categories.

[146] The best evidence for how the Neapolitans viewed their military obligation is to be found in their debate over the *lex Iulia* in 90, mentioned above. However, their hesitance to accept Roman citizenship in the first century may have little bearing on their feelings in the late third century.

[147] See above, pp. 124–5.

[148] Liv. 23.35.10–12, 23.35.16–17.

[149] According to Livy, Gracchus defeated the Capuans (23.35.13–19) and withdrew to Cumae out of fear of facing Hannibal in the field (23.36.1–2); Hannibal ordered his troops to bring siege equipment to Cumae (23.35.5–8) but soon gave up and returned to his camp at Mount Tifata (23.37.1–9).

[150] After breaking Hannibal's siege, Gracchus marched from Cumae to Luceria (Liv. 23.48.3). Naples was garrisoned under the command of Silanus, and Livy (24.7.10, 24.13.6–7) explicitly

the Cumaeans withstand Hannibal's last attempt to capture the city, in 214.[151] The order to bring in goods from the farms suggests that the Cumaeans would have been susceptible to devastation tactics, or at least that Gracchus was concerned about the potential repercussions if their farms were destroyed. That Gracchus needed to post guards to prevent his plans from getting out of Cumae may indicate that local loyalty was suspect. But the Roman garrison was not in place to prevent a Cumaean revolt in 216, either before or after Capua's defection, thus despite indications of some wavering loyalty, the citizens of Cumae ultimately stayed faithful to Rome when they had the chance to revolt.

The state of affairs in Nola, for which we have more detailed evidence, was similar to the situation in Capua, with the local ruling class politically divided, and some aristocrats entertaining defection.[152] Yet despite some flirtation with Hannibal, the Nolans ultimately did not revolt. The arrival of a Roman garrison under the command of Marcellus – at the request of the Nolan aristocracy, according to Livy – obviously limited subsequent opportunities for defection, just as in Cumae.[153] Meanwhile Hannibal brought his army to the gates of Nola and tried to instigate a pitched battle with the Romans. Marcellus initially avoided battle, but he received information from loyal aristocrats that there was still a movement to betray the city, compelling him to march out and face Hannibal in the field. Marcellus managed to catch Hannibal's troops off-guard by ordering his own soldiers to make a rapid sally out of the gates against the enemy position. The Romans won the engagement, and for the moment Hannibal gave up trying to win over the Nolans, instead withdrawing to Acerrae.[154] After the battle Marcellus conducted trials, condemning and

states that Fabius garrisoned Puteoli at the end of the year with 6,000 troops. It appears that the Romans were securing coastal towns, so it is likely that they also garrisoned Cumae at the same time.

[151] Liv. 24.13.6–7: Hannibal marched the bulk of his army from his camp at Tifata to Cumae, lingered for some time while he devastated much of the Cumaean *chora* and then withdrew to attack Puteoli and Naples.

[152] Hannibal first approached Nola after he gained possession of Capua, and after his second unsuccessful try at Naples (Liv. 23.14.5). For the chronology, see above, nn. 135–6.

[153] According to both Livy (23.14.8–13) and Plutarch (*Marc.* 10.1), the commoners were in favour of Hannibal, but the local senate was loyal to Rome. Livy reports that some members of the Nolan senate met with Hannibal in order to stall while messengers were sent to Marcellus to request military assistance. Livy's explanation for Nolan–Hannibalic negotiations is not convincing (see below, n. 166), but the evidence does show that the Nolans had the opportunity to defect to Hannibal before Marcellus secured the city with a garrison. At Marcellus' arrival, Hannibal withdrew to Nuceria (Liv. 23.15.1–2) before returning to Nola.

[154] Liv. 23.16.2–17.1; Plut. *Marc.* 11.1–4. Livy (23.16.15) admits that some of his sources probably exaggerated the magnitude of the Roman victory, but there is no reason to believe that this skirmish

executing over seventy Nolans as traitors and confiscating their property, but also handing out rewards and honours to loyal aristocrats.[155]

Marcellus' decisive actions helped to prevent Nola from revolting, and a continued Roman military presence in or near Nola from 216 to 214 further prevented revolt. In 216 Marcellus removed his troops from Nola but established a camp at nearby Suessula, where the troops remained during the winter of 216/15.[156] In the following spring Marcellus commanded two legions at Suessula, which Livy (23.32.2) says were meant specifically to guard Nola.[157] Indeed, Marcellus was performing a dual job – guarding Nola from Hannibal and guarding the Nolans themselves – for despite Marcellus' efforts the previous year, there was still dissent in Nola. That same year, the consul Fabius stationed his army at Suessula and sent Marcellus with his army to garrison Nola. These actions were taken specifically to head off a potential revolt.[158] In the late summer of 215 Marcellus marched out of Nola, leaving a garrison, and raided towns in Samnium.[159] The Samnites sent envoys to Hannibal seeking relief, and Hannibal responded by leading most of his army to Nola to devastate the territory.[160] Marcellus heard of Hannibal's approach and returned to Nola to prepare for a possible siege. Hannibal first tried to win the city over peacefully by sending Hanno to negotiate terms. Despite Hanno's promise that an alliance with Hannibal offered the Nolans better terms than an alliance with the Romans, the entreaty was rejected.[161] Hannibal next began to invest the city, compelling Marcellus to sally out from the gates, but neither side could claim a decisive victory in the subsequent skirmish. Three days after the first clash, Hannibal sent troops out to plunder the

---

is an anticipation or doublet of the later victory over Hannibal outside Nola in 215 (Liv. 23.44.1–23.46.7): Frederiksen 1984: 258–9 contra De Sanctis 1956–69: III.2.225 n. 47.

[155] The trials and executions (Liv. 23.17.1–3) followed a 'lockdown' during which Marcellus posted guards at the city gates, forbade Nolan citizens from approaching the city walls, and prevented anyone from leaving the town (Liv. 23.16.8–9, 23.17.1; Plut. *Marc.* 11.1–2). Marcellus rewarded a certain Lucius Bantius, and although this may be a moralising tale, it is not implausible that some aristocrats' loyalty was secured through material incentives (Liv. 23.15.7–16.1; Plut. *Marc.* 9.2–10.1; see above, p. 109 n. 40). He also 'handed over affairs to the senate' (Liv. 23.17.3: *summa rerum senatui tradita*), which presumably had been purged in the trials, thus effectively rewarding loyal aristocrats by consolidating their power.

[156] Liv. 23.17.3 .

[157] Livy's statement is found within a longer section (23.31.15–23.32.4) in which he records various portents, provinces for the magistrates, and edicts and judicial proceedings – that is, a passage that is likely to have been derived from pontifical records and probably, therefore, possessing much historical value. See Badian 1966: 1–2 and Astin 1989: 9–11.

[158] Liv. 23.39.5–8.   [159] Liv. 23.41.13–14.

[160] Liv. 23.42.1–13, 23.43.3–5. Hannibal figured he would both satisfy his troops and lure Marcellus away from Samnium.

[161] Liv. 23.43.9–23.44.3.

surrounding farms.[162] When Marcellus saw Hannibal's troops plundering, he immediately prepared his troops, attacked and won a close-fought battle.[163]

The Romans continued to garrison Nola through the remainder of 215 and throughout 214. When Hannibal left Campania for his winter camp in Apulia, in 215, Fabius ordered that grain be collected from Naples and Nola and brought to the Roman army wintering at Suessula;[164] he later ordered Marcellus to leave the smallest possible garrison in Nola and to send the remaining soldiers home, so as not to burden the allies.[165] Despite these precautions, in 214 a legation from Nola met with Hannibal while he attacked Naples, but loyal Nolans warned Marcellus in Cales, who marched quickly to Suessula and sent 6,000 infantry and 300 cavalry to resecure Nola. When Hannibal moved his camp from Naples to Nola, Marcellus was already prepared, and with one army at Nola and another near Suessula he was able to stymie Hannibal's efforts to take Nola.[166] Finally, even when Marcellus marched his troops north in support of the Romans' siege of Casilinum in 214, he left a garrison of 2,000 soldiers in Nola, and when the siege ended, he returned there with his army.[167]

---

[162] Liv. 23.44.3–6.

[163] Liv. 23.44.7–9, 23.46.1–9; Plut. *Marc.* 12.2–3; Zon. 9.3. In Livy's version Hannibal saw the Roman troops arranged in order and organised his troops, so that the resulting clash was a pitched battle. Plutarch and Zonaras report that Marcellus attacked while Hannibal's troops were dispersed to forage. Livy has probably exaggerated the magnitude of the battle and thus the Roman victory (see Frederiksen 1984: 259; Seibert 1993b 237–8). Still, the sources agree that Marcellus responded to Hannibal's devastation, and that Hannibal withdrew from Nola after the battle. It is striking that it only took a few days of devastating farms to compel Marcellus to come out of the city walls. When Hannibal paraded booty from local farms, landowners in the city must have agitated and put pressure on the ruling elite to act. In turn, the ruling elite must have appealed to Marcellus to protect their interests.

[164] Liv. 23.45.8, 23.46.9.

[165] Liv. 23.48.2. For a brief discussion of the strategic decision to alleviate the Nolans' burden, and of the subsequent skirmishing around Nola, see Rosenstein 2004: 36–8.

[166] Liv. 24.13.8–11 (Hannibal's negotiations with the Nolans), 24.17.1–8 (the subsequent battle and Roman victory). Some scholars reject this battle as an annalistic invention (for example, see Seibert 1993b: 259–60), and the details of Livy's narrative do present some difficulties (such as his notice that the propraetor Pomponius was in command of the force at the *castra Claudiana*). But there is no reason to reject out of hand that Hannibal made this third pass at Nola as he retired from Campania to Taras (De Sanctis 1956–69: III.2.249 n. 119; Frederiksen 1984: 259). The Nolan legation to Hannibal sounds like Livy's report of negotiations in 216, though there are some differences. For example, in this version the legates are sent by the common people, not from the senate, as Livy claims for 216. So, it is possible that the legation of 214 is a doublet of the Nolan embassy to Hannibal in 216, perhaps derived from a different source, but it is also not implausible that disaffected Nolans attempted to cut a deal with Hannibal in 214. The issue cannot be resolved decisively but, whatever the historicity of these negotiations, it is clear that the Romans maintained a strong military presence in the vicinity of Nola in 214.

[167] Liv. 24.19.5, 24.20.1–5.

As the foregoing narrative shows, Roman garrisons stationed in Nola and Suessula clearly were instrumental in controlling a very delicate and possibly explosive situation in Nola.[168] But again, this cannot fully explain why the Nolans did not revolt in 216, before the Romans had the chance to secure the town. Indeed, the Nolans first negotiated with Hannibal before Marcellus arrived with his garrison. Livy (23.14.7–10) claims that the Nolan senate carried out these negotiations only in order to buy time until they could send for help from Marcellus. This implausible explanation is clearly a Livian attempt to excuse Nolan aristocratic behaviour, which otherwise would not conform to his statement in the same passage that the upper class was resolutely pro-Roman while the masses supported Hannibal. It is far more likely that at least some Nolan aristocrats conducted legitimate negotiations with Hannibal, which fell through when the two sides could not agree on acceptable terms.[169] Indeed, this is exactly what happened in 214, at least according to Livy (23.13.8–11), as mentioned above. If so, then the whole affair underscores the contingent nature of the local politics and diplomacy facing Hannibal. Many aristocrats were probably not willing to support Hannibal at all costs, but rather fell into a swing group who could be pulled in either direction (as we saw at Capua). Although the pro-Hannibal movement won out temporarily, pro-Roman aristocrats were able to convince enough of their political supporters that revolt was not the better option, while the political wrangling allowed the Romans time to recover and take steps to prevent defection.[170]

So, even though Naples, Cumae and Nola experienced internal and external pressures to revolt – as had Capua – the three cities remained loyal to Rome despite each having had the opportunity to defect and having witnessed the successful revolt of Capua in 216. Indeed, Cumae and Nola were politically divided over the decision to remain loyal, and the latter in

---

[168] Suessula (modern Cancello) lay about halfway between Nola and Capua; its territory bordered that of Nola. Suessula lay on the route between Capua and Nola and controlled the entry to the Valley of Caudium at the Arienzo pass, where the Via Appia extended to Beneventum (Beloch 1879: 384–8; Lazenby 1978: 93; Frederiksen 1984: 35–6; Oakley 1997–2005: III.49). Controlling this strategic junction may have been the primary military objective of setting up the *castra Claudiana* in this locale. This does not deny, however, that a secondary goal was to cover Nola, especially considering Livy's explicit statement (23.32.2) that Marcellus was to use the army at Suessula to guard Nola (see p. 136), or that the nearby camp simply had the effect of checking pro-Hannibalic activity in Nola.

[169] Livy (23.14.7) states that there were men willing to propose revolt (*neque auctores defectionis deerant*), and it makes little sense for Marcellus to execute Nolan citizens if their negotiations with Hannibal were all a sham.

[170] Indeed, Livy (23.15.7) claims that Marcellus held Nola more by the goodwill of the aristocracy than by the force of his garrison. This statement certainly has a moralising quality, but if it does reflect a historical core, it underscores how Roman hegemony relied on the cooperation of local aristocrats.

particular saw the pro-Hannibalic position gain significant traction. All three cities were sensitive to the threat of devastation,[171] and all three endured military obligations to Rome that were, presumably, burdensome (though Naples' burden *may* have been relatively light).[172] So why did they not revolt? The alignment of Campanian states in the Second Punic War reflects diplomatic patterns that stretched back to the fourth century and the arrival of Roman power in the region. Thus, the policy decisions of Cumae, Naples and Nola can perhaps be understood, at least in part, in the context of their historical relationship with each other and with other Campanian cities.

Naples and Nola tended to ally with each other in conflicts dating from the fourth century, despite the fact that their territories bordered each other,[173] so we might expect to see more conflict than cooperation between the two. In fact, the fifth and fourth centuries saw the conquest of most of the Greek cities in Campania by Oscan-speaking invaders, and Nola itself had become an Oscan-speaking city by the fourth century if not earlier.[174] Greek culture did persist in Naples, but epigraphic evidence indicates that prominent Oscan families had also been integrated into Neapolitan society by the end of the fourth century.[175] Thus, the survival of Greek culture was probably the result of accommodation and compromise between the Greek Neapolitans and their would-be Oscan conquerors.[176] In this context, it makes sense for Naples to have maintained strong ties with a powerful Oscan city such as Nola, especially as a counter-weight against formidable enemies such as Capua.[177]

---

[171] As discussed above, Hannibal elicited a battle from the Neapolitans by devastating their territory. Fear of devastation weighed heavily in the debate in the Nolan senate and influenced Marcellus' tactics in defending the town; and Gracchus took specific precautions to protect the Cumaeans from potential devastation.

[172] Cumae possessed *civitas sine suffragio*, so its obligation was probably similar to that of Capua and its subordinate allies. The Nolans were probably included among the Samnites' contribution in Polybius' (2.24) account of Rome's manpower resources (see Brunt 1971: 47–8). Nola held out against the Romans during the Second Samnite War (Liv. 9.28.3–6; Diod. Sic. 19.101.3), so it is unlikely that it was granted a generous treaty. The Neapolitans, as mentioned, appear to have been granted a generous treaty, but it is not clear if they perceived their military obligations to be light (see above, pp. 133–4).

[173] Dion. Hal. 15.5.2.

[174] Nola is an Oscan name meaning 'new town', which appears on coins from the early fourth century. Frederiksen 1984: 140 argues that tombs painted in 'Samnite fashion' suggest Oscan influence by around 400 BC. For the Oscanisation of Campania, see Strab. 5.4.7; Beloch 1879: 389–92; Frederiksen 1984: 134–57; Lomas 1993: 33–4; Oakley 1997–2005: 11.654–5.

[175] See above, p. 133 n. 139.

[176] Frederiksen 1984: 139; Lomas 1993: 34; Lomas 1995b: 107–20.

[177] Strabo (5.4.7) provides some tantalising evidence. He claims that the Neapolitans admitted some 'Campani' (Καμπανῶν) as fellow townsmen (συνοίκους), so they had to treat the most hated (ἐχθίστοις) as close relatives (οἰκειοτάτοις). The status of these συνοίκοι is unclear – perhaps

In 328/7 the Neapolitans engaged in raiding the territory of Capua and the *ager Falernus*. Two sources of tension fuelled these attacks. First, both Livy and Dionysius of Halicarnassus record that there was an ongoing territorial feud between Capua and Naples.[178] Second, about a century earlier, the Neapolitans had received a number of Greeks who had fled Cumae when it was seized by the Oscan-speaking 'Campani'. The Neapolitans planned to seize Cumae, presumably now allied with Capua, and restore it to the descendants of these refugees who were still living in Naples.[179] The Capuans appealed to the Romans, who in turn sent ambassadors to Naples. But embassies from Nola, Taras and the Samnites encouraged the Neapolitans not to abandon their alliance with the Samnites; after some debate the pro-Samnite position won out and Rome and Naples were at war.[180] The so-called Neapolitan War – this local conflict between Neapolitans, allied with the Nolans and the Samnites, and the Romans, allied with the Capuans – should be seen as independent from the Second Samnite War, though it was clearly bound up in the growing Roman–Samnite friction.[181] By the outbreak of the Second Samnite War, in 326, Nola and Naples were clearly allies, as the Neapolitans had invited a large

they were not yet full citizens. More intriguing is the reference to the 'Campani'; if this means the Campanians and is not a mistake for Samnites or Oscan-speakers in general, then it may indicate hostility between the Neapolitans and the inhabitants of northern Campania, including Capua. See, however, above (n. 8) for the difficulty in determining the precise meaning of 'Campani' in Greek sources.

[178] Dion. Hal. 15.5.1: the Capuans made repeated complaints to the Roman senate about Neapolitan wrongdoing; 15.6.4: the Neapolitans hoped to capture Capuan territory; Liv. 8.22.5–9: the Romans were angry because the Neapolitans had committed hostile acts against Romans in the *ager Falernus* and the *ager Campanus*.

[179] The plan to restore the town and property to the Cumaean descendants: Dion. Hal. 15.6.4. Cumae fell in the fifth century to the 'Campani': Liv. 4.44.12, 4.52.6; Strab. 5.4.4; Dion. Hal. 15.6.4. These references to the 'Campani' probably derive ultimately from Greek sources. For the fifth century this term is probably not used to refer exclusively to the people of Capua, but instead, possibly, to a group of Oscan Samnites in northern Campania who were in the process of ethnic formation. Still, the inhabitants of Capua – who would eventually be described by the adjective *Campanus* in Roman texts – would have been numbered among the Campani. See Beloch 1879: 296–9; Rutter 1971: 58–60; Frederiksen 1984: 136–7; Musti 1988: 219–22; Pobjoy 1995: 216–23; Oakley 1997–2005: II.631–3.

[180] These affairs are described in great detail by Dionysius of Halicarnassus (15.5.1–6.5), and more briefly by Livy (8.22.5–9). Dionysius' account is derived from a Greek source, perhaps a local history, and it appears to possess much authentic information (Hoffman 1934: 131–5; Frederiksen 1984: 210–12; Oakley 1997–2005: II.640–2). Livy reports that Rome went to war with Palaeopolis, a name also recorded in the *Fasti Triumphales* (see Degrassi 1947: 108, 414–15); its location was probably the heights now known as Pizzofalcone, about a kilometre up the coastline from ancient Naples, commanding the port. Livy portrays it as an independent *polis*, but it is more likely that Neapolitan citizens occupied both sites, and Livy (or his Roman sources) simply did not recognise that Palaeopolis was effectively part of Naples.

[181] For the Neapolitan War, see Hoffman 1934: 21–35; Oakley 1997–2005: II.640–5.

contingent of Nolan and Samnite troops within its walls to protect against Roman aggression.[182]

Rome concentrated efforts around Naples in 327 and 326. The Neapolitans did not hold out for very long but rather negotiated a relatively quick surrender. The fact that the Romans guaranteed certain privileges to the Neapolitans may indicate that the surrender was voluntary.[183] The Nolan garrison retreated from Naples, perhaps as part of the Neapolitan–Roman negotiations, and Nola held out until it was stormed by the Roman dictator Gaius Poetelius in 313.[184] From this point onwards, Naples and Nola remained loyal allies of Rome, repeatedly rebuffing overtures from Hannibal (as we have seen), while numismatic evidence hints at continued bonds between the two cities.[185]

Nola and Naples, especially the latter, tended to have close relations with Cumae. Ancient literary evidence is nearly unanimous that Chalcis

[182] Liv. 8.23.1–2. Livy claims that the garrison was stationed in Palaeopolis, not Naples (but see above, n. 180). Livy also portrays the Nolan–Samnite garrison in a highly negative light, claiming that it was received more because of Nolan pressure than because of the desire of the 'Greeks' (*magis Nolanis cogentibus quam voluntate Graecorum recepta*). He later describes Nolan and Samnite cruelty, as well as the Neapolitans' longing for reinforcements from Taras to resist both the Romans and the Nolan–Samnite garrison (8.25.5–8). These details, which are not recorded by Dionysius, highlight both stereotypical Samnite ferocity and the mildness of surrender to Rome; they are probably the product of pro-Roman bias (see Oakley 1997–2005: II.644). It is more likely that the Neapolitans welcomed the Nolan contingent, especially considering how Dionysius' account (15.5.2) strongly suggests friendly negotiations between the two.

[183] Liv. 8.23.10–12, 8.25.5–8.26.1–6. According to Livy, the Romans pressured Naples in 327 and 326, but victory was secured only when two Neapolitans – Charilaus and Nymphius – negotiated a generous treaty in return for betraying the city. The conspirators bear authentic Neapolitan names, suggesting that the episode preserves historical touches rather than annalistic fabrication (Oakley 1997–2005: II.645, 682). Nymphius (Νύμφιος or Νύ(μ)ψιος, probably a Hellenised version of the Oscan name *Nium(p)sis* (related to the Latin *Numerius*)), was a common name in Naples: see Leiwo 1995: 76. For other examples of Neapolitans with the name, see Diod. Sic. 16.18.1; *IG* 14.726. Charilaus appears on Neapolitan coins (Sambon 1903: 229).

[184] Liv. 8.26.3–4: the Romans occupied one part of the city, apparently Palaeopolis, and the Nolans fled through the opposite side. It is difficult to know how much of this detail goes back to authentic sources, but the fact that Nola held out for over a decade is consistent with Livy's narrative of the flight of their significant garrison. Livy's explanation for their escape is possible as it stands, but it is more likely that their passage had been guaranteed as part of Naples' surrender terms. Livy claims that the Samnites abandoned their weapons and returned home in disgrace; a historical kernel may lie beneath Livy's scornful characterisation if disarmament was one of the negotiated conditions. For the capture of Nola: Liv. 9.28.4–6; Diod. Sic.19.101.3. There is no reason to doubt that the city surrendered to Rome in 313, but see Oakley 1997–2005: III.332–3 for a discussion of the discrepancies between the two versions.

[185] The earliest Nolan coins date to the second half of the fourth century and were modelled on nearly identical coins from Naples. They bear a female head on the obverse (sometimes Athena), and a man-headed bull (sometimes being crowned by Nike) on the reverse. Nola continued to mint coins in the middle of the third century, bearing Apollo (obverse) and the man-headed bull (reverse). The man-headed bull also continues to appear on Neapolitan coinage in the third century. The bull motif appears widely on coins from Campania and the edge of Samnium,

had founded Cumae, which in turn founded Naples.[186] As already discussed, the Cumaeans who fled their city in the late fifth century settled
in Naples, and the Neapolitans and Nolans attempted to restore their
descendants to Cumae in the late fourth century. Some Cumaean and
Neapolitan (and Nolan) coinage in the fourth century shared common
iconography, perhaps attesting to a continuation of the bonds between
mother-city and colony.[187] Cumae allied with the Capuans during the
Latin War, after which it was mulcted of land and became a *civitas sine
suffragio*.[188] Cumae may also have been allied with Capua against Naples
during the Neapolitan War, but after this point apparently fell out of
the Capuan sphere.[189] Cumae was heavily Oscanised but retained significant elements of Greek culture, supplying perhaps a cultural or ethnic link with the Neapolitans.[190] Finally, significant personal or kin ties
must have developed from the Cumaean exiles living in Naples for at least

including from Allifae, Cales, Compulteria and Teanum Sidicinum (in the north), from
Hyrium and Fenseris (obscure towns that may have been subordinate settlements of Nola), and
on a few examples from Cumae. The Neapolitan man-headed bull coins may have been issued,
at least originally, for agonistic festivals held in honour, perhaps, of the river god Archelous;
see Head 1977: 30–43, esp. 38–41 and Rutter 1979: 42–5. The widespread use of this motif may
reflect the popularity of the cult in Campania, or even simply the copying of pre-existing types
as the use of coinage spread from Greek to Oscan communities. Rutter 1979: 95–8 argues that
there were only two mints in fifth-century Campania (Cumae and Naples), and only one after
Cumae fell to the Oscans, which must have produced coins on behalf of other communities.
Still, similarity between Nolan and Neapolitan issues continued well into the third century,
suggesting some sort of common tie or identity. See Frederiksen 1984: 139–40, who calls attention (p. 140 n. 54) to the shared Nolan and Neapolitan coin types, and now Rutter 2001: 69, 72
(nos. 563 and 603–5).

[186] Liv. 8.22.5–6; Vell. Pat. 1.4.1; Ps.-Scymn. 242–3. Strabo (5.4.7) states that Naples was originally
founded by Cumae, and then refounded by Chalcis, Pithecusae and Athens. See Oakley 1997–
2005: II.633–6. A fragment of Lutatius (Serv. auct. *ad Georg.* 4.563 = Lutat. fr. 7 Peter) reports
that the Cumaeans destroyed the first settlement of Naples and refounded it. Archaeological evidence does support two separate foundations: the first during the seventh century at Palaeopolis,
and the second during the fifth century at Naples – that is, where the modern city centre is
located (Oakley 1997–2005: II.633–6; Arthur 2002: 2–6). In any case, Cumae appears to have
played a role in the foundation of Naples, regardless of the exact details.

[187] Rutter 2001: 67 (nos. 536–7). The coins again bear a female head (obverse) and the man-headed
bull (reverse), the same as the shared Nolan and Neapolitan coinage discussed above n. 185.
Rutter 1979: 40–1, 95–6 argues that these coins would have been produced by Naples on behalf
of Cumae, but suggests that the Cumaean exiles influenced the choice of iconography.

[188] Liv. 8.14.11; Cic. *Leg. agr.* 2.66; Oakley 1997–2005: II.569.

[189] Again, Dionysius (Dion. Hal. 15.6.4) reports that the Neapolitans and Nolans planned to recover
Cumae (Κύμην τ' ἀνασώσειν) from the Campani and to restore to their descendants their possessions (καὶ συγκατάξειν ἐπὶ τὰ σφέτερα τοὺς περιόντας ἔτι), which suggests that Cumae was at
that point allied with Capua (and its subordinate satellites). We do not hear about Cumae during
the Second Samnite War, with regards to the planned or actual defection of Capua and its allies.

[190] Strabo (5.4.4) comments on the persistence of Greek culture in Cumae. Its 'official' language
became Oscan, at least until the early second century when the Cumaeans petitioned Rome
for the privilege to use Latin for public business (Liv. 40.42.13). But even though Cumae was

three generations, which still may have bound the communities during the Second Punic War.[191] And of course, like Naples and Nola, Cumae remained loyal to Rome in the face of Hannibal's invasion and repeated attempts by Hannibal and his allies to win over the city.

The preceding discussion shows that Nola and Naples (and to a lesser degree Cumae) not only tended to align with each other, but they also tended to oppose the Capuan League in a series of conflicts in the fourth and third centuries, including during the Second Punic War; the diplomatic configurations are summarised in Table 2 (see p. 131). The relative consistency with which they opposed each other suggests some sort of long-standing rivalry or mutual hostility, especially between the Capuan League on the one hand and Naples and Nola on the other. Indeed, as has been discussed above, literary evidence confirms Capuan–Neapolitan border disputes.[192] Livy's statement (23.19.4) that the people of Nola (and Acerrae) did not want Marcellus to move his army from Suessula in 215 because they feared the Capuans is consistent with the suggestion of Nolan–Capuan hostility.[193] Finally, Cumaean actions during the Second Punic War hint at a similar enmity. When the Capuans tried to convince the Cumaeans to revolt, they did not simply ignore the offer but rather led the Capuans on while informing the nearby Roman consul so that he might ambush them.[194] The Cumaeans, therefore, in choosing to stay loyal, did not act with ambivalence towards the Capuans, but instead worked to damage Capuan interests. Overall, historical trends, events during the Second Punic War and specific literary references all point to the persistence of long-standing animosity between Capua and some neighbouring cities in Campania.

This is not to say that Campanian intercity rivalries and hostilities – or alliances and ties, for that matter – were necessarily immutable and constant. Indeed, the alliance between Capua and Cumae in the middle of

---

'considerably Oscanised by the time of Roman conquest', Oscan inscriptions died out in Cumae during the first century BC, while the use of Greek as an epigraphic language persisted into the Imperial period, albeit less robustly than in Naples (Lomas 1995b: 109–11, quotation at p. 110).

[191] It is unlikely that all Greek-speakers fled Cumae in the wake of the Oscan conquest, especially considering the survival of Greek in inscriptions. A second-century inscription from a chamber tomb containing an Oscanised Greek name suggests Oscan and Greek elites intermingled, as we saw in Naples (Vetter 1953: no. 112; Lomas 1995a). It does not appear as though the descendants of Cumaean exiles were restored in the 320s. Presumably, the Cumaean descendants, some of whom had relatives still in Cumae, increasingly integrated into Neapolitan families. Thus, the exiles probably acted as agents for intercommunity kin ties. Of course, such bonds could be overcome, as the Capuan example shows.

[192] See above, p. 140.   [193] See above p. 124 n. 103.

[194] Liv. 23.35.1–4, 23.35.10–11.

the fourth century shows that interstate relations might change based on contingent military or diplomatic circumstances. If this is accurate, Livy's statement that all Campanians performed a common sacrifice at Hamae, to which the Cumaeans were also invited,[195] shows that animosity could also be overcome in specific contexts, in this case a pan-Campanian conference at a shared religious sanctuary.

However, traditional bonds and rivalries must have influenced a city's ruling elite when they confronted foreign policy decisions. Earlier in this chapter I demonstrated that when Hannibal won over the Capuans, he also won over their traditional allies. But his success in gaining Capua ultimately undermined his efforts to win other Campanian allies, since Capua's traditional enemies would have been wary of the Capuan treaty with Hannibal and the threat it posed to their own interests. Thus, Capua's revolt and its treaty with Hannibal probably encouraged the loyalty of at least some members of the aristocracy in cities such as Cumae and Nola. This mirrors the situation in Apulia, but evidence for the process is much stronger for Campania. First, Hannibal won over the Capuans by promising them hegemony. These negotiations must surely have provoked resistance in neighbouring Campanian cities and so promoted their loyalty to Rome. But even if the exact nature of the Capuan–Hannibalic negotiations remained secret, Capua's subsequent acts of aggression would have made its neighbours suspicious. In this context it makes sense that Nola, Naples and Cumae sought Roman military assistance only *after* the Capuans treated with Hannibal, as their aristocrats decided that Rome was a preferable counter-weight against their traditional rival, an expansionist Capua. Second, explicit textual evidence confirms that Campanian cities feared the Capuans. Here we return to Livy's critical statement at 23.19.4, that the Nolans and Acerrans feared the Capuans – with no mention of Hannibal – should the Romans withdraw their garrison.

Intercity tension or rivalry may help to explain the loyalty of two other, less-documented Campanian cities: Acerrae and Nuceria. Acerrae was a relatively unimportant town lying approximately halfway between Nola, Naples and Capua.[196] Its citizens were *cives sine suffragio*, like the Capuans,

[195] Liv. 23.35.3: *Campanis omnibus statum sacrificium ad Hamas erat.* It is not entirely clear in this case if *Campanis* refers only to Capua (and perhaps its satellites) or to the inhabitants of Campania in a broader sense. Frederiksen 1984: 33 speculated that this was a 'federal cult' of (probably) Diana or Demeter.

[196] Polybius (3.91.1–7) fails to mention Acerrae; Strabo (5.4.11) states that there are other settlements 'even smaller' than Acerrae, implying Acerrae was relatively small. Pliny (*HN* 3.63) calls the town an *oppidum*, though he is writing at a much later time, and he tends to use the term *oppidum* imprecisely. For its location and size: Beloch 1879: 382–4; Nissen 1967: 11.754; Frederiksen 1984: 35; Oakley 1997–2005: 11.593.

but the city does not appear to have been a Capuan dependency.[197] Hannibal approached the Acerrans in 216, intending to win them over peaceably, but when they rejected his overtures, he blockaded the town. But even this threat did not compel the Acerrans to surrender, so Hannibal stormed the town, plundered it and left it at least partially destroyed.[198] The sources do not mention a Roman garrison, so the Acerrans' loyalty was not compelled at Roman spear-point. But the episode did occur after both Capua had revolted and Nola had rejected Hannibal's offers, so their actions could have influenced Acerran decision-making. We have just seen that the Acerrans requested Roman military assistance because they feared the Capuans. At the same time, there is some hint that Acerrae maintained cordial relations with Nola and Nuceria.[199] Acerran fear of Capua on the one hand, and possibly its close bonds with Nola on the other hand, probably encouraged Acerrae's decision to side with Rome. That the Acerrans let their city be destroyed rather than submit to Hannibal underscores the importance of traditional local bonds and hostilities.

A similar analysis can be applied to Nuceria, whose citizens also paid the price of resisting Hannibal with his destruction of their city. In 216 Hannibal tried to play on political divisions within Nuceria, and when this failed, he starved the inhabitants into submission. Nucerian survivors were allowed, as terms of the surrender, to take refuge wherever they wanted, with most ending up in Cumae, Naples and Nola; the city itself was sacked and burned.[200] Once again, no Roman garrison is mentioned, and once again, the episode occurred after Hannibal's negotiations with Capua and Nola.[201] Nuceria may have had economic ties to Nola and

---

[197] Acerrae was incorporated in 332, several years after Capua, apparently during an unrelated campaign: Liv. 8.17.12; Vell. Pat. 1.14.3.

[198] Liv. 23.17.1–7; App. *Pun.* 63. Livy states (23.17.6) that some Acerrans fled to nearby cities that were known to have remained loyal. We later hear (Liv. 23.19.4) that the Nolans and Acerrans sought military assistance from Marcellus, which may suggest that Acerrae was not entirely destroyed and the refugees returned home, or may indicate that the Acerrans were living in Nola when this request was made. Acerrae was restored after the fall of Capua (Liv. 27.3.6–7).

[199] Strabo (5.4.8) records that Nola, Nuceria and Acerrae traded along the Sarno River and shared the same port town, Pompeii, suggesting economic ties between these cities. The joint Nolan and Acerran request for Roman military aid may indicate only common cause, but it might also reflect some sort of alliance.

[200] Liv. 23.15.2–6. Livy records that the Nucerians were allowed to flee with only one garment each, and that the populace dispersed to Naples and Nola, except for a group of thirty aristocrats who tried to go to Capua but were refused entry, after which they went to Cumae. Later sources (Val. Max. 9.6. ext. 2; App. *Pun.* 63; Cass. Dio 15.57.34; Zon. 9.2) claim that Hannibal doublecrossed the Nucerians and instead killed them (and the Acerrans, according to Dio/Zonaras) with extreme cruelty. This later tradition is clearly embellishment.

[201] Establishing the timing of Hannibal's attempt on Nuceria is rather tricky. Despite its location in the Livian narrative, Frederiksen 1984: 257 argued that Nuceria fell *before* Hannibal won over Capua. He based this position on two points. First, the attack against Nuceria is bound up

Acerrae, as discussed above. Nuceria had also been the dominant power
over a cluster of southern Campanian cities, including Stabiae, Pompeii,
Surrentum and Herculaneum.[202] It is plausible that the Nucerians figured
that an alliance between Hannibal and Capua was potentially threatening to their own status as one of the chief cities in southern Campania.
Therefore, they chose to remain loyal to Rome, making the same decision
as the citizens of Nola and Acerrae, two cities which may have had close
links to Nuceria.

CONCLUSION

To summarise the situation in Campania by the end of 215: after the revolt
of Capua and its subordinate allies, many of the remaining Campanian
cities were compelled to choose between Rome and Hannibal, either
because Hannibal approached the cities directly or because the Capuans
tried to convince them to revolt. No other Campanian city rebelled, despite in some cases repeated overtures by Hannibal, both seductive and
threatening.

A number of Campanian communities had long felt hostility or fear
towards the powerful city of Capua, and local intercity rivalry helps to
explain why Hannibal was not more successful in Campania. When

with Livy's description of a third attack on Naples, which Frederiksen thought was a doublet
of the first attack because Hannibal's motive, to secure a port, is the same in both attempts: *ut
urbem maritimam haberet* (23.1.5) and *cupidus maritimi oppidi potiundi* (23.15.1). But Livy also
says (23.36.6) that Hannibal attacked Cumae for the same reason because he failed to secure
the port at Naples (*ut quia Neapolim non potuerat Cumas saltem maritimam urbem haberet*). The
repetition of this motive may mean that it is Livy's own thesis, or it may reflect its repetition in
his sources. Either way, the repetition does not prove securely that the third attack on Naples is a
doublet of the first (for an alternative explanation, see above, nn. 135–6), so it cannot be used to
move the attack on Nuceria to a point prior to the defection of Capua. The second point rests on
Livy's claim (23.36.6) that the Nucerian senators who went to Capua were denied entry 'because
they had closed their gates to Hannibal' (*cum ferme trigenta senatores, ac forte primus quisque,
Capuam petissent, exclusi inde,* **quod portas Hannibali clausissent,** *Cumas se contulerunt*).
Frederiksen argued that the Capuans are the subject of *clausissent*, indicating that the Nucerians
fled while Capua was still loyal to Rome. This reasoning is flawed: the subject is clearly *trigenta
senatores*, who are also the subject of every verb and participle in the sentence. Thus, Livy's logic
is that the Capuans (now allied with Hannibal) rejected the Nucerian refugees because the latter had closed their gates to Hannibal. Hannibal must, therefore, have bypassed Nuceria when
he first entered Campania, attacking Naples and securing Capua before attempting to win over
additional cities (see above, p. 103).

[202] It is not clear if Nuceria, Pompeii, Stabiae, Surrentum and Herculaneum had been organised
in a formal 'Nucerian league' before Roman conquest. But it does appear that Nuceria was the
dominant state, while these cities shared some mutual bonds. Polybius (3.91.4) mentions Nuceria
when listing the cities on the southern coast of Campania. In fact, he states that Nucerian territory reached the coast despite the fact that Nuceria was, according to Pliny (*HN* 3.62), nine
Roman miles from the sea. Polybius does not mention Herculaneum or Pompeii. Livy (9.38.2)

Hannibal won the allegiance of Capua and its subordinate cities by promising to extend Capuan hegemony, Capua's local rivals became more confirmed in their loyalty to Rome – that is, the ruling aristocracies in these cities calculated that Capuan hegemony threatened their interests more than did Roman rule. Thus, Hannibal's greatest success, winning over wealthy and powerful Capua, had the effect of limiting the overall effectiveness of his strategy. This reflects patterns observed in Apulia in the wake of Cannae, but in Campania the evidence for this process – albeit sometimes problematic – is more copious and explicit.

That is not to say that the remaining cities in Campania were completely firm in their loyalty. Rather, the aristocracies in these cities tended to be divided, with at least some aristocrats promoting a pro-Hannibalic position. In some cases (especially Nola) the loyalty of the aristocracy continued to waver, and the threat of revolt lasted for years. Initial suspicion of the Capuan–Hannibalic alliance, however, rooted in traditional hostility toward the Capuans, delayed potential revolts. This allowed pro-Roman aristocrats time to consolidate their power, usually with the help of a Roman garrison. When Hannibal did not win over all or most Campanian cities in 216, Rome had time to recover: to encourage local aristocracies, win back the loyalty of important individual aristocrats, punish aristocrats who promoted sedition, and place garrisons to protect cities against potential attacks by Hannibal or his allies. With the remaining Campanian cities more secure against revolt, both through the loyalty of the local elite and through the strategic placement and maintenance of garrisons, Rome weathered the storm of the first few years of the Second Punic War. In the years to follow, when Hannibal was forced to protect the allies he had won over lest he lose credibility, Rome's long-term strategic advantages would increasingly come into play. This will be treated at greater length in Chapter 6. For now, we will shift our analysis to the south-western peninsula (Bruttium), where Hannibal won over his most enduring Italian allies yet still failed to elicit defections from the every community in the region.

states that, during the Second Samnite War, P. Cornelius led a raid on the territory of Nuceria by landing a fleet at Pompeii. These three passages suggest that the coastal towns of Pompeii and Herculaneum were included in the territory of Nuceria. Nuceria coined money for all of these cities, and the chief Nucerian magistrate may have had some authority in subordinate cities (Afzelius 1942: 161; Toynbee 1965: 1.111; Salmon 1967: 99–100, 233 n. 4; and Frederiksen 1984: 141–2 n. 77).

CHAPTER 4

Bruttium and western Magna Graecia

INTRODUCTION

After Cannae, Hannibal waited a few days in Apulia and then proceeded to Samnium; there he gained the loyalty of Compsa as the pro-Roman aristocracy fled the city. At this point Hannibal divided his forces and marched into Campania, leaving part of his army with Mago to secure the loyalty of any remaining pro-Roman settlements 'of that region' (*regionis eius*).[1] Thence, Mago marched into Bruttium to encourage rebellion, and finally returned to Carthage and reported Hannibal's victories to the Carthaginian senate. In the meantime, Hanno took over operations in Bruttium, though his forces did not reach the area until August at the earliest.[2] Most of the Bruttians appear to have come over to the Carthaginians quite readily, though whether they did so before Mago's or Hanno's arrival is not clear. But some Bruttian communities, including the important cities of Petelia and Consentia, remained loyal to Rome, at least initially. It would take nearly a year to capture Petelia and Consentia, and only after these cities capitulated did Hannibal's commanders begin to gain the support of western Italiote cities such as Locri and Croton. Indeed, Hannibal never secured all of Bruttium and western Magna Graecia, because Rhegion, which commanded the Straits of Messina,

---

[1] Liv. 23.1.1–5. In this section Livy speaks both generally about Hannibal's entering *in Samnium*, and more specifically about his dealings 'among the Hirpini' (*in Hirpinos*). It is not clear where Mago was ordered to win over cities, though his operations were probably confined to the territory of the Hirpini. It is possible, however, that the Caudini also defected at this time, either spontaneously or because of Mago's activities (see Appendix A).

[2] For the movements of Mago and Hanno, see Liv. 23.11.7, 23.43.6, 23.46.8, 24.1.1, 23.30.1 (where Livy mistakes Himilco for Hanno); App. *Hann.* 29; see also De Sanctis 1956–69: III.2.204 n. 13, suggesting that Himilco was a lieutenant of Hanno. For the chronology: the battle of Cannae was fought on 2 August on the Roman calendar, which probably equated to around 1 July on the solar calendar (see Chapter 1, n. 2), allowing Mago/Hanno around a month, at least, to begin operations in Bruttium. If the Roman calendar was more or less synchronised with the solar calendar, Carthaginian operations would probably not have begun until around early September (solar).

148

remained loyal to Rome throughout the war. It served as a base for Roman land and sea operations in the reconquest of Bruttium and the western Italiote cities.

Hannibal should have expected to find widespread support in southern Italy. Ancient Bruttium as well as the cities of western Magna Graecia[3] were among Rome's most recent conquests and they had been less fully pacified. There was precedent, moreover, for successfully fostering rebellion in southern Italy: Pyrrhus was able to win over most of the Greek cities along the Ionian coast and perhaps some inland Italic communities after inflicting military defeat upon Roman armies in the field.[4] On the surface it is surprising that Hannibal's strategy did not bear fruit more quickly. This chapter will examine the implementation and relative success of Hannibal's strategy in Bruttium and among the Greek cities of western Magna Graecia, as well as the local factors that shaped and limited his diplomatic efforts. In particular, we will focus on local interstate rivalries – not only long-standing hostility between coastal Greeks and inland Italic peoples (Bruttians and Lucanians), but also intra-Bruttian and intra-Greek tensions – that would impede the Hannibalic strategy.[5]

THE REVOLT OF THE BRUTTIANS, 216–215

Hannibal gathered widespread support from among the various communities of the Bruttians. Livy (22.61.11) claims that 'all of the Bruttians' (*Bruttii omnes*) rebelled after the Roman disaster at Cannae, though his own testimony suggests this is an exaggeration.[6] At a later point in his narrative (25.1.2), corresponding to the year 213, he specifies that Consentia and Taurianum were among the twelve Bruttian communities that had

---

[3] For the purposes of this chapter, western Magna Graecia corresponds roughly to the Greek cities on the coast of the region of ancient Bruttium (modern Calabria; the 'toe' of Italy), stretching approximately from the boundary of Laös (but not including Laös) to the boundary of Thurii (but not including Thurii); see Strab. 6.1.5–12.

[4] See Chapter 1, p. 15 n. 33.

[5] Kukofka 1990: 9–36 emphasises a division between urbanised and non-urbanised, arguing that the less urbanised Bruttians came over to Hannibal more willingly while the more urbanised people (mainly the Italiote Greeks) tended to resist. This general conclusion does not do justice to the complexity of the situation, wherein both the Bruttians and the Greeks displayed degrees of loyalty, nor to the highly contingent nature of diplomacy in south-western Italy during the Second Punic War.

[6] Whether or not all of the Bruttians eventually came over to Hannibal, the people of Petelia did not rebel immediately in the wake of Cannae – indeed, Livy (23.20.4) praises them for being alone among the Bruttians (*uni ex Bruttiis*) in maintaining their loyalty to Rome, and they stoutly defended their city against the Carthaginians for eleven months (see below, p. 155). Consentia also remained loyal, at least for a time (Liv. 23.30.5).

revolted.[7] In 203 the consul Cn. Servilius Caepio is reported to have captured a number of Bruttian towns, including Consentia, Aufugum, Bergae, Baesidiae, Ocriculum, Lymphaeum, Argentanum, Clampetia and 'many other unimportant peoples' (*multique alii ignobiles populi*).[8] Pandosia also had defected and appears to have been captured in this same campaign.[9] Finally, in 194, the Romans founded a Latin colony at Hipponion (renamed Vibo Valentia) on territory confiscated from the Bruttians, implying that Hipponion had also sided with Hannibal at some point during the war. It is not clear, however, if the Bruttians controlled Hipponion at the outbreak of the Second Punic War (this was the more likely case), or if they occupied it during the course of the conflict.[10]

The reasons for widespread support for Hannibal in Bruttium are not difficult to locate; indeed, they probably mirrored the sources of discontent with Roman rule that have already been discussed in the previous chapters. The defeated Bruttians were mulcted of land – the price of Roman conquest – and most likely were compelled to provide troops for service alongside the legions.[11] Rome probably punished some leading aristocrats,

---

[7] Livy's chronology here is also problematic: he claims that 'out of twelve Bruttian peoples' (*in Bruttiis ex duodecim populis*) that had revolted 'in the previous year' (*anno priore*), Consentia and Taurianum returned to alliance with Rome. The passage is found in his narrative for 213, placing the revolt of Consentia, and others, in 214. Yet Livy's more detailed description of the revolt of Consentia (23.30.5) is placed on the heels of Hannibal's capture of Petelia in 215 – indeed, Livy implies that Consentia revolted only a few days after the fall of Petelia. Since some Bruttian troops helped the Carthaginians attack Petelia (Liv. 23.19.4), at least some Bruttian communities must have revolted earlier than 214. It is likely that Livy has recorded a doublet in his sources of the revolt of Consentia and other Bruttian towns, with one or more of his sources displacing events from late 216 or early 215 to 214.

[8] Liv. 30.19.10. Consentia had already returned under Roman control by 213 (see above, n. 7). Livy's notice that it was taken by force in 203 indicates that the town had fallen back into Carthaginian hands after 213, unless Livy has accidentally reduplicated its capture.

[9] Liv. 29.38.1: in this passage Livy reports that Clampetia, Consentia, Pandosia and 'other unimportant cities' (*ignobiles aliae civitates*) were taken by force by the consul (in 204). This notice and the very similar report at 30.19.10 are clearly a doublet of the same campaign in different years, though each specifying a somewhat different list of captured cities. In which year we should place the campaign is not important here. Rather, we are concerned only with identifying the Bruttian communities that had allied with Hannibal at some point during the war.

[10] On balance, it is more likely that the Bruttians already controlled Hipponion before the Second Punic War began. Strabo (6.1.5) and Livy (35.40.5–6) both indicate that the Bruttians took Hipponion from the Greeks until the Romans in turn took it away from them, though when the Bruttians came to possess Hipponion is not explicit. Diodorus Siculus (16.15.2) records that the Bruttians captured both Thurii and Hipponion in the fourth century. Thurii was soon freed from Bruttian control, and in fact sometime in the 330s Alexander of Epirus temporarily made it the head of the Italiote League. Hipponion's ultimate fate is unclear, but Diodorus later reports (21.8.1) that Agathocles (*c.* 295) seized the city from the Bruttians, who in turn retook it and probably continued to hold it throughout the third century. See also Cappelletti 2002: 232–3.

[11] Polybius (2.23–4) does not include the Bruttians or the Greeks in his famous summary of available Roman manpower in 225. This is most probably because they were not asked to contribute

while rewarding others who had either displayed or promised their fidelity. This arrangement would have contributed to aristocratic competition, perhaps exacerbating pre-existing aristocratic rivalries, and most certainly generating new political tensions.

Roman rule also deprived Bruttian communities of the free exercise of foreign policy. According to the ancient literary tradition, the Bruttians separated from the Lucanians and formed some sort of confederacy (the Bruttian League) in the middle of the fourth century.[12] Strabo records that Consentia was the chief city of the Bruttians, though Petelia was also apparently an important stronghold.[13] The early history of the Bruttians is, unsurprisingly, rather muddled, but the ancient sources do agree that they attacked and at times occupied, a number of coastal Greek communities, including Laös, Temesa, Terina, Hipponion, Sybaris/Thurii and Caulonia. In the late fourth century the Bruttians fought against both Alexander of Epirus (who was employed by Taras) and Agathocles (whom the Locrians may have employed in order to further their own territorial aspirations in the region).[14] Tensions between the Bruttians and neighbouring Italiote Greeks continued in the third century, when Rome began to interfere more directly in regional interstate affairs. The people of Rhegion requested a Roman garrison as protection against the Bruttians, Lucanians and Tarentines. Around the same time, the Romans voted to send military assistance to the people of Thurii against the Lucanians, and the campaign was probably conducted along the border between Bruttium and Lucania. In 282 the consul C. Fabricius Luscinus celebrated a triumph

troops in 225, perhaps because they were so far away: Beloch 1886: 357–9, 366; Brunt 1971: 50–1; Marchetti 1978: 142; Baronowski 1993: 199. Toynbee 1965: 1.489–96 argues that Polybius' omission is the fault of his source, Fabius Pictor, failing to mention them.

[12] Diod. Sic. 16.15.1–2 (claiming that the Bruttians formed a κοινὴν πολιτείαν); Strab. 6.1.4; Just. *Epit.* 23.1.3–5; The nature of the 'Bruttian League' is much debated. Cappelletti 2002: 222–48 argues for a relatively high level of league organisation, a type of *sympoliteia* with common currency, a single army, a league-wide council, federal legislation, and league magistrates, though with some degree of political autonomy for the various member communities. See also Salmon 1967: 288 n. 4 and Lomas 1993: 41–3, 56–7, who argue that the league was not disbanded until long after Roman conquest, perhaps even as late as the Second Punic War. Senatore 2006: 89–92 is more cautious, emphasising that the political autonomy of a number of Bruttian communities (Petelia, for example, which, as we have seen, exercised foreign policy independent of the league) denotes a much looser and less formal arrangement. See also Guzzo 1984, 1990a, who downplays the level of organisation of the Bruttian League.

[13] Strab. 6.1.3, 6.1.5; for Consentia, see also Arslan 1989; Oakley 1997–2005: 11.670–1.

[14] Polyb. 2.39.6–7; Diod. Sic. 12.22.1, 16.15.2, 19.3.3, 21.8.1; Just. *Epit.* 23.1.4; Liv. 8.24.4–6; Strab. 6.1.5, 6.1.10; for the relationship between Alexander and Taras, see Chapter 5, pp. 195–6; for Locrian hegemonic aspirations, see below, pp. 167–71. Bruttian activity fits a more general pattern of expansion by Osco-Italic peoples into Magna Graecia from the fifth to third centuries: Toynbee 1965: 93–100; Salmon 1982: 6–16; Frederiksen 1984: 134–40; Adamesteanu 1990a: 143–50; Lomas 1993: 30–49; Small and Buck 1994: 11.23–6; Guzzo 1996.

for relieving a siege of Thurii and defeating the Samnites, Lucanians and Bruttians.[15]

Archaeological evidence is consistent with this general picture. The late fourth century was a period of important change in Bruttium, similar to contemporary developments in Apulia. While the Bruttians seem to have remained relatively less urbanised, we do see in this period the emergence of more nucleated settlements.[16] Some Bruttian sites might be described as 'semi-urban', displaying significant fortifications and (sometimes) other large-scale, presumably public structures. For example, Castiglione di Paludi, situated in northern Bruttium on the slopes of the modern Sila Mountains (a few kilometres from Rossano), has the remains of impressive fortification walls, towers and small buildings, although there is no clear street plan. In a few cases, such as Petelia (modern Strongoli) and Consentia (modern Cosenza), Bruttian sites took on more urban forms.[17] This semi-urban and/or urban development resulted at least partly from acculturation, as Bruttian communities adopted practices and institutions from nearby Greeks.[18] We should also assume that the appearance of defensive walls and fortifications meant those communities faced either the real or perceived threat of conflict.

The Hellenisation of Bruttian communities is visible in other forms. Numerous Bruttian coin types bear legends in Greek letters that frequently depict Greek gods. Perhaps most interesting are those with various obverses (including Heracles, Athena, Poseidon and Zeus) and the legend BPETTIΩN on the reverse. These are sometimes thought to be examples of federal coinage, though the legend may indicate an ethnic or 'tribal' identity rather than that of a federal state.[19] In any case, the lettering and iconography suggest Greek cultural influence.[20] Individual

---

[15] For the Rhegian request for a garrison against the Bruttians, Lucanians and Tarentines, see below, pp. 178–9. For Roman military aid to Thurii and related campaigns in the area: Dion. Hal. 19.13.1; Val. Max. 1.8.6; Plin. *HN* 9.118, 34.32; Liv. *Per.* 11, 12; see also Broughton 1951–2: 1.189. In 285, or perhaps a bit earlier, the dictator M. Aemilius Barbula may have received the submission of Nerulum, a town near Thurii straddling the border between Lucania and Bruttium (Liv. 9.20.9); see Fronda 2006: 404–6 for a complete discussion.

[16] Guzzo 1984, 1990a; Lombardo 1995.   [17] Sironen 1990: 146–7; Lombardo 1995: 119–21.

[18] Greek influence is evident in late fourth-century fortifications at such sites as Serra di Vaglio, Moio della Civitella and Castiglione di Paludi (Sironen 1990: 144).

[19] Head 1977: 90–2; Crawford 1985: 66–9; Arslan 1989; Taliercio Mensitieri 1988, 1995; Caltabiano 1995; Rutter 2001: 157–61. Cappelletti (2002: 222–5) argues that the coins constitute 'l'attestazione principale ed ufficiale dell'esistenza della loro organizzazione comune a livello politico-istituzionale ed economico' (quotation at p. 222).

[20] Older scholarship tends to argue that the Bruttians began to mint coinage as early as the Pyrrhic War (or just after it, *c.* 270) and continued until Roman reconquest in the Second Punic War, while more recent scholarship tends to associate all Bruttian coinage with the Second Punic War.

Bruttian communities, including Consentia, Hipponion, Noukria, Petelia and Terina, also produced emissions with Greek legends and similar depictions.[21] Wealthy monumental tombs have been found at a number of Bruttian settlements (for example, at Cosenza, Strongoli and Tiriolo), presumably belonging to Bruttian elite individuals or families; the grave goods found in these tombs are mostly of Greek production and promote, according to Lombardo, an 'ideologia funeraria' centred on warfare and banqueting.[22] Both literary sources and inscriptions attest to bilingualism among the Bruttians.[23] One remarkable inscription from Petelia, written in Greek and datable to the end of the third or perhaps early second century, lists two brothers (Minatos Krittios Menidas and Markos Krittios Menidas) who held the office of gymnasiarch. The triple name is obviously an Italic format; the praenomen Minatos is Oscan, as is apparently the nomen Krittios; Markos is a Roman praenomen and the cognomen Menidas is Greek.[24] Thus, this inscription shows an elite family whose names suggest an integration of Greek, Oscan and Roman elements. Perhaps more importantly, the office of gymnasiarch clearly shows the adoption by the Bruttian elite (at least in Petelia) not only of Greek titles, but also of the associated institutions of the gymnasium and the *ephebia*.[25] Overall, then, we see in Bruttium around the end of the fourth century and through the third century similar patterns to those observed

Likewise for emissions from individual communities, especially Petelia: scholars now generally agree that the earliest Petelian emissions belong to the Second Punic War. Whether the coins appeared first *c.* 270 or *c.* 215, they indicate Greek-Bruttian cultural influence by the third century, if not earlier. For the historiographic debate and references, see Caltabiano 1976: 89–90, 1977: 11–17; Arslan 1989: 25–34; Taliercio Mensitieri 1995: 127–8; Rutter 2001: 157.

[21] **Consentia** (obverse) various deities including Artemis, Ares, young river god and (reverse) ΚΩΣ; **Hipponion** (obverse) various deities including Hermes, Zeus, Apollo, Athena and (reverse) FEIΠ (= *Veip*, indicating Oscan influence), ΕΙΠΩΝΙΕΩΝ; **Noukria** (obverse) Apollo and (reverse) ΝΟΥΚΡΙΝΩΝ; **Petelia** (obverse) various deities including Demeter, Apollo, Artemis, Heracles, Zeus, Ares and (reverse) ΠΕΤΗΛΙΝΩΝ; **Terina** (obverse) Apollo and (reverse) ΤΕΡΙΝΑΙΩΝ. See Caltabiano 1976, 1977; Head 1977: 94, 100–1, 105, 106–7, 112–14; Crawford 1985: 66–9, 338; Rutter 2001: 166, 175–6, 184–6, 193–6; Cappelletti 2002: 227–34.

[22] Lombardo 1995: 119–21, quotation on 120; see also Sironen 1990: 144–5.

[23] Ennius, *Ann.* 543 [Loeb]: *Bruttace bilingui* ('bilingual Bruttians').

[24] *SEG* 34.1008 (= Costabile's republication of *IG* 14.637). For a complete discussion, see Costabile 1984. The inscription reads:

Ἐπὶ γ	υμ	ν	ασιάρχ	ων
Μινάτο	υ Κρι	τ	τίο	υ	Μινά	του
Μενί	δα, Μάρκου Κρι	ττίου
Μινάτ	ου, ἡ στοὰ ἀ	νεσκευ-　　(sic)
άσθη	ἐκ τῶν κοιν	ῶν
χρημάτων

[25] De Sanctis 1956–69: III.2.204 argues that Petelia was unusually Hellenised because of its proximity to Croton. See also Kukofka 1990: 10–11.

in Apulia: the emergence of a Hellenised political elite whose status was bound up with wealth and military success, and the contemporaneous shift to more nucleated and even urban settlements, often fortified, for reasons of defence and (perhaps) because of cultural influences. In this rather martial context, it is not surprising that there would be endemic interstate conflict between Bruttians and Greeks, and we may even speculate that there were conflicts among the various Bruttian communities themselves.

Increasing Roman influence in regional politics in the early third century would certainly have interfered with, and indeed limited, the ability of Bruttian communities to make war on the cities of western Magna Graecia. Rome supplied garrisons for at least some Greek cities – for example Rhegion and Locri – and while these garrisons ultimately proved dangerous to the citizens whom they were meant to protect, they must have shifted the military balance of power in favour of the Greeks and thus challenged any martial aspirations of the Bruttian elite. Indeed, we have already seen that by the 280s Roman generals had campaigned against the Bruttians (and Lucanians) on behalf of the Greek city Thurii. This helps to explain why the Bruttians made the fateful decision to side with Pyrrhus against the Romans.[26] The decade of the 270s saw the Romans retaliate with a series of consular campaigns against the Bruttians, as well as the Lucanians, Samnites and Greeks who had also allied with Pyrrhus. Indeed, the Bruttians are listed among the defeated over whom Roman consuls celebrated triumphs in 278, 277, 276, 273 and 272.[27] A further campaign may have followed in 269, but the evidence is less clear.[28] The intensity of Roman military activity and the number of triumphs suggests that these campaigns were particularly brutal. When the Romans finally forced the Bruttians to accept an alliance, around 270, the harsh terms of their *deditio* also indicate the severity of the Roman subjugation of this region.

---

[26] Liv. *Per.* 12–14; App. *Sam.* 10.1; Dion. Hal. 20.1.2–4, 20.2.6, 20.3.1; Zon. 8.6. Dionysius specifies that the Bruttians supplied Pyrrhus with both infantry and cavalry at the battle of Ausculum in 279, though his details of the battle contain a number of internal discrepancies.

[27] Broughton 1951–2: 1.189–99 ; De Sanctis 1956–69: III.2.399–400.

[28] Dionysius of Halicarnassus (20.17) says that the consuls for 269 campaigned against brigands led by an unnamed Samnite. The narrative immediately follows an account of an uprising in Rhegion (20.16); Dionysius also states that the land plundered by the brigands had already been sold off after having been conquered the previous year (20.17.2). This has led Broughton 1951–2: 1.199 to conclude that both consuls were sent into Bruttium. Zonaras (8.7) reports, however, that the Samnite brigand (whom he identifies as a certain Λόλιυς) operated in his homeland (ἐν τῇ ἰκεείᾳ), and that the consular campaigns took place in the territory of the Caricini, in northern Samnium. The idea of further Roman campaigns in Bruttium is attractive, but the contradictory evidence does not allow the point to be pushed too far.

According to Dionysius of Halicarnassus (20.15.5–6), the Bruttians were compelled to give up half of their territory in the ancient Sila Mountains, an area particularly important for its supply of lumber and resin (Strab. 6.1.9).[29] Ultimately, the brutality of Roman conquest and the relative harshness of the Roman settlement must have generated widespread discontent, and this goes a long way towards explaining why so many Bruttian communities rebelled in short order during the Second Punic War.

But it does not explain why the two most important Bruttian communities, Petelia and Consentia, did not revolt immediately. Indeed, the Petelians resisted Carthaginian negotiations and endured a brutal, eleven-month siege before finally relenting to Carthaginian pressure. Petelian resistance became legendary, and Rome even excused their defection when they ultimately succumbed to the siege in 215.[30] Consentia fell to the Carthaginians shortly after Petelia, so the Consentians also remained faithful to Rome for about a year after Cannae and even then only surrendered under direct Carthaginian military pressure.[31]

Literary sources provide very little detail about the situation in Consentia, but fortunately the events in Petelia are relatively well documented. According to Livy, both the Carthaginians and the rest of the Bruttians were attacking or besieging (*oppugnabant*) the Petelians because they had not gone along with the rest of the Bruttians in submitting to Carthage. Faced with this threat, the people of Petelia sent an embassy to the Roman senate to ask for a garrison. After lengthy deliberations, the senate decided that there were not enough resources available to protect the city, so the legates were dismissed with both a commendation (that the Petelians had fulfilled their obligations as allies) and a recommendation (that they do whatever they thought best under the circumstances). After their appeal was refused, the ruling class of Petelia splintered into a number of factions, as some proposed to flee, some suggested siding with Hannibal and some

---

[29] Both Strabo (6.1.9) and Pliny (*HN* 3.74) place the Sila Mountain forests in the vicinity of Rhegion and Locri, probably corresponding to the highlands between modern Aspromonte (prov. di Reggio di Calabria) and Serra di Bruno (prov. di Vibo Valentia) in the far south of modern Calabria; the ancient Silas should not be confused with the modern mountains of the same name, located further north. See Map 11. For the topography, see also Nissen 1967: 1.245–6, 11.925–7; Lombardo 1996.

[30] For the siege: Polyb. 7.1.3 (quoted in Ath. 12.528a); Liv. 23.20.4–10, 23.30.1–2; Frontin. *Str.* 4.5.18; App. *Hann.* 29; Val. Max. 6.6 ext. 2; Sil. 12.431–2. Polybius reports that the Petelians surrendered with Roman approval (συνευδοκούντων Ῥωμαίων παρέδοσαν ἑαυτούς). Livy (23.20.6) says that the Roman senate told the Petelians that they had fulfilled their treaty to the last (*fideque ad ultimum expleta*) by seeking Rome's help before surrendering. Appian (*Hann.* 29) reports that after the war, the Romans restored the town to 800 faithful townsfolk who had survived the siege.

[31] According to Livy (23.30.5), once Petelia was taken, the Carthaginians marched to Consentia and received the city's surrender within a few days (*intra paucos dies*).

argued for remaining loyal to Rome. In the end, the loyalists won out, and the citizens were ordered to bring in crops from the surrounding farms and strengthen the city's defences in preparation for the impending siege.

This narrative does present some difficulties. First, it seems rather fortunate that an embassy was able to depart Petelia and return from Rome unmolested, eluding the repeated Carthaginian and Bruttian attacks on the city, let alone a siege. It is more likely that the legates were sent to Rome before Hanno's forces began to invest Petelia; perhaps Hanno had only threatened the use of force, or perhaps the Petelians were weighing diplomatic options or buying time by negotiating with the Carthaginians and the Romans at the same time. Second, Livy's depiction of Petelia's tripartite factionalism is probably overly schematised – indeed, his description of the pro-Roman group as *optimates* who did not make decisions *raptim* or *timere* smacks of literary embellishment. Still, it is plausible that the Petelian aristocracy was greatly divided, with varying levels of support for Rome, so that the arrival of Carthaginian troops in the area either brought to the surface long-standing political divisions and rivalries or created new lines of cleavage. After conquering Bruttium during and after the Pyrrhic War, Rome presumably placed pro-Roman aristocratic families in charge of Bruttian communities, possibly executing or exiling members of the local elite who sided with Pyrrhus. Such pro-Roman families would have benefited from Roman rule, and members of these families probably made up the loyalist elements of the ruling class.

But presumably, similar political circumstances could be found in communities throughout Bruttium. Why did the pro-Roman (or anti-Carthaginian) position win out in Petelia, but not in the rest of Bruttium (with the exception of Consentia)?

First, the literary record hints at particularly close relations between the Petelian elite and their Roman counterparts. Indeed, the very fact that the Petelian elite chose to endure an eleven-month siege, despite tacit permission from Rome to defect, suggests that the local elite saw their interests tied strongly to collusion with Roman rule. According to Appian (*Hann.* 29), only a few Petelians escaped the siege, 800 of whom the Romans carefully collected and restored to their city after the war.[32] It has been suggested that these 800 were the vocally pro-Roman *optimates* and their families.[33] This must remain speculation, though it may have been the case

---

[32] See above, n. 30.

[33] Caltabiano 1977: 45–7; see also Kukofka 1990: 12–14, who doubts this number as impossibly high. It is possible that the figure of 800, if at all historical, included both local elite and regular townsmen.

that the Petelians who escaped and sought Roman protection came disproportionately from the aristocracy. The careful treatment of the Petelian refugees when they were in Rome is again consistent with the picture of good relations between the Petelian and Roman aristocracies. Livy preserves a reference to a praetor, Marcus Aemilius, who may have acted as an advocate for the Petelians.[34] Again, this fits nicely with the hypothesis that there were strong ties between members of the Petelian and Roman elites that would have encouraged Petelian loyalty. Finally, we can return to the Markos Krittios Menidas mentioned in the Petelian gymnasiarch inscription. The Roman *praenomen* represents at least a cultural affectation, but it may also reflect a close relationship between the Menidas family – clearly local aristocrats – and some members of the Roman elite. Overall, while the evidence is admittedly inconclusive, there are certain indications that the Petelian elite possessed particularly close connections to Rome that may have resulted in a critical mass of the ruling aristocracy remaining loyal in the face of external pressure.

We can also consider Petelian loyalty from the opposite direction. That is, there may have been less disaffection with Roman hegemony in Petelia than among other Bruttian communities. This is not to say that all Petelians embraced Roman rule: indeed, the above discussion implies that even in a loyal city such as Petelia individual aristocrats' loyalty to Rome would have varied greatly. Rather, it may have been the case that the factors promoting Bruttian disaffection were felt less acutely in Petelia. For example, we have already noted that the Romans exacted very harsh terms at the conclusion of their campaigns in Bruttium, namely the confiscation of one half of the Sila Mountain forest. This presumably would have had a dramatic impact on southern Bruttian communities, but Petelia, situated well to the north of the Silas, probably felt the effects less directly. Indeed,

---

[34] According to Livy (23.20.5–6), the Petelians first made their entreaty for a garrison before the senate, after which the senators were again asked by Marcus Aemilius (*consultique iterum a Marco Aemilio praetore patres*). It may be that Marcus Aemilius simply introduced the Petelian embassy to the senate in his normal capacity as presiding officer (see Brennan 2000: 99–135, esp. 115–16). Livy's account calls particular attention to the praetor's role in the second appeal, however, suggesting perhaps that he pressed the issue after the senate rejected the initial appeal. Surely having the support of the presiding magistrate, as well as other prominent members of the senate, benefited foreign embassies. As for the identity of Marcus Aemilius, Broughton 1951–2: 1.238, 249 argues that this is M. Aemilius Lepidus, serving as suffect praetor because one elected praetor had been killed in Gaul and another was seriously injured. Lepidus had previously served as praetor in Sicily (218), where he commanded a large fleet at Lilybaeum (Liv. 21.49.6–8); he was charged with protecting the coast of Sicily (Liv. 21.51.1), but he also played a part in defending the Italian coast after the Carthaginians raided the territory of Hipponion/Vibo Valentia (Liv. 21.51.3–7). Brennan 2000: 287 n. 40 argues, however, that the name is a mistake for M. Pomponius (Matho), the *praetor peregrinus*.

the fact that Rome concentrated its punishment on southern Bruttium may indicate that northern Bruttian communities, such as Petelia and Consentia, resisted Roman conquest less fiercely after the departure of Pyrrhus.

Finally, we must consider that there may have been local tensions and rivalries between the Petelians and the other Bruttian communities, which may have further encouraged Petelian loyalty to Rome. I have speculated that the widespread appearance of fortifications and elite tombs that celebrate a martial ideology hint at endemic conflict between Bruttian communities (see above, pp. 152–4). Livy's account of the siege of Petelia also reveals some sort of intra-Bruttian hostility, as he states clearly (23.20.4) that the Petelians were besieged not only by the Carthaginians but also by the other Bruttians who were angry with them for not having gone along with their plans to side with Hannibal. Livy's language does not specify whether the split between the Petelians and *ceteri Bruttii* caused the hostility, or if the Petelian decision and the other Bruttians' response was the manifestation of longer-term tensions. Numismatic evidence suggests the latter. The reverses of numerous Bruttian coin types, both those minted with the legend BPETTIΩN and those minted in the names of individual communities, commonly depict a crab,[35] which Cappelletti (2002: 234–5) argues was a federal symbol of the Bruttian League. While this perhaps pushes the evidence too far, it is intriguing that no surviving Petelian coin types bear the image. If the motif did reflect some sort of common identity, bond or fraternity – however vague – then its absence from Petelian coinage may indicate an emerging Petelian identity distinct from the rest of the Bruttians by the late third century, if not earlier.[36]

Overall then, the evidence suggests that the Petelian aristocracy maintained somewhat closer ties to Rome than did the elites in other Bruttian communities, and there is good reason to believe that Petelia had suffered less from Rome's conquest of the toe of the peninsula. In addition, there are indications of simmering tensions between the Petelians and *ceteri Bruttii*. Although the picture is far from complete, these factors help to explain Petelia's stout loyalty. When Hanno marched into Bruttium in 216, many Bruttian communities, resentful of Roman rule and eager to profit from their new alliance, quickly came over to the Carthaginians.[37] The Petelians held

---

[35] The crab motif appears on coins from Consentia, Hipponion, Terina and Noukria; for references, see above, n. 21.

[36] For the chronology of Petelian coinage, see above, n. 20.

[37] Livy (24.2.1–2) reports that the Bruttians complained because they had been unable to plunder the territory of Locri and Rhegion, so they set out to attack Croton. The narrative clearly

out longer, at least in part because their ruling aristocracy was more closely bound to Rome. Their reluctance to follow the rest of the Bruttians' foreign policy then either generated hostility or inflamed long-standing tensions, and the Bruttians joined the Carthaginians in attacking Petelia. Indeed, the Petelians may have feared the consequences of the Bruttian–Carthaginian alliance and so were driven more firmly into the Roman camp.

After the capture of Petelia the Carthaginians advanced to Consentia, which fell in only a few days, according to Livy (23.30.5). There are no detailed accounts of the internal politics of Consentia, but we may surmise that the political context was similar to that of Petelia, with the local ruling elite divided over how to respond after Cannae. In fact, Consentia appears to have switched sides a couple of times during the Second Punic War,[38] perhaps indicating that the ruling class was more closely divided in its loyalties to Rome, and thus was more susceptible to immediate threats or promises by the Carthaginians (or the Romans, for that matter). The Petelian siege must have influenced the Consentians' foreign policy decision. They had witnessed its outcome and thus knew what fate awaited those who resisted the Carthaginians. The Roman senate abandoned a Bruttian ally that had requested a garrison, yet the Romans garrisoned at least one of the Greek cities in Bruttium.[39] This all undermined the credibility of whatever pro-Roman aristocrats remained; hence there was no protracted siege, and Consentia fell to the Carthaginians with relative ease. Hannibal had finally dislodged these important Bruttian towns from Rome.

THE REVOLT OF LOCRI AND SUBORDINATE COMMUNITIES, 215

After securing the last of the Bruttian settlements in 215, the Carthaginians were able to turn their sights to the Greek cities of Bruttium. By the end of the year every Greek city in Bruttium except Rhegion had fallen to the Carthaginians. Yet, despite this success, Hannibal's strategy ultimately

---

indicates that the Bruttians hoped to utilise their alliance with Hannibal in order to profit at the expense of their (in this case Greek) neighbours.

[38] Restored to Rome in 214 or 213 (Liv. 25.1.2), under Carthaginian control in 206 (Liv. 28.11.12–13) and recaptured by Rome in 204 or 203 (Liv. 29.38.1, 30.19.10; App. *Hann.* 56); see De Sanctis 1956–69: III.2.263 n. 133.

[39] Locri (Liv. 24.1.9) seems to have contained a Roman garrison from the earliest stages of the war; Rhegion (Liv. 24.1.10–13) might have had a garrison from the outbreak of the war, though Livy's narrative shows the Roman garrison arriving after the fall of Locri. There is no direct evidence that Croton was garrisoned, though Lomas (1993: 65) assumes all three cities were garrisoned at the same time.

failed in Bruttium, and indeed his inability to secure the strategic city of Rhegion contributed to this failure. Moreover, Hannibal made relatively slow diplomatic progress with the Greek cities in southern Italy, both in Bruttium and in the eastern part of Magna Graecia (with such cities as Taras and Metapontion, discussed in Chapter 5). No southern Italian Greek city came over to Hannibal's side in the immediate wake of Cannae; as late as 214 he had secured the loyalty only of the Greek cities on the coast of Bruttium (except for Rhegion). By the time he made significant inroads into eastern Magna Graecia, the tide of the war was already turning against him.[40]

Scholars have tended to appeal to shared identity, outlook and institutions (the 'Greekness') of southern Italian Greek cities, regardless of whether they emphasise Italiote discontent with Roman rule, or their supposed attraction to Rome and reluctance to revolt.[41] The flaw with this approach is that it assumes that the Greek cities were more or less monolithic in their thinking. More recently, Lomas has suggested that the decision of Italiote cities to stay loyal to Rome or to revolt was bound up in local issues rather than global concerns, but she undermines her position by then arguing that the Italiote League was at the core of the revolt of the Greek cities.[42] Thus, Lomas essentially sees the revolt of Greek cities in Magna Graecia as a pan-Italiote response. The chronology of events argues against this: Taras, once the league hegemon, did not revolt until 213, by which point most (but not all) of the Italiote cities in Bruttium had already sided with Hannibal. Overall, while the perspective of the Greeks of southern Italy must have been shaped by cultural commonality, their varied responses indicate that other local and specific factors came into play.

---

[40] For eastern Magna Graecia, see Chapter 5.

[41] For example: Reid 1915: 95 argues that the Greeks would have been inclined to Roman rule for economic reasons; Ciaceri 1928–40: III.138–9 argues that the Romans had treated the Greeks mildly, and that Italiote revolts resulted mainly from direct Hannibalic military pressure (on this point see also Kahrstedt 1913: III.443); De Sanctis 1956–69: III.2.241–2, 264–5 argues that the Greeks mistrusted the neighbouring Italic peoples who had quickly allied with Hannibal, yet ultimately decided to revolt out of a desire for liberty and a return to past glory.

[42] Lomas 1993: 60–1: 'It is notable that the cities which defected most readily to Hannibal, and which supported him the longest, included Taras, Thurii, Croton, Locri, and Metapontion, all of which were leading members of the Italiote League in the fourth century. With the exception of Rhegion, the cities that remained loyal to Rome were those of Campania and northern Lucania, which were less involved with the Italiote League, as far as is known. This may imply that the core of the revolt centred on the League' (p. 61). The Italiote League was a league of Greek cities in Italy, formed in the sixth century and modelled after the Achaean League. The league had a central treasury, a central meeting place, and regular meetings by the member states. The league was originally under the hegemony of Croton, however, in the fourth century, league hegemony passed to Taras. It is not clear how many Italian cities belonged to the league, and league

Focusing for the moment on the coast of Bruttium, what factors hampered Hannibal's success among the Italiote cities? Long-standing Greek versus native (Bruttian and Lucanian) tension certainly played a role. At the same time, internal political divisions and long-standing rivalries as well as mistrust between the Greek states themselves undermined Hannibal's strategy and delayed his acquisition of allies after Cannae. The problematic nature of the sources challenges any reconstruction of Greek–Carthaginian diplomacy.[43] Fortunately, however, the defection of Locri and Croton, and subsequent Greek–Carthaginian–Bruttian negotiations are preserved in relative detail, revealing clearly the problems Hannibal faced in trying to navigate the complex matrix of local alliances and rivalries.

Immediately following the capture of Consentia and Petelia, Carthaginian forces moved against the Greek cities of Bruttium, attacking first Rhegion then Locri. We will return to Rhegion later in this chapter, but for the moment let us focus on Locri, which remained loyal to Rome until the summer of 215. Locrian loyalty resulted in part from Carthaginian–Bruttian diplomatic relations. Livy (24.1.1) is explicit that the Greeks in Bruttium remained loyal to Rome because they knew that the Bruttians, towards whom they had long felt animosity, had sided with Hannibal. Later, the Locrians refused to treat with the Bruttians out of mistrust, and they entered negotiations only when the Carthaginians appeared on the scene.[44] Ultimately the Locrians struck a treaty with the Carthaginians, and Livy's account makes it clear that the Bruttians were excluded from the final deal.[45] Long-standing hostility and mistrust between the Greeks and the Bruttians is well attested in the literary evidence. I have already discussed Bruttian attacks on Greek cities,[46] and the Locrians must have been particularly sensitive to the Bruttian capture of Hipponion, a colony of Locri. In turn, the Locrians may at one time have seized Temesa (later the Roman colony of Tempsa) from the Bruttians.[47] Locrian fear in 216–215

---

membership varied over time; it is also unclear if the league continued to function as a formal entity after the Roman conquest following the Pyrrhic War, though less formal bonds between former members may have persisted. For the Italiote League, see Giannelli 1928; Wuilleumier 1939: 62–71; Larsen 1968: 95–7; Brauer 1986: 53–6; Lombardo 1987: 55–6; Lomas 1993: 32–7; Purcell 1994: 386–8; see also Chapter 5, pp. 193–4.

[43] The chronology of events is particularly difficult to disentangle from surviving literary accounts, as Polybius is fragmentary, Livy appears to have repeated certain episodes and Appian glosses over many events. For a reconstruction of the sequence of events surrounding Locri and Croton in 215–214, see Appendix B.

[44] Liv. 24.1.5–6.   [45] Liv. 24.1.13–24.2.1.

[46] See above, pp. 151–4.

[47] According to Strabo (6.1.5) Temesa/Tempsa was founded by the Ausones and later resettled by the Aetolians; he also mentions that the Locrians captured the location (Λοκρῶν δὲ τῶν Ἐπιζεφυρίων ἑλόντων τὴν πόλιν) but places these events in the Homeric period (he links its capture to a legend

appears to have been well founded, as Hannibal's Bruttian allies expressed disappointment at not having sacked Rhegion or Locri and initiated the attack on Croton.[48] Livy's description of events implies that the Bruttians expected to gain plunder or territory by siding with Hannibal, and it is possible that Hannibal made such promises in order to secure Bruttian loyalty.

Anti-Bruttian sentiment was not the sole factor contributing to Locrian reluctance to side with Hannibal. First, there was also a Roman garrison quartered in the city,[49] which certainly would have made the Locrians suspicious of Carthaginian motives and confirmed their loyalty to Rome. Second, the Carthaginians themselves had already attacked coastal territories in which the Locrians historically had strong interest.[50] Thus, the Locrians may have initially mistrusted the Carthaginians as they did the Bruttians. Third, the loyalty of the local elite, or at least the loyalty of enough of them, was critical to Rome's control of Locri. At one point Livy (23.30.8) states that when Locri rebelled, it was betrayed by the leading citizens (*a principibus*), but later details reveal a far more complex scenario. During negotiations with the Carthaginians, three main groups appear: those who wished to remain loyal, those who wanted to ally with Hannibal, and a third group whose opinions were swayed by the capture of their relatives.[51] After Locri's ultimate surrender to Rome in 205, Scipio ordered those who had been guilty of sedition to be killed, and their property confiscated and turned over to the loyal Locrians.[52] When Locri first fell to Carthaginian forces, a number of Locrians fled to loyal Rhegion, and the Roman garrison was able to negotiate its own escape before being captured by Hanno.[53] It is clear that Locrian loyalty to Rome was mixed, that some Locrian aristocrats remained loyal to Rome and that Rome relied on the loyalty of Locrian aristocrats to keep the city under Roman control.

about Polites, a companion of Odysseus), before the colony was founded in the seventh century. The reference to the Locrians seizing Temesa fits the historical picture of conflict between Greeks and Osco-Italic peoples, and it may reflect a historical kernel that was mythologised, though one cannot push this point too far. For Temesa, see also Strab. 12.3.23; Hom. *Od.* 1.184; Paus. 6.6.2; Plin. *HN* 3.72.

[48] Liv. 24.2.1–3.   [49] Liv. 24.1.9.

[50] A Carthaginian fleet had plundered the area around Hipponion in 218 (Liv. 21.51.3–6). Hipponion was a colony of Locri (Strabo 6.1.5), and although it had fallen to the Bruttians in the mid fourth century, the town continued to be a focus of Locrian foreign policy (see below, pp. 168–70). Until the negotiations of 215 the Locrians may have assumed that the Carthaginians would be no better than the Bruttians – or the Romans, for that matter – with regard to their own territorial or hegemonic interests.

[51] Liv. 24.1.7–8. The picture is also certainly oversimplified but probably reflects the range of opinions as to the best response to Carthaginian overtures.

[52] Liv. 29.8.2.   [53] Liv. 24.1.9–10, 29.6.5–6.

It is likely that political rivalry among the Locrian elite predated its expression in the Hannibalic War, going back to the time of the Pyrrhic incursion into Italy, if not earlier. By around 282 the Locrians had invited the Romans to quarter a garrison in their city,[54] but after the battle of Heraclea they betrayed the Roman garrison and allied with Pyrrhus, only later to betray the Pyrrhic garrison to the Romans.[55] Pyrrhus retook the city briefly and executed any Locrians who had opposed his plans, before it fell back into Roman hands.[56] The wavering nature of Locrian loyalty, at different times inviting garrisons from both Pyrrhus and the Romans, and the fact that Pyrrhus singled out individuals for punishment near the end of the war suggest that the Locrian aristocracy was politically divided. Presumably, some aristocrats sought to further their own power through Roman backing, while others reckoned that Pyrrhus was a means to political advantage. Pyrrhus killed the Locrians who opposed him, and we can surmise that Rome likewise punished aristocratic families who supported alliance with Pyrrhus and subsequently either promoted surviving loyal aristocratic families or installed new pro-Roman aristocrats in positions of power.[57]

This is consistent with Livy's description of Locrian politics during the Hannibalic War. Consider again Livy's account (24.1.7–8) of the tripartite division of the Locrian assembly.[58] Livy refers to the pro-Hannibalic party with scorn, calling them fickle and claiming that they sought not only a new alliance but also revolution (*levissimus quisque novas res novamque societatem mallent*). Looking beyond the obvious invective, it is clear that the pro-Hannibalic party in the assembly tied a foreign policy decision (siding with Hannibal) to political change. Livy (29.6.5–6) again links the decision to side with Hannibal to political rivalry in his description of the Locrian exiles in Rhegion: at least some of the exiles were aristocrats (*ab Locrensium principibus*); a rival faction drove them out of Locri and allied

---

[54] Just. *Epit.* 18.1.9; Beloch 1926: 461; Toynbee 1965: 1.260; Del Monaco and Musti 1999: 424–5.

[55] App. *Sam.* 12.1; Just. *Epit.* 18.1.9, 18.2.12; Zon. 8.6. Appian claims that the Locrians massacred the Pyrrhic garrison because they had committed abuses.

[56] Zon. 8.6; App. *Sam.* 12.1. Appian claims that Pyrrhus retook the city violently and sacked it, in response to the massacre of his garrison.

[57] At the very least, those aristocrats in power after Rome captured Locri would have been wise enough to remain faithful, lest they suffer the consequences of disloyalty. The consul P. Cornelius Rufinus' 'friends' (τῶν ἐπιτηδείων), through whom he tried to secure the surrender of Croton in 277 (Zon. 8.6.2; see below p. 174), provide a contemporary example of the intersection of foreign policy, local politics and personal bonds between Roman and local elites during the Pyrrhic War.

[58] The situation recalls the political divisions in Capua (discussed in the previous chapter), which entailed a vocal pro-Roman party cautioning against rebellion, a vocal anti-Roman party promoting rebellion, and a large group of 'swing voters'.

with Hannibal (*pulsi ab adversa factione, quae Hannibali Locros tradiderat*). The entire account implies that some Locrians saw their political fortunes linked to an alliance with Hannibal, presumably at the expense of those aristocrats, supported by Rome, who sought to remain loyal. Scipio's Locrian settlement in 205 – with the ringleaders of the revolt executed, and their property given to pro-Roman aristocrats – would have been similar to the post-Pyrrhic settlement imposed by Rome.

It was critical for Hannibal to play on those political divisions in order to gain possession of the city. Yet although anti-Roman sentiment existed in Locri when Hannibal invaded Italy, the fact that Locri did not immediately rebel shows that pro-Roman sentiment held sway. In fact, the Locrians had supported Rome since the post-Pyrrhic settlement: the city was one of the few specifically mentioned as supplying ships for the Roman navy, during the First Punic War.[59] The question, then, is how was Hannibal able to undermine the control of the pro-Roman aristocracy?

Hannibal's promise of freedom was probably attractive propaganda to the Locrians. Throughout the Hellenistic period, promises of ἐλευθερία and αὐτονομία played an important role in interstate diplomacy in the Greek world.[60] Pyrrhus had invoked similar language when he invaded Italy, demanding that Rome leave the Greek states in Italy free and autonomous and restore to the other communities whatever the Romans had taken in war.[61] Presumably, such language resonated with the Greek audience in southern Italy, and indeed the eventual Locrian–Carthaginian treaty guaranteed the Locrians the right to govern themselves by their own laws.[62] Hannibal's military success and the presence of Carthaginian forces

---

[59] Polybius (1.20.14) does not specify the number of ships that the Locrians supplied in 260, but they may have regularly contributed two vessels (Polyb. 12.5.2; Liv. 42.48.7; Del Monaco and Musti 1999: 424–5).

[60] Kukofka 1990: 16–18 cites the promise of freedom and autonomy as an important factor in finally securing the Locrians. On Hellenistic freedom propaganda more generally, see Chapter 1, pp. 35–6. As a comparison, consider T. Quinctius Flamininus' pronouncement of Greek freedom at the Isthmian Games in 196 – the first known example of a Roman use of the slogan in a diplomatic context – and the enthusiastic response that he received (Polyb. 18.46.5; Liv. 33.32.5; Plut. *Flam.* 10.4, 12.2; App. *Mac.* 9.4).

[61] App. *Sam.* 10.1: ἐδίδου δ' αὐτοῖς εἰρήνην καὶ φιλίαν καὶ συμμαχίαν πρὸς Πύρρον, εἰ Ταραντίνους μὲν ἐς ταῦτα συμπεριλάβοιεν, τοὺς δ' ἄλλους Ἕλληνας τοὺς ἐν Ἰταλίᾳ κατοικοῦντας ἐλευθέρους καὶ αὐτονόμους ἐῷεν, Λευκανοῖς δὲ καὶ Σαυνίταις καὶ Δαυνίοις καὶ Βρεττίοις ἀποδοῖεν, ὅσα αὐτῶν ἔχουσι πολέμῳ λαβόντες ('He offered them peace and friendship and an alliance with Pyrrhus if they included the Tarentines in the same treaty, if they left all the Greeks living in Italy free and autonomous, and if they gave back to the Lucanians and Samnites and Daunians and Bruttians those things which they held having taken them in war').

[62] Liv. 24.1.13: *data pax ut [Locrenses] liberi suis legibus viverent.* It is not clear if the guarantee afforded the Locrians better terms than they already had under Roman rule, though presumably Hannibal offered conditions that gave the Locrians no less political autonomy.

in Bruttium certainly discredited Rome and would have undermined the authority of local pro-Roman aristocrats.

Yet these factors were not enough to detach Locri from its alliance with Rome. When a combined Bruttian and Carthaginian force began to attack the Greek cities in Bruttium, Locri was immediately braced for a siege and its citizens scattered to their farms in order to bring food and valuables within the city walls.[63] They should have been relatively confident that they could resist a siege: the city maintained a system of defensive walls extending for a circuit of about seven kilometres and enclosing an area of about 230 hectares – among the most extensive in Magna Graecia. More recent archaeological research has revealed that city defences were reinforced from the fourth to the beginning of the third centuries; these included the construction of a number of towers along the original wall circuit and a reconstruction of the stretch of wall along the coastline that had previously offered little protection. The new fortifications correspond to inscriptions preserved from the local Temple of Olympian Zeus that record funds allocated for thirty-six years to reinforce the city, including entries for the tower building.[64] There is no evidence that the walls were breached during the Pyrrhic war: Zonaras (8.6) records that Locri was betrayed to the Romans in 275 but that later the Locrians massacred the Roman garrison and invited Pyrrhus back into the city; in both cases Locri did not fall because of a failure of the defensive works.[65] The appearance of hostile forces, therefore, was probably not the deciding factor that compelled Locri to break with Rome, and, in fact, Livy's account seems to indicate that the Carthaginian approach strengthened Locrian resolve, at least in the short term.

The proximate event that brought the Locrians to the bargaining table was the capture of a number of Locrian citizens by the Carthaginian cavalry under the command of a certain Hamilcar. According to Livy (24.1.2–5), while some Locrians repaired the city's defensive works and the majority of Locrians went out to their farms in order to gather food and valuables, Hamilcar sent his cavalry to cut them off from returning to the city. He then surrounded Locri and sent some Bruttian allies to seek surrender from the few citizens remaining inside the city's walls. While Livy may exaggerate the total number of Locrians taken, he states explicitly

---

[63] Liv. 24.1.2–3.

[64] For a brief discussion of the defences around Locri, see Costamagna and Sabbione 1990: 49–53.

[65] Appian (*Sam.* 12.1) records, however, that after the Locrians had massacred the Pyrrhic garrison, Pyrrhus retook the city and sacked it. This may imply that Pyrrhus retook Locri violently, thus breaching the walls, but the notice is not explicit.

that the captured were composed of all classes (*permixtam omnium aetatium ordinumque multitudinem*) and therefore included some aristocrats. The capture of even a few aristocrats as hostages would have had a powerful effect on the ruling class.[66] Yet even the capture of Locrian citizens did not immediately bring the city to its knees but instead convinced the remaining aristocrats to begin negotiating terms.

When the Carthaginians offered the 'friendship of Hannibal' (*amicitiam Hannibalis*) in return for the city's surrender, the Locrian aristocracy responded by calling an assembly. The Livian account (24.1.7–8) of the subsequent debate, while probably stylised, provides a glimpse of the complexities of local politics. Some wanted to remain loyal to Rome, while others sought alliance with Hannibal. Those who had relatives captured by Hamilcar and made up the 'swing vote' chose to ally with the Carthaginians because the possible restoration of their family members outweighed loyalty to Rome and the various disincentives to rebelling. Presumably, the most important voices came from the aristocracy. The debate is reminiscent of the deliberations of the Capuan senate before they reached the decision to revolt:[67] in both cases, a middle group of aristocrats held the balance between those whose feelings ran more strongly for or against fidelity to Rome, and, ultimately, local and immediate concerns shifted that balance from a pro-Roman to pro-Carthaginian position.

Livy preserves the terms of the final treaty between the Carthaginians (by Hannibal's command) and the Locrians: the Locrians would live as free men under their own laws, the city would be open to the Carthaginians, its port under the authority of the Locrians, and the alliance would rest on the promise that both sides would help each other in peace and war.[68] The reference to Locrian control of the port is a unique condition among the various known treaties that Hannibal made with Italian cities, and this

---

[66] See Kukofka 1990: 16–17. Consider also how the 300 Campanian *equites* serving in Sicily, and viewed as (real or potential) hostages of the Romans, weighed heavily in Capua's negotiations with Rome and Hannibal (Liv. 23.2.6, 23.4.7–8; for a more detailed discussion, see Chapter 3, pp. 104–5, 107, 113–14). Rome also demanded hostages from Taras and Thurii, presumably from the aristocracy, in order to secure the loyalty of those cities; mistreatment of the hostages from Taras was a key factor in the eventual Tarentine decision to revolt in 213 (Liv. 25.7.10–8.1; see also Chapter 5, pp. 211–17).

[67] See Chapter 3, pp. 106–8.

[68] Liv. 24.1.13: *Locrensibus iussu Hannibalis data pax ut liberi suis legibus viverent, urbs pateret Poenis, portus in potestate Locrensium esset, societas eo iure staret ut Poenus Locrensem Locrensisque Poenum pace ac bello iuvaret* ('Peace was granted to the Locrians at Hannibal's order: that they should live as free men under their own laws, their city should be open to the Carthaginians, the port should be in the control of the Locrians, and the alliance should stand firm in this principle, that Carthaginian help Locrian and Locrian help Carthaginian in peace and war'). Livy (24.1.9) implies that the Locrians promised to hand over the Roman garrison as a pre-condition to negotiating

suggests that Livy has preserved some specific details rather than simply reproducing a stock treaty.[69] Thus, we might look at the treaty for additional insight into specific Locrian concerns and motivations.

The guarantee that the Locrians should live in freedom under their own laws is clearly in keeping with liberation slogans of Hellenistic diplomatic rhetoric. The final, reciprocal clause that Livy mentions, that Hannibal and the Locrians would help each other in war and peace, was a typical formula for a Hellenistic military alliance (συμμαχία). Such a treaty need not have placed the Locrians in a subordinate position. In fact, Locri's restored capacity to conduct independent foreign policy after the treaty suggests that the Locrians, at least, felt that they were truly independent actors if not more or less equal partners with Hannibal. Soon after the Locrians and Carthaginians concluded their negotiations, the Bruttians unsuccessfully attacked Croton and were forced to call on the Carthaginians for help. The Carthaginians under Hanno held back from offering the Bruttians too much assistance. Meanwhile, the Crotoniates refused to surrender their city to the Bruttians because of their mutual hostility. The Bruttians managed to seize the town but could not capture the citadel. The deadlock was broken only when Locrian ambassadors appeared on the scene to broker the surrender of Croton to the Bruttians in return for the transplantation of a number of Crotoniates to Locri.[70] The narrative implies that the Locrians had acted on their own initiative in seeking permission to send the embassy, and the episode shows the Locrians in the role of arbiters.[71] By offering arbitration, Locri was acting as an independent state in the tradition of Hellenistic diplomacy.[72]

In addition to the desire to conduct independent foreign policy, hegemonic ambitions may also have drawn the Locrians into alliance with

---

their treaty with the Carthaginians, a promise that the Carthaginians accused the Locrians of breaking. Livy does not include the promise to turn over the garrison as a term of the treaty *per se*, though clearly it was, at least originally, an important component of the negotiations.

[69] See Chapter 1, n. 133.

[70] Liv. 24.2.1–11, 24.3.9–15; see also above, n. 37. Note that the Bruttians sent a delegation to the Carthaginians only after their own effort to seize Croton had failed, in order to guarantee that they would profit territorially from Croton's capture. It is clear that Hannibal promised power to all his allies, or at least that was a common expectation on the part of his allies.

[71] Liv. 24.3.14–15: *Locrenses brevi post legati, cum permissu Hannonis arcem intrassent, persuadent ut traduci se in Locros paterentur nec ultima experiri vellent; iam hoc ut sibi liceret impetraverant et ab Hannibale missis ad id ipsum legatis* ('Shortly after Locrian legates entered the citadel with the permission of Hanno; they persuaded [the Crotoniates] that they should allow themselves to be handed over into Locri and not to desire to endure the ultimate end; already they [the Locrians] had achieved that this be allowed for them, and legates had been sent by Hannibal for this purpose').

[72] Hellenistic monarchs and powerful states often acted as arbiters in interstate disputes, though smaller independent states could also function as such. It is important to recognise that the

Hannibal. There is no direct evidence that Hannibal's agents promised local dominion in return for loyalty, or that the issue was raised among the Locrian aristocracy. Still, the Locrian–Carthaginian treaty was sealed with a promise of reciprocal military assistance *pace ac bello* – in other words, it was both a defensive and offensive military alliance. The condition may be seen as a standard Hellenistic formula, yet the proviso does not appear in the other extant Hannibalic treaties, including the pact with Taras, another Italiote state. The uniqueness of the condition suggests that the Locrians hoped to use the alliance not merely to be free from Rome but also to further their own local (or regional) power.

This suggestion is certainly consistent with Locri's clear and long-standing hegemonic aspirations in Bruttium. The territory of Locri was bounded to the south by the river Halex, perhaps the modern-day Fiume Galati, which separated Locri from Rhegion.[73] To the north, the Greek settlement of Caulonia/Aulonia abutted the territory of Locri; the exact boundary was probably the Fiume Allaro or the Fiume Torbido, with one or the other to be identified with the ancient Sagra.[74] Since Locri was unable to expand to the north and south, it founded sub-colonies and acquired territory across the Bruttian peninsula, presupposing that it came to control the mountainous interior of Bruttium or that it had the naval capacity to maintain communications by sea.[75] Locri founded Hipponion (near modern Vibo Valentia) and Medma (modern Rosarno) and conquered the area known as Metaurus (Gioia Tauro).[76] Strabo (6.1.5) also records that the Locrians captured the Bruttian settlement of Temesa, a location once known for its copper mines.[77]

Medma and Hipponion were politically independent from Locri, though they seem generally to have remained under the Locrians' influence or to

---

Locrians were acting as an independent third party and were not standing for (and therefore subordinate to) the Carthaginians, and such an independent action would have been prevented under Roman rule. For interstate arbitration in the Greek world, see Gruen 1984: 96–9.

[73] Strab. 6.1.9; Costamagna and Sabbione 1990: 160; Osanna 1992: 214; see Map 11.

[74] Strab. 6.1.10; the identity of the Sagra remains, however, uncertain. See Costamagna and Sabbione 1990: 160; Osanna 1992: 214.

[75] Costamagna and Sabbione 1990: 35–7; Osanna 1992: 220.

[76] Strab. 6.1.5; De Franciscis 1960; Costamagna and Sabbione 1990: 36; Osanna 1992: 220.

[77] See Map 10 and Map 11. Strabo's account of the Locrian capture of Temesa is problematic (for explanation and references, see above n. 47). In any case, the town appears to have been under the control of the Bruttians by the outbreak of the Second Punic War. While the exact site of Temesa remains unknown, it should be located somewhere in the vicinity of the mouth of the Savuto (ancient Sabutus) River, perhaps near Serra d'Aiello. The copper resources seem to have been exhausted at a very early date: Maddoli 1982: 75–8, 221–3; contra Zancani Montuoro 1969; see also Ridgeway 1984; Muggia 2002.

have been the targets of Locrian foreign policy. Two fragments of inscriptions from a trophy at Olympia – perhaps commemorating the Battle of Sagra (mid sixth century?) at which Locri crushed the Crotoniates, or another, otherwise unknown battle (*c.* 500–480) – list Hipponion and Medma as victors alongside the Locrians.[78] Diodorus reports that Dionysius I of Syracuse recruited both Locrians and Medmaeans to resettle Messina.[79] During this period Hipponion seems to have asserted its independence, but Dionysius I and the Locrians forged a marriage alliance, and the tyrant reconquered Hipponion, giving its territory to the Locrians.[80] The Carthaginians later restored Hipponian exiles, perhaps to encourage anti-Dionysian sentiment in Italy.[81] Hipponion was overrun by the Bruttians during the fourth century[82] but was recaptured and used as a base of operations against the Bruttians by Agathocles.[83] Although ancient sources do not explicitly state that Agathocles was allied with the Locrians, the latter often maintained friendly relations with Syracuse and its tyrants.[84] Moreover, Agathocles not only attacked the Bruttians but also was planning to capture Croton.[85] Locri had previously tried to expand its control of territory in the direction of Croton: according to Strabo (6.1.10), Dionysius I captured Scylletium/Scylacium and incorporated it into Locrian territory, and Diodorus (14.106.3) records that Dionysius I captured Caulonia and gave it to the Locrians.[86] This pattern suggests that Locri would have allied with Agathocles in order to reassert control over

---

[78] Ancient literary sources for the battle of the Sagra (Strab. 6.1.10, 12; Diod. Sic. 11.90; Just. *Epit.* 20.2.10–3.9) are difficult and present contradictory evidence about its date. Modern scholars are also divided (for discussion, see Bicknell 1966). The two fragments (*SEG* 11.1211) read: τοὶ ϝειπονιἔς ἀ[νέ]θ[ε]σαν] τὸν Ϙροτονια[τὸν] καὶ Μεδμαῖοι καὶ Λ[οϙροί] and ... καὶ Λοκροὶ καὶ. They are dated on stylistic grounds to (possibly) the late sixth century (Jeffrey 1961: 286) or (more probably) the early sixth century (Bicknell 1966: 299), and thus probably too late to be associated with Sagra (contra Costamagna and Sabbione 1990: 36).

[79] Diod. Sic. 14.78.5.   [80] Diod. Sic. 14.107.2–3.

[81] Diod. Sic. 15.24.1.   [82] Diod. Sic. 16.15.1–2.

[83] Diod. Sic. 21.8.1; Strab. 6.1.5; Just. *Epit.* 23.2.1.

[84] I have already mentioned the alliance between Dionysius I and Locri. Dionysius II was born of a Locrian mother (Diod. Sic. 16.6.1–2). After being defeated by his brother-in-law Dion, Dionysius II found refuge in Locri (Diod. Sic. 16.17.1–2, 16.18.1; Just. *Epit.* 21.2.8–9), where he stayed until his abuses compelled the Locrians to drive him from their city (Just. *Epit.* 21.2.10–3.9). Justin's account of Dionysius' cruelty seems exaggerated – Dionysius stayed in Locri for six years and probably helped the Locrians defend themselves against Italic pressure (implied in Just. *Epit.* 21.3.3). The relevant point is that Locri started out on good terms with Dionysius and may even have invited him to stay there (possibly implied by Just. *Epit.* 21.2.9). His long stay in Locri suggests that his rule was at least initially welcomed, and that it took some time for relations to deteriorate.

[85] Diod. Sic. 19.4.1.

[86] The territory of Scylletium (modern Squillace) bordered Croton (Strab. 6.1.11).

Hipponion and perhaps extend its power to the north along the Ionian coast.[87] An inscription from Delphi, datable to around 280, shows that Locri maintained links with Hipponion into the third century.[88]

Caulonia may also have been a target of Locrian expansion. According to Strabo, the city was originally a colony of the Achaeans, though it may have been a Crotoniate colony.[89] In any case, the city fell under the domination of Croton but was later captured by Dionysius I; the population was exiled and its territory given to the Locrians.[90] The city seems to have been refounded by Dionysius II, and in light of his alliance with Locri, it probably remained, at least for the time being, under Locrian hegemony.[91]

To summarise the above discussion of Locrian politics and policy at the outbreak of the Hannibalic War: Rome maintained the loyalty of Locri not only by placing a garrison in the city, but also through the support of a local elite friendly to the Romans. Hannibal's military success in the first few years of the war discredited the Roman position and presumably also undermined the power of the pro-Roman Locrian elite. The capture of Locrian citizens, including members of aristocratic families, provided an opportunity for anti-Roman members of the elite, motivated in part by their own political aspirations, to voice dissent over Roman rule. Concern on the part of the relatives of hostages held by Rome lent additional support

[87] Locri was probably the base of operations for Agathocles' campaign in Italy; see Costamagna and Sabbione 1990: 40.

[88] *Fouilles de Delphes* 3.1.76 (for the date, see the commentary at *FdD* 3.1.176); the inscription reads:

[Θε]ός. Δελφοὶ ἔδωκαν δημιάρχωι Φιλώται Λοκρῶι ἐκ τῶν Ἐπι-
|ζε|φυρίων Ἱππωνιεῖ προχενίαν, προμαντείαν, ἀτέλει-
|αν π|άντων αὐτῶι καὶ ἐκγόνοις καὶ τἆλλα ὅσα καὶ τοῖς
|ἄλλ|οις προξένοις. Ἄρχοντος Ξενοχάρευς, Βουλευόν-
των Ἐλέλλα, Κράτωνος, Φιλώνδα.

[89] Strabo (6.1.10) and Pausanias (6.3.12) consider Caulonia an Achaean colony. Ciaceri 1928–40: 1.173–83 argues that Caulonia was a colony of Croton, established to check Locrian expansion; see also Lomas 1993: 19–25.

[90] Diod. Sic. 14.106.3.

[91] Diod. Sic. 16.10.2, 16.11.3; Plut. *Dion* 26.4. For Caulonia's history between its refounding and the Second Punic War: Strabo (6.1.10) says that the city was abandoned because of attacks by otherwise unnamed barbarians, and Pausanias (6.3.12) records that the city was utterly destroyed by Rome's Campanian allies during the Pyrrhic War, implying that its existence during the Hannibalic War would have been the result of non-Greek occupation. Tréziny 1989: 155–7 concludes, based on archaeological evidence, that there was a hiatus of human occupation at the site during the fourth century (Dionysius I's destruction?), but continuous occupation from later in the fourth century (Dionysius II's refounding?) through the Hannibalic War, contradicting Pausanias' account. Tréziny also argues that finds of tiles, stamped bricks, and Bruttian coinage indicate that Caulonia experienced increased interaction with Oscan-speaking peoples, but retained significant Greek characteristics. It should be counted among the Greek cities at the outbreak of the Hannibalic War: Afzelius 1944: 89 (suggesting that Caulonia was a Greek *socius navalis*); Toynbee 1965: 1.490–2; De Sanctis 1956–69: 11.250.

to the anti-Roman cause. Finally, the terms of the Locrian–Carthaginian treaty indicate, possibly, that the desire to re-establish Locri as an independent player in regional interstate affairs also informed the Locrian decision to break with Rome. In fact, the local ruling class probably saw this moment as an opportunity to satisfy Locrian hegemonic ambitions. This would fit with their long-term historical tendencies, and is consistent with the behaviour of other would-be regional hegemonic powers discussed in previous chapters (such as Capua and Arpi).

If the Locrians were motivated to defect, at least in part, out of a desire to establish some sort of regional dominion, then we might expect them to act on this impulse once they saw the opening to carry out independent foreign policy – for example, attempting to assert authority over neighbouring communities. In turn, less formidable surrounding communities may have been convinced by Locri's defection to follow suit, whether because of compulsion, such as the real or perceived threat of Locrian force, or attraction, such as traditional alliances, personal connections or other informal bonds that resulted in these smaller states tending to gravitate to the Locrian sphere. This would be similar to the dynamic observed in Campania and Apulia. Direct evidence is lacking, but patterns of revolt during the Hannibalic War are suggestive: Locri historically influenced Hipponion, Temesa, Medma and Caulonia, and all of these cities (with the possible exception Medma, whose fate during the war is unclear) defected in the Second Punic War, implying some sort of link.[92] It is attractive to conjecture that Locri's history as a local hegemonic power and its influence with these smaller communities helps to explain their posture during the Second Punic War.

THE REVOLT OF CROTON, 215

Livy's account of Croton's defection (24.2–3 and 23.30.6–7) is one of the longest and most detailed of his revolt narratives, and it reveals quite clearly the sorts of complex local conditions and pressures – some mutually contradictory – that shaped a city's decision to remain loyal or revolt in the face of Hannibalic overtures. At first the Crotoniates had been hesitant to revolt because of their long-standing hostility towards the Bruttians. A Bruttian force with at least token Carthaginian assistance seized the city and besieged its citadel, yet even this increased military pressure could not convince the

---

[92] Hipponion (later Vibo Valentia) and Temesa (later Tempsa) were refounded as Latin colonies in 194, implying their defection to Hannibal: Liv. 35.40.4–6; Strab. 6.1.5. For the defection of Caulonia: Liv. 27.12.6, 27.15.8, 27.16.9.

remaining Crotoniates to submit. Rather, other immediate conditions, including the recent revolt of Locri, proved to be decisive in persuading the Crotoniates to break with Rome. Only after the Locrians had defected from Rome, and then sent legates to take part in negotiations between the Crotoniates, Bruttians and Carthaginians, did Croton finally revolt.

Before analysing the factors that contributed to Crotoniate policy in the Second Punic War, it is necessary to clarify the narrative of events from the details that Livy presents in the two passages cited above. Livy claims that the Bruttians first sent a delegation to Hannibal before attacking Croton, to seek assurance that the city would be theirs once they captured it (24.2.5), but he referred them to Hanno. It is more likely, however, that the Bruttians went directly to Hanno, since he was the Carthaginian commander in Bruttium and later played a role in negotiations with Croton (24.2.6–7, 24.3.10–15). Indeed, it is even possible that the Bruttians attacked Croton on their own and only sought Carthaginian help when they failed to capture the citadel.[93] The Bruttians attacked Croton, and at the same time, some Crotoniates fled the city and deserted to the Bruttians (24.2.9–11).[94] A certain Aristomachus advised that the Crotoniates should surrender, but only to the Carthaginians; presumably other aristocrats argued the city should stand firm. The Bruttians were able to storm the city walls, at which point the *optimates* (according to Livy), including Aristomachus, retreated to the citadel (24.2.11). This shows that Aristomachus preferred some sort of negotiated settlement and was unwilling to surrender to hostile Bruttians. Subsequently, after the Bruttians were unable to capture the citadel, they were forced to call on the Carthaginians for military assistance (24.3.9–11). This ushered in a period of Bruttian–Carthaginian–Crotoniate negotiations, during which Aristomachus again emerged as a proponent of Crotoniate submission to the Carthaginians (24.3.11–13). When Aristomachus was unable to convince the Crotoniate aristocracy to submit to the Carthaginians, he forged a separate peace with Hanno (24.3.13). Livy claims that Aristomachus acted alone, but it is more plausible that he was joined by his aristocratic supporters. Negotiations between

---

[93] Livy makes no mention at 23.30.6–7 of the various Bruttian diplomatic missions to Hannibal and Hanno, as he elaborates in the longer version in Book 24.

[94] Livy reports that a single deserter helped the Bruttians attack Croton, though we must imagine that other individuals deserted as well. According to the deserter, Croton was unoccupied (*vasta urbe*), echoing Livy's earlier description of the city (23.30.7): *urbe a defensoribus vasta*. This is surely an exaggeration, but may point to the fact that many citizens fled upon the approach of the Bruttians. In addition, the city had been in decline for many years and the statement may reflect its generally small population, which Livy (23.30.6) places at fewer than 2,000 citizens. For the decline of Croton in the third century, see below, p. 176.

the Crotoniates, the Bruttians and the Carthaginians broke down until the arrival of Locrian ambassadors, either at the urging of the Carthaginians or (as argued earlier) because the Locrians recognised the deadlock as a chance to exercise an independent foreign policy. The Crotoniates, faced with a siege, finally opted to evacuate their city and move to Locri (24.3.14–15). Now that I have established the narrative, I can analyse more carefully the factors that contributed to the Crotoniate surrender.

The political context of Croton at the time of the Second Punic War conforms to general patterns already observed. Rome exercised its control of the city through the loyalty of a local ruling class that was divided by political rivalry and aristocratic competition. Livy tries again to paint a picture of class conflict, with the upper class supporting Rome and the lower class yearning to side with Hannibal, a situation that (according to him) beset all cities in Italy.[95] Yet his own narrative undermines the generalisation, for in the very same passage Livy notes that there was no single plan or desire among the general Crotoniate population (*Crotone nec consilium unum inter populares nec voluntas erat*). Likewise, the aristocracy was more divided than Livy would allow. Aristomachus, the 'leader of the plebeians' (*principem plebis*) who led the pro-Carthaginian movement, was certainly an aristocrat.[96] Only Aristomachus is mentioned by name, but we must assume he represented a group of aristocrats who were more willing to side with Hannibal.[97] The aristocracy further fragmented at the appearance of a large and hostile Bruttian army outside the city walls, as some Crotoniates immediately went over to the Bruttians.[98] Aristomachus (and presumably his party) advised that Croton should surrender, but only to the Carthaginians.[99] Some aristocrats remained defiantly loyal

---

[95] Liv. 24.2.8: *unus velut morbus invaserat omnes Italiae civitates ut plebes ab optimatibus dissentirent, senatus Romanis faveret, plebs ad Poenos rem traheret* ('Just as one disease had invaded all the states of Italy, the *plebs* were dissenting from the best people: the senate favoured the Romans, the *plebs* dragged the state toward the Carthaginians').

[96] According to Livy, Aristomachus took refuge with the *optimates* in the citadel while the *plebs* supposedly welcomed the Bruttians within the city walls (24.2.11). The picture of the *optimates* defending the citadel and the *plebs* welcoming the Bruttians within the city walls is over-schematised. In fact, in his shorter version of the Crotoniate revolt, Livy (23.30.6–7) states that the Crotoniates who held the citadel were those who had escaped the initial Bruttian attack, with no reference to social class, implying that a cross-section of the population fled to the citadel. In any case, Aristomachus appears in the narrative in Book 24 as an aristocrat. He also features in negotiations between the Crotoniates and the Carthaginians, an unlikely role for a non-aristocrat (Liv. 24.2.10–1, 24.3.11–13). Finally, Aristomachus' name implies his elite status.

[97] Liv. 24.2.11.

[98] Livy (24.2.9) calls attention to an unnamed deserter who gave the Bruttians vital intelligence for storming the city.

[99] According to Livy's narrative (24.2.9, 24.2.11), Aristomachus advised that Croton should surrender, though to whom is unclear. But when the Bruttians stormed the city, Aristomachus fled

even though they were trapped in the citadel. In the end, some aristocrats went over to the Carthaginians, some chose to live with the Bruttians and still others sought refuge in Locri.[100] Overall, we should envision the Crotoniate upper class not as monolithic (as Livy emphasises), but rather as greatly divided in the face of an immediate external threat: some argued to remain loyal to Rome, some sought accommodation with the Bruttians and others looked to the Carthaginians for help.

These sorts of divisions long predated the Hannibalic War. Croton had a record of political instability and factional rivalry stretching back to the late fourth century, when the Crotoniates adopted a democratic government and exiled supporters of the previous government, presumably an oligarchy. Subsequently, a civil war erupted between the democratic and oligarchic partisans, during which Croton's elected generals, Menedemus and Paron, massacred the oligarchic exiles. Menedemus then established himself as tyrant of the city and established close relations with Agathocles, who in turn seized Croton.[101] Political factionalism and rivalry presumably continued, and it probably intensified at moments of crisis, such as during the Pyrrhic War. During this conflict Croton sided with Pyrrhus, after which a group of aristocrats plotted to hand the city over to the Roman consul P. Cornelius Rufinus. These Crotoniate aristocrats were also the 'friends' (τῶν ἐπιτηδείων) of Rufinus. Their plan failed, however, when opposing aristocrats found out about it and requested a garrison from Pyrrhus' general, Milo.[102] It is likely that members of each faction sought to further their own political standing through the patronage either of the Romans or of Pyrrhus, but in any case, this is an excellent example of the intersection of local political divisions and foreign policy decisions. After the war, Rome probably punished leading pro-Pyrrhic aristocrats while rewarding pro-Roman aristocrats, such as the aforementioned friends of Rufinus. The Romans would have relied on such aristocrats in order to secure their hegemony over Croton.

'as if he had been the author of handing over the city to the Carthaginians, not to the Bruttians' (*tamquam Poenis, non Bruttiis auctor urbis tradendae fuisset*).

[100] Livy (24.3.15) reports that the entire population went to Locri (*Locros omnis multitudo abeunt*), but this is probably an exaggeration; indeed, he admits that a lone Crotoniate had fled to the Bruttians, and we should assume that at least some others had joined themselves to the Bruttians rather than face the consequences. See Lomas 1993: 65 and above, pp. 167, 172 and n. 94.

[101] The civil war and massacre occurred sometime after about 317; Agathocles captured Croton in 295: Diod. Sic. 19.4.1–2, 19.10.2–4, 21.4.1; Mele 1993: 265–8; Muggia 1999b.

[102] Zon. 8.6: Ῥουφῖνος δὲ Λευκανοῖς καὶ Βρεττίοις ἐλυμήνατο. καὶ ἐπὶ Κρότωνα ὥρμησεν ἀποστάντα Ῥωμαίων, μεταπεμψαμένων αὐτὸν τῶν ἐπιτηδείων, φθασάντων δὲ τῶν λοιπῶν ἐπαγαγέσθαι παρὰ τοῦ Μίλωνος φρουράν, ἧς ἦρχε Νικόμαχος ('Rufinus injured the Lucanians and Bruttians, and then he set out against Croton, which had revolted from the Romans, since

It is also likely, as I have discussed before, that some aristocratic families 'lost out' when other aristocrats and their families either received Roman backing or simply benefited from the political settlement following Roman conquest or reconquest. Aristomachus and his party were more willing to throw off Roman rule and submit to the Carthaginians when Croton was faced with a Bruttian attack, suggesting that they were less loyal to Rome or perceived less benefit from maintaining the political status quo. It is possible that Aristomachus' party consisted of aristocrats whose families were punished by Rome after the Pyrrhic War or failed to receive Roman backing and therefore lost out politically. Or, perhaps Aristomachus and his followers simply saw an opportunity to advance their own political careers by seeking an alliance with the Carthaginians and thus overturning the current political arrangement. In any case, two important points emerge. First, the Crotoniate aristocracy was clearly divided, and the Carthaginians could hope to exploit these political divisions. Second, Aristomachus' party could not generate enough support, at least at first, to secure an alliance between Croton and the Carthaginians, so other factors weighed more heavily in the minds of the aristocracy. Thus, the Crotoniate aristocracy remained, for the moment, loyal to Rome.

It is clear that Greek–Bruttian hostility discouraged the Crotoniates from defecting earlier. Like other Greek states on the coast of Bruttium discussed in this chapter, Croton had a long and contentious relationship with the neighbouring Italic peoples. Diodorus reports that a Bruttian siege of Croton resulted in Syracusan military support for the Crotoniates, while Polybius speaks in general terms of hostility between the Italiote League and the surrounding 'barbarians'. Livy states that the Greek cities of Bruttium remained loyal to Rome because they saw that their enemies, the Bruttians, had gone over to Hannibal's side, and he later records that the besieged Crotoniates refused to surrender to the condition that a colony of Bruttians cohabit the city.[103] There is no mention of a Roman garrison in the city, or of Crotoniate hostages held in Rome.[104] Despite the presence of Carthaginian forces in Bruttium and repeated Roman military failures, Croton remained loyal to Rome until late 215 (or early 214).[105] This underscores the degree to which fear and hatred of the Bruttians must have bolstered the pro-Roman position.

---

his friends had sent for him. But the rest had acted first to bring in a garrison from Milo, that Nicomachus commanded').

[103] Diod. 19.3.3, 19.10.3; Polyb. 2.39.6–7; Liv. 24.3.10–15, 24.4.1.

[104] Lomas 1993: 64–5 states that Croton was garrisoned, but cites no evidence.

[105] For the chronology, see Appendix B.

But other considerations won out and, eventually, the Crotoniates decided to defect. Croton was not powerful in the late third century; indeed, the surrender of Croton in 215 (or 214) in many ways marks the end of the long decline of the once mighty city. Croton had formerly been one of the most formidable cities in Magna Graecia, at one time holding hegemony over the Italiote League. But Dionysius I defeated the league and dismantled it, occupied Croton for twelve years and turned over Crotoniate territory to the Locrians,[106] and when the Italiote League re-emerged in the middle of the fourth century, league hegemony had passed to Taras.[107] According to Diodorus (21.4), the city suffered greatly at the hands of Agathocles. Livy states that only 2,000 citizens inhabited Croton, the population having been greatly reduced as a result of the Pyrrhic War and 'many great disasters' (*multis magnisque cladibus adflictam*).[108] Croton also endured attacks from the Bruttians and Lucanians, and by about 280 the Crotoniates, along with other Italiote cities, had turned to Rome for protection against Osco-Italic pressure.[109] Archaeological evidence in general supports the picture of Croton as a city in decline through the fourth and third centuries. Results from field surveys conducted in the Crotoniate *chora* indicate that the number of rural sites, presumably farmhouses, declined between about 400 and 250, correlating to a gradual decline in the economy of Croton over the same period.[110] Despite the difficulty in identifying archaeological sites in Magna Graecia as either 'Greek' or 'native Italic', there is clear evidence that the territory controlled by Croton contracted greatly from the fifth to the third centuries.[111] The Carthaginians exploited Croton's declining fortunes, promising that a union with the Bruttians would restore the population and glory of the city.[112] The Crotoniates rejected this offer, however, indicating that appeals to their power and glory carried less weight in Croton than did their enmity towards the Bruttians.

Croton was clearly not a local hegemonic power, and one might suspect that such a relatively weak state would seek the protection of a more

---

[106] Polyb. 2.39.1–7; Diod. Sic. 14.91.1, 14.101.1, 14.102.1–3, 14.103.3–14.106.3; Strab. 6.1.10; Just. *Epit.* 20.5.1–3; Liv. 24.3.8; Dion. Hal. 20.7.2–3; see Caven 1990: 124–53.

[107] Strab. 6.3.4; Caven 1990: 139; Lomas 1993: 35; for a more complete discussion, see Chapter 5.

[108] Liv. 23.30.6, 24.3.1–2; Zonaras (8.6) suggests that Croton was completely destroyed during the Pyrrhic War, though this is clearly an exaggeration.

[109] Diod. Sic. 19.3.3, 19.10.3; Lomas 1993: 50–2.

[110] Carter and D'Annibale 1993: 93–9; although the results also indicate that the decline of Croton was less dramatic than indicated in the literary sources.

[111] Osanna 1992: 167–87. At one point, the territory of Croton stretched between the Fiume Nicà and the Fiume Tacina. However, by the end of the fourth century it had contracted to the area between the Fiume Neto and the Fiume Tacina. See Map 11.

[112] Liv. 24.3.11.

powerful state under the circumstances. In fact, when notified of the Bruttian siege, the Carthaginians figured that the Crotoniates would seek their aid.[113] But surrender to either the Carthaginians or the Bruttians was unacceptable to the majority of Crotoniates who had fled to the citadel, and, for the moment, the siege actually seemed to strengthen Crotoniate resolve.[114] Even after Aristomachus and his supporters gave in and fled to Hanno, the citadel remained in Crotoniate hands, indicating that many of the besieged preferred not to defect even if Rome's discredited authority opened the door for dissent. It was only the arrival of the Locrian delegation that finally swung the remaining Crotoniates against Rome. The Locrians provided them with a more acceptable option than surrendering either to Carthage or the Bruttians, or even remaining loyal to Rome.[115] While Livy claims that the whole remaining population transferred themselves to Locri, it is more likely that only the most staunchly anti-Bruttian Crotoniates, especially aristocrats, left their city. Some Crotoniates may also have stayed behind and cohabited with the new Bruttian colonists, as I have argued. In the end, Croton did ultimately submit to a more powerful state, but that state was a local hegemonic power (Locri) rather than Rome or Carthage.

The surrender of Croton plainly illustrates the importance of local conditions in shaping the foreign policies of cities in Italy. Hannibal's victory at Cannae and the presence of Carthaginian troops in Bruttium were not enough to compel Croton to surrender, nor does there appear to have been an overriding enmity towards Rome that drove the Crotoniates to the Carthaginian cause. The Crotoniates were also not motivated by an ideological closeness to Rome. Their ultimate policy decision was instead shaped by local hostilities and the promise of immediate protection by local hegemon Locri, a Greek city with which Croton shared cultural links. The surrender of Croton also reveals a number of Carthaginian miscalculations: Hanno (and perhaps Hannibal) figured that the Bruttians would compel Croton to seek Carthaginian help, and they later assumed the appeal of renewed Crotoniate power outweighed hostile feelings towards the Bruttians. In addition, these events point to the sorts of conflicts of interest created by Hannibal's strategy. It is clear that the Bruttians took it upon themselves to attack Croton, since they were frustrated from failing to profit from their alliance with Hannibal.[116] Livy's narrative (24.3.7) clearly implies that the Bruttians expected to profit, and it has already

---

[113] Liv. 24.2.6–7.   [114] Consider the defiant Crotoniate statements: Liv. 24.3.12.
[115] On this point, see also Kukofka 1990: 21–2.   [116] Liv. 24.2.1–4.

been shown that Hannibal dangled the promise of local hegemony to attract allies in Italy. Meanwhile, the Carthaginians preferred that the Bruttians not sack Croton, but they were forced to promote a compromise settlement that would ideally not frustrate their Bruttian allies any further. Lastly, the failure of the Bruttians to capture Croton compelled the Carthaginians to provide military assistance, lest Hannibal appear incapable of following through as an ally. Hannibal could ill afford to divert manpower either to protect his new allies from Roman reprisal or to bail them out from their own failed military initiatives.[117]

HANNIBAL'S INCOMPLETE SUCCESS: RHEGION

Hannibal's string of successes in Bruttium ended with Carthaginian attempts to capture Rhegion, for Hannibal and his allies were never able to capture this city or lure it into alliance with Carthage. Rhegion had a long history of loyalty to Rome, so it may not seem surprising that it remained faithful throughout the Hannibalic War. The failure of the Hannibalic strategy in Rhegion is interesting, though, because Rhegion decided not to defect despite facing many of the same conditions that confronted the other Greek cities in Bruttium: for example, aristocratic factionalism that could be manipulated by Carthaginian appeals, the erosion of Roman credibility following Cannae, increased Carthaginian military pressure and even Hannibal's self-promotion as a Hellenistic liberator through the use of 'freedom propaganda'. Once again, the ultimate failure of Hannibal to capture Rhegion lies to a great degree in the local diplomatic matrix, especially the network of long-standing local rivalries and mutual hostilities.

The same factors that promoted loyalty in other cities in Bruttium operated as well in Rhegion. Rome obviously managed to secure the loyalty of at least some of the local elite. Although a detailed description of Rhegian politics during or immediately preceding the Hannibalic War is lacking, the situation can be inferred from the events in the first thirty years of the third century. In 282 the Rhegians requested a Roman garrison as protection against neighbouring Lucanians and Bruttians, but also against the Tarentines. The Romans responded by garrisoning the city with Campanian mercenaries under the command of Decius Vibellius (the so-called *legio Campana*) who proceeded to take over the city and massacre

---

[117] Compare Hannibal's assistance to the Capuans, after their botched attempt to ambush the Cumaeans; see Chapter 3, pp. 124–5.

its inhabitants.[118] Dio and Livy state specifically that this was not a general massacre but instead aimed at the leading citizens.[119] There is some evidence that local aristocrats were planning to turn the city over to Pyrrhus when Decius ordered the massacre, though any pro-Pyrrhic movement may have arisen after the *legio Campana* seized the city. The harsh punishment of certain Rhegian families suggests that the pro-Pyrrhic movement had gained significant traction.[120] In any case, literary accounts agree that when Rome recaptured Rhegion, the Campanian garrison was executed, and the city was restored to the surviving Rhegians.[121] It is likely that this 'restoration' involved placing pro-Roman families in charge of the city or re-establishing previously loyal families; if any pro-Pyrrhic families had not been executed by Decius Vibellius, the Romans would probably have punished them during this settlement, especially if they perceived that the pro-Pyrrhic plot had posed a serious risk. Roman restoration (or rewards) may have created a strong sense of obligation on the part of the surviving Rhegian elite, which may have contributed to the loyalty of their descendants during the Second Punic War, assuming that these same families remained prominent.

Hostility towards the Bruttians would also have bolstered the loyalty of the Rhegians, most importantly the loyalty among the pro-Roman elite. As we have seen in the discussions of Locri and Croton, anti-Italic

[118] Polyb. 1.7.6–8; Diod. Sic. 22.1.2–3; Dion. Hal. 20.4.1–8; Liv. 28.28.1–3, 31.31.6, *Per.* 12; Cass. Dio 9.40.7–11; App. *Sam.* 9.1; Strab. 6.1.6. It is difficult to establish the date of the garrison's installation because of the contradictory nature of the sources. The ancient sources agree that the garrison seized the city when Pyrrhus was in Italy. Most of the ancient sources state that the garrison was installed because the Rhegians wanted protection against Pyrrhus. However, Dionysius states that the garrison was installed in 282 to protect the Rhegians against the Lucanians, the Bruttians and the Tarentines. This is plausible, since Thurii had requested a Roman garrison for the same reason (App. *Sam.* 7.1–2; Liv. *Per.* 12). The statement is also consistent with Taras' history of employing Italic allies to exert hegemony over Italiote cities (see Chapter 5, pp. 196–7). The best reconciliation of the sources is to accept Dionysius' reference and place the installation of the garrison in 282 (the date is arrived at because Dionysius mentions the consul's name as C. Fabricius; see Broughton 1951–2: 1.189). The garrison then seized Rhegion after Pyrrhus had arrived in Italy and the Romans were preoccupied (perhaps after the battle of Heraclea, *c.* 280). See Beloch 1926: 461; Toynbee 1965: 1.100–2; De Sanctis 1956–69: 11.379; Walbank 1970: 1.52–3; Oakley 1997–2005: 1V.130.

[119] Cass. Dio 9.40.7; Liv. 28.28.2; see also Dion. Hal. 20.4.3.

[120] Cass. Dio 9.40.9–10; Dion. Hal. 20.4.4–6; both Dio and Dionysius claim that Decius had forged documents to show that the Rhegians were promising to turn over the city to Pyrrhus. This may reflect, however, pro-Roman bias, and there may have been a movement by the Rhegians to ally with Pyrrhus. Lomas 1993: 52–3 argues that the Campanian garrison was trying to forestall a Rhegian alliance with Pyrrhus, which triggered the garrison's seizure of Rhegion. However, Polybius (1.7.6) states that it was the example of the Mamertines that triggered the revolt of the *legio Campana*, not dissent among the Rhegians. Even if there were pro-Pyrrhic aristocrats, it is likely that they surfaced *after* the Campanians seized the city.

[121] Polyb. 1.7.9–13; Dion. Hal. 20.5.1–5; App. *Sam.* 9.3; Liv. 28.28.3, 31.31.6–7.

sentiment in Rhegion long predated Hannibal's invasion of Italy. Diodorus Siculus (21.52.1–5) records that, during the fifth century, a contingent of 'Iapygians' defeated the Rhegians in a pitched battle near Taras then pursued the fleeing Greeks to Rhegion and captured the city.[122] Moving closer to the period examined in this book, Rhegion requested a Roman garrison in 282 specifically out of fear of the Bruttians and Lucanians.[123] The revolt of the Campanian garrison may also be seen within the context of Greek and Italic hostility. The garrison comprised Campanian and Sidicinian mercenaries, and their commander, Decius Vibellius, had an Oscan name.[124] The quartering of Oscan-Italic troops in the city, especially considering the threat posed by the Bruttians, may have encouraged the plotters to reject the garrison and seek the assistance of Pyrrhus, a fellow Greek. At any rate, the Rhegians' experience with the Campanian garrison was far from positive, and the occupation by Oscan-speakers and the massacre of Rhegian citizens must have contributed to anti-Italic feelings. There is clear evidence for Rhegian–Bruttian hostility during the Second Punic War, as Livy (24.1.1–2) states that Greek fear and hatred of the Bruttians encouraged loyalty to Rome and discouraged the Greeks in Bruttium, including the Rhegians, from allying with Hannibal. The hostility between Rhegians and Bruttians emerged later in the Hannibalic War, when the Rhegians requested Roman troops as protection against the Bruttians, and so that they could plunder Bruttian territory.[125] By gaining the Bruttians as allies, Hannibal certainly strengthened the Rhegians' loyalty to Rome, especially from among the pro-Roman aristocracy.

Rome was able to strengthen Rhegian resolve more directly by placing a garrison in the city. It is worth noting, however, that a Roman garrison did not arrive in Rhegion until 215, only *after* the Rhegians repelled an initial assault by Hannibalic forces, at least according to Livy's chronology.[126] Livy synchronises the arrival of the Roman garrison with the fall of Locri, and his narrative implies that these troops, sent from Sicily by

[122] See Ciaceri 1928–40: II.280–4; Lomas 1993: 30–2.
[123] Dion. Hal. 20.4.1–2.
[124] Dion. Hal. 20.4.6 states explicitly that he was a Campanian (that is, from Capua), and Capua had been Oscanised by the time of the Pyrrhic War (Frederiksen 1984: 137–40). It might be tempting to see the treachery and cruelty of Decius Vibellius and the *legio campana* as fitting a literary trope of Campanian duplicity, born of Roman bitterness over the Capuan revolt in the Second Punic War and retrojected onto previous events. Yet Polybius, writing probably before the Campanian tradition was fully developed, mentions Decius by name. Even if we allow for some literary exaggeration, there appears to be a significant historical core to the seizure of Rhegion at the hands of the *legio campana*. For the possibility that Decius Vibellius is an Oscan name, see Schulze 1966: 519 n. 5.
[125] Liv. 26.50.18, 27.12.4–6.   [126] Liv. 23.51.10–12, 24.1.2, 24.1.9–13, 24.2.1.

the praetor Appius Claudius, were initially sent to relieve the Roman garrison at Locri.[127] If this is an accurate report, then these troops came to garrison Rhegion only as a secondary mission, though their arrival was probably instrumental in maintaining Rhegian loyalty in 215.[128] It is not clear if the Romans maintained the Rhegion garrison throughout the war, though events later in the Second Punic War suggest that they did not: after Hannibal's failed march on Rome in 211, he marched swiftly to Rhegion and nearly took the city by surprise, yet there is no mention of a Roman garrison's protecting the city.[129] Also, references to the mercenaries sent by Laevinus to Rhegion (210–209), apparently at the request of the Rhegians, imply that this was the only Roman force quartered in the city.[130] The proximity of this garrison's arrival to Hannibal's march on Rhegion suggests that Laevinus sent a garrison to Rhegion, at least in part, as a response to the lack of a Roman presence the previous year.[131] Thus, Rhegion quartered a Roman garrison beginning only in 215, and (probably) just intermittently thereafter. Initial Rhegian loyalty was not, therefore, compelled by an overt Roman military presence within the city walls. The fact that Rome felt the need neither to garrison Rhegion at the outbreak of hostilities, nor to hold Rhegian hostages, and the fact that the Rhegians withstood Hannibalic forces despite Roman failure in the early stages of the war, both underscore the degree to which Rhegian loyalty was the result of factors such as anti-Bruttian hostility rather than direct Roman military intervention.[132]

This is not to say that support for Rome would have been universal, and presumably there were forces at play undermining Rhegian loyalty. It is unlikely, for example, that the Rhegian ruling elite was undivided in its loyalty. Indeed, we have observed political rivalry in every allied city for which there remains an account of its internal politics, and while there are no detailed descriptions of Rhegian politics during the late third century,

---

[127] Lomas 1993: 65 claims, however, that Locri, Croton and Rhegion were all garrisoned by the time of the events described by Livy (24.13).

[128] Livy (24.1.12–13) explicitly links the arrival of Roman troops with the abandonment of the Carthaginian attack on Rhegion.

[129] Polyb. 9.7.10; Liv. 26.12.1–2.　　[130] Liv. 26.40.16–17, 27.12.4–6.

[131] It is possible, however, that after the arrival of the initial Roman garrison, Rome maintained a small force in Rhegion, and that the force sent by Laevinus bolstered the Roman military presence in response both to Hannibal's attack and to Rhegian requests for troops to attack the Bruttians. However, no Roman forces are mentioned in addition to the mercenaries.

[132] Rhegian resistance is all the more striking since it occurred after the battle of Cannae. Without a Roman garrison present, the Rhegians appear to have both the reason and the opportunity to revolt. Thus, traditional enmity towards the Bruttians was important in convincing the Rhegians to remain loyal to Rome.

we have already noted that there is some evidence that the Rhegian aristocracy was politically divided during the Pyrrhic War. Lomas (1993: 67–8) argues that the outstanding loyalty of Rhegion during the Second Punic War should be explained by Rhegion's unusual misfortune a half-century earlier, because the Campanian occupation of Rhegion, the massacre of pro-Pyrrhic aristocrats by Decius Vibellius and the subsequent recapture of the city by Rome in 270 offered Rome the chance to establish a firmly pro-Roman government in Rhegion. This is plausible, and indeed I have argued that Rome's restoration of the Rhegian aristocracy would have engendered strong loyalty on the part of those Rhegians who benefited – including perhaps even a majority of the surviving aristocratic families. It is hard to imagine, however, that the Campanian occupation did not yield at least some anti-Roman sentiment, especially since the Roman senate was responsible for sending the garrison to begin with. It is very likely that some aristocrats in Rhegion at the time of the Second Punic War were less enamoured with Roman rule, perhaps because their families were punished by Rome in 270, or simply because they were not in power and so were dissatisfied with the political status quo.

Roman military credibility must have been greatly undermined in the eyes of the Rhegians, and not simply because Rome had suffered a humiliating defeat in the field against Hannibal. Closer to home, the Rhegians witnessed Rome's inability to maintain control of other Greek cities, especially Roman-garrisoned Locri. As I pointed out above, the Romans had not prevented the Bruttians and Carthaginians from assaulting Rhegion, and although Appius Claudius' arrival drove off the attackers, at least some Rhegians must have questioned Rome's ability to provide adequate protection in the future.

Lastly, Hannibal's posture as a Hellenistic liberator and his promises of freedom may have been particularly attractive to the Rhegians. Rhegion displayed a distinctly Hellenic character long after the Hannibalic War. Strabo (6.1.2) implies that in his own day (νυνί), Rhegion was the only Greek city remaining in Bruttium, although νυνί cannot be taken too literally as a chronological indicator, since Strabo's 'present' can refer to the period spanning the whole first century BC and early first century AD.[133] In addition, is not clear on which sources Strabo is drawing in this description

---

[133] Strab. 6.1.2: νυνὶ δὲ πλὴν Τάραντος καὶ Ῥηγίου καὶ Νεαπόλεως ἐκβεβαρβαρῶσθαι συμβέβηκεν ἅπαντα ('but now all [of Magna Graecia] has come to be barbarised except for Taras, Rhegion and Naples'). Lomas (1995b: 113): '[At Rhegion] religious and euergetic documents were deliberately couched in terms drawn from the city's Greek past.' For Strabo's use of the 'present': Pothecary 1997; Clarke 1999: 281–93.

of Rhegion.[134] Still, his characterisation is consistent with the epigraphic record, which, as Lomas (1995b: esp. 111–13) argues, clearly indicates the survival of Greek language and institutions into the early Imperial era. If so, then Rhegion's Hellenic character would have been intact during the Second Punic War, and promises of ἐλευθερία and αὐτονομία might be expected to have found an approving audience.

It is surprising, therefore, that we do not hear about any anti-Roman agitation in Rhegion. This suggests that, on the whole, the aristocracy was strongly pro-Roman even if some aristocrats felt less attachment to Rome. The remarkable resolve of the Rhegians, considering that all the other Greek cities in Bruttium rebelled, implies circumstances specific to Rhegion promoted its loyalty. The deciding factor in Rhegion's loyalty may have been local diplomatic rivalries and animosities in addition to the traditional Greek–Bruttian hostility that has already been discussed. In particular, Rhegion and Locri maintained a long-standing rivalry over local hegemony.[135] The territories of the two cities abutted along the Halex River, so attempts at territorial expansion by Locri, at least to the south and west, would have come at the expense of Rhegion.[136] As rivals, the two cities tended to fall on opposite sides of a number of conflicts dating to the fifth century. In 427–426, Syracuse and Leontini were at war, and the Locrians sided with Syracuse while the Rhegians sided with the Leontinians (Thuc. 3.86.2).[137] Dionysius I of Syracuse appears to have manipulated the rivalry between Locri and Rhegion: he initially sought an alliance with the Rhegians since he feared that the Carthaginians could use both Rhegion's military and its strategic location against his interests in Sicily; he thus sent an embassy to Rhegion offering a marriage alliance that he promised would bring Rhegion territorial expansion,[138] but when

---

[134] Strabo mentions Apollodorus in the next section (6.1.3), where he discusses the interior peoples (the Lucanians) who lived around Croton and Thurii, but he also appears to have used Timaeus as a source for Rhegion, especially for stories associated with its foundation (Musti 1988: 37–40).

[135] Costamagna and Sabbione 1990: 37.

[136] Strab. 6.1.9. The Halex has been identified with the modern rivers Amendolea, Melito or Galati: Osanna 1992: 214; Osanna prefers the Galati because its geography conforms to Strabo's description and on toponymic grounds (the site was called Alica in the Middle Ages). Ciaceri 1928–40: II.190–4 also argues that the nature of the rivalry between Rhegion and Locri was territorial and hegemonical, as the two cities struggled for control of Hipponion and Medma. Strabo (6.1.6) implies the loss of territory when stating that Rhegion was once a powerful city with many dependencies in the area.

[137] There may have been an additional cultural factor, as Rhegion and Leontini were both Chalcidian colonies. Thucydides (3.86.3) reports that the Leontinians and their allies – which presumably included the Rhegians – appealed to the Athenians for help, citing an old alliance and the fact that they were all Ionian, indicating another potential bond, whether 'real' or constructed.

[138] Diod. Sic. 14.44.3–4.

the Rhegians refused his alliance, Dionysius I immediately sought and gained an alliance with Locri.[139] He then used Locri as a base of operations against the Rhegians, ultimately capturing Rhegion, ruling it for twelve years and giving the Locrians a portion of the territory that he captured in Bruttium.[140] The campaign suggests that Dionysius made promises of territory to the Locrians similar to those which he had made to the Rhegians. In fact, Dionysius of Halicarnassus (20.7.2–3) records that the Locrians invited Dionysius I into Italy because of their local squabble with the Rhegians. Later, Locri and Rhegion were again in opposing camps during the reign of Dionysius II. The Syracusan tyrant maintained a garrison in Rhegion; after he was driven from Syracuse he sought refuge in Locri, while anti-Dionysian forces drove the garrison from Rhegion and restored Rhegian independence.[141] The rivalry probably played a role in the Pyrrhic War: the Rhegians began the Pyrrhic War on the side of the Romans, and although there eventually was a plot to turn the city over to Pyrrhus, he never gained control of the city;[142] meanwhile, Locri welcomed Pyrrhus, at least at the beginning of the war.[143] These events show a consistent pattern in which Rhegion and Locri tended to oppose each other regardless of the conflict, suggesting some sort of ongoing interstate rivalry between the two.

Locri was not the only Greek city with which Rhegion had an enduring rivalry. Rhegion was strategically located overlooking the Straits of Messina and lay only a few miles away from Sicily; as such it often found itself deeply involved in Sicilian affairs. From the fifth century onwards, Rhegion and Syracuse, the most powerful Sicilian city, were more often than not on opposing sides in various conflicts.[144] As mentioned above, Thucydides (3.86) records that Rhegion sided with Leontini in the war between Syracuse and Leontini. Dionysius I and the Rhegians contested each other in a protracted struggle that resulted in the destruction of Rhegion and the establishment of a 'Syracusan empire' on the Italian

[139] Diod. Sic. 14.44.6–7, 14.106.1, 14.107.2–5.
[140] Diod. Sic. 14.100.1–2, 14.106.3, 14.107.2–5, 14.111.1–14.113.1; Dion. Hal. 20.7.3.
[141] Diod. Sic. 16.17.1–2, 16.18.1, 16.45.9; Just. *Epit.* 21.2.1–9. Dionysius ultimately was driven from Locri; however, the important point is that he was initially welcomed by the Locrians.
[142] For the failed plot to turn Rhegion over to Pyrrhus, which probably arose only after Rome garrisoned the city with the infamous *legio campana*, see above pp. 178–9. Pyrrhus tried to capture the city but failed: App. *Sam.* 21.1; Zon. 8.6.
[143] Just. *Epit.* 18.1.9.
[144] Lomas 1993: 68: '[Rhegion] had enjoyed a closer diplomatic relationship with Sicily, owing to its geographical situation, than with most other areas of Magna Graecia.' Lomas' wording is ambiguous, and it was in fact the case that Rhegion's diplomatic relationships with Sicilian cities were not always enjoyable.

peninsula.[145] Dionysius II refounded Rhegion in honour of his father but garrisoned the city; the Rhegians undoubtedly sided with Dion in his struggle with Dionysius II, and two Syracusans, Leptines and Callippus, finally liberated Rhegion by ejecting Dionysius II's garrison.[146] This should not be seen as a softening of Rhegion's relationship with Syracuse so much as Sicilian domination of Rhegion's affairs and the Rhegians' preference for any Sicilian leadership other than that of Dionysus II. Around 317, when the Syracusans were under the oligarchic rule of the Six Hundred, Syracuse besieged Rhegion; the Rhegians called on Agathocles, who not only successfully relieved the siege but also helped to topple the Syracusan oligarchy.[147]

It is likely that the Rhegion–Locri and Rhegion–Syracuse rivalries helped to dissuade the Rhegians from defecting during the Second Punic War. By the time the combined Bruttian and Carthaginian forces had besieged Rhegion, Locri had already gone over to Hannibal's side. The people of Rhegion had long clashed with the Locrians over territory in the toe of Bruttium, and they must have considered that an effective joint Bruttian and Locrian bloc would pose a serious threat to their independence, particularly in light of their additional mistrust of the Bruttians. Also, by the fall of 215, Syracuse had either switched allegiances or was leaning in that direction under Hieronymus,[148] and both Polybius' (7.4.1–9) and Livy's accounts (24.6.7–9) of the Syracusan revolt clearly indicate that Hieronymus expected territorial gain in return for an alliance with Hannibal. Thus, before the end of the year (215), all of the Bruttians

---

[145] Diod. Sic. 14.100.1–2, 14.106.3, 14.107.2–5, 14.111.1–14.113.1; Dion. Hal. 20.7.3; see Caven 1990: 127–46, for a reconstruction of the diplomatic manoeuvring and warfare between Rhegion and Dionysius, *c.* 395–386.

[146] Diod. Sic. 16.17.1–2, 16.18.1, 16.45.9; Just. *Epit.* 21.2.1–9; see Caven 1990: 213–21, for a reconstruction of Dionysius II's reign.

[147] Diod. Sic. 19.4.2–3.

[148] Polyb. 7.2.1–8.9 and Liv. 24.4.1–7.9 both provide narratives for the death of Hiero, the accession of Hieronymus and the treaty between Hannibal and Syracuse, but it is hard to establish during which months these events occurred. De Sanctis 1956–69: III.2.317–22 has worked out the chronology such that Hiero died in the spring or summer of 215, and Hieronymus was assassinated in the summer of 214. Polybius (7.2.1–2) implies that Hieronymus sent envoys to Hannibal soon after the death of Hiero. Meanwhile, at some point the Romans sent envoys to renew their previous treaty with Syracuse. According to Polybius (7.3.1–4), Hieronymus had yet to sign a treaty with Hannibal when the Roman envoys arrived, though Carthaginian ambassadors were already present in Syracuse who had informed Hieronymus of recent Roman military defeats. According to Livy (24.6.1–7), the Syracusans and Hannibal had already agreed to terms by the time the Roman envoys arrived on the scene. In either case, both narratives suggest that Hieronymus had been advised to treat with Hannibal relatively early in his short reign. If we assume an early death for Hiero (spring 215), it is possible that Syracuse had sided with Hannibal around the same time or soon after Locri had surrendered.

and also the two most powerful local Greek hegemonic powers – both long-time rivals of Rhegion – had sided with Hannibal. These new allies of Hannibal saw the Carthaginians as a means to territorial expansion, which threatened Rhegian interests. In this context it makes sense that the ruling aristocracy of Rhegion calculated that the Romans, despite their recent setbacks, still offered a better deal than the Carthaginians.

Rhegion was not immune to political rivalries and divided loyalty, but Rome was able to maintain the loyalty of enough of the local elite to prevent defection. When Hannibal gained the Bruttians as allies, he initially strengthened the resolve of the Greek cities in Bruttium to stay loyal to Rome. Hannibal was able to overcome the anti-Bruttian sentiment in Croton, Locri and other smaller Greek communities in western Magna Graecia, yet his strategy could not entirely neutralise the effects of local rivalries on the decision-making of local aristocracies. The Rhegians in particular preferred an alliance to Rome as a counter-weight against Bruttian, Syracusan or Locrian aggression. The reluctance of Rhegion to revolt when Locri, Syracuse and Croton revolted bought Rome time to garrison (or further garrison) the city. The combination of long-term conditions (local rivalries) and short-term factors (Rome's military response) proved too much for Hannibal's strategy to overcome, and Rhegion would remain staunchly loyal to Rome for the duration of the war.

CONCLUSION

Hannibal probably expected to find the communities of south-western Italy, a region where Pyrrhus had had significant success two generations before, ready to throw off their alliances with Rome, and in fact he made significant diplomatic gains in this region in the first couple of years of the war. Most of the Bruttians came over to his side rather quickly, perhaps even in the immediate wake of Cannae, and in the course of the following year nearly every Greek city along the coast of Bruttium had also been convinced to defect. Yet the Hannibalic strategy was not an unqualified success in the Bruttian theatre, even at the high-water mark of the Carthaginian war effort. Hannibal was compelled to divert a part of his army and eventually some of the few reinforcements that he would receive from Carthage, under the command of Hanno, in order to win over recalcitrant Bruttian cities (Petelia and Consentia) and to hasten the initial defection of the Greek cities. The fact that he had to bring to bear direct military pressure perhaps underscores the surprising reluctance of the citizens of these cities (or at least of their ruling classes) to revolt.

The explanation for their relative loyalty is to be located, at least in part, in the same factors that have been discussed in the previous two chapters. On one level, Roman rule relied on the loyalty of a critical mass of the local ruling elite; in those cities that exhibited the most remarkable loyalty – Petelia and Rhegion – there is at least some evidence that the local aristocracy had established closer ties to Rome through processes that were set in motion in the times of the Pyrrhic War if not earlier. On another level, Hannibal's difficulties in winning over these cities relate to the nature of the regional interstate system: the region was subject to deep-rooted ethnic tensions – Greek against Bruttian – that were also cross-cut by rivalries within these groups. There is indirect indication of regular conflict among the Bruttians, which probably slowed Hannibal's acquisition of Petelia. There is much stronger evidence for long-standing interstate rivalry between Rhegion and Locri, and Rhegion and Syracuse. The Carthaginians were able to overcome this complex system in some cases: thus, Locri and Croton eventually set aside their mistrust of the Bruttians enough to be willing to ally with the Carthaginians. But for the people of Rhegion, the union of the Carthaginians with both the hated Bruttians and two local rival states (Locri and Syracuse) with histories of aggression and hegemonic ambition proved to be a major obstacle. Once again, Hannibal's success in winning over some new allies – in this case the Bruttians and some Greek cities, mainly Locri – undermined his efforts and limited his strategy in winning over other states.

CHAPTER 5

Southern Lucania and eastern Magna Graecia

INTRODUCTION

For the last regional case study I will focus on 'eastern Magna Graecia', the band of Greek cities stretching along the coast of the Gulf of Taranto from Taras to Thurii. This strip equates more or less to the southern portion of Lucania, though Taras lay within the confines of Messapia.[1] Taras was the most powerful city in the region, and it would become one of the most important cities to ally with Hannibal during the Second Punic War, its defection setting in motion a string of revolts by other Greek cities – and perhaps also some Lucanian communities (see Appendix D). Scholars have tended to see the defection of these eastern Italiote cities in terms of a broader, even global phenomenon: an expression of Hellenic identity and an effort by proud Greeks to recapture former glory.[2] Yet Taras, Thurii, Metapontion and Heraclea defected two years after Locri and Croton, while Rhegion and Naples never revolted. The previous chapter discussed the bitter rivalry between Locri and Rhegion, and we will see later in this chapter that Taras and Thurii also harboured a long-standing rivalry.[3] Livy (25.15.7) states explicitly that the Thurians did not revolt out of a common cause with the Tarentines or because of cultural ties with the people of Metapontion.[4] Greek fraternity does not appear, therefore, to explain adequately why only some of these cities revolted, nor why they revolted when they did.

---

[1] Strabo (6.1.4, 6.1.15, 6.3.1) states that Thurii to the west and Metapontion to the east bounded the southern coast of Lucania, while Taras lay in Messapia. Metapontion also later marked the border between Augustus' *Regio* III (Bruttium and Lucania) and *Regio* II (Apulia and Calabria): Plin. *HN* 97–9. Although Taras clearly lay to the east of Lucania, the city was actively involved in both Messapic and Lucanian affairs.

[2] For example, see Hallward 1930b: 76–7; De Sanctis 1956–69: III.2.264–6; Caven 1980: 165–6.

[3] For Locri and Rhegion, see Chapter 4, pp. 183–4; for Thurii and Taras, see below pp. 225–7. The revolt of the southern Greeks should not indicate the unified activity of a reconstituted Italiote League under Tarentine hegemony: Chapter 4, p. 160; contra Lomas 1993: 60–1.

[4] In addition, Appian (*Hann.* 35) states that Heraclea revolted out of fear, and he implies that it was, at least in part, fear of Taras and Metapontion.

188

It is unnecessary to look for global explanations for the Tarentine revolt. Taras had a long history as a regional hegemonic power (like Capua, Arpi and Locri), it had frequently come into conflict with Rome and it had employed numerous foreign *condottieri* to further Tarentine interests. Overall, Taras should have been particularly inclined to seek an alliance with Hannibal and thus defect from Rome. Rather, the interesting feature of Taras' revolt is the length of time it took before the Tarentines openly sided with Hannibal. Indeed, by the time Hannibal gained control of the city (but not its citadel), the Romans had already begun to recover, and within two years of the Tarentine revolt, Capua was recaptured and the tide of the war had clearly turned in Rome's favour.

As stated above, the revolt of Taras set off a domino effect of defections, including Metapontion and Heraclea, two cities that historically fell under the Tarentine sway. This recalls a dynamic that was discussed in previous chapters, where a powerful, rebellious state encouraged, compelled or otherwise convinced nearby smaller states to follow suit. More interesting, however, is that Thurii, a long-time and bitter rival of Taras, also revolted. The analysis in Chapters 2 to 4 has shown that interstate rivalry could have a powerful influence on a state's decision to revolt, and we might expect the Thurians to have responded to the recent alliance between Taras and Hannibal by remaining faithful to Rome. As we will see, however, in the case of Thurii short-term and immediate factors outweighed the effects of such interstate rivalry. Thus, this chapter continues to look at the impact of local conditions on Hannibal's strategy and further develops the theme of the significance of hegemonic ambitions and regional interstate rivalry. Our final case study shows how specific political and military factors could overcome longer-term patterns of interstate behaviour, and consequently this reveals the limits of rivalry.

TARAS' TENUOUS LOYALTY, 216–213

Rebellions failed to materialise among the Greek cities of eastern Magna Graecia in the immediate aftermath of Hannibal's crushing victory at Cannae. Despite Polybius' (3.118.3) and Livy's (22.61.12) statements that Taras defected directly after the battle, it did not revolt until late in the winter of 213/12,[5] when a party of aristocrats led by Philomenus and Nico arranged to turn the city over to Hannibal.[6] This reluctance to revolt is

---

[5] See Appendix C.

[6] Livy (25.8.2–3) says that a total of thirteen young aristocrats formed the core of the anti-Roman party; he later mentions unspecified leaders of Taras (*principibus Tarentinis*) with whom Hannibal

remarkable considering the likelihood of particularly strong anti-Roman sentiment among the Tarentine ruling elite.

Accounts of the Tarentine revolt reveal that the local aristocracy was deeply divided; in light of the previous chapters, this is unsurprising. Yet the specific situation in Taras deserves further discussion. Some Tarentine aristocrats were more firmly attached to Rome. When the city fell to Hannibal, a group of Tarentines who, according to Polybius, 'held goodwill towards the Romans' retreated to the citadel, which was controlled by a Roman garrison.[7] His narrative makes clear that these individuals sought refuge in the citadel only after they understood that Hannibal and the anti-Roman party had seized power. Thus, the retreat to Roman protection was a calculated manoeuvre, rather than a hasty decision made in the midst of confusion. In 208, after Rome had recovered Taras, the senate voted to restore any Tarentine citizens (presumably from among the elites) who had been banished by Hannibal;[8] they would not have been exiled unless they exhibited pro-Roman behaviour during Hannibal's control of the city. Some Tarentines probably had very close relations with members of the Roman aristocracy, though the evidence is less clear.[9]

---

conferred concerning the blockade of the citadel (Liv. 25.11.12). The names of at most six of the anti-Roman aristocrats are known: both Livy and Polybius (8.24.4, 8.24.11–13) identify Philomenus and Nico as the main architects of the revolt; Polybius also names a certain Tragiscus as a prominent conspirator (for example 8.27.3); Livy adds Democrates (26.39.15). Appian (*Hann.* 32) and Frontinus (*Str.* 3.3.6) call the architect of the revolt Cononeus. Perhaps Cononeus was another conspirator not mentioned by name in the Livian or Polybian account, though the name may simply be a mistake. Livy (26.39.15) refers to Nico Perco as a member of the conspiracy; it is not clear if he is a separate individual from the Nico who led the conspiracy.

[7] Polyb. 8.31.3: ὅσοι μὲν οὖν τῶν Ταραντίνων προκατείχοντο τῇ πρὸς τοὺς Ῥωμαίους εὐνοίᾳ, γνόντες ἀπεχώρουν εἰς τὴν ἄκραν ('When they knew [what had happened], those of the Tarentines who held goodwill towards the Romans withdrew to the citadel'); see also Liv. 25.10.7; App. *Hann.* 33.

[8] Liv. 27.35.3–4.

[9] The Via Appia connected Beneventum, Taras and Brundisium, so presumably Romans passed through Taras with some frequency on this busy road: see Wiseman 1971: 29–30. Some details in the account of the revolt of Taras imply that Roman magistrates could act as patrons for Tarentine aristocrats. Philemenus apparently made a habit of presenting wild game to the Roman garrison commander. The act was an attempt to win over the confidence and favour of the garrison commander but also reveals a certain intimacy between the magistrate and the local aristocracy (Polyb. 8.25.7–8; Liv. 25.8.10). According to Polybius (8.27.4–6), Livius and his officers enjoyed drunken jests with some of the conspirators, also suggesting that amicable interaction between the magistrate and the local aristocracy was not uncommon. Livius also became drunk at an unspecified public celebration (Polyb. 8.25.11, 8.27.1–7). Such events would have provided excellent forums for public displays of loyalty by the local elite and patronage by the Roman magistrate. Caution should be exercised with these episodes, however, since they may also be moralising tales that link Livius' administrative incompetence with his immoderate behaviour. There was also an ancient historiographic tradition of associating Taras with 'Greek vice', especially drunkenness: Barnes 2005. Still, the stories may contain a kernel of truth, as it is not improbable that the Roman commander, Livius, had cordial, if not very close, relations with select Tarentine aristocrats.

The surviving evidence also indicates, however, that a portion of the elite was much more antagonistic towards the Roman cause, including, obviously, the party of Philomenus and Nico. We also learn that the two ringleaders were associated either by friendship or family connection to an unknown number of aristocrats who had been taken as hostages to Rome in order to ensure Taras' loyalty.[10] Presumably these hostages were seized in the early stages of the war from families whose loyalty the Romans questioned, suggesting that a dangerously powerful anti-Roman movement was already suspected, if not in place, at the start of the war.[11] Also, Rome had garrisoned Taras at the time of the Gallic War in 225, and the garrison was probably still in place at the outbreak of the war with Hannibal.[12] Both actions point to Roman suspicion of Tarentine loyalty, which in turn may indicate strong anti-Roman sentiment. Nico's party successfully curried political favour with their fellow Tarentines, building up their following before allowing Hannibal to enter the city; their fruitful canvassing shows that many Tarentines felt at most an ambivalence to Rome and could be swayed to the anti-Roman position.[13] Indeed, once Hannibal held the city, his Tarentine supporters went door-to-door to encourage their fellow citizens, while Hannibal addressed the citizenry in person. If Polybius' account is trustworthy, Hannibal's words were met with wild enthusiasm, suggesting that there was widespread, latent disaffection with Rome.[14]

The Tarentine political situation during the Second Punic War bears a strong resemblance to the factionalism and aristocratic rivalry on display at the time of the Pyrrhic invasion. Plutarch (*Pyrrh.* 13) records a debate among

---

[10] Liv. 25.7.11–8.1.

[11] Livy (25.7.10) says that the revolt was 'long suspected' (*Tarentinorum defectio iam diu … in suspicione Romanis esset*). The hostages were probably removed to Rome before the battle of Cannae or shortly thereafter and, if so, they would have been in Rome at least three years before the city rebelled in 213/12.

[12] Polyb. 2.24.13, 8.25.7; Liv. 25.8.13; App. *Hann.* 32. Polybius states that Rome maintained a permanent garrison in Taras at the time of the Gallic War in 225. It is possible that this garrison was removed at some point before the Second Punic War and then replaced some time before the Tarentine revolt. On balance, however, it is more probable that the garrison remained continuously from 225. For further discussion, see below, pp. 208–9.

[13] Polyb. 8.24.11–13. This recalls the political atmosphere in Capua, where the anti-Roman party was able to win over members of the aristocracy who had pro-Roman leanings (such as Pacuvius Calavius) and thus tip the political balance against the pro-Roman aristocrats. See Liv. 23.6.1–5, 23.8.1–2; see also Chapter 3, pp. 106–8.

[14] Polyb. 8.31.2–4. Livy (25.10.8–9) adds that he called attention to Rome's 'haughty rule' (*dominationem superbam*). Of course, once the Tarentines saw that Hannibal's troops controlled the city, it would have been in their interest to display enthusiasm for him. Still, it was at this point that some Tarentines escaped to the citadel, so those who remained in the city (or at least a portion of them) did so in part voluntarily.

the Tarentines over whether to invite Pyrrhus to Italy to fight against Rome. His depiction of three parties – the old and sensible who opposed war, the impetuous who sought war, and those who remained silent – is surely an oversimplification of the political setting, of the sort we have seen several times already. Still Plutarch's three parties hint at the variety of opinions that must have been expressed at the point of a momentous foreign policy decision. After the decision was made to call in Pyrrhus, a party under the leadership of a certain Nico grew dissatisfied with Milo, who commanded the Pyrrhic garrison stationed in Taras. This party set up in a nearby fortress and sent envoys to Rome seeking an alliance; later, more Tarentines came to oppose Milo, though presumably the local ruling elite was never uniform in its rejection of the Pyrrhic garrison.[15]

After Rome captured Taras in 272, pro-Roman aristocratic families, perhaps including those who sent envoys to Rome, were probably installed in power or otherwise rewarded, while those who were more staunchly anti-Roman would have been executed, exiled or at least removed from power.[16] If these assumptions are accurate, then some Tarentine aristocratic families would have benefited from Rome's settlement after the Pyrrhic War, while others would have suffered, although, whatever the Romans did to pro-Pyrrhic aristocrats in the late 270s, the fact that they took Tarentine hostages in 218 (or 216) suggests that they had not been systematically rooted out and thus still posed a threat two generations later. Indeed, we may speculate that the families and friends of Nico and Philomenus included descendants of those losing families from the 270s. Roman rule would have either laid the groundwork for new aristocratic rivalry or exacerbated pre-existing competition. Those aristocrats whose families had lost out as a result of Roman rule may have seen in Hannibal an opportunity to advance their own political standing, while Hannibal should have been able to manipulate local factionalism to win over key aristocratic allies.

Moreover, Taras had formerly been a powerful state in the region, and it had opposed Rome either directly or indirectly in a series of conflicts in the fourth and third centuries. We have seen in previous chapters that Hannibal was particularly attractive to the ruling classes of powerful cities with local or regional hegemonic aspirations. Polybius and Livy mention only vaguely that Hannibal addressed the Tarentines in kind terms,[17] though it is tempting to think that he would have played up Taras'

---

[15] Zon. 8.6.   [16] Lomas 1993: 56.
[17] Polyb. 8.31.3: Ἀννίβας φιλανθρώπους διελέχθη λόγους; Liv. 25.10.8: *ibi Hannibal benigne adlocutus Tarentinos*; see also App. *Hann.* 32: καὶ τοὺς Ταραντίνους ἑταιρισάμενος.

past – and potential future, should they side with him – glory. This must also remain speculation, but in any case, the Tarentines' hesitation about revolting is striking when one considers the city's history.

Indeed, literary evidence attests that Taras was the most powerful city along the central coast of the Gulf of Taranto. Livy (25.8.1) writes that Taras and Thurii were two of the most renowned Greek cities (*nobilissimarum Graecarum civitatium*) in Italy, while Strabo (6.3.1) comments on Taras' large harbour, formidable acropolis and extensive defensive walls that stretched 100 *stades* in circumference. Strabo also emphasises that although the city had declined greatly after its fall in the Second Punic War, it remained worthy in size.[18] Modern scholars estimate that the enclosed area of Taras exceeded 500 hectares, and its population at its height in the fourth century may have been between 110,000 and 150,000 persons.[19] The Tarentines expanded the colony's territory from a core area around the Mare Piccolo, until the *chora* extended from the Bradano River and the border with Metapontion as far south as modern-day Campomarino along the coast, and inland to the Murge, perhaps as far as Crispiano. By the outbreak of the Second Punic War, the Tarentines had come to control the port of Callipolis, far down the south-east coast of the Sallentine peninsula.[20] Taras was, in terms of territory, certainly the largest Greek city in southern Italy by the fourth century.[21]

Taras was a regional hegemonic state that, from the middle of the fourth century, tried to extend its influence over neighbouring Greek settlements. At some point it assumed the leadership of the Italiote League, which was formed under the dominance of Croton in the fifth century, disbanded by Dionysius I of Syracuse in the early fourth century and apparently revived

---

[18] Here again Strabo uses the present tense, but his description, which alternates between positive and negative observations about the city, is probably a composite of his source material, ranging from the second century BC to the first century AD (Poulter 2002: 219–21). What is important for the present argument is that Taras appears to have contained impressive architecture even after the Second Punic War, and it was probably a formidable city at the outbreak of the war.

[19] Lomas 1993: 21; Pani 2005: 22, arguing that this population had fallen by more than a half after war with Rome in the 280s and 270s.

[20] The site was also known as Anxa, modern-day Gallipoli in the Provincia di Lecce: Dion. Hal. 19.3.1–2; Pomponius Mela 2.66; Plin. *HN* 3.99–100; Lamboley 1996: 243–5.

[21] See Map 13. There has yet to be a comprehensive archaeological survey of the entire Tarentine *chora*, but the limited surveys that have been done show a marked increase in the number of rural sites (including farmsteads, cult sites and burial sites) during the later fourth century. There also appear to be a number of fortified rural sites, both 'lookout posts' and more significant settlements. The overall picture is one of population and economic growth. See Cocchiaro 1981; De Juliis 1984b: 121–2; Osanna 1992: 19; Poulter 2001: 89–96. The settlement of Magna Graecia after Rome defeated Pyrrhus does not seem to have been very severe, at least with regard to land confiscation, so Taras (and other cities that sided with Pyrrhus) probably lost little or no territory after their defeat: Lomas 1993: 56–7.

at a later time. It is unclear when the league was revived, but by the middle of the fourth century hegemony of the Italiote League had passed to Taras.[22] The status of the league after the Romans defeated Pyrrhus and, subsequently, conquered Magna Graecia is also obscure. Even if it was disbanded as a formal institution, we might expect that informal and perhaps even some formal links connected its former members. At the same time, the Tarentines would have recognised their former position vis-à-vis the league and may have been motivated to re-establish it.

Whatever the status of the Italiote League, Taras emerged as a regional hegemonic power whose interests came into conflict with Rome's as early as the fourth century. Ancient sources report that the Tarentines promised to reinforce Naples against Roman aggression during the Second Samnite War (in 328), perhaps appealing to ethnic fellowship to convince the Neapolitans not to surrender to Roman forces.[23] Even though the later hostility between Rome and Taras in the third century may be influencing the sources, there is no reason to reject out of hand that the Tarentines were involved directly in Neapolitan (and thus Roman) diplomacy at this point.[24] Whether Tarentine support failed to materialise because of logistical problems or because, as Livy claims, they never really intended to send troops, is not clear.[25] In any case, Livy is explicit that the Tarentines were angered by the surrender of Naples to Rome and saw the event as a threat to Tarentine hegemonic interests.[26] In 326 Taras tried to destabilise

---

[22] Polyb. 2.39.1–7; Diod. Sic. 14.91.1, 14.101.1; Strab. 6.3.4; Polyaenus 2.10.1; Iambl. *VP.* 263–4; Wuilleumier 1939: 64–71; Ehrenberg 1948; Walbank 1970: 1.225–6; Brauer 1986: 43–55; Lomas 1993: 35; Purcell 1994: 388; De Sensi Sestito 1994: 202–3; Poulter 2002: 130–7. The Italiote League was organised along the lines of the Achaean league. The chronology of its foundation, its initial purpose and its membership are all subject to debate, but the existence of some sort of defensive league of Greek cities in southern Italy by the early fourth century is certain. Taras assumed hegemony of the league perhaps as early as 380 – certainly before the arrival of Alexander of Epirus in the 340s – and it continued to dominate the league throughout the fourth century. If the league continued to function into the third century, Rome may have disbanded it after the Pyrrhic War, though Lomas 1993: 56–7, 61 argues that it continued to function in some form until the Second Punic War.

[23] Liv. 8.25.7–8, 8.27.2–5; Dion. Hal. 15.5.2–3.

[24] As I will discuss, from the 340s Taras sought military assistance from mainland Greek powers, and they came into direct conflict with Syracuse; also, around 330 Taras and Rome had made a treaty that limited the movement of Roman ships. By 328, therefore, the Tarentines were already interacting with states in a broader 'international' environment, while at the same time it would have made sense for Naples to seek the assistance of another powerful state, especially one that had already opposed Rome. For this early interaction between Rome, Taras and Naples, see Hoffman 1934: 41–56; Wuilleumier 1939: 70–1; Raaflaub, Richards and Samons II 1992: 19; Oakley 1997–2005: II.680–2 and 681 n. 1; Eckstein 2006: 153; Fronda 2006: 414–15 n. 79.

[25] The second explanation could be interpreted as hinting at the Tarentine expectation that a fellow Greek community would remain loyal, though it may simply be pro-Roman sources characterising the Tarentines as duplicitous.

[26] See Oakley 1997–2005: II.685–6.

the Roman–Lucanian alliance by bribing members of the Lucanian elite to take up arms alongside the Samnites against Rome.[27] The Tarentines had probably perceived that the Roman–Lucanian alliance posed an immediate threat to their interests and so they acted accordingly to disrupt it.[28] It is also worth noting that Taras attempted to assert hegemony by securing the loyalty of the Lucanian elite and playing local rival factions against each other – the same method used by Rome (and Hannibal) to secure their allies. Finally, the Tarentines tried unsuccessfully to arbitrate between Rome and the Samnites before their battle near Luceria in 320, obviously attempting to influence interstate affairs and, presumably, further their own interests.[29]

Taras also employed a series of Hellenistic *condottieri* to protect its welfare and even to advance its authority against hostile Italic peoples, other Greek cities and ultimately Rome. For example, in the 340s the Tarentines appealed to Archidamus of Sparta to help them against the Messapians who had previously overrun nearby Metapontion and Heraclea. Unfortunately for the Tarentines, Archidamus died in battle at Manduria.[30] Taras next sought the assistance of Alexander of Epirus, who fought with great success from 333 to 330 against a number of Italic peoples, until his death at Pandosia. During this campaign he drove the Messapians from Heraclea and Metapontion.[31] The capture of these two towns resulted ultimately from Tarentine initiative, and designs not only to drive off hostile Italic tribes but also to assert hegemony over Metapontion and Heraclea probably lay behind their initial decision to invite Alexander. This conclusion gains strength if we consider the three groups with whom Alexander made treaties, according to Justin: the Metapontians, the Poediculi and the Romans.[32] Metapontion's inclusion in this list is curious, and it implies that Alexander's capture was an act of conquest more than one of liberation. Since he was acting, at least in part, at the request of the Tarentines,

---

[27] Liv. 8.25.6–11, 8.29.1; Oakley 1997–2005: II.680–2.

[28] Contra Lomas 1993: 47–8, who argues that anti-Roman Lucanian aristocrats rather than the Tarentines drove the events of 326, while the picture of Tarentine anti-Roman sentiment is the product of Livy's (or his sources') hostility. Lomas does agree, however, that the Tarentines probably encouraged the Lucanian elite since Taras recognised the Roman–Lucanian alliance as a threat to its power.

[29] Liv. 9.14.1–16; for interstate arbitration in the Hellenistic world, see Chapter 4, pp. 167–8 and n. 72.

[30] Diod. Sic. 16.15.1–2, 16.62.4, 16.63.2; Plut. *Agis*. 3.2; Plin. *HN* 3.98; Lomas 1993: 41–2.

[31] Liv. 8.3.6, 8.17.9–10, 8.24.1–6, 8.24.16; Strab. 6.3.4; Just. *Epit*. 12.2.1–15; Lomas 1993: 42–3.

[32] *Epit*. 12.2.12: *gessit et cum Bruttiis Lucanisque bellum multasque urbes cepit; cum Metapontinis et Poediculis et Romanis foedus amicitiamque fecit* ('He waged war with the Bruttians and Lucanians and he captured many cities; with the Metapontians, Poediculi, and Romans he made a treaty and friendship').

they probably encouraged his seizure of Metapontion as a way to extend their authority along the coast of the Gulf of Taranto. The subsequent strained relations between Alexander and Taras also support this conclusion. Strabo (6.3.4) records that Alexander transferred a panhellenic festival (probably related to the Italiote League) from Heraclea to Thurii out of enmity towards the Tarentines. The reference shows that Taras was concerned with its hegemonic status relative to the neighbouring Greek settlements. It is also worth noting that in this same passage Strabo claims that Heraclea lay within Taras' territory, and that the Tarentines had once fought the Messapians for possession of Heraclea. This last reference, albeit nebulous,[33] again fits the general picture of Taras' repeated attempts to dominate Metapontion and Heraclea.

The Tarentines continued to employ *condottieri* later in the fourth century. In 315/14 they enrolled Acrotatus of Sparta as protection against Agathocles, the tyrant of Syracuse.[34] Agathocles had previously made a number of forays into Italy with little success and was driven from Taras on suspicion of seditious behaviour. Next the Tarentines outfitted Acrotatus with a fleet so that he could overthrow the Syracusan tyrant. Acrotatus sailed to Acragas and assumed the office of general; in the meantime, the Tarentines sent their fleet to rendezvous with him. When Acrotatus appeared more interested in establishing himself as tyrant of Acragas, the Tarentines withdrew their support and recalled their fleet. In 303/2, Taras employed Acrotatus' brother, Cleonymus of Sparta, against a coalition of Lucanians and, possibly, Romans.[35] While the exact course of events is difficult to disentangle, the basic outline of the campaign is clear: the Tarentines invited Cleonymus to Italy and supplied him with ships and money, and he then forged a coalition of Greeks and Messapians, defeated the Lucanians and possibly conquered some of the cities on the Sallentine peninsula. Diodorus states that Cleonymus forced the Lucanians to accept an alliance with Taras, and he specifies, moreover, that the Metapontians did not come to terms with Cleonymus, so the general attacked and conquered the city using his new Lucanian allies. He may also have captured

---

[33] Strabo claims that the Tarentines obtained the assistance of the 'king of the Daunians and the King of the Peucetians' (ἔχοντες συνεργοὺς τόν τε τῶν Δαυνίων καὶ τὸν τῶν Πευκετίων βασιλέα) against the Messapians in their struggle for Heraclea. If there is any historicity in this notice, it may refer to a fifth-century context (Poulter 2002: 124), with these 'kings' perhaps comparable to the 'ruler' (δυνάστης) of the Messapians mentioned by Thucydides (7.33.4). Even if Strabo has conflated fourth- and third-century material in this passage, it only confirms that Taras had a long history of hegemonic aspirations.

[34] Diod. Sic. 19.4.1–2, 19.70.4–19.71.7.

[35] Diod. Sic. 20.104.1–20.105.3; Liv. 10.2.1–14; Strab. 6.3.4; Broughton 1951–2: 1.169–71.

Thurii as well before departing from Italy after his relationship with Taras soured.[36] Even though the sources are problematic, it is clear that the Tarentines employed *condottieri* to further their hegemonic interests. In particular, Taras used Cleonymus to assert control over the Lucanians and (perhaps) the Sallentines, as well as the Greek cities of Metapontion and (possibly) Thurii. These events also demonstrate Taras' willingness to employ non-Greek allies – Messapians and later Lucanians – against other Italiote cities.

The most famous Hellenistic *condottiere* was Pyrrhus, whose Italian campaign reveals most clearly Taras' hegemonic tactics. Ancient accounts of the outbreak of the Pyrrhic War disagree over its exact causes and, more importantly, the degree to which Taras acted alone in inviting the Epirote king. Fortunately, these differences can be reconciled. Plutarch, whose relevant account is the most intact, states that seeking military assistance from Pyrrhus was a joint Italiote decision made under Tarentine leadership (*Pyrrh.* 13.5). Yet Plutarch initially lists Taras as the only Greek city to furnish contingents for Pyrrhus' army, which at the time included Messapians, Lucanians and Samnites, and he implies that other Greek cities joined Taras only after Pyrrhus' initial success.[37] Other ancient sources emphasise that Taras acted alone in inviting Pyrrhus. Appian (*Sam.* 7.1–2) reports that the Tarentines sank a Roman fleet that had violated a treaty prohibiting the Romans from sailing beyond the Lacinian promontory. They next attacked Thurii, which had previously allied with Rome, captured a Roman garrison stationed there and expelled pro-Roman Thurian

---

[36] Livy (10.2.1–2) claims that Cleonymus captured a city called 'Thuriae', on the Sallentine peninsula, but its inhabitants were restored by Roman forces under the command of the consul M. Aemilius Paullus or the dictator C. Iunius Bubulcus Brutus (Livy's sources disagreed as to the identity). 'Thuriae' might refer to an otherwise unknown Sallentine community, or Livy means Thurii. The latter solution is more attractive, especially considering that Livy, at an earlier point, specifies Thurii as a Roman ally (9.19.4). If we read 'Thurii' for 'Thuriae', the confused geography can easily be explained by the confusion of his annalistic sources and their faulty geographic knowledge. Indeed, I have already noted the disagreement in Livy's sources over the name of the Roman commander. For Thurii instead of Thuriae: Beloch 1926: 435–6 (arguing that the correct reading is Thurii, but that the reference is annalistic fabrication); Broughton 1951–2: 1.169; Oakley 1997–2005 IV.55–7 (claiming that it is difficult to choose either solution).

[37] Plut. *Pyrrh.* 13.6, 17.5, 18.4. Plutarch (18.4) states explicitly that the Roman senate considered suing for peace because they had been defeated at Heraclea and now faced an even larger army since the Italiote Greeks had joined Pyrrhus: δῆλοί γε μὴν ἦσαν ἐνδιδόντες οἱ πολλοὶ πρὸς τὴν εἰρήνην, ἡττημένοι τε μεγάλῃ μάχῃ καὶ προσδοκῶντες ἑτέραν ἀπὸ μείζονος δυνάμεως, τῶν Ἰταλικῶν τῷ Πύρρῳ προσγεγονότων ('For indeed many were clearly leaning towards peace, having been defeated in a great battle and expecting another with a larger army, since the Italiotes [or Italians?] had attached themselves to Pyrrhus'). We know, however, that the Tarentines had already supplied Pyrrhus with troops (17.5), so the remaining Italiotes joined Pyrrhus only after his initial military success.

aristocrats. The Tarantines then called on Pyrrhus for help in the resulting conflict with Rome.[38] This version is consistent with other testimony that the Romans had aided the Thurians against attacks by the Lucanians and Bruttians.[39] Dionysius of Halicarnassus (20.4.1–2) records that Rhegion had also sought Roman protection against Italic peoples; in the same passage he claims that the Rhegians feared the Tarentines, and he implies that Taras may have promoted the barbarian attacks on Thurii.[40] Overall, the sources clearly indicate that Taras was the prime mover behind Pyrrhus' invasion of Italy.

The behaviour of Taras towards Pyrrhus is consistent with the campaign of Cleonymus, when Taras tried to employ a combination of Italic allies and a Hellenistic mercenary general to extend its own regional hegemony. Two additional ancient references can be brought to bear on this point. Both Appian (*Sam.* 10.1) and Dionysius of Halicarnassus (19.9.2) record that Pyrrhus offered a settlement between Taras and Rome. Dionysius says that he proposed to arbitrate the differences between Rome and the Tarentines, Lucanians and Samnites. In Appian's version, he presented peace terms to the Romans: that the Romans, Pyrrhus and the Tarentines would make a treaty alliance; the other Greeks would live under their own laws; and the Romans would restore anything they took in war to the Samnites, Lucanians, Daunians and Bruttians. In both versions only Taras and various Italic peoples are mentioned by name, suggesting that Pyrrhus was acting on behalf of a coalition of Taras and (at least some) Italic communities. The Tarentines must have understood that both the appearance of a Roman fleet off the Sallentine peninsula and the Roman garrisons installed in Italiote cities posed serious threats to their regional hegemony. I have already mentioned that Taras may have been behind Italic attacks on Thurii, and that other Italiote states feared Taras. Overall, therefore, it looks as though the Tarentines hoped to use local Italic tribes and Pyrrhus' army as counter-weights against Roman influence and to assert (or reassert) their own power over other Italiote cities.

Ultimately, such *condottieri* proved incapable of extending, or even maintaining, Tarentine hegemony over the Italiotes, and by about 270 Rome had brought all of the cities of Magna Graecia under its control,

---

[38] See also Liv. *Per.* 12.
[39] Dion. Hal. 19.13.1, 19.16.3, 20.4.2; Liv. *Per.* 11, 12; Val. Max. 1.8.6; see also Broughton 1951–2: 1.189.
[40] See also Polyb. 1.7.6–8 (who also notes Rhegian fear of Taras); Diod. Sic. 22.1.2–3; App. *Sam.* 9.1. Unfortunately for the Rhegians, the request resulted in the sack of Rhegion by the *legio Campana*.

willingly or unwillingly. Tarentine hegemonic aspirations in the Sallentine peninsula were likewise curtailed by Roman expansion. Taras probably struggled with Brundisium for hegemony over the peninsula. Ancient sources attest that Brundisium was the most important Messapic city, perhaps even dominating the dozen or so smaller cities in the peninsula, such as Aletium, Basta, Neretum, Uzentum, Veretum, Lupiae, Rudiae, Manduria and Hyria/Uria/Oria.[41] Florus (1.20), referring to the Roman conquest of the Salento in the 260s, calls Brundisium the capital of the region (*caput regionis*); Zonaras (8.7) also emphasises that Brundisium was the focus of these Roman campaigns, implying that it was the most important centre in the region.[42] We have already noted that Taras employed Archidamus and Alexander of Epirus against the Messapians, which probably brought Taras into conflict with Brundisium. Taras' subsequent ally, Pyrrhus, enrolled Messapian contingents in his army, perhaps indicating that Taras temporarily exercised some authority over the peninsula. Soon after Pyrrhus' departure from Italy, however, Roman generals celebrated triumphs over the Sallentines and Messapians – in both 267 and 266 – and presumably all the cities of the Salento, including Brundisium, were bound by *foedera* at this time.[43] Within a few years, then, all of the potential objects of Tarentine expansion had been absorbed into the Roman sphere. The final blow came circa 244, when a Latin colony was established at Brundisium:[44] this gave Rome not only a strategic naval base for accessing Illyria, but also a powerful forward position for controlling the Sallentines and the Tarentines.[45]

This brings us back to the Second Punic War. The decision to side with Hannibal in 213/12 fits within the long-term pattern of Tarentine foreign policy, as the Tarentines had frequently turned to mercenary kings and generals to protect their interests and advance their own hegemony. Hannibal would have represented the first opportunity since the

[41] An exact list of Sallentine cities is difficult to produce, since ancient sources record various lists. See Plin. *HN* 3.99–100, 105; Strab. 6.3.5–6; see also Liv. 22.61.12, 27.15.4. La Bua 1992: 44–51 argues that Brundisium was the hegemon of a more or less formal 'Sallentine League', but the evidence for such an organisation is rather slender. See Map 14.

[42] Although Zonaras also points out that Brundisium had a fine harbour, so the Romans may have focused their efforts here because of its strategic importance rather than political status.

[43] Broughton 1951–2: 1.200–1; Degrassi 1954: 99; Camassa 1997: 796.

[44] For the foundation: Liv. *Per.* 19; Vell. Pat. 1.14.8; Broughton 1951–2: 1.217; Salmon 1969: 64; La Bua 1992: 50–1 suggests that the colony was founded in response to a revolt of the speculative Sallentine League (see above, n. 41).

[45] Sirago 1999: 157. Roman ships stationed in Brundisium afterwards were charged with policing the coast between Taras and Brundisium and certainly paid close attention to the Tarentines. See Liv. 23.32.17, 24.11.3–6.

days of Pyrrhus for the Tarentines to exercise regional power. Hannibal, like Pyrrhus, also utilised typical Hellenistic diplomatic terminology – promising that Taras would be free – perhaps providing a further point of comparison to the past *condottieri*.[46] It also makes sense that Hannibal was attractive to a significant portion of the Tarentine ruling class, given their considerable anti-Roman sentiment. The real question is why it took so long for Taras to finally revolt – much longer, in fact, than other powerful states (such as Capua, Arpi and Locri) which had defected in 216 and 215.

De Sanctis (1956–69: III.2.265) argued that economic reasons explain Tarentine loyalty between 216 and 213/12: Taras was a centre of commerce, and Roman rule supposedly afforded protection for Tarentine ships and fostered trade, thus encouraging Tarentine loyalty. The available literary evidence suggests, however, that, if anything, the Tarentine economy would have suffered in the years under Roman rule. For example, Rome's refoundation of Brundisium as a Latin colony almost certainly hurt Tarentine trade. As early as the time of Herodotus, ancient authors attest that Brundisium was important, its port superior to Taras' and well situated for trade with the southern Balkans and Asia Minor.[47] Indeed, Cassius Dio (12.49.2) records that Illyrian pirates harassed ships sailing from Brundisium, suggesting that the port functioned as a link between Italy and the East. When it was refounded as a Latin colony, the Romans extended the Via Appia from Beneventum, through Venusia and Taras, to Brundisium. The extension of the road would have strengthened the lines of communication with Rome and perhaps further solidified Brundisium's position as the dominant port for trade with the East. Strabo (6.3.7) also mentions a second road that connected Brundisium to Beneventum by way of Canusium: the so-called 'mule road', which probably followed more or less the same course as the later Via Traiana and was in use long before Strabo's time.[48] In the same passage Strabo reports that this route from Beneventum to Brundisium saved the traveller a day's journey, though the Via Appia was better for travel by carriage. At least some traders, less concerned with comfort than profit, would have used the mule road instead

---

[46] The Tarentine–Hannibalic treaty guaranteed that Taras would be free and the Carthaginians would not exact tribute or other burdens (Polyb. 8.25.2). The promise of ἐλευθερία is comparable to Pyrrhus' demand that the Italiote Greeks be allowed to live under their own laws (App. *Sam.* 10.1).

[47] Hdt. 4.99, 7.170; Strab. 6.3.6, 6.3.7; Plin. *HN* 3.101; Ennius. *Ann.* 488; Flor. 1.15. According to Lagona 1992: 83–5 Brundisium had long been an important port for trade in the Adriatic and Aegean seas; see also Poulter 2002: 302–3.

[48] Ashby and Gardner 1916: 108–11; see Chapter 2, p. 74 n. 93.

of the Via Appia, circumventing Taras altogether.[49] According to Polybius, the foundation of Brundisium had a severe and detrimental impact on Tarentine trade,[50] while the people of Taras appear to have recognised the commercial threat and founded a competing port (Fratuentium) on the Adriatic.[51]

Archaeological evidence is consistent with the previous discussion, as studies of material-culture remains suggest that the Tarentine economy was generally in decline during the third century. Guzzo (1991: 79–81), for example, notes a drastic decline from the fourth to the third century in the number of datable Tarentine graves. According to Poulter (2002: 274), 'the physical remains of structures and intense densities of ceramic finds at the majority of those sites' identified as farmsteads by Osanna and Cocchiaro did not survive the third century.[52] Much of the Hellenistic material among grave goods in the territory of Taras also disappears in the third century, while many of the fortified rural sites seem too to have been

---

[49] Of course, Roman roads served primarily a military function, and shipping goods overland was far more time consuming and costly than moving them by sea, so the economic impact of the Via Appia and the 'mule road' should not be exaggerated. Laurence 1999: 95–108 points out, however, that a significant portion of goods were transported along land routes because of the lack of available waterways, the availability of roads in all weather and seasons, etc., so the Roman road system in Italy had a significant economic impact. Laurence focused on the period from around 200 BC to AD 200, but his overall point should hold true for roads built in an earlier period. Thus, we can conclude that at least some trade would have been conducted inland over land routes, especially along major roads, and it is likely that Brundisium consequently benefited from its situation along the 'mule road' and the Via Appia.

[50] Polyb. 10.1.8–9. In this passage Polybius claims that everyone coming from the opposite coast (of the Adriatic) used to land at Taras and use the town as an emporium to exchange goods because the town of Brundisium had not yet been founded: ἀπὸ γὰρ ἄκρας Ἰαπυγίας ἕως εἰς Σιποῦντα πᾶς ὁ προσφερόμενος ἐκ τῶν ἀντιπέρας καὶ καθορμισθεὶς πρὸς τὴν Ἰταλίαν εἰς Τάραντ᾽ ἐποιεῖτο τὴν ὑπερβολήν, καὶ ταύτῃ συνεχρῆτο τῇ πόλει πρὸς τὰς ἀλλαγὰς καὶ μεταθέσεις οἷον εἰ ἐμπορίῳ· οὐδέπω γὰρ συνέβαινε τότε τὴν τῶν Βρεντεσίνων ἐκτίσθαιπόλιν ('From the furthest point of Iapygia as far as Sipontum, all who were conveyed from the opposite coast to Italy and put in at a harbour made the crossing to Taras, and they made use of this city as an emporium for the purpose of the exchange of goods and trade, for at that time Brundisium had yet to be founded'). This clearly implies that once Brundisium was founded, it supplanted Taras as the most important port in south-east Italy. Appian (*B Civ.* 1.79) preserves a curious note: that Sulla granted Brundisium immunity (ἀτέλειαν), which the city enjoyed to Appian's day – it is not clear whether this referred to immunity from a range of financial obligations and levies, or from *portoria* only: Crawford 1998: 35–6 contra Henderson 1897: 251–5. Lomas 1993: 91–2 cautions against accepting *c.* 80 as the date for the granting of this exemption and suggests that it may have been granted at an earlier point in time. If immunity had been granted at a much earlier date (and Appian thus mistaken about its origins), then it is possible that Brundisium had a further competitive advantage over Taras. This must remain, however, a tenuous speculation. Even if the grant of immunity was made in the first century BC, it may still be indicative of the long-term ascendancy of Brundisium at the expense of Taras.

[51] Plin. *HN* 3.101; Sirago 1999: 157–8: the site of Fratuentium is perhaps to be identified with modern Torre dell'Orso; it seems to have remained unimportant.

[52] Osanna 1992: sites no. 5, 7, 12, 14, 22, 26; Cocchiaro 1981: sites no. 4, 5, 7, 8, 20, 25, 26, 29, 37.

in decline.[53] It should be noted that the entire territory of Taras has not been systematically studied with an eye towards third-century developments, so the available data may represent highly local rather than general trends. Also, the decline of cultural material in the rural territory need not represent a decline in population but may indicate merely different burial, settlement or land-use practices.[54] Still, there does appear to have been significant economic change in the third century. In addition, Sirago argues that there was a consistent drop in the quality and quantity of contemporary Tarentine coinage, noting especially that didrachmae from 228 were minted at a lesser weight.[55] The foundation of the Roman colony at Brundisium appears to have shifted patterns of commerce, and in any case, the Tarentine economy underwent change – and probably decline – at the same time that Rome extended and consolidated its control of the southern peninsula.[56]

Roman rule meant other, more direct burdens. Taras was probably one of the *socii navales* expected to help to outfit the Roman navy.[57] Polybius (1.20.14) records that the Tarentines supplied an unknown number of ships during the First Punic War. Livy records that Rhegion, Paestum and Velia combined to supply a total of twelve vessels, which they owed the Romans by treaty.[58] Although Taras' exact naval obligation is unknown, we can extrapolate from the aforementioned information: as one of the largest Greek cities in Italy, it may have been required to furnish more vessels than Rhegion, Paestum or Velia – perhaps six to eight ships. We know that the Tarentines could outfit a fleet of at least twenty vessels, so their obligation to Rome may have represented a significant portion of Taras' naval capacity.[59] Polybius (2.24) does not mention any Greek cities among those allies obliged to provide Rome with infantry and cavalry in 225, but this does not mean that the Greeks never contributed troops, nor were so-called *socii navales* a mutually exclusive category from the allies under the *formula togatorum*. Rather, some allied cities supplying ships and marines

---

[53] For a general discussion of third-century material-culture evidence from the Tarentine *chora*, see Poulter 2002: 272–6. Although Poulter is cautious in drawing conclusions from the available evidence, she agrees that the picture is generally one of 'decline'. See also Alessio and Guzzo: 1989–90.

[54] Although, as mentioned above (n. 53), it has been estimated that the Tarentine population declined steeply in the third century.

[55] Sirago 1999: 157–9. See also Lomas 1993: 91–2.

[56] Brundisium's negative economic impact, real or perceived, must have been all the more frustrating to the Tarentines, considering Taras' long-standing rivalry with Brundisium; see above, pp. 198–9.

[57] For the obligations of the *socii navales*, see Ilari 1974: 105–17.

[58] Liv. 26.39.2–5.   [59] Liv. 26.39.3–19, *Epit.* 12; App. *Sam.* 7.1.

for the Roman navy were also probably obliged to supply ground troops, at least in reduced proportion.[60] Indeed, the reference to Tarentine prisoners captured at Cannae and Trasimene suggests that Taras was also bound to supply land forces, either infantry or cavalry, for the Roman army.[61] It is plausible that Taras was bound to supply ships, crews and ground troops. The Tarentines certainly resented their military burden, and this may be reflected in the terms of their treaty with Hannibal, which relieved the Tarentines of unspecified 'burdens' if they sided with him.[62] More relevant to the present discussion, supplying ships may have imposed a significant, albeit periodic, financial burden on the Tarentines.

Roman rule certainly brought with it additional financial consequences. Rome had a garrison of one legion of 4,200 infantry and 200 cavalry in Taras in 225. There was also a Roman garrison holding the city when it revolted in 213/12, and we may surmise that there had been a Roman military presence in Taras continuously since 225 (if not earlier).[63] The Tarentines probably absorbed at least part of the cost of maintaining the garrison, perhaps supplying it with food at fixed prices, if not underwriting the legion's stipend altogether.[64] Supporting the Roman garrison could have put a strain on the local population, as an episode later in the war suggests. In 211 a Carthaginian fleet arrived in Taras, having been sent to protect the Tarentines from a Roman blockade.[65] The Carthaginian marines quickly consumed Tarentine food stores, with the result that the fleet's departure made the Tarentines happier than its arrival.[66] Both the Livian and Polybian versions of the Hannibalic–Tarentine treaty also preserve a clause protecting the Tarentines from tribute and may indicate that

---

[60] Toynbee 1965: 1.491–2; Brunt 1971: 50; Ilari 1974: 112–14; Baronowski 1993: 199. It is possible that the southern Greek cities were omitted from Polybius' Roman manpower totals for 225 because their infantry/cavalry obligations were rather light and because they were so far from the theatre of war. For a similar discussion concerning the omission of the Bruttians, see Chapter 4, n. 11.

[61] Liv. 24.13.1, 25.10.8. For the historicity of references to Tarentine soldiers fighting alongside the legions: Sirago 1992: 78 contra Walbank 1970: 1.107.

[62] Polyb. 8.25.2.

[63] Polyb. 2.24.13, 8.25.7; Liv. 25.8.13; App. *Hann.* 32; see below, pp. 208–9.

[64] For the local financial burden of a Roman garrison, consider the Claudian camp near Suessula. The garrison was supplied by bringing in grain from Nola and Naples (Liv. 23.46.8–9), and Marcellus was ordered to leave the smallest possible garrison in Nola over the winter of 215/14 so that the soldiers did not burden the allies (Liv. 23.48.2): *M. Claudio proconsuli imperavit ut, retento Nolae necessario ad tuendam urbem praesidio, ceteros milites dimitteret Romam, ne oneri sociis et sumptui rei publicae essent.* See also Rosenstein 2004: 35–8.

[65] Liv. 26.20.7–11; Polyb. 9.9.11.

[66] Food stores might already have been depleted, since the town had been blockaded. Still, the episode indicates the costs to the local population associated with maintaining a foreign garrison, be it welcome or not.

Taras was subject to yearly tribute since it was captured in 272.[67] Whatever Tarentine economic disaffection there was may have been exacerbated by the presence of wealthy Romans within the city walls. The treaty also guaranteed the Carthaginians the right to plunder Roman houses once Taras was secured for Hannibal. When the city fell into Hannibal's hands, the Carthaginians did in fact pillage Roman property, and ancient accounts state that the Carthaginians carried off a significant amount of booty.[68]

The loss of trade to Brundisium, periodic costly contributions of ships and possibly troops to Rome, the probable expense of maintaining a foreign garrison, and wealthy Romans living in Taras all must have contributed to anti-Roman sentiment among the Tarentines. Overall, there is little to suggest that the Tarentines would have perceived any economic benefit from submission to Rome, so De Sanctis' argument that economic factors contributed to Tarentine loyalty between 216 and 213/12 does not rest on much support.

De Sanctis (1956–69: III.2.265) also argued that the Roman pacification of Italy protected the Tarentines from their enemies, the Lucanians and Messapians, implying that long-term hostility between coastal Greeks and inland Italic peoples, combined with the decision of the Lucanians and Messapians to ally with Hannibal, contributed to Taras' loyalty in the early stages of the Second Punic War. There may be some truth to this assertion, considering the impact of Graeco-Bruttian hostility on events in western Magna Graecia, which were discussed in Chapter 4. As we will see, however, this does not really account for the failure of the Tarentines to revolt earlier in the war.

It is true that there had been conflicts between the eastern Italiote Greeks and the Lucanians and Messapians.[69] According to Livy (27.15.9–19), when Rome recaptured Taras in 209, it was the Bruttian contingent of the Carthaginian garrison that betrayed the city to Q. Fabius Maximus,[70] and

---

[67] Polyb. 8.25.2; Liv. 25.8.8; see also Zon. 8.6. Livy later indicates that Taras paid tribute in 193 (35.16.3). According to the Polybian version of the treaty, Taras was protected from unspecified burdens. I argued above that these 'burdens' might refer to military obligations (see pp. 202–3), though the term is sufficiently vague to encompass financial obligations as well. In any case, supplying ships for the Roman navy was probably costly in terms of both men and money.

[68] For the clause guaranteeing the right to plunder Roman homes: Polyb. 8.25.2; Liv. 25.8.8; for the amount of plunder taken from the Romans living in Taras: Polyb. 8.32.1: Πολλῶν δὲ καὶ παντοδαπῶν κατασκευασμάτων ἀθροισθέντων ἐκ τῆς διαρπαγῆς, καὶ γενομένης ὠφελείας τοῖς Καρχηδονίοις ἀξίας τῶν προσδοκωμένων ἐλπίδων ('Many and all kinds of items were gathered up from the plundering, and the spoils met the expectations anticipated by the Carthaginians'); Liv. 25.10.10: *et fuit praedae aliquantum* ('and there was not a small amount of booty').

[69] For example, Hdt. 7.170; Diod. Sic. 11.52, 16.15.1–2, 16.62.4, 16.63.2; Strab. 6.3.4; Paus. 10.10.6; Plut. *Agis* 3.2; Just. *Epit.* 21.3.3.

[70] See also Liv. 27.16.10; Plut. *Fab. Max.* 22.3–8; Strab. 6.3.1.

the episode may reflect lingering Graeco-Bruttian hostility. Yet at the same time, it seems to be the case that Tarentine mistrust of Lucanians and Messapians was far less pronounced than the clear tension between the Bruttians and the western Italiote Greeks. As discussed earlier in this chapter, Taras had not infrequently allied with its Italic neighbours in order to further its own interests, even against other Greek cities (see above, pp. 194–9). Moreover, Hannibal did not garner uniform support among the Lucanians and Messapians in the early stages of the war. Livy records that the Lucanians revolted in the aftermath of Hannibal's victory at Cannae, as did the Uzentini in the Sallentine peninsula; Polybius makes no mention of either in his list of communities that defected.[71] Livy's claim is anachronistic, for he later reports that the Romans enrolled Lucanian troops in either 214 or 213,[72] while some Lucanians remained loyal to Rome until 212, after the revolt of Taras.[73] The Uzentini probably did not revolt in 216 but instead defected with the rest of the communities in the Sallentine peninsula in the summer of 213.[74] If De Sanctis is correct that the Tarentines were bitterly hostile towards the Lucanians and Messapians, then the fact that at least some of the Lucanians and the Messapians remained loyal to Rome might actually have compelled the Tarentines to seek an alliance with Hannibal *sooner*, rather than delaying their revolt.

It is true, however, that Lucania was a large region encompassing many communities, so only the most geographically proximate Lucanians would have significantly influenced Tarentine policy in the Second Punic War. While the evidence is incomplete, it appears that the Lucanians who revolted first and resisted reconquest the longest were those who inhabited the northern and western regions of Lucania – that is, those furthest from Taras.

According to De Sanctis (1956–69: III.2.251), most of the Lucanians along the Tyrrhenian coast remained loyal, but neither literary nor archaeological evidence supports this assertion. For example, in 214 the Romans stormed Blanda (modern Palecastro di Tortora) on the Tyrrhenian coast, indicating that the town had rebelled.[75] The nearby city of Laös (modern Marcellina),

---

[71] Liv. 22.61.11–12; Polyb. 3.118.3.

[72] Liv. 24.20.1–2, 25.1.3–5, 25.3.9. The details of the two battles are so similar as to suggest that Livy has duplicated the account. If there was only one battle, it is unclear whether to place it in 213 or 214. The confusion between Bruttium and Lucania suggests that the campaign took place along the border of the two regions. See De Sanctis 1956–69: III.2.263–4 and n. 135. The Lucanians could raise 30,000 infantry and 3000 cavalry, according to Polyb. 2.24.12.

[73] Liv. 25.16.5–24; App. *Hann.* 35; see also Polyb. 8.35.

[74] Liv. 25.1.1, 27.15.4; see De Sanctis 1956–69: III.2.263–4 ; La Bua 1992: 60–1.

[75] Liv. 25.20.5. Although Ptolemy (3.1.70) places Blanda inland, Pliny (*HN* 3.72), Mela (2.4) and the Peutinger Table locate it on the coast. For the association of ancient Blanda with the

once a Greek community (a colony of Sybaris) but later Lucanian, appears to have been abandoned by the end of the third century. The timing of its abandonment suggests that it also rebelled during the Second Punic War and was subsequently destroyed by the Romans, though, admittedly, caution should be exercised when tying archaeological evidence to a singular event.[76] The colony of Buxentum, near modern Policastro, was founded after the war, presumably to keep an eye on coastal Lucania and perhaps in response to Lucanian defection.[77] Further inland, the important city of Grumentum (near modern Grumento) almost certainly revolted, as did the town of Volceii (modern Buccino).[78] The main narrative accounts do not mention Potentia's status during the Second Punic War, but it is listed along with Grumentum and Volceii as *praefecturae* in the *Liber coloniarum*; Brunt accepts this as evidence that much of the nearby countryside was confiscated by 200.[79] If so, then Potentia probably revolted and was punished upon its recapture. Hannibal appears to have held Numistro (modern Muro Lucano), but the evidence for its defection is, again, somewhat ambiguous.[80] Finally, most Roman military action in Lucania took place in the western and northern sections of the region. For example, either the consul Ti. Sempronius Gracchus or a *praefectus socium* T. Pomponius Veientanus campaigned in Lucania in 213, probably along the border of

archaeological remains at modern Palecastro di Tortora: La Torre 1991: 133–55; Greco and La Torre 1999: 7–8, 31–6; Isayev 2007: 110 n. 267.

[76] Strab. 6.1.1; Plin. *HN* 3.72 (claiming that the city no longer existed). There are remains of a fourth-century wall, but no archaeological material datable to later than the third century: Guzzo and Greco 1978: 429–59; Guzzo 1983; Barone *et al.* 1986 (concluding that the site was abandoned during the Second Punic War); Greco and La Torre 1999: 50–8; Isayev 2007: 108.

[77] Livy records that the proposal to found Buxentum, among a total of five colonies, was passed in 197 and the colony was founded in 194 (32.29.3–4, 34.42.5–6, 34.45.1–5). The list of colonies founded that year includes some that were placed in cities that had remained loyal during the Second Punic War (for example, Puteoli), but also a number that were located either in cities that had revolted, or on land confiscated from them (for example Croton, Sipontum Temesa). Colonists were sent to Buxentum again in 186 (Liv. 39.22.4). See also Isayev 2007: 110 n. 265.

[78] Livy (23.37.10–1) records Roman military activity near Grumentum in 215; De Sanctis 1956–69: III.2.444 doubts the historicity of Livy's account; Seibert 1993b: 236 n. 61 accepts it cautiously. Livy (27.41.1–27.42.17) also says that Hannibal returned to Grumentum in 207 in order to recover nearby Lucanian towns that had gone over to Rome. Grumentum's loyalty in 207 is unclear. De Sanctis (1956–69: III.2.472) believes the city was still loyal to Hannibal, though he may have been trying to recover the city: Seibert 1993b: 383. In either case, Grumentum seems to have revolted at some point during the war, with Hannibal trying either to recover it or to use it as a base for attacking other cities. For the revolt of Volceii and possibly other unnamed Lucanian towns, see Liv. 27.15.2–3; for the identification of Volceii with Buccino, see A. Russi 1995: 14.

[79] *Lib. colon.* 209 L; Brunt 1971: 280–1; see also Isayev 2007: 94–5, who is more cautious in accepting the evidence from the *Liber coloniarum*.

[80] Liv. 27.2.4–10; Plut. *Marc.* 24.4–5; Frontin. *Str.* 2.2.6; Plin. *HN* 3.98; Ptol. *Geog.* 3.1.74. Plutarch says that Marcellus followed Hannibal into Lucania (in 210), where the former camped in the plains near Numistro while the latter had already occupied the heights around the city. After

Bruttium, and captured a number of small Lucanian towns.[81] In the following year Gracchus, as proconsul, was ambushed and killed near the Bruttian–Lucanian border.[82] Finally, in 209, the consul Q. Fulvius Flaccus was assigned the province *in Lucanis ac Bruttiis*, and he restored a number of Lucanian and possibly Bruttian towns.[83]

It is not surprising that the western and northern Lucanians would have been both more resistant to Roman rule and more likely to revolt. The history of western Lucania frequently involved Lucanian encroachment on coastal Greek settlements, such as Poseidonia (later Paestum) and Laös.[84] Rome's domination prevented Lucanian expansion along the Tyrrhenian coast, while the conquest of the few remaining Greek cities (such as Velia) ultimately shielded them from Lucanian aggression, albeit at the cost of their freedom and the imposition of military obligations.[85] The Romans

an inconclusive battle, Hannibal withdrew. Plutarch's account may imply that Hannibal controlled the city but set up his camp in the nearby hills as he had done near Capua. In Livy's version, Marcellus left a garrison in Numistro after Hannibal withdrew, suggesting that he did not trust the local population. According to Pliny, the territory of Numistro bordered Volceii. For the battle, see De Sanctis 1956–69: III.2.446–7 and n. 30; Seibert 1993b: 332–3. For the topography: Nissen 1967: II.902; Buck 1981: 324; Del Tutto Palma and Capano 1990.

[81] Liv. 25.1.2–5, 25.3.9: Livy first records that Veientanus was successfully campaigning in Bruttium when he was captured by Hanno, while Gracchus stormed towns in Lucania (24.47.12, 25.1.2–5). But he later reports that Veientanus was campaigning in Lucania when he was captured (25.3.9). Broughton 1951–2: I.262–3 places Gracchus in Luceria without explanation; De Sanctis 1956–69: III.2.263–4 suggests that Veientanus was under the command of Gracchus, with both operating in south-western Italy. Whatever the case, there appears to have been some Roman military activity along the Bruttian–Lucanian border, which resulted in the capture of a number of small Lucanian towns.

[82] Liv. 25.15.10–25.17.3; App. *Hann.* 35; see also Polyb. 8.35. Livy places the location of Gracchus' death in Lucania (25.16.24) but admits that some maintain that he died beside a river named Calore near Beneventum. A location in the vicinity of the Bruttian–Lucanian border makes more sense, especially since there was an ancient Calore (probably modern Tànagro) River, in Lucania near Bruttium. For the topography, see Nissen 1967: II.903; De Sanctis 1956–69: III.2.281 n. 149.

[83] Liv. 27.7.7, 27.15.2–3.

[84] Strab. 5.4.13, 6.1.1–2; Diod. Sic. 14.101.3–4; Lomas 1993: 33–4. Many Lucanian sites were fortified in the late fourth century (Isayev 2007: 151–4), suggesting conflict or threat of conflict. Archaeological evidence also suggests Lucanian penetration into Greek sites, though in some cases (for example Poseidonia) the process appears to have been one of gradual infiltration rather than violent conquest: Isayev 2007: 110–17.

[85] Velia may have been conquered in 293 during the Third Samnite War: Livy mentions that the consul Sp. Carvilius Maximus captured a city with that name (10.44.8–9, 10.45.9), but some scholars doubt that the consuls fought south of Samnium that year. Thus, Livy may be referring to another, otherwise unknown Velia rather than the more famous Italiote city, or his notice is a retrojection of Cervilius' exploits during his second consulship in 272: see Beloch 1926: 431; De Sanctis 1956–69: II.361 n. 1; Salmon 1967: 273 n. 1 (who are all sceptical of the notice); Lomas 1993: 47 (who accepts this as a reference to the famous Velia); Oakley 1997–2005: IV:379–91 (for complete discussion and bibliography). Whether Velia came under Roman control in 293 or 272 does not seriously affect the present discussion. In either case, the Velians were forced to supply ships for the Roman navy (Polyb. 1.20.14; Liv. 26.39.5), though they seemed to have enjoyed a favourable treaty with Rome (Cic. *Balb.* 55).

also directly conquered Lucanian-controlled cities, and in the case of Oscanised Paestum, they imposed a colony in 273.[86] The colony's foundation not only strengthened Roman control and checked possible Lucanian incursions, but it also must have had a profound impact on the surrounding settlement patterns.[87] Some western Lucanians probably suffered under Roman domination, as did other inland Italic peoples such as the Bruttians (especially in southern Bruttium) and Samnites, who also revolted during the Second Punic War. Indeed, western and northern Lucanians may have been encouraged to revolt by the actions of their neighbours. It is no coincidence, then, that Rome concentrated its military efforts in Lucania on areas bordering both Bruttium and Samnium.

Taras was situated in Messapia, near the far south-east corner of Lucania, and thus distant from those Lucanian communities that, according to the foregoing discussion, lent Hannibal early and robust support. Meanwhile, those Lucanians who inhabited territory closest to Taras appear to have remained loyal to Rome for a longer time than their kinsmen to the northwest. It is not likely, therefore, that the defection of the north-western Lucanians had much impact on Tarentine policy decisions; if anything, the closest Lucanians defected only after, and perhaps even because, the Tarentines did.[88] If so, then Taras' surprising loyalty until 213/12 cannot be explained by appealing to anti-Lucanian sentiment (contra De Sanctis).

The explanation for Tarentine loyalty in the early years of the war – that is, why anti-Roman sentiment among the ruling elite did not reach a critical mass until years after Cannae – must be located in specific immediate conditions. Perhaps the most important factor was the particularly robust Roman military presence in Taras and nearby locales since the outbreak of the war, if not earlier, which must have discouraged thoughts of defection. As has been mentioned, there was a large Roman garrison stationed in Taras, totalling between around 4,000 and 5,000 men. According to Livy, some time after Taras had revolted, the Roman garrison commander dispatched a force of 2,000 or 2,500 troops from the citadel to harass Tarentine foragers.[89] Given the circumstances, the entire garrison probably would

---

[86] Strab. 5.4.13; Liv. *Per.* 14; Vell. Pat. 1.14.7; Eutr. 2.16; Salmon 1969: 62–3; Mario Torelli 1988: 33–41; Isayev 2007: 91.

[87] This is seen most clearly with the later foundation of Buxentum, which seems to have resulted in the abandonment of the inland Lucanian settlements around Roccagloriosa: Gualtieri and de Polignac 1991: 196–8; Lomas 1993: 87–9; see also Isayev 2007: 148–9, 154–8, noting that three-quarters of what she calls 'Italo-Lucanian fortified centres' were abandoned in the late fourth or early third century.

[88] See Appendix D.

[89] Liv. 26.39.21–2; there is confusion in the manuscripts as to the correct figure.

not have been sent from the citadel, so the reference points to a larger figure for the entire garrison. According to Polybius (2.24.13), Rome had garrisoned Sicily and Taras with two legions (στρατόπεδα δύο) at the time of the Gallic revolt in 225; each legion had about 4,400 troops (4,200 infantry and 200 cavalry). He also reports that the Romans dispatched 'legions to Sardinia and Sicily and garrisons to Taras and the well-situated places of other regions' after the battle of Trebbia, in the winter of 218/17.[90] Polybius thus appears to make a distinction between legions (στρατόπεδα) and garrisons (προφυλακάς). It is possible that the Taras 'legion' was removed sometime after 225 and then replaced at the outbreak of the Second Punic War with a new 'garrison' of unspecified strength, but it seems more likely that the legion was still stationed in Taras at the beginning of the war and then reinforced after Trebbia. This could explain Appian's claim that the Taras garrison was 5,000 strong.[91] A garrison equivalent to at least one legion represented a formidable military presence.

Roman garrisons were also stationed in neighbouring Metapontion and further afield in Thurii, though none is mentioned for Heraclea.[92] It is impossible to tell if they were in place before the Second Punic War or if they are among the garrisons sent to 'well-situated places of other regions', but, in either case, Roman military assets were visible to the eastern Italiote Greeks from at least the earliest stages of the war. The Metapontion garrison may have drawn the attention of the Tarentines. First, Metapontion had historically fallen under Tarentine hegemony, so the Roman occupation of this nearby city would have underscored Roman ascendance and the decline of Tarentine regional hegemony.[93] Second, and perhaps more importantly, the Tarentines must have recognised that the Metapontion garrison could quickly be redeployed to reinforce the force occupying Taras.[94]

Roman strategic advantages and military activity in Apulia and the Sallentine peninsula also probably limited the opportunity for defection. Taras lay between the Latin colonies of Brundisium and Venusia, from which the Romans could quickly move troops along the Via Appia. Meanwhile, Rome actively defended the Salento. In 216, after the

---

[90] Polyb. 3.75.4: πέμποντες εἰς Σαρδόνα καὶ Σικελίαν στρατόπεδα, πρὸς δὲ τούτοις εἰς Τάραντα προφυλακὰς καὶ τῶν ἄλλων τόπων εἰς τοὺς εὐκαίρους.

[91] Appian wrote at a time when the 'paper strength' of the legion was 5,280, so his reference to 5,000 men in the Taras garrison may simply represent a round figure for a single legion.

[92] Polyb. 8.34; Liv. 25.11, 25.15, App. *Hann.* 33–4.

[93] For Tarentine hegemony over Metapontion, see above, pp. 195–9.

[94] This is in fact what the Romans did after Hannibal captured Taras but Rome still held the citadel: Polyb. 8.34.1; Liv. 25.15.5–6, 25.11.10; App. *Hann.* 35.

battle of Cannae, C. Terentius Varro returned to Apulia with an unnamed army – perhaps the *legio classica* that had been sent previously to Teanum Sidicinum; the force was relocated in 215 to Taras. In the same year the senate ordered twenty-five ships to guard the coast between Brundisium and Taras, and the fleet was later increased to fifty vessels.[95] The following year, a fleet was again stationed near Brundisium for the protection of Taras and the Salento.[96] If Livy is to be believed, the combined Roman land and sea forces effectively prevented ambassadors sent by Philip V of Macedon from landing in the Sallentine peninsula.[97] Overall, garrisons and vigorous Roman military activity in the region must have discouraged the coastal cities on the Salento, Taras included, from rebelling after Cannae.

Finally, we should not underestimate the impact that the Tarentine hostages held in Rome probably had in blunting the momentum of any anti-Roman movement.[98] Concern for hostages could have a powerful effect on a city's ruling elite, and hostage-takers played on these fears: concern for Capuan aristocrats stationed in Sicily was critical in preventing Capua from revolting sooner; the Carthaginian capture of Locrian hostages was instrumental in Locri's revolt; when the Romans attempted to recapture Arpi in 214, they took an aristocrat named Altinius hostage; meanwhile, Hannibal executed members of Altinius' family in order to discourage the Arpians from changing sides; when Hannibal captured a number of Neapolitan aristocrats, he used them as leverage in negotiations.[99] Thus, both the Romans and Hannibal employed the threat of punishment to aristocrats and their families as a means of controlling a city. Turning to Taras, it was the execution of Tarentine hostages in Rome that was the proximate event that set the city's revolt in motion.[100] This implies that so long as these hostages remained alive, they were effective collateral against Taras' defection.

Overall, the fact that the Romans stationed a large garrison in Taras and held a number of Tarentine aristocrats hostage goes a long way towards explaining Taras' failure to revolt in the immediate wake of Cannae; Rome's subsequent land and sea operations around the Salento then kept

[95] Liv. 22.57.7–8, 23.32.16–17, 23.38.8–10; Brunt 1971: 648–9; Lazenby 1978: 91.

[96] Liv. 24.11.3–5; 24.20.12–13; Brunt 1971: 649–50.

[97] Liv. 23.33.1–4.

[98] Liv. 25.7.10–13.

[99] Arpi: Liv. 24.45.8–14; Chapter 2, p. 65 n. 48; Capua: Liv. 23.4.8; Chapter 3, pp. 113–14; Naples: Liv. 23.1.9–10; Chapter 2, pp. 132–3; Locri: Liv. 24.1.4–5; Chapter 4, pp. 165–6.

[100] Liv. 25.7.10–13. The execution of the hostages is discussed more fully later in this chapter: see below, pp. 214–17.

Taras in check until 213/12. This may appear a mundane conclusion, but not when it is considered in the context of the discussion in the previous three chapters. Taras had a long history as a local hegemonic power, and such cities were typically the first to come over to Hannibal in Apulia, Campania and Bruttium. In the case of Taras, particular political and, more importantly, military circumstances eclipsed long-term tendencies. The local military landscape meant that Hannibal needed to make additional displays of force to convince the local elites of his credibility. But Roman manoeuvres that were effective early in the war came at a price, for garrisoning and hostage-taking generated further Tarentine resentment that Hannibal could exploit when he began to act more directly in southeastern Italy in 214.

THE REVOLT OF TARAS, 213/12

The local political and military landscape began to change in 214, and by 213 the situation was markedly different. The conditions that shaped Tarentine policy began, therefore, to shift in Hannibal's favour. A party of anti-Roman aristocrats seized this opportunity to convince their fellow citizens (or at least a critical mass of the decision-making elite) that alliance with Hannibal was preferable to remaining loyal to Rome, while at the same time promoting their own political status. We will now consider more specifically what factors contributed to this political, and subsequently foreign policy, volte-face.

Hannibal had grown frustrated with his limited success in Campania, especially his inability to capture a port city, and for the first time, it seems, he turned his attention more seriously to the cities along the south-eastern coast of the peninsula.[101] His treaty with Philip V of Macedon, which had been struck in 215, may have furnished further motivation to shift his focus to the south. Philip agreed, according to the treaty, to help Hannibal in whatever way was needed or agreed upon.[102] If this represented a serious offer of military support, Hannibal probably would have sought to secure

---

[101] For Hannibal's strained patience concerning affairs in Campania, see Liv. 24.13.11. Besides his frustration, Hannibal perhaps also desired a port in south-east Italy in order to link up with Philip V, with whom he had recently concluded a treaty; see Liv. 24.13.5.

[102] The text of the Hannibalic–Macedonian treaty: Polyb. 7.9; Walbank 1970: II.42–56. The clause promising help is found at Polyb. 7.9.10–11: ἔσεσθε δὲ καὶ ἡμῖν σύμμαχοι πρὸς τὸν πόλεμον, ὅς ἐστιν ἡμῖν πρὸς Ῥωμαίους, ἕως ἂν ἡμῖν καὶ ὑμῖν οἱ θεοὶ διδῶσι τὴν εὐημερίαν. βοηθήσετε δὲ ἡμῖν, ὡς ἂν χρεία ᾖ καὶ ὡς ἂν συμφωνήσωμεν ('You will be our allies for the war, which is ours against the Romans, until the gods grant success for us and for you. You will provide such aid for us as there is need and as we agree').

a port in the Salento in order to facilitate the movement of ships and troops from the East.[103] As we have seen, Philip's ambassadors were forced to land at Locri because they could not put in at Brundisium or Taras, and the strategic value of a south-eastern port would not have been lost on Hannibal or Philip.[104] Meanwhile, if Livy can be trusted, an embassy of Tarentine aristocrats approached Hannibal in Campania in the summer of 214 and promised that Taras was ready to revolt if only Hannibal would march to the city; the delegation convinced him to campaign in the immediate vicinity of Taras for the first time during the war.[105]

Whether or not the delegation is historical, Hannibal did set out for Taras, 'devastating' along the way, until he entered Tarentine territory, at which point his troops were ordered to cease ravaging in order to win over the local population peaceably.[106] Hannibal pitched camp near Taras for an unspecified number of days, hoping that this show of strength would encourage the city to defect, but the propraetor, Marcus Valerius, who commanded the fleet stationed in Brundisium, had learned of his approach and secured Taras' defences.[107] It was already autumn, so Hannibal left Taras with the grain he had collected around Metapontion and Heraclea and moved to winter quarters in Salapia, from which he began to raid the Sallentine peninsula.[108]

[103] Livy (23.33.9–12; cf. 31.7.4) preserves a version of the treaty that specifies that Philip was supposed to cross over to Italy with a fleet, lay waste to the Italian coast and then wage war on land and sea (see also Chapter 1, n. 87 for additional ancient references to the Roman tradition on this alliance). The Livian version is almost certainly an annalistic invention rather than a more complete or later modified version of the treaty recorded by Polybius. Still, the Polybian treaty does contain a clause providing for military cooperation (see above, n. 102), so there is no reason to assume that collaboration in some form, even limited in scope, was never seriously envisioned. On this point, I am in agreement with Briscoe's (1973: 73) conclusion that 'it is reasonable to interpret this as looking forward to Philip's eventual coming to Italy. It is unnecessary to think that Philip's activities were to be confined to Greece'; contra Bickerman 1952: 15–17; De Sanctis 1956–69: II.2.392–4; Walbank 1970: II.55; Gruen 1984: 374–7. For further discussion, see also Chapter 7, pp. 298–9.

[104] According to Livy (24.13.5), Hannibal recognised Taras' potential for linking with Macedon and Philip. For the difficulty that Philip's ambassadors experienced landing in Italy, see above, p. 210.

[105] Liv. 24.13.1–6. Hannibal had spent the winter of 215/14 in Apulia, but Livy implies that he decided to campaign around Taras only after he met with the Tarentine delegation in Campania. The report of this early sign of Tarentine disloyalty might be a Roman invention to foreshadow the later revolt or underscore the treacherous nature of the people of Taras. Still, that Hannibal would have received at least occasional embassies from various cities that were 'testing the water' – especially after Cannae – is not inherently implausible.

[106] Liv. 24.17.8, 24.20.9–10.   [107] Liv. 24.20.11–13.

[108] Liv. 24.20.13–16. For the time of year, see Lazenby 1978: 110. The grain from Metapontion and Heraclea may have been collected during Hannibal's march, while he devastated the countryside; see De Sanctis 1956–69: III.2.250. The cities along the Ionian coast could have supplied Hannibal with significant grain stores, as the broad plains and coastal terraces of the Metapontino possess

Hannibal spent the next campaign season in the Sallentine peninsula, and it is at this time that he probably encouraged the defection of
most of the communities there.[109] Although Livy downplays Hannibal's
achievements for the year, the defecting cities included Uzentum and
Manduria.[110] Only after capturing the cities in the Salento did Hannibal
again march toward Taras. In late 213 (either autumn or early winter)
another Tarentine delegation met Hannibal and proposed to turn over
their city.[111] Hannibal had altered the military landscape by marching
through Lucania and the Salento, and the appearance of his army and
his nearby successes seem to have impressed the Tarentines. Also, since
Manduria controlled the lines of communication between Taras and
Brundisium and was the key to holding the Sallentine peninsula,[112] when
Hannibal captured it he effectively shielded Taras from Roman forces
in Brundisium. Meanwhile, Rome had been unwilling or unable to stop
him from pillaging around Metapontion, Heraclea and the Salento, so
Hannibal had exposed weakness in Rome's regional military network
and thus encouraged disgruntled Tarentine aristocrats to come forward
and seek a treaty with him.

At the same time, Hannibal's treaty with Philip may have further
emboldened the Tarentines. The Romans found out about the treaty and
prepared for war with Philip: M. Valerius Laevinus was sent to take over
the fleet stationed in the Salento, not only to guard the coast but also to
prepare to cross over to Macedon.[113] In 214 Laevinus was still operating
around Brundisium, and (as we have seen) he responded effectively when
Hannibal first approached Taras.[114] Later in 214, however, an embassy
from the Illyrian city of Oricum arrived to inform Laevinus of Philip's
offensive against Apollonia. Laevinus brought his fleet to Oricum, where
it spent the winter; he was redeployed again in 213 and assigned Greece

great agricultural potential; see Carter 1990: 423–5; Giardino and De Siena 1999: 335–6. However,
the reference to the collection of grain may pose a chronological problem, since the grain harvest in that part of Italy should have occurred in early June, long before Hannibal's arrival in
the area; see Azzi 1922: 544–5. It may have been the case that Hannibal collected grain stored in
rural silos. This is not unprecedented: the Romans had converted Cannae into a granary earlier
in the war, and Hannibal raided the site; see Chapter 2, pp. 67–8 and n. 57.

[109] La Bua 1992: 44–8; see above, p. 205 and n. 74.

[110] Liv. 22.61.11–12, 25.1.1, 27.15.4. Livy mentions the Uzentini in his anachronistic list of cities
that revolted immediately after Cannae (22.61.11–12), and reports that the Romans recaptured
Manduria in 209, indicating its prior defection to Hannibal (27.15.4). He also records that
Hannibal spent the summer of 213 in the Salento, encouraging a number of unimportant cit-
ies (*ignobiles urbes*) to revolt. Hannibal probably won over Uzentum, Manduria and any other
Sallentine cities that may have revolted during this campaign in 213: La Bua 1992: 61–2.

[111] Polyb. 8.24.4–8; Liv. 25.8.3–6.   [112] La Bua 1992: 59–64.

[113] Liv. 23.38.4–11, 23.48.3.   [114] Liv. 24.10.4, 24.11.3, 24.20.12–14; see above, pp. 209–10.

and Macedon as his province.[115] The opening of this new war front had forced the Romans to reallocate military assets from the Salento to Illyria, which opened the door for more open Tarentine dissent.

Meanwhile, anti-Roman sentiment within Taras had almost certainly increased since the outbreak of the war, as both the economic and military burdens of Roman occupation were felt more acutely. There was already a Roman garrison of around one legion stationed in the citadel, probably in place since the beginning of the war.[116] As mentioned above, in 214 M. Valerius Laevinus had taken steps to prevent Hannibal from capturing Taras. It is worth examining his actions more carefully: according to Livy (24.20.12–13), three days before Hannibal arrived Laevinus conscripted more troops, posted guards along the city walls, kept vigilant day and night and thus left no opportunity for the city to be captured or to defect. Livy's account suggests that the newly conscripted were drawn from the local population, which may have generated resentment; at the very least, the Tarentines must have been expected to help fund the increased manpower. Perhaps more costly would have been maintenance of Laevinus' fleet, which was protecting the shores between Brundisium and Taras. It had been augmented to fifty vessels and spent at least some time harboured in Taras, where it may have posed a significant burden on the local population;[117] indeed, in 211 the sailors from a Carthaginian fleet sent to protect the Tarentines after they defected angered the locals by eating all of their food.[118] Certainly, the financial and military burden on the Tarentines would not have lessened between 216 and 213.

The single greatest contribution to anti-Roman sentiment, however, was the execution of the Tarentine (and Thurian) hostages held in Rome, probably sometime in the summer or autumn of 213. The hostages were housed in the Atrium Libertatis under the watch of two *aeditui*, the light guard possibly indicating that the Romans did not want to appear heavy-handed in their treatment. A Tarentine aristocrat named Phileas, who had been staying in Rome for an unspecified time as an ambassador, bribed

---

[115] Liv. 24.40.1–6, 24.40.16–17, 24.44.5. Laevinus' fleet was still stationed across the Adriatic in 212: Liv. 24.48.5.

[116] See above, pp. 208–9.

[117] Liv. 23.38.8–11. In the same passage, Livy informs us that Hiero of Syracuse sent money, 200,000 *modii* of wheat and 100,000 *modii* of barley to help pay for and feed the fleet. If so, then the burden on the Tarentines would have been lessened. The notice does underscore, however, the cost of maintaining a fleet. We do not know if these supplies entirely obviated the need for Tarentine contributions, nor do we know how long these supplies lasted, since the fleet lingered in the area until late 214.

[118] Polyb. 9.9.11; Liv. 26.20.7–11.

the guards and convinced the hostages to escape; they were captured the next day near Terracina and executed.[119] Their punishment appears to have been critical in turning Tarentine public opinion against the Romans.

The executions had serious consequences for Roman interests in south-eastern Italy. First, it enraged the Tarentine citizenry in general;[120] Hannibal played on this anger, agreeing to a treaty that guaranteed that the Tarentines would live under their own laws and then inveighing against Roman high-handedness in a speech to the general citizen assembly, which, according to Polybius, was enthusiastically received.[121] Hannibal had repeatedly employed Hellenistic 'liberation' propaganda in the early stages of the war, and the terms of the Hannibalic–Tarentine treaty (guaranteeing αὐτονομία) and his speech (calling to mind Roman brutality and, presumably, promising temperance on his part) both fit this Hellenistic diplomatic pattern. Indeed, Hannibal's Tarentine allies went through the streets championing the cause of freedom (ἐπὶ τὴν ἐλευθερίαν) and spreading word that the Carthaginians had come on their behalf.[122] Thus, Roman severity in the case of the hostages and the anger that it engendered both gave Hannibal and his local partners a clear opening to emphasise liberation propaganda, which apparently resonated with its intended audience.

Second, the executions particularly angered the elite friends and relatives of the hostages, who, in response, either formed the core of an anti-Roman conspiracy or joined a pre-existing party of aristocrats who were hostile to Rome.[123] While the hostages' relatives may have acted primarily out of revenge, it is clear that at least some of them saw Hannibal as an

---

[119] For the account of the hostages' execution, see Liv. 25.7.10–13. De Sanctis 1956–69: III.2.264 places the executions near the time of the Tarentine revolt, contra Lomas 1993: 70, who argues that the hostages were executed in 215. Since Hannibal captured Taras sometime in the winter of 213/12, it seems reasonable for the executions to have occurred in the autumn, allowing a couple of months for news to reach the Tarentines and take effect on public opinion. For the general discussion of the chronology of the events related to the Tarentine revolt, see Appendix C. The Atrium Libertatis was later the site of the torture of slaves during the trial of Milo (Cic. *Mil.* 59), so its use as a holding area for hostages, a detail mentioned only by Livy, is not implausible. More generally, Livy's account of the revolt of Taras closely parallels Polybius' version, though it contains additional details. Livy probably did not use Polybius directly as a source. Rather, both Polybius and Livy derive their accounts from a common source: ultimately Silenus, with Livy probably using Coelius, who in turn drew on Silenus; see Walbank 1970: II.100–1; for a detailed analysis of the parallel passages, see also Kukofka 1990: 37–55.

[120] Liv. 25.8.1.   [121] Polyb. 8.25.1–2, 8.31.1–4; Liv. 25.8.8, 25.10.6–9.

[122] Polyb. 8.31.2.

[123] There may already have been an anti-Roman movement, if we accept Livy's reference to the aristocrats who met with Hannibal in 214. Thirteen Tarentine aristocrats (we know the names of five) were the main movers behind the defection (see above, n. 6), though others may have been involved less prominently.

opportunity for their own political advancement. Thus, the five aristocrats who met Hannibal in Campania claimed to have convinced other Tarentines to prefer an alliance with Hannibal, and if true, they appear to have increased their political standing by associating themselves with Hannibal's cause.[124] As mentioned above, the conspirators in 213/12 were parroting Hannibal's liberation propaganda, presumably hoping to capitalise on what appears to have been a popular message. Some of the conspirators had previously curried favour with the Tarentine citizenry by selling food and putting on entertainment, probably at their own expense; Polybius' account (8.24.12–13) shows rather clearly that these activities were aimed at building a political following – and the tactics were working. When looked at from the Tarentine perspective, the available evidence suggests that the defection of Taras was bound up with internal political competition, with at least some of the conspirators seizing on Hannibal's arrival as a promising moment to stage a political coup.[125]

Lastly, by executing the hostages, the Romans lost a good deal of the leverage they had over potential anti-Roman aristocrats in Taras (and Thurii). Here, it is appropriate to invoke once again a brief comparison with the Capuan situation: concern for the safety of Campanian *equites* serving in Sicily, who were viewed by their relatives as hostages, was a major obstacle to Capua's defection. In the case of Capua, Hannibal addressed the situation by promising to hand over Roman hostages whom the Capuans could hold as collateral for the safety of their own citizens. In the case of Taras, the Romans solved the problem for Hannibal by executing the hostages.

The revolt of Taras provides, therefore, striking evidence for the interplay between Hannibal's strategy and the dynamics of local politics shaped by long-term developments. As discussed earlier in the chapter, the Tarentine elite was (unsurprisingly) divided, with some members particularly dissatisfied with Roman hegemony. There were also a number of long-term developments, possibly including economic decline, which should have disposed the Tarentines to defect. Yet both the formidable Roman military presence in and near the Salento and the taking of Tarentine hostages prevented an anti-Roman movement from gaining much momentum, even after Cannae. Between 216 and 213 Rome's military capacity in the Salento was diminished, giving Hannibal the chance to play on intensifying anti-Roman sympathies. The execution of the Tarentine hostages

---

[124] Liv. 24.13.1–3.
[125] Lomas 1993: 70. Nico, Philomenus and Democrates were still in power three years later when Taras fell to Rome (Liv. 27.16), so they seem to have established themselves as part of a new ruling regime.

removed an important impediment to revolt, while at the same time acting as a trigger event, allowing anti-Roman sentiment to come to the surface. This climate in turn encouraged a group of local aristocrats to believe that associating with Hannibal and encouraging defection was a viable political platform; these aristocrats drummed up political support in Taras while at the same time they negotiated with Hannibal and formulated a plan for his occupation of the city – and their seizure of power.

Yet even after his local allies had opened the gates and his troops occupied the city, Hannibal's job was not done. First, his troops engaged in vicious street fighting with the Romans.[126] Second, Hannibal and the conspirators needed (or perceived that they needed) to address the remaining citizenry in public and make the appropriate diplomatic gestures and promises, in order to quiet any remaining pro-Roman opposition. The sequence of events bears a remarkable similarity to the series of negotiations that culminated in the Capuan revolt: as discussed in Chapter 3, even after the anti-Roman movement gained ascendancy and the Capuans agreed to make a treaty with Hannibal, he still needed to visit Capua in person, address the assembled elite, and reiterate his promises – including his promise that Capuan hegemony would be restored. No such promise is recorded in Hannibal's address to the Tarentines, but considering Taras' history as a regional hegemonic power, we can plausibly conjecture that Hannibal (or perhaps his local political allies) appealed to Tarentine greatness and ambitions to win over the population,[127] or at least this consideration coloured their reception of his offers, whatever they may have been. Indeed, as we will see in the next section, the Tarentines do appear to have used their new freedom from Rome, backed up by alliance with Hannibal, to influence – and perhaps establish hegemony over – the cities of Heraclea, Metapontion and Thurii.[128]

AFTERMATH OF THE TARENTINE REVOLT: METAPONTION, HERACLEA AND THURII, 212

Even though Hannibal had occupied the city of Taras and won over many of the citizens, he failed to capture its citadel, which the Roman garrison and an unknown number of pro-Roman Tarentines continued

---

[126] Polyb. 8.30.1–9; Liv. 25.9.16–17.
[127] Perhaps such an offer formed part of the otherwise unspecified 'promises' that Hannibal made to Tarentine aristocrats in 214 and again in 213/12: Liv. 24.13.4, 25.8.6.
[128] Lomas 1993: 70–1 also suggests that Taras tried to reassert its regional hegemony during the Second Punic War.

to hold.[129] The citadel was then reinforced with troops from the garrison at Metapontion, either the whole garrison (implied by Livy), or half of the garrison (stated by Appian).[130] Hannibal built a palisade, a moat and then a second palisade along the wall that separated the citadel from the urban centre. He then ordered the construction of another wall to separate the Tarentines from the Romans camped in the citadel, while he retired to a camp a few miles from Taras to plan for storming the citadel. In the meantime, the Romans sallied from the citadel and destroyed some of the siege machinery. Hannibal came back to inspect the progress on the siege works, decided instead to blockade the citadel rather than storm it, and then he returned to his camp for the remainder of the winter.[131] Hannibal's failure to capture the citadel would have serious long-term strategic consequences, as will be discussed in Chapter 6. For the moment, however, we will focus on the immediate impact of his partial success in Taras.

The arrival of reinforcements from Metapontion surely helped to secure the citadel of Taras, but the corresponding weakening of the Roman garrison in Metapontion accelerated the Metapontian defection. Appian (*Hann.* 35) claims that the Metapontians massacred the remaining Roman garrison. Livy (25.15.5–6), who reports that the whole garrison was restationed to Taras, states that Metapontion revolted immediately once fear of the Roman garrison had been removed. Both accounts indicate that the city was held more through Roman force than through the goodwill of its ruling elite, and both accounts agree that the complete or partial reduction of Roman troop strength allowed anti-Roman Metapontians to seize control of their city and hand it over to Hannibal. Metapontion defected in short order after the Tarentine revolt, only a few weeks later in early March, though it is impossible to specify an exact date.[132] On one level, the explanation for Metapontion's defection is clear: the local ruling elite had wanted to revolt sooner but were prevented from doing so by the Roman garrison; a rapidly changing military landscape in the winter of 213/12 opened the door to revolt.

Presumably, the local ruling aristocracy was subject to comparable pressures and influenced by similar push and pull factors as we have seen in other, better-documented cases. The speed with which the Metapontians defected when they had a chance, and the ferocity with which they treated the remaining Roman garrison (if we follow Appian's account), suggest

---

[129] Polyb. 8.30.8; Liv. 25.10.6; App. *Hann.* 32.
[130] Liv. 25.15.4–6; App. *Hann.* 33, 35.
[131] Polyb. 8.33.1–8.34.1; Liv. 25.11.2–11.   [132] See Appendix C.

a high level of disaffection. Indeed, the very fact that the city had been garrisoned at some point during the war, if not earlier,[133] implies that the Romans did not trust the Metapontians, perhaps also indicating that they were particularly restive. Unfortunately, however, the sources offer little testimony about the pre-existing conditions shaping their decision to revolt, so we are left to speculate as to the precise and decisive motives.

The recent revolt of neighbouring Taras must have been a critical consideration. Obviously, the Tarentine revolt created the preconditions for defection by compelling the Romans to shift troop levels in Metapontion, but historic patterns of regional interstate diplomacy, especially between these two cities, also shed light on the Metapontian reaction. Metapontion reached its height in population and prosperity in the second half of the fourth century,[134] at which time it also faced Lucanian and Messapian pressure and fell increasingly under Tarentine hegemony. Strabo (6.1.15) claims that it was wiped out by the Samnites (ἠφανίσθη δ᾽ ὑπὸ Σαυνιτῶν); the reference is obscure, but it may reflect a historical echo of Oscan–Metapontian tension. Taras invited both Archidamus (*c.* 340) and Alexander of Epirus (*c.* 330) to Italy in order to drive the Messapians from Metapontion.[135] The Metapontians tried unsuccessfully to reject another Tarentine ally, Cleonymus of Sparta (*c.* 300), who subsequently attacked and captured the city with Lucanian reinforcements, took hostages from elite families, and demanded a huge indemnity of 600 talents of silver – approximately one year's production of wheat according to one modern

---

[133] De Sanctis 1956–69: II.366, 400 n. 87 argues that the garrisons in Metapontion and Thurii in the Second Punic War had been in place since *c.* 270 (or earlier), because they had allied with Pyrrhus. This is plausible, though it should be noted that Thurii was compelled by Taras to receive Pyrrhus and had previously invited a Roman garrison as protection (see below, pp. 226–7). Metapontion, however, may have been among the unnamed Greek cities sending ambassadors to Pyrrhus (Plut. *Pyrrh.* 13.5). It is not surprising that a weaker city, such as Metapontion, would not be mentioned by name as supplying troops for Pyrrhus.

[134] At the time of the Second Punic War, the *chora* of Metapontion was bounded by the Bradano and Cavone rivers, and stretched inland about 14 km at its furthest extent, for a total area of over 18,000 hectares. The total population may have been as high as 40,000 in the sixth century, with around 12,000 to 15,000 persons (maximum) living in the urban centre and the rest inhabiting the *chora*: Carter 1990: 405–6. Archaeological survey projects have identified a large number of 'farm sites', suggesting a dense rural population; the total number of rural farm sites appears to have remained relatively stable between *c.* 550 and *c.* 250, with peaks in the early fifth and late fourth centuries. The increase in the number of occupied farm sites in the late fourth century corresponds to other building activity, such as the construction of a new theatre and repaired city walls. Archaeological evidence shows, however, a very steep decline in the second half of the third century, as nearly all of the rural sites identified as farms appear to have been abandoned. See Carter 1990: 405–6, 2006: 195–237; Osanna 1992: 19–20; see also Lomas 1993: 37; Giardino and De Siena 1999.

[135] Diod. Sic. 16.15.12, 16.62.4, 16.63.2; Liv. 8.3.6, 8.17.9–10, 8.24.1–6, 8.24.16; Strab. 6.3.4; Plin. *HN* 3.98; Plut. *Agis* 3.2; Ath. 12.536c–d; Paus. 3.10.5; Just. *Epit.* 12.2.1–15; see above, pp. 195–7.

estimate.[136] A generation later, Metapontion followed Taras in allying with Pyrrhus, bringing the Metapontians into conflict with Rome. Presumably the city was conquered by the Romans at about the same time as Taras, around 270.[137]

The city seems not to have recovered from this series of conflicts and occupations, and archaeological evidence suggests a rapid decline starting in the third century. The University of Texas' survey of the Metapontian *chora*, originally conducted in the early 1980s with the survey continuing through the 1990s, has identified over 200 rural farm sites occupied in the period from *c.* 350 to 300 BC; the number dropped to about 150 occupied farm sites for *c.* 300–250 BC, and to only about 25 occupied farm sites for *c.* 250–25 BC.[138] Carter interpreted this as evidence for a virtual desertion of Metapontion's territory. Although it is possible that this 'rural desertion' reflects simply a different pattern of land use,[139] it is hard to avoid the conclusion that Metapontion experienced a severe decline in population in the third century, so that by the time of the Second Punic War, it had ceased to be an important city.

The specific timing of the Metapontian defection becomes clearer in light of the previous discussion. Metapontion was a weak state that had, historically, been an object of Taras' influence. When the Tarentines revolted, they may have pressured Metapontion into following suit, thus taking advantage of Rome's diminished power and their new alliance with Hannibal as a chance to re-establish their own regional hegemony. Or, what is more probable in this case, as a small state with a high level of disaffection with Rome, Metapontion seized on the opportunity to throw off Roman hegemony. If so, the Metapontians could have drawn encouragement from Taras' revolt, or (more importantly) they would have seen the Tarentines as potential allies against Roman reprisals. There is no direct evidence for this dynamic, but the close timing of the two revolts is

---

[136] Diod. Sic. 20.104.1–20.105.3; Liv. 10.2.1–14; Strab. 6.3.4; Carter 1990: 423–5.

[137] See above, pp. 198–9.

[138] The number of rural farm sites is tabulated in Carter 2006: 214, Fig. 5.20. These totals represent a modification of figures found in Carter's previous publications on Metapontion. For example, Carter 1990: 410 gives 128 rural farm sites for 350–300 BC, 73 for 300–250 BC, and 12 for 250–25 BC. The growing total number of identified sites, as indicated in the more recent publication, is the result of more of the rural *chora* having been surveyed or resurveyed since initial publications. Still, the general trend in the data has remained consistent, with rural sites showing evidence of widespread abandonment beginning in the third century.

[139] Carter 1990: 412. Indeed, more recently, Carter 2006: 242–7 has suggested that during the period between 250 and 50, the large number of smaller, more 'egalitarian' farms were replaced by fewer, larger 'capitalistic' farms of the sort Cato describes; in addition some stretches of the Metapontian *chora* may have been confiscated and turned over to the Roman state.

suggestive, as is Appian's account of the Heraclean revolt, which, even though problematic, hints at cooperation between Metapontion and Taras (see below).

Indeed, Heraclea revolted soon after Metapontion, in middle or late March 212. Neither Polybius nor Livy records the city's revolt, so we must rely on Appian (*Hann.* 35).[140] Despite the almost complete lack of details in the Appianic account, two important features of the event can be observed. First, Appian does not mention a Roman garrison either defending the city or intimidating the local population, nor do we hear of any atrocities committed against Roman citizens living or quartered in the city. This is striking given the relative frequency of reports of brutality against Romans when cities defected.[141] Arguments based on omissions are admittedly dangerous, but the lack of such references may indicate that the local impact of Roman hegemony was slight. The Heracleans had joined the Tarentines and their allies in siding with Pyrrhus,[142] but they do not seem to have opposed Rome very stiffly and received a very favourable treaty from Rome by about 278, which they enjoyed until the Social War.[143] Overall, therefore, Heraclea did not suffer dramatically from the spread of Roman hegemony into southern Italy, which may help to explain why the local elite was comparatively well disposed to Rome. In fact, the lack of a garrison may suggest that the Romans by and large trusted the Heracleans. This relates to the second feature of the Appianic account.

The second important point is that Appian also claims that the Heracleans revolted 'out of fear more than out of inclination' (δέει μᾶλλον ἢ γνώμῃ), and his account implies that it was Taras and Metapontion, presumably with Hannibal's support, that intimidated them.[144] While Appian is certainly promoting an oversimplified, pro-Roman version of the story, there may be some plausibility in his account. Like Metapontion, Heraclea was a weaker city that had long been subject to Tarentine influence until the arrival of Roman power.[145] According to Strabo (6.1.14), who claims to be citing Antiochus, Heraclea was founded in 433 near the site of Siris as a joint colony of Thurii and Taras. It was soon considered of

---

[140] For the date and discussion of the difficulties presented by Appian's account, see Appendix C.

[141] For example, Roman citizens or garrison troops were attacked in Capua, Taras and Metapontion; see Chapter 3, pp. 104–5 (Capua); above, pp. 204, 217–18 (Taras and Metapontion).

[142] De Sanctis 1956–69: II.366, 391.

[143] Cic. *Balb.* 21–2, *Arch.* 6; Quilici 1967: 162.

[144] See Appendix C for the arguments preferring the manuscript reading of 'Tarentum' over an emendation of 'Thurii'.

[145] Quilici 1967: 162.

Tarentine foundation, at which point its name was changed to Heraclea, perhaps to emphasise a strong association between Taras, Heracles and Heraclea.[146] In the same passage Strabo also preserves a variant tradition that the Tarentines alone founded Heraclea. Diodorus (12.36.4) preserves a slightly different version: Heraclea was founded with colonists from Taras and the remnants of Siris, also with no reference to Thurii. Whatever the situation of its initial foundation, Taras came to dominate Heraclea. The Tarentines employed both Archidamus and Alexander of Epirus to drive the Messapians from Heraclea (see above, pp. 195–6). Strabo (6.3.4) states that Heraclea was in Tarentine territory when Alexander moved a panhellenic festival from there to Thurii.[147] Finally, as mentioned above, Heraclea also joined Taras and Metapontion in allying with Pyrrhus.

When Taras revolted and the neighbouring city of Metapontion followed suit, the Heracleans were forced to decide whether to stay loyal to a distant Rome or to submit to the nearer regional hegemonic power, Taras. Indeed, if the Tarentines saw their alliance with Hannibal as a chance to reassert local hegemony, as I speculated above (pp. 199–200, 217), then it is plausible that they threatened Heraclea in some way. Meanwhile, Roman authority in the region clearly appeared to be waning, with the recent loss of Taras, Metapontion and the Salento. Bearing more directly on Heraclea, Rome was incapable of preventing Hannibal from devastating and collecting supplies in the Heraclean *chora* when he first seriously tried to elicit Taras' defection in 214.[148] Heraclea's reluctance to defect until 212 despite the (apparent) lack of a Roman garrison to guarantee its loyalty suggests that pro-Roman sentiment was relatively strong – or at least that the local ruling class was ambivalent with respect to Rome and

---

[146] The original colony of Siris was supposedly founded by 'Trojans' (perhaps Greeks from Asia Minor) sometime in the seventh century, and it was later destroyed sometime in the sixth century; it lay on the ancient river of the same name: Ath. 12 523d (= Archil. fr. 18 D); Lycoph. 978–92; Hdt. 8.62.2; Arist. *Ath. Pol.* 7.9.3; Strab. 6.1.14; Just. *Epit.* 20.2.3–9; Quilici 1967: 153–5; Head 1977: 83–5; Adamesteanu 1981; Tocco Sciarelli 1980. For the association of Taras with Heracles: Taras was a Spartan colony, and Heracles was an important Peloponnesian hero; the association is most visible in the fourth century, when Taras began to mint a significant amount of coins with Heracles on the reverse and Athena or Heracles on the obverse. Similar emissions are found in Heraclea, Metapontion, Croton and Naples, and they have been interpreted as examples of federal coinage of the Italiote League. Yet Heracles also features prominently on contemporary Tarentine statuary and pottery, and Taras appears to have become a sort of 'Heracles centre' in the fourth century. Thus, the iconography on coins may also have expressed Tarentine power. See Wuilleumier 1939: 522–6; Head 1977: 39–40, 53–69, 71–3, 75–80, 95–100; Rutter 1997: 95; Poulter 2002: 135–6.

[147] Lomas 1993: 111 observed that many of the magistrates listed on the 'Heraclea Tables' have Messapic names, suggesting that the Heracleans reached some sort of accommodation with the neighbouring Italic peoples who threatened coastal Greek settlements.

[148] Liv. 24.20.15.

Hannibal. The significantly different military landscape between 214 and 212, and especially the threat posed by Taras, altered their calculations. Thus, immediate conditions convinced the Heracleans to defect.

Hence, by the spring of 212 Heraclea and Metapontion had followed Taras by defecting. Both cities had traditionally fallen under Tarentine hegemony, and their decisions to revolt in the Second Punic War reflect a pattern observed in other regions: the defection of the regional hegemonic state tended to encourage smaller, neighbouring states to do the same, for example in Campania (Capua and its subordinate allies) and Apulia (Arpi and its subordinate allies). But the details of the revolts of these two small cities also reveal how this process could play out differently depending on the specific relationship between hegemonic and subordinate city. Metapontion appears to have been more hostile to Rome and, thus, relatively more amenable to Tarentine hegemony. Only the presence of a Roman garrison prevented revolt, so that the combination of Taras' revolt and the weakening of the garrison brought about rebellion in short order. Heraclea, meanwhile, appears to have been initially more tentative but crumbled under Tarentine pressure, suggesting that their relationship, at least in the late third century, was based more on compulsion than attraction.

The last Italiote city along the Gulf of Taranto to revolt was Thurii, in the spring of 212, perhaps around 15 May.[149] According to Livy (25.8.1, 25.15.7), the primary reason for Thurii's defection was the execution of Thurian hostages, who were involved in the same unsuccessful attempt by the Tarentine hostages to escape from Rome in autumn 213. Subsequently, friends and relatives of the executed Thurians formed a conspiracy and betrayed their city to Mago and Hanno (25.15.7–8). Appian (*Hann.* 34) preserves a very different tradition: the Thurians sent ships laden with supplies to help relieve the pro-Roman forces besieged in the citadel of Taras, but the Tarentines, with Carthaginian help, captured all the Thurian vessels and held the crews hostage, which compelled the Thurians to send envoys in order to negotiate their release. The Tarentines convinced the envoys to bring Thurii over to Hannibal in exchange for the hostages' freedom; after the negotiations concluded, all Thurian hostages were released, and both the envoys and former hostages convinced their fellow townsmen to open the gates for Hanno. Although Appian claims that the envoys and former hostages forced (Βιασάμενοι) their relatives to hand over the

---

[149] See Appendix C for a chronological discussion. On the revolt of Thurii, see also Kukofka 1990: 57–60.

city, it makes more sense that the Thurians would have been compelled to receive Hanno before their hostages were restored. The two accounts can be reconciled. Thurian hostages were executed in Rome at the same time as the Tarentine hostages, but Thurii did not immediately revolt. Rather, Thurii remained loyal after the Tarentine revolt, and the Thurians sent supply ships (presumably at Rome's request) to relieve the besieged Roman garrison. The ships and crews were captured, leading to several rounds of Tarentine, Thurian and Carthaginian negotiations and, consequently, Thurii's defection.[150]

The Thurian revolt offers a particularly intriguing case study of the relationship between local conditions, especially interstate rivalry, and the overall limited success of the Hannibalic strategy. There is clear evidence that Thurii and Taras were long-time interstate rivals. As we have seen in the previous three chapters, the defection of one rival (in this case Taras) should have had the effect of discouraging the other rival (Thurii) from revolting. In addition, Thurii seems to have maintained a close relationship with Rome, at least in the early third century. Thus, the Thurian revolt is striking, and it reveals the limits of long-term rivalries and alliances in influencing the decision-making of a city's ruling elite.

Like Taras, Thurii was a powerful city that probably attempted to assert its own regional influence. Livy (25.8.1) lists Thurii along with Taras as the two greatest (*duarum nobilissimarum*) Greek cities in Italy at the time of the Second Punic War. Thurii was founded near the site of Sybaris, which Croton had destroyed, and it controlled at its height an extensive *chora*, dominating a territory that stretched north to around present-day Trebisacce and the Fiume Saraceno, south beyond Rossano di Calabria to the Fiume Trionto, and inland as far as Spezzano and the confluence of the Coscile and Esaro. The city also controlled the major inland communication routes of the Crati and Coscile rivers.[151] At the Capo Trionto, the coastal plain narrows greatly, and the terrain is more rugged and

---

[150] Appian's reference to captured Thurian supply ships is consistent with Livy's report (25.15.4–5) that the Roman senate commissioned a special purchase of grain from Etruria to be conveyed to the Roman garrison besieged in Taras. Livy claims that the supplies made it through and relieved the beleaguered garrison. It is possible that (a) the Thurian ships were used to carry the grain, with Livy exaggerating the success of the mission (i.e. all the ships reached the citadel) and Appian the failure (i.e. all were captured); or (b) the senate commissioned the grain and sent a separate convoy after the failure of the Thurian mission. Since Livy roughly synchronises (*interim*) the Etrurian grain commission with Hanno's mission to bring food to Campania, which provides a *terminus ante quem* for the Thurian defection (see Appendix C), solution (b) fits the timeline better. Still, Livy's synchronising is imprecise enough to allow for either solution.

[151] The site of Thurii is between the present-day Crati and Coscile Rivers, near the town of Sibari. The urban structures and planning can be reconstructed with the help of archaeological remains

mountainous, but to the north, although the coastal plain narrows somewhat, the unbroken flat land stretches around the Gulf of Taranto. Any
expansion of the Thurian hinterland would naturally be to the north, into
the territory of Heraclea and thus in conflict with the Tarentine sphere of
influence.

Indeed, Thurii and Taras (and its subordinate cities Metapontion and
Heraclea) consistently opposed each other almost from the Thurian foundation in 444/3. Thurii was technically a panhellenic colony, but a large
number of Athenian colonists dominated the new city,[152] which came
into immediate conflict with Taras. Perhaps the initial hostility between
largely Athenian Thurii and the Spartan colony Taras was rooted in the
contemporary tensions between their respective mother cities. The two
colonies soon fought for control of the territory between Metapontion and
Thurii, occupied previously by Siris; ultimately, Taras gained control of the
Siritide through the colony of Heraclea.[153] An inscription on a Tarentine
trophy erected at Olympia commemorates a victory over Thurii, possibly
for possession of the Siritide.[154]

The Thurian rivalry with Taras manifested itself again in the fifth century when the Peloponnesian War expanded more directly into Magna
Graecia. During the so-called Sicilian expedition Thurii received the
Athenian fleet under Alcibiades, but neither Taras nor Heraclea provided any aid. According to Thucydides (7.33.4–6), the Thurians and the
Metapontians were allies of the Athenians, and the Metapontians reinforced the Athenian expedition with two ships and a contingent of troops
'according to their *symmachia*' (κατὰ τὸ ξυμμαχικόν).[155] Diodorus (13.3.3–4)
does not include references to the Metapontians allying with, or otherwise
helping the Athenians. This version is tempting to follow because, if it is
the more accurate in this case, it would show a strikingly consistent alliance pattern as early as the fifth century: Thurii versus Taras, Heraclea

---

[152] Dion. Hal. *Lys.* 1; Strab. 6.1.13; Diod. Sic. 11.90.3, 12.9.1–11.3; Hdt. 5.44–5.

and Diodorus' (12.9.1–11.3) unusually detailed account of the city's foundation. See Ehrenberg
1948; Osanna 1992: 138–48; Lomas 1993: 23–5; Greco 1999b: 413–30; Map 13.

[153] Strab. 6.1.14; Diod. Sic. 12.36.4; see also Strab. 6.1.15, which describes efforts by the 'Sybarites'
to prevent Taras from seizing the territory of Siris, and thus effectively controlling most of the
Gulf of Taranto. Tarentine designs to control the Siritide, therefore, predated the foundation of
Thurii.

[154] Meiggs and Lewis 1969: no. 57: Σκῦλα ἀπὸ Θουρίον Ταραντῖνοι ἀνέθεκαν Διὶ Ὀλυμπίοι δεκάταν
('Spoils from the Thurians, the Tarantines dedicated a tenth to the Olympian Gods').

[155] Thucydides says that an anti-Athenian party had been expelled from Thurii, so the Athenians
were able to conclude a *symmachia* alliance with the Thurians. He later reports (7.57.11) that both
Thurii and Metapontion were drawn into the conflict at a time of political instability, implying
perhaps that a pro-democracy party had taken power in Metapontion.

and Metapontion. It is more prudent, however, to follow Thucydides, whose testimony suggests that Metapontion had not yet succumbed to Tarentine hegemony. In either case, the accounts agree that Thurii and Taras opposed each other at this juncture in the Peloponnesian War.[156]

Tensions between the two cities continued in the late fourth and early third centuries. Near the conclusion of his campaign in Italy, Alexander of Epirus tried to transfer a panhellenic festival – probably related to the Italiote League – from Heraclea (which Strabo identifies as within Tarentine territory) to Thurii, out of enmity towards his former ally, Taras.[157] Heraclea, of course, was not literally part of Taras, but the two were closely linked, and Alexander was clearly exploiting the rivalry between Taras and Thurii by transferring the festival. Later, Taras employed Cleonymus the Spartan to attack Thurii.[158] These campaigns came at a time when Thurii faced increased pressure from inland Italic peoples, as literary evidence attests to repeated Lucanian and Bruttian attacks against the Thurians into the third century.[159] Archaeological evidence indicates that a number of small sites along the Thurian frontier were abandoned or were replaced by non-Greek settlements, which is consistent with a general phenomenon of the contraction of Greek settlements in the 'toe' of Italy and their reoccupation by Bruttians.[160] The combined threats posed by Italic tribes and the Tarentines compelled Thurii to seek Roman protection in the 280s. Around 285 the dictator M. Aemilius Barbula may have received the submission of Nerulum, a town near Thurii on the Lucanian–Bruttian border, and in the same year, the people of Thurii donated a statue in Rome in honour of a certain C. Aelius for his actions against the Lucanians; in 282 the consul C. Fabricius Luscinus celebrated a triumph for relieving a joint Samnite, Lucanian and Bruttian siege of Thurii.[161] At around this time Thurii agreed to a treaty with Rome and received a Roman garrison. This angered the Tarentines, who must have viewed the Roman–Thurian alliance, and the Roman garrison, as a threat to their regional influence. So once again, the Tarentines attacked Thurii, driving out the Roman garrison and exiling pro-Roman Thurian aristocrats.[162] These events can be

---

[156] Gomme 1945–78: IV.413–14, 439 accepts that Metapontion aided Athens and does not make reference to Diodorus' version.

[157] Strab. 6.3.4.   [158] Liv. 10.2.1; see above, n. 36.

[159] Dion. Hal. 19.13.1, 19.16.3, 20.4.2; Liv. *Per.* 11, 12; Val. Max. 1.8.6; see also Broughton 1951–2: 1.189.

[160] For the contraction of Thurian settlements, see Osanna 1992: 146.

[161] Dion. Hal. 19.13.1; Val. Max. 1.8.6; Plin. *HN* 9.118, 34.32 (identifying C. Aelius as a tribune of the plebs, but perhaps referring to C. Aelius Paetus, consul in 286); Liv. 9.20.9, *Epit.* 11–12; see Broughton 1951–2: 1.189; Fronda 2006: 404–6.

[162] App. *Sam.* 7.1–2; Liv. *Per.* 12.

viewed in the context of heightened tensions between Rome and Taras leading up to the Pyrrhic War, but they must also be seen as an extension of long-standing interstate rivalry between Thurii and Taras.

Rome's conquest of southern Italy removed the potential for the Tarentine–Thurian rivalry to play out in terms of open conflict, though the underlying sentiment probably remained, and in the Second Punic War, we still see attempts by Taras to assert hegemony over its regional rival. As discussed above, Thurii was compelled to defect when the Tarentines (and Carthaginians) captured Thurian sailors and held them hostage. It was the Tarentines who met with Thurian envoys sent to negotiate the release of the hostages, so either the Tarentines held the hostages, or they were acting as arbiters between Thurii and Hannibal – in either case the Tarentines clearly used the situation to influence Thurian policy. Livy emphasises that Rome's execution of Thurian hostages was the key event triggering Thurii's revolt, but even here the Tarentines played an important role: the hostages were executed after a failed attempt to escape, mentioned above, and the initiative to escape came from a Tarentine aristocrat named Phileas. Thus, both the Appianic and Livian versions show the Tarentines exerting pressure on the Thurians to revolt, suggesting that they aimed to extend their influence over the neighbouring Italiote cities.[163]

Yet long-standing interstate rivalry with Taras and renewed Tarentine efforts to influence Thurii probably deterred some Thurians from seeking to defect. The capture of Thurian sailors by Taras was the final straw that pushed the Thurians to defect, but even at this point they seem to have chafed at the notion of submitting to Tarentine domination. This explains why they surrendered to Hanno rather than to the Tarentines: by allying with the Carthaginians and granting Hanno entrance to their city, the Thurians protected themselves from potential Tarentine threats, perhaps thinking that Hannibal would not allow Taras to attack another of his allies. Finally, Livy (25.15.7) states that the Thurians were not moved to defect so much out of a sense of kinship with the Tarentines and Metapontians, but because of their anger at the Romans. Again, Livy emphasises Rome's execution of the Thurian hostages, but his rejection of Greek kinship as an important motivating factor hints at the tension between Thurii and Taras, which should have inclined the Thurians to remain loyal once the Tarentines defected.

Meanwhile, there appears to have been significant support for the Romans by the Thurian aristocracy, though the evidence for Thurian sentiment is somewhat ambiguous. On the one hand, the Romans stationed a garrison in Thurii and had taken a number of local aristocrats hostage; this suggests that they doubted Thurian loyalty, perhaps implying that some Thurians harboured strong anti-Roman sentiments. The anti-Roman movement that eventually won out in 212 centred at least in part on relatives of the hostages held in Rome.[164] Presumably, these families were considered less trustworthy at the start of the war. On the other hand, the locals continued to help the Roman cause even after the Romans executed Thurian citizens. Livy (25.15.7–17) states that the anti-Roman faction closed the gates on the garrison after it had sallied out unsuccessfully against a Carthaginian army; but later, the garrison commander Atinius and a few of his men were admitted, and these men were allowed to escape by sea before the Thurians handed over their city to Hanno. Appian (*Hann.* 34) says that they escaped by sea to Brundisium. Both accounts agree that some, if not all, of the Roman garrison was allowed to enter *after* it was defeated, indicating that there was still support for Rome until just before Thurii fell to the Carthaginians. In the same section Livy adds that the anti-Roman party prevailed only after some debate, again implying that some aristocrats remained openly loyal to Rome until the city's final surrender to Hannibal. Although the city was garrisoned, Livy (25.15.9) claims that it was only a moderately sized force (*modico praesidio*), and the Roman commander Marcus Atinius was overly confident in anticipation of battle with the Carthaginians, not because of his very few (*perpaucos*) troops, but because of the training and expected loyalty of the Thurians themselves. The Thurians tried to send grain to the Roman garrison in Taras, they fought alongside Atinius' troops, and they allowed the Roman garrison and its commander to escape: these all suggest at least ambiguous feelings towards Rome on the eve of Thurii's revolt.[165]

These very displays of loyalty probably meant that the Thurians felt the burdens and obligation of Roman rule more acutely in 213 and 212, as the focus of the war shifted to the southern theatre. Thus, the sending of a fleet with supplies to relieve the garrison in Taras probably was not an entirely voluntary act. Likewise, though the Thurians fought loyally alongside Marcus Atinius, he also seems to have conscripted and trained local citizens, which may have represented an increased military obligation. In both cases, the combined Roman and Thurian projects were defeated, which certainly would have undercut Roman credibility while it probably increased Thurian resentment.

---

[164] Liv. 25.15.8; App. *Hann.* 34.　　[165] See Lomas 1993: 70–1.

Overall, a cluster of short-term developments and immediate factors convinced the Thurians to defect. There is no doubt that the execution of Thurian hostages in Rome led to the creation of, or (more likely) a significant upsurge in anti-Roman sentiment in Thurii, just as it had in Taras. Yet it is striking that Thurii did not revolt until May 212, a couple of months after the Tarentine revolt and several months after the hostages' execution. The timing perhaps suggests that the execution had less impact on the Thurians than it did on the Tarentines, possibly indicating a closer attachment to Rome and/or hostility towards Taras. Still, Roman heavy-handedness would have lent credibility to any anti-Roman aristocrats who argued that Hannibal offered better prospects for protecting Thurian interests. In the months following the executions Roman demands increased while Thurian citizens suffered in a series of Roman-led ventures. Thurii was then forced to the bargaining table when Taras captured some Thurian sailors. Their traditional rivalry must have made the Thurians wary of the negotiations with Taras. At this point, Hannibal exploited the situation with some particularly shrewd diplomacy: he ordered the Tarentines to release the Thurian sailors whom they held as hostages.[166] Hannibal had surely learned about the execution of the Tarentine and Thurian hostages in Rome.[167] By ordering the sailors' release, he at once improved his standing with the Thurians, by showing that he could protect them against Tarentine abuse, and by highlighting Roman cruelty. The cumulative effect of these events was to give the anti-Roman movement enough momentum to win sway, and Thurii defected. Thus, immediate circumstances and short-term events appear to have been the considerations that weighed most heavily in the Thurian decision to defect. Whatever pre-existing anti-Roman sentiment there was among the Thurian ruling class, the events of 213 and 212 greatly amplified it and gave Hannibal the opportunity he needed to win over the city.

Lomas argues, however, that Thurii's continued and active support for Hannibal in the years following its defection suggests that it was not compelled by the immediate circumstances to switch sides against its will.[168] According to Appian (*Hann.* 57), Thurii remained loyal to Hannibal until 204, when he resettled 3,500 Thurian citizens in Croton. In 210 the Thurians and Metapontians either killed or captured survivors from a Roman fleet that had been defeated in an engagement with the

[166] App. *Hann.* 34.
[167] Since the anti-Roman conspiracy in Taras included relatives of the executed Tarentine hostages, Philomenus and Nico would probably have told Hannibal about the situation.
[168] Lomas 1993: 70–1.

Tarentines.[169] The Thurians were also instrumental in helping Hannibal ambush Roman troops near Petelia, preventing Rome from recapturing Locri in 208.[170] Thus, the Thurians did provide Hannibal with valuable military assistance, and they remained in the Hannibalic camp until nearly the end of the war – long after Taras, for example, had been recaptured. Lomas believes that this reflects deep-seated resentment against Roman rule, which in turn would imply that the Thurians defected relatively wilfully in 212, once they had the chance.

Yet Lomas fails to account for other details in Hannibal's relationship with the Thurians from 212 to 204. First, as mentioned above, there was some debate over what course to pursue after Hanno and Mago had defeated Marcus Atinius' garrison; when the Thurians ultimately decided to allow Atinius and the remaining Romans to escape rather than handing them over to the Carthaginians, local pro-Roman aristocrats probably fled alongside them, as they had in Locri and Taras.[171] Furthermore, in 210 Hannibal resettled a significant portion of the population of Herdonia in Thurii and Metapontion after executing Herdonian aristocrats whom he suspected of plotting with the Romans.[172] Thus, the Thurian population received an influx of inhabitants who were particularly loyal to Hannibal. Despite all of this, there is evidence that some Thurians remained loyal to Rome even after the city defected. For example, according to Livy (26.39.7), before the aforementioned naval battle in 210 between the Tarentine and Roman fleets, Decimus Quinctius enrolled rowers from around Thurii and Croton. When Hannibal evacuated Thurii in 204, he did not move the entire population but rather selected 3,000 citizens from the city and 500 rural inhabitants who were particularly friendly to the Carthaginians and moved them to Croton.[173] Both references suggest that the population of Thurii was not uniformly in support of Hannibal. Finally, by 210 the Romans had recaptured Capua and Syracuse, treating both conquered cities harshly, and Hannibal had destroyed Herdonia and punished members of the ruling elite; in 209 Roman troops massacred the population of Taras.[174] The Thurians probably reckoned that they had little choice but to

---

[169] Liv. 26.39.18.   [170] Liv. 27.26.3–6.

[171] For Locri: Liv. 29.6.5–6; for Taras: Polyb. 8.31.3; Liv. 25.10.7; App. *Hann.* 33; see also Liv. 27.35.4 for Tarentine citizens banished by Hannibal, presumably because they were loyal to Rome.

[172] Liv. 27.1.14–15. Livy claims that he resettled the entire population, but it is more likely that a good number of Herdonians simply fled, returning to reoccupy their city once Hannibal had departed. Those who followed Hannibal would have included, presumably, the most pro-Hannibalic (or anti-Roman) elements of the local population. See Chapter 2, pp. 59–60.

[173] App. *Hann.* 57.

[174] Capua: Liv. 26.15–16; App. *Hann.* 43; Taras: Liv. 27.16; Plut. *Fab. Max.* 22; Syracuse: Liv. 25.31; Plut. *Marc.* 19; Herdonia: Liv. 27.1.3–15.

stay the course once they had sided with Hannibal since both Hannibal and Rome set examples by severely punishing disloyalty. Overall, the subsequent actions of Thurii in support of Hannibal do not seem to bear much on its initial decision to revolt, so they do not lend support to Lomas' argument that the Thurian revolt resulted more from long-term resentment than short-term events and developments.

The foregoing analysis of the Thurian revolt demonstrates the limits of interstate rivalry in shaping local policy decisions. As stated earlier, the patterns observed in previous chapters suggest that Thurii should have been more confirmed in its loyalty to Rome once its long-time enemies, mainly Taras but also the Bruttians, had sided with Hannibal. Mistrust of the Tarentines certainly seems to have had an effect, probably delaying Thurii's defection for a few months in 212, but in the end, other considerations outweighed local rivalry. The increased military and economic burden of Roman rule and, especially, the Roman execution of Thurian aristocrats convinced the local elite that siding with Hannibal was a better deal, despite the recent Tarentine alliance with Hannibal; friendly Hannibalic gestures made this calculation less objectionable. Thurii was compelled to revolt, therefore, by a series of events that created an increasingly unfavourable military and diplomatic landscape, and immediate circumstances overcame the longer-term tendency of Thurii to align against Taras.

CONCLUSION

By the summer of 212 Hannibal had finally achieved nearly complete success in eastern Magna Graecia and the Salento: all of the Greek cities along the Gulf of Taranto had defected, he had won over most (if not all) of the Sallentine communities, save of course Brundisium, and some southern Lucanians may have come over as well. The jewel in the crown was Taras, the largest and most formidable city in the region, capable of providing Hannibal with ships and, more importantly, a strategic port. Taras had the potential to be a very valuable ally. Indeed, the Tarentine revolt paid early dividends: it encouraged Metapontion and Heraclea to defect, and the Tarentines' capture of Thurian sailors set the stage for successful Carthaginian negotiations with Thurii.

Yet Hannibal's record in the region was not perfect. He failed to capture Taras' citadel, which was controlled by the remnants of a Roman garrison and by pro-Roman Tarentine citizens. Consequently, Hannibal was never able to utilise the port facilities since the citadel commanded Taras' harbour. Perhaps more importantly, his success came more than three years after the battle of Cannae, so that by the time he won over most of the region, Rome had already begun to reclaim ground in other theatres that had been lost in 216 and 215 (for example, Arpi in Apulia was recaptured in 213). Finally, holding Taras would prove, at least to some degree, to be more of a burden than a benefit. Rome recaptured Taras by 209, and ultimately, much of Hannibal's success in eastern Magna Graecia was short-lived.

A faulty strategic decision may have helped to postpone his success in Taras and the surrounding region. In 214, when Hannibal was engaged in Campania, a small party of Tarentines approached him and guaranteed that Taras would revolt if only he would move his camp closer to their city.[175] This reference indicates that the Tarentines needed Hannibal to 'show them the goods' before they would seriously entertain rebellion, and it also suggests that Hannibal did not decide to make a serious effort at winning over Taras before the envoys arrived in 214. This appears to have been a strategic blunder on Hannibal's part since, as this chapter demonstrates, Taras was a particularly promising candidate for defection, considering its history of regional hegemony and conflict with Rome. Instead of focusing immediately on the Campanian theatre, Hannibal perhaps should have marched towards Taras and secured a solid bloc of southern Italy. This error in turn forced Hannibal to divide his attention – and resources – between different parts of Italy where he had achieved incomplete success, which contributed to his overall defeat in the war. In the following chapter I will examine how Hannibal's partial success in a number of regions in Italy actually played to Rome's strategic advantages, and we will come back to the question of Hannibal's possible strategic mistakes in Chapter 7.

Returning our attention to this chapter, we have observed that the implementation and relative success of the Hannibalic strategy in eastern Magna Graecia was conditioned by local circumstances such as the internal political competition among various ruling aristocracies and the traditional bonds and rivalries between communities that often long predated the Second Punic War. This conclusion is consistent with what was observed in Chapters 2 to 4, but the distinct way in which the process played out with the communities in eastern Magna Graecia provides an interesting contrast to our previous regional case studies. In Apulia, Campania and Bruttium, Hannibal's success was incomplete in that he could only win over some – not all – of the cities in a given region. In eastern Magna Graecia he succeeded in eliciting the defection of all the states, but only after a significant delay. In the first three regions Hannibal quickly won over the regional hegemonic power, suggesting (as argued above) that such states saw him as an opportunity to reassert their regional influence, so their ruling aristocracies were more attracted to his diplomatic overtures. In the case of Taras, however, despite the fact that it was clearly the most powerful state in the region, Hannibal won the city over only with some difficulty, after a delay of three years following Cannae. The reasons for the delay are to be found primarily in the specific military situation as well as the political circumstances (i.e. Romans holding Tarentine hostages). This underscores the fact that hegemonic ambition was necessarily an overriding concern, and thus Hannibal could not simply expect any powerful city to defect regardless of the circumstances.

Likewise, the Thurian defection shows the limits of local interstate rivalry. In Chapters 2 to 4, we observed that the defection of a powerful state tended to convince its local rival states to remain loyal to Rome. Thurii and Taras had clearly been rivals for regional hegemony from the fifth century onwards, yet the Thurians defected in the Second Punic War after their rival, Taras, had allied with Hannibal. This is not to say that tension between Taras and Thurii disappeared – in fact, the evidence suggests that it continued to inform Thurian policy. Rather, immediate conditions and considerations outweighed interstate rivalry: recent abusive Roman treatment of Thurian citizens, a decline in regional Roman military credibility, Carthaginian and Tarentine pressure, and clever Hannibalic diplomacy combined to make the Thurians reconsider the desirability of honouring their alliance with Rome. Thus, while local interstate rivalries certainly shaped how states responded to Rome, Hannibal and each other, the process was not deterministic. Instead, interstate rivalry was, in the minds of local aristocrats, only one of many concerns that Hannibal needed to address when trying – ultimately unsuccessfully – to convince a critical number of Rome's allies to defect.

CHAPTER 6

The Roman reconquest of southern Italy

INTRODUCTION

By the summer of 212, with the defection of Thurii, Hannibal had secured the loyalty of the remaining cities of Magna Graecia; most of the communities in the Sallentine peninsula had also come over to the Carthaginians, as well as some southern Lucanian communities. Yet even as these new allies were acquired, his position was already crumbling in other regions of Italy. Rome began to reconquer important rebel cities as early as 214, and by the time Taras revolted Hannibal's situation in both Campania and Apulia was perilous. When Taras fell to the Romans in 209, all of the rebellious Campanian and Apulian cities had already been retaken. By 207 Hannibal was operating in an increasingly restricted territory, mostly limited to Bruttium. When the Romans defeated his brother, Hasdrubal, at the Metaurus River in that same year, the war in Italy was essentially over. It was only a matter of time, barring a military miracle, until the Romans drove Hannibal from Italy and captured and punished the few states that still held out.

This chapter examines the Roman reconquest of southern Italy, from the high-water mark of Hannibal's Italian campaign in 215 and 214, through the fall of the few remaining rebellious cities such as Locri and Thurii in 205 and 204, and Hannibal's retreat from Italy in 203. We will focus on the period before the battle of the Metaurus, when the Italian campaign, although having turned in Rome's favour, still hung in the balance. First, I will discuss briefly and in general terms how Hannibal's partial strategic success in the early years of the war – that he won over some but not all states in a number of regions of southern Italy – played directly into the Romans' long-term strategic advantages and contributed to their ultimate victory. Second, we will look at the same four regions examined in Chapters 2 to 5 to see how these general patterns unfolded with local variations, as each individual case was shaped by particular local political and military factors.

'HOLDING THE WOLF BY THE EARS': HANNIBAL'S STRATEGIC CONUNDRUM AFTER 216–215

As we saw in the previous four chapters, Hannibal was not unsuccessful in his efforts to elicit defections by Rome's Italian allies. A significant number of Apulian and Campanian cities came over to Hannibal after Cannae, as did most of the Bruttians, some Lucanians, and eventually the majority of cities in Magna Graecia. At this juncture, we should also recall his achievements in Samnium and the Sallentine peninsula, two regions that are not examined in detail in this book. Hannibal enjoyed significant success among the Samnites, winning over most of the Hirpini and Caudini, though largely failing to elicit defections from the Pentri (see Appendix A). The majority of the inhabitants of the Sallentine peninsula came over to Hannibal in 213, as discussed in Chapter 5 (pp. 212–13). Indeed, as Lazenby (1996b: 44) notes: 'it is possible to calculate that by 212 over 40% of the allies were no longer available to Rome, and the majority of Campanians, whom Polybius classifies as citizens, were also unavailable'. Based on the estimates of Roman-allied manpower presented in the first chapter, this represents approximately 200,000 men of military age of whom Hannibal deprived the Romans.[1]

Yet Hannibal faced the bitter irony that his impressive military and diplomatic success placed him in a strategic situation that was probably more difficult to manage than it would have been had he failed to elicit as many allied revolts. On the one hand, he had not won over enough Italian communities to overcome Rome's advantage in manpower, nor even to mitigate it to a significant degree. On the other hand, Hannibal now found himself committed to protecting a host of new allies, which surely drained resources from his main objective of bringing the Romans to terms. This state of affairs played into Rome's long-term strategic advantages. This has already been discussed in the first chapter, but it is worth reviewing and expanding on the main lines of argument.

Even after Cannae the Romans could draw on a massive reservoir of citizens and allies. Turning again to Polybius' figures, after the loss of 40 per cent of potential allied manpower, Rome might still hope to draw on more than 200,000 men of military age from the remaining, loyal *socii*. One might suspect, however, that some 'loyal' allies took advantage of Rome's

---

[1] See Chapter 1, pp. 37–9: there were around 410,000 available men from allied states, and around 50,000 from the Campanians, if we assume that Polybius' figures (adjusted by Brunt) are more or less accurate. The exact figure is not of particular importance here, but rather the scale of allied defections is significant.

weakened position by hesitating or even refusing to fulfil their manpower obligations, even if they did not openly side with Hannibal. Meanwhile, the Romans would have been less capable of compelling them to do so. Even if we assume an extreme hypothetical scenario wherein no allied communities except for Latin colonies supplied troops, there still would have been far more than 200,000 potential Roman and Latin soldiers available, even *after* factoring in the tens of thousands lost at Trebbia, Trasimene and Cannae. In addition, this figure does not take into account any extraordinary measures that the Romans could take to raise 'emergency' troops. For example, in the darkest moments after Cannae, they raised an additional 25,000 troops, including conscripts from the *ager Picenus et Gallicus*, two legions of slave volunteers (*volones*), and criminals given their freedom in exchange for military service.[2] Thus, Roman military resources remained formidable despite Hannibal's stunning, early success.

Indeed, Rome regularly fielded at least twenty legions each year for nearly a decade in the middle of the war (214–206), around 90,000 infantry and cavalry each year (assuming 'paper strength' legions), not including any associated allied units.[3] Even Brunt (1971: 418), whose more conservative figures assume that the wartime legions were regularly undermanned, argues for an average of around 70,000 Roman citizens under arms per year between 214 and 206. It is usually assumed that allied soldiers made up at least half of a Republican army,[4] though as suggested above, given the extraordinary circumstances of the Second Punic War, perhaps allied troop numbers were lower than usual. Still, citizens of the Latin colonies, since they were technically *peregrini*, served in the allied units rather than the legions. There is little to suggest that the Latins provided an inadequate number of allied troops. In a famous episode in 209, recounted by Livy (27.8–10), twelve of the thirty Latin colonies refused to send their required troops because they lacked the men and money. The Romans were surprised by the refusal, suggesting that the colonies had been supplying troops as expected up to that point.[5] More importantly, Livy also

---

[2] Liv. 22.57.10–12, 23.14.2–4. The *volones* totalled 8,000 men, so the legions were slightly under strength. Livy reports that 6,000 criminals were enrolled, and he claims that Pera set out for Campania in 216 with all 25,000 men. Brunt 1971: 648–51 argues, however, that Pera left Rome with only the 8,000 *volones*, leaving the new cohorts and released prisoners to guard the city.

[3] For the number of legions in the field each year, Brunt 1971: 418 Table x. In theory, the typical Roman legion of the middle Republic comprised about 4,500 men (about 4,200 infantry and 300 cavalry), though larger legions of 5,000 men could be assembled: Polyb. 6.19.

[4] Keppie 1998: 21–3.

[5] Indeed, if we can trust Livy's account of the grievances discussed in their local meetings, the Latins complained because the Romans continued to draft their men, while Latin soldiers levied earlier in the war had not been returned (27.9.5).

reports (27.10.3–4) that the other colonies promised to make up the short-fall, and there is no further indication that the Romans were unsatisfied with the number of troops that they received. The episode reveals how the long war must have put pressure on loyal allies, but it also indicates that the Roman army continued to draw on adequate allied resources. Lastly, a large number of citizens and allies were required to man the Roman navy. Any final tally will have to remain speculative, but we can reasonably argue that Rome fielded armies and navies totalling around 200,000 Roman and allied men each year between 214 and 206, with the bulk serving in the Italian theatre.[6] We may conclude, therefore, that both the Roman army and navy continued to receive significant support from allied manpower.

After his victory at Cannae Hannibal was unable to deal with this disparity in manpower, especially given both the failure to resupply his army from abroad and the Roman generals' overall unwillingness to engage him in subsequent major pitched battles. Hannibal also did not receive enough reinforcements from his new Italian allies, besides the 14,000 Gauls who are said to have joined before the battle of the Trebbia.[7] There are several scattered references to Italians providing military service for Hannibal and his lieutenants. Livy (30.19.6), Diodorus (27.9.1) and Appian (*Hann.* 59) report that Hannibal massacred many 'Italians' in his army because they refused to follow him to Africa upon his retreat from Italy in 203. The story is undoubtedly exaggerated, if not entirely fictitious, to exemplify Hannibal's supposed cruelty. Still, it assumes that Hannibal's army did contain men from Italian communities that had defected.[8] Some Italians appear to have remained with Hannibal and fought for him at Zama, mostly Bruttians, according to Livy and Appian.[9] In 214 Hanno commanded an

---

[6] Brunt 1971: 422 estimates the total Roman-allied military contribution by multiplying the number of legionaries each year by a factor of 2.5 or 3. My own rough calculations follow more or less along the same lines, though I suspect that Brunt somewhat underestimates the allied contributions to the Roman cause.

[7] For the calculation, see Lazenby 1978: 56.

[8] Appian (*Hann.* 60) and Livy (30.20.5) agree that Hannibal also left some troops to garrison a few towns in Bruttium. Appian reports that these garrisons were attacked and slain by the people of Petelia and other Italians. Livy claims that these men were left behind because they were the 'useless throng' (*inutile turba*) of Hannibal's army, whom he stationed in cities just to give the appearance of a garrison (*specie praesidii*). It is possible that these were not garrisons at all, but instead Bruttians – perhaps some soldiers along with civilians who had taken refuge with Hannibal – who tried to filter back into nearby communities when they learned that he was going to quit Italy. The reference to hostilities between the 'garrisons' and the Petelians might echo the intra-Bruttian tensions that were discussed in Chapter 4 (p. 158).

[9] Liv. 30.33.6; App. *Pun.* 40. Polybius (15.11.2) reports only that Hannibal's second line at Zama was composed of 'Libyans and Carthaginians, in addition to all who came from Italy with him'

army of 17,000 infantry made up mostly of Bruttians and Lucanians, and 1,200 cavalry including 'very few' (*pauci admodum*) Italians.[10] Hanno also raised fresh troops from the Bruttians in 207.[11] Campanians appear to have been with Hannibal's army in 210, after Capua and its satellites had been recaptured.[12] Livy (23.39.6) mentions that 'very many Campanians were captured' (*Campani permulti capti*) when the Romans seized some towns along the border of Samnium and Campania; clearly they were helping to garrison these towns.[13] We also find Bruttians forming part of the Carthaginian garrison in Taras.[14] Therefore, some Italians, perhaps mostly Bruttians, did in fact join up with Hannibal's army, fighting in the field and serving as garrison troops. Yet their total numbers appear to have been insignificant. Hannibal's ranks certainly did not swell enough to off-set the attrition of the long war, let alone compensate decisively for Roman manpower advantages.[15] At the same time, Hannibal was compelled to station either his own Carthaginian, Spanish and Numidian troops or his allied Italian contingents in many rebel cities, offsetting any influx of Italian volunteers to his army.[16] The very possession of Italian allies meant

---

(Λίβυας καὶ Καρχηδονίους, ἐπὶ δὲ πᾶσι τοὺς ἐξ Ἰταλίας ἥκοντας μεθ' αὑτοῦ). Polybius' version is ambiguous but not inconsistent with the other accounts specifying that there were Italian elements in Hannibal's army. Livy places these Bruttian soldiers in the second line at Zama; Appian puts them in the third line.

[10] Liv. 24.15.1–2.   [11] Liv. 27.42.15–16.

[12] Livy (26.34.6–7) states that the Roman senate designated a separate punishment for those Capuans, Atellani, Calatini and Sabatini who were 'among the enemy' (*apud hostis*), presumably meaning with Hannibal's army. It is not clear, however, what function they served in the army. It is possible that they were not soldiers, but rather refugees who fled to Hannibal's army for protection.

[13] A large number of Capuans, 2,000 men according to Livy, helped to garrison Casilinum (Liv. 24.19.1). This is not surprising given Capua's claim to the town (see Chapter 3, pp. 125–6). It is interesting to note that we only hear about Campanian garrisons in the vicinity of their own territory, suggesting perhaps that they were unwilling to serve Hannibal far from home.

[14] Liv. 27.15.17–18.

[15] Lazenby 1978: 215 calculates that Hannibal left Italy with a scant 12,000 men. Even if we accept that he in fact massacred several thousand Italians before sailing – an unlikely act – and left several thousand more as 'garrisons', the men in Hannibal's army in 203 would total fewer than the number he led into the Po Valley in 218, around 26,000 (see Chapter 1, pp. 37–8). For a different assessment, see now Hoyos 2004a: 128–9, arguing that the 'part played by Italian troops in his operations from 216 on is not to be underestimated'.

[16] There are references to Carthaginian garrisons, in some cases quite large, in the following locations: **Arpi**, 5,000 men (Liv. 24.46.1–2); **Capua** (Liv. 24.12.3, 25.15.3, 26.5.6, 26.12.10; App. *Hann.* 36, 43); **Casilinum**, 700 Carthaginians and a large number of Capuans (Liv. 23.20.1, 24.19.10–11); **Compsa** (Liv. 23.1.3); **Locri**, Carthaginians under Mago (Liv. 27.28.14–16, 29.6.11–14, 29.7.8–10); **Metapontion** (Liv. 27.42.15–16); **Salapia** 500 Numidian cavalry (Liv. 26.38.11–14); **Taras** a Bruttian 'cohort' and Carthaginians (Polyb. 8.34.13; Liv. 25.11.8, 27.15.9, 27.15.17–18, 27.16.5–6); generic reference to garrisons in Bruttium (Liv. 27.41.1); Campanians garrisoning small Samnite towns, see above, this page. The last two examples suggest that Hannibal's practice of garrisoning even small towns was widespread.

that precious troops had to be frittered away protecting them from Roman reprisals, shoring up the position of pro-Carthaginian elites, and even forcibly preventing some cities from switching sides back to Rome.

More importantly, the Italian cities that had defected became targets in Rome's counter-strategy of fighting a war of attrition. The Romans could afford to garrison cities of wavering loyalty and thus forestall additional allied revolts. They also stationed multiple armies throughout Italy, which could simultaneously shadow the movement of Hannibal's main field army, protect sensitive and strategic locations, discourage still loyal allies from defecting (especially in northern Italy),[17] as well as bring direct military pressure to bear against rebellious cities. Roman reconquest typically involved brutal consequences. Members of the local aristocracy faced trials, the confiscation of land and even execution; a significant portion of the general citizenry might be put to the sword; captured cities were not infrequently plundered by the legions. Since one of the ways that Hannibal won over Italian allies was by holding out the promise of autonomy and freedom, he could ill afford to allow Rome to recapture such cities, for whenever one of his allies fell into Roman hands and suffered often vicious punishment, it underscored his inability to make good on his promises. This in turn further undermined his credibility vis-à-vis his remaining Italian allies.

These military-diplomatic challenges were made more daunting because of the checkerboard pattern of alliances that emerged between 216 and 212, as individual southern Italian communities responded differently to the post-Cannae interstate landscape. As we saw in the previous chapters, the decision of each city to ally with Hannibal or remain loyal to Rome was shaped mainly by specific local concerns. Regions such as

---

[17] Note, for example, that two legions were stationed in Etruria each year from 212 to 201, even though the region saw very little active fighting after Trasimene in 217. The legions served to check the Gauls to the north, but also to limit the opportunities for Etruscan cities to defect. Late in 209 there were rumours that cities in Etruria were planning to revolt, led by the Arretines (Liv. 27.21.6–8). The situation worsened in 208, so a propraetor was ordered to bring one legion against the city: a large number of aristocratic hostages were taken to Rome, Arretium was garrisoned, and the Romans kept a back-up plan to move one of the urban legions to Etruria if the circumstances so warranted (Liv. 27.24.1–9). In 207 the senate sent M. Livius Salinator to conduct further investigations to see which cities in Etruria and Umbria had discussed plans to revolt and join Hasdrubal when he marched into Italy or had aided him in any way (Liv. 28.10.4–5). Whether or not any Etruscan or Umbrian cities (including Arretium) actually defected is not important. It is strong testimony to Rome's vast resources that troops could be stationed on an otherwise quiet front, with additional legions in reserve that could be sent, if need be, all the while continuing to commit major assets to multiple 'hot spots' in the Italian theatre and beyond. The senate's and magistrates' decisive actions, coupled with the force of the legions, seem to have averted a potentially serious rebellion on the northern front.

Apulia, Bruttium/western Magna Graecia, and Campania were divided, with, in some cases, loyal *socii* and Latin colonies situated side by side with rebellious communities. The Romans were able to stabilise the situation immediately after Cannae by garrisoning some loyal cities and by fortifying camps in the vicinity of others. These also served as bases from which the Romans could launch a variety of operations aimed at neighbouring defectors: from lightning raids and 'devastation' campaigns to large-scale campaigns of reconquest. Moreover, their manpower reserves allowed the Romans to concentrate forces in multiple locations and thus attack multiple squares on the checkerboard at the same time.

Hannibal could not possibly hope to respond to every Roman operation against his allies. He was forced, therefore, to move his army from region to region, more often than not in reaction to Roman military actions rather than himself proactively seizing the military initiative. He repeatedly faced the dilemma of choosing between two or more allied .cities, marching in defence of one while leaving the other(s) exposed to Roman force. Similarly, the defence of his allies at times compromised 'offensive' operations. For example, between 214 and 212 Hannibal was torn between trying to win over the powerful port city of Taras in the far south and defending his most important ally, Capua, from extraordinary Roman military pressure; his efforts to shore up the situation in Campania probably delayed his diplomatic success with the Tarentines.[18] Roman commanders, meanwhile, could exploit Hannibal's inability to be everywhere at once, yielding occasionally spectacular results. Thus, in 209 the consul Quintus Fabius Maximus ordered the proconsul Marcus Claudius Marcellus to keep Hannibal busy in Apulia; he then ordered the Roman garrison in Rhegion to besiege nearby Caulonia. Both actions drew Hannibal away from Taras, allowing Fabius to storm the city in his absence.[19] Livy (27.51.13) states that Hannibal decided in 207 to concentrate all of his forces in Bruttium, because he could not defend all of his allies since they were widely scattered. Whether Hannibal actually thought this, or whether the statement is Livy's editorialising, it certainly captures the strategic reality.

Since he could not protect all of his allies directly by stationing his army nearby or marching his army into the vicinity and driving off any Roman forces that may have threatened, Hannibal was compelled to leave

---

[18] The dilemma of Taras and Capua, which bedevilled Hannibal, will be discussed in greater detail below, pp. 246–7.

[19] This coordinated campaign struck a major blow against Hannibal's position in Magna Graecia. It will be discussed at greater length later in this chapter (see pp. 264–5).

garrisons in a number of cities, as discussed above. Garrisoning allied cities, however, not only consumed troops but also burdened his allies and, in some cases, became a source of resentment. This was especially true in cases where the local ruling class began to waver in its loyalty, perhaps forcing the garrison to use more oppressive tactics to maintain control. The citizens of some rebellious cities must have come to see the Carthaginian garrisons more as a problem than a solution: an unwanted symbol of occupation rather than of protection.

Hannibal had little choice but to leave some cities to fend for themselves, relying on the local elite to show resolve in the face of mounting Roman pressure, bolstered only by their disenchantment with Rome and occasional gestures of Hannibal's support. Here too, the specific local conditions that shaped the effectiveness of the Hannibalic strategy in the immediate wake of Cannae would come back to haunt him later in the war. As demonstrated in the previous chapters, the local aristocracies of southern Italy were deeply divided by factionalism, family rivalries and fierce political competition. Whether to remain loyal or to defect – perhaps the first legitimate, independent foreign policy decision in generations – would have been a hotly contested debate crosscut by political rivalry and other internal tensions. The momentous decision to revolt could only be reached if a critical mass of aristocrats became convinced that Hannibal presented the better option for themselves and their city. In the typical pattern this occurred where a 'swing group' of aristocrats shifted their support decisively from the more 'hard core' pro-Roman elite to their pro-Hannibalic (or anti-Roman) opponents. Some local aristocrats capitalised on the situation, calculating that pro-Roman aristocrats who may have relied on Roman backing would lose credibility and political standing when their city defected, while they could hope to profit politically from associating with Hannibal. Municipal elites did not, therefore, back Hannibal out of a deep sense of personal loyalty, nor were they bound to him by a greater ideology; rather, they were drawn to Hannibal for opportunistic and often self-serving reasons.

As will be examined in greater detail later in the chapter, this local aristocratic support proved ephemeral: so long as Hannibal was successful, they might be counted on to remain faithful, but when his fortunes in Italy began to wane, his popularity and credibility among local aristocrats rapidly dissolved. When this happened, those elites who associated themselves closely with the Hannibalic cause also lost local political credibility, while members of the 'swing group' looked for opportunities to (re)ingratiate themselves with the Romans. Meanwhile, Hannibal sometimes tried to respond to his fragmenting support among the local elite, using both the carrot and the stick. Yet this often yielded unwelcome consequences. When, for example, Hannibal executed the family of Dasius Altinius of Arpi on the suspicion that he had been in contact with the Romans, the heavy-handed actions engendered resentment and alienation among some local (that is, Arpian) elites.[20] At the same time, the Romans could play on local aristocratic factionalism and exploit political rivalries, just as Hannibal had done earlier in the war.

Maintaining the political support of the ruling class in important cities, such as Capua, Locri, Arpi and Taras, presented an additional set of challenges. As discussed in the previous chapters, the ruling elites of these cities were motivated by hegemonic aspirations. Hannibal explicitly guaranteed the Capuans hegemony in return for their loyalty, and similar concerns probably influenced the ruling classes of Locri, Arpi and Taras. He was obliged, therefore, not only to protect these cities, but also to convince them that he would help to restore and extend their local hegemony. This at times constrained Hannibal's actions and compromised his overall strategy. For example, he found himself fighting distracting campaigns in order to placate the ambitions and concerns of the Capuans.[21] When he failed to deliver on his promises to such important cities – when it became clear that rebelling from Rome would not yield an extension of territory or hegemony over rival cities – his aristocratic support eroded and he eventually lost a number of his most powerful allies. In addition, when a large city such as Capua fell to the Romans, its smaller satellite towns were more likely to surrender as well.

Thus, the middle years of the war (215 to 207)[22] saw Hannibal juggling various, often conflicting strategic aims: protecting his allies, winning new territory for some of them, trying to win over additional allies, conquering recalcitrant states, and both punishing and encouraging those states whose loyalty was wavering. He had neither the manpower nor the time to balance all of the competing concerns, and one by one the states that revolted in the wake of Cannae slipped out of his control. Some cities more or less willingly submitted to Rome, others were brought forcibly under the Roman yoke once more; a few states (such as Locri and Thurii) even held out and resisted Rome until the dying years of the war, yet ultimately they

---

[20] Liv. 24.45.14; App. *Hann.* 31; see below, pp. 256–7.

[21] Thus, Hannibal was caught up in Capua's attempts to capture Cumae in 215: Liv. 23.35.1–4, 23.35.13, 23.36.2–8, 23.37.1–10; see discussion in Chapter 3, pp. 124–5.

[22] For present purposes, the middle period of the war comes to a close in 207 with the battle of the Metaurus, and Hannibal's subsequent decision to retreat to Bruttium.

too were reconquered. This serves to remind us how the general patterns discussed in the preceding pages played out with local variations, underscoring the continued importance of local conditions and contingent factors in shaping the course of the Second Punic War. At the same time, the partial success of the Hannibalic strategy in the wake of Cannae set the context for the subsequent actions of southern Italian communities, which will be examined in more detail for the remainder of this chapter. As Hannibal sat in his camp on Mount Tifata late in the winter of 216/15, after he had captured Casilinum and was coerced by the Capuans to make another unsuccessful attack on Cumae, perhaps he reflected on his incomplete diplomatic success the previous year and pondered the challenges ahead in satisfying these new allies, now that he had them. If he did, perhaps he also anticipated the words of Terence's Antipho: *'auribus teneo lupum'.*[23]

CAMPANIA, 215–211

Whether or not Hannibal uttered such sentiments as he gazed down from Mount Tifata, he must have recognised the strategic and symbolic significance of holding Campania, arguably the most important front in the Italian theatre. With the capture of Casilinum early in 215, the battle lines in Campania were drawn: Hannibal controlled Capua and its subordinate allies, Rome held the remaining cities in the region, and all of Italy looked on.[24] Because the region was a strategic focus for both the Romans and Hannibal, the Roman reconquest of Campania receives much attention in the primary sources. As such, it provides an excellent case study for examining the intersection of specific local conditions, general Roman strategic advantages, and individual strategic decisions within a particular political-military regional landscape after Cannae.

Rome's advantage in manpower was of fundamental importance. Six legions were stationed in Campania in four out of the six years after the battle of Cannae: 216, 215, 212 and 211. In 216 and 215 the six legions included the two legions of *volones* ('volunteers'). There were four legions stationed there in 214, as the Romans moved the *volones* to Apulia, perhaps anticipating their major operations in south-east Italy the following year. Only two

[23] Ter. *Phorm.* 506–7: *immo, id quod aiunt, auribus teneo lupum: nam neque quo pacto a me amittam neque uti retineam scio* ('No indeed, I'm holding the wolf by the ears, as they say: for I don't know how to let go or how to keep hold').
[24] Livy repeatedly emphasises the importance of Campania as an example to observers throughout Italy: 22.57.9–12, 23.14.2–4, 23.17.7.

legions were stationed in Campania in 213, but in that year Hannibal was far off in the neighbourhood of Taras, where the Romans were also focusing their war efforts. In any case, two legions still represented a significant force, especially considering the absence of Hannibal's army from the region.[25] The effects of Roman manpower were visible in Campania almost immediately after Cannae. During the first critical months, the dictator M. Iunius Pera marched towards Casilinum with at least 8,000 newly raised troops, perhaps as many as 25,000 men.[26] Meanwhile, C. Terentius Varro gathered the survivors from the Cannae legions, approximately 14,500 men,[27] and handed them over to the praetor M. Claudius Marcellus, who led them into southern Campania, near Nola and Suessula.[28] Thus, even in the wake of Cannae the Romans had enough men to hold the line in northern Campania while simultaneously controlling two of the main routes out of southern Campania.[29] When Casilinum had fallen, the Romans stationed an army near Sinuessa, which controlled the Via Appia at the coastal pass near the Mons Massicus.[30] They also garrisoned a number of Campanian cities, including Cumae and Naples, which probably helped to forestall additional defections.[31] Q. Fabius Maximus fortified Puteoli late in 215/14, and we hear later that the city was protected by a garrison of 6,000 Roman troops.[32] By the time of the siege of Capua (212), Rome was able to bring to bear three armies against its rebellious ally.[33] Overall, the Romans made good use of their manpower reserves to stabilise the Campanian front after Cannae. They were able to raise new troops and hold strategic points in Campania, thus limiting Hannibal's movements, while protecting their own allies and taking the offensive against rebellious cities.[34]

The Roman military response in the wake of Cannae was not the only challenge that Hannibal faced. His position in Campania was particularly

[25] For the distribution of Roman legions, see Toynbee 1965: 11.647–51; De Sanctis 1956–69: 111.2.614–19; Brunt 1971: 416–22.
[26] The lower figure is more probable; see above, n. 2.
[27] For the estimated number of survivors, see Liv.22.49.13–18, 22.50.11, 22.52.4, 22.54.1–4, 22.60.9–19; Polyb. 3.117.2; Walbank 1970: 1.440; Lazenby 1978: 90–1.
[28] Liv. 22.57.1, 23.31.3–4.
[29] Until Hannibal captured Casilinum late in the winter of 216/15, the Romans still held the town, which overlooked the crossing of the Volturnus at the juncture of the Via Appia and Via Latina. Marcellus established himself at the so-called *castra Claudiana* on modern-day Monte Cancello (above Suessula), which commanded both the route between Capua and Nola and the Via Appia to Beneventum through the pass at Arienzo: (Beloch 1879: 384–8; Lazenby 1978: 93; Frederiksen 1984: 35–6; Oakley 1997–2005: 111.49). Not only did the *castra Claudiana* control this strategic juncture, it also allowed Marcellus to guard Nola (Liv. 23.32.2; see also Chapter 3, pp. 136–8).
[30] Liv. 23.35.5.   [31] Liv. 23.15.2; see Chapter 3, pp. 136–8 and n. 168.
[32] Liv. 24.7.10, 24.12.4, 24.13.7.   [33] Liv. 25.22.7–9.
[34] On this point, see also Frederiksen 1984: 241–2.

vulnerable to political divisions and wavering loyalty among the ruling aristocracies in the cities he had won over, especially Capua. He had convinced the city to revolt only after very difficult negotiations in which he promised to (re-)establish Capuan hegemony, and even then there remained some aristocratic opposition. While a few aristocrats, such as Vibius Virrius, were rather vocal in supporting the Carthaginian cause, many Capuans were less enthusiastic, and Hannibal was at times coerced to pursue policies to bolster their loyalty. In 215, for example, he was compelled to leave winter quarters early in order to assist the Capuans after the consul Ti. Sempronius Gracchus routed them at Hamae; later that spring Hannibal attacked Cumae at the request of the Capuans.[35] Indeed, as early as 216, in the months immediately following the Capuan revolt, Hannibal already suspected the loyalty of his new allies.[36]

Meanwhile, the Romans played on the political divisions and the varying degrees of loyalty among the aristocracies in rebellious Campanian cities, employing a range of psychological warfare tactics. Early in 215 the Roman senate voted to bring the 300 Capuan *equites* back from Sicily and give them Roman citizenship, transferring their municipal rights to Cumae.[37] This act was designed to weaken the resolve of Capuan aristocrats loyal to Hannibal by emphasising the potential rewards granted to faithful allies. Such rewards were, of course, juxtaposed with Roman reprisals against the disloyal. Between 215 and 213 the Romans repeatedly devastated Capuan territory or otherwise interfered with their agricultural production.[38] The devastation of 215 is particularly interesting. Q. Fabius Maximus waited until he had heard that Hannibal had left Campania for winter quarters in Apulia, then he moved the Roman camp close to Capua and began to devastate the territory. This episode highlights Rome's manpower advantage and the difficulties Hannibal faced in protecting his allies. While it is impossible to know how much physical damage was caused by Roman devastation, the tactic worked well enough to compel

---

[35] Liv. 23.36.1–7; for a complete discussion of both episodes, see Chapter 3, pp. 124–5.

[36] Hannibal marched to Casilinum after he received word that the Romans were bringing newly conscripted legions there. While strategic considerations certainly motivated Hannibal, Livy (23.17.7) states that he feared that Capua would waver if the Romans drew their camp nearby: *ne quid tam propinquis hostium castris Capuae quoque moveretur, exercitum ad Casilinum ducit* ('He led his army to Casilinum lest anything should be stirred also at Capua by the camp of the enemy being so near'). By beginning a siege in the fall, Hannibal was not able to winter his troops in Apulia, where he had set up a supply base.

[37] Liv. 23.31.10–11. Their status as *municipes* of Cumae was to be dated retroactively to the day before the revolt of Capua. This made them technically not citizens of Capua at the time of the city's defection and therefore exempt from any punishment meted out against Capuans.

[38] Liv. 23.46.8–11, 23.48.1–3, 25.13.1.

the Capuans to respond by sending out troops from within the city walls in order to protect farms and territory.[39] Roman actions probably exacerbated Capuan political divisions by convincing some aristocrats that siding with Hannibal had been a poor choice. Indeed, Livy (24.47.12–13) states that 112 Capuan nobles presented themselves in 213 to the praetor Cn. Fulvius Centumalus, who was in command of the Roman camp at Suessula, and they surrendered on the stipulation that when Capua fell, their property would be restored. This points to the sort of personal motivations on the part of local aristocrats that the Romans could exploit in order to wear down the resolve of Hannibal's allies. Perhaps the clearest example of a Roman attempt to undermine Capuan resolve by contrasting the price of disloyalty with the benefits of rejecting Hannibal occurred in 212. As the Romans prepared to surround Capua with siege walls, the senate sent word to the consuls that any Capuans who left their city before 15 March would have their property restored, while those who remained would be considered enemies. The edict was announced to the Capuans, indicating that they were the target audience and suggesting that it was aimed specifically at grinding down their will to resist.[40]

Hannibal often found himself torn between protecting Capuan interests and prosecuting the war in south-east Italy. I have already mentioned how Fabius Maximus exploited this situation in 215, waiting for Hannibal to move to his winter camp in Apulia before devastating the Capuan countryside. In 214 the large number of legions that Rome levied frightened the Capuans, who suspected that the Romans were preparing to mount a siege of their city, so they sent legates to Hannibal, still wintering in Apulia, to beg him for protection. If he failed to respond to such entreaties he risked appearing to have abandoned his allies. Thus, Hannibal quickly led his army to Campania and re-established his camp at Mount Tifata.[41] Yet this in turn freed Roman forces to conduct a series of campaigns in southern Italy, including attacks against Aecae and Herdonia in Apulia.[42] Hannibal found himself torn between trying to secure Taras and trying to protect and ameliorate the Capuans in the summer of 214, when he was informed that he could easily capture Taras if only he drew his army near.[43] At the

[39] Liv. 23.46.10.
[40] Liv. 25.22.11–13; Diod. Sic. 26.17.
[41] Liv. 24.12.1–5. Livy reports that Hannibal tried to attack the Roman garrison at Puteoli after he had set up camp above Capua. The attempt perhaps reflects his continued desire to gain a port. The assault on Puteoli may also have been designed to draw Roman pressure from Capua, or, if he had been able to capture the city and its Roman garrison, provide Hannibal with additional bargaining leverage.
[42] Liv. 24.20.5–8; see below, n. 79.   [43] Liv. 24.13.1–2.

time, Hannibal was clearly growing impatient with his inability to capture more cities in Campania, so late in the summer of 214 he withdrew to Taras and spent the next year in Calabria.[44] Yet, during Hannibal's operations near Taras, the Romans again took advantage of his absence and recaptured Casilinum; members of the Capuan garrison who were taken captive were imprisoned in Rome.[45] These sorts of Roman campaigns, which were made possible by Hannibal's absence, further strained the relationship between Hannibal and the Capuans.

Indeed, the Capuans must quickly have come to realise that their alliance with Hannibal did not bring about the promised extension of Capua's hegemony, but rather that their city was in worse straits than before the war. The Capuans had temporarily gained possession of Casilinum, but the Romans retook the town within two years. It is worth noting that when the Romans began to draw up siege equipment before the gates of Casilinum, a number of the Capuans garrisoning the town lost their will to fight and begged for permission to return home, which Fabius Maximus apparently granted to some.[46] This is perhaps the first indication that Capuan morale was flagging. Hannibal had failed to secure Cumae, which seems to have been envisioned as a primary target of Capuan expansion. The Romans may also have temporarily captured Calatia, one of the subordinate towns of the 'Capuan League', perhaps in 212 or early 211.[47] As we have seen, the Capuans also suffered from repeated Roman devastation of their territory. In 214, while Hannibal was near Taras, Fabius marched into Samnium, devastated Samnite territory and captured a number of towns by force, including Compulteria/Conpulteria, Trebula, Austicula, Telesia and Compsa. Some of these towns, Trebula and Compulteria/Conpulteria for example, were located not far from the border between Campania and Samnium, which matches Livy's description of Fabius' campaign as 'nearby Capua' (*circa Capuam*).[48] In the same passage Livy mentions that Campanians

---

[44] Liv. 24.17.8; for Hannibal's campaign around Taras, 214–213, see Chapter 5, pp. 211–13.

[45] For the siege and capture of Casilinum, see Liv. 24.19.1–11.

[46] Liv. 24.19.8–9.

[47] Liv. 26.5.5. The manuscript, accepted by Madvig among others, reads that Hannibal seized the 'fortress Galatia' (*castellum Galatiam*) after driving out its garrison, in 211, immediately before he attacked the Roman armies besieging Capua. Conway emends the text to *castellum Calatiam*. If this emendation is correct and the reference is historical, then the Romans probably captured Calatia and garrisoned it in late 212 at the earliest, when they began making final preparations for the siege of Capua.

[48] Liv. 23.39.5–6, 24.20.3–5. Livy records two separate campaigns, in 215 (against Compulteria, Trebula and Austicula) and 214 (against Conpulteria, Telesia and Compsa). The repetition with variant spelling of Compulteria/Conpulteria suggests that Livy drew on multiple sources that placed the campaign in different years, failing to recognise they referred to the same event. If this

were captured (*captivi Campanorum*) in large numbers – these probably included Capuan citizens. Thus, alliance with Hannibal had gained the Capuans nothing but had cost them in terms of devastated territory and killed or captured citizens. Moreover, reports of the Roman reconquest of these Samnite–Campanian border towns will have reached Capua, especially since Capuan citizens would probably have been among those captured. Such reports would only have reinforced the sense that Hannibal could not – or, given his absence, *would* not – protect his allies.

Patterns established in the first few years after Cannae continued, and the strategic problems that Hannibal faced in Campania came to a head in 212/11, when the Romans began to besiege Capua. According to Livy (25.13.1–8), in 212 the Capuans were suffering from deprivation and sent legates to Hannibal in Taras in order to request food. Hannibal was busy trying to capture the citadel of Taras, so he could not deal with the request personally. Yet he did not want to appear as though he was abandoning the Capuans, so he ordered Hanno to quit Bruttium and go to Campania with supplies. Hanno marched his army via Samnium, gathered grain that had been collected during the summer from Hannibal's allies, collected wagons and pack animals from surrounding farms and set up a day to meet the Capuans with the provisions. Loyal colonists at Beneventum informed the consuls of Hanno's actions, and the Romans ambushed the camp where the supplies were being distributed. If Livy (25.14.11–14) can be trusted, thousands of Capuans and Carthaginians were killed or captured, and all the grain, pack animals and plunder collected by Hanno was captured. Meanwhile, Hanno fled to Bruttium. The mission was an utter failure, and Hannibal lost precious men and materiel while trying to balance his own immediate strategic goals with an important ally's local concerns.

Hannibal continued to be torn between his desire to secure the citadel of Taras and the necessity of protecting Capua. The Capuans sent another legation to Hannibal, which reported the disaster that befell Hanno and expressed concern that the Romans would soon take the city. Hannibal replied with the appropriate niceties, promising that he would not abandon Capua, and he sent 2,000 cavalry to protect Capuan farms from Roman devastation.[49] He then marched by way of Beneventum to Capua,

is a doublet, the campaign should probably be placed in 214: De Sanctis 1956–69: III.2.203 n. 9, 245; Salmon 1967: 300–1. For the location of Compulteria/Conpulteria (near modern Alvignano) and Trebula (modern Treglia, in the heart of the Monti Trebulani), see Nissen 1967: II.799–801; Solin 1993: 13–24, 145–53.

49 Liv. 25.15.1–3. This must be the cavalry under the command of Mago, which we later see successfully thwarting the Roman devastation operations (Liv. 25.18.1–3).

where he fought a successful pitched battle against the assembled Roman armies. After the battle, however, he left Capua in order to pursue the consul Ap. Claudius Pulcher's legions.[50] Livy claims that a carefully calculated plan to draw him away from Capua worked to perfection: the two Roman consuls marched in opposite directions – Ap. Claudius Pulcher towards Lucania and Q. Fulvius Flaccus in the direction of Cumae – and after Hannibal chose to go after Claudius, the consul led him on a wild goose chase into Lucania then doubled back to Capua. We later hear that Hannibal broke off his pursuit in order to crush a small Roman force in Lucania[51] and then marched to Apulia when Apulian legates informed him that the praetor Cn. Fulvius Flaccus was conducting campaigns in the vicinity of Herdonia against cities that had gone over to Hannibal.[52] Once again, these peregrinations show Hannibal moving from one hot spot to another, trying to protect various allies while simultaneously attempting to strike the Roman army a direct blow.[53]

While Hannibal campaigned in Lucania and then in Apulia, both consuls renewed their operations against Capua. In addition, the praetor C. Claudius Nero left a token garrison at his camp near Suessula and led the bulk of his army to Capua. Thus, by the end of the campaign season, the Romans had surrounded Capua with three camps and began to encircle it with a ditch and rampart.[54] In the meantime, the consuls took measures to guarantee that there would be enough grain and other provisions to maintain these armies over the winter. They stored grain at Casilinum, a fortress at the mouth of the Volturnus River was reinforced (*castellum communitum*), and garrisons were stationed in both the fortress and Puteoli to control coastal waters and the river. Shipments of grain were brought from Sardinia and Etruria to Ostia, conveyed to Campania and stored at Puteoli and the Volturnus fortress.[55] The Etrurian grain was purchased, no doubt at a fixed rate, by the praetor M. Iunius Silanus, who commanded two legions.[56] These preparations reveal yet another long-term

[50] Liv. 25.19.4–8. [51] Liv. 25.19.8–17.
[52] Liv. 25.20.6–7.
[53] Hannibal may have handed Flaccus a crushing defeat (Liv. 25.21.1–10), if we accept that this first battle of Herdonia is historical and not a confused doublet of Hannibal's victory in 210 over the praetor Cn. Fulvius Centumalus (Liv. 27.1.3–15). For a full discussion, see below, p. 258 n. 93. Whatever the historicity of the battle in Apulia, Livy (25.19.7–8) makes it clear that Hannibal made a conscious decision to pursue one of the consular armies when he learned that their camps in Campania had been abandoned. This shows that Hannibal was desperate to force another pitched battle, perhaps hoping for a decisive victory, or at least to elicit more revolts.
[54] Liv. 25.22.7–9. [55] Liv. 25.20.1–3.
[56] Liv. 25.3.1–4, 25.20.3.

Roman strategic advantage that was not discussed earlier in the chapter. Although Hannibal was able to supply his army by capturing Roman stores and gathering crops from the countryside, Rome still had significant logistical superiority. In this particular instance, the Romans utilised their manpower advantage to gather supplies from distant locales, to control land and sea routes and to transport the supplies to Roman forces 'at the front'.[57] In addition to these siege preparations, the Romans tried to undermine Capuan resolve by promising to restore the property of any man who abandoned Capua before 15 March, as discussed above. Finally, Roman activities in Campania in the second half of 212 were more or less unhindered because Hannibal was compelled to respond to allied interests in Apulia. Indeed, according to Livy (25.22.1), the consuls' successful siege preparations in Campania allowed the Romans to overcome Hannibal's battlefield victories elsewhere in Italy.

Before the circumvallation was completed, the Capuans managed to send Hannibal another legation, pleading for relief from the siege, but he was busy in the south-east of the peninsula, first trying to capture the Tarentine citadel and secondly hoping to win over Brundisium. Thus, he sent the legates home with vague promises that he would return.[58] In the next year (211) the Capuans managed to get word to Hannibal, only with immense difficulty, that they were suffering greatly from the Roman siege.[59] He debated long and hard whether he ought to attend to Taras or Capua before finally choosing to relieve the Capuans. The decision was mainly for political reasons: Hannibal knew that the Romans wanted to make an example of Capua, and that his allies would take the outcome of the Capuan revolt as a precedent for his ability to protect them.[60] Accordingly, he made a rapid march to Capua with picked troops and managed to get a message through to his besieged allies to coordinate a simultaneous assault on the Roman camps.[61] According to Livy (26.5.1–13), a battle of some magnitude followed, in which the Romans were trapped between the onrushing Carthaginians and a Capuan sally from within the walls. Polybius (9.3.1–4.6) describes a much less significant encounter. In

---

[57] It is also worth noting how Rome's naval advantage came into play in this case.

[58] Liv. 25.22.14–16. This last legation took place very late in the year, if we can trust Livy's synchronising of the construction of siege works around Capua, the fall of Syracuse and the end of the consular elections (Liv. 25.23.1, 25.41.7–8). A precise synchronisation need not be pushed too far, as the exact arrangement of events at the end of Book 25 may owe itself to Livy's dramatic sensibilities. Hannibal apparently wintered in Bruttium (Liv. 26.5.1). His focus on Taras and Brundisium may indicate a continued frustration at not possessing an adequate seaport.

[59] Liv. 26.4.1–3.   [60] Liv. 26.5.1–2.

[61] Liv. 26.4.3–6.

either case, Hannibal was unable to lift the siege, and he retired unsuccessfully from Capua.[62] In frustration, he tried one last tactic to make the Romans raise their siege: he made a rapid march to Rome, expecting that this would draw the Roman armies from Campania.[63] This famous diversion, the only time Hannibal marched on Rome, failed to elicit the desired response, and at this point he seems to have given up on Capua. Instead, he marched into Bruttium and made a surprise attack on Rhegion, capturing a number of Rhegian citizens but failing to capture the city.[64]

In the final stages of the Capuan revolt Roman military pressure and Hannibal's declining fortunes translated into a clear erosion of local elite support and even open political dissent. The Capuans also suffered the deprivations of a siege, which no doubt weakened Capuan resolve and fed anti-Hannibalic sentiment.[65] Hannibal seems to have recognised his tenuous standing, since he made a point of sending messengers to the Capuans before he marched on Rome, telling them of his plans and promising that he had not abandoned their cause.[66] This gesture may have been too little and too late: earlier in the summer, the *meddix tuticus* Seppius Loesius complained that the Capuan elite had betrayed the city by siding with Hannibal, suggesting that high-ranking aristocrats were beginning to switch sides.[67] Even the Carthaginian garrison felt abandoned by Hannibal: its commander, Hanno, sent a letter to Hannibal complaining that he abandoned them and begging him to break the siege. The letter was carried by seventy Numidians who pretended to be deserters, but the Romans captured them. The messengers were scourged, and their hands were cut off and sent back to Capua.[68]

The terror tactic was the final straw. Seppius Loesius called a meeting of the Capuan senate. Some senators argued that legates should be sent to the Roman camp, while others argued that they should hold out longer.

---

[62] Liv. 26.7.1–2; Polyb. 9.4.7–8.   [63] Polyb. 9.4.7–8; Liv. 26.7.1–5.
[64] Hannibal's route from Capua to Rome, thence to Rhegion: Polyb. 9.5.7–9, 9.7.1–10; Liv. 26.7.1–3, 26.8.10–12.2; The attack on Rhegion: Polyb. 9.7.9–10; Liv. 26.12.1–2. Concerning Hannibal's retreat from Rome to Rhegion, Polybius (9.7.10) records that he marched διὰ τῆς Δαυνίας καὶ τῆς Βρεττίας, leading some editors to emend Livy's version (26.12.2) from *per Samnium et Lucanos in Bruttium* to *per Samnium* **Apuliamque** *et Lucanos in Bruttium*. Walbank 1970: II.127, following De Sanctis 1956–69: III.2.329, argues that such a circuitous route makes little sense, and so he emends Polybius' Δαυνίας to Σαυνίτιδος or Λευκανίας. This also obviates the need to emend Livy's text. Goldsworthy 2002: 234–5, however, accepts the route through Apulia. On the whole, the Walbank/De Sanctis solution is more attractive. See also Lazenby 1978: 122–3; Seibert 1993b: 304–11.
[65] Indeed, Livy (26.6.16) claims that the Capuans were starving, and even if we allow that this is an exaggeration, the Roman siege surely took a heavy toll on the local population.
[66] Liv.26.7.5–8; Polyb. 9.5.1–6.   [67] Liv. 26.6.13–17.
[68] Liv. 26.12.10–19.

The leader of the latter group was Vibius Virrius, who was foremost in engineering the revolt.[69] Twenty-eight senators killed themselves rather than face surrender to Rome, but the rest voted to send an embassy to propose a surrender, and on the next day, the gates of Capua were opened.[70] The combination of Hannibal's inability to satisfy Capuan interests, the deprivation caused by Roman devastation and the siege, the loss of Capuan citizens captured in battle over the previous years, and the growing sense that Hannibal was unwilling or unable to provide protection – let alone ensure Capuan hegemony – forced a major shift in the political calculation of the local elite. That some Capuans still vigorously opposed surrender shows that the aristocracy was still not uniform in its sentiments. It is clear, however, that the large group of 'swing voters' in the senate, the aristocrats who had been convinced by Vibius Virrius' arguments and Hannibal's promises, had swung back and now favoured cutting the best deal possible with Rome.[71]

The smaller, subordinate Campanian towns surrendered soon after Capua fell to the Romans. According to Livy (26.14.9), fifty-three Capuan senators were found guilty of fostering rebellion and sent to Cales and Teanum Sidicinum to await punishment. Livy later reports (26.16.5–6) that the local senators were scourged and beheaded, after which the proconsuls Ap. Claudius Pulcher and Q. Fulvius Flaccus returned to Capua and received the surrender of Atella and Calatia. In the same passage he records that over seventy senators in total were executed; this higher figure may include local senators from both Capua and the satellite towns that were captured subsequently.[72] Livy does not mention Sabata in this passage but later (26.34.6–7) lists the Sabatini along with the Capuans, Atellani and Calatini as having surrendered to the Romans, so we may presume that Sabata surrendered around the same time as the other 'Capuan League' members. Appian (*Hann.* 49) and Zonaras (9.6) preserve another tradition, that the Atellani abandoned their city and joined Hannibal's army in one body, possibly to be settled in Thurii. The versions can be reconciled. Livy (26.34.6) refers to certain Capuans, Atellani,

[69] Liv. 26.13.1–19; for Vibius' role in the initial revolt, see Chapter 3, pp. 105–7, 119–21.

[70] Liv. 26.14.1–6.

[71] Fifty-three senators who had voted to revolt did not commit suicide along with Vibius and his followers. These may have included some of the aristocrats who had been convinced by Vibius in the first place. For a brief discussion of Capuan politics during the period of the city's revolt, see Frederiksen 1984: 242–3.

[72] Livy (26.16.6) also claims that over 300 'Campanians' – aristocrats – who were imprisoned or sent as hostages in other cities were also killed. In the context of this passage, it is likely that Livy is referring to leading men from all of the Campanian cities, not just Capua.

Sabatini and Calatini who 'were among the enemy' (*apud hostis*) after the Capuan League had surrendered. It is clear that some Campanians had joined Hannibal's army or simply fled to Hannibal when Rome attacked their cities. It is to these individuals that Zonaras and Appian may refer.[73]

The leading citizens of the Atellani and Calatini (and presumably the Sabatini) whom the Romans executed because they had been most responsible for revolt probably formed the core of the initial pro-Hannibalic party that held sway in 216. Like their Capuan counterparts, they would have argued against surrender. Indeed, the ringleaders must have suspected that they faced certain and extreme punishment if their city fell to the Romans. The ruling class of the subordinate Campanian states probably endured comparable conditions as did their Capuan counterparts, and the political environment was probably very similar. By 211 many of the aristocrats in these smaller towns would have lost faith in Hannibal's ability to protect them. Moreover, as discussed in Chapter 3 (see pp. 122–3, 128–30), Capua was the most powerful city in Campania and the smaller satellite towns tended to follow its lead in foreign policy. Perhaps Capua's surrender convinced the elite in Sabata, Atella and Calatia that further resistance was futile, but whatever the exact reasoning, that these smaller states followed Capua's lead fits the historical patterns that were discussed in Chapter 3. By the end of the campaign season in 211 Hannibal no longer possessed allies in Campania. The war along this high-profile front of the Italian theatre was over.

APULIA, 215–210

At the same time as Hannibal was trying to hold the line in Campania, he also struggled to keep hold of his allies in Apulia. In fact, as we saw in the last section, from 216 to 211 Hannibal often moved between Campania and Apulia trying to shore up allied support in both regions. The long-term failure of the Hannibalic strategy played out in much the same way in the two regions. Apulian cities were among the very first to defect after Cannae, but within the first two years after the battle the Romans not only consolidated their own position in the region but also began to take back some smaller cities. In 213 they managed to reconquer Arpi, Hannibal's most powerful ally in the region, and as Hannibal's fortunes declined, he lost the critical support of local ruling aristocracies. Indeed, the Apulian

---

[73] For discussion of difficulties with the sources for the surrender and punishment of the Campanians, see Ungern-Sternberg 1975: 77–95.

case study exposes some of the clearest examples of local aristocrats who were drawn to Hannibal only so long as he was successful, because they figured that associating with him would further their own interests. When Hannibal's fortunes declined, his support from these local nobles evaporated. The Roman reconquest of Apulia also highlights the strategic importance of the Latin colonies. Venusia and especially Luceria served as bases of operation and were key to the Roman war effort in the region.

As in Campania, the Romans maintained a large number of troops in Apulia between 216 and 214, which not only helped to prevent further defections but also put military pressure on Hannibal's local allies. It is difficult to disentangle the exact location of Roman forces at the end of 216, after the remnants of the defeated army, the *legiones cannenses*, were reunited at Canusium. By the following year (215) the Romans appear to have been more confident in the loyalty of Canusium, since they no longer stationed legions there. The *legiones cannenses* had been led out of Apulia to the Claudian camp near Suessula, after which they were sent to Sicily for the remainder of the war. The two legions in Sicily were conveyed to Italy, and thence to Apulia under the praetor M. Valerius Laevinus. This force replaced C. Terentius Varro's army – this was perhaps the legion of marines stationed in Ostia at the beginning of 216 – which was sent to Taras. Varro, meanwhile, was commissioned to levy troops in Picenum.[74] Livy later reports (23.33.5) that Laevinus and his two legions made their camp near Luceria. Laevinus avoided significant campaigning in Apulia, though one may speculate that he foraged in Hannibal's allies' territory. Instead, he raided part of Samnium, storming a few small Samnite villages and taking, according to Livy (23.37.12–13), 5,000 captives and a great amount of plunder, which was carried back to Luceria. Although Livy may have inflated the scale of Laevinus' success, the additional detail in the same passage that Samnite ringleaders were beheaded is grimly plausible.

Already in 214 the Romans took advantage of Hannibal's competing concerns and inability to protect all of his geographically distant allies. When the Romans took up winter quarters in the fall of 215, they sent two legions under Ti. Sempronius Gracchus to Luceria, and they moved the two legions under Laevinus to Brundisium, thus beginning to encircle Apulia with armies.[75] Over the winter Gracchus' troops skirmished with Hannibal's, probably in minor clashes between foraging parties.[76] Despite the additional military threat to his Apulian allies, Hannibal broke winter

[74] Liv. 23.31.1–6, 23.32.1–2, 23.32.16–18; see De Sanctis 1956–69: III.2.238–9; Lazenby 1978: 92–3.
[75] Liv. 23.48.3.   [76] Liv. 24.3.16–17.

quarters and marched to Capua at the request of Campanian envoys.[77] He did not leave Apulia unguarded but stationed a large garrison in Arpi, 5,000 men strong.[78] With Arpi strongly garrisoned, the Romans focused instead on retaking its satellite allies: the praetor Q. Fabius Maximus II (the son of the famous Cunctator), operating again out of Luceria, took Aecae and probably Ausculum by storm, and he made a permanent camp near Herdonia, whose territory he undoubtedly plundered.[79]

Hannibal returned to Apulia late in 214, after concluding a disappointing campaigning season. Livy's account of Hannibal's exact route is somewhat confusing: he had spent at least part of 214 trying unsuccessfully to win over Taras, and then at some point before wintering he sent his cavalry to round up horses and cattle from Apulia and the Sallentine peninsula. Finally, Hannibal set up winter quarters near Salapia, an area which, according to Livy (24.25.15), afforded him good foraging grounds.[80] In addition, his decision to winter in Salapia rather than Arpi may indicate concern not to overburden an ally that had already supported a large garrison for the year. Hannibal's various operations in the area may have served as a show of strength to the Apulians who, since 216, had witnessed only Roman success in the area.

The Romans stepped up their war effort in Apulia in 213 by assigning four legions to the region. The combination of Rome's military strength and Hannibal's failure to protect his allies wore down the resolve of his most important ally in the region, Arpi. Two legions under the praetor M. Aemilius Lepidus were stationed at the Roman camp in Luceria. Q. Fabius Maximus (the younger), now consul, was assigned Apulia as his province, in command of two legions probably stationed at the permanent camp near

---

[77] Liv. 24.12.1–3. The Romans had levied an extraordinary number of legions for the year, and the Campanians feared a siege of Capua. Livy states that Hannibal hastened from Arpi to Capua before the Romans could prevent him from doing so (presumably by sending another army to shadow him).

[78] Liv. 24.46.1–2. Livy mentions the garrison in his account of the year 213. Hannibal spent the campaign season away from Apulia, then he returned and wintered in Salapia in 214/13. It is most likely, therefore, that Hannibal left the garrison in Arpi in 214.

[79] Liv. 24.20.3–8, 25.21.1. Livy states that the elder Fabius Maximus advanced into Samnium and captured a number of towns, then he stormed Blanda in Lucania and Aecae in Apulia. He also states that Fabius Maximus II, whom he misidentifies as a propraetor, captured a place called Acuca. The name may be a mistake for Aecae; otherwise nothing is known about it. Livy has probably conflated the two Fabii, and it makes more sense to ascribe the capture of Aecae to Fabius Maximus II, whose province was in the vicinity. Livy states that Fabius Maximus II fortified a permanent camp near Herdonia, but does not say if he attacked the city. In any case, since Herdonia was still under Hannibal's control in 210, Fabius Maximus II probably did not capture it. Ausculum is not mentioned explicitly, but given that Fabius captured Aecae and campaigned in the vicinity of Herdonia, it is likely that Ausculum was also targeted.

[80] For Hannibal's movements: Liv. 24.17.8, 24.20.9–16.

Herdonia.[81] While the younger Fabius was at Suessula *en route* to Apulia, and while Hannibal was still stationed in Salapia, he was approached by an aristocrat from Arpi, Dasius Altinius, with an offer to betray the city. After the Roman command council debated, it was decided to arrest Dasius and deport him to Cales.[82]

The Dasius Altinius episode, reported by both Livy (24.45.1–47.11) and Appian (*Hann.* 31), illuminates very well the difficulties that Hannibal faced in maintaining the loyalty of allied elites. Both ancient accounts agree that Dasius Altinius was from an old, aristocratic family – the sort of family that may have held power since the first contact between Arpi and Rome.[83] It had been Dasius who had convinced the Arpian elite to side with Hannibal after Cannae. He probably did not act alone but represented a party of aristocrats who saw personal advantages and the chance for political power in siding with Hannibal. But their loyalty would only hold so long as Hannibal was successful, and indeed, both Appian and Livy are explicit that Carthaginian reverses and the apparent revitalisation of Rome led Dasius to consider a second betrayal.[84] The arrival of a second Roman army permanently camped nearby would have underscored Roman power, and we can surmise that Hannibal's garrison began to cause resentment among the Arpian citizenry as the years passed.[85]

Dasius' disappearance caused a stir among the Arpians, and after a search failed to turn up the leading citizen, messengers were sent to inform Hannibal. It is not clear who warned Hannibal, but Livy's account implies that it was the Arpians themselves. Livy is explicit, however, in stating that they warned Hannibal because they feared a rebellion.[86] Clearly, Hannibal continued to enjoy some political support in the city,

[81] Liv. 24.44.1–3, 24.44.9–10.   [82] Liv. 24.45.1–10; App. *Hann.* 31.

[83] See Chapter 2, pp. 61–2.

[84] Liv. 24.45.3: [*Dasius*] *post Cannensem cladem, tamquam cum fortuna fidem stare oporteret, ad Hannibalem descisset traxissetque ad defectionem Arpos; tum, quia res Romana contra spem votaque eius velut resurgere ab stirpibus videatur, novam referre proditionem proditis polliceatur* ('[Dasius] after the Cannae disaster, as if fortune should determine loyalty, went over to Hannibal and dragged the Arpians to defect. Then, because the Roman situation seemed like it was rising up from its roots, against his hopes and wishes, he promised to repay betrayals with a new betrayal').

App. *Hann.* 31: τότε δ' αὖ δυσπραγοῦντος Ἀννίβου ἔλαθεν ἐς Ῥώμην διιππεύσας καὶ ἐπὶ τὴν βουλὴν ἐπαχθεὶς ἔφη δύνασθαι τὸ ἁμάρτημα ἰάσασθαι καὶ μεταβαλεῖν αὖθις ἐς Ῥωμαίους τὴν πόλιν ('But now with Hannibal in turn having bad luck, Dasius rode unnoticed to Rome and was introduced in the senate, and he stated that he could repair the harm and turn the city [Arpi] back over to the Romans').

[85] Indeed, when Fabius Maximus II later entered Arpi, the citizenry turned on the garrison; see Liv. 24.47.7.

[86] Liv. 24.45.11: *metuque rerum novarum extemplo nuntii missi* ('and out of fear of a revolution messages were sent straight away').

presumably including some of the local aristocracy, even as some pro-Hannibalic aristocrats began to lose their resolve. Hannibal investigated the Arpian situation personally and then ordered members of Dasius' immediate family to be burnt alive.[87] Livy claims that the executions were a ruse to obscure Hannibal's true designs to confiscate Dasius' property. The story of the ruse, meant to exemplify Carthaginian cruelty, is clearly a reflection of Roman hostility, whether it is Livy's own judgment or drawn from his sources. At the same time, it is not implausible that Hannibal executed Dasius' family. The act would have been aimed not only at punishing the family but also at deterring other local aristocrats from plotting against him. One suspects, however, that the executions further undermined Hannibal's credibility among the Arpian elite.[88] If there had been resentment towards the Carthaginians, he may well have worsened it in his handling of the Dasius affair.

In the meantime Fabius Maximus II arrived in Apulia, moved his camp close to Arpi and began to invest the city.[89] Dasius' defection encouraged the Romans that they could avoid a prolonged siege and win the city through betrayal. They were able to penetrate one of the city gates at night, and the next day they entered the city in force. The Roman soldiers were met by 3,000 armed Arpians and, behind them, the Carthaginian garrison of 5,000. The Carthaginians had arranged the forces as such because they suspected further rebellion,[90] but the formation did not work, as the Carthaginian cause was by now completely discredited. Instead of fighting, the Romans and Arpians parlayed. The townsfolk brought out the chief magistrate of the city. Presumably, he had formerly supported Hannibal, at least tacitly, but he now shifted his loyalty to Rome. After further negotiations the Arpians turned on the Carthaginians. Perhaps more surprisingly, the Spanish contingent of the garrison also came over to the Romans.[91] Thus, the failure of Hannibal to defend his allies eroded the confidence of not only the Italians, but also some of his own troops.

After capturing the city, the Romans took steps to shore up their control. Appian records that a Roman garrison was stationed in the city. The fate of the Carthaginian troops is less clear: Livy (24.47.9–11) claims that they were allowed to return to Hannibal in Salapia, while Appian (*Hann.* 31) reports that they were massacred. Livy (24.47.10) downplays any Roman violence, but it is more likely that the most prominent supporters of Hannibal from

---

[87] Liv. 24.45.12–14; App. *Hann.* 31.   [88] De Sanctis 1956–69: III.2.262–3.
[89] Liv. 24.46.1–2.   [90] Liv. 24.47.2.
[91] Liv. 24.47.4–9.

among the Arpian aristocracy were punished. That the Romans continued to station troops in Arpi suggests that they recognised that the loyalty of local aristocrats could still be swayed according to the vagaries of war. The capture of Arpi was a major victory for the Romans, which essentially broke Carthaginian power in Apulia.[92] Hannibal still had control of Salapia and Herdonia, but he would spend little time in Apulia for the remainder of the war, instead focusing on Taras, Capua and other fronts. He may have marched into Apulia in 212: according to Livy, he pursued one of the Roman consuls from Capua into Lucania, defeated another Roman force there and then swept into Apulia and crushed a Roman force operating near Herdonia.[93] He may also have passed through Apulia in 211, after his march on Rome; this route is doubtful, but even if he did swing through Apulia at this time, the purpose of his brief appearance was not to support his allies there.[94] Only in 210 did Hannibal return to Apulia for any length of time.[95] He may have suspected that his neglect had weakened his allies' resolve, especially considering the outcome of the Capuan revolt the previous year.[96] Despite this show of strength, Hannibal was already losing the support of the remaining two pro-Carthaginian cities, Salapia and Herdonia.

As discussed in Chapter 2 (see pp. 60–1), Hannibal had capitalised on a political rivalry to gain the allegiance of a party of the local elite in Salapia, through whom he controlled the city.[97] But his absence from Apulia and the string of Roman victories weakened the position of the pro-Carthaginian

[92] Livy (26.41.15) ascribes a speech to Scipio, supposedly given to veteran troops in 210, which compares the victory over Arpi to the capture of Capua and Syracuse.

[93] Liv. 25.19.1–17, 25.20.1, 25.20.5–7, 26.21.1–10. The historicity of the so-called First Battle of Herdonia is questionable because (1) the details of the battle are very similar to a second battle near Herdonia reported by Livy (27.1.3–15) and Appian (*Hann.* 48); (2) the similarity of the commanders' names; and (3) the silence of sources corroborating Livy's account of the first battle. De Sanctis 1956–69: III.2.444–7 and n. 28 argued that the episode has been duplicated; Broughton 1951–2: I.271 n. 2 and Lazenby 1978: 114 argued that both battles are historical. The historicity of the First Battle of Herdonia does not affect the present analysis: if it is historical, then Hannibal's decision to enter Apulia was meant only to relieve the siege of Capua by attacking elsewhere to lure the Romans away (Lazenby 1978: 114); if the battle did not occur, then Hannibal did not show himself in Apulia during the 212 campaigning season. All are in agreement that the Second Battle of Herdonia is historical.

[94] See above, n. 64.

[95] Liv. 26.28.5–13, 26.29.1–10, 27.1.1. It is not clear where Hannibal had wintered in 211/10, though, as we have seen, he operated in Bruttium late in 211. By summer 210 Hannibal had probably worked his way back at least as far as Lucania. The consul Marcellus was assigned the war with Hannibal as his province and was later active in Samnium. The Romans also maintained two legions in Apulia. The disposition of troops, especially Marcellus', suggests that Hannibal was in either Lucania or Apulia.

[96] Liv. 26.38.1–2; Polyb. 9.26.2. According to De Sanctis 1956–69: III.2.443, Hannibal was concerned with holding the Carapelle–Sele line in order to protect his allies to the south.

[97] Liv. 26.38; App. *Hann.* 45–7.

elite and provided an opportunity for their political opponents to seek out Roman assistance. According to Livy, the heads of the rival factions were Blattius and Dasius. Blattius supported the Roman cause and hoped to hand over the city to them, but he did not feel that he had enough political support. He therefore approached his rival Dasius, who had supported the city's defection to Hannibal. Dasius warned Hannibal of the plans; Hannibal investigated the matter but dismissed the allegations as the product of personal political hostility. Finally, Blattius was able to win over Dasius, convincing him to hand over the city. It is striking that Blattius approached his rival and risked exposing himself as a traitor to Hannibal. We can make sense of this if we consider the contingent nature of Hannibal's aristocratic support. The initial decision to side with Hannibal split along lines of aristocratic rivalry at a time when the Carthaginian was ascendant. Now that Hannibal had been discredited, pro-Roman aristocrats probably began to look for opportunities to switch sides. In this context Blattius may have felt confident that he could approach his rival. Whatever the exact process, the city was handed over to the consul M. Claudius Marcellus; most of the Carthaginian garrison of 500 Numidian cavalry was killed.

The situation was similar in Herdonia.[98] Messengers informed Hannibal that loyalty in the city was wavering because of the loss of Salapia, and because of reports that he had quit Apulia and abandoned his allies there. The city was further pressured when the Roman propraetor Cn. Fulvius moved his camp closer, trying to win the city by betrayal. Fulvius himself had received reports that the loyalty of the city was in doubt, presumably from pro-Roman factions within the walls. Hannibal made a forced march to Herdonia and caught Fulvius off guard, destroying the Roman army. After the battle Hannibal conducted investigations, and executed the ringleaders of the potential revolt. But Hannibal still doubted that he could maintain the loyalty of the city, so he took the extreme step of destroying Herdonia and removing the population to Metapontion and Thurii. By the end of 210 Hannibal had to admit defeat in Apulia.

Hannibal did march into Apulia a few more times and even tested the resolve of a few Apulian cities, though with no success. In spring 209 Hannibal tried to tempt Canusium to revolt but retreated quickly when Marcellus emerged from winter quarters and marched into the vicinity.[99] In

---

[98] For events surrounding Herdonia in 210, see Liv. 27.1.1–15; App. *Hann.* 48. For the historicity of the multiple accounts of the battle of Herdonia, see above, n. 93.

[99] Liv. 27.12.7–8. Marcellus may have wintered near Venusia, and he would do so in 208 (Liv. 27.22.2). The proximity of the Roman army should have suppressed any possible chance of revolt, though at this stage it seems unlikely that Hannibal seriously threatened the loyalty of the town.

208 Hannibal retreated into Apulia, where he ambushed and killed
Marcellus. He tried to use Marcellus' ring to gain access to Salapia.
The townsmen, however, knew about the ruse and trapped a number of
Hannibal's men within the gates; Hannibal retreated in defeat.[100] Finally,
Hannibal marched again into Apulia in 207, in the vicinity of Canusium.
He was probably on his way to join forces with his brother, but when news
of the battle of the Metaurus River reached Hannibal, the Carthaginian
retreated from Apulia for good.[101] The exact process differed somewhat
from Campania, but the general patterns – and end result – were largely
the same.

TARAS AND SOUTH-EASTERN ITALY, 212–207

In the year following the loss of Herdonia and Salapia, Hannibal suffered
a major setback in the far south of the peninsula when Taras was captured
by Q. Fabius Maximus, who was consul for the fifth time overall, and for
the third and final time during the Second Punic War. Hannibal's relatively
recent strategic success in the region, starting with the defection of Taras in
213/12, had somewhat offset Roman advances elsewhere in the Peninsula.
In 209, however, his strategic revival in south-east Italy began to unravel.
Hannibal's long-term failure in this region is bound up largely with the story
of Taras, where unique military and topographical circumstances gave rise
to yet another variation on the general patterns discussed in this chapter.

Hannibal held the city, but the Romans remained in control of the citadel. Although negligence on the part of the Roman garrison commander
Marcus Livius may have contributed to Hannibal's capture of Taras, a
swift Roman military response and a diligent policy of resupply prevented
Hannibal from capturing the citadel. Troops from the Roman garrison in
Metapontion were quickly sent to reinforce Livius' garrison. This realloca-
tion of troops allowed the Metapontians to revolt, but the reinforcements

---

[100] Liv. 27.28.1–13; App. *Hann.* 51. Neither account explicitly mentions a Roman garrison, though
Livy's account *may* imply some Roman guards remained: the best men 'in the garrison' (*in praesidio*) guarded the gate (27.28.8), and Hannibal employed Roman deserters speaking Latin to
try to win them over (27.28.9). Whether the guards were Roman or Latin-speaking Salapians,
however, is not clear. Meanwhile, the context of the passage suggests that the Salapians were
active in rejecting Hannibal's offer. For example, Livy (27.28.7) states that their own townsfolk
(*oppidanos*) were posted as guards along the walls. He adds (27.28.6) that the Salapians were also
afraid that Hannibal wanted to punish them for betraying him. Overall, the Salapian response
indicates that Hannibal was so discredited that they rejected him on their own initiative, without much (or any) Roman military coercion.

[101] Liv. 27.41.1–27.42.17, 27.51.12–13. For an attempt to make sense of Hannibal's movements before
the battle of the Metaurus, see Lazenby 1978: 184–6.

did convince Hannibal that he could not take the citadel by storm. Instead, he ordered that the citadel be blockaded and left a garrison to protect the city from potential Roman counter-attacks launched from the citadel. He also convinced the Tarentines that the Roman garrison could be starved into submission if they supplied ships to cut off the harbour. He then marched to winter quarters.[102]

Roman logistical advantages, however, foiled Hannibal's plans to starve out Livius' garrison, and indeed the Tarentines in the city may have suffered greater deprivation than did the soldiers holding the citadel. The Romans made a concerted effort to support the citadel garrison by sea. Before the spring of 212 the people of Thurii sent ships laden with supplies to relieve the Roman troops in Metapontion, and it appears that Taras was the ultimate destination for at least some of the supplies.[103] Livy (25.15.4–6) provides more explicit evidence: in the spring of 212 the Roman senate commissioned a special purchase of grain from Etruria to support the Taras garrison, at least some of which later reached its destination. An episode late in the summer of 211 suggests that supplies continued to reach the garrison. The Tarentines requested a Carthaginian fleet not only to help prevent supplies from reaching the Roman forces, but also to protect the Tarentines' own incoming seaborne grain shipments. The request indicates both that provisions were getting through to the citadel, and that the Romans used the citadel, which commanded the harbour, to cut off Tarentine supplies. It is not clear how successful the Carthaginian fleet was in securing the harbour for the Tarentines. Livy (26.20.7–11) claims the Carthaginians succeeded in cutting off the Romans from the harbour, but Polybius (9.9.1) is silent on the matter. Whatever they accomplished, the Carthaginian sailors also used up a great deal of supplies – Livy claims that the amount they consumed more than offset the amount of food allowed to reach the townsfolk under their protection – so the Tarentines requested that the fleet leave. Thus, the Tarentines appear to have suffered a severe shortage of food, perhaps worse than that endured by the Roman garrison. In 210 the Romans sent another supply fleet under the prefect Decimus Quinctius, but the Tarentine fleet badly defeated it and thus prevented the cargo from reaching the Roman garrison.[104] Sometime after the

---

[102] For events immediately following Hannibal's capture of Taras, including the Romans' strategic response and Hannibal's decision to blockade the citadel: Polyb. 8.34.1–13; Liv. 25.11.10–20, 25.15.5–6, App. *Hann.* 35. For additional discussion, see Chapter 5, pp. 217–18.

[103] Polyb. 8.34.1; App. *Hann.* 34. The ships and crews were captured by the Tarentines, an event that helped to trigger the revolt of Thurii; see Chapter 5, pp. 223–4, 229.

[104] Liv. 26.39.1–19. For Decimus Quinctius' praenomen and title, see Broughton 1951–2: 1.281 n. 5.

naval battle, Marcus Livius ordered 2,500 troops under the command of a certain Gaius Perseus to attack a large body of Tarentine citizens who were foraging in the surrounding countryside. The Romans reportedly killed many of the foragers and drove the rest back within the city walls.[105] Livy claims that both the Tarentines and the Romans were equally frustrated in their efforts to obtain new supplies. Still, the Tarentines captured a few of the Roman supply ships, while the Romans probably had a chance to forage after defeating the Tarentines. Later in 210 the Roman senate again authorised the purchase of grain from Etruria, which was brought to Taras along with additional troops to reinforce the citadel.[106] Finally, in 209 a fleet was sent from Sicily with grain supplies for the Roman army, under the command of the consul Fabius Maximus, who was encamped near Taras.[107] Fabius was also given a special sum of one hundred pounds of gold to convey to the Tarentine citadel.[108] There is no doubt that he brought both the grain and gold to the besieged garrison. Overall, Rome's determination in transporting money, reinforcements and especially food to the citadel ruined Hannibal's prediction to his Tarentine allies that the Roman garrison would soon succumb to hunger.

As mentioned before, Hannibal had also left a garrison of both infantry and cavalry to protect the Tarentine townsfolk from the Romans and pro-Roman Tarentines in the citadel.[109] But this produced predictably ambiguous results. In addition to the obvious drain on his manpower, the prolonged quartering of foreign troops within the city over time probably engendered feelings of resentment from the local population. This may have been especially true in the case of Taras. The terms of their treaty with Hannibal suggest that the Tarentines were sensitive to issues of sovereignty, particularly with reference to foreign garrisons.[110] Moreover, at least part of the garrison was composed of Bruttian troops.[111] Although Taras had a history of employing various Italic peoples, even against other Greek cities, the Tarentines probably felt some degree of enmity towards various Italic peoples – a common hostility shared throughout Magna Graecia and discussed at various points in this book.[112] If so, then the garrison

[105] Liv. 26.39.20–3.   [106] Liv. 27.3.8–9.

[107] Liv. 27.7.12–13, 27.7.16, 27.8.13–19. There is some confusion in Livy whether the supply fleet was commanded by the proconsul M. Valerius Laevinus or his prefect M. Valerius Messalla; Broughton 1951–2: 1.287–8.

[108] Liv. 27.10.18.   [109] Polyb. 8.33.7–8; Liv. 25.11.8.

[110] Polyb. 8.25.2; Liv. 25.8.8. Livy's version of the treaty specifically stipulates that there was to be no Carthaginian garrison against the will of the Tarentines and certainly indicates their suspicion of foreign garrisons.

[111] For the Bruttian contingent, see Liv. 27.15.9; App. *Hann.* 49.

[112] See Chapter 4, pp. 151–4, 160–2, Chapter 5, pp. 195–9, 204–5.

may have stirred up ethnic tensions. On a practical level, the garrison must have strained the Tarentine food supply, a critical issue, as discussed above. Finally, the Carthaginian garrison was simply not very effective in protecting the Tarentines. Roman troops were able to harass Tarentine foragers with no recorded Carthaginian response. The Carthaginian fleet sent to protect Taras in 211 did more harm than good, while the Tarentines bore the brunt of naval defence in 210. Indeed, when the city fell to Fabius, the anti-Roman Tarentines, Bruttian soldiers and Carthaginian soldiers displayed conflicting interests. The Bruttians betrayed Taras and the Carthaginians tried to surrender; meanwhile, the Tarentines tried to put up some defence.[113] Overall, by 209 there appears to have been little common cause between the Tarentines and the garrison that was supposed to be helping them.

I argue that one additional yet important factor also undermined Hannibal's credibility in the eyes of the local elite: his failure to satisfy Tarentine hegemonic aspirations.[114] Whether or not Hannibal explicitly promised that he would establish Taras as a regional hegemonic power, his initial successes in the wake of the Tarentine revolt must have been encouraging. Traditional Tarentine satellites Metapontion and Heraclea revolted, and Taras asserted influence over long-time rival Thurii. In addition, most of the Lucanians who had remained loyal to Rome came over to Hannibal, perhaps also under Tarentine influence.[115] After this, however, hopes of renewed Tarentine power and regional hegemony started to fade. In 212 Hannibal made one last attempt to storm the Tarentine citadel, and when this failed, he marched to Brundisium, where he mistakenly believed the port would be betrayed to him.[116] Strategic considerations undoubtedly influenced this failed operation, though it is tempting to speculate that he was also trying to capture a city that challenged Tarentine regional interests.[117] If so, then Hannibal's failure to capture the port may have been interpreted as proof of his inability to help restore Tarentine glory. The razing of Herdonia and resettlement of its citizens to Thurii and Metapontion cannot have helped his reputation.[118] Although he had soundly defeated a Roman army before resettling the Herdonians, the final fate of the city must have been unnerving for his allies. Finally, in 209, before the final assault in Taras, Fabius Maximus recaptured

[113] Liv. 27.15.17–16.6.   [114] See Chapter 5, pp. 192–9, 210–11, 216–17.
[115] See Chapter 5, pp. 205–8 and Appendix D.   [116] Liv. 25.22.14–15.
[117] The colony of Brundisium helped Rome maintain control of the Sallentine peninsula, and its busy and strategic port appears to have hurt Taras' commercial interests: see Chapter 5, pp. 200–2.
[118] Liv. 27.1.14. The Tarentines surely would have heard about this from Metapontion.

Manduria, the most important town in the Sallentine peninsula, and Fulvius Flaccus received the surrender of some Lucanian towns. Both were historical targets of Tarentine expansion.[119] From a military perspective, the Romans were tightening the noose around Taras; the operations also would have served harsh notice that alliance with Hannibal did not bring with it Tarentine hegemony over neighbouring peoples.

I have already discussed how Hannibal was often caught between competing strategic interests, especially the difficult choice to focus military resources in one area of Italy at the expense of defending his allies in another area. Most striking was his annual decision between 214 and 211 whether to defend Capua or focus on Taras. The Romans exploited this sort of dilemma in 209, with a spectacular coordinated military effort that divided Hannibal's attention between Taras and Caulonia. The consul for the year, Q. Fabius Maximus, was assigned Taras as his province. He marched first into the Sallentine peninsula and, as I have just mentioned, captured the strategic city of Manduria.[120] Fabius encouraged M. Claudius Marcellus to keep Hannibal busy in Apulia so that he would be able to besiege Taras.[121] Marcellus twice engaged Hannibal near Canusium, with both battles ending as costly Roman defeats.[122] Fabius also ordered the Roman garrison at Rhegion to make a raid into Bruttium and lay siege to Caulonia.[123] In the meantime, as mentioned above (p. 262), a fleet was prepared to convey extra supplies from Sicily to Taras in order to aid Fabius Maximus in his planned attack on Taras. It is clear from these wide-ranging plans that the Romans had decided to besiege Taras by the beginning of the campaign season. Indeed, according to Livy (27.12.3), Fabius Maximus

---

[119] Liv. 27.15.2–4; see also above, n. 114.

[120] Liv. 27.15.4. The other consul, Q. Fulvius Flaccus, was assigned Lucania and Bruttium as his province. Flaccus operated in northern Lucania and received the surrender of some Lucanian communities (including the *Volceientes*) and the Samnite tribe of the Hirpini (Liv. 27.15.2–3). Livy oddly lists the surrender of the Volceii and Lucanians separately. This may indicate that the *Volceientes* cut their own deal with Rome, separately from the other Lucanians. It is also possible that Livy did not recognise that they were Lucanian, perhaps confusing Volceii with Etruscan Volci/Vulci. The Hirpini inhabited the most southern reaches of Samnium, bordering on Lucania, while Volceii lay in northern Lucania (near modern Buccino), where Flaccus probably campaigned. See Chapter 5, pp. 205–7 and n. 78 (Volceii); Salmon 1967: 46–8; Appendix A (Hirpini). Livy also mentions that members of the Bruttian elite sought the same mild terms that the Lucanians had received, suggesting that Flaccus had enticed these communities to surrender by offering attractive conditions. It is not clear whether the Bruttians were from communities still allied with Hannibal, or those that had surrendered previously (see Liv. 25.1.2) and sought milder terms.

[121] Liv. 27.12.1–2.

[122] Liv. 27.12.7–14.14. Livy claims that Hannibal won the first battle, and the Romans won the second. It is likely, however, that Hannibal was victorious on both occasions: Lazenby 1978: 175.

[123] Liv. 27.12.4–6.

believed that if he could recaptured Taras, Hannibal would retreat from Italy. If this is an accurate report, then it is not surprising that so much of the Roman war effort in 209 was focused on the Tarentine campaign. It is also clear that the simultaneous Roman operations, especially the attack on Caulonia, were designed to lure Hannibal away from Taras. The plan worked, albeit at a heavy cost. After the two battles near Canusium, Hannibal marched into Bruttium to relieve the siege of Caulonia,[124] either not recognising that the Romans would attack Taras or believing that the Tarentines could hold on long enough for him to relieve Caulonia.[125] In either case, Hannibal left the Tarentines to defend themselves. The defence of Taras was further compromised because the Punic fleet had crossed to Corcyra to help Philip attack the Aetolians.[126] Hannibal's long-term strategic weakness was drawn into sharp focus: he could assist only one ally at the often tragic expense of another.

Fabius captured Taras after only a brief siege. Had the Tarentines been able to hold out longer, Hannibal might have been able to return to Taras and relieve the siege (see above, n. 125). His absence, combined with the Roman control of the citadel, allowed Fabius to station troops very near the city and thus completely surround it. Fabius himself pitched camp near the entrance of the harbour, while ships laden with siege weapons were drawn up to the city walls.[127] The Romans then stormed the walls on the eastern side of the city when the Bruttian contingent of the Carthaginian garrison betrayed the city to Fabius.[128] Bruttian willingness to betray Taras may reflect lingering hostility between the Bruttians and the Greeks, though it also indicates that the garrison was demoralised. In fact, after Fabius' troops entered the city, both the Bruttians and Carthaginians

---

[124] Liv. 27.15.1, 27.15.8, 27.16.10.

[125] Hannibal heard of the attack on Taras while he was near Caulonia (Liv. 27.16.9–10), suggesting that he did not know of the Roman attack sooner. However, it is unlikely that Hannibal would not have suspected a Roman attempt on Taras. If Plutarch (*Fab. Max.* 22) is to be believed, the siege of Taras took only about a week; Hannibal may have figured that even if Taras were attacked, it would hold out longer than a week, so that he could relieve the siege of Caulonia and return to defend Taras. As it was, he almost managed to get back to Taras in time. For the Roman campaign to recapture Taras in 209, see Kukofka 1990: 99–111.

[126] Liv. 27.15.7. Livy seems to mean that the Carthaginian ships were stationed in Taras and then moved to Corcyra: Lazenby 1978: 175. If the fleet had been in Taras, it was probably only putting in for a short time on its way to help Philip. It is not likely that any Carthaginian fleet would have stayed long in Taras, given the unpopularity of the previous Carthaginian fleet to dock in the port.

[127] Liv. 27.15.4–6.

[128] Liv. 27.15.9–12; App. *Hann.* 49; Plut. *Fab. Max.* 21. Livy includes the fanciful tale that the commander of the Bruttians betrayed the city because he was in love with a Tarentine woman whose brother served in the Roman army and who helped to sway his loyalty, though he later (27.15.18) claims that many Bruttians were involved in the plot.

appear to have given up without a fight.[129] Most of the Tarentine citizenry
also put up only token resistance. After joining combat with the Romans
in the *agora*, they fought half-heartedly before retreating and hiding in
private homes.[130] When Livy (27.16.6) describes the massacre that ensued,
he states that the Romans killed Carthaginians, Bruttians and Tarentines,
whether they were armed or not, implying that not all Tarentines put up
armed resistance. Livy does note that the leaders of the anti-Roman party
fought bravely (26.16.3), and he also claims that the fighting in the *agora*
was spirited at first (26.16.1). It is not surprising that the leaders who had
urged alliance with Hannibal, facing certain punishment by the Romans,
were more willing to fight on. The initial Tarentine resistance probably
represents the last ditch effort by the minority of citizens who still clung to
Hannibal, for whatever reasons. The near total collapse of Taras' defence
suggests that the city could have been taken more or less peacefully had
the Roman troops been more disciplined.

Taras was the linchpin to Hannibal's control of southern Lucania, the
Sallentine peninsula and eastern Magna Graecia, to the degree that he still
had any possessions in these regions. It was also a vital link to his one major
'international' ally, Philip V of Macedon.[131] So, unsurprisingly, Hannibal
did not immediately concede the city after it fell to Fabius Maximus.
After spending a few days in the vicinity, he retreated to Metapontion
and devised a plan to ambush Fabius: a Metapontian envoy was sent to
Fabius promising that the ruling aristocracy would betray the city and its
Carthaginian garrison.[132] Fabius did not take the bait, since he was tipped
off, according to Livy (26.16.13–16), by bad auspices and confirmed his suspicions by torturing the messengers. Hannibal lingered in Metapontion
for an unspecified time, perhaps wintering in the vicinity.[133]

Over the following two years, the Romans leveraged their manpower
advantage to secure Taras. In 208 the praetor Q. Claudius Flamen was
assigned two legions and the province 'Taras and the Sallentinians'
(*Tarentum et Sallentini*).[134] The army appears to have stayed near Taras and

---

[129] Liv. 27.16.5–6.   [130] Liv. 27.16.2.

[131] Livy's report (27.15.7) of a Carthaginian fleet leaving Taras in 209 to help Philip attack the
Aetolians shows that Hannibal was still trying to make good on this alliance.

[132] Liv. 27.16.11–12.

[133] Liv.27.25.12–14; A. Russi 1995: 14. The sources do not indicate the exact location of Hannibal's
winter quarters in 209/8, though it appears to have been somewhat close to Taras rather than in
Bruttium.

[134] Liv. 27.22.2–3. Livy supplies the name 'Q. Claudius Flamen', but the cognomen is otherwise
unknown, and perhaps the name should be amended to Quinctius Claudius Flamininus. See
Broughton 1951–2: 1.290 n. 1; Badian 1971: 107–9; Palmer 1996: 83–90 (defending 'Flamen');
Brennan 2000: 728 n. 33.

then wintered in the Sallentine peninsula. Meanwhile, Hannibal killed the consul M. Claudius Marcellus and mortally wounded his colleague T. Quinctius Crispinus in an ambush somewhere near Bantia and Venusia.[135] Yet he was unable to capitalise much on this success, as the Romans twice attacked Locri, one of his principal allies in Bruttium – once before the ambush and once after; the attacks on Locri drew Hannibal away from Taras.[136] Q. Claudius was redeployed in 207 and once again assigned the province of Taras and the Sallentines.[137] During these two years Rome probably subjugated any Messapian communities that had not already surrendered.[138] Hannibal's movements in 207 are difficult to disentangle from the sources, but he may have made one last, failed attempt to capture Taras. While wintering in Bruttium in 208/7, he made a raid in the direction of Taras and the Salento and engaged a Roman force, but he quickly retreated at the approach of a second Roman army.[139] In the spring he gathered his troops and marched near Grumentum in Lucania. Livy (27.41.3–27.42.8, 27.42.14–16) claims that he suffered two setbacks, losing battles in Lucania and Apulia, before doubling back to Metapontion to gather reinforcements.[140] Hannibal marched north to meet his brother and perhaps reached Larinum, where he learned about the battle of Metaurus.[141] At this point he retreated to Bruttium, first turning in the direction of Metapontion one last time.

Hannibal's last few possessions in the region fell to the Romans soon thereafter. According to Livy (27.51.13), after Metaurus, Hannibal resettled the entire population of Metapontion in Bruttium.[142] This is probably an exaggeration, but it is not implausible that the bulk of the population fled under his protection. In the same passage Livy also claims that Hannibal resettled all of the Lucanians who were still allied with him. This contradicts his later statement (28.11.15) that the 'whole population'

---

[135] Polyb. 10.32; Liv. 27.25.13–14, 27.26.7–27.27.14; Val. Max. 1.6.9; App. *Hann.* 50; Plut. *Marc.* 29, Zon. 9.9. On the topography and chronology, see Lazenby 1978: 178–9.

[136] Liv. 27.25.11–13, 26.3–6, 28.13–17.   [137] Liv. 27.36.13, 27.38.8, 27.40.11–14.

[138] La Bua 1992: 68–9.   [139] Liv. 27.40.1–12.

[140] Livy claims that the reason for his movements was to recapture Lucanian towns that had submitted to Rome. This may be partly accurate, though he was surely planning to meet with his brother Hasdrubal, who had descended the Alps and reached the Po valley the same spring. According to Livy, the Romans won two smashing victories over Hannibal; this is undoubtedly the product of pro-Roman bias by Livy or his sources. After doubling back to Metapontion, Hannibal supposedly received reinforcements from the Metapontians and the Bruttians. For further discussion on these campaigns and the garbled Livian narrative, see De Sanctis 1956–69: III.2.553–4 (who rejects the historicity of the march); Lazenby 1978: 185–6 (who accepts the march as historical).

[141] Liv. 27.40.10; see Lazenby 1978: 185, 190.

[142] See also App. *Hann.* 54; Kukofka 1990: 122–5.

of Lucania peacefully returned to alliance with Rome in 206. One need not be too concerned about these contradictory details. Livy, in his notice for 207, possibly conflated the Lucanian surrender with the relocation of Metapontion and failed to notice this when he reported the Lucanian surrender again in 206. Or, more probably, only some of the Lucanians (those in the region of Taras, perhaps) were resettled in 207, with remaining communities surrending to Rome the following year. We do not hear specifically about the fate of Heraclea. It is possible that Hannibal evacuated the city along with Metapontion, in 207. Cicero claims (*Arch.* 6, *Balb.* 21–2), however, that Heraclea continued to enjoy a favourable treaty until the Social War, and the city does not appear to have been colonised after the war. The city was visited by Delphic *theoroi* in 198 or 194 and is mentioned in the list of *theorodokoi* of Delphi. This all indicates that Heraclea maintained a degree of political autonomy that was denied to other Greek cities such as Metapontion, Thurii, Croton and Caulonia, suggesting that the Heracleans returned to their alliance with Rome more willingly.[143] We can only speculate as to the date: probably after the recapture of Taras but before Hannibal resettled the Metapontians.

Unlike the other cities of eastern Magna Graecia, which fell to Rome soon after Taras was recaptured, Thurii remained in revolt until 204. This is even more striking when we consider that Thurii initially resisted defecting: they were the last of the Greek cities to side with Hannibal. As discussed in Chapter 5 (pp. 229–31), the Thurians' stubborn resistance into the very late years of the war must be understood in its particular military and political context, namely the influx of pro-Hannibalic refugees from Herdonia, who may have felt that they had little choice but to hold out as long as possible. Moreover, Rome's treatment of rebellious Greek cities, with the aforementioned exception of Heraclea, had generally been fierce – Taras, Syracuse and Locri each suffered greatly when reconquered – and this probably discouraged the Thurians from giving up on Hannibal. I have argued in this chapter that Hannibal's failure to respond to Roman reprisals undermined the resolve of local aristocrats. But Roman punishments and brutal post-reconquest settlements offered diminishing returns. As the war dragged on, some local aristocrats surely figured that they were no worse off staying the course with Hannibal than trying to negotiate with Rome. Finally, as Hannibal controlled a smaller and smaller corner of south-western Italy, he would have found it easier to keep his field army in close proximity to his remaining allies – another

---

[143] Manganaro 1964: 419–26; Quilici 1967: 162; see also Kukofka 1990: 125, 158–9.

strategic irony. For a city such as Thurii, if it did not realign with Rome by, say, 207 or 206, the tipping point was reached and the only credible option left to the surviving ruling class was to hold out and hope for the best. Once again, therefore, Thurii stands somewhat as a counterexample to general patterns of state behaviour that have been discussed. Yet at the same time, it reminds us how specific and contingent local circumstances could exert powerful influence on state behaviour.

WESTERN MAGNA GRAECIA AND BRUTTIUM, 215–203

Hannibal's strategy was perhaps most successful in the 'toe' of Italy, where he secured a large number of communities early in the war, both Greeks and Bruttians, many of whom remained loyal to him until the very last years of the conflict in Italy. Indeed, as far as the sources indicate, Hannibal's Italian possessions after 206 did not extend beyond the boundaries of Bruttium, with the exception of Thurii.[144] Moreover, throughout the entirety of the war, only one city in this region did not defect: Rhegion. The staunch support that Hannibal received in the region, together with the very slow pace of the Roman reconquest, is yet another local variation on the general themes discussed in this chapter. I will consider why the Bruttians and two important Greek cities (Locri and Croton) held out so long and examine how Rhegion made ongoing contributions to Rome's military efforts in the region, ultimately playing a key role in the reconquest of Locri.

It must be recognised that the Romans did not throw as many resources into Bruttium as they did into other fronts in the Italian theatre, at least until late in the war, after Campania, Apulia and south-eastern Italy had already been subdued. In fact, the Romans did not station any legions in Bruttium *or* Lucania between 216 and 209, with the exception of the two legions of *volones*, which were stationed in Lucania between 214 and 212.[145] Although the *volones* never campaigned in Bruttium, they badly defeated Hanno's army, made up of mostly Lucanian and Bruttian infantry.[146] In 209 the consul Q. Fulvius Flaccus was given two legions to wage war

---

[144] Thurii was situated, however, close to Bruttium. As the territory controlled by Hannibal contracted, he concentrated his army in a tighter field of operation centred in Bruttium, and Thurii effectively fell within this zone at the end of the war.

[145] The *volones* commended themselves well under Ti. Sempronius Gracchus (cos. 213, procos. 214, 212), but when he was ambushed and killed in Lucania in 212, they deserted and dispersed: Liv. 24.44.1, 24.47.12, 25.1.5.

[146] The battle took place near Beneventum in 214: Liv. 24.14.1–2, 24.15.1–2, 24.16.2–9; Val. Max. 5.6.8; Zon. 9.4. Later in the same year Hanno won a smaller engagement in Lucania, possibly near the border of Bruttium: Liv. 24.20.1–2.

'among the Lucanians and Bruttians' (*in Lucanis ac Bruttiis*), but he seems to have operated only in Lucania.[147] Only in 208 do we find Roman legions active in Bruttium, when the consul T. Quinctius Crispinus led two legions from his base in Lucania into Bruttium in order to besiege Locri. Although Quinctius broke off the attack, withdrew from Bruttium and was mortally wounded in the same ambush that claimed Marcellus, his legate L. Cincius Alimentus (the Roman historian) renewed the siege later in the summer, with equipment brought over from Sicily.[148] We also hear of a Roman force operating in the vicinity of Petelia.[149] The Roman garrison in Rhegion, composed mostly of men from Agathyrna and Bruttian deserters, made raids into Bruttian territory.[150] Overall, however, there was little Roman military presence in Bruttium before 208, which helped Hannibal maintain the loyalty of his allies in the region.[151]

There is no doubt that anti-Roman sentiments ran high among the Bruttians, with widespread discontent erupting into open defection in the wake of Cannae. As discussed in Chapter 4 (pp. 154–5), the Bruttians had been subject to major confiscations of territory after they were initially conquered. In the short term, alliance with Hannibal proved profitable for the Bruttians – or more accurately, one group of Bruttians, drawn from an unknown number of communities. They seized control of Croton,

---

[147] Liv. 27.7.7, 27.14.2: According to Livy, he received the surrender of some towns in northern Lucania, and also met with representatives of the Bruttians who sought the same terms of surrender. It is not clear if these towns had already surrendered in 213 (see Liv. 25.1–2) and now desired better terms, or if these were representatives of different towns still loyal to Hannibal.

[148] Liv. 27.25.11–14, 27.26.3–6, 27.28.13–17.

[149] Liv. 27.26.5–6. The chronology is badly garbled in Livy's narrative. A plausible sequence, adopting more or less Lazenby's (1978: 178–80) reconstruction, is as follows: Crispinus marched to Bruttium to initiate the siege but withdrew when he heard that Hannibal's army was nearby. He may have already contacted Cincius to bring siege supplies from Sicily. Hannibal followed the consul into Lucania and ambushed Crispinus and Marcellus. While Hannibal made an attempt to recapture Salapia, Cincius began (or continued) the siege of Locri. Meanwhile, another Roman force had been sent from Taras to Locri, but it was trapped and destroyed near Petelia.

[150] We know of two such raids, in 210 and 209: Liv. 27.12.4–6, 27.15.8, 27.16.9–10. Livy (26.40.18) and Polybius (9.27.10–11) state, however, that the people of Rhegion wanted such a force so that they could devastate Bruttian lands, implying perhaps that the raids were more common than the sources make explicit. For the composition of the garrison in 210: Liv. 26.40.16–18, 27.12.4–5, Polyb. 9.27.10–11.

[151] After 208 the Romans began to focus more on Bruttium, with four to six legions operating in or near the region. **207:** Consul C. Claudius Nero commanded two legions in Bruttium and Lucania, and proconsul Q. Fulvius Flaccus commanded two legions in Bruttium. **206:** Consuls L. Veturus Philo and Q. Caecilius Metellus commanded two legions each in Bruttium. **205:** Consul P. Cornelius Scipio was given two legions for Sicily but was active in capturing Locri, consul P. Licinius Crassus Dives commanded two legions for Bruttium, and Q. Caecilius Metellus was redeployed with his two legions for Bruttium. **204:** P. Sempronius Tuditanus commanded two legions in Bruttium, and P. Licinius Crassus Dives was redeployed with his two legions in Bruttium. For references, see Broughton 1951–2: 1.294–6, 298, 301–2, 305, 308.

possibly on their own accord but certainly with the tacit permission of the Carthaginians.[152] The Bruttians appear to have served in the armies of Hannibal and Hanno in greater proportion than other Italians.[153] The opportunity for military service may have been welcome, especially considering the martial ethos of the Bruttian elite.[154] In addition, the willingness to serve in relatively large numbers late into the war may also reflect anti-Roman sentiment.

The depth of the Bruttians' pro-Hannibalic/anti-Roman sympathies should not, however, be overestimated. As early as 213, a number of Bruttian communities had already surrendered to Rome.[155] One of these communities was Consentia, which seems to have switched sides more than once during the war,[156] indicating the degree to which Bruttian loyalties were contingent. The same can be said about Bruttian military service for the Carthaginians. The garrison at Rhegion, which raided Bruttian territory, was composed partly of Bruttian soldiers. Livy (27.12.5) is clear that these were Bruttian 'deserters' (*perfugae*), presumably men who either gave up on Hannibal's cause or simply saw a chance to profit by working for the Romans and Rhegians. Even if we allow that the Bruttians adhered particularly strongly to Hannibal, relative to other Italian groups that defected during the Second Punic War, they still appear to have been willing to switch sides if presented with adequate incentive or coercion. In this light, the Roman decision not to allocate significant military resources to Bruttium earlier in the war must be seen as a critical factor in their enduring support for Hannibal. This point is reinforced when we look again at the Bruttian towns that surrendered in 213. Livy (25.1.3–4) claims that more would have submitted if the *praefectus socium*, T. Pomponius Veientanus, who had been ravaging Bruttian territory, had not been captured after foolishly stumbling into a battle with Hanno. In other words, direct Roman military pressure *did* succeed in undermining the loyalty of Hannibal's allies in Bruttium, and had the Romans been able

---

[152] See Chapter 4, pp. 171–3.   [153] See above, pp. 237–9.

[154] See Chapter 4, pp. 152–4. This suggestion should not be pushed too far, however, since it is far from certain that the Bruttians were significantly more martial than other Italic peoples. Livy (29.6.2–3) claims that the Bruttians acted as brigands (*latrociniis*) by their nature (*ingenio*); this is clearly ethnic stereotyping in a historiographic tradition hostile to upland folk as unsettled, violent and barbarian.

[155] Liv. 25.1.1–2, 25.3.9.

[156] Livy (28.11.12–13) reports that in 206 the consul Q. Caecilius Mettellus ravaged the territory of Consentia and took a great deal of booty. Livy later reports that Consentia voluntarily submitted to the Romans in 204 (29.37.1–2) and in 203 (30.19.10). Livy has clearly recorded a doublet. But even if we accept that Consentia surrendered only once to Rome, in 204 or 203, it still means that it defected after Cannae, submitted to Rome in 213, switched sides again at some point and then submitted a second time.

to press the Bruttians earlier in the war, his hold on the region would probably have been broken sooner.

Even though the Roman war effort in the toe of the peninsula was limited,
at least until the tide had turned badly against Hannibal, the Carthaginian
cause did not go unchallenged. Hannibal had successfully won over nearly
the entire region by 215, but he was never able to pry Rhegion away from the
Romans. Instead, this strategic city remained unwavering in its alliance and
provided Rome with a valuable beachhead for the reconquest of Bruttium.
The city contributed to (albeit minor) Roman military operations in the
middle years of the war, chiefly as a base of operation and as a *socius navalis*. In the later stages of the war Rhegion would prove instrumental in the
reconquest of Locri, Hannibal's most valuable ally in the region.

Rhegion contributed to Roman naval operations along the coast of
Bruttium and even as far as the coast of the Gulf of Taranto. It was the
finest natural port between Naples and Taras, possessing a far superior
harbour than neighbouring Locri, the best port under Hannibal's control.[157] Although it was not a decisive factor, Hannibal was frustrated by
his own incapacity to obtain seaports, hampering his ability to receive
reinforcements.[158] In addition, Rhegion was strategically situated, controlling the Straits of Messina and the easiest access between Italy and
Sicily. Rhegion's fortunate geography probably helped the Romans to
interfere with Hannibal's use of Locri's port, since it could potentially
control the shipping lanes from Carthage to southern Italy via Sicily.[159]
In 210 the Romans launched a small fleet from Rhegion to carry supplies
from Sicily to the Roman garrison besieged in the Tarentine citadel.[160]
The fleet was under a Roman commander (a certain Decimus Quinctius)
but composed of ships supplied by the allies, including the Rhegians. This
calls attention to another of Rome's long-term strategic advantages: the
so-called *socii navales* absorbed most of the manpower and financial burden of outfitting Rome's navy.[161] In 208 the Romans mounted a combined

---

[157] Thiel 1954: 61–2.

[158] It is possible that Hannibal wanted a seaport in south-east Italy so that he could link up more
easily with Philip V. See Chapter 5, pp. 211–12.

[159] For example, in 210 the Romans stationed a small fleet of twenty vessels in Rhegion, in order to
protect supply ships conveying supplies from Sicily to the citadel of Taras. This clearly indicates
how Rhegion dominated the shipping lanes from Sicily and along the coast of southern Italy. See
Liv. 26.39.1–3.

[160] Liv. 26.39.1–19. The venture proved disastrous when a Tarentine fleet routed and sank the Roman
ships; most of the sailors were captured in the vicinity of Thurii.

[161] For Rhegion as a *socius navalis*, see Afzelius 1944: 89; Toynbee 1965: 1.491 n. 8. The Rhegians were
probably obliged to supply at most about four ships and the necessary rowers and sailors. Of
the twenty ships under Decimus Quinctius' command, five were assigned to him by Marcellus

naval and land assault on Locri, using a fleet from Sicily that would have crossed the Straits of Messina, probably putting in at Rhegion along the way.[162]

The Romans also launched a series of raids into Bruttium from Rhegion. Some aimed at punishing or seizing rebellious Bruttian communities, while others were diversionary actions that formed part of larger, coordinated operations. In 210 the consul M. Valerius Laevinus led a band of 4,000 Greek mercenaries from Sicily to Rhegion, to be used for raiding and plundering Bruttium. According to Livy, the Rhegians themselves had been seeking additional soldiers for such a purpose.[163] Livy does not provide explicit details about their devastation campaigns, but such operations seem to have been conducted successfully. We hear later that the mercenary ranks swelled to around 8,000 by 209 with the addition of Bruttian deserters;[164] presumably, they saw an opportunity to join when the Greek mercenaries raided Bruttium.[165] According to Appian (*Hann.* 44), a Bruttian town called Tisia betrayed its Carthaginian garrison and handed itself over to the Romans.[166] If this episode is historical, the timing of the surrender suggests that it was linked to the campaign launched

---

and he added another three from the allies. He then added an additional twelve ships from Paestum, Velia and Rhegion – probably four ships each (see Liv. 26.39.2–6). This contribution may represent a maximum. In 191 the Rhegians supplied an unspecified number of ships for the war against Antiochus (Liv. 35.16.3, 36.42.1–3), but in 171 they supplied only a single trireme for the war against Perseus (Liv. 42.48.7).

[162] Liv. 27.26.3–6.

[163] Liv. 26.40.16–18; Livy claims that the mercenaries were debtors, criminals and exiles from a number of Sicilian cities, who were living as bandits, operating around Agathyrna.

[164] Liv. 27.12.4–6.

[165] Livy says that the Bruttians came 'from the same place' (*indidem*), which would mean, in the grammar of the passage, that they fled from Sicily, whence the other mercenaries came. It is possible that these were Bruttian mercenaries fighting for Sicilian communities or once serving in Carthaginian armies, or perhaps they were simply brigands who crossed over to Sicily. In the broader context, however, it makes more sense to assume that the Bruttians had simply deserted from nearby locales in the toe of the peninsula. See also below, n. 171.

[166] The victory was short-lived, however, as Hannibal recaptured Tisia the following year. Appian's account is fascinating, providing that it contains some elements of historical fact. Tisia appears to have been geographically close to Rhegion, since the Roman garrison moved there upon Hannibal's approach. The plot to betray the first Carthaginian garrison involved introducing 'Roman' soldiers into the city who were operating in the vicinity. Such forces were probably the mercenaries from Rhegion. If so, then this campaign was probably launched from Rhegion. The operation encouraged Bruttians to abandon Hannibal, either individually or as a community, and it indicates Rhegion's potential as base for the reconquest of south-western Italy. Appian states that the Tisians had grown weary of their treatment at the hands of the Carthaginian garrison. Again, if true, this highlights the necessary risks that Hannibal took by leaving garrisons in allied cities. It would be dangerous to place too much emphasis on this episode, given that it appears only in Appian's account. At the same time, it is an intriguing case that is consistent with many of the themes that have been discussed above.

from Rhegion.[167] In 209 the same band of mercenaries in the service of Rhegion, their numbers now enlarged, enthusiastically ravaged Bruttian territory before embarking on a siege of Caulonia.[168] As we have seen, this attack was part of a coordinated series of Roman military ventures, not a random raid against a target of opportunity by a mercenary rabble, for Q. Fabius Maximus had arranged for the siege of Caulonia and other operations in Apulia in order to draw Hannibal away from Taras. The plan was costly, as Hannibal marched rapidly to Caulonia and captured all of the attackers, but in so doing, he left Taras vulnerable, and it quickly fell to Fabius Maximus.[169] All in all, Rhegion's loyalty was an important element in Rome's first, albeit limited, military operations in Bruttium.

In the long term, Rhegion would play a significant part in Rome's reconquest of the biggest prize in Bruttium: Locri. Initial attempts to reconquer Locri did not meet with much success, however, and the Locrians remained staunchly allied with Hannibal until very late in the war. In 208, for example, T. Quinctius Crispinus mounted a major yet failed campaign to capture Locri through a combined land and sea assault. He led his consular army of two legions from Lucania in the direction of the city. In the meantime he ordered that a large number of various siege weapons be brought from Sicily, and he arranged for ships to attack the city from the port.[170] As mentioned above, the naval expedition probably took advantage of Rhegion's harbour facilities, and we may speculate that the Rhegians also supplied some ships.[171] Crispinus broke off his land attack when he heard that Hannibal had drawn his army near, in the vicinity of the Lacinian promontory.[172] Crispinus' legate, L. Cincius Alimentus, pressed the siege. The Carthaginian garrison commander, Mago, feared that the city was lost, until he received word that Hannibal was making a forced march back to Locri and had sent ahead a contingent of Numidian cavalry. A surprise sally by the garrison, coordinated with the arrival of the

---

[167] Appian places the Tisia episode between the recapture of Capua and Salapia, or somewhere in 211 or 210, if his narrative is chronologically sound: De Sanctis 1956–69: III.2.444 n. 26; Kukofka 1990: 82 (arguing that Hannibal recaptured the city when he attacked Rhegion in 211, after his march on Rome). It makes more sense, in my opinion, to locate the Tisia campaign in 210 or even 209, and thus to assume that Appian's narrative is not entirely accurate chronologically. In any case, it is very probable that the Roman operation to take Tisia was launched from Rhegion.

[168] Liv. 27.12.4–6; App. *Hann.* 49. Appian mistakenly claims that the Romans captured Caulonia.

[169] Liv. 27.12.1–6, 27.15.8, 27.16.10–11; see above, pp. 264–6.

[170] Liv. 27.25.11.

[171] In the same passage, however, Livy states that the ships came 'from the same place' (*indidem*), i.e. Sicily.

[172] Liv. 27.25.12.

Numidians, threw the Romans into a panic, and they fled to their ships and withdrew.[173]

One may wonder why the Locrians remained so loyal to Hannibal for so long. The specific, local political conditions must be considered. Let us return to the sequence of events in 215, when the Locrians decided to throw in their lot with Hannibal. This tough decision was reached after a series of internal political debates and negotiations with the Carthaginians and Bruttians, and there appears to have been a group of aristocrats solidly opposed to rebellion.[174] Livy (29.6.5–6) provides an additional detail: some aristocrats from the 'pro-Roman' party were driven out by opposing aristocrats and took up residence in Rhegion. Thus, those aristocrats who were most likely to oppose defection, and around whom anti-Carthaginian sentiment might later have crystallised during the war, had been eliminated from the Locrian decision-making elite from 215 until the city fell in 205. The remaining aristocrats would have been more 'pro-Hannibalic' from the start and probably expected to have the most to lose by surrendering. They were likely to suffer the most severe punishment should Roman rule be re-established. As was discussed with regard to Thurii,[175] the unattractiveness of surrender may have been reinforced by the Romans' harsh treatment of captured Italiote cities. In addition, the Locrian population was increased by Crotoniate citizens who fled their city in 214 when it was handed over to the Bruttians. With no city to go back to (at least in their minds), these refugees as well may have determined that it was better to hold out as long a possible and hope for the best.

The military landscape was also an important factor in shaping the Locrians' resolve. As discussed above, the Romans put less direct military pressure on the communities of Bruttium and western Magna Graecia, so there was less impetus for cities that had defected to submit to Rome. When the Romans did bring force to bear against the Locrians, Hannibal responded immediately to defend them. Consider again the amphibious campaign of 208: that Hannibal happened to be in the neighbourhood of Lacinium compelled the Roman consular army to retreat, and later in the same campaign season Hannibal hastened to relieve the siege. Indeed, it is telling that had Hannibal not marched back into Bruttium, the Roman siege would have been successful – or at least that is what Mago supposedly

---

[173] Liv. 27.26.3–5, 27.28.13–17. For further discussion of the chronology, see above, n. 149. Lazenby 1978: 179–80 speculates that this is when Cincius Alimentus was captured by Hannibal. Livy is no doubt drawing on Cincius' account for the details of this campaign.

[174] For a complete discussion of Locrian factional politics and the decision to side with Hannibal, see Chapter 4, pp. 162–6.

[175] See Chapter 5, pp. 230–1 and above, pp. 268–9.

thought, according to Livy (27.28.14–16). Similarly, Hannibal responded to the attack on nearby Caulonia. Even though this may have cost him Taras, it may also have reinforced his local reputation among the Greek cities of Bruttium as a guarantor of freedom. Finally, after 207, Hannibal concentrated his army in Bruttium, which made it easier for him to forestall defections from among the few cities he still controlled. Overall, Hannibal seems to have done a better job of defending and controlling his allies in south-western Italy, most importantly the city of Locri.

Events unfolded in 205 that greatly altered the local political and military landscape, setting the stage for Rome's reconquest of this important, long-time Hannibalic stronghold. Rhegion's loyalty was instrumental to Roman success. The Romans began the year skirmishing and plundering in Bruttium, apparently in the vicinity of Locri, where they captured a number of Locrian citizens.[176] These captives were taken to Rhegion and entered into negotiations with the pro-Roman Locrian aristocrats who had been exiled a decade before. The exiles recognised an opportunity to take back control of their city, so they promised to ransom the captives in exchange for promises to help to betray the city.[177] Livy (29.6.7) emphasises that the aristocratic exiles were motivated by personal enmity towards their political rivals (*cupiditate inimicos ulciscendi arderent*), underscoring once again how Italian affairs during the Second Punic War were crosscut by local political rivalry and factionalism. The Locrian exiles then went to P. Cornelius Scipio and personally convinced him of the plan's potential for success. Scipio in turn ordered his legate Q. Pleminius to take 3,000 troops from Rhegion and assist with the effort to capture Locri.[178]

The Roman soldiers were able to enter the city with the aid of the former captives who had been ransomed, but they met stiff resistance from the Carthaginian garrison. The Romans eventually seized the town's main citadel (the Carthaginians held the smaller citadel) and the two sides engaged in street skirmishes.[179] The Carthaginians gathered reinforcements 'from nearby places' (*ex propinquis locis*), presumably from the

---

[176] Liv. 29.6.2–3. [177] Liv. 29.6.4–8.

[178] Liv. 29.6.8–9. It is worth noting the highly personal nature of these negotiations. Not only did the Locrian exiles make a personal appeal to Scipio, but some exiles were already with him in Sicily. It is possible that Scipio was holding them as hostages, but this does not seem to fit the context. Rather, some of the exiles appear to have been personally close to Scipio. This makes sense if we consider that the exiles would have been mostly pro-Roman aristocrats. Their families probably had some sort of formal or informal ties to Roman aristocratic families, including it seems the Cornelii Scipiones. We will come back to this theme, and to this episode, in Chapter 7.

[179] Liv. 29.6.10–17; see also App. *Hann.* 56, with a much telescoped version.

Locrian countryside or even nearby Bruttian communities.[180] At this point, however, the Locrian citizenry threw their support behind the Romans. According to Livy (29.6.17), the relatively small Roman force could not have held on to the citadel had not the Locrian citizenry decided to support them instead of the Carthaginians. In the same passage Livy says that the Locrians chose the Romans' side because they resented the behaviour of the Carthaginian garrison.[181] This is plausible, in light of the arguments in this chapter. Still, it is remarkable how long it took for Locrian disaffection to emerge. Indeed, this serves as a reminder of the degree of Locrian support for Hannibal and bitterness towards Rome that were discussed earlier in this chapter. The Locrian volte-face in 205 is clearly the product of immediate circumstances: the capture of Locrian citizens, the betrayal of the city's defence and the entry of Roman soldiers within the walls rapidly eroded support for Hannibal and the will to continue resisting. Meanwhile, whatever underlying resentment against Hannibal or the Carthaginian garrison there was now rose to the surface.

In the meantime Hannibal began to march his army in relief of the siege, once again responding promptly to a threat to Locri.[182] He sent an advanced force to attack the landward side of the city, but the Roman garrison was able to hold out until Scipio arrived with a fleet carrying reinforcements, which landed in the city's harbour. The fleet had crossed over from Messina, so once again, Rome's control of Rhegion facilitated the movement of men and materiel.[183] Once Scipio reinforced the city, he made a surprise sortie, caught Hannibal off guard and drove him from the walls. A discouraged Hannibal moved his camp from the city and sent word to the Carthaginian garrison to abandon the smaller citadel.[184] Lazenby (1978: 199) suggests that Hannibal's only concern was to retrieve his garrison, not to retake Locri, making this a successful operation. Whatever the interpretation, the Romans had dislodged the Carthaginians from Locri and finally scored a major victory in Bruttium and western Magna Graecia.

From the fall of Locri in 205 until his departure from Italy in 203, Hannibal was restricted to a tiny corner of southern Italy, encompassing Thurii, Petelia and Croton and some inland Bruttian territory. The

---

[180] Liv. 29.6.17.
[181] *nec sustinuissent Romani nisi Locrensium multitudo, exacerbata superbia atque avaritia Poenorum, ad Romanos inclinasset* ('Nor would the Romans have held out if the mass of the Locrians had not been favourably disposed to the Romans, since they were exasperated by the arrogance and greed of the Carthaginians').
[182] Liv. 29.6.17–17.1.   [183] Liv. 29.7.1–7.
[184] Liv. 29.7.8–10.

sources do not record when Caulonia fell, though we can speculate that it was sometime in 205, given its proximity to Locri.[185] Thurii was abandoned in 204. Appian (*Hann.* 57) records that Hannibal selected 3,500 citizens and country folk who were particularly loyal and resettled them in Croton. Appian also reports that Hannibal began to suspect his Bruttian allies after 207, even accusing them of various plots.[186] Whatever the value of Appian's claims, most of the remaining Bruttian towns submitted to Rome in 204 and 203.[187] When the messengers arrived from Carthage to give Hannibal his recall orders, only Croton and Petelia and a handful of small Bruttian communities remained loyal. He distributed garrisons among these holdouts, embarked the remains of his army and ruefully prepared to set sail for Africa.[188]

The Roman reconquest of Bruttium and western Magna Graecia marked the final stages of the Second Punic War in Italy. The general patterns discussed at the beginning of the chapter were, unsurprisingly, replicated as Rome slowly reabsorbed the Greek and Bruttian cities that had defected in the early stages of the war. Yet the unique features of the war in this region highlight certain particular themes. First, Rome's relatively light military footprint in the region, coupled with the strong Carthaginian presence, allowed for more enduring pro-Carthaginian regimes. Indeed, Hannibal increasingly concentrated his forces in Bruttium and responded quickly to the first few serious Roman threats. This reinforces one of the main thrusts of this chapter, that the disparity in manpower was fundamental to Rome's long-term strategic success. Where the Romans could apply constant military pressure, Hannibal had a difficult time protecting and maintaining the loyalty of his allies. This section also showed how local political conditions and contexts shaped the course of the war. For example, Locri's specific political landscape, which emerged from unique circumstances in the early stages of the war, allowed Hannibal to enjoy firmer aristocratic support. Finally, even in this region with little military presence and widespread defections, the Romans still maintained the loyalty of Rhegion; this strategic city provided the Romans with logistical and military support, and gave Rome an important toehold in the eventual reconquest of the region. Once again, Hannibal's incomplete strategic

---

[185] See Muggia 1999a.
[186] App. *Hann.* 54, 57.
[187] Liv. 29.38.1, 30.19.10: Consentia, Aufugum, Bergae, Baesidiae, Ocriculum, Lymphaeum, Argentanum, Clampetia, Pandosia and other unimportant cities (*ignobiles aliae civitates* and *multique alii ignobiles populi*).
[188] Liv. 30.19.5–9; App. *Hann.* 59–61.

success in the first few years of the war laid the groundwork for his long-term strategic failure.

CONCLUSION

This chapter has considered how local and contingent variables intersected with long-term military and strategic conditions in shaping the course of the Second Punic War in Italy after the main battle lines were drawn in the wake of Cannae when a significant number of allied revolts erupted. The Romans enjoyed a massive advantage in terms of manpower, which set the overall tone of the war. Thus, even when a large number of Italian states defected, which surely must have seemed encouraging to Hannibal in 216 and 215, it did not counteract Rome's primary strategic advantage. Instead, it left him responsible for a number of allies that he could not in the end defend. In fact, Hannibal's strategic strengths – his tactical flexibility and creativity as a field general, for example – were greatly compromised when he found himself instead fighting a largely defensive war, reacting to Roman military initiatives and responding to allied concerns. Moreover, each ally had unique and sometimes conflicting interests, and each region presented Hannibal with a different set of strategic and diplomatic challenges. As a result, the overall decade-long collapse of his Italian project played out somewhat differently from region to region and city to city, depending on local variables. Finally, we observed that Hannibal's various strategic difficulties were exacerbated by the 'checkerboard' of loyal and rebel states that emerged after Cannae. Yet this pattern was itself largely determined by local political, military and economic circumstances, inter-state ties and rivalries, and competing concerns, which were discussed in Chapters 2 to 5. The very same local conditions that limited the effectiveness of the Hannibalic strategy early in the war continued, therefore, to bedevil him for the remaining years of the conflict.

CHAPTER 7

Conclusions

The previous five chapters have brought the Second Punic War into focus from the perspective of the Italian states and suggest that Hannibal's lack of success as a diplomat was an important component of his overall defeat in the Italian theatre of the war. Because Rome enjoyed a significant manpower advantage, Hannibal needed to elicit massive allied revolts in a short period of time. Rome's Italian allies were willing to come over to Hannibal's side, but only on their own terms, and Hannibal struggled to get all the communities in any given region to revolt at the same time. Moreover, it was difficult for Hannibal to maintain the loyalty of the Italian communities that did revolt. The arguments presented in this book reveal that local conditions and motivations significantly influenced the decisions of various Italian states to remain loyal to Rome, thus shaping the course and ultimately the outcome of the Second Punic War. In short, Hannibal's failure resulted from military disadvantage that he could not overcome through diplomatic means because of local, circumstantial factors.

Why was Hannibal unable to unify the Italians against Rome, or even to keep his new Italian allies unified during the eventual war of attrition? Goldsworthy has stated that the communities that did join Hannibal lacked a sense of common identity or purpose.[1] This was indeed the case, though it is perhaps more accurate to say that there were too many mutually exclusive identities and agendas. Hannibal's invasion of Italy and his initial military success over the Roman army temporarily suspended the cohesive structures of Roman rule and brought to the fore local tensions that had been suppressed beneath the surface of Roman hegemony. In some cases, these local tensions long predated Roman conquest. The Italian communities were little motivated by global ideological impulses, such as 'loyalty to Rome', or by the cause of the Carthaginians. Instead, local conditions and factors had

[1] Goldsworthy 2000: 223.

280

greater impact in shaping decision-making in individual communities, and it was difficult for Hannibal to appear attractive in all local contexts. Local interstate rivalries introduced further difficulties, as some Italian cities were more concerned with pressure from a local expansionist hegemonic power than with the imposition of Roman rule. When Hannibal gained a powerful city as his ally, such as Capua, Arpi, Locri or Taras, he pushed that ally's rival cities more firmly into the Roman camp. Even playing on political factionalism proved tricky. If Hannibal backed the rule of one group of a city's aristocrats in return for their loyalty, there was likely to be a rival faction of aristocrats who would be prone to seek the restoration of Roman rule in return for political backing. Moreover, some local aristocrats tied their political power to Hannibal's success, and when Hannibal's fortunes declined their resolve was easily broken. Overall, the variety of local contexts hindered Hannibal's efforts to accommodate the desires of every Italian community, despite the flexibility of his diplomacy. In the short term, therefore, local conditions limited the effectiveness of Hannibal's Italian strategy of eliciting allied revolts, and as the war dragged on, long-term Roman advantages came increasingly into play. Thus, Hannibal could not elicit the defection of enough of Rome's allies sufficiently quickly to overcome Rome's manpower advantage and achieve his strategic objective.

ENDURING INTERSTATE RIVALRY AND REALIST THEORY

The existence and impact of local interstate rivalries has featured prominently in my analysis of the failure of Hannibal's Italian strategy. As we have seen, there was deeply rooted mistrust and hostility between a number of neighbouring communities in Italy, with grudges sometimes long predating Roman conquest. In some cases cities had fought against each other in a series of conflicts, regardless of Rome's involvement or noninvolvement. These rivalries were suppressed when Rome conquered the peninsula and took away the power of individual states to wage war on each other, but they rose to the surface again when Hannibal gave Italian communities the chance to make independent foreign policy. Indeed, such rivalries appear to have shaped foreign policy decisions, as antipathy towards a local rival strongly influenced an ally's choice to remain loyal to Rome or defect to Hannibal.

Political scientists have begun to discuss the effects of so-called 'enduring rivalries' on international relations and state behaviour.[2] Goertz

---

[2] See, for example, Goertz and Diehl 1992, 1993, 1995; Bennett 1996; Gartzke and Simon 1999; Stinnett and Diehl 2001; Thies 2001; Thompson 2001.

and Diehl (1993: 148) observe that '[i]t is clear that some dyads become involved repeatedly in conflict'. It is possible, indeed probable, that conflicts between such feuding states are interconnected. As Thompson (2001: 557–8) puts it:

> Moreover, their conflicts are not independent across time – another frequent and major assumption in conflict studies. They are part of an historical process in which a pair of states create and sustain a relationship of atypical hostility for some period of time. What they do to each other in the present is conditioned by what they have done to each other in the past. What they do in the present is also conditioned by calculations about future ramifications of current choices. Rivalries thus represent a distinctive class of conflict in the sense that rivals deal with each other in a psychologically charged context of path-dependent hostility in ways that are not necessarily observed in conflicts that occur in more neutral contexts.

This observation may strike a historian as intuitive if not obvious: it makes sense that states with a history of hostilities, mutual grievances, perceived injustices, slights and brutality would be more likely to go to war with each other should a new conflict arise. In fact, past conflicts would have fuelled further controversies and conflicts. Likewise, it seems common sense that a given state's political elite would take rivalry into account when forming policy, as they might, for example, tend to mistrust an enduring rival's ally or assume that hostile intent lurks behind a rival's every action. Thus, a state might take a rival's diplomatic offer less seriously, or opt to attack a rival pre-emptively for fear that the rival is already plotting a similar course of action, or seek out additional alliances from third parties in anticipation of an assumed war with the rival, and so on.

The difficulty lies in identifying enduring rivalries: when are repeated conflicts between two states related (i.e. an enduring rivalry), and when are they simply independent events? Political scientists have tended to adopt two strategies for determining if a dyad of two competing states should be classified as an enduring rivalry. First, they try to establish a threshold frequency of conflicts, a minimum number of confrontations within a given timeframe, usually wars but sometimes also diplomatic challenges, beyond which the two competing states are determined to be rivals. The danger of this approach is that it lends itself to circular argument: the frequency of conflicts proves the existence of an enduring rivalry, which in turn explains the frequency of conflicts. Moreover, since this approach focuses mostly on militarised conflicts, it does not allow for the possibility that two states in a dyad could perceive each other as rivals over relatively long 'dormant' periods, when no military or diplomatic challenges are offered. Some argue that simply tallying the number of 'conflicts' between two states does little to prove that such conflicts are necessarily interconnected. In other words, that two states frequently go to war does not automatically indicate that they choose to fight *because* they are rivals, Rather, it may be the case that the underlying conditions that led to the initial conflict were never resolved, resulting in repeated clashes over the same issues. According to this line of thinking, an interstate rivalry can only be firmly identified when the motives of the relevant state actors are understood. Thus, the second strategy in identifying interstate rivalry is to historicise interstate behaviour, '[relying] on an intensive interpretation of historical evidence and a conceptualization of rivalry that emphasizes perceptions rather than militarized conflict'.[3] This approach tends, however, to be highly subjective, unless one is fortunate enough to have access to comprehensive information about the perceptions of the decision-makers.

Neither approach is fully applicable to the present discussion of interstate rivalries in Roman and pre-Roman Italy. As we have seen throughout this book, ancient literary sources are generally focused on Rome, allowing us only brief glimpses of Italian interstate affairs that did not directly involve the Romans. We may occasionally hear about tensions or hostilities between communities, but typically only when the Romans are drawn into the struggle, and even then the information is not infrequently coloured by Roman perceptions. For the years when Roman foreign policy was less active in a given geographic region of the peninsula, the sources can be frustratingly silent about what sorts of local diplomatic and military activities were being carried out there. Thus we are told a good deal about Apulia, for example, in the 320s and 310s, when the area became a major front in the ongoing wars between the Romans and the Samnites, but for the previous and subsequent decades, when Roman armies were not operating in the region, the sources say very little. Moreover, as discussed in the first chapter, the ancient sources for the fourth and third centuries are rather patchy in their coverage and quality. Overall, we must assume that many more conflicts between local states, whether actual wars or merely diplomatic challenges, took place than have been recorded in the extant sources. Without these data it is impossible to apply any sort of numerical test or to set a minimum threshold of conflict frequency to determine if two states were rivals. Put simply, the lack of empirical data would render almost any ancient enduring rivalry invisible under such a test. In addition, even when we do hear about local interstate relations (i.e. involving

---

[3] Thompson 2001: 583.

other states besides Rome) we are rarely afforded enough details about local politics and policy formation to carry out an intensive investigation of motives and perceptions. In the end, we are left to draw plausible inferences from the available evidence, however reticent it may be.

Yet despite these limitations, we can indeed conclude that enduring rivalries existed in ancient Italy. With respect to the analysis in Chapters 2 to 5, a strong case can be made that a number of pairs of states were dyads locked in respective enduring rivalries: for example, Naples and Capua, Taras and Thurii, Locri and Rhegion. This deduction derives from a number of interrelated observations: the pairs tended to fight each other repeatedly or at least take opposing sides in larger conflicts; occasional references in the primary sources to grudges or feelings of mutual hostility; and the length of time over which such animosities and conflicts manifest themselves.[4]

The identification of such ancient examples of enduring rivalries is not, however, an end in itself. Rather, recognising that deep-rooted interstate structures such as enduring rivalries at least sometimes conditioned the behaviour and policies of ancient communities has the potential to throw new light on important questions. Our regional case studies have demonstrated, for example, that such interstate rivalries played an important role in shaping the course and outcome of the Second Punic War in Italy, which adds another layer to our understanding of Rome's victory in this pivotal struggle. Long-standing mutual animosities resurfaced when Hannibal temporarily freed Italian cities from the yoke of Roman hegemony. The

---

[4] Comparative evidence from the early Imperial period can also be introduced, which further attests to the existence, endurance and occasional ferocity of such interstate rivalries. For example, Tacitus (*Hist.* 1.65) reports that the people of Lugdunum and Vienna Allobrogrium, in Gaul, fought against each other during the civil discord of AD 68–9. Lugdunum had sided with Nero and Vienna with Galba; the recent dynastic struggle triggered a pre-existing 'old feud' (**veterem ... discordiam** *proximum bellum accenderat*). In Tacitus' estimation, the atrocities that each side committed against the other made it clear that the recent war was not the source of their enmity. Rather, he calls attention to the 'rivalry, jealousy and mutual hatred' (*aemulatio et invidia et ... conexum odium*) between the two communities. The rivalry between Lugdunum and Vienna traced back at least to the 40s BC (Cass. Dio. 46.50.4–5); it was apparently crosscut by ethnic tension and reinforced by recent grievances. Tacitus (*Hist.* 3.57) mentions another intriguing example that is more directly relevant to the present discussion: in AD 69 Puteoli supported Vespasian, and Capua sided with Vitellius. In Tacitus' words, the citizens of these towns 'intermingled municipal rivalry with civil war' (*municipalem aemulationem bellis civilibus miscebant*). We are not told the origins of this rivalry. It is perhaps too much of a stretch to connect the events of AD 69 with those of the third century BC, when Puteoli emerged as an important port and the two cities chose opposing sides in the war with Hannibal (see Chapter 3, pp. 112 n. 55, 127, 132–3). Still, this case is explicit evidence for latent interstate rivalry lurking beneath the surface of the *Pax Romana*, even in Italy, long after the Social War and the political unification of the peninsula. Both examples can be adduced as further proof of the potential for local communities to harbour deep grudges for long periods, which could rise to the surface when the veneer of unity, imposed by Rome, was stripped away.

re-emergence of suppressed rivalry was not an automatism leading inevitably to diverging policy decisions. Indeed, as we saw in Chapter 5 with the revolt of Thurii and Taras, specific events and conditions could compel rivals to act in common cause. Hannibal could not, however, overcome all such local interstate tensions. Thus enduring rivalries undercut his chances to unite a critical mass of Italian communities against Rome and contributed to the failure of his Italian strategy.

Such mutual animosities, interstate grudges and enduring rivalries surely shaped other events and developments in Roman history, which might force modern historians to reconsider present interpretations. For example, the repeated campaigns against the Samnites in the late fourth and early third centuries are typically taken as examples of Rome's pathological aggression and extreme bellicosity, the reasons for which are often located in peculiar Roman political or social structures.[5] It may be the case, however, that the frequent, almost continual warfare between the Romans and various Samnite communities was bound up in some sort of enduring rivalry, where prior wars between the two made subsequent wars more likely. If so, then our understanding of the nature of Roman expansion in Italy might have to be seriously re-evaluated. This concluding chapter is not the place to explore thoroughly this particular suggestion. Rather, I use it to illustrate the avenues of inquiry on which the present analysis and conclusions might touch, demonstrating as well how modern international-relations theories and models can be profitably applied to the ancient world.

The suggestion that enduring rivalries significantly impacted on interstate relations in ancient Italy appears on one level, however, to undermine one of the fundamental assumptions of my analysis: that ancient Italy was essentially an anarchic international system conforming more or less to Realist patterns of interstate behaviour. Realists argue that states are rational actors seeking to maximise their resources, power and security in a highly competitive international environment. Realist theory allows little room for other considerations to shape foreign policy. It denies, for example, that democracies are less likely to go to war with each other than with states governed by different types of political regimes. Thus, the past behaviour between states should not influence subsequent foreign policy decisions made in the context of evolving international conditions, different threats and the loss or acquisition of new resources. As Goertz and Diehl (1993: 150) put it: 'one of the central aspects of rationality is that the

---

[5] See Chapter 1, n. 34.

past is largely irrelevant in making decisions in the present', so 'the concept of enduring rivalries implicitly contests a fundamental aspect of most standard rational actor models'.

Yet it is possible to reconcile an assumption that states in ancient Italy functioned within a Realist framework with my conclusion that interstate rivalries played an important role in shaping interstate relations in Italy during the fourth and third centuries. The key lies in recalling the primitive nature of ancient diplomacy and policy-making.[6] As discussed in Chapter 1, interstate 'negotiations' (such as they were) often took the form of public grievances, demands for retribution and threats, which tended to exacerbate tensions rather than resolve them. Ancient states did not maintain permanent embassies or consulates in foreign lands. There were no professional diplomatic corps, though individuals, invariably aristocrats and often with personal connections to foreign states, may have been employed as ambassadors to those communities.[7] Even in such cases diplomatic missions were carried out by relative amateurs. Long-distance communications were very limited, and most states must have possessed woefully inadequate up-to-date intelligence. The ruling elite of one state generally had, therefore, little idea of what was going on in other states, even neighbouring communities.[8] In addition, the stakes of interstate relations could be very high, especially for small states, as the wholesale destruction of a defeated city or the enslavement of its citizenry was an all too possible outcome of war.[9] This surely led the decision-making elite to view interstate relations pessimistically and assume the most dire and threatening scenarios.

---

[6] For the primitive nature of ancient, especially Roman, diplomacy, see Eckstein 1987: xviii–xix; Eckstein 2006: 59–63, 121.

[7] For example, C. Julius Caesar selected a certain Marcus Mettius as his ambassador to Ariovistus because Mettius enjoyed guest-friendship (*hospitio utebatur*) with the German king (Caes. *B Gall.* 1.47). Personal connection to a foreign state or region was a criterion for diplomatic and military appointments in both classical Athens and Sparta: Mitchell 1997: 73–110.

[8] See for example Liv. 39.23.3–4: in 186 the Roman senate learned only by accident that the colonies of Buxentum and Sipontum had been abandoned when the consul Sp. Postumius Albinus returned to Rome after investigating the Bacchanalia and reported the fact. Thus, as late as the second century the Romans were apparently badly informed about the goings on in other cities within Italy.

[9] Before the advent of more advanced siege weapons and techniques in the late fourth and third centuries, the destruction or enslavement of whole cities were infrequent but not unheard of occurrences in Italy. The most famous is the Roman destruction of Veii, with the slaughter and enslavement of its entire population (*c.* 396): Liv. 5.21.12–5.22.8. The Romans also reportedly massacred the population of Tarquinia (353) and Luceria (314): Liv. 7.19.1–4, 9.26.1–5. Even if a city was not destroyed, warfare might have resulted in significant loss of citizens to death or enslavement. Livy's tenth book records the enslavement of nearly 70,000 persons by the Romans just between the years 297 and 293: see Oakley 1993: 22–6 for specific references and discussion suggesting that the scale of enslavement is plausible. Some reports of the capture of individual cities give

Given the atmosphere of fear, perceived threat and mistrust, as well as the general ignorance of each other's true aims and intentions, it is natural that ancient states would look to the past as a guide to formulating foreign policy. If a state perceived that it had been wronged by a rival before, it would be less likely to trust that rival's intentions in subsequent affairs.[10] This mistrust would have, at least at times, contributed to new conflicts and hostilities, which in turn only reinforced the image of the rival state as untrustworthy and dangerous. This is not to say that a state could never be convinced that its rival was no longer a threat, or that changes in the inter-national balance of power could not compel old enemies to form a new friendship out of common interest. Yet it is likely that some states became locked in a cycle of mistrust and conflict, which over time developed into an enduring rivalry. Similarly, states that helped each other in the past, albeit out of cynical self-interest, may sometimes have found their interests best served by maintaining their alliance and through ongoing mutual aid. Past acts of friendship were surely invoked as evidence of a state's reliabil-ity and good intentions, just as former hostilities and old grievances and insults would have been taken as a sign that a state could not be trusted. Since the stakes of war were so high, especially for weaker states, whom to trust was a vital question. Indeed, considering the lack of reliable informa-tion available on which to make foreign policy decisions, trust based on prior dealings must have been a fundamental consideration. In the ancient context, therefore, reliance on the past does not contradict the model of states as rational actors. Thus, the existence of enduring interstate rivalries in ancient Italy is perfectly compatible with the Realist approach that has informed my analysis throughout this book.

rather large numbers of both deaths and enslavements, such as Rusellae (approximately 2,000 killed and 2,000 captured), Milionia (3,200 killed and 4,700 captured), Perusia (4,500 killed and 1,700 captured and ransomed) and Cominum (4,800 killed and 11,400 captured): Liv. 10.31.3, 10.34.3, 10.37.3, 10.43.8. If these high figures are broadly accurate in scale, then casualties and enslavements probably included non-combatants. Moreover, the Romans were not the only peo-ple to treat defeated cities harshly. Dionysius I of Syracuse, for example, conquered Caulonia and exiled the population, handing over the territory to the Locrians (Diod. Sic. 14.106.3). For earlier examples from southern Italy, Croton and allies destroyed both Sybaris and Siris in the sixth century: Beloch 1894; Rainey 1969; Rutter 1970; Lomas 1993: 24, 30. Thucydides lists more than thirty city-states that were reportedly destroyed in the fifth century (Champion and Eckstein 2004: 9 n. 28). Presumably other notorious cases from the Greek world, such as Athens' destruc-tion of Melos or Sparta's destruction of Plataea, were known in some parts of Italy.

[10] Although the situation is not exactly parallel, consider Caesar's justification for going to war with the Helvetians (*B Gall.* 1.7). Caesar decided to refuse the Helvetians' request for passage, all but guaranteeing a war, because the same tribe supposedly had defeated a Roman army and its general nearly a half-century earlier, and because, he argued, men with such an unfriendly spirit could not refrain from doing harm and injury. In effect, prior conflict could be used to discredit present intentions, leading to additional conflict.

COULD HANNIBAL HAVE WON? THREE
HYPOTHETICAL SCENARIOS

The foregoing discussion reinforces the enormity of Hannibal's task in trying to detach a critical mass of Rome's Italian allies and, ideally, convince
them to unite in common cause against the Romans. Yet Hannibal did
win over a significant number of Italian communities, despite their often
divergent interests, mutual mistrust and local rivalries. He appears to have
come tantalisingly close to achieving his strategic objectives, with ultimate success dangling just out of reach. His close brush with victory invites
counterfactual speculation on what he should, or could, have done better
in prosecuting the war during its pivotal phase. In this section we will consider some alternative paths that Hannibal might have taken, which *might*
have brought him closer to elusive victory in Italy. In so doing, the following discussion will highlight once again the strategic challenges that local
conditions would have posed regardless of specific decisions that Hannibal
made or might have made during the contested phase of the war.

The tradition of second-guessing Hannibal traces back at least as far as
Livy's implicit assessment (22.51.1–4) that the Carthaginian general would
have won the war had he marched on Rome immediately after Cannae,
and it may go back all the way to just after the Second Punic War.[11] As suggested in Chapter 1, had Hannibal in fact made an incursion into Latium,
this might well have compelled the Romans to commit themselves to
another pitched battle, thereby offering him another shot at the elusive
conclusive victory that would have brought Rome to its knees. Even if the
Romans simply refused to surrender, it is hard to imagine that yet another
major victory on the heels of Cannae, this time in central Italy and possibly in the heart of the *ager Romanus*, would have failed to bring about an
even greater number of allied defections. It may be unrealistic, however,
to fault Hannibal for not embarking on a forced march in the direction
of Rome immediately following what must have been an emotionally and
physically taxing campaign in Apulia. According to Polybius, Hannibal
was marching towards Rome in 217, but after the battle of Trasimene he
rejected approaching the city because he felt assured of success.[12] Since he
was confident that battlefield success would guarantee victory, it is not
surprising that he avoided a potentially risky strategy of advancing on the
city after an even greater triumph at Cannae. In any event, marching on

---

11 Indeed, Cato the Elder may have been the first author to make the case; see Chapter 1, n. 106.
12 Polyb. 3.82.9, 3.86.8.

Rome does not appear to have been an important aspect of Hannibal's Italian strategy of eliciting widespread allied rebellions.

But could he have done anything differently within the scope of this strategy that would have improved his chances of winning the war? It is possible that he missed opportunities to bring about allied defections on a larger scale. Hannibal's strategic success was restricted to southern Italy, and even then his accomplishment was limited by local conditions and contingent factors that were mostly out of his control. In addition, he failed to elicit serious rebellions from communities north of the Apulia–Campania line, including the Etruscans, Umbrians, central Samnites (Pentri) and peoples of the Abruzzo (such as the Frentani). There is no reason to expect that the peoples of northern or central Italy should have felt any more loyalty or affinity to Rome than did their southern counterparts, and his failure to win over allies in central and northern Italy (south of the Po) surely constituted a major blow to his Italian strategy.[13]

It is rather surprising that Hannibal did not fare better with the communities in Etruria and Umbria. In particular, Etruria features prominently in the early years of the Second Punic War, but we hear very little about the region between the battle of Trasimene and the emergence of significant unrest in later stages of the war. In 208 the senate was informed that a widespread Etruscan revolt was in the making, started by the people of Arretium. The threat was deemed serious enough that the senate sent the consul designate, M. Livius Salinator, to inspect the situation. Salinator spent his consulship (207) and subsequent proconsulship (206) investigating which Etruscan and Umbrian cities had planned to help Hasrubal, and more seriously which had actually given him assistance. Those suspected of disloyalty were later put on trial, and the guilty, including *multi nobiles Etrusci*, were executed or exiled and their property was confiscated. Hostages were also taken to prevent further plots.[14] The consul M. Cornelius Cethegus was still overseeing the matter in 204, which indicates the seriousness of the affair.[15] The disturbances in Etruria and Umbria may have arisen out of war-weariness, or from specific conditions or events occurring later in the conflict. For example, the Romans had made multiple requisitions of grain, undoubtedly at fixed prices, which

---

[13] At the start of the Second Punic War, Rome could call on approximately 360,000 Roman and Latin citizens and 410,000 men from allied cities to perform military service (see Chapter 1, pp. 37–9). The Etruscans, Umbrians, Sarsinates, Marsi, Marrucini, Frentani and Vestini represented approximately 100,000 available troops, or more than 20 per cent of the potential allied military manpower (see Baronowski 1993).

[14] For the Etruscan 'revolt', see: Liv. 27.21.6–8, 27.22.5, 27.22.12–13, 27.24.1–9, 28.10.4–5.

[15] Liv. 29.36.11–12.

presumably burdened the local communities.[16] Also, starting in 212 and continuing for the remainder of the war, the Romans stationed two legions in Etruria, which may possibly have further strained local resources and generated additional resentment. The disturbances of 208 and subsequent years were bound up with Hasdrubal's march into northern Italy, which surely sparked any underlying discontent.

This does not mean, however, that the Etruscan communities were immune to defection before the arrival of Hasdrubal. Indeed, the very fact that legions were stationed in Etruria as early as 212 may indicate that Rome doubted the loyalty of the Etruscans. As discussed in Chapter 1, the Romans were still consolidating their power in Etruria and Umbria as late as the middle of the third century, with the destruction of Volsinii (264) and Falerii (241), and the foundation of Spoletium (241). The southern and eastern borders of Etruria and Umbria were bounded by a string of Latin colonies and stretches of the *ager Romanus*, yet the north-eastern and north-central areas of the two regions remained relatively unchecked. On the one hand, the inhabitants of northern Etruria and Umbria may have been comparatively undisturbed by Roman hegemony and therefore less inclined to risk defection. On the other hand, the comparatively light Roman presence and absence of colonies possibly emboldened the Etruscans and Umbrians; the cities in northern Etruria certainly had ample opportunity to revolt in the early stages of the war.[17] The presence of Gallic troops in Hannibal's army was potentially off-putting to some Etruscans and Umbrians, since the fierceness of the recent Gallic threat in 225 supposedly drove them to rally in large numbers in support of the Romans at Telamon. Yet we should not push this too far, given the long history of the Etruscans' willingness to ally with Gallic peoples against the Romans.[18] Overall, it is surprising that Hannibal did not make any significant gains among the Etruscans or Umbrians.

Striking also was Hannibal's limited success among the peoples of the central Apennines. The Samnites had consistently opposed Rome, not

---

[16] In 212 special commissions were set up to buy and ship Etruscan grain to Campania and Taras: Liv. 25.15.4–6, 25.20.1–3.

[17] Regarding Umbria, Bradley 2000: 103–54 argues that the Romans introduced a significant number of settlers into the region through the granting of viritane allotments and especially the foundation of Latin colonies. He concludes that 'the size of [the Latin] colonies would have dwarfed all but the largest neighbouring Umbrian communities … The colonies would also be able to fulfil a very powerful military role, preventing any disturbances or revolt in central and southern Umbria' (p. 138). Bradley does note that the Romans confiscated some of the richest agricultural land in the region.

[18] See Chapter 1, n. 68.

only in the three so-called Samnite Wars but also in the decade following Pyrrhus' invasion. Hannibal received support from the Caudini and the Hirpini, yet the Pentri remained mostly loyal to Rome throughout the Second Punic War.[19] Livy (22.24.11–14) reports that a certain Numerius Decimius of Bovianum supported the Romans in 217 with a large force of Pentri. If this notice is accurate, then Numerius Decimius represents the sort of local aristocrat whose loyalty was critical for the Roman cause. We may speculate that the Romans had favoured Decimius' family in some way, which could account for his and his town's apparently remarkable support. Yet there is little evidence that the Pentrian elite as a whole felt distinct affinity towards Rome. Moreover, as discussed before, the Romans enjoyed similar support from the aristocratic Mopsii of Compsa, yet Compsa and other communities of the Hirpini ultimately went over to Hannibal. Thus, the existence of a single loyal local aristocrat (or aristocratic family) could not necessarily guarantee an entire community's loyalty, so the steadfastness of Numerius Decimius does not entirely account for the Pentrian's apparent loyalty during the Second Punic War, when other Samnite tribes defected.

It is possible that the Hirpini and Caudini harboured particular bitterness and resentment about their treatment at the hands of the Romans and so were more receptive to Hannibal's overtures. Indeed, both tribes had suffered territorial confiscation and were tightly ringed by colonies and the *ager Romanus*. Yet the Pentri had also lost territory: Allifae and Aesernia were both confiscated, and the latter was resettled as a Latin colony.[20] The Carricini, a northern Samnite tribe, disappear from the historical record after the Samnite Wars, and they may have been absorbed into the Pentri and the neighbouring Frentani.[21] The acquisition of territory from the Carricini may have blunted long-term Pentrian discontent, thus tipping the scale against revolt when the local ruling class faced the difficult decision of what to do after Cannae.[22] If so, then the divergent reactions of the Samnites during the Second Punic War exemplify once

---

[19] See Appendix A.   [20] Festus, *Gloss. Lat.* p. 262 L; Salmon 1967: 277–9, 288–90.
[21] Salmon 1967: 290.
[22] Lloyd 1995: 208–10 observes that the leading Pentrian centres, such as Bovianum, show evidence of urbanisation, stable and sizeable populations, a high degree of economic activity, and impressive public and private buildings from the fourth to the second centuries. Lloyd, in his discussion of the Pentri, states that '[d]uring the 3rd and 2nd centuries the economic life of Samnium developed considerably and the elites clearly prospered' (quotation at p. 209), and he posits that Roman conquest may have compelled Pentrian elites to shift their economic practices and, in the end, develop strategies for extracting more wealth from their land. What role, if any, these developments played in shaping Pentrian loyalty during the Second Punic War must be left an open question.

more how specific local conditions and historical developments limited the effectiveness of Hannibal's strategy in Italy. Even so, Pentrian loyalty was not uniform, as Fagifulae, a Pentrian town near the border of the Frentani, defected.[23] This is the only Pentrian community mentioned by name to have revolted, but it hints at possibly more significant underlying dissatisfaction that Hannibal could have better exploited, especially given the long history of fierce Samnite resistance to Rome. Perhaps Hannibal should have marched north after the battle of Cannae, along more or less the same route that he took when he first entered Apulia in 217 – along the Adriatic coast through the territory of the Frentani and Marrucini towards the *ager Picenus* – instead of marching west through southern Samnium into Campania. Fagifulae lay along that route, and had Hannibal passed once more through the vicinity he might have brought about the defection of more Pentrian communities.

This route also would have allowed Hannibal to make inroads among the Abruzzese peoples – the Marsi, Paeligni, Marrucini, Vestini and Frentani – all of whom remained firmly loyal to Rome throughout the Second Punic War. It is difficult to tease out the reasons for their loyalty because the region saw little fighting during the war and therefore tends to be passed over in the sources. In the longer view, the peoples of the Abruzzo had stiffly resisted the Romans in the late fourth century before succumbing and signing treaties.[24] Some of them may have joined forces with the Samnites in the 290s, but after this time all of the Abruzzese tribes remained faithful to the Romans until the Social War.[25] In 302 the Romans defeated the Marsi and confiscated some of their territory. In the year prior to that, the Romans had founded Alba Fucens, in the territory of the Aequi but near the border of the Marsi. Another colony, Hadria, was founded in 289 in the south of Picenum near the border of the Vestini.[26] These colonies were strategically placed to hinder potential cooperation between the Aequi, Samnites, Picentes and the various Abruzzese tribes. The strategic situation was further secured by construction of the Via Valeria, begun in 306, which cut through the territory of the Marsi

---

[23] See Appendix A.

[24] The Marsi, Paeligni, Marrucini and Frentani were granted treaties in 304: Liv. 9.45.18; Diod. Sic. 20.90.3–4, 20.101.5. The Romans made a treaty with the Vestini, allegedly at the latter's insistence, in 302 or 301: Liv. 10.3.1. See also Salmon 1967: 252–5; Oakley 1997–2005: IV.26.

[25] The author of the *De viris illustribus* (32, 34) lists the Marsi on the Samnite side in 295, though Oakley 1997–2005: IV.288 doubts the accuracy of this notice. Salmon 1967: 265 n. 2, following Afzelius 1942: 180, suggests that the Vestini may have joined forces with the Samnites.

[26] Foundation of Alba Fucens: Liv. 10.1.1–6; Vell. Pat. 1.14.5; Oakley 1997–2005: IV. 35; confiscations from the Marsi: 10.3.3–5; Oakley 1997–2005: IV.69; foundation of Hadria: *Liv. Per.* 11.

and Paeligni.[27] Otherwise, the imprint of Roman hegemony appears to have been light. The mulcting of territory was restricted, it seems, to the Marsi and Paeligni. Meanwhile the Frentani probably benefited when the Romans defeated the Carricini, as mentioned above. In addition, archaeological surveys conducted in the Biferno River valley have produced evidence suggesting that Larinum, the principal city of the southern Frentani, near the border of northern Apulia, emerged as an important and wealthy urban centre in the third and second centuries.[28] These developments may help to explain the steadfast loyalty of the Frentani in Rome's struggles against both Pyrrhus and Hannibal.[29] We are left to speculate on the reasons for the loyalty of the other Abruzzese peoples. It is possible that the relative unintrusiveness of Roman hegemony in the Abruzzo gave the locals less cause for complaint, while the strategic landscape probably strongly discouraged those groups that had suffered (e.g. the Marsi) from risking defection during the Second Punic War. Yet, as we saw in Chapters 2 to 5, there must have been some underlying disaffection even among those Abruzzese communities that were most inclined towards Rome. Also, strategic factors that discouraged allied defections could be overcome. The solid loyalty of the Abruzzese tribes was certainly a contributing factor in Rome's ability to survive the war.[30] If Hannibal had marched north after the battle of Cannae, he might have better exploited local disaffection, while at the same time shifting the strategic balance and, if necessary, applying firmer military pressure against recalcitrant communities.[31]

---

[27] Via Valeria: Liv. 9.43.25. Strategic situation of colonies: Salmon 1969: 59–62 and Oakley 1997–2005: IV.37, who refers to Alba Fucens as the 'Roman bulwark in western Abruzzo'. The Via Valeria connected Rome to Carseoli and Alba Fucens.

[28] Lloyd 1995: esp. 197–207. There is evidence for regular street planning and increased monumentalisation of urban centres, and the increased number of rural sites datable to the third and second centuries suggests that Larinum's *chora* was densely populated. There are also signs that local elites grew more prosperous over the same period. Larinum may have become politically independent from the rest of the Frentani (Lloyd 1995: 181–3), though the relationship between this urban centre and the other Frentanian communities is unclear.

[29] In fact, during the Pyrrhic War, the Frentani fought particularly bravely on the Romans' side at the battle of Heraclea: Plut. *Pyrrh.* 16.10; Dion. Hal. 19.12; Flor. 1.18.7. Lloyd 1995: 211–12 notes, intriguingly, that the use of Latin spread from Larinum into more rural Frentanian territories as early as the second century, which may indicate a relatively high degree of 'Romanisation'. There is not enough evidence, however, to project these developments back to the third century (or earlier), or to invoke 'Romanisation' to explain the loyalty of the Frentani during the Second Punic War.

[30] According to Polybius (2.24), the various Abruzzese tribes could supply as many as 4,000 cavalry and 20,000 infantry for the Roman army. This is one of the smaller potential contributions mentioned in Polybius' list but still represents an important asset.

[31] Hannibal did pass through the region in 217, on his march from Trasimene to Apulia, reportedly devastating the territories of the Marrucini, the Frentani (Polyb. 3.88.3), and possibly the Marsi and Paeligni (Liv. 22.9). According to Livy (26.11), Hannibal also swept through the territories of the Paeligni, Marrucini and Marsi in 211, after his march to Rome. Yet Hannibal does not appear

Of course, had Hannibal elected to move north rather than to march into Campania, Capua and its satellites probably would not have spontaneously defected. This would have been a blow, yet perhaps not as critical as it appears at first glance. As we saw in Chapters 3 and 6, Hannibal's alliance with Capua was frustrating and yielded ambiguous benefits, and he often found his operational flexibility constrained by his obligation to his highest-profile allies. We can assume that the same Apulian states would have defected after Cannae, most importantly Arpi. We might also assume that events would have played out the same way in south-western Italy, where Hanno won over Locri, Croton and most of the Bruttians. Perhaps the southern Hirpini would still have defected as well. It is unlikely, however, that Hannibal could have reached Etruria before the Romans responded by stationing legions to block his advance. In this scenario, therefore, Hannibal would have found himself defending allies in the central Apennines and along the eastern coast of the peninsula, holding more of a north–south line, rather than the east–west line from Arpi to Capua. He might have been better situated to pressure additional states in Apulia to join him, such as Canusium and Teanum Apulum, allowing him to consolidate his position in the south-east. Still, there is no guarantee that such gains, even had they materialised, would have offset Rome's long-term strategic advantages. It is doubtful that this scenario would have resulted in large-scale defections from among the Etruscans and Umbrians, and Hannibal might still have been trapped defending a 'checkerboard' of southern Italian allies from Roman reprisals while trying in vain to elicit one more conclusive battle.

Hannibal's best chance to win over states in the northern half of the peninsula probably came not in 216 but in the previous year. In the days leading up to Trasimene, Hannibal's army passed through Etruria, devastating the countryside and taking plunder in order to lure the Romans into battle. After crushing Flaminius at Trasimene, Hannibal led his army methodically through Etruria and southern Umbria to Picenum, all the while accumulating plunder and killing local inhabitants. He reached the coast within a couple of weeks and proceeded south to Apulia, after which he would not again pass through Etruria. Livy (21.58.1–2) states that Hannibal broke winter quarters in 217 and marched into Etruria with the specific intention of winning over the Etruscans, though this may be an

to have put pressure on the Abruzzese tribes in the critical juncture after Cannae, when Roman credibility was at its lowest. Even if we accept the historicity of Livy's version of Hannibal's route from Rome to Rhegion in 211, this movement through the Abruzzo occurred after the tide of the war had turned in Rome's favour.

assumption on the Roman historian's part. In any case, Hannibal appears to have been genuinely surprised that his heavy-handed tactics combined with his victory in the field did not bring about immediate allied defections: Polybius (3.90.12–14) implies that he marched into the *ager Falernus* in 217 out of frustration because no ally had yet defected even though he had twice defeated the Romans and could march about Italy with seeming impunity. He clearly miscalculated the degree to which the allies adhered to Rome or were overawed by Roman power.

Perhaps Hannibal should have chosen a different route. Indeed, he could have lingered in the vicinity of Etruria for the remainder of the summer and perhaps through the winter, while possibly taking a lighter approach with the allies. By keeping his army north of Rome and presenting himself as a credible and appealing alternative, he could have tapped into underlying allied discontent and convinced some of them to break away. Even if major defections had not materialised immediately, his army's presence only a few days' march from Rome would have put additional pressure on the Roman political elite. This political situation might have prevented Fabius Maximus from convincing the Romans to adopt his delaying strategy, resulting in a more aggressive and careless Roman response to the disaster. Yet even if Fabius' dictatorship had unfolded along similar lines, there is little doubt that the Romans would have mounted a massive campaign against Hannibal in 216. In this second hypothetical scenario, the battle of Cannae would have been fought in Etruria rather than Apulia and, assuming for the sake of this exercise a similar outcome, massive defections in northern Italy probably would have followed. Additionally, two major defeats so near to Rome might have finally convinced the senate to accept terms, while Hannibal would have been in a much better position to march on the city and force a conclusive showdown.[32] Finally, had Hannibal focused his efforts in 217 and 216 in Etruria instead of Apulia and Campania, it is unlikely that the Romans would have concentrated as many troops in southern Italy (such as the legions stationed in Campania). Thus, after his hypothetical victory at the 'Etruscan Cannae', Hannibal

---

[32] The distance from Trasimene to Rome is about half of that between Rome and Apulia, so the march itself would have been much more practical. Hannibal would still have needed to deal with the urban legions stationed in the city. On the other hand, the city's defences were probably stronger in 216 than they were in 217. In fact, when Q. Fabius Maximus was chosen as dictator after Trasimene, he immediately set about bolstering the city's defences, which included destroying bridges spanning the Anio and Tiber rivers (Liv. 22.8.6–7). If this notice is accurate, it suggests that the Romans themselves were concerned that Hannibal was going to march against the city. If he had moved quickly, he might have been able to approach Rome before the defences had been adequately reinforced.

would still have been free to march east and then south into Apulia and to send Hanno into Bruttium in order to foster rebellions in those two regions. Perhaps additional central Italian peoples such as the Pentri or the Frentani would have joined in as his army passed through their territory. Presumably, peoples such as the Etruscans would not have defected *en masse*, since their actions would have been conditioned by the same sort of local rivalries that limited Hannibal's strategic success in southern Italy. Still, widespread revolts in both southern and northern Italy might have been enough to tip the scales in Hannibal's favour. If so, then perhaps the war was lost not in the days after Cannae, as Livy's Maharbal claimed, but rather in the wake of Trasimene.

The third alternative scenario involves Hannibal in adopting an audacious and surprising course of action, given our focus in the first two scenarios on central and northern Italy. Immediately after the battle of Cannae he could have mounted a serious operation against the city of Canusium, where the remnants of the Cannae legions had gathered.[33] Peddie (1997: 198–9) argued that Hannibal lost the military initiative by not pursuing the Cannae legions. More tangibly, if the operation had proved successful, Hannibal would have taken an additional 10,000 Roman soldiers out of service, while gaining control of an important, recalcitrant Roman ally. He might also have captured or killed the surviving consul, C. Terentius Varro. Such a high-ranking hostage could have proven an exceptionally valuable bargaining chip in any subsequent negotiations. At the very least, news of the loss of both consuls and additional legionary casualties would have further undermined Roman confidence and contributed to allied unrest. Assuming that Rome still did not accept surrender terms, Hannibal next would have marched south in the direction of Taras, in order to win over the southern Greek states. Thus, in this third hypothetical scenario Hannibal would have tried to consolidate his position in the south before turning his attention to Rome, Campania or northern Italy.

A Tarentine revolt was by no means guaranteed: the Romans maintained a strong garrison in Taras and held a number of local aristocrats hostage in Rome as insurance against possible defection. Yet strong anti-Roman sentiment persisted among a significant portion of the political elite, and as early as 214 Hannibal was approached by Tarentine aristocrats offering to hand over their city. Moreover, Hannibal made a strong impression when he approached Taras in 214 and especially when he campaigned

---

[33] See Chapter 2, pp. 65–6, 95–6.

successfully in the Sallentine peninsula in 213. In so doing, he bolstered the anti-Roman movement in Taras, despite the fact that the Roman military presence in the region was arguably stronger than it had been in 216.[34] If Hannibal had marched soon after Cannae into the vicinity of Taras and campaigned in the Sallentine peninsula in 216 or 215, there is a good chance the city would have defected in short order. Metapontion and Heraclea might have followed suit soon thereafter, though Thurii probably would not have revolted, given its long-standing rivalry with Taras. At the same time, Hannibal could have left Hanno to protect his allies in Apulia while wooing over those who remained loyal to Rome: Teanum Apulum and Canusium (if the latter had not fallen earlier). The better move, however, would have been to send Hanno into Bruttium as soon as possible, to try to win over as many southern Italian communities as quickly as he could. This would have left any holdout loyalist states isolated.

In this third scenario Hannibal would have thus secured a long band of southern Italy by 215, including much of Apulia and Messapia, most of the Italiote states from Taras through Locri, and much of Bruttium. He could then have focused on winning over the few recalcitrant coastal states, such as Thurii and Rhegion, before turning his attention north. Rhegion played a key role in the Roman reconquest of Locri and served as a base of operations against the Bruttians (see Chapter 6, pp. 276–7). By securing the city, Hannibal could have deprived the Romans of this strategic base. Perhaps more importantly, Rhegion commanded the Straits of Messina and could have acted, therefore, as a critical bridge between his southern Italian conquests and Sicily. We must assume in our scenario that Hieronymus of Syracuse would still have allied with Hannibal in 215. If so, then by directing his war efforts to far southern Italy in 216 and 215, Hannibal would probably have found himself in command of a more or less unified bloc of allies stretching from Arpi to Syracuse, even if Rhegion and Thurii had resisted or he had chosen to ignore them for the time being.

Potential gains in the south of course would have been at least partially balanced by losses in other regions of Italy. There was always the danger that recalcitrant states could serve as Roman bridgeheads, while conquering them might use up too much time and resources. Hannibal would also have needed to secure the citadel of Taras in order to make freer use of this major port. Marching south would have cost Hannibal any realistic chance of eliciting defections in northern and central Italy, including

[34] See Chapter 5, pp. 208–13.

Campania and possibly from among the central Samnites, at least for the present time. He would have had to hope that subsequent opportunities would arise to put pressure on the communities to the north of his southern bloc. In the meantime the Romans would not have acquiesced to the establishment of southern Italy as a sort of Carthaginian protectorate, and Hannibal's new allies would have been vulnerable to Roman reprisals, especially if he had failed to quickly establish a more manageable line of defence by securing the loyalty of the Hirpini and northern Lucanians.

At the same time, however, winning over the communities along the southern coast of the peninsula might have placed Hannibal in a better position early in the war to receive reinforcements by sea from Carthage or Philip V of Macedon. In the best-case scenario, Hannibal's early successes in the south might have convinced Philip V to commit significant, perhaps decisive resources to the Italian war.[35] But even if Philip V had remained on the sidelines, the very different strategic circumstances – Hannibal in control of much of the south, including ideally Taras – would have made the treaty in 215 between Philip and Hannibal appear as a much more credible military threat to the Romans, which in turn might have convinced them to divert additional assets to the East and to pursue the Macedonian war with greater vigour.[36] The Romans might even have abandoned their patient strategy in Italy out of fear, however exaggerated, of possible Macedonian intervention, opting instead to drive Hannibal from the peninsula before Philip's army arrived and thus increasing the chances for another major disaster on the battlefield. Had Hannibal at least been able to receive substantial reinforcements from Macedon or Carthage – and it is admittedly uncertain that either planned to lend more than token assistance[37] – then he could have better endured a longer war of attrition. This is not to say that he would necessarily have won such a war, but his chances of coming out on top would have been greatly improved if he had had additional manpower to defend the states that defected while

---

[35] On the possibility of Philip's committing forces to Italy see Chapter 5, n. 103. Livy (23.33.1–3) says that Philip waited to see which side was winning before he decided to send an embassy to Hannibal. The passage is hostile to Philip, but such a cautious policy is not implausible.

[36] Indeed, we should not underestimate how threatening the treaty must have looked to the Roman senate in 215, given the military situation at that juncture in the war, whatever Philip's real intentions might have been: Badian 1958: 56 n. 4; Seibert 1995; Eckstein 2008: 84–5. Roman fear would have grown only more acute had Hannibal secured an easier sea lane to the East.

[37] Hoyos 2004a: 129–32 notes, however, that large Carthaginian forces were sent to reinforce Spain and Sicily. Perhaps the Carthaginian senate never planned to send many reinforcements directly to Italy, though it may have been the case that they changed plans in response to Hannibal's early success. That is, the Carthaginian senate may have figured that Hannibal would reinforce himself from the Italians, so forces originally earmarked for Italy were rerouted to other theatres.

he tried to elicit further revolts and waited for an opportunity to force a conclusive battle.

All three scenarios introduce serious strategic risks, and none guarantees victory. The first two focus on ways that Hannibal could have elicited revolts in central and northern Italy, which he needed to do if he hoped to bring Rome to its knees. His best strategy might have been, in my opinion, to remain in northern Italy after Trasimene, only marching south after he had begun to win over allies in Etruria. Yet it must be stressed that this strategy would probably have worked only if he had been able to defeat the Romans again (winning his 'Etruscan Cannae') and then march to the south at some point to elicit rebellions there. Otherwise, Hannibal would have found himself in a very similar situation, having successfully won over a significant number but not a critical mass of Rome's Italian allies. Marching south after Cannae might have been the better course of action for fighting a long war of attrition, but such a plan relied heavily on outside support from Carthage or Philip V, which might not have been forthcoming. It does not seem to be the case that Hannibal overlooked a glaringly obvious strategy that would have sewn up victory, nor does he seem to have made a specific blunder within the context of his Italian strategy that cost him the war. Whatever course of action Hannibal had chosen, he would have needed a series of events to break his way in order to overcome Rome's vast advantage in manpower (discussed in Chapter 1, pp. 37–42 and Chapter 6, pp. 235–43). In all three scenarios he would have found it difficult to convince enough Italian communities to join with him in common cause, not only because of their fear of Rome or their scepticism of his enterprise – both of which must have been reinforced by the Romans' strategic response after Cannae – but also because he could not have made them look beyond their own local interests and, in some cases, rivalries and mutual mistrust. Winning over all of the communities in even a single region was a daunting task, requiring time and energy to seduce the recalcitrant or force them to switch sides. Additional resources spent in one region meant that Hannibal had to make at least short-term strategic sacrifices in others. Given this conclusion, perhaps it is fairer to commend Hannibal for doing as well as he did, rather than condemn him for overlooking alternative strategies or failing to capitalise on missed opportunities.[38]

The three counterfactual scenarios presented in the foregoing discussion are certainly intriguing to contemplate, but they are not, I believe, merely

---

[38] For a similar assessment, see Lazenby 1996b.

entertaining diversions. Rather, they illustrate the strategic disadvantages that Hannibal faced and the sorts of local conditions and conflicting parochial interests that frustrated his Italian campaign.

OVERCOMING LOCAL CONDITIONS: THE ROMAN GENIUS?

It stands to reason that the Romans contended with the same types of divergent and contradictory interests at the regional and sub-regional levels. The various communities of Italy still remained fiercely independent, and did not share a strong sense of common identity or purpose with Rome as late as the outbreak of the Second Punic War, as discussed in Chapter 1. Yet the Romans managed to forge the various Italian polities into a formidable and resilient alliance network that repelled three major external threats during the third century (Pyrrhus, the Gauls and Hannibal) and subsequently enabled Rome to conquer the Mediterranean. Several factors allowed the Romans to overcome divisive local conditions, such as enduring interstate rivalries, but, as we shall see, the road to Rome's success was long and difficult.

It must be recognised that local conditions surely slowed the pace of the Rome's conquest of Italy. This assertion is consistent with the course of Roman imperialism in the late fourth and early third centuries: rarely did all of the polities in the same geographic region fall under Rome's hegemony simultaneously. Instead, the Romans sometimes found themselves campaigning repeatedly in the same region, at times defeating the same community more than once before it finally succumbed. The loyalties of neighbouring communities were not infrequently split. Sometimes communities had allied with Rome more or less voluntarily, while their neighbours had to be forced to submit unwillingly to Roman hegemony. Overall, Rome's conquest of the peninsula was a long, slow and piecemeal process. All of this fits well with the picture I have drawn of competitive, mistrusting and rivalrous Italian communities whose independent aims and concerns worked against efforts to unite them.

In Chapter 1 I argued that these very same centrifugal forces created preconditions that encouraged Rome's interference throughout Italy. In the long run this actually facilitated the extension of Roman power throughout the period of intense expansion, *c.* 350–270. The rhythm of Roman warfare during this stage is striking to the modern observer: nearly every year the Romans went to war, at times fighting simultaneously on multiple, geographically far-flung fronts. The motives behind such relentless campaigning were several and overlapping. There is no doubt that Romans, both individual citizens and as a community, recognised and enjoyed the economic benefits of their mostly successful wars, including booty, slaves and territory.[39] Warfare was also the central mechanism through which Roman aristocrats won glory and prestige; war-making and the *cursus honorum* were closely bound up.[40] It is surely the case that some wars were waged on strategic grounds, to maximise security or in response to perceived threats,[41] while others were no doubt fought for mostly opportunistic reasons. Whatever moved the Romans to go to war – and indeed, complex, multilayered and fluctuating motives probably lay behind each conflict[42] – they would have sought to explain and justify their policies. It would have been undesirable simply to show up at the enemy's gates without pretext or alleged provocation, even if opportunism and self-enrichment were the 'real' impetus.[43] The highly competitive interstate environment in Italy in the late fourth and early third centuries provided both numerous opportunities and ample justifications to go to war.

Smaller states might be driven to rely on an outside power to balance against a local expansionist power. The sources preserve many examples of communities calling on the Romans to help against an enemy.[44] Rome certainly did not have a monopoly on providing military assistance,[45] but the Romans must have gained a reputation as fierce allies.[46] Once they

---

[39] William V. Harris (1971, 1979: 54–104, 1990) has been the most forceful proponent of the position that economic motives chiefly drove Roman imperialism during the Republic. See also Oakley 1993: 18–28.

[40] Aristocratic ethos and war, see: Harris 1979: 9–41; Bleckmann 2002; Beck 2005.

[41] Security concerns or fear as a motivating factor, see: Sherwin-White 1980, 1984; Dyson 1985; Eckstein 1987: esp. xiv–xvi, 2006.

[42] Rich 1993, 1996 stresses the complexity of the motives and decision-making behind Roman warfare and imperialism, including occasional periods of inactivity. For a concise summary of various older views, see Gruen 1984: 5–7.

[43] Even Harris 1979: 166–75 admits that the Romans generally sought at least a pretext for war that made their cause appear more sympathetic.

[44] See Chapter 1, n. 47 for examples of Italian communities appealing to Rome for help in the period before the Second Punic War. To these we may also add the appeal of the Mamertines, which sparked the First Punic War (Polyb. 1.10.1–2), and the appeal of the Saguntines (Polyb. 3.15.1–5; Liv. 21.6.1–4). See also now Champion 2007, pointing out the collaborative role of the 'periphery' of Hellenistic states in the development of Roman overseas imperialism in the second century.

[45] Recall, for example, how Naples requested and received a garrison from Nola in 327 or 326, for protection *against* the Romans: see Chapter 3, n. 182.

[46] For an interesting example of Republican Rome's reputation to outsiders, see the first book of Maccabees. According to the author of this account, Judas Maccabeus sought an alliance with Rome because he had learned that the Romans were brave fighters who had defeated many powerful enemies, but who also treated their friends well and granted alliances to anyone who asked (1 Macc. 8.1–16, esp. 1–2). 1 Maccabees was probably written in the late second century BC for a Jewish audience (Attridge 1984: 171). This vision of the Romans perhaps reflects, therefore, what the author and/or his audience thought about them, not merely what the Romans wanted to hear

interfered in a local dispute, they could justify further intervention as fulfilling their obligation to their allies. As the Roman circle of alliances and friendships grew to encompass more and more states – whether peacefully or by the sword – the chances that a given ally would be wronged by a neighbouring polity (or at least that the Romans could claim such a provocation) only increased, providing the Romans with more openings to expand their power. Also, Roman expansion intersected with local enduring interstate rivalries. If the Romans favoured one member of a dyad, then this is likely to have increased tensions between the rivals, leading perhaps to subsequent conflicts and in turn repeated Roman intervention. Finally, the Romans did suffer occasional setbacks between about 350 and 270: they lost battles, and occasionally former allies switched sides.[47] These events too could justify subsequent hostilities to redress perceived wrongs, restore honour, and so forth. Overall, the divisive and disuniting local factors and conditions, which we have focused on throughout this book, fed into and contributed to an intensely competitive and anarchic environment that provided a steady stream of conflicts for Rome to become involved in. They offered both opportunities and rationales for the patchwork conquest of the entire peninsula.

At the same time, Rome was by far the most populous state in Italy already in the middle of the fourth century.[48] This gave a huge military advantage that enabled the Romans to neutralise the Italian communities' tendency to fight with each other. Rome could not only overwhelm most individual opponents, but also recover from occasional defeats that might cripple other states. Individual Italian communities could resist Roman power for only so long; sooner or later they were compelled to submit to Rome or else suffer dire consequences. Local grievances, grudges and rivalries might have conditioned state behaviour, but the overriding concern was security and survival. Once Rome established its dominance in a region, there was less room for the subordinate states there to exercise free foreign policy and attack each other without risking Roman retribution. Yet the slow pace and patchwork nature of Rome's conquest of the peninsula indicate how difficult it was for Rome to deal with conflicting local interests, rivalries, and the like. Moreover, it must be stressed that

(see Yarrow 2006: 16–17, 133–8). Of course, the Romans did not always live up to this reputation, at times failing to fulfil their obligations to friends and allies: consider most famously their tardy response to the Saguntine appeal (for references and discussion, see Rich 1976: 18–55 esp. 42–3, 1996: 28–30).

[47] For example, between 326 and 314 the loyalty of Apulian communities, especially Luceria, varied in response to, among other things, Rome's changing fortunes: Fronda 2006: 415–17.

[48] See Chapter 1, n. 70.

Rome did not entirely eliminate these centrifugal tendencies but rather suppressed them primarily through military force.

Rome's large citizen population and corresponding military strength were both closely related to inclusive policies that integrated many conquered communities, especially in central Italy, into a sort of Roman 'super-state'. The most important of these was the policy of granting Roman citizenship to outside groups. The willingness to share citizenship is reflective of the general openness of central Italian societies to outsiders, at least in comparison with the highly exclusive societies of contemporary ancient Greece.[49] Roman inclusiveness traces back to the very early history of the Republic, if not before. The Romans' foundation legends emphasised their willingness at a very early date to incorporate various outside groups in order to form a larger city-state.[50] The Romans may have shared the rights of *conubium*, *commercium* and *migratio* with Latin communities in the early fifth century. After the Latin War, Roman citizenship was extended to many Latin communities, which were incorporated into the Roman citizen body and remained, at the local level, self-governing *municipia*. Additionally, some non-Latin communities were later incorporated as Roman *municipia*. The status of *civitas sine suffragio* ('citizenship without the vote'), which provided partial citizen rights and privileges, was granted to a number of non-Latin communities especially in Campania. Similarly, the Romans founded 'Latin colonies', whose settlers were granted the rights of Latin citizens, regardless of where these colonies were planted or the ethnic origins of the settlers. This constellation of political concepts and policies gave the Roman state a huge potential for growth because it detached citizenship from ethnic or linguistic origins: Roman citizenship became a bundle of rights and obligations that could be extended in whole or in part to whomever the Romans wished. This masterstroke also encouraged cooperation on the part of incorporated peoples and created bonds between the conquerors and conquered. This does not mean that all conquered communities desired Roman or Latin citizenship, or that incorporation did not carry additional burdens or generate resentment.[51] Yet the extension of citizenship was one mechanism that must have encouraged the development of some sort of common

---

[49] Eckstein 2006: 245–57.
[50] The image of Rome as an inclusive society willing to incorporate foreigners at an early date was a major theme in literature of the late Republican and early Imperial periods and constituted an important aspect of Roman self-perception: Dench 2005: 93–151.
[51] Indeed, as we saw in Chapter 3 (pp. 114–18), the people of Campania who possessed citizenship without the vote appear to have viewed this status with ambiguity.

identity – or at least common interest – among those groups who were incorporated.[52]

Other circumstances and policies may have rendered Roman hegemony more tolerable for those communities that were not formally incorporated as *municipia*. Rome's practice of making bilateral treaties with individual communities corresponded at times to the self-interested security concerns of the weaker party.[53] This is because such treaties offered protection for weaker states, especially those threatened by an aggressive, expansionist neighbour. As mentioned above, there are numerous examples of the Romans fighting on behalf of a vulnerable ally against nearby hostile communities, either in response to an appeal for help or on their own initiative.[54] Even if the Romans used such circumstances for cynical purposes to further their own ambitions, their weaker ally may have been generally satisfied with the arrangement as well. In addition, since Rome's subject allies were not able to make war on each other, weaker allies continued to be shielded from stronger members of the alliance network after the initial period of conquest. Smaller and weaker states may have felt, therefore, that Roman hegemony offered them some real advantages. Presumably these states would have preferred legitimate independence and the option to pursue their own foreign policy, and they may well have chafed under the burdens imposed by Roman rule, such as military obligations.[55] But given the lack of any realistic alternative, the relative security provided by Roman hegemony may have offset these negatives from the perspective of those small states that benefited the most. This arrangement was probably much less attractive, however, to regional hegemonic powers that lost the opportunity to expand their own influence and territory as Rome made more and more alliances with surrounding communities. It is perhaps no coincidence, therefore, that the most powerful states in each of the four regions discussed in Chapters 2 to 5 went over to Hannibal more readily.

State-level bonds such as alliances and shared citizen rights encouraged links at the personal level, as well. It was discussed in Chapter 1

---

[52] The willingness of the Capuans and their satellites to revolt in the Second Punic War shows that any common identity between the Romans and incorporated, self-governing communities could give way to local self-interest under certain circumstances. At the same time, the otherwise firm loyalty displayed by *municipia* and Latin colonies suggests that shared citizenship created some type of cohesion.

[53] On Rome's practice of making treaties with their allies, see Chapter 1, n. 51.

[54] See above, n. 44.

[55] The sources of Italian discontent with Roman hegemony were discussed in Chapters 2 to 5, *passim*.

that Roman hegemony relied in large part on the collaboration of local ruling classes, while members of these local aristocracies forged personal ties with Roman *nobiles* and their families. For aristocrats who lived in communities possessing some form of Roman or Latin citizenship, the mutual right of *conubium* opened the possibility of marriage alliances with Roman elite households. There is strong evidence, for example, of widespread intermarriage between the Capuan and Roman ruling classes, as discussed in Chapter 3. There is also evidence for *hospitium*, formal guest-friendship entailing hereditary mutual obligations, between Roman and Italian aristocratic families during the fourth and third centuries: the brother of Q. Fabius Maximus Rullianus (cos. 310) had been educated in the house of guest-friends (*apud hospites*) in Etruscan Caere;[56] Ti. Sempronius Gracchus (cos. 215, 213) shared *hospitium* with a Lucanian aristocrat named Flavus;[57] Titus Manlius Torquatus (cos. 235, 224) shared *hospitium* with a Marsic aristocrat named T. Staiodius.[58] Other less formal bonds of friendship surely connected Roman and non-Roman aristocrats. Thus, I refer again to the aristocratic faction in Croton who were the 'friends' (ἐπιτηδείοι) of P. Cornelius Rufinus (cos. 277).[59] The garrison commander in Taras during the Second Punic War, Gaius Livius, was caught off guard by the plot to betray the city to Hannibal because he had grown friendly with some of the conspirators and frequently banqueted 'with his intimates' (μετὰ τῶν συνήθων), presumably including local aristocrats.[60] We might expect some personal connections to grow out of the Roman backing of specific local aristocratic families, such as the Mopsii of Compsa,[61] or from public deeds performed by Roman magistrates that occasionally benefited Italian communities.[62] There must have been personal connections between aristocrats from different Italian

---

[56] Liv. 9.36.2–3.

[57] Liv. 25.16.5–6.

[58] *CIL* I² 1764 = *ILLRP* 1066; see J. R. Patterson 2006b: 141. The inscription is a fine example of a *tessera hospitalis*: it is a small bronze ram's head cut in half, bearing the two men's names ('T. Staiodius N. f.' and 'T. Manlius T. f.') and the word HOSPES written in between. Both parties would possess a corresponding *tessera* so that when they or their descendants met, the two halves could be matched to verify the relationship of *hospitium*. The identification of T. Manlius is a plausible speculation, but even if the individual was not the twice consul, the *tessera* still attests to *hospitium* between Roman and non-Roman elites.

[59] Zon. 8.6.2.

[60] Polyb. 8.24.4–8.30.12, esp. 8.25.5–7, 8.27.1–7. Polybius' account assumes frequent friendly interaction between the Roman garrison commander and his officers and members of the Tarentine aristocracy. For the revolt of Taras, see Chapter 5, pp. 211–17.

[61] Liv. 23.1.1–3; see Chapter 1, p. 32.

[62] Pliny (*HN* 34.32) reports that the people of Thurii erected a statue in Rome to Gaius Aelius, in 285, for his role in protecting the Thurians from attacks by the Lucanians. Note that the statue

cities other than Rome. Rome's dominant position and 'global' reach ensured, however, that the Roman aristocracy was involved in these connections on a much grander scale. Moreover, personal connections and bonds, both formal and informal, between Roman and Italian aristocrats no doubt grew more numerous over time,[63] and the phenomenon was surely widespread already by the outbreak of the Second Punic War. It is likely that such deepening personal links between members of the ruling classes throughout Italy not only reinforced allied loyalty towards Rome but also at least temporarily blunted the intensity of local hostilities and rivalries. As Rome emerged as the most powerful state in the peninsula, it became the centre of a web of both personal and state-level connections that bound the individual allied polities to the dominant power. In this context local rivalries receded into the background.

A number of cautionary observations must be stressed. The communities in Italy were still driven by self-interest and, with the exception of those communities that had been incorporated into the Roman state, we cannot observe much in the way of a shared 'pan-Italian' identity. The Romans had not created a unified nation-state; the allies did not desire to 'become Roman'. Moreover, the Romans had not altogether eliminated the centrifugal forces (factionalism, localism, rivalry, hostility and mistrust) that prevented Hannibal from uniting the Italians in common cause against Rome, though these forces may have been somewhat weakened over time. Rather, the extensive and complex network of personal relations between Roman and local elites combined with Rome's overwhelming power vis-à-vis any single Italian community suppressed divisive forces beneath the surface. This was a fragile arrangement, prone to revert to multipolar interstate anarchy once the balance was disrupted.[64]

One final note: Rome's achievement took a long time. The conquest of individual states, the incorporation of some communities, the formation of multiple layers of personal and state-level bonds, and ultimately

---

honoured Aelius individually. Although it was supposedly set up by the Thurian people, one suspects that leading citizens were behind the dedication: perhaps these were aristocrats who were in some way already linked to Aelius, or perhaps they hoped to win his favour or friendship. In either case, those who dedicated the statue may have earned additional gratitude from the dedicatee and strengthened their mutual links.

[63] See below, pp. 315–19.

[64] Indeed, the widespread rebellions that erupted after Cannae remind us of the potential frailty of Rome's imperial enterprise in Italy, and Hannibal's Italian strategy presupposed that the subject allies could be easily detached. Such fragility was not uncommon in the ancient world even among the most powerful states: Eckstein 2006: 245–6, 309–10. The rapid disintegration of Carthage's empire in Africa at the start of the Mercenary War is an excellent example (Polyb.1.70.7–9).

the suppression of divisive local factors unfolded over decades. But time was not a luxury that Hannibal possessed. By marching into Italy and, more importantly, defeating the Romans in a series of battles, he was able to capitalise on the inherent brittleness of their hegemony. He played on the allies' feelings of resentment and took advantage of the very factionalism and parochial self-interest that had been checked by Roman power. He gave cover for fiercely independent and competitive communities to exercise independent foreign policy and pursue their own expansionistic ambitions. He did not have the time, however, to put in place structures to overcome the centrifugal tendencies that he had set loose by temporarily removing Rome's overwhelming grip on the peninsula. Thus he was unable to unify enough Italian communities in common cause to counteract Rome's strategic advantages. Such coordination and cooperation among the Italians would not be seen until the Social War (discussed below, pp. 324–9).

ROME AND THE ITALIANS, *CIRCA* 200–90

When Hannibal failed to break the Romans' will after the battle of Cannae, his hopes of winning the war began to fade, and with them faded also any hopes of independence for the various communities in Italy. The subsequent reconquest of those areas that rose in rebellion between 216 and 213/12 was the final stage in the Roman conquest of Italy. The period from the end of the Second Punic War until the outbreak of the Social War (91–88) was characterised by a changing dynamic in the relationship between Rome and the allies, as the fiercely independent, competitive and often rivalrous tendencies of the Italian communities slowly gave way in response to the geopolitical reality. This is not to say that there was no continuity, and indeed some of the trends and developments in Roman–Italian (and intra-Italian) relations visible in the fourth and third centuries continued after the Second Punic War. At the same time, the war marked a pivotal point, and when the next major conflict finally broke out in Italy more than a century later, with the Social War, the rebellious Italian communities behaved in a very different manner.

As control over the Italians was slowly re-established between 214 and 200, Rome had occasion to impose a wide-ranging series of settlements on the many communities that had revolted, and even on some that had remained loyal. Particular post-war conditions surely varied from city to city, as specific historical circumstances, namely the disparate paths by which individual rebellious communities fell back into Roman hands (discussed in Chapter 6), influenced the treatment of the defeated. Local political and military contexts, even the disposition of the Roman commander overseeing the recapture, were all unique, guaranteeing that each and every reconquered community suffered the consequences of war in varying degrees. Some fortunate communities were even spared the more extreme exercise of Roman brutality. Despite the myriad local variations, however, there was a general pattern to the settlements imposed by Rome on formerly rebellious communities, which typically entailed harsh terms and severe punishments.

The settlements following reconquest often involved the confiscation of territory from previously rebellious communities. We do not know precisely which lands were mulcted at this time, though the available evidence suggests that the confiscations were extensive.[65] The territory of Capua became *ager publicus* and was placed under the administration of a Roman prefect; sections were sold off in 205 and 199, and small coastal sections were used for the foundation of citizen colonies.[66] Arpi was deprived of its port at Sipontum, which was later refounded as a Roman colony, and Herdonia and Aecae may also have lost territory.[67] Significant portions of Lucania were seized in a broad band, stretching from Buxentum to Grumentum and south to the Gulf of Taranto.[68] Colonies planted along the coast of Bruttium (discussed below) indicate several confiscations in that region. At least part of the territory of Taras was converted into *ager publicus*.[69] In the interior of the peninsula both the Hirpini and Caudini were further mulcted of territory in addition to lands already lost during the Samnite Wars.[70] These massive confiscations obviously increased the size of the Roman state, providing land for the rapidly growing Roman citizen body, whose population rebounded and increased dramatically after the war.[71] Post-reconquest settlements also greatly weakened former

---

[65] For a summary, see Lomas 1993: 86–8; Nagle 1973.

[66] Liv. 28.46.4–6, 32.6.3.

[67] Liv. 31.4.49, 34.45.3; Toynbee 1965: II.659; Nagle 1973: 377–8.

[68] Nagle 1973: 375–6; for further discussion and references, see also Chapter 5, pp. 205–6.

[69] Liv. 44.16.7–8. The colony of Neptunia was founded in 123/2 on land that had been taken from the Tarentines after the Second Punic War: Vell. Pat. 1.15.4; Plut. *C. Gracch.* 8.3; Plin. *HN* 3.99; *CIL* I².590; Lomas 1993: 88.

[70] Liv. 40.38.3, 40.41.3–4; Salmon 1967: 299.

[71] According to Brunt 1971: 69–83, the Roman population (men of military age) increased from 240,000 citizens in 203 to 430,000 citizens in 124. Such a net increase, which included military deaths in addition to normal civilian mortality, represents a very high rate of increase for a premodern, pre-industrial society: Rosenstein 2004: 145–6. Whatever the reasons for the dramatic growth in the Roman population (Italians moving to Rome, natural increase and the manumission of slaves have been variously invoked to explain the phenomenon), it was surely facilitated by the vastness of the *ager Romanus*.

regional powers such as Arpi, Capua and Taras, who had posed as the most credible rivals to Rome within their own areas.[72]

Perhaps more significantly, the new round of confiscations facilitated the last wave of Roman colonisation before the Gracchan period. Between 200 and 177 around twenty new Latin and Roman colonies were founded, located mostly in the northern and southern extremes of the Italian peninsula.[73] Five citizen colonies of 300 settlers each were founded along the western coast of Italy in 194: Puteoli, Liternum and Volturnum in Campania (the latter two on land confiscated from Capua); Salernum on the southern edge of Campania, south of the Sorrentine peninsula; and Buxentum in Lucania.[74] In the same year citizen colonies were also placed in Sipontum on the coast of Apulia, and in Croton and Tempsa on the coast of Bruttium.[75] Two large Latin colonies were also founded in Bruttium: Copia (at the site of Thurii) in 193 and Vibo Valentia in 192.[76] Etruria received two or three new citizen colonies: inland Saturnia in 183, and coastal Graviscae in 181 and (perhaps) Pyrgi in about 194.[77] To the north-west, citizen colonies were founded in 184 at Potentia in the *ager Picenus* and Pisaurum in the *ager Gallicus*.[78] Further to the north-west, in the Veneto, a Latin colony was planted at Aquileia in 183.[79] To the northeast, a series of large colonies were founded to secure the frontier against the Gauls and Ligurians: the Latin colony of Bononia with 3,000 settlers in 189, and three citizen colonies of 2,000 settlers, Parma (183), Mutina

---

[72] Indeed, Capua ceased to exist as a self-governing entity: the community lost its political privileges and was placed under the direct administration of a Roman prefect. In addition, the Romans planned to scatter the urban population and leave the buildings as dwellings for ploughmen (*aratorum sedes*), in Livy's famous words (26.16.7). Cicero (*Leg. agr.* 2.88) preserves nearly identical terms and invokes similar language, saying that the buildings of Capua would be preserved so that ploughmen worn out from working the fields (*aratores cultu agrorum defessi*) could use them as shelters. See also App. *Pun.* 43; Zon. 9.6; Val. Max. 3.8.1; Sil. 13.347–8. For whatever reasons, the Romans did not follow up on some of the punishments, for it appears as though massive deportation and evacuation of homes probably never took place. In 189 and 188 the Capuans appealed to the senate and were re-enrolled as Roman citizens: Liv. 38.36.5–6, 39.3.4, 41.9.9. Literary and archaeological evidence suggests continuous occupation throughout the *ager Campanus*, and even some second-century urban improvements in Capua and its former satellites. See Frederiksen 1984: 249–50, 264–75; see also Manzo 2002.

[73] For the following summary of colonial foundations in the second century, before the Gracchi, see Salmon 1936: 47–50, 1969: 95–111.

[74] Liv. 34.45.1–2; Vell. Pat. 1.15.3.

[75] Liv. 34.45.3–4.

[76] Liv. 34.53.1, 35.9.9, 35.40.5; Vell. Pat. 1.14.8. Vibo Valentia was founded with 4,000 settlers, Copia with over 3,000 settlers.

[77] Liv. 39.55.9, 40.29.1. The date of the colonization of Pyrgi is a matter of dispute. Salmon initially argued that it belonged to the early second century (1936: 48–9) but later placed it in the middle third century (1969: 64, 79).

[78] Liv. 39.44.10–11; Vell. Pat. 1.15.2.   [79] Liv. 39.55.4–6, 40.32.2.

(183) and Luna (177).[80] Livy mentions an additional citizen colony founded in 199 at a place called Castrum, which may be the same as the *castrum/ castra Hannibalis* near Scyllatium in Bruttium, though the identity of the colony is not secure.[81] Similarly, Livy reports that a Latin colony with 3,000 settlers was founded at Luca *circa* 180, though this foundation is sometimes doubted.[82] Some colonies, both old and new, were reinforced with additional settlers, including Venusia (200), Narnia (199), Cosa (197), Placentia (189), Cremona (189), Sipontum (186), Buxentum (186) and Aquileia (169).[83] Strategic, economic and punitive motives have been cited to explain this rash of founding colonies in the decades following the Second Punic War,[84] but whatever lay behind the foundations, one effect must have been the further tightening of Rome's control over the nominally independent communities of Italy. Not only was the centre of Italy now crosscut by a wide band of Roman territory and Roman and Latin colonies, but also the extremities of the peninsula were ringed by colonies and cut through by stretches of *ager Romanus*. Communities in areas where the Roman colonial presence had been rather limited before the war, such as Bruttium in the south and northern Etruria in the north, now found themselves guarded by *propugnacula imperii*.

The colonies and stretches of *ager Romanus* were, in turn, connected by a system of Roman military roads, which also underwent major construction and expansion in the second century.[85] Much of the construction during the first half of the second century took place in the northern half of the peninsula and was related to the fierce campaigns waged against the Cisalpine Gauls and Ligurians. Thus, in 187 the Via Aemilia was built between Ariminum and Placentia, and an additional connecting road

---

[80] Liv. 37.47.2, 37.57.7, 39.55.6–8, 41.13.4.
[81] Liv. 32.7.3; see also Vell. Pat. 1.15.4. It is assumed that *Castrum* was on the coast since Livy mentions a *portorium* associated with the place, and this is consistent with Pliny's (*HN* 3.95) description of the *castra Hannibalis* as the harbour near Scyllatium. Nissen 1967: II.946 accepts that the *Castrum* which received 300 colonists in 199 was the same as the *castra Hannibalis*, but Salmon 1936: 47 n. 5 is more sceptical.
[82] Liv. 41.43.13; see also Vell. Pat. 1.15.2. Gargola 1995: 69–70 accepts the foundation of a Latin colony at Luca. The foundation originally was rejected by Salmon (1933, 1936: 50, 1969: 109), but he later changed his position (1982: 95).
[83] Liv. 31.49.6, 32.2.6–7, 33.24.8–9, 37.46.9, 37.47.2, 37.57.7–8, 39.23.3–4, 43.17.1.
[84] For a brief, albeit older, discussion of the views on the motives behind Roman colonisation between the Second Punic War and the Gracchan era, see Salmon 1936: 51–5. Salmon argues that the colonies were founded mainly for strategic reasons, to guard the peninsula from outside threats such as the Ligurians, Gauls or Antiochus of Syria. Subsequent scholarship has tended to agree that colonies in the middle Republic served a primarily strategic function; see Salmon 1969: 95–111; Galsterer 1976: 41–64; Gargola 1995: 51; Bispham 2006: 83 (implicit).
[85] The following summary of Roman road building during the second century is based on Wiseman 1970 and Laurence 1999: 11–42; see also Coarelli 1988.

('Via Flaminia minor') was built between Bononia and Arretium. By 150 the Via Cassia had been built between Rome and Arretium and extended through Faesulae to Pisa. The Via Annia connected Bononia, Patavium and Aquileia by 153. Additional roads were built in the second half of the century: a connecting road linked Ariminum to the Via Annia (133), and a major road (Via Popillia?) connected Capua and Rhegion (*c.* 130),[86] thus bringing a Roman trunk road through Bruttium. Gaius Gracchus is supposed to have sponsored a wide-scale road-building programme, though the sources may exaggerate his role in what was otherwise a more complicated process involving the expansion and improvement of the road network.[87] The roads built in the second century were more elaborate and costly than their predecessors,[88] reflecting greater Roman ambitions and standing as impressive monuments to Roman power. Taken together, the roads, colonies and the expansion of Roman territory marked by centuriation all must have served as constant and very tangible reminders to the Italians of Rome's virtual stranglehold on the peninsula, a position that had grown only more pronounced since the Second Punic War.[89]

Meanwhile, Rome's empire continued to expand apace.[90] Roman hegemony in Sicily, Sardinia and Corsica was re-established by the end of the Second Punic War. New conquests were added to the north: the Gauls and Ligurians between the Po river and the Alps were largely conquered by around 170, though fighting continued until 155. More striking was the expansion of Roman influence beyond the peninsula. Put simply, Rome emerged as the most powerful state in the Mediterranean by 168.[91] Large stretches of Spain were subject to Rome even if the inhabitants had not

---

[86] Identification of this road as the Via Popillia depends largely on *CIL* 1².638, a milestone found near the Forum Popillii (modern Polla) in Lucania. The dedicator's name is missing from the inscription, but he claims to have been a praetor in Sicily during some sort of disturbance of slaves, probably the slave revolt of 135. It was formerly thought that P. Popillius Laenas (pr. 135, cos. 132) was the most likely candidate (see Broughton 1951–2: 489 and 490 n. 3), though more recently T. Annius Rufus (pr. 131) has been proposed as the identity for the unnamed praetor (see Wiseman 1964, 1969; Brennan 2000: 152–3).

[87] Plut. *C. Gracch.* 6–7; App. *B Civ.* 1.23; Laurence 1999: 40–1.

[88] The censors paved a short stretch of the Via Appia outside Rome in 187, the first reference to road paving outside the city (Liv. 38.28.3). In 174 the censors embarked on an elaborate building programme that included paving the streets within Rome and laying gravel beds on the roads outside the city (Liv. 41.27.5); see also Wiseman 1970: 149.

[89] For an intriguing discussion, using Cisalpine Gaul as a case study, of the powerful symbolism of marking the landscape with roads and especially centuriation, see Purcell 1990. In reference to centuriation, Purcell says that 'doing this to a landscape is a spectacular display of the conquerer's power' (p. 16).

[90] The general outline of Roman expansion during the second century is well known. For a good summary of events down to *c.* 130, see Derow 1989; Errington 1989; Harris 1989.

[91] For an excellent analysis of this process employing political science theory, see Eckstein 2008.

yet been completely subdued, Carthage was reduced in power, and the kingdom of Massinissa became a Roman ally. In the Greek East, Illyria and the kingdom of Macedon were both divided into smaller client states. Overseas expansion continued after Rome had achieved Mediterranean hegemony. By 146 Carthage and Corinth had been destroyed and Macedon and Africa were henceforth governed as Roman provinces. By 133 most of Spain had submitted to Rome, and within a few years the province of Asia was created out of the Attalid kingdom.

Polybius (1.1.5) famously remarked how the Romans had conquered the whole world in less than fifty-three years, an unparalleled achievement in his estimation. Rome's victory in the Second Punic War, the post-war consolidation of Roman power in Italy and the awesome expansion of the *imperium Romanum* must have had a tremendous psychological impact on the Italians as well. They surely recognised that Rome emerged from the Second Punic War even more powerful vis-à-vis the Italian allies than it had been in the half-century before the war. Moreover, since the allies continued to shoulder a significant military burden, supplying the troops that enabled Rome to conquer the Mediterranean world, they had some first-hand knowledge of the geographic vastness of Rome's extra-peninsular empire. Rome's capacity to outlast Hannibal no doubt made a lasting impression. It might have been argued by an observer in the middle of the third century that Pyrrhus 'let the Romans off the hook' when he decided to invade Sicily, thereby abandoning his allies in southern Italy and giving the Romans the chance to recover. But Hannibal did not leave Italy too soon. Rather, he stayed for fifteen long years, and he continued to fight and win battles late into the war. Yet the Romans still came out on top. Edward Bispham (2007: 113) succinctly states what many Italians must have reckoned: 'if Hannibal had been unable to remove the Roman yoke, who else could?' Perhaps more to the point, who else was there? Invasions by Philip V, Antiochus and Perseus never materialised.[92] Whether or not

---

[92] Livy is our main source for rumours and Roman fears that Hellenistic monarchs were planning to invade Italy. The legate M. Aurelius Cotta allegedly advised that the Romans should attack Philip before he did what Pyrrhus had done before (31.3.4–6, 42.11.4–5); the consul P. Sulpicius Galba supposedly invoked this fear in a speech, claiming that war with Philip was inevitable, with the only choice being whether to fight it in Italy or in Macedon (31.7). There were wild rumours circulating Rome that Antiochus was planning to send a fleet to Sicily once he crossed to Illyria (35.23.1–4). More serious were reports that Hannibal had joined Antiochus' court and advised him to invade Italy (34.40, 36.7–8; see App. *Syr.* 7, 14). Eumenes II of Pergamum allegedly came to Rome and reported that Perseus was planning to carry out the Italian war that his father never had a chance to wage (Liv. 42.11). It does not matter for present purposes whether these rumours and reports were really in circulation, or whether they are later fabrications to justify Roman pre-emptive interventions in the East.

anyone in Italy really believed or hoped that Philip or Antiochus or Perseus was planning to invade, it must have been ever more evident that Roman overseas expansion progressively decreased the chances that another credible outside balancer such as Hannibal or Pyrrhus would appear. Such potential liberators were now met and defeated abroad before they could ever cross into Italy.

Roman power was also impressed upon local Italian elites more directly in the late-war and post-war periods as part of the typical settlement following reconquest. Local aristocrats were unsympathetically punished, especially those who were held to be the most responsible for the city's decision to revolt. Sentences ranged from the confiscation of property to execution. Thus, for example, over fifty Capuan senators were arrested and executed, as well as an unknown number of aristocrats from other rebellious Campanian cities. The Romans later conducted further trials and handed out additional punishments on a family-by-family basis: some were enslaved or had their property confiscated.[93] Local leaders in rebellious Samnite towns were beheaded.[94] In Taras much of the population was put to the sword or enslaved, while the leaders of the revolt were, according to Livy (27.16.1–9), killed in battle.[95] After he recaptured Locri, Scipio Africanus called a general assembly and chastised the Locrians for rebelling. He then executed the leaders of the revolt and handed over their property to the 'leaders of the other faction' (*alterius factionis principibus*) on account of their remarkable loyalty to Rome.[96] Punishment was even visited upon areas where allied communities remained more or less loyal. As discussed above, the Romans executed an unknown number of Etruscan aristocrats and confiscated their property on the suspicion that they were planning to defect. Similarly, Marcellus executed members of the aristocracy of Nola during the war in order to forestall defection.[97] Executions and confiscations are not mentioned in every account of recapture, but this is not surprising, given the sources' general interest (especially on Livy's part) in playing up Hannibal's supposed cruelty. The frank and unapologetic references that we do have, however, suggest that this sort of treatment of the defeated was typical and justified from a Roman perspective. We must assume that comparably brutal punishments were widely meted out.

Scipio's Locrian settlement is a particularly illustrative case because we hear not only about the punishment of disloyal local aristocrats but also about rewards handed out to local loyalists. The anti-Roman faction

---

[93] Liv. 26.14.6–9, 26.15.7–10, 26.16.5–7, 26.33.1–3, 26.34.1–4; see Chapter 6, pp. 252–3.
[94] Liv. 23.37.12–13; see Chapter 6, p. 254.   [95] See also Chapter 6, pp. 225–6.
[96] Liv. 29.8.1–2.   [97] See Chapter 3, pp. 135–6.

whom Scipio punished must have achieved political dominance early in the war, since Locri had in fact defected. Scipio's settlement fundamentally altered the local political scene by eliminating, or at least weakening, the formerly dominant party, while strengthening their aristocratic rivals. The new ruling party, therefore, would have owed its position, at least partly, to Scipio's administration. Scipio's actions at Locri were surely not an isolated case. Rather, we may plausibly speculate that similar rewards were handed out alongside punishments in many of the formerly rebellious communities. Italian aristocrats who demonstrated their loyalty during the Second Punic War would have been rewarded and their local political positions further strengthened by the Roman post-war settlement.[98] Even when a community did not revolt during the war, the conflict itself was an occasion for local aristocrats to call attention to their loyalty to Rome and, therefore, receive some type of reward or honour,[99] or at least come out ahead after the war. Less loyal factions would have been greatly weakened if not eliminated altogether. This recalls a dynamic that was discussed in Chapter 1: Rome's slow conquest in the fourth and early third centuries had also created both 'winners' and 'losers' among the local ruling aristocracies. Rome's victory in the Second Punic War must have similarly produced winners and losers, relatively speaking, among the local Italian ruling classes. The scope of the Second Punic War in Italy and the widespread allied defections, however, gave the Romans the opportunity to replay this dynamic at a much-accelerated rate compared with its slow unfolding during the initial phase of Roman conquest.

In this way, within a relatively short span of time, the Romans were able to influence and alter the political landscape in communities throughout

---

[98] The Magii family from Capua is a fascinating case. Decius Magius was among the most vocal critics of Hannibal in the days leading up to the Capuan revolt. According to Livy (23.10), Hannibal had him arrested and sent by ship to Carthage, but the ship was blown off course, allowing Decius to escape, eventually to Egypt. Elements of the story may be fanciful, and it appears that Decius remained in or returned to Italy. His great-grandson Minatius Minucius (the great-grandfather of Velleius Paterculus, according to the author) was a leading citizen in Aeculanum who during the Social War personally raised a large body of troops from the Hirpini and helped the Romans retake several cities. Minatius was subsequently rewarded with a special grant of citizenship and a viritane land allotment, and his two sons were both elected to the praetorship (Vell. Pat. 2.16.1–3; see Sumner 1970: 257–61). This family's remarkable history of success is clearly tied up with its displays of loyalty in times of crisis. This explains why Decius escaped the severe Roman punishment visited on many of his aristocratic townsmen. We may speculate that he and possibly his children were rewarded in some way, allowing them to establish themselves in a new city.

[99] The Roman senate publicly honoured Busa of Canusium for her loyalty in providing food and shelter for the survivors of Cannae: Liv. 22.52.7; Chapter 2, pp. 62–3 n. 38. Marcus Anicius of Praeneste, the garrison commander at Casilinum, was honoured with a statue set up in the forum of his home town: Liv. 23.20.1–2; Chapter 3, n. 79.

the peninsula, sometimes radically shaping or reshaping numerous local governing classes. Extensive post-war settlements meant that many local aristocrats (individuals, families or even groupings or 'parties') in cities all through Italy had received some form of Roman support, so their position was bound up closely with Roman favour. The Romans continued to back favoured individuals or factions in the second century. The lack of a major war on Italian soil limited the opportunities for wide-scale intervention, yet local disputes provided some openings. Thus, in 175 or 174 the senate received an embassy from the people of Patavium, whose city had erupted in factional warfare (*certamine factionum*).[100] The senate sent one of the consuls, who quickly suppressed the disturbance. Livy's account suggests that the disturbance was a class struggle,[101] so the consul's settlement may represent the Romans backing a local ruling class against 'the people' or a 'people's party'. One suspects that the situation was rather more complicated. We may speculate that the discord was the product of fighting between rival aristocratic families or factions, and the ambassadors probably represented only one side in the struggle. If so, then the consul probably dealt with the affair by picking one side in the dispute – perhaps the faction represented by the ambassadors – and punishing the rival party.[102] The Patavian affair is clear evidence of Rome's continued backing of local aristocrats after the Second Punic War.[103]

The Roman senate intervened in a series of local land disputes, sometimes on its own initiative and sometimes at the urging of the parties involved. In 168, when the people of Pisa complained to the senate that the Roman colonists at Luna had illegally taken possession of Pisan land, the senate sent a board of five to investigate.[104] In 117 the senate sent the brothers Quintus and Marcus Minucius Rufus to arbitrate between the people of Genua and their subordinate neighbours, the Langenses Viturii. The former apparently had accused the latter of occupying Genuan public lands. We know about the case from a long inscription (*CIL* I².584) recording the judgment of the Minucii, to which we will return shortly. The senate instructed proconsuls

---

[100] For the Patavian affair: Liv. 41.27.3–4. Livy places events in his narrative of 174 but claims that the consul Aemilius was involved, referring probably to M. Aemilus Lepidus (cos. 175). Livy has erred either with respect to the year or the consul's name.

[101] According to Livy (41.27.4), the Patavian ambassadors reported that they could not control the 'madness of the people' (*rabiem gentis*).

[102] The Patavian affair recalls the events in Volsinii in 264; see Chapter 1, pp. 26–7.

[103] Mouritsen 1998: 71 argued that 'we have no examples of Rome actually intervening on behalf of allied nobles in the second century'. Presumably he excluded the case of Patavium because it lay north of the Po River, though this is a clear example of Rome's supporting some or all of the ruling class in an allied town.

[104] Liv. 45.13.10–11.

to fix the boundaries between Ateste and Patavium in 141 or 116,[105] and between Ateste and Vicetia in 135.[106] Q. Fabius Labeo was sent to settle a boundary dispute between Nola and Naples probably sometime after his consulship in 183.[107] The Roman magistrates' decision could have a significant effect on the local landowners, and it is hard to imagine that prior ties between members of the local elite and the responsible Roman magistrate did not result in favorable rulings. Indeed, the difference between arbitration and the granting of favours was potentially negligible. On this point, the Minucii may have been chosen to arbitrate between the Genuans and Langenses Viturii precisely because they had personal ties to the region,[108] and one suspects that their settlement benefited those Genuan elites with whom their family was connected.[109] In this way Romans continued to provide periodic support – rewards and honours, sympathetic judgments, or the like – for members of the local ruling classes throughout the second century. Also, the relatively large number of cases of Roman arbitration in local land disputes may indicate that this sort of intervention became a more frequent practice in the second century.

More generally there was increased interaction between Romans and Italians in the period after the Second Punic War.[110] Thus, we see a deepening and widening of personal connections and relationships between Roman and Italian elites of the sorts that were discussed above (pp. 304–6) in reference to the fourth and third centuries. For example, Livy

---

[105] *CIL* 1².633, 634, 2501; Broughton 1951–2: 1.478, 530.

[106] *CIL* 1².636; Broughton 1951–2: 1.489.

[107] Cic. *Off.* 1.33; Val. Max. 7.3.4; Broughton 1951–2: 1.378. Both Cicero and Valerius Maximus report the same story: Fabius allegedly swindled the Nolans and Neapolitans by convincing both to make concessions and then, once the boundary between the two communities had been fixed, he took the tract of land that was left over and gave it to the Roman people. The precise date of this arbitration is unknown, and it is possible that the Q. Fabius Labeo in question is different from the consul of 183.

[108] J. R. Patterson 2006b: 144; Bispham 2007: 139 n. 111.

[109] The judgment of the Minucii protected Viturian private property and established grazing rights for the Genuans and Vituii. The main part of the judgment involves, however, Genuan state lands supposedly possessed by the Viturii (ll. 13–23) for which rents had to be paid into Genuan treasury (ll. 25–7, 35–6). Any Viturii who were imprisoned because of the land dispute were free (ll.43–4), but the ruling assumes that the Viturii had been justly condemned for wrongs (*ob iniourias*). Overall, it appears that the Genuans received a more favourable ruling in this arbitration. It is tempting to speculate that members of the Genuan aristocracy, perhaps the local commissioners mentioned at the end of the inscription (l. 46), were behind the decision to call in the Romans, figuring that they would come out ahead economically or politically from the conflict's resolution.

[110] So concludes Bispham 2007: 114: '[the Italians] were experiencing a stronger degree of interaction with Rome than they had been used to, both in the form of what we might crudely call interference, and in terms of political, social and economic processes, mediated at the levels of state and individual'.

(42.1.9–10) mentions that *hospitium* between Roman and Italian elite families was already common by 173, as Roman aristocrats would open their homes to Italian elites in whose homes the Romans themselves would stay. In his account of events in 172 Livy (42.17.2–3) mentions a certain Lucius Rammius of Brundisium, who maintained *hospitium* with distinguished men from Rome and other communities, including foreign royalty.[111] Cicero (*Rosc. Am.* 15) mentions that the father of one of his clients, Sextus Roscius, a leading citizen of Ameria in Umbria, maintained *hospitium* and 'private relations and intimacy' with the Metelli, Servilii and Scipiones.[112] The *Pro Roscio* was composed in 80, so it is likely that Sextus Roscius' friendships with Roman *nobiles* had already been established before the Social War. Sallust (*Iug.* 8.1, 40.2) speaks of Roman nobles of the second century who were influential among the allies (*potentes apud socios*) or who had friends (*amicos*) among the Latins and Italian allies. Appian (*B Civ.* 1.38) reports that on the eve of the Social War the senate dispatched individual Roman aristocrats to specific Italian cities with which each man had personal ties of some sort.[113] According to Diodorus Siculus (37.15.2), when the Roman army under Marius faced a Marsic army in 90, the soldiers on both sides recognised many friends and relatives by marriage. If accurate, this anecdote attests to widespread Roman–Italian intermarriage as well as friendships by the time of the Social War.

A number of overlapping factors explain the intensification in contacts between Romans and Italians. Formal *hospitium* was hereditary, so connections made between two aristocrats would be passed on to subsequent generations, potentially perpetuating links between their descendants. Similarly, aristocratic intermarriage could create family alliances that lasted for generations. Thus, the original contract between two individuals, which might effectively link two families, could yield an ever-widening circle of descendants who shared some bond. Occasional grants of Roman citizenship to individuals or groups of Italian allies opened the door for new intermarriage links between Roman and Italian elites.[114] Meanwhile,

---

[111] He is called Erennios (Ἐρέννιος) by Appian (*Mac.* 11.7–8), and appears to be the same individual as Gaios Dazoupos Rennios of Brundisium (Γάιος Δάζουπος Ῥέννιος Βρενεσινός) mentioned in an inscription found at Dodona (Cauer² no. 247); see Roberts 1881: 113–15; Giles 1887: 170.

[112] *Nam cum Metellis, Serviliis, Scipionibus erat ei non modo hospitium verum etiam domesticus usus et consuetudo.*

[113] ὡς δ'ἐπύθοντο, περιέπεμπον ἐς τὰς πόλεις ἀπὸ σφῶν τοὺς ἑκάστοις μάλιστα ἐπιτηδείους, ἀφανῶς τὰ γιγνόμενα ἐξετάζειν ('When they [the Romans] heard tell, they sent around into the cities those from their own number the most suitable to each city, to inquire secretly into the things taking place').

[114] Such grants were no doubt rare, but perhaps more frequent than the few surviving references imply. In 101 Marius offered citizenship to two cohorts of allied soldiers from Camerinum, and in

Italian communities remained, it seems, generally open to outsiders, and Rome in particular appears to have received a large number of immigrants during the second century despite restrictions placed on immigration and the periodic expulsion of foreigners.[115] The extension of the *ager Romanus* and the foundation of new colonies in further corners of the peninsula increased the opportunities for personal contact and interaction between allies and Roman or Latin citizens. Roman roads, although built originally for military purposes, facilitated travel and communications between Rome and communities throughout Italy,[116] while the overall prevailing peaceful conditions in the peninsula further encouraged movement between communities. The Italians continued to bear a significant military burden in the second century, fighting in Rome's overseas wars. The military also functioned, therefore, as a potential locus for Roman and Italian interaction, especially at the elite level.[117] Overall, there was great

---

100 a colonial law (the *lex Appuleia*) authorised Marius to enfranchise three settlers in each of the citizen colonies to be founded (i.e. to enrol non-Romans in the colony whereby they would gain citizenship): Cic. *Balb.* 44, 46; Val. Max. 5.2.8; Cuff 1975; Mouritsen 1998: 90. In 216 the senate offered Roman citizenship to the Praenestine soldiers who had shown valour at Casilinum, but the offer was turned down for other rewards: Liv. 23.20.2. In 189–188, the people of Campania had their citizenship restored after appealing to the senate: Liv. 38.36.5–6, 39.3.4, 41.9.9. Through the patronage of the Fulvii, the poet Ennius obtained a grant of citizenship in 184, probably being enrolled in one of the citizen colonies founded that year: Cic. *Brut.* 79, *Arch.* 22, *De or.* 3.168; Liv. 39.54.16; Piper 1987: 39–40. The *lex Acilia* of 111 gave non-Romans who successfully prosecuted a Roman magistrate for extortion the option of obtaining Roman citizenship (see below, p. 322). It is commonly held that Latin citizens were granted the right to obtain Roman citizenship *per magistratum* in 124 (for example: Tibiletti 1953; Piper 1988; Keaveney 2005: 84–5) or at a later date before the Social War (Sherwin-White 1973: 111–12). Some scholars argue, however, that this right dates to the mid first century BC or even later (for example: Bradeen 1959; Galsterer 1976: 93–100; Mouritsen 1998: 99–108).

[115] Livy (39.3.4–6, 41.8.7–12) reports that the senate responded positively to two separate appeals (in 187 and 177) by the Latin colonies, who expressed concern that too many Latin citizens were moving to Rome in order to become Roman citizens under their right of *migratio*. In both cases the Romans imposed regulations to control the flow of Latin immigrants to the city. If Livy is to be believed, the Romans deported 12,000 Latins in 187. The Romans also passed a law *c.* 125 that was aimed more generally at expelling foreigners from the city: Cic. *Brut.* 109, *Off.* 3.47; Festus p. 388 L. This last expulsion was probably motivated by politics more than anything else. Still, it suggests at least that the Romans believed their city contained many foreigners. It strikes me as too sceptical to argue that these sentiments were based entirely on perception without any reflection of reality, so we must assume that Rome continued to receive a visible number of outsiders.

[116] Wiseman 1971: 24–32.

[117] Pfeilschifter 2007 makes a strong case against the army as an agent for significant integration and Romanisation of Italy, and we should not exaggerate the degree to which it encouraged Roman and Italian interaction. Still, there must have been some interaction between Romans and non-Romans serving together, and allied elites who served as unit commanders probably had contact with Roman aristocrats. Consider the case of T. Turpilius Silanus (see Sall. *Iug.* 66.3–4, 67.3, 69.4; Plut. *Marc.* 8; App. *Numidica* 3). The consul Metellus placed Turpilius, a Latin citizen, in command of the garrison at Vaca during the Jugurthine War. Plutarch reports that Turpilius and Metellus were guest-friends, as their fathers had been. This is a clear example

potential for Roman and Italian aristocratic interaction in the century following the Second Punic War.

Local elites had strong incentives to take advantage of conditions that favoured interaction between Roman and Italian aristocrats. Put simply, it behoved Italian aristocrats to build up or strengthen relations with powerful Roman *nobiles*. As we have seen, Roman aristocrats could offer local elite friends direct and indirect political advantages: financial backing, military support, honours and gifts of symbolic value, favourable judgments and settlements, advocacy in Rome or other acts that benefited the local contact or his community. A local aristocrat who had received Roman backing in the past, perhaps as part of the post-war settlement of his community, might have felt that his local standing was intertwined with Roman favour, and he would have sought to reinforce pre-existing connections in order to safeguard his position. Local aristocrats who had 'lost out' after the Second Punic War may have harboured resentment against their local political rivals and the Romans. But Rome's dominance could not be ignored, and they and their descendants would have found it advantageous to reconcile themselves to the political situation and forge stronger ties with the Roman aristocracy. I am not arguing that local aristocrats sought closer ties with Rome because they were drawn to Roman culture, or in order to 'become Roman' or to achieve greater political integration, though individual Italians may have valued and sought Roman citizenship for any number of reasons. Rather, they were motivated by political expediency, in large part to gain political advantages at the local level. Italian aristocrats stood to benefit from their relations with the Roman elite within the competitive political milieus of their own communities.

The same factors no doubt encouraged more intensive interrelations among various local ruling classes, and thus Italian aristocrats increasingly forged personal ties with their counterparts in other Italian communities. Having prestigious associates, whether they were friends, clients, *hospites*, family members or dependants, was itself a source of prestige and a marker of elite status for an Italian aristocrat, regardless of where such friends came from: his own community, Rome, a neighbouring city or a far-off land. Thus, Rammius of Brundisium cultivated personal relations for political gain with aristocrats from Rome, from cities in the Greek East, and

---

of the intersection of aristocratic interaction and military service extending over multiple generations. Although Turpilius and Metellus had a pre-existing relationship, military service could sometimes lead to the creation of new friendships. Of course, such relationships did not always turn out well for the subordinate party: Turpilius was flogged and executed for cowardice.

presumably from other Italian states.[118] Cicero's *Pro Cluentio* illustrates not only the sorts of complex and far-ranging aristocratic interconnections that must have become more and more common after the Second Punic War, but also the mechanisms that promoted them. Cicero's client Aulus Cluentius Habitus was from Larinum in southern Abruzzo (near Apulia), the son of a prominent local citizen of the same name. The younger Cluentius had been accused of poisoning his stepfather, Oppianicus the Elder; the charges were brought by his stepbrother, Oppianicus the Younger, who was married to a woman from Teanum Apulum, about thirty kilometres to the south of Larinum. Oppianicus had two close friends (*familiarissime*), the brothers Gaius and Lucius Fabricius, who came from Aletrium, only about seventy kilometres from Rome. Cicero owned property in Aletrium, and the two brothers had previously come to his house in Rome and appealed to him personally as a neighbour. Moreover, Cicero had once defended the freedman client of the Fabricii brothers in an unrelated case. We also learn that the elder Cluentius had secured the patronage of a Roman senator, Marius Babrius. We see in this case a variety of overlapping personal connections stretching over generations and involving individuals from neighbouring and distant communities.[119] I suspect that the increasing frequency of such connections at the elite level, over time, wore down some of the old grudges between Italian communities and ultimately helped to bring an end to the enduring interstate rivalries that still exerted influence during the Second Punic War, an idea that we will return to later in this chapter (pp. 327–9).

Rome emerged from the war as a superpower relative to the various communities in Italy. Regarding relations at the level of both state and individual, 'there seems to be little doubt that Rome bulked larger on the horizon for them than any of their immediate neighbours'.[120] The Italians grew more accustomed to dealing with Romans in various contexts on multiple levels.

---

[118] Liv. 42.17.3–5. Livy states that Rammius was motivated to meet Perseus out of 'hope for a more intimate friendship and after that fortune' (*spem amicitiae interioris inde fortunae*). In this context 'fortune' (*fortuna*) might mean anything from money or property to status, rank or position. Indeed, there was little practical difference between political rewards (some sort of symbolic title or honour, for example) and financial benefits, since wealth and politics were so closely bound together.

[119] This speech obviously post-dates the Social War, after which the extension of citizenship no doubt made such interrelations easier. It is not clear, for example, whether Oppianicus could have married a woman from another town in the days before every Italian possessed the right of *conubium* through Roman citizenship. At the same time, the speech illustrates how far-ranging and complex aristocratic links could be. Presumably there existed similar clusters of contacts throughout Italy in the period before the Social War.

[120] Keaveney 2005: 22.

Meanwhile, Rome's widespread interference in local affairs during the Second Punic War and its increasingly dominant position after the war gave rise to an even greater sense of entitlement vis-à-vis the other Italian communities.

As discussed in Chapter 1, the Romans probably conceived of Italy as their exclusive sphere of influence, a coherent whole defined against 'outsiders', as early as the first part of the third century. This notion further crystallised during the second century.[121] Thus, according to Polybius (30.19.6–8), when the Roman senate learned that Eumenes II of Pergamum had landed in Brundisium (in 167) on his way to Rome to defend himself, a quaestor was sent to meet him there, who was instructed to ask Eumenes if he needed anything from the senate. If the king responded that he did not require anything, the quaestor was to order him to depart from Italy (ἐκ τῆς Ἰταλίας) as soon as possible. If Polybius' account is accurate, a relatively low-ranking Roman magistrate was sent to a city that technically lay outside the *ager Romanus*, where he commanded a foreign head of state to vacate the Italian peninsula. Meanwhile, contemporary Romans appear to have been interested in further defining 'Italy' as a geographic, historical and cultural concept. Thus, Cato the Elder's *Origines*, begun in 167, purported to detail the history of each and every Italian community. The *lex Agraria* (111)[122] repeatedly invokes the term *terra Italia* and differentiates between lands that are located *in terra Italia* and those *extra terra Italia*.[123]

Time and again, the senate displayed a willingness to extend its authority over the Italian allies in certain circumstances and to regulate the peninsula whenever they saw fit, regardless of the legal status of the communities involved. For example, on several occasions the senate sent praetors or propraetors to regions of Italy that were not war zones on what we might call 'policing activities'. These included the suppression of slave uprisings in Etruria (196), Apulia (185 and 184) and Campania (104), and taking over investigation into the Bacchanalia from the consuls once the perceived crisis had passed (184 and 181).[124] Further evidence of senatorial

---

[121] Williams 2001: 95–8.   [122] *CIL* 1².585.

[123] See for example lines 49–50. See also *CIL* 1².638, the milestone set up near the Forum Popillii in Lucania (see above, n. 86). The dedicator claims to have captured 917 'runaway slaves of the Italians' (*fugiteivos Italicorum*) when he was praetor in Sicily and returned them to their owners. The precise meaning of *Italici* is uncertain, but its use indicates the existence of some sort of Roman concept of 'Italians'.

[124] Bacchanalia investigations: Liv. 39.41.6–7, 40.19.9–10, 40.35.8–9; investigations into brigandage by shepherds or slaves or both in Apulia: Liv. 39.29.8 (7,000 men condemned), 39.41.6; slave revolt in Etruria: Liv. 33.36.1–3; slave revolt in Campania: Diod. 36.2. Other praetorian commands include 'to hold Apulia and the Bruttians' (*ad Apuliam Bruttiosque obtinendos*) and 'against the Etruscans' (*in Tuscos*) in 190: Liv. 37.2.6, 9; both commands prorogued in 189: Liv. 37.50.13; the *praetor urbanus* suppressed a slave revolt in Latium in 198: Liv. 32.26.4–18; Zon. 9.16.

interference in allied internal affairs is provided by the so-called *senatus consultum de Bacchanalibus* (186),[125] which records a variety of regulations placed on the worship of Bacchus. According to the preamble to the edict, the senate's regulations governed the *foideratei*.[126] Various attempts have been made to identify the *foideratei*, but the most straightforward explanation is that the term refers to those who were bound to Rome by treaties, the *socii*.[127] If so, then the edict represents an attempt by the Roman senate to assert its authority more widely within Italy by regulating cult practice among non-Romans.[128] The *lex Acilia* (123 or 122)[129] provides clearer evidence of the senate's interference in local affairs. According to the law, non-Romans who successfully prosecuted a Roman magistrate for extortion were given the choice of Roman citizenship and exemption from military service, or the right of *provocatio*, exemption from military service and exemption from 'local duties *in his own city*'.[130] Taken with the cases of Roman arbitration that were discussed above, a clear picture emerges: the senate was increasingly comfortable with exercising authority over the Italian peninsula as if it were Rome's exclusive realm, regardless of the citizenship status of the Italian communities with which it dealt.

At the same time, Roman intervention in local affairs and the enormous power imbalance between Rome and the other individual Italian communities produced a counter-current within the expansion of interconnections between Roman and Italian aristocrats. Overall, members of the Roman ruling class were growing more powerful than their Italian counterparts. Thus, Italian aristocrats might hope to receive favours and benefits from their associations with Roman *nobiles*, but they could offer fewer tangible advantages to their Roman friends in return.[131] Thus, although they

[125] *CIL* 1².581 = *ILLRP* 511; see Liv. 39.8–19.

[126] Lines 2–3: *De Bacanalibus quei foideratei | esent, ita exdeicendum censuere ...* ('Concerning the Bacchanales who are *foideratei*, [the senate] resolved that it must be decreed as follows ...').

[127] Thus for example Gruen 1990: 37 n. 11; Bispham 2007: 116–23; contra the argument that *foideratei* should be interpreted as 'members of the cult' rather than 'allies': Rudolph 1935: 162; Fronza 1946/7: 214–15; Galsterer 1976: 169; Mouritsen 1998: 53–4; Rich 2008: 65–6. That *foideratei* should include allies perhaps finds support in Livy's version of events, which reports (39.14.7–8, 39.17.4) that edicts were sent out through all Italy (*per totam Italiam*) to regulate the cult. On Roman treaties in general, see Chapter 1, n. 51.

[128] Gruen 1990; contra Mouritsen 1998: 52–7 and now Rich 2008: 65–6, who argue that the edicts governed only individuals residing on *ager Romanus*.

[129] *CIL* 1².583.

[130] Line 79: *munerisque poplici in su[a quoiusque ceiv]itate* (following the line numbering and editing used by E. H. Warmington (ed.), *Remains of Old Latin IV: Archaic Roman Inscriptions*, Loeb Classical Library vol. 359, no. 59).

[131] Roman *nobiles* may have valued having many aristocratic connections, since having prominent friends and relatives was presumably a source of prestige and a marker of status for Roman as well as for Italian elites.

theoretically shared the same social rank, local aristocrats found themselves in an increasingly subordinate position vis-à-vis their Roman counterparts. By the end of the second century many members of the Italian
elite were essentially clients of the great Roman noble houses.[132] This situation increased the potential for unfulfilled mutual expectations, leading
to feelings of frustration and to resentment and heightened tensions. Livy
(42.1) reports an early example: in 173, the consul L. Postumius Albinus
was on his way to Praeneste and sent word ahead that the local magistrates
were to come out to greet him formally, and he insisted on being housed
and entertained at public expense. He made these high-handed demands
because he was angry with the Praenestines for failing to show him appropriate respect when previously, as a *privatus,* he had gone to sacrifice at
the temple of Fortuna.[133] The sources record other abuses and imperious
behaviour by Roman aristocrats, and even a few cases would have served
to remind the Italian elite of their inferior and dependent status.[134]

It is illuminating to read the revolt of Fregellae (c. 125) in the context of
the foregoing discussions. Most of details of the Fregellan affair have been
lost, but we do know that the Latin colony was destroyed by the praetor L. Opimius, who earned neither a military triumph nor an ovation
for his achievement.[135] Praetors or propraetors were assigned a number of
policing tasks in Italy during the second century, as was discussed above
(pp. 321–2), so the choice of Opimius to lead the campaign is revealing
of Rome's opinion of the affair. Compare this with Rome's dealing with
another isolated revolt of a small community: Falerii in 241. In this case,
the senate sent both consuls for that year to suppress the disturbance, and
both celebrated triumphs upon their successful return.[136] The Faliscan
War was thus promoted as a major operation against an independent

---

[132] For the absorption of *hospitium* into patron-clientage: Badian 1958: 11–12, 154; Wiseman 1971: 34–7; Nicols 1980: 549.

[133] Livy (42.1.12) condemns Postumius for abusing his consular authority, claiming that this epi-sode set a precedent for future abuses by Roman magistrates, which continued to grow more burdensome for the Italians. That Postumius was the first magistrate to behave in this way is doubtful. Still, the story assumes that commonplace abuses were believable to Livy's audience.

[134] For various versions of the view that Romans treated the Italian allies with increasing arrogance, see McDonald 1944; Harris 1971: 105–13; Sherwin-White 1973: 104–8, 127–9; David 1996: 140–5; Keaveney 2005: 31–2. The view has been rejected by Galsterer 1976: 153–71, whose more moder-ate tone is followed by Bispham 2007: 131–60. Still, Bispham admits: 'There were disgraceful incidents, but they were not routine, and we cannot extrapolate to posit "background noise" of Roman brutality. Yet reality is one thing, perception of reality is another. Only a few high-profile incidents are needed to create the impression of a widespread problem, and those living under the shadow of potential harsh treatment do not often allow themselves the luxury of histo-rians' detachment and statistical comforts' (p. 157).

[135] Liv. *Per.* 60; Vell. Pat. 2.6.4; Val. Max. 2.8.4; see Broughton 1951–2: 1.510 for further references.

[136] See Chapter 1, pp. 26–7.

foreign state that warranted the attention of Rome's highest elected magistrates *cum imperio*. Somewhat more than a century later, however, the suppression of Fregellae fell to a single magistrate of lesser rank. By sending a praetor to take care of the Fregellan revolt, the Romans treated it as a relatively minor situation, even an internal matter.[137] That the Fregellans chose to rebel and risk the almost certain obliteration of their community hints at the level of Italian disaffection in the generation before the Social War.

It is to the Social War that we now turn, for this conflict reveals how interstate relations in Italy had been transformed since, and because of, the Second Punic War. The causes of the Social War have been widely debated,[138] but whatever were the origins of the conflict, it is clear that the Italians' decision to revolt was motivated by widespread resentment and underlying disaffection. Various Roman land-reform schemes proposed and/or put in motion since the tribunate of Tiberius Gracchus threatened to be very disruptive and were probably the cause of much allied concern. More debatable is how Italian desires to obtain Roman citizenship fit into the picture, namely whether the Italians revolted in order to gain citizenship or out of frustration at Rome's reluctance to extend enfranchisement.[139] These questions cannot be resolved here, but fortunately they do not bear significantly on the arguments in this section. Why the Italians revolted is

---

[137] Brennan 2000: 220–1 finds it striking that a praetor rather than a consul was assigned to take care of this 'major affair', ultimately concluding that 'the exact *provincia* which allowed for this man's appointment against Fregellae must remain one of the numerous mysteries of this ill-attested period'. Yet the mystery dissolves if we recognise that the Fregellan situation, although a serious matter and involving a difficult siege, was not a 'major affair' worthy of consular attention. Opimius tried to play up the seriousness of the campaign in order to be awarded a triumph. His request for triumph was denied, however, no doubt out of typical aristocratic competition, but also because the enemy was an allied state (Val. Max. 2.8.4). This is consistent with my suggestion that by the later second century Italy was deemed a praetorian prerogative in most cases, including the suppression of a rebellious allied city.

[138] See, for example, Salmon 1962; Brunt 1965; Badian 1970–1; Sherwin-White 1973: 134–49; Nagle 1973; Gabba: 1994: 104–13; David 1996: 40–56; Mouritsen 1998; Pobjoy 2000; Keaveney 2005: 47–98. Most scholars hold that Italians desired Roman citizenship in order to obtain economic benefits (the right of *commercium*), political advancement within the Roman system or protection from abuses (the right of *provocatio*). In this view, the Social War was fought either to force the Romans to grant these rights or out of frustration at the Romans' refusal to share these privileges more widely. Mouritsen and Pobjoy argue, however, that the Italians were motivated by the desire for freedom from Roman domination rather than out of (frustrated) aspirations to obtain Roman citizenship.

[139] See above, n. 138. Mouritsen 1998 presents a fascinating revisionist analysis of the causes of the Social War, which suggests that the emphasis on the Italians' alleged desire for Roman citizenship is a teleological historiographic construct whose modern roots can be traced to Mommsen and other scholars writing in the age of nineteenth-century nationalism. I am sympathetic to some, but not all, of Mouritsen's positions, especially his caution against confusing the outcome of the Social War (enfranchisement of the defeated Italians) with its possible causes.

less relevant to the present discussion than how they behaved immediately leading up to the Social War and during its early stages.

According to Appian (*B Civ.* 1.38), when the Romans heard about Italian disaffection in 91, they sent men into various cities with which each was acquainted in order to find out what was going on. One of these men witnessed suspicious activity (a hostage exchange) in Asculum and reported it to a certain Quintus Servilius, a praetor who held a command in the area, perhaps with some sort of special *imperium*.[140] Appian claims that praetors had been sent to various regions in Italy, and, if this is an accurate report, then the Romans clearly had strong suspicions that something serious was afoot. The arrival of Roman magistrates *cum imperio* might have heightened local tensions. Servilius went to Asculum, presumably to investigate, and proceeded to treat the locals abusively. The Asculans figured that the Italians' plans had been discovered so they killed Servilius, his legate Fonteius and other Roman citizens who happened to be in the town. The violence in Asculum triggered revolts among neighbouring communities, and soon widespread defections erupted in Campania, Apulia, Lucania, the central Apennines including the Marsi, Paeligni, Hirpini and Samnites, and the Adriatic coast including the Picentes, Vestini, Marrucini and Frentani (*B Civ.* 1.39).[141] The Umbrians and Etruscans were eager to revolt in the following year (90) – indeed, they may have briefly defected[142] – but the Romans won back their loyalty by offering them citizenship (*B Civ.* 1.49). Some Cisalpine Gauls also joined the Italian cause (*B Civ.* 1.50). The geographic scope of the defections rivalled, if not exceeded, that of the Second Punic War: revolts broke out in areas that had been largely or entirely loyal during the war with Hannibal, and, perhaps most surprisingly, a Latin colony (Venusia) was among the first cities to defect. The extent of the defections indicates the depth of allied disaffection and desperation.

Possibly even more striking is the level of coordination and planning on the part of the Italians. To be sure, the precise sequence of events in 91 has a somewhat *ad hoc* and contingent feel: Servilius' specific actions sparked local resentment, and the panicked and angry response of the people of Asculum set off a domino effect. Despite the fact that the Asculans

---

[140] Vell. Pat. 2.12.6; Liv. *Per.* 72; App. *B Civ.* 1.38; Diod. Sic. 37.13.2; Brennan 2000: 371–2.

[141] On the outbreak of the war, see also Diod. Sic. 37.2.1–5, 37.13.1–2; Liv. *Per.* 71, 72; Vell. Pat. 2.15; Flor. 2.6; Just. *Epit.* 38.4.13; Obsequens 114–15; see Salmon 1959: 159–69; Gabba 1994: 114–15; Mouritsen 1998: 129–51 (with caution).

[142] Appian (*B Civ.* 1.49–50) states that the Etruscans and Umbrians were tempted to revolt, but decided against it when the Romans passed the *lex Iulia*. Other sources, however, report that they actually revolted but were quickly defeated: Liv. *Per.* 74; Oros. 5.18.17; Flor. 2.6.5–6. Mouritsen 1998: 153–6 argues that Appian has distorted the chronology and therefore inverted the cause-and-effect relationship between the *lex Iulia* and the aborted Etruscan-Umbrian revolt.

appear to have jumped the gun, however, we should not lose sight of the Italians' very deliberate and premeditated activity. According to Appian (*B Civ.* 1.38), the Italians had resolved ahead of time to revolt in order to achieve their political ends, whatever we think those goals to have been. They had also conducted secret diplomacy and exchanged hostages with each other in order to guarantee future good faith before the revolts broke out. Once the war started, the Italians quickly raised a large field army and had troops ready to guard rebellious cities from Roman reprisals (*B Civ.* 1.39) – the Italians clearly remembered lessons from the Second Punic War. Most importantly, they formed some sort of league under the name Italia, whose capital was Corfinum (renamed Italica). The league had a deliberative body of 500 aristocratic members and a smaller war council; fourteen annual magistrates were chosen, two 'consuls' and twelve 'praetors,' to command the Italian armies;[143] money was minted bearing the league's name in either Latin (*Italia*) or Oscan (*Viteliú* or *Vítelliú*).[144] These activities followed almost immediately upon the outbreak of war, if we are to believe our literary sources, but this sort of organisation must have taken significant time and effort. The plans for setting up the league and conducting the war, which appear to have been rather complex, must have been well in place before the hostilities began.

It is telling that most of the communities that revolted during the Social War tended to do so swiftly and readily after the Asculan riots. It is true that some Italians were compelled to defect: a rebel army under Gaius Papius plundered southern Campania and thus frightened Nuceria and the surrounding towns into submission, while Gaius Vidacilius besieged towns in Apulia that did not willingly join the Italian cause.[145] The Italians attacked or besieged with varying degrees of success colonies and other allied cities that had remained loyal to Rome, such as Aesernia, Acerrae, Pinna, Salernum, Stabiae and Surrentum.[146] Yet the majority of the rebel communities were not

---

[143] App. *B Civ.* 1.38; Diod. Sic. 37.2.4–7; Strab. 5.4.2; Vell. Pat. 2.16.4. Mouritsen 1998: 139–40 argues that 'this federal structure represented a clear alternative to the Roman system', one that demonstrated 'well thought-out political ideals, which differed greatly from that of the centralized Roman state'. I agree with Pobjoy's (2000: 192) assessment that our knowledge of the short-lived state of Italia is too sparse to make such an evaluation. Still, that the rebel Italians organised themselves into a state with any sort of political identity is remarkable.

[144] Pobjoy 2000: 198–205. See also *CIL* 9.6086 = I².848 = *ILLRP* 1089, which is a sling bullet found near Asculum, bearing the inscription 'ITALI | T(itus) | LAF(renius) PR(aetor).' Titus Lafranius was one of the rebel generals, and the use of the term '*Itali*' for the rebel soldiers 'suggests that they were being represented (and perhaps representing themselves) as possessing a unified identity' (Pobjoy 2000: 191).

[145] App. *B Civ.* 1.42; contra Mouritsen 1998: 131 n. 2, who argues that Nuceria 'seems to have joined the revolt without hesitation'.

[146] App. *B Civ.* 1.41–2; Diod. Sic. 37.19–21.

forced to defect, and many of them revolted before the Italians had achieved any notable battlefield successes, at least if the patchy narrative sources can be trusted. Indeed, some cities rebelled despite unfavourable military circumstances: Nola, for example, went over to Gaius Papius in spite of being occupied by a Roman garrison.[147] There was neither an outside balancer such as Hannibal or Pyrrhus, nor a single major internal power such as Taras or Capua, around which a wider rebellion might gain momentum.[148] Nor did the Italians wait on the sidelines for the Romans to lose a series of major battles before they rebelled, as they had done during the Second Punic War. In other words, the revolts of the Social War were not primarily the product of a bandwagon effect. Rather, they show a large number of communities located throughout the Italian peninsula behaving proactively and cooperating to achieve a common goal, the defeat of Rome.[149]

This level of cooperation suggests, I believe, that the local interstate rivalries that plagued Hannibal had largely faded in the century following the Roman reconquest of Italy. Patterns of Italian loyalty during the Social War lend support to this contention. For example, Canusium in Apulia was a rebel stronghold and nearby Salapia also revolted. Yet Salapia tended historically to align with Arpi against Arpi's regional rival Canusium.[150] The disposition of Apulian cities during the Social War suggests that there had been at least a partial breakdown in older patterns of regional alliances and rivalries. A similar development is visible for the cities of Campania. Thus, Nuceria had formerly been one of the chief cities in southern Campania, dominating Stabiae, Surrentum, Pompeii and Herculaneum.[151] Nuceria and nearby cities, including Stabiae and Surrentum, remained loyal during the Social War until they were captured by the rebels. Pompeii, however, was among the most prominent of the rebel communities.[152] More intriguing, perhaps, is the case of Nola and Naples, two cities with a very

---

[147] App. *B Civ.* 1.42.

[148] The Italians did solicit military aid from Mithridates, but only after the tide of the war had turned decidedly in Rome's favour and the Italian cause appeared desperate. More to the point, even this initiative came from the Italians: they contacted Mithridates, not the other way around. In general, the Italian rebellion spread quickly and, on the whole, spontaneously. See Diod. Sic. 37.2.11; Ath. 5.213c (= Poseidonius, *FGrH* 87 fr. 37).

[149] That they shared a common strategic/political goal leaves open the possibility that the initial motives of individual groups varied. Some may have desired from the start to establish a counterstate in order to be free from Roman dominion, while others may have been frustrated at being blocked from greater inclusion in the Roman system.

[150] See Chapter 2, pp. 85–91 and Table 1. It is possible that Salapia was one of the unnamed Apulian cities that was forced to revolt by Gaius Vidacilius: App. *B Civ.* 1.42. Gaius Cosconius' violent recapture of Salapia suggests, however, that the city had willingly joined the revolt: App. *B Civ.* 1.52; Diod. Sic. 37.2.8–9.

[151] See Chapter 3, pp. 145–6.

[152] Pompeii is identified separately as one of the first communities to defect (App. *B Civ.* 1.39), and it was probably the base of rebel operations in Campania, at least until Nola was betrayed to the

long history of cooperation and close relations.[153] Naples remained loyal to
Rome during the Social War, while Nola willingly joined the Italians and
was one of the last rebel cities to fall.[154] Moreover, Nola and Naples had
been involved in some sort of territorial dispute during the second century,
which the Roman senate sent Q. Fabius Labeo to settle.[155] What appears
to have happened in Campania during the second century is the erosion
of some long-standing local interstate bonds, and this suggests that traditional rivalries within the region also probably weakened. This does not
mean that local interstate tensions completely disappeared, and indeed the
squabble between Nola and Naples indicates that new tensions might arise
between former allies. At the same time, the powerful interstate rivalries
that were discussed in Chapters 2 to 5 do not seem to have come into play
during the Social War.[156] Through a variety of mechanisms and over time
the Romans had blunted some of the Italians' fiercest competitive tendencies, which had hamstrung Hannibal during the Second Punic War.

I am not arguing in this section that the Social War marks the appearance of a strong pan-Italian cultural or ethnic identity, and it certainly
does not reveal any underlying sense of Roman–Italian unity. The rebels'
self-identification with terms such as *Italia*, *Itali* and *Víteliú/Vítelliú* does
indicate the emergence of at least some sort of common political identity,
though the Augustan ideal of *tota Italia* was still a long way in the future,
if in fact it was ever fully realised. Nor am I arguing that local and contingent factors did not continue to have a strong influence on state behaviour
during the Social War. The decision to revolt was not to be taken lightly,
and it is doubtful that local ruling classes were uniform in their opinion
as to which was the best course to follow.[157] The fact that neighbouring
cities within the same geographic region reacted differently to the events
at Asculum suggests that the decision to revolt or to remain loyal might
hinge on specific circumstances. All the same, however, I believe that the

---

rebels (App. *B Civ.* 1.42). The town suffered a brutal siege by Sulla and was later refounded as a
Sullan veteran colony: App. *B Civ.* 50.

[153] See Chapter 3, pp. 139–43.

[154] As noted above, the people of Nola betrayed a large Roman garrison and handed their city over
to one of the Italians' regional commanders; they also executed a Roman praetor, L. Postumius,
who was apparently in charge of the garrison (App. *B Civ.* 1.42; Liv. *Per.* 73). It was one of the last
rebel cities to fall (Diod. Sic. 37.2.11), and it too received a Sullan veteran colony after the war.

[155] See above, n. 107.

[156] Not a single Italiote Greek city rebelled, as far as we know, so the rivalries between Rhegion and
Locri (see Chapter 4, pp. 183–4) and Thurii and Taras (Chapter 5, pp. 225–7) did not come into
play. Diodorus (37.2.13–14) reports that rebels tried to seize Rhegion but were prevented by the
Roman governor of Sicily. The strategic connection between Rhegion and Sicily recalls discussions in Chapter 4 (pp. 184–5) and Chapter 6 (p. 277).

[157] Gabba 1994: 115–18. For example, the people of Pinna (a town of the Vestini) appear to have
been divided: the city remained in the hands of loyalists, but rebels (including presumably some

outbreak of the Social War and its opening stages indicate a remarkable shift in Italian attitude. The Italian states that decided to revolt had been able to organise, plan, coordinate themselves and work together towards a common purpose to a remarkably high degree compared with how disunited the rebellious communities were in the Second Punic War. Indeed, it would have been extremely difficult for Hannibal to achieve the same level of cooperation from such a broad cross-section of Italian communities given their highly competitive and mutually mistrusting nature. Yet much had changed in the long century between the Second Punic War and the Social War, and Italy was a very different interstate environment *circa* 90 BC than it was on the eve of Hannibal's march across the Alps.

EPILOGUE

Somewhere in the vicinity of Croton, sometime in the late summer or early fall of 203, Hannibal boarded a ship and departed for Africa. He had spent fifteen years in Italy, at that point one-third of his life and half of his adulthood. He would never return. What was he thinking as he looked back at the shores of Bruttium receding behind him? Did he blame the gods? Did he reproach the Carthaginian government for failing to support his war effort adequately? Did he curse himself for not attacking Rome when he had the chance, while his soldiers were still bloodstained from the battle of Cannae? This is what Livy (30.20.1–9) tells us. Even though his story is fictitious, the scene may well capture the moment. For the laments of Livy's Hannibal evoke the frustrating reality of his long and difficult struggle in Italy. It had begun so auspiciously but now culminated not in a spectacular clash of arms but rather with his unceremonious recall to Africa.

Africa would provide the setting for the war's denouement. The signature event of the Italian theatre occurred thirteen years prior, near the beginning of the war, on the plains of Apulia. It was here that Hannibal had won his most famous victory. This victory in turn unleashed centrifugal forces that had characterised Italian relations over the *longue durée*. He possessed neither the military resources nor the time to overcome the disuniting tendencies – the local rivalries, mutual hostilities, mistrust, factionalism, and so on – that surfaced when he temporarily broke Rome's grip on the peninsula. After the war Hannibal still held fast to the view that Rome could only be defeated in Italy, reports Livy (36.7). The assessment is sound, whether it belongs to Livy or Hannibal. Could he have won?

Pinnans) held some of the children of the loyalists hostage and threatened to kill them if the city was not handed over: Diod. Sic. 37.19.3–21.1.

Should he have marched on Rome? Would reinforcements from Carthage have made any difference? Was there any way he could have overcome the local conditions, especially the mistrust, hostility and rivalry between Italian communities that compromised his strategy? We will never know for sure, though in retrospect it seems clear that his chances were slim.

Hannibal's experiences in Italy were painfully ironic. He planned to defeat the Romans in battle and cause massive disruptions in the complex web of bilateral alliances binding the Italian communities to Rome. He succeeded, but in so doing created a new set of strategic conditions that he could not control and that ultimately contributed to his defeat. He had hoped to alter radically the balance of power in Italy and the western Mediterranean, and he succeeded in this as well, yet the outcome was not what he had envisioned. For Rome emerged, albeit after fifteen long and trying years, even more powerful than before, both in relation to the Italian allies and in the broader Mediterranean context. When he had descended the Alps in 218, he had found a collection of fiercely independent and competitive polities bound under Roman hegemony. By the time he left Croton in 203, he had cleared the way for a more thorough Roman (re)conquest of the peninsula, accelerating processes and mechanisms by which the Italians were attached to Rome at both the state and individual level. His defeat paved the way for Rome's conquest of the Mediterranean and, ultimately, the establishment of Roman 'global' supremacy that would endure for centuries. One wonders if the aging Hannibal, living in exile in the Hellenistic world, pondered the coming of Rome. If so, did he fully appreciate the pivotal role that he had played in the transformation of interstate relations both within and beyond Italy?

And what of the communities of southern Italy, which have been the focus of this book? Some had remained loyal throughout the Second Punic War. Many more defected. They were all reconquered, sometimes with ease, sometimes after putting up stiff and occasionally lengthy resistance. A few even managed to hold out until after Hannibal had quit Italy. All of these communities, both loyal and disloyal, felt the effects of the war. In the wake of the battle of Cannae, their ruling classes must have known that whatever path they decided upon would have serious consequences for their own political futures. But surely they had no idea that their specific histories, especially the many local rivalries which had shaped and influenced their policy choices, were going to play a decisive role in an event of a truly global scale.

Appendix A
The war in Samnium, 217–209

Hannibal achieved some measure of success in eliciting defections from among the Samnites, especially in southern and western Samnium (the lands of the Hirpini and Caudini, respectively).[1] Several communities of the Hirpini came over to Hannibal in the immediate wake of the battle of Cannae. According to Livy (23.1.1–3), Hannibal was invited to Compsa, which then fell into his hands peacefully. After this, Hannibal placed part of his army under the command of Mago, whom 'he ordered either to receive the cities of this region that were then defecting from the Romans, or to compel those to defect that were refusing to'.[2] The passage clearly illustrates that other Hirpinian communities began to fall away from Rome at about the same time as Compsa. In 215 the Romans reportedly conducted raids against the Hirpini in the vicinity of Nola, obviously against towns that had defected. It is likely that they had rebelled in the previous year. Besides Compsa, the names of only a few rebellious Hirpinian towns are known: Vercellium, Vescellium, Sicilinum, Meles and Marmoreae.[3]

Similarly, we hear of the Romans capturing towns that belonged to the Caudini or laying waste to their territory, indicating that several had defected. M. Claudius Marcellus and Q. Fabius Maximus conducted campaigns in the vicinity of Caudium in 215 and 214, during which the Romans took Compulteria/Conpulteria, Trebula Balliensis, Austicula and

---

[1] Samnium during the Second Punic War: Salmon 1967: 295–302.
[2] Liv. 23.1.4: *Magonem regionis eius urbes aut deficientis ab Romanis accipere aut detractantis cogere ad defectionem iubet.* Interestestingly, if Livy's statement is accurate, it indicates varying levels of loyalty among the Hirpini, with some communities adhering more stubbornly to their alliance with Rome.
[3] Liv. 23.37.12–13, 23.41.13–14, 27.1.1–2. Vercellium and Vescellium may be a doublet for the same community, and one (or both, if they are a doublet) could be identified as the town of the Vescellani mentioned by Pliny (*HN* 3.105). Sicilinum is otherwise unattested. Meles is sometimes associated with modern Melizzano, in the vicinity of Beneventum. Marmorae is obscure; it may have been located somewhere near Meles, as the two places were captured together. See also Salmon 1967: 300–1.

Telesia.[4] With the exception of Telesia,[5] we cannot know for certain when these communities defected, though obviously the operations of Marcellus and Fabius provide a *terminus ante quem*. It is possible that the Caudini spontaneously revolted at the news of Hannibal's victory at Cannae or when he marched in the direction of Compsa, or perhaps Mago, during his aforementioned operations in 216, won them over to the Carthaginian side, though Livy's language implies that Mago's activities were restricted to the Hirpini. It is also possible that the Caudini defected later in 216, after Capua revolted. Indeed, all of the rebellious communities of the Caudini mentioned by name in the sources were situated on the very western edge of Samnium, near the border of Campania. We may speculate that the presence of Hannibal's army in the vicinity of Capua, as well as Mago's force not too far away in the land of the Hirpini, encouraged the Caudini to revolt. Whatever the exact sequence, it is likely that most of the Caudini defected sometime in 216,[6] not long after the battle of Cannae.

Despite Hannibal's success in winning over the majority of the Caudini and Hirpini, he failed to have much success in eliciting defections from among the Pentri, in northern Samnium. Livy, in his famous list of allies who rebelled after Cannae (22.61.10–12), mentions that 'the Hirpini … [and] the Samnites except for the Pentri' defected, suggesting that all of the Pentri remained loyal.[7] Livy may, however, overstate the case, for there is some evidence that Pentrian loyalty during the war was not completely steadfast. At a later point in his narrative Livy mentions (24.20.5) that the Romans recaptured a town named 'Fugifulae', in 215. This is probably the same as Fagifulae, a Pentrian town located near the border of the Frentani.[8] That Fugifulae/Fagifulae is the only Pentrian community

---

[4] Liv. 23.39.5–7, 23.41.13–14, 24.20.3–5. Livy says that Marcellus made attacks against the Hirpini and the *Samnites Caudinos* in 215. He reports that Fabius campaigned against the Caudini in two different years: in 215 (capturing Compulteria, Trebula and Austicula) and 214 (capturing Conpulteria, Telesia and Compsa). The repetition with variant spelling of Compulteria/ Conpulteria suggests that Livy drew on multiple sources that placed the campaign in different years and failed to recognise that they referred to the same event. If this is a doublet, the campaign should probably be placed in 214: De Sanctis 1956–69: III.2.203 n. 9, 245; Salmon 1967: 300–1. For the location of Compulteria/Conpulteria (near modern Alvignano) and Trebula (modern Treglia, in the heart of the Monti Trebulani), see Nissen 1967: II.799–801; Solin 1993: 13–24, 145–53.

[5] According to Livy (22.13.1), Hannibal captured Telesia in 217.

[6] Not all Caudinian communities defected, however. For example, Caiatia remained loyal to Rome: Salmon 1967: 299.

[7] *Hirpini … Samnites praeter Pentros* … Livy's phrasing is interesting: here and elsewhere he differentiates the Hirpini from the Samnites, the latter presumably referring only to the Pentri and Caudini. Polybius also sometimes separates the Hirpini from the Samnites (for example, 3.91.9). See Salmon 1967: 290; Dench 1995: 209–10.

[8] Ancient Fugifulae/Fagifulae was located in the vicinity of modern S. Maria a Faifoli; see Nissen 1967: II.792–3, De Sanctis 1956–69: II.214 n. 32; De Benedittis 1991; Barker 1995a: 8 site A143;

mentioned by name to have revolted does suggest, however, that this area of Samnium did not see widespread defections.[9] This fits in general Livy's indication that the Pentri adhered to Rome.

It appears that the Romans had largely reconquered Samnium by the middle years of the Second Punic War. As was just discussed, the campaigns in 215 and 214 resulted in the capture of several Caudinian and Hirpinian towns. Meles and Marmoreae were seized in 210, and in 209 the consul Q. Fulvius Flaccus received the surrender of the remaining Hirpini.[10] We do not hear any additional specific information about the Caudini. If any communities remained in revolt after the Roman campaigns in the region in 215 and 214, most were probably brought back under control by around 210, when the neighbouring Campanians and Hirpini were also recaptured. A few undocumented pockets of Samnite resistance may have held out, but in the main, the Second Punic War in Samnium was over.

contra Salmon 1967: 299 n. 2 (who argues that Fugifulae is not Fagifulae, but rather an otherwise unknown town in or near Lucania).
[9] This does not mean, however, that there did not exist underlying disaffection, which Hannibal did not tap into for whatever reasons.
[10] Liv. 27.1.1, 27.15.2–3.

Appendix B
Chronology of events in Bruttium, 215

Immediately following the capture of Consentia and Petelia, Carthaginian forces moved against the Greek cities of Bruttium, attacking first Rhegion then Locri. Polybius records that the siege of Petelia lasted eleven months, and this date is followed by Frontinus, while Livy mentions only an unspecified number of months.[1] Walbank (1970: II.30–1) argues that the siege would have ended late in the summer of 215, perhaps in September, assuming (1) a couple of months passed from the battle at Cannae until the investment of Petelia, and (2) the Roman calendar was in line with the solar calendar.

This position is difficult to reconcile with Livy's claim that Carthaginian forces landed at Locri, which fell after Petelia, then marched to Hannibal in Campania and finally returned to Bruttium by the end of the campaign season.[2] If Locri fell a few weeks after Petelia, then the reinforcements could not have arrived until late September or early October. Hanno would not have reached Hannibal with the reinforcements until mid- or late October, and he would not have returned to Bruttium until (probably) sometime in November. Even if the Roman calendar were running well ahead of the seasons, by a month or even six weeks (Derow 1976), then Hanno would have returned to Bruttium in October, still very late in the campaign season. It is unlikely, though not impossible, that the Carthaginians conducted operations so late in the year.[3]

Livy's narrative itself presents certain internal impossibilities: he claims that the Carthaginian reinforcements landed at Locri before the fall of the city and compelled the Locrians to close their city to the Romans and side

---

[1] Polyb. 7.1.3; Liv. 23.10.410, 23.20, 23.30.15, 24.1; Frontin. *Str.* 4.5.18; cf. Val. Max. 6.6; Sil. 12.431–2.
[2] De Sanctis 1956–69: III.2.665 places the defections of Croton, Locri and Caulonia early in the summer of 215, before the arrival of the reinforcements.
[3] Late-season military activity was possible: for example, the battle of Trebbia was fought in mid-January, and since the climate in southern Italy was relatively mild, the Carthaginians may have been able to operate later in the season. But even if we allow that the Roman calendar was running early, it is difficult to fit all of the events that Livy reports reasonably into the campaign season.

with Hannibal, and then later he claims the same reinforcements returned to Bruttium and were used to help capture Locri.[4] In Book 23 the fall of Croton precedes the surrender of Locri, while in Book 24 the order is reversed.[5] This account, as it stands, makes no sense, and it is clear that Livy has duplicated some events and anticipated in Book 23 the rebellion of Locri in Book 24. There is, fortunately, a plausible reconstruction of events.

If we accept the eleven-month reference as correct, then the earliest Petelia could have fallen, counting inclusively, is May 215, if the Roman calendar was running ahead of the solar calendar (as I have assumed throughout this book), or June 215 if the Roman calendar was synchronised with the solar year and Cannae occurred on or about 2 August (solar). Since we are forced to estimate dates for most of these events, whether or not the calendar was running early will not make a great deal of difference. The fall of Petelia preceded the defection of Locri, and if events followed in short order, then we may estimate that Locri fell at the earliest in June, if the calendar was ahead of the seasons (or July, if the calendar was accurate). An earlier date for the capture of Locri finds support in Livy's mention (24.1.2) of the Locrians hastily bringing in grain and other goods into the city from the fields. If Hanno attacked the city in late summer or early autumn, then we would have to suppose that the Locrians knew that Carthaginian forces had been operating in the area and yet took no steps to prepare for a siege until much later. Livy's note also suggests that Locrian preparations occurred around the time of the grain harvest (unless the grain being brought in was from rural storehouses), which corresponds better to an earlier date for the attack on Locri.

Next, the Carthaginian reinforcements arrived after the fall of Locri, perhaps also in June or early July, if the calendar was ahead of the seasons (or July or early August, if the calendar was accurate). This is consistent with the terms of the Carthaginian–Locrian treaty, which guaranteed the Carthaginians access to the city but left the port under the control of the Locrians (Liv. 24.1.13). The Carthaginians may have known that a fleet with reinforcements was on the way and informed the Locrians of their desire to land at Locri. Since the Carthaginians did not yet possess a major port, the Locrians were in a position to bargain. By controlling the port, the Locrians guaranteed that the Carthaginians would not maintain a permanent naval presence that could potentially strain Locrian resources, as later happened in Taras (Liv. 26.20.7–11).

---

[4] Liv. 23.41.10–12, 23.43.5–6, 23.46.8, 24.1.1–10.   [5] Liv. 23.30.6–8, 24.2.1–3.15.

Marcellus' attack on Samnium in the summer of 215 drew complaints from Hannibal's Samnite allies.[6] This would have occurred about the same time that Locri fell and the Carthaginian reinforcements arrived in Italy. Hanno marched to Campania in mid or late summer to help Hannibal with the assault on Nola. After the assault failed, as Hannibal moved to winter quarters in Apulia, Hanno returned to Bruttium with the reinforcements, perhaps in the autumn of 215.[7] Livy (24.1.1) also reports that upon Hanno's return to Bruttium, he attacked first Rhegion and then Locri. An attack on Rhegion later in the year makes perfect sense chronologically, especially if we accept that Hanno was compelled to move against Rhegion by the Bruttians, who were frustrated by not having profited from previous campaigns against the Greeks. The attack on Locri must be rejected, as the city had already surrendered by this point. It may be that the reference to Locri belongs to the summer, before the city had defected, and Livy has telescoped events.

Croton surrendered to the Carthaginians some time after Locri capitulated. It is possible that Croton did not fall until Hanno returned to Bruttium in the autumn. This would correspond well to the details of Livy's narrative (24.3.9–11), where the Bruttians attacked Croton on their own and were forced to ask for Hanno's assistance when they could not capture the formidable citadel. The Bruttians could have attacked Croton while Hanno was in Campania, and then, upon his return to Bruttium, sought his intervention in the campaign. This can be summarised in the following chart:

Date	Event	Source
1 July (2 August) 216	Cannae	
May–June (June–July) 215	Petelia falls after 11-month siege	App. *Hann.* 29, Polyb. 7.3.1
Summer 215	Locri surrenders	Liv. 24.1.1–13, 23.30.8, 23.41.12
	Reinforcements land	Liv. 23.41.10–12
	Marcellus attacks Samnium	Liv. 23.41.13–23.42.1
Late summer 215	Hannibal attacks Nola with Reinforcements from Locri	Liv. 23.43.5–6
	Bruttians attack Croton (?)	Liv. 24.2.1–11, 24.3.9–11
Autumn 215	Hannibal to winter quarters (Arpi)	Liv. 23.46.8, 24.1.1
	Hanno returns to Bruttium	
Autumn–winter 215/14	Croton surrenders	Liv. 24.3.10–15

Dates in parenthesis assume that the Roman calendar was synchronised with the solar calendar.

---

[6] Liv. 23.41.13–42.1.   [7] Liv. 23.46.8.

Appendix C
Chronology of events from the defection of Taras through the defection of Thurii, 213–212

The defection of Taras set off a string of revolts, including Metapontion, Heraclea and Thurii. Unfortunately, the sources for the Tarentine revolt contain a certain amount of confusion. Polybius' full narrative of the Tarentine revolt (8.24–34) is located in a fragmentary book and lacks reference to specific dates. Livy's fuller account (25.7.10–11.20) places the revolt after the beginning of the consular year 212 (25.3.1) and possibly before 26 April 212 (25.12.1). He also states, however, that most of his sources dated the event to 212, but some placed it in 213 (25.11.20). He later mentions that the Roman garrison commander in Taras held the citadel for five years (27.25.4), and since the city was recaptured in 209 (27.12.1–3, 27.15.4–16.9), this also suggests that the revolt fell in 213. Appian (*Hann.* 35) also implies that Taras revolted in 213, placing it in the year before Tiberius Sempronius Gracchus died, which occurred in 212 (Liv. 25.16). Polybius' Book 8 covered Olympic years 141.1–141.4, which included both the consular years 214/13 and 213/12. Hannibal besieged the citadel of Taras during the winter (Polyb. 8.34.13), and he probably captured it sometime late in winter.

It is possible that (a) he captured Taras in the winter of 213/12 but before the beginning of consular year (15 March) 212/11, or (b) if the Roman calendar was running about a month ahead of the solar calendar and 15 March (Roman) fell around 15 February (solar),[1] then Taras could have fallen just after the start of the consular year 213 but still late in the winter season. The confusion in Livy's sources reflects the overlap of Olympic years and consular years, with the sources choosing either 213 or 212.[2] I will estimate that Taras defected around 15 February (solar), though an exact date is impossible to determine.

---

[1] Derow 1976: 272–3.
[2] See De Sanctis 1956–69: III.2.322–4; Walbank 1970: II.5, 100–11; Lazenby 1978: 110 (placing events between 15 March and 26 April 212).

Even though Hannibal captured the city, he failed to control Taras' citadel, which was occupied by a Roman garrison and some Tarentines sympathetic to the Roman cause.[3] The garrison was soon reinforced by Roman troops who had been stationed in Metapontion.[4] Hannibal ordered preparations for a siege and eventually for the storming of the citadel. He retired to a camp a few miles from Taras, returned to inspect the progress on the siege works, and finally decided to blockade the citadel; he then returned to his camp for the remainder of the winter.[5] Polybius and Livy agree that the reinforcements from Metapontion arrived after the completion of the wall cutting off the citadel but before Hannibal finally retired to winter quarters. We can estimate, therefore, that the troops left Metapontion and arrived in Taras a few weeks after the Tarentine defection, sometime late in the winter of 213/12 – perhaps in late February or early March according to the solar calendar. I will estimate 7 March (solar).

Appian (*Hann.* 35) places the revolts of both Heraclea and Metapontion after the revolt of Thurii; his brief description of Heraclea is particularly problematic. In the oldest manuscript Heraclea is erroneously located between Metapontion and Taras.[6] Schweighaeuser emended Ταραντίνων to Θουρίνων, which solves the geographical error but introduces further chronological and logical complications.[7] In the same passage Appian claims that Heraclea defected out of fear; the implication is that it was fear of Metapontion and Taras (or Thurii if we accept the emendation). But Thurii probably did not defect until early May (see below), meaning that Heraclea's defection would not have occurred until sometime later, if we accept Schweighaeuser's emendation. It is hard to imagine that this relatively small and apparently ungarrisoned city held out so long, when the rest of the region began to defect. It makes more sense that the defections occurred in geographic order, first Taras, then Metapontion and Heraclea, especially considering that Heraclea was only a short distance from Metapontion. It also makes more sense that Taras (rather than Thurii) and Metapontion, presumably backed by Hannibal, put pressure on Heraclea,

---

[3] Polyb. 8.31.3; Liv. 25.10.6; App. *Hann.* 32.

[4] Polyb. 8.34.1; Liv. 25.15.4–6; App. *Hann.* 33, 35.

[5] Polyb. 8.33.1–8.34.13; Liv. 25.11.2–11, 25.11.1820.

[6] προσέθετο δὲ καὶ ἡ μεταξὺ Μεταποντίνων τε καὶ Θουρίων Ἡράκλεια, δέει μᾶλλον ἢ γνώμῃ ('Heraclea, between Metapontion and Tarentum, was added, out of fear more than inclination'). In fact, Heraclea lay just to the west of Metapontion (that is, on the other side of Metapontion from Taras along the coast), between the ancient Siris and Amiris rivers: Plin. *HN* 3.97. The ancient site has been identified a few miles from modern Policoro: Quilici 1967: 157–9; Osanna 1992: 97.

[7] The emendation has been adopted in the Teubner edition; Loeb has also adopted Θουρίων in the Greek, but Horace White's translation curiously reads Tarentum.

considering Taras' history as an expansionistic regional power (see Chapter 5, pp. 192–200). There is thus no need to emend Ταραντίνων in the manuscript. Livy (25.15.5–7) places the revolt of Metapontion before the revolt of Thurii, and although he neglects to mention the Heraclean revolt, we can interpolate that it occurred soon after Metapontion's but before Thurii's; I will estimate around 21 March (solar).

Finally, I must establish the date for the defection of Thurii. Appian (*Hann.* 34–5) places the Thurian revolt immediately after the Tarentine revolt but before the revolts of Metapontion and Heraclea, though this sequence was rejected in the preceding discussion. Livy more plausibly places the Thurian revolt after that of Metapontion, and I argued that this also occurred after the revolt of Heraclea. Appian and Livy agree that Thurii surrendered to Hanno, who was in command of Carthaginian forces in Bruttium. Livy's full narrative of the Thurian revolt is placed after the consuls and praetors took office in 212 and were then delayed in Rome until 26 April, providing a tentative *terminus post quem*. If the Roman calendar were running early, then 26 April would correspond to early April or late March by the solar year. Livy (25.13.1–2) also records that the Capuans were afraid that the consuls were planning to invest their city, and they sent legates to Hannibal while he was still near Taras, presumably in winter quarters. Hannibal commanded Hanno to march out of Bruttium and collect supplies for the Capuans; Hanno pitched camp near Beneventum and collected grain from allies who had stored it the previous year, suggesting that the current grain crop was not yet ready for harvest and allowing us to estimate a *terminus ante quem* of around mid-June (solar). The Roman consuls defeated Hanno and captured the grain supplies that he had collected. Hanno retreated into Bruttium, and the consuls marched into Campania when the crops were still young (*in herbis*), probably in early May (solar).[8] The Thurians probably negotiated with Hanno after he returned to Bruttium, meaning the fall of Thurii occurred around mid-May, perhaps 15 May (solar).

---

[8] Liv. 23.13.3–5, 25.14.11–14; 25.15.18: *Consules a Benevento in Campanum agrum legiones ducunt non ad frumenta modo, quae iam in herbis erant*; see Azzi 1922: 544–5.

Appendix D
Defection of the southern Lucanians, 212

The rebellion of the Greek cities of eastern Magna Graecia was followed by the ambush and death of the proconsul Tiberius Sempronius Gracchus.[1] An exact chronology is difficult to establish, but Livy places Gracchus' death after the defection of Thurii, which occurred in May 212 (see Appendix C). Livy also reports that he was ambushed as he planned to return from Lucania to Beneventum; the consuls had marched from Beneventum to Capua as the crops were ripening in Campania, perhaps in early May; so they may have returned in the late spring or early summer.[2] I will estimate some time in June, though the date is far from secure.

Some Lucanian aristocrats who were still loyal to Rome, led by a certain Flavus (Flavius, according to Appian), decided to seek the favour of the Carthaginians. They met with Mago and negotiated a treaty by which the Lucanians would live as free men under their own laws in friendship (*amicitiam*) with the Carthaginians; in return, the Lucanians promised to deliver Gracchus. Flavus and his party lured Gracchus into their trap by promising that they could secure the surrender of all the Lucanians who had previously sided with Hannibal. The whole episode again underscores the personal nature of politics and, at times, diplomacy during the Second Punic War. According to Livy (25.16.6, 15, 23), Flavus was a guest-friend (*hospes*) of Gracchus, and the proconsul so trusted the Lucanian that he met Flavus with only a token bodyguard. More interesting is his statement (25.16.5–6) that Flavus suddenly decided to switch allegiance, even though he had achieved political prominence by associating with the Romans. Flavus and his party may have felt that, with Hannibal's recent success in Lucania, the pro-Hannibalic Lucanian elite would gain political influence while their own prestige had been undercut. The timing of these events suggests that Flavus and the other previously pro-Roman aristocrats may

---

[1] Liv. 25.15.18–16.7; Polyb. 8.35.1; App. *Hann.* 35; see also Walbank 1970: II.109–10.
[2] Liv. 25.15.18–16.1; see De Sanctis 1956–69: III.2.322–4.

also have been influenced by the defection of the Italiote cities. In particular, we might speculate that the Tarentines were behind the Lucanian plot, since they had a history of manipulating the Lucanian elite in order to destabilise Lucanian–Roman relations and thus secure Taras' local hegemony.[3] Whatever the case, the episode emphasises that Hannibal's allies in Italy were not attached ideologically to the Carthaginian cause but based their decisions more on the immediate political and military landscape.

[3] Liv. 8.25.6–11, 8.29.1.

Bibliography

Adamesteanu, D. (1981) 'Siris: il problema topografico', in *Siris e l'influenza ionica in Occidente: atti del ventesimo Convegno di studi sulla Magna Grecia, Taranto, 12–17 ottobre 1980* (Taranto), 61–93.

(1984) 'Centri e territori', in Neppi Modona (1984), 53–8.

(1990a) 'Greeks and Natives in Basilicata', in Descoeudres (1990), 143–50.

(1990b) 'Rossano di Vaglio', in Salvatore (1990), 79–80.

Adcock, F. E. (1928) 'The Conquest of Central Italy', *CAH*, vol. vii: 581–616.

Afzelius, A. (1942) *Die römische Eroberung Italiens (340–264 v. Chr)*. Aarhus.

(1944) *Die römische Kriegsmacht während der Auseinandersetzung mit den hellenistischen Grossmächten*. Copenhagen.

Alessio, A. and Guzzo, P. (1989–90) 'Sanctuari e fattorie ad est di Taranto. Elementi archaeologici per un modello di interpretazione', *Scienze dell'Antichità* 3–4: 363–96.

Allen, J. (2006) *Hostages and Hostage-taking in the Roman Empire*. Cambridge.

Alvisi, G. (1970) *La viabilità romana della Daunia*. Bari.

Antonacci Sanpaolo, E. (2001) 'Landscape Changes: Romanization and New Settlement Patterns at Tiati', in Keay and Terrenato (2001), 27–38.

Arslan, E. (1989) *Monetazione aurea ed argentea dei Brettii*. Milan.

Arthur, P. (1991a) *Romans in Northern Campania: Settlement and Land-use around the Massico and the Garigliano Basin*. London.

(1991b) 'Territories, Wine and Wealth: Suessa Aurunca, Sinuessa, Minturnae and the Ager Falernus', in Barker and Lloyd (1991), 153–9.

(2002) *Naples: From Roman Town to City-state*. London.

Ashby, T. and Gardner, R. (1916) 'The Via Traiana', *PBSR* 8: 104–71.

Astin, A. E. (1989) 'Sources', *CAH*, 2nd edn, vol. viii: 1–16.

Attema, P. (2000) 'Landscape Archaeology and Livy: Warfare, Colonial Expansion and Town and Country in Central Italy of the 7th to 4th c. BC', *BABesch* 75: 115–26.

Attridge, H. A. (1984) 'Historiography', in M. Stone (ed.), *Jewish Writing of the Second Temple Period* (Philadelphia), 171–6.

Austin, M., Harries, J. and Smith, C. (1998) *Modus Operandi: Essays in Honour of Geoffrey Rickman*. London.

Azzi, G. (1922) 'Il clima del grano in Italia', *Nuovi Annali del Ministero per l'Agricoltura* 3: 453–624.

Badian, E. (1958) *Foreign Clientelae*. Oxford.

(1966) 'The Early Historians', in Dorey (1966), 1–38.

(1970–1) 'Roman Politics and the Italians (133–91 BC)', *Dialoghi di archeologia* 4–5: 373–409.

(1971) 'The Family and Early Career of T. Quinctius Flamininus', *JRS* 61: 102–11.

Bagnall, N. (1990) *The Punic Wars*. London.

Baker, G. P. (1929) *Hannibal*. New York.

Barceló, P. (1998) *Hannibal*. Munich.

Barker, G. (ed.) (1995a) *The Biferno Valley Survey: the Archaeological and Geomorphological Record*. London.

(1995b) *A Mediterranean Valley: Landscape Archaeology and Annales History in the Biferno Valley*. London.

Barker, G. and Hodges, R. (eds.) (1981) *Archaeology and Italian Society. Prehistoric, Roman and Medieval Studies*. BAR International Series 102. Oxford.

Barker, G. and Lloyd, J. A. (eds.) (1981) *Archaeology and Italian Society: Prehistoric, Roman and Medieval Studies*. London.

(1991) *Roman Landscapes: Archaeological Survey in the Western Mediterranean Region*. London.

Barker, G. and Rasmussen, T. (1998) *The Etruscans*. London.

Barnes, C. (2005) *Images and Insults: Ancient Historiography and the Outbreak of the Tarentine War*. Stuttgart.

Barone A., Greco, E., Lafage, F. and Luppino, S. (1986) 'Marcellina (Laos). Dix ans de recherche, un bilan préliminaire', *MEFRA* 98: 101–28.

Baronowski, D. (1993) 'Roman Military Forces in 225 BC (Polybius 2.23–4)', *Historia* 42: 181–202.

Barré, M. (1983) *The God-list in the Treaty between Hannibal and Philip V of Macedonia: a Study in Light of the Ancient Near Eastern Treaty Tradition*. Baltimore, MA.

Basile, B., De Stefano, G. and Lena, G. (1988) 'Landings, Ports, Coastal Settlements and Coastlines in Southeastern Sicily from Prehistory to Late Antiquity', in Raban (1988), 15–33.

Beaumont, R. L. (1936) 'Greek Influence in the Adriatic Sea before the Fourth Century BC', *JHS* 56: 159–204.

Beck, H. (2005) *Karriere und Hierarchie: Die römische Aristokratie und die Anfänge des cursus honorum in der mittleren Republik*. Berlin.

(2008) 'Prologue: Power Politics in Fourth-Century Greece', in J. Buckler and H. Beck, *Central Greece and the Politics of Power in the Fourth Century BC* (Cambridge), 1–30.

Beck, H. and Walter, U. (2001) *Die frühen römischen Historiker* (2 vols.). Darmstadt.

Bell, A. J. E. (1997) 'Cicero and the Spectacle of Power', *JRS* 87: 1–22.

Beloch, K. J. (1879) *Campanien: Topographie, Geschichte und Leben der Umgebung Neapels im Alterthum, nebst einem Atlas von Campanien mit beischreibendem Texte*. Berlin.

(1880) *Der italische Bund unter Roms hegemonie: staatsrechtliche und statistiche forshungen.* Leipzig.

(1886) *Die Bevölkerung der griechisch-römischen Welt.* Leipzig.

(1894) 'Siris', *Hermes* 29: 604–10.

(1926) *Römische Geschichte bis zum Beginn der punischen Kriege.* Berlin.

Bennett, D. S. (1996) 'Security, Bargaining, and the End of Interstate Rivalry', *International Studies Quarterly* 40: 157–83.

Bernardi, A. (1947) 'Dallo stato-città allo stato municipale in Roma Antica', *Paideia* 1: 213–27.

Bernstein, A. (1994) 'The Strategy of a Warrior State: Rome and the Wars against Carthage, 264–201 BC', in Murray *et al.* (1994), 56–84.

Bickerman, E. (1944) 'An Oath of Hannibal', *TAPhA* 75: 87–102.

(1952) 'Hannibal's Covenant', *AJPh* 73: 1–23.

Bicknell, P. (1966) 'The Date of the Battle of the Sagra River', *Phoenix* 20: 294–301.

Bintliff, J. and Sbonias, K. (eds.) (1999) *Reconstructing Past Population Trends in Mediterranean Europe (3000 BC–AD 1800).* Oxford.

Bispham, E. (2006) '*Coloniam deducere*: How Roman was Roman Colonization during the Middle Republic?', in Bradley and Wilson (2006), 73–160.

(2007) *From Asculum to Actium: the Municipalization of Italy from the Social War to Augustus.* Oxford.

Blagg, T. F. C. and Millett, M. (eds.) (1990) *The Early Roman Empire in the West.* Oxford.

Blake, H., Potter, T. W. and Whitehouse, D. (eds.) (1978) *Papers in Italian Archaeology, vol. I: Recent Research in Prehistoric, Classical and Medieval Archaeology.* Oxford.

Bleckmann, B. (2002) *Die römische Nobilität im Ersten Punischen Krieg: Untersuchungen zur aristokratischen Konkurrenz in der Republik.* Berlin.

Bloch, R. (1947) 'Volsinies étrusque: essai historique et topographique', *MEFRA* 59: 9–39.

(1950) 'Volsinies étrusque et romaine. Nouvelles découvertes archéologiques et épigraphiques', *MEFRA* 62: 57–123.

(1953) 'Découverte d'une nouvelle nécropole étrusque auprès de Bolsena', *MEFRA* 65: 39–61.

(1963) 'Gli scavi della Scuola francese a Bolsena (1946–1962)', *Studi etruschi* 31: 399–424.

(1973) *Recherches archéologiques en territoire volsinien.* Paris.

Blume, F., Lachmann, K. and Rudorff, A. (eds.) (1967) *Die Schriften der römischen Feldmesser*, reprint (2 vols.). Hildesheim.

Bottini, A. (1981) 'L'area melfese fino alla conquista romana', in Giardina and Schiavone (1981), 151–4.

(1990) 'La conca di Castelluccio e il problema di Nerulum', in Salvatore (1990), 159–64.

Bottini, A., Fresa, M. P. and Tagliente, M. (1990) 'L'evoluzione della struttura di un centro daunio fra VII e III secolo: l'esempio di Forentum', in Tagliente (1990a), 233–55.

Bottini, A. and Tagliente, M. (1986) 'Forentum ritrovato', *Bollettino Storico della Basilicata* 2: 65–7.

(1990) 'Due casi di acculturazione nel mondo indigeno della Basilicata', *PP* 45: 206–31.

Bracco, V. (1978) *Volcei.* Florence.

Bradeen, D. (1959) 'Roman Citizenship per magistratum', *CJ* 54: 221–8.

Bradford, J. (1957) 'The Ancient City of Arpi in Apulia', *Antiquity* 31: 167–9.

Bradley, G. (2000) *Ancient Umbria: State, Culture, and Identity in Central Italy from the Iron Age to the Augustan Era.* Oxford.

(2006) 'Colonization and Identity in Republican Italy', in Bradley and Wilson (2006), 161–87.

Bradley, G. and Wilson, J-P. (eds.) (2006) *Greek and Roman Colonization: Origins, Ideologies and Interactions.* Swansea, Wales.

Brauer, G. (1986) *Taras: Its History and Coinage.* New Rochelle, NY.

Brennan, T. (2000) *The Praetorship in the Roman Republic* (2 vols.). Oxford.

Briquel D. and Thuillier, J.-P. (eds.) (2001) *Le censeur et les Samnites: sur Tite-Live, livre IX.* Paris.

Briscoe, J. (1971) 'The First Decade', in Dorey (1971), 1–20.

(1973) *A Commentary on Livy, Books XXXI–XXXIII.* Oxford.

(1981a) *A Commentary on Livy, Books 34–37.* Oxford.

(1981b) 'The Historiography of the Century of the Roman Republic', *CR* 31: 49–51.

(1989) 'The Second Punic War', *CAH*, 2nd edn, vol. VIII: 44–80.

Brodersen, K. (1993) 'Appian und sein Werk', *ANRW* II.34.1: 339–63.

Broughton, T. R. S. (1951–2) *The Magistrates of the Roman Republic* (3 vols.). Cleveland, OH.

Brunt, P. A. (1965) 'Italian Aims at the Time of the Social War', *JRS* 55: 90–109.

(1971) *Italian Manpower.* Oxford.

Bucher, G. S. (1987) 'The *Annales Maximi* in the Light of Roman Methods of Keeping Records', *AJAH* 12: 2–61.

Buck, R. J. (1981) 'The Ancient Roads of Northwestern Lucania', *PP* 36: 317–47.

Burck, E. (1971) 'The Third Decade', in Dorey (1971), 21–46.

Burgers, G.-L. (1998) *Constructing Messapian Landscape: Settlement Dynamics, Social Organization and Cultural Contact in the Margins of Graeco-Roman Italy.* Amsterdam.

Caltabiano, M. (1976) 'La monetazione "annibalica" di Petelia', *NAC* 5: 85–101.

(1977) *Una città del sud tra Roma e Annibale: la monetazione de Petelia.* Palermo.

(1995) 'La rete relazionale dei Brettii riflessa nel documento monetale', in de Sensi Sestito (1995), 153–83.

Camassa, G. (1984) 'πόλις Χαλκῖτις ἐν Μεσσαπίᾳ', *ASNP* 14: 829–43.

(1997) 'Brundisium', *DNP*, vol. II: 796.

Campbell, D. (2000) *The Writings of the Roman Land Surveyors: Introduction, Text, Translation, and Commentary.* London.

Camporeale, G. (1970) *La Collezione alla Querce. Materiali archeologici orvietani.* Florence.

(2002) 'Volsinii', *DNP*, vol. xii.2: 314–15.

Capini, S. and Di Niro, A. (eds.) (2001) *Samnium: Archeologia del Molise*. Rome.

Capozza, M. (1997) 'La tradizione sui conflitti sociali a Volsini nel III secolo a.C.: dai servi agli oiketai attraverso i liberti', *Athene e Roma* 40: 28–41.

Cappelletti, L. (2002) *Lucani e Brettii: ricerche sulla storia politica e istituzionale di due popoli dell' Italia antica (V–III sec. a.C.)*. Bern.

Carlsen, J., Ørsted, P. and Skydsgaard, J. E. (eds.) (1994) *Landuse in the Roman Empire*. Rome.

Carratelli, G. (ed.) (1996) *The Greek World: Art and Civilization in Magna Graecia and Sicily*. New York.

Carter, J. C. (1981) 'Rural Settlement at Metaponto', in Barker and Hodges (1981), 167–78.

(1990) 'Metapontum – Population and Wealth', in Descoeudres (1990), 405–41.

(2006) *Discovering the Greek Countryside at Metaponto*. Ann Arbor, MI,

Carter, J. C. and D'Annibale, C. (1993), 'Il territorio di Crotone. Ricognizione topographiche 1983–1986', in Napolitano (1993), 93–9.

Cassano, R. (ed.) (1992) *Principi imperatori vescovi: duemila anni di storia a Canosa*. Venice.

Caven, B. (1980) *The Punic Wars*. New York.

(1990) *Dionysius I: Warlord of Sicily*. New Haven, CT.

Cazanove, O. de (2001) 'Itinéraires et étapes de l'avancée romaine entre Samnium, Daunie, Lucanie et Étrurie', in Briquel and Thuillier (2001), 147–92.

Champion, C. (ed.) (2004) *Roman Imperialism: Readings and Sources*. Malden, MA.

(2007) 'Empire by Invitation: Greek Political Strategies and Roman Imperial Interventions in the Second Century BCE', *TAPhA* 137: 255–75.

Champion, C. and Eckstein, A. (2004) 'Introduction: the Study of Roman Imperialism', in Champion (2004), 1–10.

Chaniotis, A. (2005) *Warfare in the Hellenistic World*. Malden, MA.

Chaplin, J. D and Kraus, C. S. (eds.) (2009) *Livy*. Oxford Readings in Classical Studies. Oxford.

Chelotti, M. (1996) 'L'élite municipale della Apulia tra città e campagna', *CCG* 7: 283–90.

Chouquer, G., Clavel-Lévêque, M., Favory, F. and Vallat, J-P. (1987) *Structures agraires en Italie centro-méridionale: cadastres et paysages ruraux*. Rome.

Ciaceri, E. (1928–40) *Storia della Magna Grecia*, 2nd edn (3 vols.). Milan.

Clarke, K. (1999) *Between Geography and History: Hellenistic Constructions of the Roman World*. Oxford.

Coarelli, F. (1988) 'Colonizzazione romana e viabilità', *Dialoghi de archeologia* 6: 35–48.

Cocchiaro, A. (1981) 'Contributo per la carta archeologica del territorio a sud-est di Taranto', *Taras* 1: 53–75.

Coraluppi, L. (2002) 'Osservazioni critiche sul testo delle orazioni de Lege Agraria di Cicerone', in Michelotto (2002), 103–17.

Cornell, T. J. (1982) 'Review of Wiseman', *JRS* 72: 203–6.

(1989a) 'The Conquest of Italy', *CAH*, 2nd edn, vol. VII.2: 351–419.

(1989b) 'The Recovery of Rome', *CAH*, 2nd edn, vol. VII.2: 309–50.

(1989c) 'Rome and Latium to 390', *CAH*, 2nd edn, vol. VII.2: 243–308.

(1995a) *The Beginnings of Rome*. London.

(1995b) 'Warfare and Urbanization in Roman Italy', in Cornell and Lomas (1995), 121–34.

(1996) 'Hannibal's Legacy: the Effects of the Hannibalic War on Italy', in Cornell *et al.* (1996), 97–117.

(2004) 'Deconstructing the Samnite Wars: an Essay in Historiography', in Jones (2004), 115–31.

Cornell, T. and Lomas, K. (eds.) (1995) *Urban Society in Roman Italy*. New York.

Cornell, T., Rankov, B. and Sabin, P. (eds.) (1996) *The Second Punic War: a Reappraisal*. London.

Costabile, F. (1976) *Municipium Locrensium: Istituzioni ed organizzazione sociale di Locri romana (attraverso il corpus delle iscrizioni latine di Locri)*. Naples.

(1984) 'I ginnasiarchi a Petelia', *ASCL* 51: 5–15.

Costamagna, L. and Sabbione, C. (eds.) (1990) *Una città in Magna Grecia: Locri Epizefiri*. Reggio Calabria.

Costanzi, V. (1919) 'Osservationi sulla terza guerra sannitica', *RFIC* 97: 161–215.

Cottrell, L. (1961) *Hannibal: Enemy of Rome*. New York.

Crake, J. E. A. (1963) 'Roman Politics from 215–209 BC', *Phoenix* 17: 123–30.

Crawford, M. (1964) 'War and Finance', *JRS* 54: 29–32.

(1975) *Roman Republican Coinage*. Cambridge.

(1978) *The Roman Republic*. Cambridge, MA.

(1985) *Coinage and Money under the Roman Republic*. London.

(1992) *The Roman Republic*, 2nd edn. Cambridge, MA.

(1998) 'How to Create a *municipium*', in Austin, Harries and Smith (1998), 31–46.

Cuff, P. J. (1975) 'Two Cohorts from Camerinum', in B, Levick (ed.), *The Ancient Historian and his Materials: Essays in Honour of C. E. Stevens* (Farnborough), 75–91.

Curti, E. (2001) 'Toynbee's Legacy: Discussing Aspects of the Romanization of Italy', in Keay and Terrenato (2001), 17–26.

Curti, E., Dench, E. and Patterson, J. R. (1996) 'The Archaeology of Central and Southern Roman Italy: Recent Trends and Approaches', *JRS* 86: 170–89.

Daly, G. (2002) *Cannae: the Experience of Battle in the Second Punic War*. London.

David, J.-M. (1996) *The Roman Conquest of Italy*, trans. A. Nevill. Oxford. Originally published as *La Romanisation de l' Italie* (Paris 1994).

De Beer, G. (1969) *Hannibal*. New York.

De Benedittis, G. (1991) 'Fagifulae', in Capini and Di Niro (1991), 259–60.

De Felice, E. (1994) *Larinum. Forma Italia 36*. Florence.

De Franciscis, A. (1960) 'Μέταυρος', *Atti e Memorie della Società Magna Grecia* 4: 21–67.

Degrassi, A. (ed.) (1947) *Inscriptiones Italiae*, vol. XIII.I. Rome.

(ed.) (1954) *Fasti Capitolini*. Torino.

De Juliis, E. (1975) 'Caratteri della civiltà daunia dal VI secolo all' arrivo dei Romani', in *Atti del Colloquio internazionale di preistoria e protostoria della Daunia, Foggia, 24–29 aprile 1973: Civiltà preistoriche e protostoriche della Daunia* (Florence): 286–97.

(1984a) 'L'età del Ferro', in Mazzei (1984a), 166–72.

(1984b) *Gli Ori di Taranto in età ellenistica*. Milan.

(1985) 'Canne', in Nenci and Vallet (1985), vol. IV: 359–63.

(1990) 'Canosa', in Tagliente (1990a), 69–77.

(2000) *Taranto*. Bari.

Delano-Smith, C. (1967) 'Ancient Landscapes of the Tavoliere, Apulia', *Transactions of the Institute of British Geographers* 41: 203–8.

(1976) 'The Tavoliere of Foggia (Italy): an Aggrading Coastline and its Early Settlement Patterns', in D. A. Davidson and M. L. Shackley (eds). *Geoarchaeology: Earth Science and the Past* (London), 197–212.

(1978) 'Coastal Sedimentation, Lagoons, and the Ports of Italy', in Blake *et al.* (1978), 25–33.

(1987) 'The Neolithic Environment of the Tavoliere', in G. D. B. Jones (1987), 1–26.

Delbrück, H. (1975) *History of the Art of War within the Framework of Political History*, vol. I: *Antiquity*. London. Translation by W. Renfroe of *Geschichte der Kriegskunst im Rahmen der politischen Geschichte* (3rd edn, Berlin 1920).

De Ligt, L. (1990) 'The Roman Peasantry: Demand, Supply, Distribution between Town and Countryside I: Rural Monetization and Peasant Demand', *MBAH* 9: 24–56.

(1991) 'The Roman Peasantry: Demand, Supply, Distribution between Town and Countryside II: Supply, Distribution, and a Comparative Perspective', *MBAH* 10: 33–77.

(2004) 'Poverty and Demography: The Case of the Gracchan Land Reforms', *Mnemosyne* 57: 725–57

Del Monaco, L. and Musti, D. (1999) 'Lokroi Epizephyrioi', *DNP*, vol. VII: 421–6.

Del Tutto Palma, A. and Capano, A. (1990) 'L'iscrizione di Muro Lucano', in Tagliente (1990a), 105–10.

De Martino, F. (1984) 'Gromatici e questioni graccane', in Giuffrè (1984), vol. VII: 3125–50

Dench, E. (1995) *From Barbarians to New Men*. Oxford.

(2004) 'Samnites in English: the Legacy of E. Togo Salmon in the English Speaking World', in H. Jones (2004), 7–22.

(2005) *Romulus' Asylum: Roman Identities from the Age of Alexander to the Age of Hadrian*. Oxford.

De Palo, M. and Labellarte, P. (1987) 'Canne: recenti ritrovamenti dell' abito indigeno', in *Profili della Daunia antica* (CRSEC Foggia) (Foggia), 101–31.

Derow, P. S. (1976) 'The Roman Calendar, 218–191 BC', *Phoenix* 30: 265–81.

(1989) 'Rome, the Fall of Macedon and the Sack of Corinth', *CAH*, 2nd edn, vol. VIII: 290–323.

De Sanctis, G. (1956–69) *Storia dei Romani*, 2nd edn (4 vols.). Florence.

De Santis, M. (1966) 'La città di Aecae', *Archeologia* 4.36: 299–303.

Descoeudres, J.-P. (ed.) (1990) *Greek Colonists and Native Populations: Proceedings of the First Australian Congress of Classical Archaeology Held in Honour of Emeritus Professor A. D. Trendall, Sydney, 9–14 July 1985*. Oxford.

De Sensi Sestito (1994) 'Il federalismo in Magna Grecia', in L. A. Foresti, A. Barzanò, C. Bearzor, L. Prandi and G. Zecchini (eds.), *Federazioni e federalismo nell'Europa antica*, vol. I: 195–216.

(ed.) (1995) *I Brettii*, vol. I: *Cultura, lingua e documentazione storico-archeologica*. Rubbettino.

De Simone, C. (1988) 'Iscrizioni messapiche della Grotta della Poesia (Melendugno, Lecce)', *ASNP* 17: 325–415.

(1992) 'Lingue e culture nelle Puglie nel III–II sec. a.C.', in Uggeri (1992), 25–8.

Desy, P. (1989) 'Il grano dell'Apulia e la data della battaglia del Trasimeno', *PP* 44: 102–15.

Develin, R. (1976) 'Appius Claudius Caecus and the Brindisi Elogium', *Historia* 25: 484–7.

(1985) *The Practice of Politics at Rome, 366–167 BC*. Brussels.

Diana, B. (1989) 'L'atteggiamento degli Etruschi nella guerra annibalica', *RSA* 19: 93–106.

Dillon, S. and Welch, K. (eds.) (2006) *Representations of War in Ancient Rome*. Cambridge.

Dodge, T. A. (1891) *Hannibal*. Boston.

Dorey, T. A. (1956) 'The Debate on the Carthaginian Peace Terms in 203 BC', *Orpheus* 3: 79–80.

(ed.) (1966) *Latin Historians*. London.

(ed.) (1971) *Livy*. London.

Dorey, T. A. and Dudley, D. R. (1972) *Rome against Carthage*. New York.

Drews, R. (1988) 'Pontiffs, Prodigies, and the Disappearance of the Annales Maximi', *CP* 83: 289–99.

Dyson, S. L. (1985) *The Creation of the Roman Frontier*. Princeton.

Eckstein, A. M. (1979) 'The Foundation Day of Roman Coloniae', *California Studies in Classical Antiquity* 12: 85–97.

(1982) 'Two Notes on the Chronology of the Outbreak of the Hannibalic War', *RhM* 126: 257–68.

(1987) *Senate and General: Individual Decision-making and Roman Foreign Relations, 264–194 BC*. Berkeley.

(2003) 'Thucydides, the Outbreak of the Peloponnesian War, and the Foundation of International Systems Theory', *International Historical Review* 23: 757–74.

(2006) *Mediterranean Anarchy, Interstate War, and the Rise of Rome*. Berkeley.

(2008) *Rome Enters the Greek East: From Anarchy to Hierarchy in the Hellenistic Mediterranean, 230–170 BC*. Oxford.

Eder, W. (ed.) (1990) *Staat und Staatlichkeit in der frühen römischen Republik*. Stuttgart.

Ehrenberg, V. (1948) 'The Foundation of Thurii', *AJPh* 69: 149–70.

Erdkamp, P. (1992) 'Polybius, Livy and the "Fabian Strategy"', *Anc Soc* 23: 127–47.

(1998) *Hunger and the Sword: Warfare and Food Supply in Roman Republican Wars (264–30 BC)*. Amsterdam.

Errington, R. M. (1972) *The Dawn of Empire: Rome's Rise to World Power*. Ithaca, NY.

(1989) 'Rome against Philip and Antiochus', *CAH*, 2nd edn, vol. VIII: 244–89.

Erskine, A. (1993) 'Hannibal and the Freedom of the Italians', *Hermes* 121: 58–62.

Finley, M. I. (1971) 'Archaeology and History', *Daedalus* 100: 168–86.

(1986) *Ancient History: Evidence and Models*. New York.

Fischer-Hansen, T. (1993) 'Apulia and Etruria in the Early Hellenistic Period: a Survey', in Guldager Bilde, Nielsen and Nielsen (1993), 53–90.

Forsythe, G. (2005) *A Critical History of Early Rome: From Prehistory to the First Punic War*. Berkeley.

Fracchia, H. (2004) 'Western Lucania, Southern Samnium, and Northern Apulia: Settlement and Cultural Changes, Fifth–Third Centuries BC', in H. Jones (2004), 69–84.

Franke, P. (1989) 'Pyrrhus', *CAH*, 2nd edn, vol. VII.2: 456–85.

Frederiksen, M. (1959) 'Republican Capua: a Social and Economic Study', *PBSR* 27: 80–130.

(1976) 'Changes in the Patterns of Settlement', in Zanker (1976), 341–55.

(1977) 'Review of Ungern-Sternberg', *JRS* 67: 183–4.

(1984) *Campania*. Rome.

Frederiksen, M. and Ward-Perkins, J. B. (1957) 'The Ancient Road Systems of the Central and Northern Ager Faliscus. Notes on Southern Etruria, II', *PBSR* 25: 67–208.

Frier, B. (1999) *Libri Annales Pontificum Maximorum: the Origins of the Annalistic Tradition*, 2nd edn. Ann Arbor, MI.

Fronda, M. (2006) 'Livy 9.20 and Early Roman Imperialism in Apulia', *Historia* 30: 397–417.

(2007a) 'Hegemony and Rivalry: the Revolt of Capua Revisited', *Phoenix* 61: 83–108.

(2007b) 'Review of Dillon and Welch', *CB* 83: 306–8.

Fronza, L. (1946/7) 'De Bacchanalibus', *Annali Triestini* 17: 205–28.

Gabba, E. (1958) 'L'Elogio di Brindisi', *Athenaeum* 36: 90–105.

(1994) 'Rome and Italy: the Social War', *CAH*, 2nd edn, vol. IX: 104–28.

Gallini C. (1973) 'Che cosa intendere per ellenizzazione. Problemi di metodo', *Dialoghi di archeologia* 7: 175–91.

Galsterer, H. (1976) *Herrschaft und Verwaltung im republikanischen Italien*. Munich.

Gargini, M. (1998) 'Forentum', *DNP*, vol. IV: 590.

Gargola, D. (1990) 'The Colonial Commissioners of 218 BC and the Foundation of Cemona and Placentia', *Athenaeum* 78: 465–73.

(1995) *Lands, Laws, and Gods: Magistrates & Ceremony in the Regulation of Public Lands in Republican Rome*. Chapel Hill, NC.

Garlan, Y. (1994) 'Warfare', *CAH*, 2nd edn, vol. vi: 678–92.

Garnsey, P. (1998a) 'Mountain Economies in Southern Europe: Thoughts on the Early History, Continuity and Individuality of Mediterranean Upland Pastoralism', in P. Garnsey, *Cities, Peasants and Food in Classical Antiquity* (Cambridge), 166–79.

(1998b) 'Where Did Italian Peasants Live?', in P. Garnsey, *Cities, Peasants and Food in Classical Antiquity* (Cambridge), 107–33.

Gartzke, E. and Simon, M. (1999) ' "Hot Hand": a Critical Analysis of Enduring Rivalries', *The Journal of Politics* 61: 777–98.

Giampaolo, D. (1990) 'Benevento: il processo di aggregazione di un territorio', in Salvatore (1990), 281–92.

Giannelli, G. (1928) *La Magna Grecia da Pitagora a Pirro*. Milan.

Giardina, A. and Schiavone, A. (eds.) (1981) *Società romana e produzione schiavistica*, vol. i: *L'Italia: Insediamenti e forme economiche*. Bari.

Giardino, L. (1990) 'L'abitato di Grumentum in età repubblicana: problemi storici e topografici', in Salvatore (1990), 125–41.

Giardino, L. and De Siena, A. (1999) 'Metaponto', in Greco (1999a), 329–63.

Giles, P. (1887) 'Emendation of Livy XLII.17 and of Appian Maced. XI. 7, 8', *CR* 1: 170.

Giuffre, V. (ed.) (1984) *Sodalitas: Scritti in onore di Antonio Guarino* (10 vols.). Naples.

Goertz, G. and Diehl, P. (1992) 'The Empirical Importance of Enduring Rivalries', *International Interactions* 18: 151–63.

(1993) 'Enduring Rivalries: Theoretical Constructs and Empirical Patterns', *International Studies Quarterly* 37: 147–71.

(1995) 'The Initiation and Termination of Enduring Rivalries: the Impact of Political Shocks', *American Journal of Political Science* 39: 30–52.

Goldsworthy, A. (2000) *The Punic Wars*. London.

Gomme, A. W. (1945–78) *A Historical Commentary on Thucydides*, 2nd edn (5 vols.). Oxford.

Greco, E. (1981) *Magna Greca*. Bari.

(1990) 'Problemi della romanizzazione della Lucania occidentale nell'area compresa tra Paestum e Laos', in Salvatore (1990), 265–8.

(ed.) (1999a) *La città greca antica: Istituzioni, società, e forme urbane*. Rome.

(1999b) 'Turi', in Greco (1999a), 413–30.

Greco, E. and La Torre, G. F. (1999) *Blanda, Laos, Cerillae: guida archeologica dell'alto Tirreno cosentino*. Paestum.

Grelle, F. (1981) 'Canosa: le istituzioni, la società', in Giardina and Schiavone (1981), 181–225.

(1992) 'La Daunia fra la guerre samnitiche e la guerra annibalica', in Uggeri (1992), 29–42.

(1993) *Canosa Romana*. Rome.

Grenier, A. (1905) 'La transhumance des troupeaux en Italie et son rôle dans l'histoire', *MEFRA* 25: 293–328.

Groag, E. (1929) *Hannibal als Politiker*. Vienna.

Gruen, E. (1984) *The Hellenistic World and the Coming of Rome*. Berkeley.

(1990) 'The Bacchanalian Affair', in E. Gruen, *Studies in Greek Culture and Roman Foreign Policy* (Leiden), 34–78.

Gualandi, M.L., Palazzi C. and Paoletti, M. (1981) 'La Lucania orientale', in Giardina and Schiavone (1981), 155–79.

Gualtieri, M. (1987) 'Fortifications and Settlement Oraganization: an Example from Pre-Roman Italy', *World Archaeology* 19: 30–46.

(1990) 'Roccagloriosa: strutture insediative di una comunità lucana di IV sec. a.C.', in Tagliente (1990a), 41–8.

(1993) (ed.), *Fourth Century BC Magna Graecia: a Case Study.* Jonsered.

(2004) 'Between Samnites and Lucanians: New Archaeological and Epigraphic Evidence for Settlement Organization', in H. Jones (2004), 35–50.

Gualtieri, M. and de Polignac, F. (1991) 'A Rural Landscape in Western Lucania', in Barker and Lloyd (1991), 194–203.

Guldager Bilde, P., Nielsen, I. and Nielsen, M. (eds.) (1993) *Aspects of Hellenism in Italy: Towards a Cultural Unity?* Copenhagen.

Guzzo, P.G. (1976) 'Attività dell' ufficio scavi sibari nel 1975', in *La Magna Grecia nell' età romana, atti del quindicesimo convegno di studi sulla Magna Grecia, Taranto, 5–10 ottobre 1975.* Naples: 615–31.

(1983) 'Per lo studio del territorio di Laos', *BA* 68: 57–66.

(1984) 'Lucanians, Brettians, and Italiote Greeks in the Fourth and Third Centuries BC', in Hackens, Holloway and Holloway (1984), 191–246.

(1990a) 'Il politico fra i Brezi', in Tagliente (1990a), 87–92.

(1990b) 'Myths and Archaeology in South Italy', in Descoeudres (1990), 131–41.

(1991) 'Documentazioni ed ipotesi archaeologiche per la più antica romanizzazione di Bari, Brindisi, Taranto', in Mertens and Lambrechts (1991), 77–88.

(1996) 'The Encounter with the Bruttians', in Carratelli (1996), 559–62.

Guzzo, P.G. and Greco, E. (1978) 'S. Maria del Cedro, fraz. Marcellina, loc. S. Bartolo (Cosenza): Scavo di una struttura di epoca ellenistica (1973 e 1975)', *NSA* 32: 429–59.

Habinek, T. (2007) 'Cincius Alimentus, L. (810)', *Brill's New Jacoby.* Online.

Hackens, T., Holloway, N. and Holloway, R. (eds.) (1984) *Crossroads of the Mediterranean*, Providence, RI.

Hackens, T., Holloway. N., Holloway, R. and Moucharte, G. (1992) *The Age of Pyrrhus.* Louvain.

Hahn, I. (1972) 'Appian und Hannibal', *AAntHung* 20: 95–121.

Halstead, P. (1987) 'Traditional and Ancient Rural Economy in Mediterranean Europe: Plus ça change?', *JHS* 107: 77–87.

Halward, B.L. (1930a) 'Hannibal's Invasion of Italy', *CAH*, vol. VIII: 25–56.

(1930b) 'The Roman Defensive', *CAH*, vol. VIII: 57–8.

Hamilton, C. (1999) 'The Hellenistic World', in Raaflaub and Rosenstein (1999), 163–91.

Hantos, T. (1983) *Das römische Bundesgenossensystem in Italien.* Munich.

Harris, W.V. (1965) 'The Via Cassia and the Via Traiana Nova between Bolsena and Chiusi', *PBSR* 33: 113–33.

(1971) *Rome in Etruria and Umbria*. Oxford.

(1979) *War and Imperialism in Republican Rome, 327–70 BC*. Oxford.

(1989) 'Roman Expansion in the West', *CAH*, 2nd edn, vol. VIII: 107–62.

(1990) 'Roman Warfare in the Economic and Social Context of the Fourth Century', in Eder (1990), 494–510.

Head, B. (1977) *Historia Nummorum*, 2nd edn. Oxford.

Henderson, B. (1897) 'Grant of *immunitas* to Brundisium', *CR* 11: 251–5.

Herring, E. (2000) ' "To See Oursels as Others See Us!" The Construction of Native Identities in Southern Italy', in Herring and Lomas (2000), 45–77.

Herring, E. and Lomas, K. (eds.) (2000) *The Emergence of State Identities in Italy in the First Millenium BC*. London.

Heurgon, J. (1942) *Recherches sur l'histoire, la religion et la civilisation de Capoue préromaine des origines à la deuxième guerre punique*. Paris.

Hof, A. (2002) *Romische Aussenpolitik vom Ausbruch des Krieges gegen Tarent bis zum Frieden mit Syrakuse (281–263 v. Chr.)*. Olms.

Hoffman, W. (1934) *Rom und die griechische Welt im 4. Jahrhundert*. Leipzig.

Holleaux, M. (1957) *Rome et la conquête de l'Orient*. Paris.

Horden, P. and Purcell, N. (2000) *The Corrupting Sea: a Study of Mediterranean History*. London.

Hornblower, S. (1983) *The Greek World, 479–323 BC*. London.

Hoyos, B. D. (1983) 'Hannibal: What Kind of Genius?', *G&R* 30: 171–80.

(1985) 'Treaties True and False: the Error of Philinus of Agrigentum', *CQ* 35: 92–109.

(2004a) *Hannibal's Dynasty: Power Politics in the Western Mediterranean, 247–183 BC*. London.

(2004b) 'Review of Bleckmann', *CR* 54: 487–8.

Humbert, M. (1978) *Municipium et civitas sine suffragio: l'organisation de la conquête jusqu'à la guerre sociale*. Rome.

Huss, W. (1985) *Geschichte der Karthager*. Munich.

Iker, R. (1995) 'L'Epoca Daunia', in Mertens (1995a), 45–74.

Ilari, V. (1974) *Gli Italici nelle strutture militari romane*. Milan.

Isayev, E. (2007) *Inside Ancient Lucania: Dialogues in History and Archaeology*. London.

Jeffrey, L. H. (1961) *The Local Scripts of Archaic Greece*. Oxford.

Jehne, M. and Pfeilschifter, R. (eds.) (2006) *Herrschaft ohne Integration? Rom und Italien in republikanischer Zeit*. Frankfurt.

Jendel, M. and Deschênes-Wagner, G. (eds.) (2004) *Tranquillitas: Mélanges en l'honneur de Tran tam Tinh*. Quebec.

Jones, G. D. B. (ed.) (1987) *Apulia*, vol. 1: *Neolithic Settlement in the Tavoliere*. London.

Jones, H. (ed.) (2004) *Samnium: Settlement and Cultural Change*. Providence, RI.

Jonkers, E. J. (1963) *Social and Economic Commentary on Cicero's de Lege Agraria Orationes Tres*. Leiden.

Kahrstedt, U. (1913) *Geschichte der Karthager*, vol. III. Berlin.

Keaveney, A. (2005) *Rome and the Unification of Italy*, 2nd edn. Exeter.

Keay, S. and Terrenato, N. (eds.) (2001) *Italy and the West: Comparative Issues in Romanization*. Oxford.

Keppie, L. (1983) *Colonization and Veteran Settlement*. Rome.

(1998) *The Making of the Roman Army from Republic to Empire*. London.

Klebs, E. (1889) 'Busa', *RE* III: 1072–3.

Klotz, A. (1951) 'Die Benutzung des Polybios bei römischen Schriftellern', *SIFC* 25: 243–65.

Kromayer, J. (1903) *Antike Schlachtfelder; Bausteine zu einer antiken Kriegsgeschichte*. Berlin.

Kugler, J. and Lemke, D. (1996) *Parity and War*. Ann Arbor, MI.

Kukofka, D.-A. (1990) *Süditalien im Zeiten Punischen Krieg*. Frankfurt.

La Bua, V. (1992) 'Il Salento e i Messapi di fronte al conflitto tra Annibale e Roma', in Uggeri (1992), 43–69.

Lagona, S. (1992) 'I porti della Puglia in età annibalica', in Uggeri (1992), 83–91.

Lamboley, J.-L. (1996) *Recherches sur les Messapiens IVe–IIe siècle avant J.-C.* Rome.

Lancel, S. (1999) *Hannibal*, trans. A. Nevill. Oxford. Originally published as *Hannibal* (Paris 1995).

Larsen, J. A. O. (1968) *Greek Federal States: Their Institutions and History*. Oxford.

La Torre, G. F. (1991) 'Blanda alla luce delle prime ricerche. Palecastro, Tortora (Cosenza)', *Bollettino di Archeologia* 8: 133–55.

Launey, M. (1949) *Recherches sur les armées hellénistiques* (2 vols.). Paris.

Laurence, R. (1994) *Roman Pompeii: Space and Society*. London.

(1999) *The Roads of Roman Italy*. London.

Lazenby, J. (1978) *Hannibal's War*. Norman, OK.

(1996a) *The First Punic War*. Stanford, CA.

(1996b) 'Was Maharbal Right?', in T. Cornell *et al.* (1996), 39–48.

Lazzeroni, R. (1991) 'Osco e latino nella Lex Sacra di Lucera', *SSL* 31: 95–111.

Lefkowitz, M. (1959) 'Pyrrhus' Negotiations with the Romans, 280–275 BC', *HSPh* 64: 147–77.

Leidl, C. (1996) *Appians Darstellung des 2. Punische Krieg in Spanien (Iberike c. 1–38, §1–158a). Text und Kommentar*. Munich.

Leiwo, M. (1995) *Neapolitana: a Study of Population and Language in Graeco-Roman Naples*. Helsinki.

Lemke, D. (1996) 'Small States and War: an Expansion of Power Transition Theory', in Kugler and Lemke (1996), 77–91.

Lepore, E. (1984) 'Società indigena e influenze esterne con particolare riguardo all' influenze greca', in Neppi Modona (1984), 317–24.

Letta, C. (1994) 'Dall' "oppidum" al "nomen": i diversi livelli dell'aggregazione politica nel mondo osco-umbro', in L. Foresti *et al.* (eds.), *Federazioni e federalismo nell' Europa antica*, vol. 1: 387–405.

Lloyd, J. A. (1995) 'Pentri, Frentani and the Beginnings of Urbanization (c. 500–80 BC)', in Barker (1995a), 181–212.

Lo Cascio, E. (1994) 'The Size of the Roman Population: Beloch and the Meaning of the Augustan Census Figures', *JRS* 84: 23–40.

(1999) 'The Population of Roman Italy in Town and Country', in Bintliff and Sbonias (1999), 161–71.

Lomas, K. (1993) *Rome and the Western Greeks, 350 BC–AD 200: Conquest and Acculturation in Southern Italy*. London.

(1995a) 'KAR[IS] BRIT[TIUS]: a Reinterpretation of Vetter no. 112', *CQ* 45: 481–4.

(1995b) 'Urban Elites and Cultural Definition: Romanization in Southern Italy', in Cornell and Lomas (1995), 107–20.

(1996) 'Herdonia', *OCD*, 3rd edn, 689.

(2000) 'Cities, States and Ethnic Identity in Southeast Italy', in Herring and Lomas (2000), 79–90.

Lombardo, M. (1987) 'La Magna Grecia dalla fine del V secolo a.C. alla conquista romana', in Pugliese Carratelli (1987), 55–88.

(1992) (ed.) *I Messapi e la Messapia nelle fonti letterarie greche e latine*. Galatina.

(1995) 'L'organizzazione e i rapporti economici e sociali dei Brettii', in De Sensi Sestito (1995), 109–23.

(1996) 'Sila', *DNP*, vol. XI: 544–5.

Longo, F. (1999) 'Poseidonia', in E. Greco (ed.) *La città greca antica*. Rome: 365–84.

Luce, T. J. (1977) *Livy: the Composition of his History*. Princeton, NJ.

Maddoli, G. (ed.) (1982) *Temesa e il suo territorio*. Taranto.

Manzo, A. (2002) 'L'*Ager Romanus*. Dalla *deditio* di Capua alla redazione della *Forma Agri Campani* di Publio Cornelio Lentulo', in G. Franciosi (ed.), *La romanizzazione della campania antica 1* (Naples), 125–59.

Manganaro, G. (1964) 'Città di Sicilia e sanctuari panellenici nel III e II sec. a.C.', *Historia* 13: 414–39.

Marangio, C. (ed.) (1988) *La Puglia in età repubblicana: atti del I Convegno di studi sulla Puglia romana, Mesagne, 20–22 marzo 1986*. Galatina.

Marchetti, P. (1973) 'La marche du calendrier de 203 à 190 (années varr. 551–564)', *AC* 42: 473–96.

(1976) 'La marche du calendrier romain et la chronologie à l'époque de la bataille de Pydna', *BCH* 100: 401–32.

(1978) *Histoire économique et monétaire de la deuxième guerre punique*. Brussels.

Marchi, M. L. and Sabbatini, G. (1996) *Venusia*. Rome.

Marcotte D. (1985) 'Lucaniae. Considérations sur l'éloge de Scipion Barbatus', *Latomus* 44: 721–42.

Marin, M. D. (1970) *Topografia storica della Daunia antica*. Bari.

Mazzei, M. (ed.) (1984a) *La Daunia Antica: Dalla preistoria all' altomedioevo*. Milan.

(1984b) 'Arpi preromana e romana, i dati archeologici: analisi e proposte di interpretazione', *Taras* 4: 7–46.

(1987) 'Nota su un gruppo di vasi policromi decorati con scene di combattimento, da Arpi (FG)', *AION(archeol)* 9: 167–88.

(1990) 'Arpi', in Tagliente (1990a), 57–64.

(1991) 'Indigeni e Romani nella Daunia settentrionale', in Mertens and Lambrechts (1991), 109–24.

Mazzei, M. and Lippolis, E. (1984) 'Dall' ellenizzazione all' età tardorepubblicana', in Mazzei (1984a), 185–252.

Mazzei, M. and Steingräber, S. (2000) 'Fürstengräber, Luxushäuser und Delphine: archäologische Neuentdeckungen im Daunischen Arpi (Nordapulien)', *Antike Welt* 31: 261–8.

McDonald, A. H. (1944) 'Rome and the Italian Confederacy', *JRS* 34: 11–33.

Mearsheimer, J. (1995) *The Tragedy of Great Power Politics*. New York.

Meiggs, R. and Lewis, D. (eds.) (1969) *A Selection of Greek Historical Inscriptions to the End of the Fifth Century BC*. Oxford.

Mele, A. (1993) 'Crotone greca negli ultimi due secoli della sua storia', in Napolitano (1993), 235–91.

Mertens, J. (1992) 'Sulle tracce di Annibale negli scavi di Ordona', in Uggeri (1992), 93–101.

(ed.) (1995a) *Herdonia: Scoperta di una città*. Bari.

(1995b) 'Le mura e la rete viaria urbana', in Mertens (1995a), 139–52.

(1995c) 'Topografia generale', in Mertens (1995a), 135–8.

Mertens, J. and Lambrechts, R. (eds.) (1991) *Comunità indigine e problemi della romanizzazione nell' Italia centro-meridionale (IVo–IIIo sec. Av. C.)*. Rome.

Mertens, J. and Van Wonterghem, F. (1995) 'Dall'età repubblicana all'età augustea: lo sviluppo urbanistico, i monumenti', in Mertens (1995a), 153–84.

Mertens, J. and Volpe, G. (eds.) (1999) *Herdonia: Un itinerario storico-archeologico*. Bari.

Michelotto, P. G. (ed.) (2002) *Logios aner: Studi di antichità in memoria di Mario Attilio Levi*. Milan.

Mitchell, L. (1997) *Greeks Bearing Gifts: the Public Use of Private Relationships in the Greek World, 435–323 BC*. Cambridge.

Mommsen, T. (1887–8) *Römisches Staatsrecht*. Leipzig.

(1888–94) *Römische Geschichte*, 8th edn (4 vols.). Berlin.

(1967) 'Die *libri coloniarum*', in Blume, Lachmann and Rudorff (1967), vol. II: 143–226.

Montgomery B. (1968) *A History of Warfare*. London.

Moreno, R. (1981) 'Appendice: I dati archeologici', in Giardina and Schiavone (1981), 227–9.

Morley, N. (1997) 'Cities in Context: Urban Systems in Roman Italy', in H. Parkins (ed.), *Roman Urbanization: Beyond the Consumer City* (London), 42–58.

Mouritsen, H. (1998) *Italian Unification: a Study in Ancient and Modern Historiography*. London.

(2006) 'Hindsight and historiography: Writing the History of pre-Roman Italy', in Jehne and Pfeilschifter (2006), 23–37.

Moxon, I., Smart J. and Woodman, A. J. (eds.) (1986) *Past Perspectives: Studies in Greek and Roman Historical Writing*. Cambridge.

Muccigrosso, J. (2003) 'The Brindisi Elogium and the Rejected *lectio senatus* of Appius Claudius Caecus', *Historia* 52: 496–501.

Muggia, A. (1999a) 'Kaulonia', *DNP*, vol. VI: 363–4.

(1999b) 'Kroton', *DNP*, vol. VI: 870–1.

(2002) 'Temesa', *DNP*, vol. XII.1: 107.

Münzer, F. (1920) *Römische Adelsparteien und Adelsfamilien.* Republished 1963, Stuttgart.

Murray, W., Bernstein, A. and Knox, M. (eds.) (1994) *The Making of Strategy: Rulers, States and Wars.* Cambridge.

Musti, D. (1988) *Strabone e la Magna Grecia: Città e popoli dell' Italia antica.* Padua.

Nagle, B. (1973) 'An Allied View of the Social War', *AJA* 77: 367–78.

Napolitano, M. (ed.) (1993) *Crotone e la sua storia tra IV e III secolo a.C.* Naples.

Nardella, F. (1990) 'Dati per un quadro insediativo della Daunia settentrionale preromana', in Tagliente (1990a), 65–8.

Nenci, G. and Vallet, G. (eds.) (1977–) *Bibliografia topografica della colonizzazione greca in Italia e nelle isole tirreniche* (17 vols.). Pisa.

Neppi Modona, A. (ed.) (1984) *La civiltà dei Dauni nel quadro del mondo italico: Atti del XIII convegno di studi Etruschi e Italici, Manfredonia, 21–27 Giugno 1980.* Florence.

Nicols J. (1980) '*Tabulae patronatus*: a Study of the Agreement between Patron and Client-Community', *ANRW* II.13: 535–61.

Nissen, H. (1967) *Italische Landeskunde*, reprint (2 vols.). Amsterdam.

Oakley, S. P. (1993) 'The Roman Conquest of Italy', in Rich and Shipley (1993), 9–37.

(1997–2005) *A Commentary on Livy, Books VI–X* (4 vols.). Oxford.

(2009) 'Livy and his sources', in Chaplin and Kraus (2009), 439–60.

Ogilvie, R. M. and Drummond, A. (1989) 'The Sources for Early Roman history', *CAH*, 2nd edn, vol. VII.2: 1–29.

Osanna, M. (1992) *Chorai coloniali da Taranto a Locri: Documentazione archaeologica e ricostruzione storica.* Rome.

Paget, R. F. (1968) 'The Ancient Ports of Cumae', *JRS* 58: 152–69.

Pais, E. (1920) 'Il "Liber Coloniarum" ', *RAL* 16: 55–93, 377–411.

(1923) 'Serie cronologica delle colonie romane e latine della età regia fino all'impero: I', *Memorie della classe di scienze morali e storiche dell'Accademia dei Lincei* 8: 311–55.

Palmer, R. E. A. (1996) 'The Deconstruction of Mommsen on Festus 462/464L', in J. Linderski (ed.), *Imperium sine fine: T. Robert S. Broughton and the Roman Republic* (Stuttgart), 75–101.

Pani, M. (1979) 'Economia e società in età romana', in G. Musca (ed.), *Storia della Puglia* (Bari), vol. I: 99–124.

(1991) 'Colonia Vibina', *ZPE* 87: 125–31.

(2005) 'Il Processo di Romanizzazione', in A. Massafra and B. Salvemini (eds.), *Storia della Puglia* (Bari), vol. I: 17–48.

Parelangèli, O. (1960) *Studi messapici. Iscrizioni, lessico, glosse e indici.* Milan.

Parente, A. R. (2000) 'Dazos e Pullos sulle moneta di Arpi e Salapia', *NAC* 29: 235–49.

Parkins, H. (ed.) (1997) *Roman Urbanism: Beyond the Consumer City*. London.

Pasquinucci, M. (1979) 'La Transhumanza nell'Italia romana', in E. Gabba and M. Pasquinucci, *Strutture agrarie e allevamento transumante nell' Italia romana (III–I sec. a.C.)* (Pisa), 79–182.

Patterson, J. R. (2006a) 'Colonization and Historiography: the Roman Republic', in Bradley and Wilson (2006), 189–218.

(2006b) 'The Relationship of the Italian Ruling Classes with Rome: Friendship, Family Relations and their Consequences', in Jehne and Pfeilschifter (2006), 139–53.

Patterson, M. L. (1942) 'Rome's Choice of Magistrates during the Hannibalic War', *TAPhA* 73: 319–40.

Peddie, J. (1997) *Hannibal's War*. Thrupp, England.

Peruzzi, E. (2001) 'Il latino di Lucera', *PP* 56: 229–56.

Pfeilschifter, R. (2007) 'The Allies in the Republican Army and the Romanisation of Italy', in Roth and Keller (2007), 27–42.

Piper, D. J. (1988) 'The *ius adipiscendae ciuitatis Romanae per magistratum* and its Effect on Roman–Latin Relations', *Latomus* 47: 59–68.

Platner, S. and Ashby, T. (1929) *A Topographical Dictionary of Ancient Rome*. London.

Pobjoy, M. (1995) 'Rome and Capua from Republic to Empire', unpublished dissertation, Oxford.

(1997) 'The Decree of the Pagus Herculaneus and the Romanisation of "Oscan" Capua', *Arctos* 31: 175–95.

(2000) 'The First Italia', in Herring and Lomas (2000), 187–211.

Poccetti P. (ed.) (1988) *Per un'identità culturale dei Brettii*. Naples.

Pothecary, S. (1997) 'The Expression "Our Times" in Strabo's Geography', *CPh* 92: 235–46.

Poulter, A. (2002) 'Transforming Tarantine Horizons: a Political, Social and Cultural History from the Fourth to the First Century BC', unpublished dissertation, Oxford.

Proctor, D. (1971) *Hannibal's March in History*. Oxford.

Pugliese Caratelli, G. (1987) *Magna Grecia, lo sviluppo politico, sociale ed economico*. Milan.

Purcell, N. (1990) 'The Creation of the Provincial Landscape: the Roman Impact on Cisalpine Gaul', in Blagg and Millett (1990), 7–29.

(1994) 'South Italy in the Fourth Century BC', *CAH*, 2nd edn, vol. VI: 381–403.

Quilici, L. (1967) *Siris-Heraclea*. Rome.

Quilici-Gigli, S. (1994) 'The Changing Landscape of the Roman Campagna: Lo sfruttamento del territorio in età imperiale', in Carlsen *et al.* (1994), 135–43.

Raaflaub, K. (1996) 'Born to Be Wolves? Origins of Roman Imperialism', in Wallace and Harris (1996), 273–314.

(2005) *Social Struggles in Archaic Rome: New Perspectives on the Conflict of the Orders*. Expanded and updated edn. Oxford.

Raaflaub, K., Richards, J. and Samons II, K. (1992) 'Appius Claudius Caecus, Rome, and Italy before the Pyrrhic War', in Hackens *et al.* (1992), 13–50.

Raaflaub, K. and Rosenstein, N. (eds.) (1999) *War and Society in the Ancient and Medieval Worlds*. Cambridge, MA.

Raban, A. (ed.) (1988) *Archaeology of Coastal Changes: Proceedings of the First International Symposium 'Cities on the Sea – Past and Present', Haifa, Israel, September 22–29, 1986*. Oxford.

Rainey, F. (1969) 'The Location of Archaic Greek Sybaris', *AJA* 73: 261–73.

Rankov, B. (1996) 'The Second Punic War at Sea', in Cornell *et al.* (1996), 49–57.

Rawson, E. (1971) 'Prodigy Lists and the Use of the Annales Maximi', *CQ* 21: 158–69.

Reid, J. S. (1913) 'Problems of the Second Punic War: I. The Prelude to the War and II. Polybius as Geographer', *JRS* 3: 175–96.

  (1915) 'Problems of the Second Punic War: III. Rome and its Italian allies', *JRS* 5: 87–124.

Reugg, Bro. S. D. (1988) 'Minturnae: a Roman River Seaport on the Garigliano River, Italy', in Raban (1988), 209–28.

Riccardi, A. (1991) 'Appendice: Ricerche sistematiche ad Azetium (Rutigliano-Bari)', in Mertens and Lambrechts (1991), 89–92.

Rich, J. (1976) *Declaring War in the Roman Republic in the Period of Transmarine Expansion*. Brussels.

  (1993) 'Fear, Greed and Glory: the Causes of Roman War-making in the Middle Republic', in Rich and Shipley (1993), 38–68.

  (1996) 'The Origins of the Second Punic War', in Cornell *et al.* (1996), 1–37.

  (2005) 'Valerias Antias and the Construction of the Roman Past', *BICS* 48: 137–61.

  (2008) 'Treaties, Allies and the Roman Conquest of Italy', in P. de Souza and J. France (eds.), *War and Peace in Ancient and Medieval History* (Cambridge), 51–75.

Rich, J. and Shipley, G. (eds.) (1993) *War and Society in the Roman World*. London.

Richardson, J. S. (1986) *Hispaniae: Spain and the Development of Roman Imperialism, 218–82 BC*. Cambridge.

Ridgeway, D. (1984) 'Review: Temesa', *CR* 34: 278–80.

Ridley, R. T. (1983) 'Falsi triumphi, plures consulatus', *Hermes* 42: 372–82.

Roberts, E. S. (1881) 'Inscriptions from Dodona II', *JHS* 2: 102–21.

Rosenstein, N. (1990) *Imperatores Victi: Military Defeat and Aristocratic Competition in the Middle and Late Republic*. Berkeley.

  (1993) 'Competition and Crisis in Republican Rome', *Phoenix* 47: 313–38.

  (2004) *Rome at War: Farms, Families, and Death in the Middle Republic*. Chapel Hill, NC.

Roth, R. (2007) 'Varro's *picta Italia* (RR I.ii.1) and the Odology of Roman Italy', *Hermes* 135: 286–300.

Roth, R. and Keller, J. (eds.) (2007) *Roman by Integration: Dimensions of Group Identity in Material Culture and Text*. Portsmouth, RI.

Rudolph, H. (1935) *Stadt und Staat im römischen Italien: Untersuchungen über die Entwicklung des Munizipalwesens in der republikanischer Zeit*. Leipzig.

Russi, A. (1976) *Teanum Apulum: Le inscrizioni e la storia del municipio*. Rome.

(1980) 'Iscrizione inedite dell'ager Arpanis nel convento di S. Matteo presso S. Marco in Lamis. Contributo alla storia di Arpi romana', in *Civiltà e culture antiche tra Gargano e Tavoliere: atti del convegno archeologico, Convento di S. Matteo, 28–29 settembre 1979* (Manduria), 91–102.

(1987) 'Su un caso di duplicazione in Livio IX 20', *MGR* 12: 93–114.

(1992) 'Alla ricerca di Forentum', *MGR* 17: 145–57.

(1995) *La lucania romana: profilo storico-istituzionale*. San Severo.

Russi, V. (1982) 'Mass. Finocchito (Castelnuovo della Daunia)', *Taras* 2: 181–4.

Rutter N. K. (1970) 'Sybaris: Legend and Reality', *G&R* 17: 168–76.

(1971) 'Campanian Chronology in the Fifth Century BC', *CQ* 21: 55–61.

(1979) *Campanian Coinages, 475–380 BC* Edinburgh.

(1997) *The Greek Coinages of Southern Italy and Sicily*. London.

(2001) *Historia Nummorum: Italy*. London.

Sabin, P. (1996) 'The Mechanics of Battle in the Second Punic War', in Cornell *et al.* (1996), 59–79.

Salmon, E. T. (1933) 'The Last Latin Colony', *CQ* 27: 30–35.

(1936) 'Roman Colonisation from the Second Punic War to the Gracchi', *JRS* 26: 47–67.

(1955) 'Roman Expansion and Roman Colonization in Italy', *Phoenix* 9: 63–75.

(1959) 'Notes on the Social War', *TAPhA* 89: 159–84.

(1962) 'The Causes of the Social War', *Phoenix* 16: 107–19.

(1963) 'The Coloniae Maritimae', *Athenaeum* 41: 3–38.

(1967) *Samnium and the Samnites*. Cambridge.

(1969) *Roman Colonization under the Republic*. Ithaca, NY.

(1982) *The Making of Roman Italy*. Ithaca, NY.

Salvatore, M. (ed.) (1990) *Basilicata: l'espansionismo romano nel sud-est d'Italia: Il quadro archeologico: atti del convegno, Venosa, 23–25 aprile 1987*. Venosa.

Sambon, A. (1903) *Les monnaies antique de l'Italie*. Paris.

Sauer, E. (ed.) (2004a) *Archaeology and Ancient History: Breaking down the Boundaries*. London.

(2004b) 'The Disunited Subject: Human History's Split into "History" and "Archaeology"', in Sauer (2004a), 17–45.

Scheers, S. (1995) 'La circolazione monetaria', in Mertens (1995a), 327–36.

Scheidel, W. (2004) 'Human Mobility in Roman Italy, I: the Free Population', *JRS* 94: 1–26.

(2006) 'The Demography of Roman State Formation in Italy', in Jehne and Pfeilschifter (2006), 207–26

Schmiedt, G. (1985) 'Le centuriazioni di Luceria ed Aecae', *L'Universo* 65: 260–304.

Schulze, W. (1966) *Zur Geschichte lateinischer Eigennamen*, 2nd edn. Berlin.

Scullard, H. H. (1967) *The Etruscan Cities and Rome*. Ithaca, NY.

(1973) *Roman Politcs 220–150 BC*, 2nd edn. Oxford.

(1989) 'Carthage and Rome', *CAH*, 2nd edn, vol. VII.2: 486–569.

Seibert, J. (1993a) *Forschungen zu Hannibal*. Darmstadt.

(1993b) *Hannibal*. Darmstadt.

(1995) 'Invasion aus dem Osten: Trauma, Propaganda, oder Erfindung der Römer?', in C. Schubert, K. Brodersen and U. Huttner (eds.), *Rom und der griechischen Osten: Fetschrift für H. H. Schmitt* (Stuttgart), 237–48.

Senatore, F. (2006) *La lega sannitica*. Capri.

Serrati, J. (2006) 'Neptune's Altars: the Treaties between Rome and Carthage (509–226 BC)', *CQ* 56: 113–34.

Shean, J. F. (1996) 'Hannibal's Mules: the Logistical Limitations of Hannibal's Army and the Battle of Cannae, 216 BC', *Historia* 45: 159–87.

Sherwin-White, A. N. (1973) *The Roman Citizenship*, 2nd edn. Oxford.

(1980) 'Rome the Aggressor?', *JRS* 70: 177–81.

(1984) *Roman Foreign Policy in the East, 168 BC to AD 1.* Norman, OK.

Silvestrini, M. (1976) 'Dalla "nobilitas" municipale all' ordine senatorio: esempi da Larino e da Venosa', *CCG* 7: 269–82.

Sirago, V. (1992) 'Lacerazioni politiche in Puglia durante la presenza di Annibale', in Uggeri (1992), 71–81.

(1999) *Puglia Antica*. Bari.

Sirago, V. and Volpe, G. (eds.) (1993) *Puglia romana: con una bibliografia orientiva a cura di Giuliano Volpe*. Bari.

Sironen, T. (1990) 'The Lucanians and the Bruttians and the rural population of Magna Graecia (4th and 3rd cent. BC): with special reference to the territories of Metaponto and Croton', in Solin and Kajava (1990), 143–50.

Skydsgaard, J. (1974) 'Transhumance in Ancient Italy', *ARID* 7: 7–36.

Small, A. (1991) 'Late Roman Rural Settlement in Basilicata and Western Apulia', in Barker and Lloyd (1991), 204–22.

(1994) 'Grain from Apulia: the Changing Fortunes of Apulia as a Grain-producing Area in the Hellenistic and Roman Periods', in Jendel and Deschênes-Wagner (2004) 543–55.

Small, A. and Buck, R. (1994) *The Excavations of San Giovanni di Ruoti* (2 vols.). Toronto.

Small, A., Small, C., Campbell, I. *et al.* (1998) 'Field Survey in the Basentello Valley on the Basilicata–Puglia Border', *EMC* 62: 337–71.

Solin, H. (1993) *Le iscrizioni antiche di Trebula, Caiatia, e Cubulteria*. Caserta.

Solin, H. and Kajava, M. (eds.) (1990) *Roman Eastern Policy and Other Studies in Roman History: Proceedings of a Colloquium at Tvärminne, 2–3 October 1987.* Helsinki.

Spurr, M. S. (1986) *Arable Cultivation in Roman Italy: c. 200 BC–c. AD 100*. London.

Staccioli R. A. (1972) 'A proposito della identificazione di Volsinii etrusca', *PP* 27: 246–52.

Staveley, E. (1989) 'Rome and Italy in the Early Third Century', *CAH*, 2nd edn, vol. VII.2. 420–55.

Stazio, A. (1972) 'Per una storia della monetazione dell'antica Puglia', *ASP* 25: 39–47.

Stinnett, D. and Diehl, P. (2001) 'The Path(s) to Rivalry: Behavioral and Structural Explanations of Rivalry Development', *The Journal of Politics* 63: 717–40.

Sumner, G. V. (1970) 'The Truth about Velleius Paterculus: Prolegomena', *HSPh* 74: 257–97.

Tagliente, M. (ed.) (1990a) *Italici in Magna Grecia: Lingua, insediamenti e strutture.* Venosa.

(1990b) 'Banzi', in Tagliente (1990a), 71–4.

Tagliente, M., Fresa, M. P. and Bottini, A. (1991) 'Relazione sull' area daunio-lucano e sul santuario di Lavello', in Mertens and Lambrechts (1991), 93–104.

Taliercio Mensitieri, M. (1988), 'Osservazioni sulla monetazione dei Brettii', in Poccetti (1988), 223–42.

(1995) 'Aspetti e problemi della monetazione del koinòn dei Brettii', in De Sensi Sestito (1995), 127–51.

Terrenato, N. (1998a) 'The Romanization of Italy: Global Acculturation or Cultural Bricolage?', in C. Forcey, J. Hawthorne and R. Witcher (eds.), *TRAC 97: Proceedings of the Seventh Annual Theoretical Roman Archaeology Conference* (Oxford), 20–7.

(1998b) '*Tam firmum municipium*', *JRS* 88: 94–114.

(2004) 'The Historical Significance of Falerii Novi', in H. Patterson (ed.), *Bridging the Tiber: Approaches to Regional Archaeology in the Middle Tiber Valley* (London), 234–5.

Thiel, J. H. (1946) *Studies on the History of Roman Sea-Power in Republican Times.* Amsterdam.

(1954) *A History of Roman Sea-Power before the Second Punic War.* Amsterdam.

Thies, C. (2001) 'A Social Psychological Approach to Enduring Rivalries', *Political Psychology* 22: 693–725.

Thompson, W. (2001) 'Identifying Rivals and Rivalries in World Politics', *International Studies Quarterly* 45: 557–86.

Thomsen, R. (1947) *The Italic Regions from Augustus to the Lombard Invasions.* Copenhagen.

Tibiletti, G. (1953) 'La politica delle colonie e città Latine nella Guerra Sociale', *RIL* 86: 45–63.

(1955) 'Lo sviluppo del latifondo dall' epoca Gracchana all'impero', in *Relazioni del X Congresso Internazionale di Scienze Storiche* (Florence), vol. II: 235–92.

Tinè, F. and Tinè, S. (1973) 'Gli scavi del 1967–1968 a Salapia', *ASP* 16: 221–48.

Tocco Sciarelli, G. (1981) 'L'espansione di Siris tra l'Agri e il Sinni', in *Siris e l'influenza ionica in Occidente: atti del ventesimo Convegno di studi sulla Magna Grecia, Taranto, 12–17 ottobre 1980* (Taranto), 223–35.

Torelli, Marina (1978) *Rerum Romanarum fontes ab anno ccxcii ad annum cclxv a. Ch. n.* Pisa.

Torelli, Mario (1969) 'Contributi al Supplemento del CIL IX', *RAL* 24: 9–48.

(1984) 'Aspetti storico-archeologico della romanizzazione della Daunia', in *La civiltà dei Dauni nel quadro del mundo italico, atti del XIII Convegno di studi etruschi e italici: Manfredonia, 21–27 giugno 1980* (Florence), 325–36.

(1988) 'Paestum Romana', in A. Stazio and S. Ceccoli (eds.), *Poseidonia-Paestum: Atti del XXVII convegno di studi sulla Magna Grecia, Taranto-Paestum, 9–15 ottobre 1987* (Taranto 1988, Naples 1992), 33–115.

(1990a) 'I culti di Rossano di Vaglio', in Salvatore (1990), 83–93.

(1990b) 'Numerius Papius, sannita di Forentum', in Tagliente (1990a), 265–8.

(1992) 'Il quadro materiale e ideale della romanizzazione', in Cassano (1992), 608–19.

(1993a) *Studies in the Romanization of Italy*. Edmonton, AB.

(1993b) 'Historical and Archaeological Aspects of the Romanization of Daunia', in Torelli (1993a), 141–58.

(1993c) 'Da Leukania a Lucania', in *Da Leukania a Lucania: la Lucania centro-orientale fra Pirro e I Giulio-Claudii* (Venosa), xiii–xxviii.

(1999) *Tota Italia: Essays in the Cultural Formation of Roman Italy*. Oxford.

Toynbee, A. J. (1965) *Hannibal's Legacy* (2 vols.). Oxford.

Tränkle, H. (1971) *Cato in der vierten und fünften Dekade des Livius*. Mainz.

(1972) 'Livius und Polybios', *Gymnasium* 79: 13–31.

(1977) *Livius und Polybios*. Stuttgart.

Travaglini, A. (1988) 'Presenza di moneta romana repubblicana in Puglia', in Marangio (1988), 65–76.

Tréziny, H. (1989) *Kaulonia*, vol. 1: *Sondages sur la fortification nord, 1982–1985*. Naples.

Uggeri, G. (ed.) (1992) *L'Età annibalica e la Puglia: atti del II convegno di studi sulla Puglia romana, Mesagne, 24–26 marzo 1988*. Mesagne.

(1998a) 'Fagifulae', *DNP*, vol. IV: 399.

(1998b) 'Falerii', *DNP*, vol. IV: 400–2.

Ungern-Sternberg, J. von (1975) *Capua im Zweiten Punischen Krieg: Untersuchungen zur römischen Annalistik*. Munich.

(1988) 'Überlegungen zur frühen römischen Überlieferung im Licht der Oral-Tradition-Forschung', in Ungern-Sternberg and Reinau (1988) 237–65.

(2005) 'The Formation of the "Annalistic Tradition": the Example of the Decemvirate', in Raaflaub (2005), 75–97.

Ungern-Sternberg, J. von and Reinau, H. (eds.) (1988) *Vergangenheit in mündlicher Überlieferung*. Munich.

Untermann, J. (2000) 'Messapisch', *DNP*, vol. VIII: 50–1.

Vandermersch, C. (1985) 'Monnaies et amphores commerciales d'Hipponion: à propos d'une famille de conteneurs magno-grecs du IVe siècle avant J.-C.', *PP* 40: 110–45.

Vasaly, A. (1993) *Representations: Images of the World in Ciceronian Oratory*. Berkeley.

Vetter, E. (1953) *Handbuch der italischen Dialekten*, vol. 1. Heidelberg.

Vitucci, G. (1953) 'Intorno a un nuovo frammento di elogium', *RFIC* 81: 43–61.

Volpe, G. (1988) 'Primi dati sulla circolazione della anfore repubblicane nella Puglia settentrionale', in Marangio (1988), 77–90.

(1990) *La Daunia nell' età della romanizzazione: paesaggio agrario, produzione, scambi*. Bari.

Volpe, G. and Mertens, J. (1995) 'Il territorio, la viabilità, la produzione agraria', in Mertens (1995a), 291–320.

Walbank, F. W. (1970) *A Historical Commentary on Polybius*, 2nd edn (3 vols.). Oxford.

Wallace, R. and Harris, E. (1996) *Transitions to Empire: Essays in Greco-Roman History, 360–146 BC, in Honor of E. Badian.* Norman, OK.

Walsh, P. G. (1982) 'Livy and the Aims of "Historia": an Analysis of the Third Decade', *ANRW* II.30.2: 1058–74.

Walt, S. (1987) *The Origin of Alliances.* Ithaca, NY.

Waltz, K. (1959) *Man, the State, and War: a Theoretical Analysis.* New York.

  (1979) *Theory of International Politics.* New York.

  (1988) 'The Origins of War in Neorealist Theory', *Journal of Interdisciplinary History* 18: 615–28.

  (2000) 'Structural Realism after the Cold War', *International Security* 25: 5–41.

Warrior, V. M. (1991) 'Notes on Intercalation', *Latomus* 50: 80–7.

Weissbach, F. H. (1909) 'Forentum', *RE* VI: 2853.

Will, E. L. (1982) 'Greco-Italic Amphoras', *Hesperia* 51: 338–55.

Williams, J. (2001) *Beyond the Rubicon: Romans and Gauls in Republican Italy.* Oxford.

Wiseman, T. P. (1964) 'Viae Anniae', *PBSR* 32: 21–37.

  (1969) 'Viae Anniae Again', *PBSR* 37: 82–91

  (1970) 'Roman Republican Road-building', *PBSR* 38: 122–52.

  (1971) *New Men in the Roman Senate, 139 BC–AD 14.* Oxford.

  (1979) *Clio's Cosmetics: Three Studies in Greco-Roman Literature.* Leicester.

  (1986) 'Monuments and the Roman Annalists', in Moxon, Smart and Woodman (1986), 87–100.

Wuilleumier, P. (1939) *Tarente.* Paris.

Yarrow, L. M. (2006) *Historiography at the End of the Republic. Provincial Persepctives on Roman Rule.* Oxford.

Yntema, D. (1986) 'La ricerca topografica nel territorio oritano', *ASP* 39: 3–26.

  (1993) *In Search of an Ancient Countryside: the Amsterdam Free University Field Survey at Oria Province of Brindisi South Italy (1981–1983).* Amsterdam.

  (1995) 'Romanisation in the Brindisino, Southern Italy', *BABesch* 70: 153–77.

Zancani Montuoro, P. (1969) 'Dov' era Temesa', *RAAN* 44: 11–23.

Zanker, P. (ed.) (1976) *Hellenismus in Mittelitalien.* Göttingen.

Index

CPSIA information can be obtained at www.ICGtesting.com
Printed in the USA
BVOW01s1108161214

379633BV00001B/162/P